THE RISE OF CHRISTIAN BELIEFS

THE RISE OF
CHRISTIAN BELIEFS
The Thought World of Early Christians

Heikki Räisänen

Fortress Press / Minneapolis

THE RISE OF CHRISTIAN BELIEFS
The Thought World of Early Christians

Cover images, left to right: Christ as teacher (detail from the early Christian Sarcophagus of Lot, Catacomb of San Sebastiano, Rome, © Scala / Art Resource, NY); Jesus as the good shepherd (fresco from the Catacomb of San Callisto, Rome); funerary stele of Licinia Amias, one of the most ancient Christian inscriptions (from the area of the Vatican necropolis, Rome); eucharistic bread (fresco from the Catacomb of San Callisto, Rome).
Cover design: Joe Vaughan
Book design: Zan Ceeley, Trio Bookworks

Additional resources can be found online at www.fortresspress.com/raisanen

Library of Congress Cataloging-in-Publication Data

Räisänen, Heikki.
  The rise of Christian beliefs : the thought world of early Christians / Heikki Räisänen.
    p. cm.
  Includes bibliographical references and index.
  ISBN 978-0-8006-6266-0 (alk. paper)
  1. Church history—Primitive and early church, ca. 30–600. 2. Theology, Doctrinal—History—Early church, ca. 30–600. 3. Christianity—Origin. I. Title.
  BR162.3.R35 2009
  270.1—dc22
                                           2009011219

Manufactured in the U.S.A.

13   12   11   10   2   3   4   5   6   7   8   9   10

To the members of the "Center of Excellence" in Biblical Studies,
University of Helsinki / Åbo Akademi University, 1994–2005

Contents

PART II ~ BASIC PROBLEMS AND SOLUTIONS

4. Last Things First: God, History, and Beyond 79

5. After Death: The Destiny of the Individual 114

9.   The Empowering Presence: Experiences and Doctrines of the Spirit   228

10.   True Israel? From Jewish to Christian Identity   247

Figures

It is a great pleasure to bring *The Rise of Christian Beliefs* to the public. To scholars and readers familiar with New Testament studies, Heikki Räisänen will need no introduction. Indeed, his earlier books on topics ranging from *Paul and the Law* (1983; 2d ed., 1987) to *The Messianic Secret in Mark's Gospel* (1990) and his proposal to move *Beyond New Testament Theology* (1990; 2d ed., 2000) have done much to set contemporary scholarly discussions on their current paths.

The Rise of Christian Beliefs offers the same rich texture of precise observation and judicious interpretation that has characterized Professor Räisänen's earlier works. The field of vision is now expanded to take in the whole of early Christian beliefs in their historical context. Here a distinctive vision of the task of New Testament theology—addressed to the interested non-Christian as much as to the Christian, from the perspective of the history of religions—has reached a comprehensive and definitive expression.

Professor Räisänen has also written with general readers and students in mind, providing in initial chapters a discussion of the cultural environment of early Christianity and of the sources at our disposal. To complement the text, Fortress Press has included a historical timeline, maps, and numerous illustrations. Further resources for students and faculty, including study questions for each chapter and a guide to writing research papers, are available on a companion website, www.fortresspress.com/raisanen.

Neil Elliott
for Fortress Press

It is with relief that I give this book up for publishing, for I have been working on it far too long. It is an attempt to put into practice a program that I presented in 1990 in *Beyond New Testament Theology* (SCM Press; second edition, 2000): the program of creating an alternative to "New Testament Theology" by outlining an overall picture of early Christian thought from a history-of-religions point of view. At that time I had already done some preliminary work toward that goal, so that the process of writing the present book has been going on for a quarter of a century. Even so, the product is far from finished. In particular, I could (and perhaps should) still have spent much more time dealing with the boundless new literature—but coping with the mass of publications in all relevant fields is a hopelessly monumental task in any case. I felt that unless I let the book go now, I never would. So, for better or for worse, here it is.

During the process I have had various kinds of readers in mind. I have imagined, perhaps foolishly, that my work might be of interest to quite

different groups—to fellow scholars, to students (undergraduate and advanced), and even to the elusive "general reader." (It is my conviction that, as war is said to be too important to be left to generals, so the Bible is too important to be left to Biblical scholars and theologians.) The result is that the book is not of a piece. If I have a contribution to make to the scholarly discussion (as I hope), it will be found in chapters 4 to 12, in which I try to paint a big picture of the early Christian thought world. This main portion of the book is preceded by three introductory chapters. Their aim is to locate Christian thought in the world in which it arose (chapters 1 and 2) and give (in chapter three) a general survey of the literature that will constitute the source material of the book. The (elementary) information given in these chapters will hopefully aid the nonexpert to better understand the picture painted in the main part. They also give me the possibility to state some of my own academic judgments, so that I will not have to argue about authorship, dates, and the like in the main part. A reader xviii with some experience in biblical studies may well skip these chapters and jump from the introduction directly to chapter 4.

In an overall account of a manageable size it is impossible to give detailed reasons for positions taken on various issues. I have had to keep the scholarly discussion brief, though trying to give some space to sketching the "state of the question" at the most important junctures. When my assessment differs from what may be taken as the critical consensus, I make this known. To give the diligent reader the chance to trace my steps and weigh the evidence on which I rest my case, I have included in the notes an overdose of references to my own previous studies.

I could never have finished this book without the help of friends who introduced me to the discussions on the cutting edge in their fields, wrote insightful studies to draw on, commented on drafts of my chapters, shared some of the burdens of administration, or provided personal support and inspiration along the way. They include, among others, Lars Aejmelaeus, Ismo Dunderberg, Anne-Marit Enroth-Voitila, Raimo Hakola, Karl-Johan Illman (†), Jutta Jokiranta, Jarmo Kiilunen, Kari Kuula, Risto Lauha, Outi Lehtipuu, Petri Luomanen, Antti Marjanen, Matti Myllykoski, Martti Nissinen, Juha Pakkala, Karl-Gustav Sandelin, Raija Sollamo, Kari Syreeni, Risto Uro—but a much longer list could be given. The reader will find the names of many of these persons appearing repeatedly in the notes, but their significance has been far greater than can be directly inferred from my text.

I thank the Academy of Finland for appointing me as Research Professor/Academy Professor for the periods 1984–1994 and 2001–2006. Without this possibility to focus on research it would not have been possible to lay the ground-work for this book. The Academy also granted my research unit on "Formation of Early Jewish and Christian Ideology" at the University of Helsinki, complemented with a side branch at Åbo Akademi University, the status of a "Center of Excellence" in 1994–2005. The honor was accompanied by certain financial resources that made those years something of a golden age for us. In a sense, the appearance of this book brings the work of the Center to its natural, if delayed, conclusion: it was stated in our plans that I was writing an overall account that would summarize much of the work of the Center. Naturally I am alone responsible for the views presented here, but it is equally clear that on a number of issues I lean firmly on work done by my colleagues and pupils. Nowhere is this more obvious than in my utilization of the texts from the Nag Hammadi library. I have come to greatly appreciate the Christians who produced those texts. My grasp of them remains limited, but if I have understood anything at all, I have to thank Antti Marjanen, Risto Uro, and Ismo Dunderberg for it.

Thanks are due to Adele Yarbro Collins and Gerd Theissen, who acted as external advisors to the Center and also encouraged me in this personal project. Gerd's pioneering work *A Theory of Primitive Christian Religion* (SCM Press, 1999) has proved an inspiring forerunner; we share the starting point and agree on many crucial judgments, while taking a different methodological approach and also a different stance to the issue of unity and diversity. I thank Todd Penner and Caroline Vander Stichele, who organized a scholarly discussion of my program at the Rome meeting of the Society of Biblical Literature in 2001 and edited the volume *Moving Beyond New Testament Theology?* (Finnish Exegetical Society/Vandenhoeck & Ruprecht, 2005), which emerged out of that discussion and has spurred me to move on. Many other colleagues have strengthened me in my vision; I feel indebted to Chris Tuckett, Sandy Wedderburn, Steve Wilson, and Dieter Zeller in particular.

No scholar of my generation, however, has shaped my academic thinking as profoundly as Ed Sanders. While the influence of his work will be seen throughout this book, Ed has also supported and inspired me in many other ways over the years. At the final stage he kindly scrutinized several chapters of the book. His penetrating comments led to many improvements and saved me from some mistakes.

During all these years, my family has been a constant source of strength, joy, and inspiration. No words can fully express my gratitude.

Finally, warm thanks to the team of Fortress Press, in particular Neil Elliott and Zan Ceeley, for enthusiastic support for the project and tireless efforts to improve it.

Acknowledgments

A preliminary version of chapter 4 appeared as "Last Things First: 'Eschatology' as the First Chapter in an Overall Account of Early Christian Ideas" in *Temenos*, vol. 39–40 (2003–2004): 9-49, published by The Finnish Society for the Study of Religion. Used by permission.

A preliminary version of chapter 5 appeared as "Towards an Alternative to New Testament Theology: 'Individual Eschatology' as an Example," pages 167–85 in *The Nature of New Testament Theology: Essays in Honour of Robert Morgan*, edited by Christopher Rowland and Christopher Tuckett (London: Blackwell, 2006). Used by permission.

A preliminary version of chapter 6 appeared as "Sold under Sin? Early Christian Notions of the Human Condition," pages 289–300 in *Kontexte der Schrift, Vol. 2: Kultur, Politik, Religion, Sprache—Text: Für Wolfgang Stegemann zum 60. Geburtstag*, edited by Christian Strecker (Stuttgart: Kohlhammer, 2005). Used by permission.

A preliminary version of chapter 7 appeared as "Towards an Alternative to New Testament Theology: Different 'Paths to Salvation,'" pages 175–203 in *Aufgabe und Durchführung einer Theologie des Neuen Testaments*, edited by Cilliers Breytenbach and Jörg Frey, WUNT 205 (Tübingen: Mohr Siebeck, 2007). Used by permission.

A preliminary version of chapter 8 appeared as "True Man or True God? Christological Conceptions in Early Christianity," pages 331–51 in *Ancient Israel, Judaism, and Christianity in Contemporary Perspective: Essays in memory of Karl-Johan Illman*, edited by Jacob Neusner, et al. (Lanham: University of America Press, 2006). Used by permission.

A preliminary summary of chapter 10 appeared as "Early Christians and Jewish Identity," pages 554–72 in *Houses Full of All Good Things: Essays in Memory of Timo Veijola*, edited by Juha Pakkala & Martti Nissinen (Helsinki: The Finnish Exegetical Society/Göttingen: Vandenhoeck & Ruprecht, 2008). Used by permission.

Primary Sources

1 Apoc. Jas.	*First Apocalypse of James*
1 Apol.	*Apologia i / First Apology* (Justin)
1 Clem.	*1 Clement*
1 En.	*1 Enoch (Ethiopic Apocalypse)*
1 Macc.	*1 Maccabees*
1QH	Qumran Hymns
1QM	Qumran War Scroll
1QpHab	Qumran Pesher Habakkuk
1QS	Qumran Rule of the Community
2 Apoc. Jas.	*Second Apocalypse of James*
2 Apol.	*Apologia ii / Second Apology* (Justin)
2 Bar.	*2 Baruch*
2 Clem.	*2 Clement*
3 En.	*3 Enoch*
4 Ezra	*4 Ezra*
4Q174	Qumran Florilegium (Midrash on Eschatology)
4Q186	Qumran Horoscope
4Q491	4Q War Scroll[a]
4Q521	Qumran Messianic Apocalypse
4Q MMT	Qumran Halakic Letter
4QpNah	Qumran Pesher Nahum
4QShirShab	Qumran Songs of the Sabbath Sacrifice
11QMelch	Qumran Melchizedek
11QT	Qumran Temple Scroll
Abr.	*De Abrahamo / On Abraham* (Philo)
Acts Thom.	*Acts of Thomas*
Adv. nat.	*Adversus nationes* (Arnobius)
Agr.	*De agricultura / On Husbandry* (Philo)
All.	*Legum Allegoriarum / Allegorical Interpretation* (Philo)
An.	*De anima / On the Soul* (Tertullian)
Ann.	*Annales* (Tacitus)
Ant.	*Jewish Antiquities* (Josephus)
Apoc. Ab.	*Apocalypse of Abraham*
Apoc. Adam	*Apocalypse of Adam*
Apoc. Jas.	*Apocryphon of James*
Apoc. John	*Apocryphon of John*
Apoc. Paul	*Apocalypse of Paul*
Apoc. Peter	*Apocalypse of Peter*
Apoc. Zeph.	*Apocalypse of Zephaniah*
Apol.	*Apologeticum / Apology* (Tertullian)
Apol.	*Apologia* (Aristides)
Apol.	*Apologia / Apology of Socrates* (Plato)
Ascen. Isa.	*Ascension of Isaiah*
Autol.	*Ad Autolycum / To Autolycus* (Theophilus of Antioch)
b. Ber.	*Babylonian Berakot*
Bapt.	*De baptismo / Baptism* (Tertullian)
Barn.	*Epistle of Barnabas*
B.J.	*Bellum judaicum / Jewish War* (Josephus)
Carn. Chr.	*De carne Christi / The Flesh of Christ* (Tertullian)
CD	*Damascus Document*
Cels.	*Contra Celsum / Against Celsus* (Origen)

Cher.	*De Cherubim / On the Cherubim* (Philo)
Civ.	*De civitate Dei / The City of God* (Augustine)
Clem.	*De clementia* (Seneca)
Comm. Isa.	*Commentariorum in Isaiam libri XVIII* (Jerome)
Comm. Jer.	*Commentariorum in Jeremiam libri VI* (Jerome)
Comm. Jo.	*Commentarii in evangelium Joannis* (Origen)
Comm. Matt.	*Commentarium in evangelium Matthaei* (Origen)
Comm. not.	*De communibus notitiis adversus Stoicos / Against the Stoics, on common conceptions* (Plutarch)
Conf.	*De confusione linguarum / On the Confusion of Tongues* (Philo)
Congr.	*De congressu quaerendae eruditionis gratia / On the Preliminary Studies* (Philo)
Contempl.	*De vita contemplativa / On the Contemplative Life* (Philo)
Decal.	*De decalogo / On the Decalogue* (Philo)
Dial.	*Dialogus cum Tryphone / Dialogue with Trypho* (Justin)
Dial. Sav.	*Dialogue of the Savior*
Diatr.	*Diatribai / Dissertations* (Epictetus)
Did.	*Didache*
Diogn.	*Epistle of Diognetus*
Eleg.	*Elegiae* (Propertius)
Ep.	*Epistulae* (Pliny the Younger)
Ep. Apos.	*Epistle of the Apostles*
Ep. Pet.	*Epistula Petri* (Pseudo-Clementine)
Eph.	*To the Ephesians* (Ignatius)
Exc. Theod.	*Excerpta ex Theodoto / Excerpts from Theodotus* (Clement of Alexandria)
Flacc.	*In Flaccum / Against Flaccus* (Philo)
Flor.	*Epistula ad Floram / Letter to Flora* (Ptolemy)
flor.	*floruit /* flourished
frg.	fragment
Fug.	*De fuga et inventione / On Flight and Finding* (Philo)
Gig.	*De gigantibus / On the Giants* (Philo)
Gorg.	*Gorgias* (Plato)
Gos. Jud.	*Gospel of Judas*
Gos. Mary	*Gospel of Mary (Magdalene)*
Gos. Pet.	*Gospel of Peter*
Gos. Phil.	*Gospel of Philip*
Gos. Thom.	*Gospel of Thomas*
Gos. Truth	*Gospel of Truth*
Haer.	*Adversus haereses / Against Heresies* (Irenaeus)
Haer.	*Refutatio omnium haeresium / Refutation of All Heresies* (Hippolytus)
Her.	*Quis rerum divinarum heres sit / Who Is the Heir?* (Philo)
Hercul. Oet.	*Hercules Oetaeus / Hercules on Oeta* (Seneca the Younger)
Hist.	*Historiae* (Tacitus)
Hist. eccl.	*Historia ecclesiastica / Church History* (Eusebius)
Hom.	*Homilies* (Pseudo-Clementine)
Homil.	*Paschal Homily* (Melito)
Hyp. Arch.	*Hypostasis of the Archons*
Inf. Gos. Thom.	*Infancy Gospel of Thomas*
Inst.	*Divinarum institutionum libri VII / The Divine Institutes* (Lactantius)
Interp. Know.	*Interpretation of Knowledge*
Jub.	*Jubilees*
L.A.B.	*Liber Antiquitatum Biblicarum*
Leg.	*Legatio pro Christianis* (Athenagoras)
Luct.	*De luctu / Funerals* (Lucian)
LXX	Septuagint
m. 'Edu.	Mishnah *'Eduyyot*
m. Sanh.	Mishnah *Sanhedrin*
Macc.	Maccabees
Magn.	*To the Magnesians* (Ignatius)
Mand.	*Mandates* (Shepherd of Hermas)
Marc.	*Adversus Marcionem / Against Marcion* (Tertullian)
Mart. Pol.	*Martyrdom of Polycarp*
Max. princ.	*Maxime cum principibus philosopho esse disserendum / That a Philosopher Ought to Converse Especially with Men in Power* (Plutarch)
Metam.	*Metamorphoses* (Apuleius)
Metam.	*Metamorphoses* (Ovid)
Migr.	*De migratione Abrahami / On the Migration of Abraham* (Philo)
Mos.	*De vita Mosis / On the Life of Moses* (Philo)
Nat. hist.	*Naturalis historia / Natural History* (Pliny the Elder)
NRSV	New Revised Standard Version
Oct.	*Octavius* (Minucius Felix)
Odes Sol.	*Odes of Solomon*
Opif.	*De opificio mundi / On the Creation of the World* (Philo)

Or.	Oratio / Discourse (Dio Chrysostom)
Pan.	Panarion (Adversus haereses) / Refutation of All Heresies (Epiphanius)
par.	parallel(s)
Pelag.	Adversus Pelagianos (Jerome)
Phaed.	Phaedo (Plato)
Phaedr.	Phaedrus (Plato)
Phil.	Philippians (Polycarp)
Phld.	To the Philadelphians (Ignatius)
Praem.	De Praemiis et poenis / On Rewards and Punishments (Philo)
Praescr.	De praescriptione haereticorum / Prescription against Heretics (Tertullian)
Pss. Sol.	Psalms of Solomon
Q	(The Sayings Gospel) Q
QE	Quaestiones et solutiones in Exodum / Questions and Answers on Exodus (Philo)
QG	Quaestiones et solutiones in Genesin / Questions and Answers on Genesis (Philo)
Quaest. conv.	Quaestiones convivales / Table Talk (Plutarch)
Rec.	Recognitions (Pseudo-Clementine)
Res.	De resurrectione carnis / The Resurrection of the Flesh (Tertullian)
Resp.	Respublica / Republic (Plato)
Rom.	To the Romans (Ignatius)
RSV	Revised Standard Version
Sera	De sera numinis vindicta / Delays of Divine Vengeance (Plutarch)
Sib. Or.	Sibylline Oracles
Sim.	Similitudes (Shepherd of Hermas)
Sir. Prol.	Sirach Prologue
Smyrn.	To the Smyrnaeans (Ignatius)
Spec.	De specialibus legibus / The Special Laws (Philo)
Spect.	De spectaculis /On the Spectacles (Tertullian)
Strom.	Stromata / Miscellanies (Clement of Alexandria)
Suav. Viv. Epic.	Non posse suaviter vivi secundum Epicurum/ Epicurus Makes a Pleasant Life Impossible (Plutarch)
T. Ab.	Testament of Abraham
T. Benj.	Testament of Benjamin
T. Dan	Testament of Dan
T. Job	Testament of Job
T. Jud.	Testament of Judah
T. Levi	Testament of Levi
T. Mos.	Testament of Moses

T. Sim.	Testament of Simeon
T. Zeb.	Testament of Zebulun
Test. 12 Patr.	Testaments of the Twelve Patriarchs
Testim. Truth	Testimony of Truth
Thom. Cont.	Book of Thomas the Contender
Trall.	To the Trallians (Ignatius)
Tranq. An.	De tranquillitate animi / On the Peace of Mind (Seneca the Younger)
Treat. Res.	Treatise on Resurrection
Treat. Seth	Second Treatise of the Great Seth
Tri. Trac.	Tripartite Tractate
Trim. Prot.	Trimorphic Protennoia / The Three Forms of the First Thought
Tusc.	Tusculanae disputationes (Cicero)
Urb. cond.	Ab urbe condita / History of Rome (Livy)
Val.	Adversus Valentinianos (Tertullian)
Virt.	De virtutibus / On the Virtues (Philo)
Vis.	Visions (Shepherd of Hermas)
Vit. Apoll.	Vita Apollonii (Philostratus)
Vit. Phil.	Vitae Philosophorum / Lives of Philosophers (Diogenes Laertius)
Vit. pud.	De vitioso pudore / On Compliancy (Plutarch)

SECONDARY SOURCES

AAR	American Academy of Religion
AASF	Annales Academiae scientiarum fennicae
AB	Anchor Bible
ABD	Anchor Bible Dictionary
AGJU	Arbeiten zur Geschichte des antiken Judentums und des Urchristentum
ANRW	Aufstieg und Niedergang der römischen Welt
ATD	Das Alte Testament Deutsch
BETL	Bibliotheca ephemeridum theologicarum lovaniensium
BEvT	Beiträge zur evangelischen Theologie
BHT	Beiträge zur historischen Theologie
Bib	Biblica
BibInt	Biblical Interpretation (series)
BJS	Brown Judaic Studies
BKAT	Biblischer Kommentar, Altes Testament
BNTC	Black's New Testament Commentaries
BWANT	Beiträge zur Wissenschaft vom Alten und Neuen Testament
BZNW	Beihefte zur Zeitschrift für die neutestamentliche Wissenschaft

CBQ	*Catholic Biblical Quarterly*
ConBNT	Coniectanea biblica: New Testament Series
CRINT	Compendia rerum iudaicarum ad Novum Testamentum
EBib	Etudes bibliques
EKKNT	Evangelisch-katholischer Kommentar zum Neuen Testament
ER	*Encyclopedia of Religion.* Ed. Mircea Eliade
EvT	*Evangelische Theologie*
FB	Forschung zur Bibel
FRLANT	Forschungen zur Religion und Literatur des Alten und Neuen Testaments
GTA	Göttinger theologische Arbeiten
HDR	Harvard Dissertations in Religion
HNT	Handbuch zum Neuen Testament
HSS	Harvard Semitic Studies
HTKNT	Herders theologischer Kommentar zum Neuen Testament
HTR	*Harvard Theological Review*
ICC	International Critical Commentary Series
JBL	*Journal of Biblical Literature*
JR	*Journal of Religion*
JRH	*Journal of Religious History*
JSJSup	Journal for the Study of Judaism Supplement
JSNT	*Journal for the Study of the New Testament*
JSNTSup	Journal for the Study of the New Testament: Supplement Series
JSOTSup	Journal for the Study of the Old Testament: Supplement Series
JSPSup	Journal for the Study of the Pseudepigrapha Supplement Series
JTS	*Journal of Theological Studies*
KEK	Kritisch-exegetischer Kommentar über das Neue Testament (Meyer-Kommentar)
KJV	King James Version
MNTC	Moffatt New Testament Commentary
NHS	Nag Hammadi Studies
NovTSup	Supplements to Novum Testamentum
NTAbh	Neutestamentliche Abhandlungen
NTD	Das Neue Testament Deutsch
NTOA	Novum Testamentum et Orbis Antiquus
NTS	*New Testament Studies*
OTL	Old Testament Library

QD	Quaestiones disputatae
RBL	*Review of Biblical Literature*
RNT	Regensburger Neues Testament
SAC	Studies in Antiquity and Christianity
SBL	Society of Biblical Literature
SBLDS	Society of Biblical Literature Dissertation Series
SBLMS	Society of Biblical Literature Monograph Series
SBS	Stuttgarter Bibelstudien
SBT	Studies in Biblical Theology
SE	*Studia evangelica*
SHAW	Sitzungen der Heidelberger Akademie der Wissenschaften
SJLA	Studies in Judaism in Late Antiquity
SJT	*Scottish Journal of Theology*
SNT	Studien zum Neuen Testament
SNTSMS	Society for New Testament Studies Monograph Series
STDJ	Studies on the Texts of the Desert of Judah
SUNT	Studien zur Umwelt des Neuen Testaments
Sup	Supplement
TANZ	Texte und Arbeiten zum neutestament-lichen Zeitalter
TDNT	*Theological Dictionary of the New Testament*
THKNT	Theologischer Handkommentar zum Neuen Testament
ThTo	*Theology Today*
TPINTC	TPI New Testament Commentaries
TRE	*Theologische Realenzyklopädie*
TZ	*Theologische Zeitschrift*
VCSup	Vigiliae christianae Supplement
VTSup	Vetus Testamentum Supplements
WBC	Word Biblical Commentary
WMANT	Wissenschaftliche Monographien zum Alten und Neuen Testament
WUNT	Wissenschaftliche Untersuchungen zum Neuen Testament
WW	*Word and World*
ZNW	*Zeitschrift für die neutestamentliche Wissen-schaft und die Kunde der älteren Kirche*
ZTK	*Zeitschrift für Theologie und Kirche*

Introduction

The aim of this book is to give an overall account of early Christian beliefs. Such books are in short supply.[1] To be sure, a number of works cover much of the same ground, but do so from a different perspective and with a different aim. They include histories of early Christianity, which describe the emergence and development of the movement during its first century or centuries;[2] accounts of the social world of early Christianity;[3] and introductions to the New Testament or to early Christian literature at large.[4] I draw on their findings but am content with a more limited task. The "external" history and the history of the literary products form the necessary background for the mapping of the religious ideas on which I am going to focus. The love-hate relationship of this book to works called "theologies of the New Testament" will be discussed shortly.

My focus will be on the ideas of early Christians, but I want to emphasize the close connection of this thought world within its wider cultural context. Therefore the book starts with a section called "Roots and Starting Points." This section attempts to give a brief introduction to the wider world in which Christianity arose: the story of the rise and development of Christian beliefs involves among other things a shift from the Jewish bedrock of the Christian movement (chapter 1) to interaction with the world of Greco-Roman thought (chapter 2). Chapter 3 adds a survey of the literature produced by early Christians, placed within the framework of the crucial events in their history. These introductory chapters are mainly written for readers less familiar with the study of Christian beginnings. More advanced readers may wish to skip the earlier chapters and move directly to chapter 4; however, some academic judgments that will affect the presentation are stated in chapters 1–3, so that I will not argue about issues of authorship, dates, and the like in the main portion of the book.

The term *Christian* smacks of anachronism but is difficult to avoid; it would be cumbersome to dispense with it altogether. It should be understood here in a weak sense: the noun *Christian*

2   denotes all persons in whose symbolic worlds Jesus of Nazareth held a central place, one way or another; the adjective refers to their qualities and views. Using the term does *not* imply that there already was in existence a distinct new religion;[5] at what point one can meaningfully speak of Christianity in that sense remains disputed. In many connections it is convenient to speak rather of (members of) the "Jesus movement," or of followers of Jesus, especially with regard to those branches of the movement that preserved a basically Jewish identity. Nevertheless I have, for pragmatic reasons, retained the conventional "(early) Christian" as an umbrella term.[6] Thus I shall at times speak even of Jewish-born followers of Jesus as "Christians," but it should be understood that they may (or may not) be members of a group that still exists within the confines of Judaism.

Focusing on beliefs, or religious ideas, may seem a narrow task, for clearly the cognitive aspect is only one of several dimensions in a religious tradition.[7] A full discussion of early Christian religion would indeed have to include many other aspects,[8] but it is not my intention to provide a full discussion; that would vastly exceed my powers. I am consciously concentrating on a relatively small part—and the size and richness of that part alone makes me painfully aware of my limitations. I do not claim that the cognitive aspect is the most important one in religion. On the contrary, I think that Ninian Smart is right in claiming that "histories of religion have tended to exaggerate the importance of scriptures and doctrines"; while this is "not too surprising since so much of our knowledge of past religions must come from the documents which have been passed on by the scholarly elite," it is clearly unbalanced for histories of faith to concentrate on doctrinal disputes. But Smart

also warns us not to go to the other extreme, neglecting "the essential intellectual component of religion."[9]

A. J. M. Wedderburn makes a related point in his history of early Christianity: however much one may "deplore the way in which the New Testament has been studied for its ideas alone, in isolation from the social and cultural realities in which those ideas are rooted, it would be equally one-sided to ignore *the impact and the formative influence of those ideas upon the life* of the early Christian community."[10] And not just on the life of *early* Christians, of course. I think that my limiting myself to an analysis of religious thought is justified in view of our history: surely ideas and concepts loom large enough among the Christian influences on Western and other cultures to keep some general interest in them alive.[11] Yet I do not want to explore ideas as if they were floating in the air. On the contrary, they are to be firmly rooted precisely in the "social and cultural realities": in the experience of those who gave verbal expression to the ideas.

The Relationship to "New Testament Theology"

My views of how to conceive the task of dealing with beliefs, stated in earlier publications, has proved controversial. I therefore wish to clarify the issues by restating my views and briefly discussing some other opinions.

In its focus on religious ideas this book bears a family resemblance to the genre of New Testament Theology. It is, however, a somewhat distant cousin—some might say, a black sheep in the family[12]—indeed, it has been conceived of as an alternative to these theologies. This means taking up a program sketched as early as 1897 by William Wrede but badly neglected during most of the twentieth century.[13] As Gerd Theissen points out, New Testament theologies present "an internal Christian perspective," being "written for Christians, as a rule for those who are to become clergy." An alternative account, by contrast, seeks to approach the content of early Christianity "in such a way that it is accessible to men and women whether or not they are religious"; this is a cultural task, rather than a religious one, as the texts and convictions in question "are part of the basic cultural information of human history."[14] If it is assumed (and this seems largely to be the default assumption, though a broader view is possible)[15] that theology must present an internal faith perspective,[16] then a work of this kind falls outside theology into the field of comparative religion or *Religionswissenschaft*[17]—even though no clear boundary can be drawn, let alone a black-and-white contrast established, between the two.[18]

This way of defining the task means—to use catchwords that are unfortunately easily misunderstood and exposed to caricatures (sometimes vicious)[19]—that the approach has to be "descriptive" and, within the confines of what is possible, even strive for "objectivity."[20] The word *descriptive* was once introduced into the hermeneutic discussion to denote a contrast to a *confessional* understanding, which implied that exegesis should be in agreement with doctrine, or at least come forward with an edifying religious message. In this vein, I use the word simply in the sense that the emerging construction is *not prescriptive* or normative.[21] It does not follow that the topics "described" are understood to be static; a dynamic process can perfectly well be the object of "description."[22] Nor does *objective* mean that

one claims to be in possession of the Truth! The point is simply that one attempts to analyze the sources independently of whether one approves or disapproves of the ideas found in them.[23]

In the descriptive method, the tool kit of the scholar does not contain such supernatural or metaempirical concepts as revelation, inspiration, act(s) of God(s), or "Word of God." Such insider language belongs to a possible (but not mandatory) theological assessment of the findings in another context. A descriptive account must deal with the religious ideas of the early Christians as human constructs and apply to them methods similar to those that it would apply to any other texts,[24] an approach that I have called "fair play." Delbert Burkett makes the point very clear in a recent textbook:

> In an academic setting, we approach the New Testament in such a way that both Christians and interested non-Christians can participate. We seek to understand the New Testament without necessarily ascribing normative status to it. This approach is like that of a Christian student who wishes to study the scripture and religion of Islam or Hinduism. The student may want to have a description of these religions without necessarily adopting them. In an academic setting, then, we treat Christianity, Islam, Hinduism, and all other religions in the same way: we seek to understand them, not necessarily to adopt or practice them.[25]

Neither the existence nor nonexistence of God(s) is taken for granted. Conceptions of the divine, not God(s), are the object of the investigation.[26] What are accessible to scholarly analysis are human experiences and their interpretations; discussions about what may or may not lie behind those experiences belong to another context.[27]

4

Here the problem arises of how one should deal with the word *god*. Should it be capitalized and if so, when? I have decided to follow John Barclay's somewhat unusual practice of capitalizing the word in *all* contexts, whether in reference to the God of Jews and Christians or to the God/esses of Gentiles. Barclay's explanation of his reasons reflects the spirit of fair play at its best: "I have felt it better to equalize all parties in this matter, rather than succumb to the Jewish and Christian presumption that only their Deity is truly 'God,' while the rest are merely 'gods' (or worse)." Alternatively, it would have been possible to employ the lower case ("god," "gods") throughout; Barclay chose to use the upper case "since it customarily conveys respect for the beliefs and practices of the relevant worshippers."[28]

The specific features of this book, then, include the following.

- *It is not limited to the New Testament canon, but deals with all material down to the last decades of the second century*, occasionally casting a glance at even later developments. Wrede noted that "no New Testament writing was born with the predicate 'canonical' attached";[29] the canon is a later construction that came gradually into existence in a complicated process during the second to fourth centuries. While "New Testament theology" can by definition limit itself to the documents that make up our present New Testament, a descriptive-historical presentation must take into account all available evidence on equal terms.[30] The canon is not a starting point of the inquiry; instead, the beginnings of the process that later led to the formation of the canon are one of the topics to be considered within the account.[31]

- *It makes no distinction between "orthodoxy" and "heresy"* (except as historical notions). The blurring of the orthodox and the heretical follows from the previous point. It is imperative to include the important texts found in the twentieth century—the *Gospel of Thomas* and other writings from the Nag Hammadi library—as significant witnesses in their own right. The conservative Jewish Christians who came to stay outside what became mainstream Christianity likewise deserve a place. Yet doing away with canonical boundaries is not just a question of sources, for the canonical *point of view* must not guide the account either.[32] New Testament theologies tend to give very much space to Paul—as the canon, of course, does—and regard him as more or less normative.[33] In the present book Paul is seen as *one* (prominent) person among many (though I am afraid that he may still have too dominant a position!). Paul's Christian opponents, and those he opposed, should be taken just as seriously as Christians as the apostle himself.[34] Presumably all sides in a conflict had a point, and fair play demands that scholars try to put themselves into the shoes of each. The same applies to the later conflicts between proto-orthodox (the term will be explained shortly) and gnostic Christians. One has to avoid judging the conflicts from the point of view of the victors alone, recognizing (in contrast to a strictly confessional approach) that the development of religious beliefs "is not teleologically guided by any predetermined direction or destiny."[35]

- *It considers the roots of early Christian ideas in their cultural and religious environment.* To emphasize this (uncontroversial) point, a (very) brief outline of the Jewish and Greco-Roman context is prefixed.

- *It does not focus on "doctrines"* (though the development that led to the fixation of Christian doctrines, mostly after the period in question, is not without interest), *but on the formation of beliefs in interaction with the experience* of individuals and communities. The term *Rise* in my title indicates that this is understood as a living, dynamic process.[36] This process can be described as reinterpretation of traditions in new situations in light of new insights and experiences.[37] But it should be noted that "experience" here refers more to *social* experience than to private inner emotions.[38] It is often impossible to penetrate into the individual experience of any single author or group, so much so that in working out my account I have found myself putting more emphasis on the traditions and less on the experiences than I had originally assumed. But on a general level the impact of social experiences, often conflict experiences, is crucial, at least in heuristic terms. Such experiences include the Jewish War, the rejection of the Christian message by Jewish recipients, the pressure from suspicious pagan neighbors, and the persecutions by the state.

- *It concentrates on great lines and main problems and opts for a thematic organization.* New Testament theologies are often organized according to writings: Paul, the Synoptic Gospels, the Johannine writings, and so on. Comparisons among the different writings tend to be accidental,[39] and Paul is likely to receive exaggerated attention, as the New Testament contains so many writ-

ings from his pen. It is also possible to organize an overall account in chronological or tradition-historical terms, but here the fragmentary nature of the early sources causes problems;[40] one is forced to resort to very hypothetical constructions.[41] Some have suggested that we have lost no less than 85 percent of Christian literature from the first two centuries—and that includes only the literature we know about![42] "We have to be careful that we don't suppose it is possible to reconstruct the whole of early Christian history and practice out of the few surviving texts that remain. Our picture will always be partial—not only because so much is lost, but because early Christian practices were so little tied to durable writing."[43] In view of such considerations a thematic structure seems justified. Nevertheless, I have also tried to pay attention to diachronic developments in the subsections of the thematic chapters, where I do distinguish between earlier and later sources. In addition, one may assume that modern readers can profit more from a sketch of the great lines and main issues than from an exposition of the profiles of individual authors. Yet any choice of organizing the material has its advantages and disadvantages.[44] In order to offer the reader at least a glimpse of the diachronic development as I see it, as well as of the character of the main sources and authors, I have prefixed to the thematic main part a (very compressed) chapter on events, persons, and sources.

- *It tries to do justice to the diversity of early Christianity.* Today even conservative authors admit that within the New Testament alone a considerable theological

6

diversity prevails. This is felt to be a problem that should be solved either by showing that discrepancies are only apparent[45] or that beneath the diversity a fundamental unity can be established after all. A more radical solution is to identify what is often called "a canon within the canon," the basic truth or principle with the aid of which the various parts of the New Testament are evaluated. But as W. G. Kümmel pointed out at the end of his *New Testament Theology*, the problem of unity and diversity is a theological one: it arises only for believers who are convinced that they encounter in these writings "the knowledge of God's revelation in Christ." The question of a common message "does not thrust itself upon us from the involvement with the proclamation of these witnesses themselves, who stand in no direct connection with one another, but from the awareness of their common membership in the canon."[46] While there is nothing inherently impossible in the question about unity being asked even in a historical perspective, the diversity seems so obvious that unity can be sought only on a rather abstract level; quite often authors of New Testament theologies end up with assertions of basic unity that stand in tension to their own presentations of the diversity.[47] When the perspective is widened to comprise even noncanonical materials, a further increase in diversity is a natural consequence.

+   *It acknowledges intellectual and moral problems in the sources.* With regard to the former, a case in point is the question of possible inconsistencies or contradictions in Paul's thought; this question has almost become a watershed between theological and *religions-*

wissenschaftlich approaches to Paul.[48] As for the latter, the striking reluctance of New Testament theologies to even mention the notion of eternal torment in hell, imposed on the majority of humankind according to central New Testament texts,[49] is difficult to explain in any other way than as an apologetic attempt to assuage an ugly side in the biblical message. A *religionswissenschaftlich* approach has no inhibitions on such points (though I fail to see why sharp ethical criticism could not be applied even within a theological approach). *Relative* value judgments that deal with the human decisions and attitudes of those who produced the relevant texts, or with the effects of these texts, are by no means prohibited in a descriptive account as I understand it.[50]

+   *It hints at the subsequent reception and influence of the ideas,* thus helping to build a bridge toward the present. This cannot be done in any systematic way, but happens on an eclectic basis in the form of a few examples.[51]

THE STRUCTURE OF THE PRESENT WORK

The choice of starting point deserves a comment. Obviously, it would not be wise to start an account of *early* Christian ideas with an exposition of the Trinity. The decision to choose anthropology as the starting point, favored by interpreters inclined to existentialist theology, also seems to lead to undue modernizing. Monotheism as the common basis for Judaism and nascent Christianity would be a possibility, and the same is true of Christology; self-evidently Jesus has a central place in Christianity. Without denying the legitimacy of other options, I shall nevertheless start with "eschatology" (after three background chapters). The quotation marks indicate that the term is not used quite in the sense it has in traditional dogmatics. There eschatology, the doctrine of the "last things," is explained in the last chapter, as a kind of appendix. In an account of early Christian religion, by contrast, "the end" arguably belongs to the *first* chapter. For a vivid expectation of a great and decisive *turn of history*, brought about by the God of Israel, was basic to the genesis of the new religious movement from which Christianity was to develop.[52] Early Christology can be understood as part of eschatology (rather than vice versa): expectation of a redeemer figure was often connected with the expectation of the turn of history, and the understanding of Jesus as the Messiah/Christ has to do with this. A comprehensive account of eschatology, which also encompasses its transformation into something else (the great turn of history comes to be replaced by fulfillment in the beyond), could easily grow almost to an overall presentation of early Christianity.[53] This is an important reason for starting my account with the expectation of the great turn.

Indeed, most of the topics to be dealt with hang together with eschatology and its transformation; their treatment in different chapters, rather than directly in connection with eschatology, is due to pragmatic reasons. Nowhere is this clearer than in chapter 5, "After Death: The Destiny of the Individual," which deals with the notions of judgment and afterlife. All this could well have found a place in the previous chapter; but then that chapter would have grown unreasonably long. In chapter 4 the focus is on collective expectation, in chapter 5 on the destiny of the individual, though some overlapping has been unavoidable.

Chapters 6 and 7 deal with sin and salvation. This pair of terms is likely to evoke associations of individualistic piety in modern minds, but originally the notion of "salvation" hangs closely together with collective, national eschatology: the plight from which Israel is expected to be saved is attacks of enemy troops or occupation by a hostile power. The transformation of this concrete salvation into something more spiritual, either in this life or in a transcendent reality beyond this world, hangs together with the transformation of eschatology, hinted at above. Instead of enemy armies, one comes to think of sin(s) or hostile cosmic powers as the main threats to human life. The obstacles and means of salvation are obviously interrelated: the path to salvation envisaged by an author depends on his understanding of the human condition. In this case, too, pragmatic considerations about size caused me to deal with the topics separately: first the human condition, then the salvation. The focus of chapter 7 will be on the preconditions or means of salvation: how and why can one find a place in the number of the saved (or stay there)?

Only after having dealt with salvation do I turn to the person and work of the Savior. Once more, separating the issues is, in itself, artificial; one's view of who Jesus was and what he achieved has very much to do with one's vision of salvation. In this case, too, it is obvious that pragmatic considerations have dictated the course of the work. What may be a surprise, though, is my decision to postpone the chapter on Christology not only after eschatology but even after soteriology (to use the conventional doctrinal terms). I find the order a matter of taste; my decision reflects to a degree my conclusion that there is a certain ambiguity in Jesus' place in the scheme of

8 salvation as presented by certain early Christian authors. Notwithstanding the undeniable centrality that the person of Jesus has in Christian doctrine, one may claim that it is subordinated to the vision of salvation. In addition, the order of the chapters reflects the changes of emphasis that took place in Christian thought during the early generations: in the proclamation of Jesus and in the thought world of his first followers, eschatology (the imminent expectation of the kingdom of God) is the focal point; in the theology of Paul, the doctrine of salvation (participation in the body of Christ) stands in the center; it is only in the Gospel of John that the questions who Jesus is and what his relationship to God the Father is (questions that will stay on the theological agenda during the next two or three centuries, if not ever after) become truly central.

A short chapter on the spirit follows, intended to cast light on the experiential side of early Christianity. As may be expected, it has connections to all previous chapters: the "pouring out" of God's spirit on the followers of Jesus in the form of ecstatic phenomena was taken to be an end-time event; the spirit was conceived of as the power of Christian life, necessary to salvation; Jesus was seen as a bearer of the spirit par excellence. Some small signs of the personification of the spirit, which would later lead to the construction of the doctrine of Trinity, are also to be seen.

Chapters 10 and 11 deal with the forging of Christian identity. Once again, the place of the chapters in the whole is not self-evident.

This is especially true of chapter 10, on Christian identity vis-à-vis Judaism. One may feel that this issue should have been treated earlier. In the formation of Christian tradition, as in religious traditions in general, practice surely preceded theology. The formation of Christian beliefs had very much to do with practical issues connected with one's relation to the Jewish Torah, and a number of theological issues can be understood only in that connection; Paul's famous "doctrine" of justification by faith is a case in point. (Here, as often, "doctrine" is a misnomer, as the discourse of justification seems to have arisen as an attempt to legitimize a practical step: the acceptance of Gentile members into the Christian community without requiring circumcision and observance of biblical dietary rules of them.) It would have been proper to deal with these matters as early as possible; on the other hand, I just could not interrupt the flow from eschatology via soteriology to Christology. I can only emphasize that I regard the subject matter of this chapter as absolutely pivotal for any attempt to understand how Christianity emerged and, for better or for worse, separated from Judaism.

Many of the early Christians came to feel that they were a "third race," to be distinguished both from Jews and from Gentiles. Their ambivalent relationship to Greco-Roman paganism, including its religious practices and its ethical and philosophical achievements, is discussed separately, in chapter 11. A final chapter is devoted to the development toward Christian orthodoxy that took place in the second century.[54]

Timeline

General History & Literature	Jewish & Christian History	Jewish & Christian Literature*
B.C.E.		
	c. 1000–587 Time of the monarchy in Judah	
	587 Jerusalem destroyed by the Babylonians; Exile	
	539 Fall of Babylon to Cyrus of Persia; Exiles permitted to return	
	539–331 Persian (Achaemenid) period	
c. 530–500 Pythagoras		
	520–515? Rebuilding of the temple	
		c. 500–400? Deuteronomistic history edited and completed
c. 483–423 Empedocles		
	c. 450 Ezra in Jerusalem	
427–347 Plato		
c. 400–320 Diogenes of Sinope, founder of Cynicism		c. 400–300? Main parts of Jewish scripture (the Hebrew Bible) completed
341–270 Epicurus		
337–323 Alexander the Great		
	332 Conquest of Palestine by Alexander	
	c. 300–200 Palestine under the Ptolemies of Egypt	
		c. 250– Beginnings of the Septuagint translation
		before 200 early parts of *1 Enoch*
	c. 200–140 Palestine under the Seleucids of Syria	
		c. 180 Ben Sira
	175–164 Antiochus IV Epiphanes rules Syria	
		c. 170–140? *Jubilees*
	167 Desecration of the temple by Antiochus; Maccabean uprising	
		c. 165 Book of Daniel
	164 Reconsecration of the temple	
	140–63 Hasmonean rule	

continues on following page

*Many of the dates in this column are tentative. Jewish writings and authors are marked with shaded boxes.

General History & Literature	Jewish & Christian History	Jewish & Christian Literature
	135–104 John Hyrcanus (conquers Samaria)	
	c. 100–50 First settlement of Qumran	c. 100 Wisdom of Solomon
		c. 100? *Rule of Community* (1 QS), *Damascus Document* (CD) and other writings from Qumran
63 Augustus born	63 Jerusalem falls to Pompey	
63–43 Cicero		
58–50 Julius Caesar's Gallic campaigns		
55 Caesar invades Britain		c. 50 *Psalms of Solomon*
		c. 50? *War Scroll* (1 QM)
49 Civil War between Pompey and Caesar		
48 Pompey killed		
44 Caesar assassinated (15 March)		
42 Caesar included among Gods of Rome		
40 Virgil, *Fourth Eclogue*	40 Parthians invade Syria	
	37 Herod captures Jerusalem; installed as client king of Judea	
31 Battle of Actium	31 First abandonment of Qumran settlement, due to earthquake	
31 B.C.E.–14 C.E. Octavian (Augustus) rules Rome		
30 Tribunician power for life bestowed on Octavian		
27 Octavian receives title of Augustus		
	20 Herod begins Second Temple	
	c. 6? Jesus of Nazareth born	
	4 Herod dies	
B.C.E. ~~~~➤ **C.E.**		
	4 B.C.E.–6 C.E. Archelaus, ethnarch of Judea Reoccupation of Qumran	
	4 B.C.E.–34 C.E. Philip, tetrarch of Northeastern Palestine	
	4 B.C.E.–39 C.E. Herod Antipas, tetrarch of Galilee	
c. 4–96 Apollonius of Tyana		
	6 Judea becomes Roman province; the Census; Judas the Gaulanite revolts	
		c. 10–30? *Testament of Moses*

General History & Literature	Jewish & Christian History	Jewish & Christian Literature
14 Augustus dies; accepted among Gods of the state		
14–37 Tiberius, emperor		
	18–37 Caiaphas, high priest	
	19 Expulsion of Jews from Rome	
		c. 20–50 Philo, writings
	26–28? John the Baptist's ministry	
	26–36 Pontius Pilate prefect of Judea	
	c. 28 Jesus baptized by John John executed by Antipas	
	c. 28–30(?) Jesus' mission	
	c. 30 Jesus' crucifixion	
	c. 30 Followers of Jesus regather in Jerusalem	
	c. 32–35(?) "Hebrews" and "Hellenists" in Jerusalem Stephen killed "Hellenists" in Antioch Conversion of Paul	
	36 Pilate recalled to face charges of maladministration	
37–41 Caligula, emperor	37 Caiaphas deposed	
	38 Anti-Jewish riot in Alexandria	
	c. 30–50? Simon Magus, in Samaria, *flor.*	
	40 Caligula's anti-Jewish policy provokes unrest in Palestine	
40–65 Seneca, *flor.*	c. 40–62 James, brother of Jesus, in control in the congregation of Jerusalem	
41–54 Claudius, emperor	41–44 Agrippa I king of Judea and Samaria	
	42(?) James, son of Zebedee, martyred	
43 Rome invades Britain		
	44 Agrippa dies Judea becomes a province	
c. 45–125 Plutarch	c. 45 Theudas attempts an unarmed rebellion	
	c. 46–48 Paul and Barnabas's missionary journey	
	c. 49 Apostolic conference in Jerusalem	

continues on following page

General History & Literature	Jewish & Christian History	Jewish & Christian Literature
	c. 49 "Antiochian incident" (Paul's conflict with Peter and others)	
	49 Expulsion of Jews from Rome	
	49–58 Paul's missionary journeys	
		c. 50(?) *Book of Enoch* compiled
		c. 50–56 Paul, letters to the churches: 1 Thessalonians (c. 50), 1 and 2 Corinthians, Galatians, Philemon, Philippians, Romans (c. 56)
51–52 Gallio, proconsul of Achaia		
	c. 53–56 Paul in Ephesus	
54–68 Nero, emperor		
	c. 56–57 "The Egyptian" attempts rebellion	
	c. 58 Paul taken prisoner in Jerusalem	
		c. 60–70? Sayings Gospel (Q)
	c. 60–80? Menander, *flor.*	c. 60–80? 4 Maccabees
	c. 62 Paul martyred in Rome	
	62 James of Jerusalem murdered	
	63(?) Peter in Rome(?)	
64 Great fire in Rome	64 Neronian persecution	
	66–74 First Jewish War	
68 Nero commits suicide	68 Qumran settlement destroyed	
69–79 Vespasian, emperor; policy of Romanization and urbanization in provinces		
	70 Jerusalem falls to Titus	c. 70 Gospel of Mark
		c. 70–80 Colossians
	after 70 Establishment of Academy at Javneh under Johanan ben Zakkai	
	74 Masada captured	
	c. 75 Imposition of "Fiscus Judaicus"	c. 75–79 Josephus, *Jewish War*
		c. 75–100 2 Thessalonians
79 Vesuvius erupts, destroys Pompeii and Herculaneum		
79–81 Titus, emperor		
		c. 80–90 Gospel of Matthew
		c. 80–95 1 Peter
		c. 80–100? Epistle of James
80 Colosseum dedicated		
80–120 Epictetus, *flor.*		

General History & Literature	Jewish & Christian History	Jewish & Christian Literature
81–96 Domitian, emperor		
		c. 85–95 Ephesians
89 Philosophers and astrologers banished from Rome		
		c. 90 Gospel of John
		c. 90–100 Gospel of Luke
		c. 90–100 Epistle to the Hebrews
		c. 93 Josephus, *Antiquities of the Jews*
	c. 95–115? harassments of Christians in Asia Minor	c. 95 Revelation of John
96–98 Nerva, emperor		
98–117 Trajan, emperor		
	112–113 Pliny-Trajan correspondence	c. 100 *1 Clement*
		c. 100? Epistle of Jude
		c. 100 *4 Ezra*
		c. 100 *Odes of Solomon*
		c. 100 *Didache; Gospel of Thomas* (final form)
		c. 100–110? Acts of the Apostles
		c. 100–150 *Gospel of Peter, Apocalypse of Peter*
		c. 100–120? Christian editing of the *Testaments of the Twelve Patriarchs*
		c. 100–150? *Gospel of the Ebionites, Gospel of the Hebrews, Dialogue of the Savior, Gospel of Mary*; Christian editing of *Ascension of Isaiah*
114–17 Roman war against Parthia; Roman Empire reaches maximum extent		
c. 115–120? Tacitus, *Annals*	115–17 Jewish uprisings in Cyprus, Egypt, Cyrenaica, and Mesopotamia	c. 115? *Letters of Ignatius*
117–38 Hadrian, emperor		
c. 120? Suetonius, *Lives of the Caesars*		c. 120? 1 John
		c. 120? Epistle of *Barnabas* Possible date of earliest Gospel fragments found in Egypt Papias (fragments)
		c. 120–130? *Letter of Polycarp to the Philippians*
		c. 120–130? 2–3 John

continues on following page

General History & Literature	Jewish & Christian History	Jewish & Christian Literature
		c. 120–140? 2 Peter
		c. 120–140 Pastoral epistles (1–2 Timothy, Titus)
		c. 120–150 Basilides, *flor.*
		c. 125 Quadratus, earliest Apologist
	c. 130 Justin Martyr converts	c. 130 Aristides, *Apology*
	132–35 Second Jewish War: Bar Kokhba revolts Aelia Capitolina founded	
138–61 Antoninus Pius, emperor		
		c. 140 *Shepherd of Hermas*
		c. 140–60 Valentinus, *flor.*
		c. 143 Marcion, *Contradictions*
	144 Marcion expelled from Roman community; begins missionary activity. Marcionite congregations flourish until early third century	
		c. 150? *Acts of Thecla*
		c. 150 Ptolemy, *Letter to Flora*
		150–160 Justin Martyr, *Apologies* and *Dialogue with Trypho*
		c. 150–170 Heracleon, *Commentary on John*
	c. 150– "monarchic episcopate" emerges	c. 150–200 *Epistle to Diognetus*
		c. 150–200 *"Ebionite History"* (*Rec.* 1.27-71, within the *Pseudoclementines*)
		c. 150–200? *Gospel of Truth*, the *Apocryphon of John*, and many other documents from the Nag Hammadi Library
		c. 150–200? *Protevangelium of James*
	155/156 Polycarp martyred	
		160–70 Melito of Sardis, *flor.*
161–80 Marcus Aurelius, emperor		
165 Plague spreads from Mesopotamia	165 Justin martyred	
165–66 Lucian, *On the Death of Peregrinus*	165–70 Sporadic persecutions in province of Asia	
c. 170 Apuleius, *Golden Ass*	c. 170 Montanist movement starts in Phrygia	
		c. 170–85 Tatian, *flor.*
171–80 Marcus Aurelius, *Meditations*		
		c. 175 Hegesippus, *Memoirs*

General History & Literature	Jewish & Christian History	Jewish & Christian Literature
	177 Persecution at Lyons	177–80 Athenagoras, *Supplication for the Christians*
178 Celsus, *True Reason* against Christians	178 Irenaeus, bishop of Lyons	
	180 Scillitan Martyrs at Carthage	180 Theophilus of Antioch; *To Autolycus*
	c. 180 Catechetical School at Alexandria (Pantaenus)	c. 180 Irenaeus, *Against Heresies*
	c. 180 Marcus the "Magician"	
180–92 Commodus, emperor		c. 180–200 Clement of Alexandria, *flor.*
		c. 185–254 Origen
		c. 195–220 Tertullian, *flor.*
		c. 200–235 Hippolytus, *flor.*
		c. 200 Mishna
	c. 200– position of women declines	c. 200? *Acts of Paul, Acts of Peter Infancy Gospel of Thomas*
		c. 220 "Circuits of Peter" (within the *Pseudoclementines*)
c. 222 Philostratus, *Life of Apollonius*		
249–51 Decius, emperor	249–51 General persecution of Christians	
		c. 250? *Gospel of Philip*
	256–336 Arius	
	295–373 Athanasius	
		after 300 *Pseudoclementines* (Homilies, Recognitions)
	303–11 Persecution of Christians	
306 (324)–337 Constantine the Great, emperor		
	313 Christianity officially tolerated, then favored by Constantine	
	325 Council of Nicaea	
		c. 350-420 Jerome
		354–430 Augustine
		c. 375 Epiphanius, *Refutation of All Heresies*
	381 Council of Constantinople	c. 380–410 Pelagius, *flor.*
		c. 450? Palestinian Talmud completed
	451 Council of Chalcedon	
		c. 550? Babylonian Talmud completed

PART I

ROOTS
&
STARTING POINTS

1.1 Palestine in the time of Jesus

Second Temple Judaism

In 587 or 586 B.C.E., Babylonian troops conquered Jerusalem, carried out a massacre among its inhabitants, destroyed the temple, and put an end to the existence of the small state of Judah as an independent kingdom. Several thousand members of the upper class were deported to Babylon. The catastrophe initiated a far-reaching ideological process, when some literate members of the exiled community set out to rebuild its identity with the aid of a theological reinterpretation of Israel's past. This process resulted in a thorough change in worldview and religious practice.[1]

A word on the nomenclature is in order here.[2] "Judah" is unequivocally a political term, referring to a territory in central Palestine with Jerusalem as its center; in discussions of the Persian period it is often also called "Yehud." By contrast, "Israel" is used in many different senses. As a political term it can denote either the territory ruled in the tenth century B.C.E. by the kings David and Solomon or, after the split of that kingdom, its northern part that had Samaria as its last capital. This northern kingdom fell to the Assyrians in 722 B.C.E. and its upper-class members were deported to Assyria. The surviving southern kingdom, Judah, could now also be called "Israel," and its inhabitants "Israelites"; this was, however, a religious or spiritual (rather than political) designation, which implied the idea of a people in a special relationship to its God, Yahweh, a relationship built (according to the master story in the Hebrew Bible) in premonarchic times when "Israel" had consisted of an alliance of twelve "Israelite" tribes. As a religious ("eschatological") idea, even the notion of "greater Israel" could be maintained: ten of the tribes had been dispersed and lost in the disaster of 722, but the hope gained ground that Yahweh would one day gather "all Israel" back together. In light of this linguistic development it is possible to speak of "*Israel's* religious past" even with regard to the conditions in the monarchy of *Judah*. It was all-important to the exiled (and returning) "Judeans" to maintain continuity (even if it was largely imagined continuity) with the Israel and Israelites—the beloved people of Yahweh—of the past.

THE AFTERMATH OF THE EXILE

When the Persian ruler Cyrus conquered Babylon in 539 B.C.E., he permitted the Judeans, or Jews,[3] to return to their homeland. Some took the opportunity. The returnees came to be involved in conflicts with the mass of the population that had stayed in the land, but with support from the Persian king they managed to assert themselves, gain power, and even build a modest new temple. Its dedication, traditionally dated in 516 B.C.E.,[4] marks the beginning of what is generally called Second Temple Judaism.[5] Its religion came to be very different from what had been the case before the exile.

In early times, Yahweh had been the main Deity and the official God of the state, but worship in Judah did not differ very much from that in surrounding regions.[6] The official religion was centered on the temple in Jerusalem and its sacrificial cult. Like other Near Eastern peoples, the Israelites favored the cult of their own national Deity, but other Gods and Goddesses were also worshiped, probably without major problems. In the new situation, when national existence was threatened, this "tolerant monolatry" (worship of one God) was challenged. During and after the exile Israel's religious past was radically reinterpreted by the scribes who constituted what scholars call the Deuteronomistic school.[7] The disaster that had happened was interpreted as a punishment for the worship of God/esses other than Yahweh. The Deuteronomists thus created a (historically quite distorted) picture of the past, in which Israel was constantly at war with the demands of its own religion. This "intolerant monolatry" was finally transformed into exclusive monotheism with separatist tendencies that amounted to a thorough break with Israel's own past.[8] "The differences are so substantial that the very fundaments of religion had been changed."[9] Israel's relationship with Yahweh was reinterpreted as a covenant modeled on Near Eastern treaties of kings with their vassals; from now on his law (Torah) was the center of Israel's religion.[10] Collective repentance of past sins was called for so that God would fulfill his promises to the ancestors and turn the fortunes of his people.

The tradition ascribes a crucial part in the process to Ezra, a scribe who arrived in Jerusalem from Babylon, possibly in 458 B.C.E. He introduced in Judah a book of the Torah, making the people commit itself to this law by way of a common confession. The historical value of the biblical account of Ezra is controversial (and generally overestimated in scholarship),[11] but the story reflects the fact that the roots of the Torah as a document lie in the Babylonian exile, where the "nomistic" editors of Deuteronomy and the Deuteronomistic History played a decisive role. Ezra appears as an embodiment of the scribal class that came to possess a leading role as innovators of the religion.[12] The increased esteem of written texts and the vast literary activity, out of proportion with the modest resources available, point in the same direction. Identity was established and religious boundaries were drawn on the basis of a written law and written prophecies.

In the religious world of Deuteronomy, the temple and the cult were subordinated to a written text that demanded constant study and interpretation. Yahweh himself acted as a heavenly scribe who twice wrote the Decalogue on stone (Deut. 5:22; 10:4) and ordered the storage of the tablets in a special wooden ark.[13] Gradually, the written Torah grew round this core, when legal material from various sources was put together; it came to be thought that this Torah as a whole had been revealed by Yahweh to Moses, the famous leader who had once led the people to freedom from slavery in Egypt.

The efforts of the scribes (including priestly scribes) led to the gradual emergence of an extensive sacred scripture that Jews came to call the "TaNaK"[14] and Christians the "Old Testament"; modern scholars speak of the "Hebrew Bible." "In the Persian period, the various strands of the Torah were woven together for the final time, and the resulting product became the 'constitution,' or foundation document for all forms of Judaism."[15] The Torah amounted to a compromise between the interests of the scribes and those of the priests, for it combined laws that focused on the temple and cult with others that lacked such concerns. Somewhat later, the words of prophets (and some stories about them) were gathered and edited into an authoritative collection that complemented the Torah. Finally, a collection of "writings" (wisdom literature and cultic psalms) came to be added to the Torah and the prophets (cf. Sir. prologue 8-10). By the time of the early Christians this tripartite scripture formed the authoritative basis of Jewish life and thought and was probably taken for granted by most Jews (including Christian Jews[16]), even though no formal decision had been taken to mark out its limits.[17] Not only was the scripture considered to be divinely inspired; God himself was regarded as its real author, who spoke in his own voice through its words. However, various interpreters expounded scriptural texts according to their particular traditions or predilections. "From the start, what came to be 'scripture' was treated as tradition, to be interpreted in the context of other traditions and of one's circumstances."[18]

An enormously influential innovation took place when, beginning with the Torah, the scrip-ture was gradually translated into Greek in the Egyptian Diaspora (dispersion).[19] The translation, which is known as the Septuagint ("seventy," according to a legend about seventy-two translators),[20] gave the vast population of Greek-speaking Jews direct access to their scriptural tradition. The Septuagint came to be the scripture of Greek-speaking Christians.

JEWISH HISTORY IN HELLENISTIC AND ROMAN TIMES

Alexander the Great's conquest inaugurated the Hellenistic period, characterized by a blend of the Greek civilization with the various local cultures.[21] Judea was now ruled first by the Ptolemies of Egypt and then by the Seleucids of Syria. All varieties of Judaism in this period, in Judea as well as in the Diaspora, were integral parts of the culture of the ancient world. Nevertheless, some varieties had imbibed more influences from outside than others, so that valid distinctions can still be drawn between the Judaism of the Diaspora and that of Judea.[22]

The Maccabean Uprising

By the second century B.C.E. we find in Judea two parties, sometimes called the Hellenizers and the Devout. The Hellenizers had gained the upper hand in Jerusalem. Regretting the consequences of cultural separation, they wanted to reform Judaism (not to destroy it) by erasing some of its distinguishing characteristics and by "making a covenant with the Gentiles" around them (1 Macc. 1:11). This process seemed to carry on peacefully under the Syrian rulers, even during the early reign of Antiochus IV Epiphanes. It is

22   impossible to reconstruct the events that put an end to the peace, but somehow an inner-Jewish power struggle in unstable political circumstances led to a situation that Antiochus construed as rebellion. In 167 B.C.E., Jerusalem was taken by his forces and many of its inhabitants were killed. Jewish worship was suppressed and the temple polluted with the alien cult of Zeus Olympios (referred to as the "desolating sacrilege" or "abomination of desolation" in Dan. 9:27; 11:31; 12:11). A decree of the king prohibited the practice of Jewish religion in Judea (though not in the Diaspora). Possession of Torah scrolls, celebration of the Sabbath, and circumcision were to be punished by death.

Ironically, this very attempt to destroy traditional Jewish identity seems to have saved it, for it evoked a massive reaction. The mass of the people joined the strict party of the Devout, led by the family of the Hasmoneans, nicknamed Maccabees, in order to defend the old ways. Their efforts, "history's first recorded struggle for religious liberty,"[23] came to be engrained in the collective memory of the Jews, ensuring that in the future any attempt to delete ancient religious customs would meet with stern opposition. Jews would live their lives according to the law of Moses.

At some point during the rebellion, the goals of the Maccabees changed. Even after they had reconquered the temple (it was rededicated in 164) and put an end to the persecution, they continued to fight—now for political independence. Taking advantage of the power struggle between rival claimants to the Seleucid throne, they succeeded, surprisingly enough, in founding a kingdom that lasted for a full century. They even undertook to bring all of the land of ancient Israel, including many Gentile areas in Galilee and elsewhere, under the law of Moses. John

Hyrcanus, who reigned 135–104 B.C.E., took the important Samaritan cities Samaria and Shechem, and destroyed the Samaritan temple on Mount Gerizim. The deep-seated enmity between Samaritans and Jews, reflected in the New Testament, goes back to these events. Hyrcanus also conquered Idumaea and forced its inhabitants to convert to Judaism by subjecting them to circumcision. Yet the Hasmonean dynasty of the Maccabees never succeeded in securing the support of all Jews. Many of the devout who had supported them when religious freedom was at stake later abandoned them, disapproving of their worldly ways. The pious were particularly appalled by the Hasmoneans' usurpation of the office of the high priest, to which their family could make no legitimate claims.

Rome and Judea

In 63 B.C.E. the Roman general Pompey took advantage of the disorder caused by strife between two claimants to the Hasmonean throne and conquered Jerusalem. He turned part of the Hasmoneans' territory over to the Roman province of Syria and appointed one of the claimants as high priest and "ethnarch" ("ruler of the nation," a lesser title than "king"). But due to the turmoil of the civil war, in which the Roman republic came to be caught, and the military threat posed to Rome by the Parthians in the East, a new dynasty rose to power in Judea. To help combat the Parthians, the Romans installed a strong man, Herod, as king of Judea. Herod, later called "the Great," ruled in 37–4 B.C.E. with the backing of Rome as a client king who had autonomy in his own territory.

Herod has had bad press, but modern historians take a balanced view. Broadly speaking, his reign was a success. It is true that he tolerated no opposition and proceeded ruthlessly against any who might threaten his rule, having many members of the aristocracy and even of his own family executed.[24] On the other hand, his services to the Jews were many. He remitted taxes during times of famine. He carried out large building projects that brought employment; his most spectacular achievement was the rebuilding of the temple. Herod's temple was a magnificent structure that by far surpassed the previous shrines in size and splendor and became a major site of pilgrimage. Herod lived as a Jew and defended Jewish worship outside Palestine. Peace reigned during his rule, and the economic situation created by him was beneficial to the nation.[25]

After Herod's death his kingdom was divided among his sons. Archelaus received Judea, Samaria, and Idumaea; Galilee and Perea fell to Herod Antipas; and the territories north and east of the Sea of Galilee to Philip. After only a decade Archelaus was deposed and his territory was again made a Roman province. In this connection, a census (6 C.E.; dated somewhat too early in Luke 2:1-3) was taken in order to introduce Roman taxation. There were riots, and the seeds were sown for small revolutionary movements that were later to lead the nation into a disastrous war.[26]

Rome now moved to rule Judea (not Galilee, see below) through foreign administrators (called procurators or prefects), and things got worse. Some of these governors, such as Pontius Pilate (26–36 C.E.), were brutal, others corrupt; most were ignorant of local customs. Thus, when he took over the office, Pilate ordered his troops to bring standards with the bust of the emperor on them into Jerusalem. A large crowd of Jews gathered outside his residence in Caesarea, where they sat for five days and nights. When Pilate's soldiers finally drew their swords, the Jews fell to the ground and exclaimed that they were ready to die rather than to transgress the law. Pilate backed down and ordered that the standards be removed.

A greater threat came from the emperor himself: in about 41 C.E. it occurred to Caligula to have his statue placed in the temple of Jerusalem. A very large crowd appealed to the Syrian legate, asking that he slay them first. The legate hesitated; the problem was solved when the report arrived that Caligula had been assassinated.

Rome governed Judea (and later Galilee) remotely, content with the collection of tribute and the maintenance of stable borders. Palestine was not colonialized (until in the aftermath of the Bar Kokhba revolt, 132–135 C.E.): Jewish cities were not repopulated by Roman settlers nor was Jewish farmland given to veterans.[27] The prefect resided in Caesarea and utilized local aristocrats, especially the high priest, who also presided over a council (the Sanhedrin); the day-to-day control of Judea was in his hands. Towns and villages were run as they had always been: by a small group of elders, some of whom served as magistrates. During major festivals the prefect came to Jerusalem with troops to ensure that the crowds did not get out of hand. The Feast of Passover in particular was a potential source of trouble, as it reminded people of the liberation of their ancestors from the grip of another superpower in bygone times—the exodus out of Egypt.

Although the possibility of serious trouble was always there, Palestine was not in Jesus' time (contrary to a common view) constantly on the edge of revolt. "Foreign rule was not judged bad by everyone all the time."[28] Many preferred the rule of a distant empire with its guarantee of certain stability to the rule of a despot closer at hand.[29] Cooperation with Rome was beneficial for the aristocracy concerned with its possessions; the priestly elite were willing to make compromises,

Lyon

Adriatic Sea

ILLYRICUM

THRAC

MACEDONI

Corsica

Ostia •• Rome

Philipp

Thessalonica •

Sardinia

Tyrrhenian Sea

• Pompeii

Aege Se

Athens
Cenchreae
Delphi •
Corinth •
Olympia •
Epidauros •
ACHAIA

Hippo •

Carthage •

Sicily

Fair Havens

Mediterranean

Cyrene •

Lepis Magna •

AFRICA

CYRENAICA

LIBYA

0   300 Miles

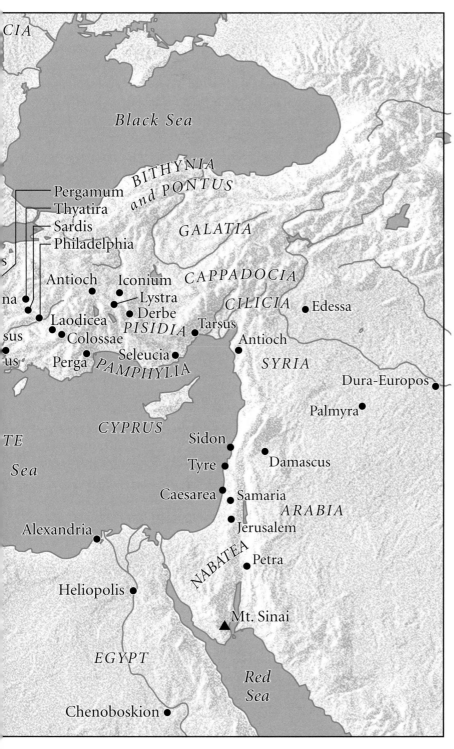

1.2 The Mediterranean environment of early Christianity

26 such as arranging a daily sacrifice in the temple for the welfare of the emperor and the Roman nation. The Jewish historian Josephus, though biased, may nevertheless be correct in his claim that even the majority were prepared to be obedient to Rome. They felt that "fighting against Rome was foolish at best and sinful at worst."[30] God would redeem Israel, but Israel could do nothing to hasten the appointed time (a point once made by Jeremiah and advanced after the war by Josephus). The dominant political stance of the Jews both in the land of Israel and in the Diaspora was accommodation: Jews must support the state until God sees fit to redeem them.[31] It was religious ideals more than a response to economic, political, or social injustice that spurred Jews to acts of resistance. When, in the early 40s, Jewish peasants neglected their farms and were willing to die, this was not because of the exploitation of the land or the economic injustice imposed by the wealthy, but in protest over Caligula's plan to erect a statue of himself in the temple. A small minority was prepared to engage in an armed fight against the Romans.

Galilee

In Galilee in Jesus' time, Herod Antipas was as independent as his father had been. There was no official Roman presence; it is unwarranted to speak of "Roman occupation" in Galilee in the first century (the second century is a different matter).[32] It would have been quite exceptional for Rome to station troops in a client king's territory.[33] The troops in Galilee were those of Antipas, and the taxes collected went to him (though he paid tribute to Rome). By Antipas's time, Galilee had become "a relatively peaceful region."[34] The focus of Jewish anti-Roman activity was in Judea; the Sicarii (see below) concentrated their terrorist activity in Jerusalem.[35]

It has been common among New Testament scholars to posit a profound cultural and religious difference between Judea and Galilee; it is often held that Gentiles were numerous, perhaps even in the majority, in the Galilee of Jesus' day.[36] It is also claimed that Galilee was thoroughly suffused with Greco-Roman culture, an assumption based largely on a particular interpretation of archaeological remains. This picture of Galilee has played a prominent role in recent research on Jesus and on the putative source of his sayings known as "Q";[37] it has produced images of Jesus as a Cynic-like social critic[38] and of members of the Q community (increasingly located in Galilee) as a "multiethnic, multicultural mix."[39]

This picture of a hellenized Galilee can be challenged. According to Mark Chancey, it exists "despite the evidence, not because of it."[40] Chancey's thorough surveys show that the image that results "from an integration of information provided by Josephus and the Gospels with the discoveries of modern excavations is entirely different."[41] Gentiles were a small segment of the populace, even in Sepphoris (in remarkable contrast to cities in the neighboring areas such as Caesarea Maritima, Ptolemais, or Paneas);[42] the vast majority of the archaeological finds that suggest Gentile presence or Greco-Roman cultural influence comes from later periods (a turn took place when a Roman legion, with support personnel, arrived in Galilee c. 120 C.E.).[43] In the first century, Galilee was still almost wholly Jewish.[44] On the whole, the populace seems to have shared the common Jewish concerns: circumcision, Sabbath observance, purity, and loyalty to the Jerusalem temple. It is unwarranted to posit (though this is often done) a widespread Galilean antipathy to the temple.[45]

Many assume that Jesus' world faced a severe social and economic crisis: that "institutionalized injustices" caused by the Romans and the Jewish aristocracy—double taxation, heavy indebtedness and loss of land—made the life of the small landholders miserable.[46] Others emphasize that while the situation was bad, it should not be exaggerated.[47] The burden of taxation was heavy, but hardly excessive by the standards of the day.[48] "What was *peculiar* to the situation was not taxation and a hard-pressed peasantry, but the Jewish combination of theology and patriotism."[49]

The topic remains controversial. For the present purpose it is enough to note that there were in any case a number of poor people whose life conditions were harsh, even if Jewish farmers were "by no means at the point of destitution."[50] All people in the countryside could not be farmers; inevitably there were numerous landless people, as the parcels of land divided among his sons after the death of a farmer quickly became too small to support a family. Like his father, Antipas took care of unemployment through big building projects, and for quite some time the *pax Romana* even permitted him "to control a strong economy." This began to change toward the end of his rule when the building program was completed and Antipas himself entered a period of political instability. Then the rural areas would have experienced a changed economic situation, "an atmosphere of perceived if not real decline in the standard of living," resulting in increasing hostility on the part of the peasants toward the wealthy and powerful.[51]

Toward Disaster

Herod's grandson Agrippa was given the old territories of Antipas, when his personal friend Caligula was made emperor. After Caligula's death, the new emperor Claudius made Agrippa king of Judea, and from 41 to 44 C.E. he ruled over a territory comparable to that of Herod the Great. After his early death, however, Judea became once again a province subject to Roman governors. The incompetent administration of the latter eventually led to a catastrophe.

The repressive administration of a new governor, Fadus, triggered a major protest action. A "popular prophet" called Theudas persuaded a large number of people to follow him to the Jordan River, expecting him to divide the waters in two (a symbolic act recalling earlier acts of liberation by Moses at the Red Sea or Joshua at the Jordan). The governor had them attacked and slain. A decade later, during the governorship of Felix, another prophet known as "the Egyptian" headed with a mass of people for the Mount of Olives, promising to make the walls of Jerusalem fall down at his mere command (thus repeating the miracle of Jericho in Joshua's time). Felix arranged a massacre (the Egyptian managed to flee). Both incidents seem to have been cases of unarmed rebellion, based on the expectation that God himself would intervene as of old.[52]

A sacrilegious act—taking money from the temple treasury—by one governor, Gessius Florus, led to public protests. These were followed by a massacre and crucifixions—and soon a revolt, first signaled by cancellation of the sacrifice for the emperor, broke out in 66 C.E. Other causes, such as ethnic tensions between Jews and Gentiles in the country, economic problems,[53] and general social unrest, played a part. The majority might have preferred the status quo, tolerating any inconvenience it entailed, but the zeal of the self-appointed revolt leaders from the ranks of the Sicarii and the Zealots (see below) could not be restrained. And in a critical situation their zeal could easily become contagious, for "Jewish memory of their free and autonomous past, suitably embroidered and idealized,

28 was a constant reminder of how much below that model state was their present situation. . . . Religious beliefs and expectations were clearly a prime mover behind the revolt when it came."[54]

The Jews had some initial success, but they were unable to form a united front and spent much of their time fighting one another. The revolt came to a disastrous end that threatened the very survival of Judaism: Jerusalem was sacked and the temple burned in 70 c.e.

These events marked the end of an era, but more trouble was to come. A series of revolts broke out in 115–117 in Egypt, Mesopotamia, and Cyprus, caused by the political tension between Jews and Gentiles and fueled by messianic speculations. There was much bloodshed; many Jewish communities were destroyed. A last in-surrection took place in 132–135 in Judea. Its leader, Bar Kokhba, had messianic pretensions and was apparently supported mainly by the landless poor in Judea. The outcome was deplorable: Jerusalem was turned into a Roman city, renamed Aelia Capitolina, which Jews were not allowed to enter. On the temple site a pagan cult was set up; circumcision and other Jewish practices were forbidden.[55]

JEWISH RELIGION

Judaism, like other ancient religions, was based on shared practice (rather than doctrinal theology). The main religious institution was the

1.3   The Roman army taking the spoils from the Temple in Jerusalem. Full-size cast of the bas-relief on the Arch of Titus in the Roman Forum. Museo della Civilta Romana, Rome. Photo: © Vanni/Art Resource, NY.

temple of Jerusalem, and the main activity that took place there was animal sacrifice. There were daily, weekly, and monthly sacrifices, and others at the major festivals. If a person wanted to seek atonement for a trespass or express his gratitude for blessings, he brought a sacrifice. Sacrifice was no empty ritual; the act was suffused with deep religious symbolism. Possibly most male Jews in the land of Israel came to the temple at least once a year. During festivals, temple worship was a social occasion, because much of the meat derived from the individual worshiper's sacrifice of quadrupeds went to the person who brought it and was consumed by him along with family and friends.

The priests were also obliged to teach the Torah to the people, although it is not clear how they did this; there may have been public read-

ings of the law.[56] The temple served as a place of prayer, too, and at some point prayer had become part of its daily liturgy (cf. Acts 3:1).[57] The Ten Commandments and the Shema (the confession "Hear, O Israel: the Lord is our God, the Lord alone," based on Deut. 6:4) were recited; the nucleus of the *Shemone Esreh*, the "Eighteen Benedictions" (which bear similarity to the Lord's Prayer) also derives from Second Temple times.

By the first century it had become common to gather for worship on the Sabbath in a *synagogue* (the term means "gathering" and, by extension, a place of gathering).[58] Reading and interpreting the Torah was the focus of these meetings. The synagogues had other functions, too, as meetinghouses for social and administrative purposes. For Palestine one may have to distinguish between the synagogues as public

30 assemblies on one hand and as "semi-public" associations on the other,[59] even though the reading and teaching of the Torah had a prominent position in both.[60] The latter type had been inspired through influences from the Diaspora, where synagogues had been organized after the model of the voluntary associations (collegia) of the Greco-Roman world (and were regarded as such clubs by the authorities). In the Diaspora the synagogues served to mark out Jewish identity and to strengthen group cohesion.

Independently of where they gained their knowledge (whether at the temple, in a synagogue, or perhaps at home), it is clear that Jews had access to the Torah in one form or another. "Writings from many different quarters show a knowledge of the law and an intense interest in understanding and interpreting it." The same applies to other books of the Hebrew Bible. The written word and its interpretation were very important even while the temple stood.[61]

Jewish identity in the time of the Second Temple was based on the notion of common ancestry and the concepts of election and covenant. God had chosen Israel to do his will; he had made a covenant with the people and set forth its terms in the Torah ("guidance," commonly rendered as "law").[62] Being Jewish was understood to consist in responding to God's call by faithfully obeying these commandments; the designation "covenantal nomism," coined by E. P. Sanders (see below p. 155), aptly characterizes the common denominator of the ideology of the various Jewish groups, all their differences notwithstanding. For differences there were; diverse groups could engage in bitter debates on the right interpretation and practical application of the Torah. In view of such inner-Jewish polemics, Jacob Neusner and others prefer to speak of "Judaisms" in the plural.[63] Yet such usage places too much emphasis on the language of insiders[64] keen on enhancing the social identity of their group by maximizing the differences between the in-group and relative out-groups.[65] In comparison with the outside Gentile world, the Jewish groups have so much in common that it is reasonable to speak, now as before, of a common Jewish identity that

1.5   Moses reading the Law. Fresco, c. 239 C.E.
Synagogue, Dura Europos, Syria.
Photo: © Art Resource, NY.

included, and mostly tolerated, variation. Different groups were united on a social level because they held to distinct convictions and practices that marked the Jews off from other people.[66] The most prominent of such identity markers were the abstention from idolatry, circumcision, food laws, and the observance of the Sabbath.

The Jews "saw themselves as the heirs and continuators of the people of preexilic Israel"; they also felt, despite all cultural and political differences, an affinity for fellow Jews throughout the world (a feeling normal for minority groups then and now). "This self-perception manifested itself especially in the relations of Diaspora Jewry to the land of Israel and the temple." Diaspora Jews responded positively to the efforts of the Hasmoneans and Herod the Great to obligate every Jew to contribute one half shekel

1.6   Scale model of Jerusalem and the Second Temple at the time of King Herod the Great. The picture shows the temple compound. Holy Land Hotel, Jerusalem. Photo: © Erich Lessing/Art Resource, NY.

32   to the temple of Jerusalem every year; by Herodian times at the latest, they also streamed in the thousands to Jerusalem to participate in the festival rituals of the temple.[67]

Groups

Certain groups stood out from "common Judaism"[68] through their lifestyles and particular beliefs. Josephus singles out the groups of Sadducees, Pharisees, and Essenes, which he represents as equivalents to the philosophical schools known to his Greek and Roman readers. The two first groups loom large also in the Christian Gospels. The Essenes are (strangely enough) absent from the New Testament texts, but their putative connection with the Dead Sea Scrolls has made them play an important part in any construction of the context of early Christianity.

We are not well informed about the Sadducees. A connection with the priestly aristocracy is very probable (the name is derived from Zadok, the alleged ancestor of the high-priestly family), but one cannot take for granted that all Sadducees were either wealthy or associated with the priesthood.[69] The Sadducees seem to have maintained conservative theological views (recognizing only the Pentateuch as authoritative scripture?), denying the relatively recent idea of resurrection. They have a bad reputation even in Jewish tradition, but there is no real evidence that they were corrupt. According to Josephus, they were less lenient than the Pharisees. Similarly, Acts 4–5 depicts them as the chief persecutors of the early Christian movement, while a Pharisee, Gamaliel, argues for leniency. In times of crisis the high priesthood found itself in a difficult position between the Romans and the people. "The Romans expected not only the high priest, but also the aristocrats in general to control the populace and to maintain order. The aristocrats did this with fair success, and the populace was generally willing to heed them."[70]

The Pharisees were a lay movement keen on studying the law. The nature of the movement is highly controversial in scholarship.[71] The Pharisees have had an extraordinarily bad press as hypocrites in Christian circles, due to the polemical caricatures drawn of them in the Gospels, particularly in the Gospel of Matthew. On the whole, however, there is no reason to doubt their sincerity. They were "known for the precision with which they interpreted the law and the strictness with which they kept it."[72] They emphasized the responsibility of each individual in the hope that every Jew could apply the decrees of the Torah in his or her own life.

In general, the Pharisees seem to have shared common Jewish religious ideas. Belief in resurrection set them apart from the Sadducees, but resurrection (though a relatively new doctrine) was not a Pharisaic invention; by the first century C.E. it was already quite popular. It is more noteworthy that the Pharisees developed a substantial body of nonbiblical "traditions of the fathers" about how to observe the Torah.[73] Some of these traditions made observance more difficult, but others made the law less restrictive.[74] They also had significant school differences among themselves; Hillel and Shammai were two prominent teachers to whom contrary opinions on several issues are attributed in the tradition, Hillel having the reputation of being more lenient and Shammai stricter in his decisions. For the most part, the Pharisees made special rules only for themselves and did not try to force them on everybody else (although they had probably once done that during the Hasmonean period, when they had also been a political force).[75] But they were respected popular teachers who had influ-

1.7   Qumran. Photo: John Collins.

ence on the opinions of people, even though they did not have a popular following on many points of their legal program.[76]

Before the discovery of the Dead Sea Scrolls and the ruins of Qumran, the Essenes were known from descriptions by Josephus, Philo, and Pliny; they give the picture of a small movement (some 4,000 members) withdrawn from society and preoccupied with strict observance of the law and purity.[77] The origin of the movement lies in the dark; it may have resulted from a schism in the movement of the Devout in Hasmonean times. In light of the ancient descriptions, there are good grounds to believe that those who inhabited the Qumran site[78] were members of the Essene movement,[79] though only a small part of all Essenes could have lived at Qumran (at its largest, the site was able to accommodate a few hundred persons).

The most important documents from the large Qumran library include the following.[80] The *Rule of the Community* (1QS)[81] contains instructions concerning communal life. Extant fragments show that the *Rule* was industriously copied (not without adaptations to new circumstances),[82] which proves its importance. The *Damascus Document* (CD)[83] reports on the origins of the movement, referred to as the "new covenant in the land of Damascus" (CD 6.19), and its interpretation of the Torah. The *War Scroll*

34   (1QM) describes the eschatological war between the sons of light and the sons of darkness. The *Hymns* (1QH) are devoted to thanksgiving; they open a window to the piety of the group. The *Pesharim* are commentaries on biblical books, of which those on *Habakkuk* (1QpHab) and *Nahum* (4QpNah) provide hidden glimpses of the early history of the movement. The *Halakic Letter* (4QMMT) casts light on issues of legal interpretation (halakah), as does the *Temple Scroll* (11QT), in which decrees concerning the temple are in focus. Finally, the *Songs of the Sabbath Sacrifice* (4QShirShab) acquaints the reader with aspects of liturgy at Qumran.

Research on the scrolls is at present in a state of turmoil. Until quite recently it was customary to speak of a self-contained, independent "Qumran community" with a distinctive social and religious outlook.[84] Its early phase was connected with the "Teacher of Righteousness," a figure mentioned in some of the scrolls. He appears to have been a Zadokite priest who was persecuted by a Hasmonean "Wicked Priest." The Teacher seems to have opposed the usurpation of the high priesthood by the Hasmoneans and rejected the temple, which he considered corrupt and defiled. It used to be thought that he withdrew with a small group of supporters to the desert (Qumran), where they led a monastic life and observed a divinely revealed solar calendar, different from that used in Jerusalem.[85] They worshiped Israel's God without animal sacrifices, being themselves the embodiment of a new, pure temple (1QS 9.4-5 and elsewhere). Their strictly hierarchical lifestyle is described (it was thought) in the *Community Rule(s)* (1QS), while the life of the larger Essene movement is reflected in the *Damascus Document* (CD). This writing presupposes a town-dwelling group that was not physically isolated from the greater society; members could marry and, surprisingly enough, sacrifice in the Jerusalem temple.[86]

Recent research has cast doubt on parts of this picture. Archaeological investigation indicates that Qumran was settled only from about 100–50 B.C.E. onward[87]—too late not only for the Teacher of Righteousness to have been the founder of the settlement,[88] but even for 1QS to have been "first written for the desert community at Qumran."[89] It may not be taken for granted any more that the community (*yahad*) of which the *Community Rule* (1QS) speaks is identical with the settlement at Qumran.[90] John Collins claims that "there is no evidence that any of the scrolls were written specifically for a community that lived by the Dead Sea."[91] Experts continue to debate the issue,[92] but it seems wise at present to avoid the term "Qumran community" (found in most textbooks and studies) and speak instead of the Essene movement. Those who produced or used texts like 1QS—whether they were a large community or a small cell and whether they lived at Qumran or elsewhere—were part of this movement. In any case the beliefs and practices reflected in these texts show a distinct family resemblance both with each other and with the beliefs and practices of the Essenes as portrayed by Josephus and Philo; therefore the assumption of a common religious worldview in a broad sense still seems justified.

Central texts from Qumran reflect the ideas and ideals of people—the Essenes—who were convinced that they alone constituted the true Israel. They could trust in God's promises, whereas the mass of the people had forfeited this privilege. The Essenes were the minority chosen by God to enter his "new covenant." They pledged themselves to return to "every commandment of the law of Moses," but this total obedience also included observance of secret additions to the Torah revealed to their Teacher and to the "sons of Zadok." The study of scripture was a central undertaking; a hard line was taken in the application of its laws. Members were to follow strict regulations on food and purity; they regarded even the Pharisees as compromisers ("those looking for easy interpretations": 4QpNah 1.2). Some of the texts display a sharply dualistic worldview, combined with antagonism toward outsiders. A strong end-time expectation involved an apocalyptic war between the sons of light (the Essenes) and the sons of darkness. Aided by heavenly troops, the sons of light would destroy both their Israelite enemies and the Gentiles, take control of Jerusalem (1QM), and rebuild the temple (11QT). It is claimed that the end time had actually begun; in their cultic gatherings members of the movement were already communicating with angels. They were predestined for salvation; outside the movement no salvation was possible. Some texts even refer to "everlasting hatred" toward the men of darkness (1QS 9.21).[93] On the other hand, the conviction of being chosen by God had brought about a humble sense of gratitude, "a feeling of personal unworthiness and an intense perception of God's graciousness."[94] On the whole, texts from Qumran make the impression of an intriguing combination of "internal self-absorption, fanaticism, vitriol and hatred of others, trust in God's grace, and love and devotion to him and his elect."[95]

The conviction of representing a holy remnant or the true Israel within a sinful people who had fallen away from God's covenant, which therefore no longer protects them from judgment, links the Essenes with other pious circles who likewise authored "sectarian" literature but whose social reality is unknown.[96] Among such circles, those who produced and cultivated writings con-

nected with the name of Enoch, the mythical ancient hero who had been taken to God without having to die, stand out. The Enoch literature, which combines vivid end-time expectation (largely expressed in apocalyptic visions granted to the ancient seer)[97] and the certainty of election over against a sinful majority, forms a substantial part of the context of the Jesus movement.

The comprehensive book of *1 Enoch* has been preserved in an Ethiopic translation. It consists of several originally independent units.[98] An intriguing issue, in view of the study of early Christianity, is the dating of the so-called *Similitudes of Enoch* (*1 En.* 37–71); one's understanding of the "Son of Man" passages of the Gospels partly depends on whether one regards the *Similitudes* as pre-Christian.[99]

A similar sense of a general apostasy and need of a fresh start characterized the activity of John the Baptist, a prophet whose rugged appearance reminds one of Elijah. In the late 20s of the first century c.e., he heralded a call to repentance and offered a baptism for the remission of sins as the means of avoiding God's impending judgment.[100] Those willing to change their ways were to undergo in the Jordan a bath that symbolized (or effected?) the purification from sin and the beginning of new life. Unlike the repeated ablutions undertaken by all Jews (especially diligently by the settlers of Qumran), John's baptism was probably a once-and-for-all act, an initiation rite of sorts. John did not, however, found a community, though he was surrounded by a circle of disciples (out of which Jesus of Nazareth was to emerge). According to Josephus, Antipas feared John's ability to gather great crowds (a potential source of rebellion) and had him executed, but the movement initiated by him stayed alive for quite a while, at times making a worthy rival for the Jesus movement in some places.

36   All groups would have been happy with the termination of Roman rule, and many looked forward to a restoration of Israel's glory—in God's own time, with or without a Messiah. Some, however, were more impatient than others and more given to direct armed resistance. An open conflict took place in 6 C.E., when Judea became a Roman province and a census was taken. Josephus reports that one Judas, a Galilean, aided by a Pharisee called Zadok, "threw himself into the cause of rebellion" (*Ant.* 18.3-10) and started "an intrusive fourth school of philosophy." Its slogan, "No king but God!" testifies to a program designed to attack the Romans and their supporters. Josephus goes on to tell that this school "agrees in all other respects with the Pharisees except that they have a passion for liberty that is almost unconquerable." He also suggests that this Fourth Philosophy gave rise to the Sicarii ("dagger-men") in the 40s.[101] The Sicarii would conceal a dagger (*sica*) inside their clothing and among throngs stab to death those Jews who, in their opinion, had betrayed the battle for freedom (they generally avoided clashes with Romans). They were active in the first phase of the revolt of 66 C.E., but after the early death of their leader, Menahem, they retreated to the mountain fortress of Masada and were not involved further in the war. In the end they committed suicide rather than be captured by the Romans.

The Zealots fought a religiously motivated battle for freedom in the spirit of Phinehas.[102] This group first became apparent during the revolt, being active in Jerusalem before and during the siege. It consisted mostly of peasants who fled to Jerusalem from Galilee, where the Romans swept southward. The Zealots fought bravely and fanatically, and most of them perished in the battle. However, they and other related groups in Jerusalem wasted a vast amount of energy in fighting one another, rather than the Romans.

The rebellion proved disastrous for many of these groups. The Essenes seem to have been wiped out in the war. The priests and the Sadducees lost their prestige with the disappearance of the temple. The groups that grew and developed were those who had potential to continue without a functioning sacrificial cult, such as the Pharisees and the scribes (who may or may not have belonged to the Pharisees). The rabbis, who in the long run—only after several centuries, according to recent research[103]—emerged as winners, combined a concern for purity with fervor for the study of scripture.[104]

DIASPORA JUDAISM

As a consequence of the Babylonian exile and of migration waves in subsequent centuries, the great majority of Jews lived in the Roman period outside Palestine. Rome and Alexandria were the most important centers, but there were Jews virtually everywhere in the empire (a vast number of Jews lived in Mesopotamia). Roman authorities (largely respecting the services that some of the Jewish leaders had rendered) took a tolerant attitude, granting the Jews the right to observe their ancestral customs,[105] including freedom from civic religion and a virtual freedom from the cult of the emperor, which would have clashed with their religious principles.[106] Life in an alien environment had the effect of binding Jews closer together and strengthening their ethnic identity, but naturally they were exposed to influences from the surrounding world. Greek philosophy had a great impact on Jewish thinking in the Diaspora, for instance on ideas of immortality and providence. Many Jewish authors (for example, Josephus) tried to present Judaism to Gentiles in an attractive light as a "philosophy." They tended to emphasize ethics and morality, suggesting that the ideal way of life recommended by Greek legislators and philosophers had been put into practice by the Jews, in fact by them alone. Such apologetics reached its peak in Philo of Alexandria, who tried to prove that the God of Judaism was very like the God of Plato and that the stories of the Bible contained hidden philosophical truths that were to be discovered through allegorical exegesis. Diaspora Judaism was to become a very important channel through which a rich treasure of Greco-Roman culture could flow into nascent Christianity.

There is no evidence for an organized Jewish mission to the Gentiles, though some individual Jews or small groups seem to have engaged in such an activity.[107] Still, several Roman authors refer to the willingness of Jews to win Gentiles to their side, if not for religious reasons then at least for political and social support; indeed, a number of Gentile sympathizers, often known as "God-fearers," showed a remarkable interest in the synagogues.[108] Most of them, shunning circumcision, did not convert and thus did not need to deny their Gods and their worship. They attended the synagogues, however, and quite a few observed some Jewish practices such as the Sabbath and some food laws.

On the other hand, the social separation of the Jews and their abstention from the public cultic ceremonies (which meant that they refused to participate in all major communal events) also raised the suspicion and sometimes the anger of their neighbors. Tensions were enhanced through the attempt of some Jewish communities to demand civic equality with

their Gentile neighbors despite their rejection of major aspects of the civic life; they thereby "antagonized certain elements of the local population by demanding both tolerance and equality."[109] This resulted in several riots and bloodshed in Alexandria, Caesarea, Antioch, and in many cities of Asia Minor during the first century C.E.; a climax was reached in Alexandria and Cyrene in the uprising of 115–117 C.E.

Jewish Writings from the Period

Apart from books that have become part of the Hebrew Bible, the most important Jewish writings from the Second Temple period (writings to which reference will often be made in subsequent chapters) include the following.[110]

From Palestine

The collection known as *1 Enoch* was introduced above (p. 35). Sirach (Ben Sira, also known as Ecclesiasticus) is a book about wisdom by a Jerusalemite scribe, composed in Hebrew around 180 B.C.E. It was translated into Greek by his grandson in 132 B.C.E. The Greek version is preserved in the Septuagint; in recent times large parts of the Hebrew text have been found.

Jubilees (second century B.C.E.) retells the early stories of the Pentateuch from the creation to Moses, as revealed to Moses on Mount Sinai. The author shows special interest in religious festivals and sacred time. He is an adamant spokesman for the sectarian solar calendar that was used at Qumran; numerous fragments of the work have been found at Qumran, where it apparently had a scriptural status.

38 First Maccabees (written c. 100 B.C.E.) is an account of the Maccabean rebellion. In the *Psalms of Solomon* (first century B.C.E.) a group of devout Jews (traditionally often identified as Pharisees, sometimes as Essenes, but such labeling is precarious) reacts to the capture of Jerusalem by Romans (63 B.C.E.) and looks forward to liberation.

The *Testament of Moses*, also known as the *Assumption of Moses*, was probably written in Palestine during the first century C.E. Presented as Moses' farewell speech before his death, the work predicts in apocalyptic style the subsequent history down to the time of King Herod and his sons, the sufferings that would ensue, and God's final victory.

Fourth Ezra, a great apocalyptic work from the end of the first century C.E., has been preserved in a Latin translation. Faced with the destruction of Jerusalem by the Romans, "Ezra" boldly wrestles with the question of theodicy in a series of dialogues with an angel whom he encounters in visions; another set of visions predicts the Roman rule and its overthrow by a Davidic Messiah. *Second Baruch*, preserved in Syriac, is an apocalypse from the early second century C.E. that deals with similar issues. The *Apocalypse of Abraham* (late first century C.E.?) tells of Abraham's rejection of idolatry and of his visions in which he sees the destruction of Jerusalem and the final victory of the righteous.

Pseudo-Philo's Biblical Antiquities (first century C.E.) freely retells the history of Israel from Adam to David.[111] The *Ascension of Isaiah* is a composite work that contains comprehensive Christian additions (see below p. 66). The oldest part is a Jewish legend of the martyr's death suffered by the prophet Isaiah (*Martyrdom of Isaiah*), composed in the first century C.E. at the latest.

For the library of Qumran (the Dead Sea Scrolls) see above, p. 33–34.

From the Diaspora

Tobit (c. 200 B.C.E., possibly from the eastern Diaspora) is a story about the fortunes of an exiled Jewish family in Assyria. The *Letter of Aristeas* (second century B.C.E., from Alexandria) tells the story of the origins of the Septuagint. The Wisdom of Solomon is a piece of hellenized wisdom literature, also from Alexandria (c. 100 B.C.E.).

Philo of Alexandria (early first century C.E.) was a wealthy intellectual, a Platonist Jewish philosopher who excelled in allegorical exegesis of the Septuagint. Most of his works (more than forty treatises) were preserved for posterity by Christians.[112] Philo embodies many Hellenistic-Jewish traditions on which many early Christians in the Greek-speaking world also drew; a little later, he had a direct impact on Christian intellectuals in Alexandria (Clement, Origen).

Second Maccabees (first century B.C.E.?) retells the Maccabean story for a Diaspora audience. Drawing on the same material, 4 Maccabees combines Hellenistic philosophy with Jewish piety; the philosophical exposition is clothed as a rhetorically powerful speech honoring the memory of the Maccabean martyrs. The work was probably composed in Antioch toward the end of the first century C.E.

Joseph and Aseneth is a story of Egyptian provenance about the conversion to Judaism of Joseph's Egyptian wife; its date could be anywhere between the second century B.C.E. and first century C.E. The *Testament of Job*, too, was composed in Egypt, in the first century either B.C.E. or C.E. A free reworking of the biblical story (Job is presented as an Egyptian king), it seems less interested in the fortunes of the Jewish nation than in individual piety. Yet another work that probably comes from Egypt is the *Testament of Abraham* (c. 80–120 C.E.). Abraham is granted a vision of heaven and of the judgment of souls.

The *Sibylline Oracles* are predictive poems from various times, composed in Greek hexameter. The Sibyl, an aged woman uttering ecstatic prophecies, was a prominent pagan figure, and Sibylline collections were a pagan phenomenon. Nevertheless, both Jews and Christians ascribed to her inspired end-time oracles with Jewish or Christian content, and the twelve books that are now connected with her name are all either Jewish or Christian. Books 1 and 2 are a Jewish work from Phrygia (from about the turn of the era) that has been subjected to an extensive Christian redaction. Book 3 was written in Egypt in a Jewish community that could, surprisingly enough, hail a Ptolemaic king as a savior. The earliest part of the work dates from the second century B.C.E., the latest probably from the end of the first century C.E. Book 4, from the late first century C.E., presumably comes from Jewish baptist circles. Book 5 reflects the atmosphere that fostered the Jewish revolt in the Diaspora in 115 C.E.

The writings of Flavius Josephus, the only Jewish historian whose works are extant to any degree worth mentioning, are an indispensable (though obviously tendentious) source for Jewish history during the first century C.E. He wrote (c. 75–79 C.E.) in Rome an account of the *Jewish War* (abbreviated *B.J.*), in which he had himself been involved in Galilee as a general; he was captured by Vespasian and during the siege of Jerusalem rendered service to the Romans. Josephus absolves Roman leadership from blame for the destruction of the city and places the guilt on the shoulders of the revolutionary leaders, described as tyrannical brigands. In a polemical autobiography (*Life*) he later defends his actions against the attacks of a rival historian. The *Jewish Antiquities* (abbreviated *Ant.*) tells the story of his people from the creation of the world to the eve of the Roman war, emphasizing divine providence. Although the account of the postbiblical times is very uneven, it is an important source for a generally poorly attested period. An apologetic and polemical tract, *Against Apion*, is designed to refute the slanders of an anti-Jewish Alexandrian author; it amounts to a panegyric for Jewish people and Jewish tradition.[113]

Uncertain Provenance

The *Testaments of the Twelve Patriarchs* is a collection of addresses given by each of the sons of Jacob on their deathbeds to their descendants, containing mainly ethical exhortation and eschatological promises. Much of the exhortatory material is "virtually timeless and could have been composed by either Jew or Christian anywhere in the Hellenistic and Roman eras," and there is "no evidence to tie the framework of the *Test. 12 Patr.* to any specific location."[114] The collection (whose textual history is quite complicated) is mostly considered an originally Jewish work, in itself a conglomerate of successive layers, which was later subjected to Christian revision(s) (see below, p. 66). However, the issue of provenance is highly controversial.

Second Enoch is an apocalypse, preserved in a Slavonic version, whose date and provenance are quite uncertain. It is a story about Enoch and his descendants; a large part describes Enoch's journey through the seven heavens.

Rabbinic Literature

The vast corpus of rabbinic literature is obviously relevant to our purposes, but difficult to use, as it contains material from different periods, and it is

40   hard to trace the oldest layers that may go back to the first and early second century c.e. The earliest part, the Mishnah ("repetition" or "teaching"), was collected and edited around 200 c.e. It may be characterized as an anthology of discussions by various legal authorities.[115] The Mishnah forms the core of the much larger collection of the two (Palestinian and Babylonian) Talmuds ("teaching"). Rabbinic material is also available in the exegetical and narrative Midrash ("exposition") collections. The dating of the interpretive traditions found in the Targums (Aramaic translations of the texts of Hebrew Bible, based on the practice of translating the biblical lections in synagogue services)[116] is controversial, and the usefulness of the Targums in reconstructing Second Temple Judaism is problematic.[117]

It used to be thought that the rabbinic literature stands in direct continuity to the traditions of the Pharisees, but the assumed connection is not without problems. With due caution, the rabbinic literature, too, can (and must) be used in the efforts to create a context for the nascent movement of the followers of Jesus.

2

Greco-Roman Religion and Philosophy

Religion

Civic Cult and Private Worship

The religious landscape in the Greco-Roman world was governed by flourishing traditional cults.[1] Public acts of worship included those performed in the name of the people by magistrates and state priests, those in which all citizens participated, and those carried by local associations as part of the total community. There was no weekly feast day, but a large number of feast days spread at irregular intervals over the year. The festivals of the Gods were great joyful occasions with processions,[2] music, sacrifices, and banqueting; they were also matters of civic self-respect, which supported a city's identity. The God/ess of any particular city protected its order of life. Traditional rituals gave people a sense of security and identity. Persons who refused to participate (as the Christians were to do) were a seriously disturbing element.

Only a temple could ensure the lasting presence of a God in a city. The central rites of the temple service were oriented toward the image of the Deity. The sacrificial praxis was "a social and religious reality of the first order in the whole of classical antiquity"[3] (Judaism differed only in that the sacrifices were limited to the Jerusalem temple). The normal form of sacrifice for Greeks and Romans was the so-called slaughter-sacrifice, which was followed by a common meal. The tables for the regular meals of the Gods were in the precincts of the temples, where much of the social life took place.

No high preconditions existed for participation in the sacrificial celebration; there were a minimum of prescriptions regarding purity that could sometimes include sexual continence for brief periods of time. But Plutarch surely gives expression to a common sentiment: "what is delightful in the feasts is not the quantity of wine or the roasted flesh, but the good hope and the belief that the God is present with his help and accepts what is taking place" (*Suav. Viv. Epic.* 1102a).

The connection that was perceived to exist between a statue and a God was different

42

in different cases. One may distinguish three different attitudes: that of "the thoroughgoing image-worshiper" for whom the image may well be divine; that of "the devotee who views the god as somehow present in the image, but only for the duration of the ritual"; and that of persons who do not worship the image, but worship *before* the image, thinking that images are helpful foci for veneration as "reflections and reminders of the deity's characteristics."[4] In this vein, a person might sit in quiet prayer for a long time at the feet of a sacred image and tell his or her problems to the God.[5]

In Homer, the Gods both look and behave like human beings.[6] But the Gods remain distinguished from humans by superior knowledge, superior though not unlimited power (they are subject to Fate), and immortality. "Taken together they represent the fundamental forms of a pluriform ordered reality which confronts the human person with a great variety of demands."[7] The number of such Gods could be endlessly multiplied, the more so as abstract terms too could be personified as divine figures (for example, Dike, the Goddess of justice). Still, the number of well-known Deities who enjoyed general veneration remained rather small.

Pagan religiosity was basically tolerant; adherence to a particular God did not exclude participation in the worship of another. There was even an openness toward new Deities. "Threats, defeats, victories, anomalies of nature, and social conflicts were explicit causes for intervention in the traditional status of the cult. Under state regulation, the Romans took up 'alien gods' and 'experimented' with new forms of worship," when the occasion arose.[8] The influence of foreign Deities grew in the first century C.E., but the new forms of belief and worship were "as a rule supplements rather than alternatives to ancestral

piety."[9] In philosophy, a tendency toward inclusive monotheism made itself felt. The various Gods were taken to be different manifestations of the one true God, often conceived of in pantheistic terms.

Between the public and private sphere, as it were, stood the private associations (collegia) with their sacrifices and feasts. Most associations were cult societies that one could enter by choice. Many Greek and Near Eastern cults appear to have established themselves in Rome initially in the juridical form of the cult association. Although Philo severely criticizes the life of the associations in Alexandria for drunkenness and revelry (*Flacc.* 136–37), many synagogues seem to have established themselves officially as collegia in the Diaspora. Christian communities in Greco-Roman cities, too, appeared to the outside observer to be associations of a newly imported Near Eastern Deity: members met in private houses, where they celebrated common meals.

After a scandal connected with the Bacchanalia in 186 B.C.E., when "the joys of wine and food" led to "excesses of every sort," culminating in deeds of rape and murder, according to Livy (*Urb. cond.* 39.8.3-8), the Senate repeatedly intervened to control the organizing of associations. Limits were placed on the cults of the Great Mother, Bacchus, and Isis. Claudius expelled the Jews (or some of them) from the city of Rome, probably in 49 C.E., because of social unrest; the consequences of this action (mentioned in Acts 18:2) are reflected in Paul's letter to the Romans from the mid-50s.[10]

A family venerated its own Gods, the *di penates*, "traveling Deities," which accompanied people as their living situations changed. The domestic ritual took on a particular intensity at the daily meal. A small portion of everything on the table belonged to the Gods. It would have been very difficult to accept an invitation to a meal in someone's home without becoming involved in sacrificial actions.

Mystery Cults

Mystery cults differed from both public and domestic religion in that they were practiced in secret, often at night; they also imposed on the participants a command to keep silent about what happened in the celebrations. Many features of the public cult reappeared in the mysteries: sacrifices, ritual meals, rites of purification, processions, veneration of the statues of Gods.

Mystery cults were known in Greece of old, the most famous being the mysteries in Eleusis. In Hellenistic and Roman times, several cults that came from Egypt or from the East gained great popularity, in particular the cults of Osiris and Isis, Attis and Cybele, and Mithras.

Each cult was based on its own myth, which narrated what happens to a God. In most cases, the God has to undergo suffering, but this leads to victory in the end. The God's destiny is dramatically reenacted in a ceremony in which the initiands participate, sharing in the God's labors and, most importantly, in his victory. Thereby a hope for salvation (*soteria*) is granted to them. The salvation can be of an inner-worldly nature (protection from sickness or dangers), but it can also consist in a prospect of a blessed life after death. Mysteries aimed at an "intensification of vitality and of life expectation,"[11] "a change of mind through experience of the sacred."[12] While seemingly relating to historical events, the myths were taken to make known eternal and immutable truths. The author of a fourth-century C.E. text puts it in a lapidary manner: "These events [the reference is to the story of Attis] never occurred, but they exist always" (Sallustius, *De diis et mundo* 4.9).

2.1   Statue of Mother Goddess Artemis, protector of the people of Ephesus (cf. Acts 19:28, 34).

The cult of Attis involves a Mother Goddess, the Great Mother (*magna mater*), known by various names but in this connection usually called Cybele. Her love for young Attis eventually results in the latter's death, which is, in one popular version of the myth, preceded by his castration. In one conclusion the Goddess asks Zeus to restore Attis to life, but is granted only that the corpse of the youth will remain incorrupt, so that

44   his hair will continue to grow and his little finger can move (Arnobius, *Adv. nat.* 5.7).[13] The most striking feature of the cult of *magna mater* was the ritual self-infliction of wounds by some participants, who could go as far as self-castration. The wild, orgiastic religious fervor made a deep impression on the minds of many people; the cult became very popular.

While Attis was not really restored to life, according to the myth, the Egyptian Osiris/ Serapis can with better grounds be called a dying and rising God.[14] The Goddess Isis searches for her dead beloved Osiris, who has been torn or cut to pieces. Isis gathers the pieces together and buries them. Thanks to the correct burial, Osiris can now become the lord and judge in the world of the dead. Initially, Osiris functioned as the prototype of the dead pharaoh, but in the course of a "democratisation of the royal privilege"[15] it came to be believed that each deceased person

2.2   A scene from Greek mythology: the Goddess Isis receives Io, a priestess fleeing the anger of the Goddess Hera, in Egypt. Roman fresco from the Ekklesiasterion, the Isis Temple in Pompeii. Museo Archeologico Nazionale, Naples, Italy. Photo: © Erich Lessing/Art Resource, NY.

became an Osiris, provided that the burial rites were correctly carried out.

When the cult moved to the Greco-Roman world, the divine mother Isis received increasing attention. Her cult was promoted by merchants and travelers and gained a foothold in Rome from 200 B.C.E. onward, though it had to fight there for a long time against strong opposition. During the first century C.E. the cult began to make progress. Isis was exalted to the status of an all-embracing Deity; for example, as the great healer she possessed the medicine of immortality. In aretalogies, the mighty deeds of the goddess are listed in long litanies with self-descriptions, as in an inscription from Cyme:

> I am Isis, the mistress of the whole land . . .
> I am she who discovered fruit on behalf
>   of human beings . . .
> I am she who separated earth from
>   heaven . . .
> I have shown mortals the initiations.
> I have taught them to honor the images
>   of Gods . . .
> I am she who is called the legislatrix.

In his *Metamorphoses*, Apuleius (second century C.E.) gives an account, partly in veiled language, of his initiation into the mysteries of Isis. Preparatory actions included a short instruction in the contents of the mystery, a purifying bath, and abstention from meat and wine for ten days. Then the initiand was clothed in linen and brought at sunset into the holy space. The injunction to silence prevented Apuleius from directly describing the cultic act itself, but he gives several hints: "I have come to the borders of death and have set my foot on the threshold of Proserpina, I have traveled through all the elements and then returned, at midnight I have seen the sun shin-

ing in dazzling white light, I have come into the very presence of the Gods below and the Gods above, and I have adored them close at hand" (*Metam.* 23.8). A descent into the underworld and an ascent to the heavenly heights is being depicted. Through the initiation, Apuleius is born as a divine being. In the service of Isis, he now has to follow her instructions and act in a moral way so that he can one day stand before Osiris, the judge of the dead. The combination of initiation with moral seriousness made the mysteries of Isis highly attractive to many people.

For political reasons, the name of Osiris was changed by the Ptolemaic rulers to Serapis to denote the supreme God that both Egyptians and Greeks could worship. Serapis was identified with Zeus and praised as a savior who helped all humans. Among the characteristics of his cult, common meals stand out; papyrus tickets to such meals have been preserved.

The cult of Mithras spread mainly among civil servants and soldiers. Most of the archaeological discoveries have been made in Rome and Ostia on the one hand and in the military centers along the Roman border on the other. Loyalty to the Roman imperial house was a fundamental trait of this cult, which Christians came to see as an especially dangerous rival. Justin Martyr could not but notice the similarities of the ritual meals of the worshipers of Mithras to the Eucharist, when in admitting a new member they "set out bread and a cup of water with a particular form of words" (*1 Apol.* 66.4).[16] Archaeological discoveries show that more luxurious meals were also held.

The mysteries had their critics, too. They asked, Is one's destiny in the afterlife really decided only by the fact of having been initiated, without taking into account one's character and conduct?[17] The Stoic philosopher Epictetus, for

46   one, emphasized the necessity of a right attitude: the mysteries have effect only if one has prepared oneself inwardly and approached the rites after purification with sacrifices and prayers (*Diatr.* 3.21.14-15).

For the old history-of-religions school,[18] the mystery cults were crucial. Christian sacraments were genetically derived from the rites of these cults (initiation, washings, unctions, meals); the myth of the dying and rising of a divinity in (some of) them was taken to be a significant influence on earliest Christianity's image of Christ. Today scholars speak of the dying and rising divinities in the mysteries with much more reserve; this type does not apply to many divine figures, and "there is no evidence at all that any of these gods was thought of as 'rising' in any proper sense of the term."[19] In a thorough investigation of the possible background of "dying and rising with Christ" in mystery religions, A. J. M. Wedderburn could find "no evidence that the initiates in any of their rites believed that in their initiation they were experiencing in themselves the death and resurrection of their deity, let alone that this idea was common to all or many of them."[20] But undoubtedly mystery language was adopted (even by Diaspora Judaism), and the similarity of many phenomena remains intriguing.[21] Many points of resemblance are probably due, not to borrowing one way or the other, but to the fact that both mystery religions and Christianity "responded in a similar fashion to the religious challenges of the Greco-Roman world," offering to devotees who had made a personal decision to undergo the pertinent rites "similar experiences, rituals and ways of salvation and transformation."[22]

Other Religious Phenomena

The phenomena dealt with here are often called "popular religion" or the like.[23] This is somewhat misleading, as the beliefs in question and the practices connected with them were widespread, criticized at the most by a small intellectual minority.

It was common to search for miraculous divine aid when faced with sickness or other hardships of life. Asclepius was the God of healing par excellence; among his many shrines the one in Epidauros, Greece, was particularly famous for its cures and contained a massive collection of accounts of healing that had taken place there.[24] Other Gods and various heroes and miracle workers also promised healing. Acts 14:8-18 gives a vivid picture about the popular belief that Gods could come down to visit mortals and help them: the inhabitants of the Lycaonian city of Lystra in Asia Minor, who had witnessed a healing miracle, wanted to bring sacrifices to Barnabas and Paul, whom they took to be Zeus and Hermes in human guise.

Exceptional men, such as Pythagoras, Empedocles,[25] or Apollonius of Tyana,[26] were also ascribed supernatural powers—gifts of healing or miraculous foreknowledge.[27] The expression *divine man* was applied, at least occasionally, to such figures. Many traits in the portrait of Jesus in the Gospels or in that of the apostles in *Acts* literature recall the figure of the divine man, though scholars continue to debate the usefulness of this category in modern research.[28]

The foretelling of the future and the interpretation of signs were also important religious skills. Asclepius could be asked where a lost boy might be found. Here the cult of healing touches the field of divination, to which belong, for example, the acts of putting questions to an oracle and of interpreting dreams. The concept of divination implies that sharing in the divine knowledge makes it possible to glimpse hidden future things. The Greek word *manteia*, probably derived from *mainomai* ("to rave"), indicates that such glimpses were often possible only in exceptional emotional states that outsiders were likely to consider madness. Divination would help people make decisions in situations that were still open. The Stoics vigorously defended divination, but the Epicureans dismissed it with contempt.

The focus of this province of religion was the oracle. The most famous oracular site was the sanctuary of Apollo in Delphi, where a prophetess called the Pythia answered questions by way of brief ambiguous utterances, which then needed to be interpreted by experts. Another important prophetic figure was the Sibyl, understood to be an aged woman who could utter ecstatic prophecies. A collection of oracles allegedly spoken by the famous Sibyl of Cumae were kept in the temple of Jupiter in Rome; these books were to be consulted by the Senate (probably by taking out at random one of the leaves), when no other signs had given clear information and a decision had to be made. Nothing of these Roman books has been preserved; a later collection of Sibylline oracles exists, but it is virtually a work of Jews and Christians who took over the genre and adapted it to their purposes (see above, p. 39).

Dreams were considered an important premonitory source. It was generally thought that significant dreams were sent from heaven and therefore were equal to oracles. However, like oracles, they needed interpretation. Books were written on that topic (*Onirocritica* [*The Interpretation of Dreams*] by Artemidorus has been preserved).

Astrological beliefs were widespread and horoscopes widely studied. Except for Trajan, all the Roman emperors from Tiberius to Hadrian used astrology, but astrologers were several times expelled from Rome as a potential source of unrest—another indication of their significance. The dwellers at Qumran had to study astronomical data in order to be able to calculate the calendar, but it is not easy to tell to what extent this study amounted to astrology: one fragment (4Q186) consists of three horoscopes. The church fathers had continually to fight against astrology; this very fact is evidence of its abiding power.

Astrology made Fate seem an overpowering force. However, it was thought (illogically, it would seem) that one could tamper with Fate through the use of magic.[29] Magic was based on the conviction of the existence of intermediary superhuman beings (demons) and on the assumption that "everything in the universe is interconnected, linked together by the bond of sympathy which can also turn into antipathy."[30] Magical practices included prophylactic magic, magic that inflicts harm (called black magic today), magic that had to do with love, and revelatory magic.[31] It was supposed that the best magicians were found in the East, in Persia, and also in Egypt; Jews also had a certain reputation (cf. Acts 13:6).[32]

Cult of Rulers

The cult of rulers was a phenomenon that took very different forms in the various areas of the Mediterranean world. Its birth was aided by such precedents as paying divine honors to men who had helped the inhabitants of a city in difficult situations, as the Spartans did to a general who had won important victories over the Athenians (c. 400 B.C.E.). Where help and rescue, which are "basic functions of the divine," are experienced, "the one who brings these is often acknowledged to be himself a manifestation of the divine power."[33] Such a helper could be called "savior" (*soter*) and "benefactor" (*euergetes*).

48   Divine power could also manifest itself in particularly favored human beings: in philosophers, poets, seers, and miracle workers. Empedocles claimed that honors were appropriately paid to him as a God, but they did not include sacrifices, altars, or the like. Nevertheless, his case shows that the boundaries between Gods and humans were porous. Another sign of this is that human beings could be declared "heroes" after their death: they could ascend to heaven and become a kind of demigod. Heroes were men of an earlier age who had performed exceptional deeds in their lifetimes, and it was believed that they still possessed some power after their death. The cult of a hero was centered on his tomb, where sacrifices were offered.[34] The founder of a city or a colony was almost always given heroic status after his death. If one combines the bestowal of quasi-divine honors for living benefactors and the cultic veneration of dead heroes, one arrives at the cultic veneration of living human beings because of their exceptional achievements—which brings us close to the cult of rulers. The difference is that the forms of veneration are now taken over from the cult of the Olympic Deities.[35]

In some Greek cities in Asia Minor, during his lifetime Alexander the Great was sporadically paid the cultic honors due to a great benefactor; after his death, his cult was intensely promoted by his followers, the Diadochi. The myths and legends that quickly formed around his person came to serve later rulers as a model for their self-portrayal.[36] In Egypt, the Ptolemies created a dynastic cult centered on the ruling family, which was imposed from above, with the aim of providing a sacral foundation for political power. The ancient Egyptian royal ideology, which considered the pharaoh to be the son of a God, was of great help here. In Syria (where the earlier history and the political structures differed from those in Egypt), the parallel processes in the case of the Seleucids took longer.

When Rome began to bring one territory after another under its rule, the inhabitants of Greece and Asia Minor reacted in their accustomed manner: they transposed the varied cult of rulers, which by now had a lengthy tradition, to the Romans. One option was the veneration of the Dea Roma, the Goddess of Rome; another was the attribution of honors to individual representatives of Rome. This was a way of coping with the new situation: an order was established in the world by transposing to the Roman power the well-tried categories of the Hellenistic cult of benefactors and rulers.[37]

Rome's own traditions provided no basis for the cult of rulers; influences from the East were necessary for such a cult to arise. In the Eastern part of the empire, traits of the Hellenistic ruler cult were transferred to Julius Caesar, who was called in inscriptions, for example, "descendant of Ares and Aphrodite, the God who has appeared visibly, and universal savior of the life of human beings."[38] After his death, Caesar was declared a God by the Senate. Octavian (Augustus), who perhaps prompted the decision, came as Caesar's adopted son to be called *Divi filius*, "the son of a God," or even *theos ek theou*, "a God of a God." What happened with the deceased Caesar provided the standard model for the deification of Roman emperors: unless they had made themselves very unpopular, resolutions of the people and the Senate included them after their death in the list of the civic Gods (*apotheosis, consecratio*). Octavian imposed on himself a prudent reservation: he did not allow things in Rome to go quite so far as a formal veneration with images, a temple, and priests, but he accepted the cultic honors that were offered him in the East. After his death, he was given a place among the Gods by the Senate. Very soon myths and legends comparable to those connected with Alexander formed around his life, too. The *pax Romana*, the "Roman peace," was seen as Augustus's great achievement that earned him "genuine gratitude and veneration." Although this peace undeniably had many negative aspects, it did impress so many people that it "led to the mythical exaltation of Augustus as the creator of peace and the ruler over a peaceful realm."[39]

One of those emperors who were not deified after their death was, seemingly paradoxically, Gaius Caligula, who had himself tried to compete directly with the ancient Gods in his lifetime. He ordered statues of himself as a God (an incarnation of Jupiter) to be erected in the Forum and established a temple dedicated to his own divine person. When the non-Jewish population of Jamnia in Palestine set up an altar for Caligula, this was at once torn down by the Jewish inhabitants. Enraged, Caligula ordered that an enormous statue of himself be set up in the temple of Jerusalem. The murder of the emperor in 41 C.E. prevented the disastrous plan from being realized.

Unlike Caligula, Nero apparently kept the imperial cult within the customary boundaries. But in retrospect his figure took on a mysterious dimension, connected with his early death and his burial in the presence of only very few. In the East, Nero's rule was not experienced as especially oppressive, and he had even maintained good relationships with the Parthian people. A legend claimed that Nero did not commit suicide at all, but fled to the land of the Parthians, from where he would one day return with a mighty army to regain his power. Jewish and Christian apocalyptic was to take up this idea, which it provided with an ominous color. The Jewish Sibylline Oracles (*Sib. Or.* 5.361-65) make Nero

God's satanic opposite number: "There will come to pass in the last time about the waning of the moon a war which will throw the world into confusion. . . . A man who is a matricide will come from the ends of the earth in flight and devising penetrating schemes in his mind. He will destroy every land and conquer all. . . ."[40]

50

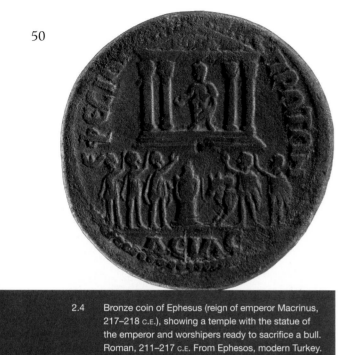

2.4   Bronze coin of Ephesus (reign of emperor Macrinus, 217–218 C.E.), showing a temple with the statue of the emperor and worshipers ready to sacrifice a bull. Roman, 211–217 C.E. From Ephesos, modern Turkey.

Photo: © British Museum/Art Resource, NY.

Vespasian was the first to introduce the imperial cult to the Western provinces. Coming from an undistinguished family, he tried thus to secure his legitimation. Domitian, too, undoubtedly promoted the cult of the emperor. The first imperial temple in Ephesus was built in his lifetime; his statue there was five to seven meters high. Nevertheless, it is questionable whether he demanded any greater divine honors than either his predecessors or successors.[41] He was sometimes called *dominus et deus noster*, "our Lord and God," though he may not have encouraged such titles.[42] Domitian did not receive the rite of *consecratio*. A strong hostility reigned between him and the Senate from the outset; this is why the historians and writers who shared the Senate's view are against him. Historical scholarship has long been working on a revision of the very somber picture of Domitian that these sources provide. Domitian was an autocrat, but he did have considerable achievements in the fields of administration, organization, and the legal system.[43]

The ritual forms practiced in the imperial cult correspond to those found in the exercise of religion in general: sacrifices, temples with images and priests, processions, feasts, athletic contests—with one or another particularity. The image of the emperor was the central point of reference for the imperial cult, but "most imperial sacrifices were offered to the gods on behalf of the emperor."[44] The image did not have the primary function of representing the emperor or of expressing the omnipotence of the ruler, but served as a symbol of the unity of the state composed of many ethnic groups. The cult was originally not something demanded, but something freely offered, as a *reaction to the experience of being helped*. At other periods there was a stronger social pressure to set up such cults, and they were also promoted by the imperial court itself. Nevertheless, the cult of the emperor never made any exclusive claims for itself, nor did it become a genuine competitor to the traditional belief in the Gods. "Language sometimes assimilated the emperor to a god, but ritual held back."[45] Therefore, as a rule, conflicts of loyalty did not arise. Christians were the obvious exception to the rule.

PHILOSOPHY

Conventional religion was not necessarily concerned with morality, let alone with intellectual search for truth; that was the province of philosophy. Even the question of the existence of a God was discussed in antiquity only in the framework of philosophy; critique of religion was also one of philosophy's concerns. In the Roman period, philosophy focused on practical issues: how to live a good life. Cicero's eloquent prayer to philosophy (*Tusc.* 5.5) carries strong religious overtones: "O philosophy, guide of life, discoverer of virtue, victress over the vices! What would we be without you—indeed, what would human life be at all without you?—We take our refuge in you, we ask you for help and we entrust ourselves to you. . . . Whose help should we seek rather than yours? For it is you who have given us rest in our life, and taken away from us the fear of death."

We might call the activities of philosophers pastoral care or spiritual guidance, or even psychotherapy. Intellectual discourse was only one part of the way of life recommended in a particular school of thought, for philosophy required more: a choice of a way of life.[46] Not surprisingly, at least some versions of early Christianity came to be seen as philosophical schools of sorts.

Plato and His Followers

Plato (427–347 B.C.E.) was persuaded that the soul was uncreated, immortal, immaterial, and the true vehicle for human identity. The body can corrupt the soul; therefore, the soul must separate itself from the body as far as possible. This view, which was designed to lead to moderately ascetic ethics, lived on in what has come to be called "Middle Platonism," a current that flourished from the first century B.C.E. to the early second century C.E.[47] In it, a sharp distinction was made between the intelligible world on one hand and the sense-perceptible world on the other. In the former, the world of God, everything is eternal, unchanging, and perfect; this is the world of the Ideas, eternal models (perceptible only by the mind), of which the things of the sense-perceptible world are images. (Thus "treeness," the Idea of a tree, is real, whereas the trees standing in the forests are reflections of it in the transient world.)

A central tenet was a belief in the immortality of the soul (and, in part at least, in reincarnation). Liberated from the body, good souls would ascend to the heavenly regions after death. The *daimones* were intermediate beings who were able to communicate with human beings on behalf of the Gods. Platonism displayed an open attitude toward other philosophical schools (except the Epicureans). Thus it adopted the concept of Logos (to some degree) from the Stoics and a mystical attitude from the Neopythagoreans. Middle Platonism provided essential intellectual presuppositions for Philo and the early Christian apologists.

2.5   Plato. Greek bust, c. 350 B.C.E. Marble. Photo by Alfredo dagli Orti. Staatliche Antikensammlung, Munich, Germany. Photo: © Bildarchiv Preussischer Kulturbesitz/Art Resource, NY.

52 *Stoics, Cynics, Others*

STOICS. The Stoics, of whom the best-known are Seneca,[48] Epictetus, and Marcus Aurelius, connected ethics with a vision of the world and nature. The cosmos is a great unity, but nothing exists beyond the world and its material principles (no world of ideas, no transcendent creator). The divine primal matter consists of a subtle fire that is also called *pneuma* ("breath," "spirit")—a vitalizing, creative power that penetrates the universe with its fiery warmth. The *pneuma* consists of a subtle matter and becomes concentrated in the *Logos* ("reason")—the principle that structures reality. The all is filled by the divine Logos and its power; its works are visible in nature.[49] The Deity (often called Zeus) sends reason to guide humans and leads those who have insight to live life well; but the divine is not thought of as being transcendent; it is immanent. Still, with astonishing suitableness this Deity governs the world, which is a beautiful and harmonious whole; consequently religious feelings can be joined to the practice of philosophy. "As a divinity which does not behave well is unthinkable, the given world is for the Stoics the best possible one: it is created and maintained beautifully and appropriately by the divine providence."[50]

Stoics generally took a conservative attitude to the civic cult, which they did not want to alter. Old myths were reinterpreted allegorically. The goal of humans is to live in agreement with nature. Social and other differences between humans are not crucial, as all people participate in the cosmic order. This equality does not affect social reality, however. The wise person is internally independent of anything that binds humans to the world. One accepts whatever happens as something dictated by divine will and necessity. We must learn to distinguish between what is at our disposal and what is not. Freedom, which is the goal of a good life, becomes a question of one's inner attitude to the given facts that one cannot alter.

CYNICS. "Cynics" (the name derives from the Greek word for "dog") went further in their contempt for the world. Their prototypical representative was Diogenes of Sinope, who led "a dog's (shameless) life." Cynics would live a simple life as poor wanderers with no needs; similarities to the lifestyle of the wandering charismatics among the early followers of Jesus have not escaped scholars.[51] Their nonconformist and provocative behavior amounted to a sharp critique of bourgeois values, as they sought their freedom and happiness in a conscious self-marginalization. There were close mutual influences between Stoicism and Cynicism; modern scholars speak of "Cynic-Stoic popular philosophy." In the early imperial period, Cynicism took on a new momentum.

Epictetus notes that the true Cynic must be aware that he is sent to people as a messenger of Zeus to show them their error and tell them about the truth (*Diatr.* 3.22.23-25). A Cynic will be exposed to blows from all sides, but he bears ill-treatment and insults with the impassiveness of a stone—and will even love those who torment him (*Diatr.* 3.22.100; 3.22.54).

EPICUREANS. The Epicureans constituted a philosophical school with a founding personality, concern to preserve the tradition, a common life, and the ideal of friendship.[52] During his lifetime and even more after his death, Epicurus grew into the role of a *soter*, a rescuer and "savior" of human beings. Cultic veneration was paid to his image. Indeed, Epicurus promised that anyone willing to devote himself to the correct philosophical way of life would become like a God. Whereas the Stoics stressed that only the wise man is free and "a king," Epicureans emphasized more strongly the similarity between the Gods and the thinking human person who knows how to translate insight into praxis.

Epicureans practiced *askesis* and *therapeia*, training in a way of life based on philosophy, and the healing and helping guidance of the soul by means of individual conversations (one has even spoken of a "confessional" praxis). "There can be no question that Epicurean schools had a well-developed group charisma, and that it was this that made them especially attractive."[53] The Epicureans often had the reputation of being atheists, though they did not deny the existence of Gods. What they denied was the correctness of customary notions of Gods. The widespread idea of the divine held by the masses is actually atheistic, since its mythical narratives attribute to the Gods all kinds of things that are utterly foreign to their dignity and their being. The Gods lead a blessed life outside time and are not concerned with what happens on earth. The prayers addressed to them do not reach them. There is no divine providence, history has no goal. Still, Epicureans recommended (inconsistently, it might seem) prayers to the Gods and even sacrifices, participation in the general cult, and care for religious customs. There is no reason to fear the Gods, or death for that matter. A happy life means health of body and firmness of soul. The highest goal is pleasure, a statement that was inevitably misunderstood. Pleasure does not mean sensual and bodily satisfaction; the most desirable condition is passive pleasure, that is, the absence of pain. True and lasting pleasure demands a modest, reflective, rational way of life. For all their differences, Stoics and Epicureans converged in an astonishing fashion in the advice

they gave for the practical conduct of life. Interestingly, it is these two groups of philosophers that debate with Luke's Paul in Athens (Acts 17).

Neopythagoreans. Pythagoras of Samos had founded a philosophical and religious movement in southern Italy in the sixth century B.C.E.[54] The Pythagorean community was later famous for its communal living and sharing. Purificatory rites, which included a daily bath, were central. Oral tradition played a decisive role in the transmission of Pythagorean teaching, which included the immortality and transmigration of the souls, the eternal cyclic recurrence of events, and the kinship of all living things.

From the first century B.C.E. onward, interest in Pythagoreanism revived. The basic features of Neopythagoreanism included interest in a symbolism of numbers, a belief in the transmigration of souls, and an emphasis on the need for the purification of the soul, to be accomplished through ascetic practices. Apollonius of Tyana considered himself a Pythagorean. His biography by Philostratus portrays him as the embodiment of the Pythagorean ideal: an ascetic way of life, rigorous morality, loyalty to the Gods, doing good to fellow humans (even by way of performing miracles).

Was There a Gnostic Religion?

Plato had used the noun *gnosis* and even the adjective *gnostikos* to describe theoretical knowledge (which he distinguished from practical knowledge or skills). What he meant was a special kind of knowledge; he did not imply that there was a

54 special group of people with an exclusive access to this knowledge. The adjective *gnostikos* in this latter sense crops up in Irenaeus's hostile report on groups who called themselves by this name. Church fathers then began to apply the name "gnostics" also to other groups who did not call themselves so,[55] but whose doctrines bore more or less resemblance to the doctrines of those who did. Modern scholars have claimed that there was in antiquity a pre-Christian "gnostic religion" marked by distinct traits of thought and practice. These included rejection of the world (a creation by an evil demiurge), determinism, elitism, hatred of the body (the soul was to be freed from its bondage), and moral extremism (in the form of either asceticism or libertinism).[56] On this view, there existed also a "gnostic myth" of the Savior that early Christian writers such as Paul and John would have known and adapted to their purposes.

It is hardly an exaggeration to say that recent scholarship has demolished this construction.[57] "Gnosticism" has proved to be too diffuse a category to be of help as an analytic tool; the designation "creates a misleading impression of a relatively unitarian movement."[58] The Nag Hammadi texts, which have been of tremendous help for the study of Gnosticism, do not present anything like a unified picture. The features ascribed to the "gnostic religion" turn out to be sweeping generalizations, gleaned from different documents that may not have much to do with one another. Yet, despite the remarkable differences, there are some common characteristics among many[59] of the texts and currents that have traditionally been called "gnostic." Two such characteristics stand out: the "notion of (an) evil or ignorant world creator(s) separate from the highest divinity," and the presupposition that "the human soul or spirit originates from a transcendental world and, having become aware of

that, has the potential of returning there after life in this world."[60] Writings that exhibit these two features may rightly be said to have a gnostic orientation.

In the gnostic view, there are two different Gods: the true, highest God on one hand, and the demiurge, the creator of the world, a lower divine being, on the other. The demiurge is ignorant: he does not know the true God, but asserts that he himself is the only God. The degree of opposition between these two Gods varies considerably in the sources. Humans are placed in the area between the two Gods. The human body stems from the demiurge, but within it dwells a divine spark (spirit or soul) that connects humans with the true God. The purpose of the body is to mislead humans to forget their divine origin; sexuality serves the same alienating purpose. The divine element ought to be freed from the shackles of the material body by saving knowledge, through an awakening experience that makes the person aware of his or her true origin and enables the soul to ascend to the divine realm after the person's death. The knowledge of the origin of humans involves knowledge of the creation of the world, which is a prominent topic in many gnostic writings.

While it therefore is no longer feasible to speak of Gnosticism as an independent religion comparable, say, to Judaism or to the mysteries of Isis, it does seem possible to speak of a gnostic current of thought, comparable to (and in fact influenced by) Middle Platonism. Both can be seen as sets of ideas or interpretive traditions that were not limited to any one school or sect; their influence could be felt in many different contexts.[61]

The influence of Platonism on the gnostic way of thinking is obvious. The dualism of matter and spirit was a major Platonic conviction, and Plato had in *Timaeus* (28a–29a) already presented the idea of a demiurge who used the divine reality as his model in creating the sense-perceptible world. Plato, however, had not provided this notion with a negative color. On the contrary, he had held that the All was the best possible precisely because it had been shaped by the demiurge.[62]

There is no unambiguous evidence for the gnostic way of thinking before the second century c.e. It can therefore at least be debated whether this current of thought arose as a particular way of interpreting the early *Christian* tradition (in which case it would belong to the *development* of early Christianity rather than to its context). This may well be the case at least as regards *Valentinianism*, one of the two major gnostic Christian traditions.[63]

As for the other tradition, known as *Sethianism* (in which Seth, the third son of Adam in the Hebrew Bible, plays a major role), a plausible case for a non-Christian (though *not* necessarily *pre*-Christian) origin can be made. Some Sethian writings seem to lack clearly Christian elements altogether (though no certainty has been reached on this question). The roots of this tradition could then perhaps be found in alienated Jewish circles that had turned their biblical legacy on its head.[64] Several Nag Hammadi documents would represent later christianized versions of this approach. The existence of pre-Christian pagan gnostic movements is very uncertain.[65] Only later did two clearly independent religions, Manicheism and Mandaeism, develop on the basis of gnostic thought.

3

Events, Persons, Sources

Pivotal events in the colorful story of early Christianity include the life and death of Jesus; the Easter visions of his followers; the constitution of the congregation in Jerusalem; the death of Stephen and the dispersion of his Hellenist circle; the mission to Gentiles and the conflicts around it; the sack of Jerusalem and its temple in the Jewish War; the gradual separation of the Jesus-believers from Judaism; the persecution of Christians by Roman authorities; and the formation of the proto-orthodox church and its rejection of gnostic Christians in the course of inner-Christian debates. The documents that make up our source material reflect in various ways these events and their consequences. What follows is a thumbnail sketch of my understanding of these developments, which includes a short presentation of the most important sources.

JESUS:
MISSION, MESSAGE, FATE

It all began with Jesus of Nazareth.[1] He announced the coming of the "kingdom of God," but the meaning of this key concept (or symbol) is open to many interpretations. Notoriously, all reconstructions of the message of Jesus are to be met with caution. The Gospels consist of various layers of tradition and redaction, and it is precarious to try to trace with any great precision "what Jesus really said." Nevertheless, one can venture the claim that he acted as an eschatological preacher who proclaimed a turn of history.[2] His choosing of *twelve* special companions indicates that the turn was to involve a restoration of Israel (or of its repentant part). While Jesus may or may not have regarded himself as the Messiah, the redeemer-king awaited by many, he seems in any case to have reserved for himself a special role in this end-time drama.

Jesus was arrested by Jewish authorities and executed by the Romans as "the king of the Jews." His talk of the kingdom must have evoked associations of the end of Roman rule in the minds of many—not least in the emotion-laden atmosphere of Jerusalem at Passover time. Indeed, it may have been overeager pilgrim crowds that brought a rebel's death on Jesus, the Jewish authorities being nervous about possible Roman intervention and the Romans willing to present a warning example to the crowd (therefore public crucifixion rather than, say, clandestine murder).[3]

No doubt the coming of the kingdom as proclaimed by Jesus would have brought with it the end of Roman rule in Judea (and everywhere). Yet Rome does not seem to have been the real target of his proclamation.[4] He announced a reversal in which the last would the first. The recipients of this message were ordinary people plagued by hunger and illness. The poor and penitent would inherit the kingdom.[5]

The message about the kingdom contained a strong appeal to the hearers to change their lives. The nearness of the kingdom demanded a full commitment to God from those willing to follow Jesus, and implied judgment for those who refused to repent. But Jesus was also known as a powerful miracle worker and exorcist. His ability to heal the sick attracted crowds, who then also listened to his message of the kingdom.

The Gospels give a contradictory picture of Jesus' relation to central Jewish symbols; his attitude to the law appears to range from extreme conservatism to quite radical statements. Considering the subsequent uncertainty of Jesus' followers during the next decades precisely about the application of the Torah, one may infer that he made no clear pronouncements in either direction. His humane interpretation of the Sabbath laws aroused objections from the Pharisees, but need not have transcended the limits of what was socially possible in some Jewish circles.[6] In any case the question of the law was *not* the lethal issue that led to Jesus' execution. The fears caused by his eschatological proclamation seem a much more plausible reason.[7]

THE EASTER EXPERIENCES

Jesus' message did not die with him. This is most of all due to the "Easter experiences" of his followers: their visions of Jesus soon after his death. Paul gives a list of the earliest and most important ones: Jesus appeared to Cephas (Peter), to the Twelve, to "more than five hundred brothers," to

3.1   Christ heals a blind man. Relief (third century C.E.) on an early Christian sarcophagus from Mezzocamino, Via Ostiense, Rome. Cat. 41. Museo Nazionale Romano, Rome. Photo: © Erich Lessing/Art Resource, NY.

58 James (the brother of Jesus), and to "all the apostles" (1 Cor. 15:3-8). This list had been handed on to him by the community (of Antioch?). Astonishingly, no early narrative accounts of such foundational experiences, not even the very first appearance to Peter[8] or the appearance seen by James,[9] have survived. The extant accounts are quite contradictory. David Friedrich Strauss already inferred that "no one of the narrators knew and presupposed what another records. . . At an early period, there were current only uncertain and very varied reports."[10] Christopher Evans's assessment of the situation is accurate:

> The impression given in some accounts is of a figure who has been resuscitated to a fully physical, visible and tangible state, and in other accounts of one who is not immediately recognizable . . . except through specific acts and words.[11] The manner of the Risen One's "coming" and "going," his being present and being absent, are presented in different ways and without explanation. While the risen Christ of Luke

3.2   Crucifixion. Fifth century c.e. One of the earliest depictions of this subject. Cypress wood carving from the door. S. Sabina, Rome. Photo: © Scala/Art Resource, NY.

moves towards ascension,[12] the ascended Christ of Matthew stays with men until the end of the age,[13] but not as the bodily risen one.[14]

The one element in common is that the appearances "issued an explicit command to evangelize the world, yet the early decades . . . make it difficult to suppose that the apostles were aware of any such command." Evans concludes that "the principal difficulty here is not to believe, but to know what it is which offers itself for belief." "There is a marked contrast between the centrality of the Easter faith in the New Testament, and the almost fortuitous character of the traditions which now support it."[15]

The Gospels narrate in conflicting ways appearances both in Galilee and in Jerusalem. Matthew states what Mark (Mark 14:28; 16:7) implies: the disciples fled to Galilee and saw the risen Jesus there (Matt. 28:16-20). By contrast, Luke and John make Jesus appear in Jerusalem, where the disciples have stayed (Luke 24:36-53; John 20:19-29). It is reasonable to conclude that the first experiences took place in Galilee, "since the appearances in Galilee can hardly be explained if we assume the priority of those in Jerusalem."[16] These events then caused part of Jesus' followers to return to Jerusalem (while others remained in Galilee[17]) and to form there a community of their own.

The New Testament Gospels also tell in different versions the story that certain women (Mary Magdalene is singled out) found Jesus' tomb empty (Mark 16:1-8 and par.). The origin of this tradition is highly controversial in scholarship,[18] and so is its significance (if any) in the thought worlds of the Jesus-believers in pre-Gospel times. What seems clear is that such a tradition was *not* the foundation of the resurrection faith—the visions were.[19]

Significantly enough, Paul sees no difference in principle between his own, admittedly late, vision of the risen Christ and that experienced by those who were "in Christ" before him (1 Cor. 15). The way he speaks in the same connection of the glorious "spiritual" body in store for the Christians at *their* resurrection suggests that his "seeing" Christ may have been a luminous visual experience. It is reasonable to assume that the earlier encounters of others with the risen Christ would have been of a similar nature;[20] it is probably no coincidence that visions of *Christ* and experiences of the *spirit* can merge (cf. John 20:21-22).[21] In this light, it is tempting to connect Paul's reference to the appearance to more than five hundred with Luke's stylized account of the "pouring out" of the spirit in Acts 2.[22] Extraordinary phenomena ascribed to the action of the spirit, such as glossolalia, continued to occupy a central place in the life of the congregations.

The Easter experiences did not make a similar impact on all followers of Jesus. Q puts all emphasis on the teachings of Jesus during his lifetime, and in the surviving fragments from the Ebionites Jesus' baptism receives more attention. But on the whole the Easter visions, interpreted as encounters with the resurrected Jesus, were a crucial incentive in the formation of the earliest congregations. In light of Jesus' proclamation of the kingdom, his followers interpreted these experiences as the beginning of the end-time events. They now propagated the message of the imminent turn of history in a transformed shape: Jesus had been raised to a heavenly throne and was soon to return to establish God's kingdom. His raising from the dead was believed soon to initiate a general resurrection (cf. 1 Cor. 15:20; Rev. 1:5).[23]

The Beginnings of the Gentile Mission

Reliable information of the life and thought of the early community in Jerusalem is sparse.[24] Apparently the Jesus-believers understood themselves as a special group within Judaism; they continued to participate in the temple cult and to observe the Torah. What distinguished them was primarily their belief in the importance of Jesus and their enthusiastic consciousness of the possession of the spirit. The circle of the Twelve was reestablished to symbolize the expected restoration of Israel, the practice of end-time baptism (once learned from John the Baptist) was resumed, and the common meals Jesus had celebrated with his followers were continued as sacred community meals.

Despite some friction with the priestly aristocracy, the Jesus-believers had some initial success. They attracted a number of others, and after some time there were in Jerusalem *two* communities of Jesus-believers. Beneath Luke's account in Acts 6–8 traces of an old division can be found: along with the Aramaic-speaking community of "Hebrews," led by Peter (and the "Twelve"?), a community of Greek-speaking "Hellenists," led by Stephen and a circle of "Seven," had come into existence. The latter were Diaspora Jews who had come to Jerusalem and there joined the new movement. Soon enough a tension developed between them and the "Hebrews."[25] Luke plays down the conflict as a practical matter that concerned the care of widows, but the division seems to have been more serious.[26] There were evidently ideological differences, which are reflected in a fateful conflict of some of the Hellenists with some non-Christian Jews. Stephen was killed in a riot and some members of his circle

60   left Jerusalem, while the Hebrew leaders were able to stay. It is not quite clear what the offense was. Luke's account of the accusations against Stephen (Acts 6:13-14) singles out attacks against the law and the temple.[27] The Stephen group may have shown some laxity with regard to the Torah, and their attitude toward the temple may have been problematic, but the particulars remain conjectural.

Some of the Hellenists landed in the Syrian city of Antioch, where they established a circle of their own (probably within a local synagogue), attracted some Gentiles who joined their circle, and, according to Acts 11:26, came to be distinguished from other Jews by the nickname "Christians" (the "Messiah party").[28]

The Jesus movement had thus gained uncircumcised male members; Gentiles had been made part of God's Israel *as* Gentiles! As so often in religious history, practice probably preceded theory. There are indications that Gentile receptivity to the new message[29] and ecstatic experiences on their part[30] played a role, apparently even a decisive role. The spirit experiences may have triggered a bold reinterpretation of Jewish tradition: God had shown that Gentiles could be accepted as members of his people without being circumcised; thus at least some requirements of the Torah could be sidestepped if fellowship with Gentile converts demanded it.

Paul had "persecuted" (whatever the word means here[31]) some Hellenists (or their converts) in Damascus; when a vision of the risen Jesus changed his life, he immediately knew that he himself had been called to be a messenger to the Gentiles (or so he claims in retrospect in Gal. 1:15-17). This suggests that the issue of the acceptance of Gentiles without circumcision was the decisive bone of contention between Paul and those he had harassed.

Whatever the precise nature of the early troubles in Jerusalem, the legacy of the Hellenists, which the fugitives brought to Antioch and to other places (such as Samaria[32] and Damascus), turned out to be a decisive factor in the development of the movement. Antioch became an important center, whose influence radiated in different directions.[33] Paul, too, found his way to the city and became a missionary of the Antiochian congregation. Paul was to make an immense contribution to the Christian mission, but the Hellenist heritage was also disseminated by others independently of him. The message reached Rome long before Paul wrote of his plans to visit the city, and it is reasonable to assume that some Hellenists or their followers had brought it there—possibly through "mouth-to-mouth propaganda," without any planned missionary efforts.[34] The Johannine circle too seems to go back to efforts by some Hellenists, and traces of their influence may be found all over early Christianity.[35] The Hellenists surely laid foundations for many currents that become visible in our sources only during the next generations.

CONFLICTS AROUND THE GENTILE MISSION

There is a grain of truth in the claim that Paul was the founder of Christianity as we know it.[36] He is clearly different from Jesus; among New Testament authors it is he who best embodies the reorientation that took place during the early decades of the Jesus movement. Paul did not initiate this new development—one could even better call the Hellenists around Stephen the "founders of Christianity"—but he came to put his indelible stamp on it through his formidable missionary effort and his wide literary output in the form of correspondence with his congregations in various critical situations.

Paul had started his religious life as the member of a rigorous wing of the Pharisees (Gal. 1:13-14). His loyalty to the traditions of the fathers had kindled in him a zeal that led him to oppose fanatically the followers of Jesus. In the middle of this activity, a vision of Jesus changed his life.[37] Paul drew the inference that the Jesus-believers were, after all, right in their messianic claims—and in their convictions about the Torah and the Gentiles as well.

The vision sparked off a colorful career. Paul later broke with the Antiochians (see below) and continued his work as a freelance apostle (envoy). His mission lasted some thirty years. He traveled widely, hurrying from one city to another in an eschatological fervor. He founded communities in Greece and Asia Minor, preached a law-free message of Jesus the Christ and Lord, and encouraged Jewish and Gentile believers to share meals without regard to biblical dietary regulations. He faced grave opposition both from the synagogue and from more traditional Jewish Christ-believers. Most Jews regarded him as an apostate; even for many Jewish-born Christ-believers he was a suspect heretic. Only wishful thinking can make a "good Jew" of Paul. Yet he himself never ceased to regard himself as a Jew, and one of the rather few true Jews at that.

Paul was continually engaged in conflicts. The most serious issue was his relation to the congregation of Jerusalem. Some visitors from the Holy City (branded by Paul as "false brethren" spying on the freedom of his community) took offense at the table fellowship practiced in Antioch and demanded the circumcision of Gentile believers (Gal. 2:4). Paul had to go to Je-

rusalem (c. 49 C.E.) to defend his practice before the pillars of the church (James, the brother of Jesus; Peter; and John, the son of Zebedee, one of the Twelve) in a meeting that is often called (somewhat pompously) the "apostolic council," though something like "the Jerusalem conference"[38] would be more accurate.[39] It was agreed that Paul could continue his work among the Gentiles and accept them without circumcision. Luke's version of the meeting adds an extra demand: Gentile converts were to observe a minimum of Jewish religious obligations set forth in the "apostolic decree" (Acts 15:20, 29). This, however, seems to be part of Luke's tactics of playing down conflicts between Paul and Jerusalem (see below).[40]

Concrete questions about the nature of the Jewish-Gentile fellowship in the congregations were evidently not solved in the Jerusalem meeting. They soon turned out to be problematic and caused a fateful clash in Antioch (Gal. 2:11-14).[41] Peter had come to Antioch and adopted the local practice: Jewish and Gentile Christians ate together. However, the appearance of some "men from James" caused him to withdraw from this table fellowship.[42] Other Jewish Christians followed suit, among them even Paul's superior and close companion, Barnabas. Paul reacted fiercely, publicly accusing Peter of hypocrisy (Gal. 2:14). It is very difficult to find out what exactly the problem was for the envoys of James,[43] but apparently table fellowship *within a Gentile framework* was unacceptable to strict Jewish Christians.[44] Political pressure may well have been involved; the trouble in Antioch may also be seen "as a Jewish-Christian response to a rise in nationalist sentiments among Jews in Judaea, which placed them in some danger."[45] It seems that Paul lost the fight and, as a consequence, broke both with Barnabas and with the

62 Antiochian congregation, working from now on as an independent missionary.

It is often thought that the above-mentioned Apostolic Decree was an attempt by the Jerusalem community to clarify, in the aftermath of this conflict, the conditions of Jewish and Gentile Jesus-believers living together.[46] Indeed, Acts gives the impression that the purpose of the decree is to regulate the practical relations between (conservative) Jewish Christians and Gentile Christians in that it lays down the minimum amount of the Torah that the latter are to observe. It is, however, difficult to understand the decree as any kind of summary of the Torah. Interpreters usually connect it with the stipula-

tions concerning foreigners in Leviticus 17–18, but even this connection is tenuous.[47] It is more likely that the decree came into existence without regard to the issue of the coexistence of Jewish and Gentile believers. In other words, it was a stipulation that even Gentile Christians were to observe in any case—not just for the sake of the more conservative believers but even for their own sakes. Since the decree in Acts 15 is directed to the Antioch church and the congregations in Syria and Cilicia, it was probably a measure first adopted in that area.[48]

Paul regarded the Antiochian incident as a precedent for what happened later in Galatia, where some Judaizers encouraged Gentile Chris-

3.3   Busts of the Apostles Peter and Paul, profiles turned towards each other. Bas-relief (unfinished), fourth century c.e. Museo Archeologico Nazionale, Aquileia, Italy. Photo: © Erich Lessing/Art Resource, NY.

tians to be circumcised. Presumably these Jewish Christians, who became the target of Paul's fierce attack, shared the Jerusalem point of view. In Romans 15:31 Paul later expressed his fear that the collection he had gathered for Jerusalem from his Gentile or mixed Jewish-Gentile congregations might not be accepted by the Jerusalem congregation—a fear that probably came true.[49]

In critical situations, Paul kept contact with his congregations through letters, a number of which have been preserved. The Corinthian correspondence (1 and 2 Corinthians)[50] bears witness to all kinds of practical problems among the new, mainly Gentile converts, and to prominent critics who challenged Paul's personal authority. The heavily polemical Galatians is a virulent attack on more conservative missionaries and contains very negative statements on the Torah. Paul's later letter to the Romans, to a group of house churches he had not founded himself, has a more conciliatory tone. The picture is rounded by an early letter to the Thessalonians (1 Thessalonians), a late one to the Philippians, and a personal note to a private individual, Philemon.[51]

Paul (and perhaps some of his closest associates?)[52] presented a radically critical assessment of Jewish religious practice (at least when applied to association with Gentile fellow-believers). Others were content with quietly dropping some practices, an act often justified with allegorical interpretation of scripture. This seems to have been the path taken by the Hellenistic mission at large.

Paul's final encounter with the Jerusalem community proved fateful. He was arrested and brought to Rome, where he was evidently executed (in the persecution by Nero?). There is sad irony in that not too long before this time, Paul had assured the Romans that state authorities are a cause of fear only to those who do evil (Rom. 13:1-7).

The congregation in Jerusalem maintained a distinctly Jewish identity. James was, since the 40s, the unquestioned leader.[53] His devotion to the Torah was admired even by non-Christian Jews. He was nevertheless executed by a high priest in 62 C.E., ostensibly for transgressing the law, but in reality for obscure political reasons.[54] James's high reputation as a central Christian figure is reflected in that he is referred or appealed to as an authority even in unexpected connections.[55] Peter took a more moderate course and evidently played an important mediating role. In his name, too, a number of pseudepigraphic works were composed.[56]

Jesus Remembered

In Paul's writings, sayings of Jesus do not loom large, but quite a few of his contemporaries were keen on treasuring teachings of the Master and stories of his actions. The collection of the Sayings Gospel, Q[57] (nowadays often located in Galilee[58]), was in process in Paul's time, even if the final editing took place somewhat later.[59] Q is much more than just a "source" for the canonical Gospels (Matthew and Luke); it is a programmatic writing that reflects the ideas and ideals of a particular group of Jesus-followers. Some were probably wandering charismatics who continued the mission started by Jesus, but the composition of the document presupposes a settled milieu;[60] it may have been produced by village scribes who put their stamp on it.[61] Loyalty to the Torah was important to them, but their community was engaged in a conflict with the local synagogue (apparently led by Pharisees), where its message had been rejected.[62]

Other anonymous teachers and preachers, first in Palestine, then also in Syria and elsewhere,

64 were also concerned with remembering and re-telling what Jesus had said and done. Traditions were formed during the first generation; small collections of, for example, miracle stories and parables were put together; more comprehensive accounts of Jesus' passion also came into being. Such materials have been preserved in the various Gospels that were produced during the next generation.[63]

FROM THE JEWISH WAR TO THE EARLY SECOND CENTURY

The next period is characterized by the repercussions of the Jewish War on one hand and the worsening of the relations of the Jesus-believers to the Roman state on the other. The grouping of documents in what follows is somewhat arbitrary; there is often also great uncertainty concerning date, authorship, and provenance.

The execution of James and other leading figures, and in particular the destruction of Jerusalem, which rendered the city insignificant, were blows from which the church of Jerusalem never recovered. Conservative Jewish Christianity of the "James" type was isolated and lost its central position, though other members of the family of Jesus still had prominent roles in the Jerusalem community that survived down to the time of Hadrian (cf. Eusebius, *Hist. eccl.* 4.5), finally disappearing in the aftermath of the Bar Kokhba rebellion. A. J. M. Wedderburn notes that "the development of the church now took a different course to what one would have expected had the Jerusalem church retained its influence and authority. . . . It is a sobering thought that it was the Roman legions that in large measure snuffed out the rival to Pauline Christianity and ensured the triumph of the latter."[64] The center of gravity in early Christianity inevitably moved to Rome.

The relation to the state gradually became an issue for the Christians, too. Jewish synagogues had been tolerated by the state. As long as the authorities did not distinguish between Jews and Christians, the Christian groups could take advantage of the same privilege. At the same time, they could become victims of any disciplinary measure taken against Jews, such as their expulsion from Rome by Claudius, probably in 49 c.e. But when the magistrates gradually became aware of the difference, no doubt largely due to the increase of non-Jewish adherents, Christians lost this protective cover. The Neronian persecution in Rome in 64 c.e. was the first sign of the changing situation. Sporadic persecutions broke out toward the end of the century, yet it was not the authorities who were responsible for bringing Christians to court, but rather the local population. Contrary to a common view, the imperial cult seems not to have been a central issue.

The More Liberal Wing

In the Gospel of Mark, episodes from the life story of Jesus and a lengthy account of his last days form the framework into which a relatively small amount of teachings and instructions have been inserted.[65] This Gospel follows the model of ancient biographies,[66] though in some respects resembling works of ancient historiography.[67] This writing, the earliest of the three Synoptic Gospels,[68] composed by an unknown author,[69] combines a Hellenistic Christian mission theology with Palestinian traditions about Jesus. Parts of the material have been shaped in the midst of a law-free Gentile mission akin to that of Paul,[70] even though many of Paul's theological emphases are missing. The tribulations connected with the Jewish War are reflected in an apocalyptic speech ascribed to Jesus (Mark 13), which the author has edited. The necessity of perseverance in the midst of sufferings is a central theme. The Gospel has been traditionally located in Rome, but in view of the nearness of the events of the war, either Syria or northern Palestine is a more likely candidate.[71]

Paul's heritage was cherished in pseudonymous epistles. Colossians, a cento of Pauline phrases and reminiscences,[72] combats in Paul's name a "heresy" that looks rather like the ideology of Revelation. Ephesians in turn draws heavily on Colossians, using phrases and clauses from that letter. From the perspective of a Gentile Christian, the author celebrates the fall of the wall that had separated Jews from Gentiles. In sharp contrast to these letters, which represent a "spiritualized" interpretation of Paul's legacy, 2 Thessalonians comes forward with a strong apocalyptic message. The pseudonymous 1 Peter writes in the name of Peter, but seems to draw on Paul's letters, with which it shares many theological features (indeed, it is more akin to Paul than to Peter). The author writes in a situation of local discrimination and harassment.

The anonymous Epistle to the Hebrews (actually a homily, possibly composed in Rome around the turn of the first century) was later often ascribed to Paul.[73] The author is an educated Christian who makes lavish use of typological exegesis: institutions of the Hebrew Bible are interpreted as types of Christ. The temple cult is obsolete, for it has been fulfilled in the work of Christ, who is portrayed both as the sacrificial victim and as the sacrificing high priest. Faced with the possibility that some members of the community will turn away, the author claims that they will have no chance of forgiveness.

The *Epistle of Barnabas* (in fact an anonymous treatise) was probably written in the early decades of the second century, either in Syria or in Alexandria. It combines a resurgence of imminent expectation of the end with an allegorical and typological exposition of scripture akin to that found in Hebrews.[74]

First Clement is attributed, probably rightly, to a prominent member of the Roman church at the turn of the century.[75] Clement writes by order of the Roman church, which wants to intervene in a conflict of authority that has arisen in Corinth. In elevated rhetorical style, the letter calls for "harmony and concord," drawing both on the Septuagint and on Stoic philosophy to make its point. The name of Clement had much prestige,[76] and a body of pseudepigraphic literature grew around him, including *2 Clement*, a miscellaneous homily from the latter part of the second century, and the *Pseudo-Clementine* romance (see below).

The More Conservative Wing

The heritage of the Jerusalem church may have lived on in what came to be called "Ebionite" circles, but their views are known from somewhat later times in later sources (see below). A somewhat milder conservatism persists in the Gospel of Matthew,[77] plausibly seen as an ideological continuation of Q.[78] For all its openness to the Gentile world (as expressed in the universalist mission command in Matt. 28:19-20),[79] Matthew also exhibits a strongly critical attitude to that world (cf. 18:17; 5:46-47). Matthew takes over the narrative framework of the Pauline Gospel of Mark, but corrects Mark's picture of Jesus' liberal attitude to the Torah.[80] He portrays Jesus as a powerful teacher by including the main contents of Q into the framework of Mark and presenting Jesus' teachings in five great speeches,

66 starting with the Sermon on the Mount. A debate is ongoing whether Matthew's community[81] still finds itself in the confines of the synagogue. My position is that a break has taken place.[82] Most locate the Gospel in Syria,[83] often more precisely in Antioch.[84]

The *Didache*, "The Teaching of the Twelve Apostles," is a (likewise probably Syrian) combination of a moral tractate and a manual of church order that draws on sayings of Jesus, making use of the Gospel of Matthew.[85] The writing has some strikingly archaic features, notably in its Eucharist liturgy. It provides interesting information about the wandering prophets (in the tradition of Jesus and Q) who still visit congregations—and may cause problems.[86]

The Revelation of John is an apocalypse whose present form stems from Asia Minor at the time of Domitian (81–96 C.E.), but which makes use of older materials in its powerful, drastic visions. It too carries on the legacy of the itinerant Palestinian prophets, combining an imminent earthly eschatology with a glowing hatred against Rome (for religious rather than political reasons)[87] and a fierce criticism of the liberal social practice of some Christian circles in the Asian cities.

The pseudonymous Epistle of James, a collection of moral instructions attributed to the famous brother of the Lord, is difficult to locate or to date (anywhere between 75 and 125?). Its message is rooted in Hellenistic Jewish wisdom and contains negative statements about wealth and the rich, and a strong sense of communal sharing. The author draws on sayings of Jesus resembling those in the Sermon on the Mount. He is highly critical of Pauline soteriology (as he understands it). The Epistle of Jude is another letter written in the name of a brother of Jesus, perhaps toward the end of the first century. It consists of a vicious attack against some other Christians.

The *Testaments of the Twelve Patriarchs* are a special case (see above, p. 39). If (as is likely) the original collection was a Jewish (composite) work, some Christians adopted it and subjected it, especially its eschatological passages, to another redaction. They added predictions about Jesus, the "man who renews the law in the power of the Most High" (*T. Levi* 16.3).[88] Another Jewish work that underwent a Christian revision is the *Ascension of Isaiah*. It contains clearly Christian parts, the earliest dating perhaps from the end of the first century C.E., that reflect a distinctive early form of Christianity. They describe the coming of the Savior, the corruption of the church, and the final end-time events.[89]

The Gospel of Luke and the Acts of the Apostles come from one and the same author. He is conventionally called Luke (after a companion of Paul to whom the work was attributed in patristic tradition), though we do not know who he really was. Luke–Acts may be placed in the borderline area between this generation and the next[90]—and also between the liberal and the conservative wings of the Christianity of the time. Luke modeled the story of Jesus on Hellenistic biography. Like Matthew, he used Mark's Gospel as the basis of his work and also included the conservative Q materials; on the whole he too preserves a conservative outlook on the Torah. Ideological continuity between biblical Israel and his own religion is all-important, but actual Torah observance is replaced with the observance of the Apostolic Decree. In the Gospel, Luke paints an impressive, almost melodramatic picture of Jesus as the great friend of sinners, a picture to which our other sources offer only modest parallels. In Acts he is at pains to present the early Christians as living in perfect harmony, which requires him to take a lot of historical freedom,[91] so much so that he comes to portray Paul as the most conservative of all the early leaders, letting Peter and James (!) make all the liberal decisions that were required for the Gentile mission to flourish. Luke's work should only be used with caution in attempts to reconstruct the earliest history of Christianity.

FURTHER DEVELOPMENTS

When we move toward the second century, the allocation and grouping of the sources becomes even more difficult. The chronological criteria are not absolute. For example, the Gospel of John may be a little earlier than the Acts of the Apostles. Its introduction is postponed to the present section because of its thematic and ideological proximity to those varieties of early Christianity that are here classified as "mystical" and "gnostic."

The Conservative Wing

In their refutations of heretics, several church fathers from Irenaeus on[92] report on Ebionites,[93] Jewish-born Christians who had preserved a firm Jewish identity and continued to observe the Torah, including circumcision and food laws. They were not a monolith; we have to reckon with varieties and developments.[94] Nevertheless, the family resemblances between the circles introduced below seem sufficient to justify the use of the common umbrella term to distinguish these more or less conservative Jewish Christians of the second and third centuries from their first-century counterparts.[95] The Ebionites hated Paul[96] and maintained an archaic view of Jesus as an ordinary man.[97] The church fathers

(above all, Irenaeus, *Haer.* 1.26.2) report that they used a version of the Gospel of Matthew, but the preserved fragments from the writing that scholars have termed the *Gospel of the Ebionites* show that it draws (in a harmonizing manner) on both Matthew and Luke. The related *Gospel of the Hebrews* shows influence of Jewish wisdom traditions.[98]

Important, relatively early Jewish Christian sources with an Ebionite coloring have been isolated from the fourth-century *Pseudo-Clementine* romance.[99] First, there is an anti-Pauline story of early Christianity, critical of Luke's Acts of the Apostles, which is embedded in a selective history of Israel (*Ps.-Clem. Rec.* 1.27-71), probably from the latter half of the second century.[100] Lacking a better designation,[101] I shall call it the *Ebionite History*. This work probably stands "in some sort of direct genetic relationship to earliest Jewish Christianity."[102] Another source used in the composition of the *Pseudo-Clementines* is the *Circuits of Peter* (c. 220).[103] A more abstruse version of Jewish Christianity was represented by the Elchasaites. They appealed to a sacred book given by a huge angel, the Son of God (accompanied by a female "Holy Spirit") to a righteous man called Elchasai. They did missionary work, promising the remission of sins to those who listened to the message of this (originally Jewish?) book and were baptized a second time.[104]

Other Christians took up elements of old Jewish Christian traditions without necessarily observing Jewish customs. A potential example is Cerinthus (in Asia Minor around the turn of the first century), who shared both the Ebionite view of Jesus as a mere man (to be distinguished from "Christ") and the millenarian view of a coming kingdom on the earth; yet there is no early evidence that he observed Jewish practice.[105]

68 ### *"Mystical" and Platonist Strands*

Converts to the Jesus movement from Greco-Roman paganism inevitably understood the contents of the new tidings in light of their previous values and convictions. The same is surely true of many converts from the circles of Diaspora Jews, who had long been open to influences from Greco-Roman culture. These previous convictions had been strongly affected by Middle Platonist and Stoic philosophy. Many took for granted the distinction between body and soul and the immortality of the soul, notions suited to lead to a lack of interest in concrete end-time events on the earth. Such persons came to understand the Christian message in a more "spiritual" way than the first followers of Jesus (who had expected a kingdom on the earth and a resurrection of the body) had done. Clear signs of spiritualizing interpretation in a Platonic vein are already seen in the views of those Corinthian Christians, whose ideas of the afterlife caused problems for Paul (who, for all his polemics, was himself not free from Platonic influences either). The Corinthian spiritualists may have received support from Paul's Alexandrian fellow missionary, Apollos.

The Gospel of John is ascribed in later tradition to John, son of Zebedee, one of the Twelve, but the real author is unknown. It is usually thought that the enigmatic beloved disciple was regarded by the Johannine community as its founder and authority,[106] but one can argue that this figure is a purely literary character in John's narrative.[107] The Gospel uses some early Palestinian Jesus traditions; it also draws on traditions cherished by the Hellenists and by the church in Antioch.[108] Yet from such traditional beginnings a quite distinctive theology is developed. The three Johannine Epistles show that this theology was cultivated in a Johannine circle, to some extent comparable to the philosophical schools of

the time. Strikingly, no external references to this circle or its literary products exist before mid-second century; it must have lived rather isolated from the rest of early Christianity.[109]

The Gospel of John paints a portrait of Jesus that is rather different from the Synoptic pictures.[110] Jesus gives long speeches that aim at revealing his identity as the divine Savior (often in an "I am" discourse, for example, John 6:35, 48; 8:12; 11:25; 14:6). He is a heavenly figure who has become "flesh" but whose divine glory tends to overshadow his humanness. Echoes of traditional end-time language are heard (cf. 5:28-29), but concrete eschatology has been replaced by what might be called individualist mysticism (cf. 14:20); no wonder that this work became the favorite Gospel of gnostically oriented Christians. Evidently the Gospel has a prehistory,[111] but no generally accepted theory about its sources has been established.[112] The work may have been completed by the end of the first or the beginning of the second century. It has traditionally been located in Ephesus, but today many scholars prefer Syria. In the background looms a serious conflict with the local synagogue.

The First Epistle of John (actually a tractate) refers to a split in the Johannine circle,[113] a consequence of disagreements concerning the person of Jesus. Some members have left the community. The author encourages those who have stayed, assuring that they have true faith and that the separatists are to be blamed.[114] Two brief letters, 2 and 3 John, evidently written by a single author who calls himself "the Elder," attempt to handle the repercussions of the same crisis.[115]

The Odes of Solomon, a collection of 42 communal hymns, were composed probably in Syriac[116] around 100 C.E. by Christians of Jewish origin in Syria. Many of these meditative songs are modeled on psalms from the Hebrew Bible. In a language rich with images and metaphors, they celebrate the appearance of the Messiah and the "present experience of eternal life and love from and for the Beloved."[117] Sometimes the singer speaks in the first person as the living Lord (for example, *Odes Sol.* 8.8-19; 17.6-17; 31.6-13; 42.3-20)—an intriguing parallel to the "I am" discourses in John's Gospel.

Ignatius, the bishop of Antioch early in the second century,[118] is known from seven letters that he wrote while he was being brought to Rome as a prisoner destined for the arena. He paradoxically combines the emergence of a mystical strand of Christianity, akin to John, and an emphasis on discipline and hierarchical order, underlining the role of the bishop in church life. Ignatius pleads for the unity of the church and vigorously fights some other Christians who hold a docetic view of Christ (the view that Christ was only apparently a really human being). He looks forward to his own martyr's death with a fanatic fervor, wishing to be ground as "God's wheat" by the teeth of wild beasts in order to become the "pure bread of Christ" (Ign. *Rom.* 4.1).

The *Gospel of Thomas* is an esoteric collection of secret and often mysteriously baffling sayings of "the living Jesus," which has been dated both very early (c. 50 C.E.) and quite late (mid-second century). No doubt the writing consists of several layers; dating the final form around the turn of the first century to the second has much to commend it.[119] Part of the earlier material is independent of the canonical Gospels; later layers go further in a spiritualizing, mystical, and moderately ascetic direction.[120] The kingdom of God is understood as an invisible reality that enlightened individuals can find within themselves. Other writings, too, are attributed to the apostle Thomas, a figure of great authority in Syrian Christianity. The book of *Thomas the Contender* is a strictly ascetic writing, probably from around 200 C.E., describing post-Easter dialogues be-

tween Jesus and his disciples and apparently drawing on the *Gospel of Thomas.*

The *Dialogue of the Savior* (written perhaps in Syria during the first half of the second century) bears some resemblance to the *Gospel of Thomas*; probably both draw on a common tradition. The writing presents Christian theology

3.4   The last page of the *Gospel of Thomas*, followed by the damaged opening lines of the *Gospel of Philip*. Photo courtesy of the Institute for Antiquity and Christianity, Claremont, California.

70 in a Platonic vein, presupposing the divine origin of the human soul and envisaging its return to its heavenly home.

The *Gospel of Mary* (Magdalene), written early in the second century, presents an interpretation of Jesus' teachings as a path to inner spiritual knowledge, rejects a soteriological interpretation of his death, and argues forcefully for the legitimacy of women as bearers of divine revelation.[121] The *Authoritative Teaching* (from Egypt, in the second century) is "a heavily metaphorical exposition of the origin, condition, and ultimate destiny of the soul."[122] The *Apocryphon of James* (late second century, possibly from Egypt) describes Jesus' dialogues with his disciples 550 days after his resurrection.

Radical Paulinism

Marcion, a wealthy shipowner or overseas merchant from Pontus, has often been considered a gnostic, though he emphasizes faith more than knowledge. He took up and developed the radical side of Paul, starting with the latter's scathing criticisms of the Torah in Galatians. Marcion was morally offended by many passages in Jewish scripture and decided that the church should get rid of it and of its God, who was an inferior demiurge, far below the true God who was manifested in Christ (at this point Marcion does resemble gnostic Christians). Marcion replaced Jewish scripture with a new collection of authoritative texts: ten letters of Paul and the Gospel of Luke (purged of some "Jewish" features that Marcion did not accept). As his views were rejected in Rome, where he was active in the 140s, Marcion founded a church of his own. This church, in which strict asceticism was practiced, flourished quite a long time as a formidable rival to the emerging orthodox church. "For many in the second century, whether Christian believ-

ers or outside observers, the word 'Christianity' would have meant 'Marcionite Christianity.'"[123]

Popular Strands

The *Gospel of Peter* provides a window into the popular Christianity of the (early?) second century. The work, of which a peculiar section that narrates the passion of Jesus is preserved, is mostly rightly regarded as a literary pastiche of texts borrowed by memory from the canonical Gospels, especially Matthew, and embellished by (partly fanciful) oral traditions.[124]

The wish to fill gaps in the story of Jesus gave rise to a number of popular infancy gospels, in which miraculous features abound. The circumstances surrounding Jesus' birth are described in detail in the *Protoevangelium of James*, in which Jesus is totally eclipsed by his mother, Mary. The *Infancy Gospel of Thomas*, perhaps from the end of the second century, portrays the boy Jesus as a child prodigy who performs massive miracles, but also excels as a teacher and revealer of divine secrets. Parallels abound from legends surrounding Krishna and the Buddha, as well as from various fairy tales.[125]

Apostolic novels[126] (traditionally called "apocryphal acts") imitate the style of Hellenistic romances. They are Christian entertainment literature where animals talk, help Christians, and can even receive baptism; all this is told about a famous lion in the *Acts of Paul*. The *Acts of Peter* (composed toward the end of the second century in Asia Minor or in Rome) depicts Peter as a mighty miracle worker who makes a dog talk and a smoked tuna swim, and defeats the notorious Simon Magus in a duel of wonder-workers. The *Acts of Paul* was composed by a presbyter in Asia Minor at the end of the second century.[127] It portrays Paul as a preacher of rigorous sexual continence,[128] which is presented as the precondition of resurrection (a recurring motif in the popular "acts"). The work also contains an independent piece (possibly from the the middle of the second century): the *Acts of Thecla*, a woman who leaves her fiancé, joins the apostle, makes a career as a missionary who vastly overshadows Paul, and eventually experiences a miraculous rescue from martyrdom.[129] Other relatively early works (possibly from the beginning of the third century) include *Acts of Andrew*, *Acts of John*, and *Acts of Thomas*.[130]

Prophecies and Revelations

The *Apocalypse of Peter* (Egypt, early second century?) introduces popular Greek notions of the afterlife, in particular gruesome punishments in hell, into Christian tradition.[131] The *Shepherd of Hermas* consists of a series of visionary revelations (divided into *Visions*, *Mandates*, and *Similitudes*) experienced by Hermas, a Roman Christian from the first half of the second century.[132] Most of these visions (often complex allegories) are explained to Hermas by a shepherd who turns out to be the "angel of repentance." The work advocates a rigorous ethic of perfection; if one sins after baptism, there is one (but only one) opportunity to receive forgiveness through repentance. Much of Hermas's material stems from Hellenistic Jewish moral teaching, while many significant details come from the Greco-Roman milieu.[133]

The ecstatic side of early Christianity was vigorously reactivated in the latter part of the second century in a renewal movement, which its adherents called simply "Prophecy" and its opponents the "New Prophecy," but which has later come to be known as Montanism after one of its early leaders, Montanus. The movement had egalitarian features, for in its initial phase two women prophets, Maximilla and Priscilla, had leading positions. The Montanists revitalized the expectation of an imminent end and considered the utterances and texts of their prophets to be as authoritative as those of the apostles. They maintained strict morality and denied the possibility of a second repentance after baptism. The movement spread rapidly, but was eventually declared heretical because of the irrational nature of its prophecy and its claim for authority; no doubt the visible role of women played a part, too.[134]

Proto-Orthodox

The term *proto-orthodox* is used here "to denote the views that later came to a position of dominance in Christianity," views that can be said to represent a kind of "incipient orthodoxy."[135] While Justin (c. 150) and Irenaeus (c. 180) may be regarded as the first full-blown representatives of proto-orthodox theology, their work is anticipated by authors who stress the apostolic tradition and set out to defend the faith against both inner-Christian and outside criticisms. The Pastoral Epistles (1 and 2 Timothy, Titus), written in Paul's name, reflect "Pauline" communities that are adapting to the values of the larger society: a marginalization of women is in progress. More rigid structures of church order and a treasure of doctrine are emerging; ascetic and gnostic tendencies are opposed. Polycarp, the bishop of Smyrna, collected Ignatius's letters and provided a cover letter for the collection. Like Ignatius, he warns against docetic teachers. Polycarp himself died as a martyr (c. 156). The account of his death in the arena (the *Martyrdom of Polycarp*) is one of the earliest pieces of martyrological literature, even though its present form is hardly earlier than mid-third century.

Second Peter, written during the first half of the second century, possibly in Rome,[136] likewise appeals to established truth (2 Pet. 1:12). In the

72 name of Peter, the author attacks "scoffers" who criticize the expectation of the parousia, since nothing has happened during the bygone century. The author takes Paul's authority, too, for granted but insists that the difficult letters of the latter are to be interpreted in the right way (that is, not advocating imminent expectation in Paul's time!).[137]

The *Epistle of the Apostles*, probably composed in Egypt in the mid-second century, presents dialogues between the risen Jesus and the twelve apostles, from which a kind of overall account of the faith evolves. The divinity of Jesus and the reality of his bodily resurrection are emphasized.[138]

Only a few fragments survive from the *Preaching of Peter*, an early second-century tractate on monotheism, paganism, and Judaism, reminiscent of the sermons in the Acts of the Apostles and therefore seen as a possible intermediary between early Christian missionary proclamation and Christian apologetic literature.[139] The increase of local persecutions gave a stimulus for specifically apologetic literature that defended the faith on both legal and intellectual grounds. Several such writings were formally addressed to the emperor (though he was not expected to read them; they were written for other Christians to arm them with arguments in debates). Quadratus and Aristides presented apologies to Hadrian, Athenagoras to Marcus Aurelius and Commodus. The apologists also include Melito, bishop of Sardis, who around 170 praised Augustus's establishment of peace as divine preparation for the gospel; Theophilus, bishop of Antioch, who wrote *To Autolycus* around 180; and the anonymous author of *The Epistle to Diognetus*, probably from the end of the second century.

The most ambitious apologetic work was, however, that of Justin, who presided over a philosophical school in Rome and addressed his two *Apologies* to Antoninus Pius around 150 C.E. Justin argued that charges of atheism against the Christians were instigated by demons; ancient Greek philosophers foresaw Christian truth. In *Dialogue with Trypho*, he defended this truth against Jewish criticisms, trying to show that the Old Testament speaks of Jesus Christ throughout. Justin died as a martyr in 164.

Tatian, a Syrian from Mesopotamia, was converted by Justin in Rome. After a break with the Roman church, in 172 he returned to his home country. He wrote a fiercely polemical *Address to the Greeks* and composed a Gospel harmony, the *Diatessaron*, which wove together the four Gospels that would become canonical. This work remained in church use in Syria down to the fifth century. Tatian also advocated asceticism.

Christians with Gnostic Leanings

Attempts to combine elements of the Jesus-movement traditions with key convictions from the wider culture, including Platonic philosophy, gradually become more visible in the sources. Along with the dualism of matter and spirit (manifested in the dichotomy between the human body and the divine soul embedded in it), the assumption of two different Gods gains prominence. Such assumptions used to be connected with Gnosticism, which was known through the polemical accounts of Irenaeus and other church fathers (Hippolytus, Tertullian, and Epiphanius in particular). The discovery of the Coptic Nag Hammadi library in Upper Egypt in 1945 has made possible a fairer treatment of gnostic Christians on their own terms.[140] Scholars have also increasingly, with good reason, ceased to apply the label "gnostic" to some writings that used to be so called, such as the *Gospel of Thomas*, the

Gospel of Mary, and the *Dialogue of the Savior* (listed above as representatives of a Platonist or mystical strand in early Christianity). The shift that has taken place in the study of Gnosticism was briefly characterized in the previous chapter (see above, p. 54). There I adopted a bipolar definition of gnostic thought, comprising the notion of (an) evil or ignorant world creator(s) and the idea that the human soul has its origin and goal in a transcendent world.

In writings that can with some plausibility be called gnostic, knowledge (a liberating insight, often connected with mystical piety) has a more central position than in Christian writings in general. Knowledge and faith are not necessarily alternatives, however. Sometimes faith belongs to a less mature stage, but faith and knowledge can also complement each other. Humans are citizens of two worlds: the body comes from an inferior demiurge (or demiurges),[141] but an inner divine spark connects them with the true God. Humans must be made conscious of their true origin (in general through a savior figure, mostly identified with Christ) so that they become able to return to the divine Fullness (*Pleroma*). The concern for human origins leads to a speculative interest in the origins of the visible world in the form of complex mythology. In general, gnostic teachers do not simply reject more conventional notions of Christianity; they want to provide a deeper spiritual interpretation of the tradition on a higher level for those with ears to hear. An early representative of gnostic Christian thought is Saturninus (Saturnilos) from Antioch in Syria (whose system is only known from descriptions in hostile sources).[142]

Basilides, who was active in Alexandria in the early second century, is traditionally listed as a gnostic. But if one focuses on the authentic fragments of his work[143] that have survived in patristic citations, rather than the polemical reports of Irenaeus and Hippolytus (which disagree with each other), what seems to emerge is simply a Christian theologian and exegete open to Platonism and Stoicism.[144] Another early Egyptian teacher associated with Gnosticism was Carpocrates, whose followers came to be generally regarded (rightly or wrongly) as ethical libertinists.

The two most significant early movements among gnostically inclined Christians are Valentinian and Sethian Christianity. Valentinianism was relatively well known even prior to the new discoveries; by contrast, only the Nag Hammadi library has made it possible to set forth the central ideas of Sethianism.

Valentinus led a philosophical school in Rome around the middle of the second century. Unlike his contemporary Marcion, he remained a member of the Roman church, and it is even related that he once ran for the office of bishop.[145] Irenaeus was worried that the Valentinians did not separate themselves clearly into a group of their own but participated in the common meetings of the Christians; in his view this made their heresy especially dangerous. The difference between Valentinians and other Christians was thus far from obvious.[146] Of Valentinus's own works a few fragments have been preserved.[147] An eloquent poem called *Harvest* (frg. 8) gives expression to a Stoic notion of the all-pervasive spirit that holds all things together and supports cosmic harmony, indicating that Valentinus's worldview was neither very negative nor strictly dualistic.[148] While the fragments do not contain much that could be designated gnostic, one of them (frg. 1) indicates that Valentinus was familiar with creation traditions similar to those found in the Sethian *Apocryphon of John* (see below).

74 Valentinians appealed to many writings that were to become part of the New Testament. Heracleon wrote in the mid-second century a large commentary on the Gospel of John, displaying great skill, for example, in allegorical exegesis. Ptolemy, possibly to be identified with a person with the same name whose martyr's death around 150 is mentioned by Justin (*2 Apol.* 2),[149] provided in his *Letter to Flora* an acute analysis of the biblical law in light of the Sermon on the Mount.

Some disciples developed Valentinus's ideas in the direction of an elaborate gnostic system.[150] Theodotus comes pretty close to the description by Irenaeus in this regard.[151] In the circles around Marcus "the Magician," women assumed a more active role; the Marcosians were also more clearly characterized by their distinctive rituals than other Valentinians. But while they tended toward "a separate cult movement," for a long time the majority of Valentinians apparently did not form a church of their own, but remained within the community of other Christians.[152]

The following are the most important Valentinian texts from the Nag Hammadi library.[153] The *Gospel of Truth*, possibly from the latter half of the second century, is (despite its title) not a gospel but a homily. It deals mainly with the question how one can find the Father of the All and the place of eternal Rest with him through the revelation of Christ. The writing is also greatly occupied with moral exhortation. The *Treatise on the Resurrection* (also known as the *Letter to Rheginus*) from the late second century discusses questions of survival after death.[154] The *Tripartite Tractate* (third century?) presents a cosmogonic myth akin to that in the Sethian *Apocryphon of John*. Thus there must have been some affinity between the Valentinian and Sethian mythologies.[155] The *Tripartite Trac-*

tate also stands out by emphasizing the lust for power of the demiurge and his assistants. The *Interpretation of Knowledge* is a homily that tries to heal a conflict situation in a congregation divided over spiritual gifts. The *First Apocalypse of James*, a dialogue of the risen Christ with James, has its roots in Jewish Christianity, where James was the great figure. The work is followed by a *Second Apocalypse of James*. The *Gospel of Philip* (which may, however, be late)[156] is a compilation of mixed, sometimes contradictory, statements pertaining primarily to the meaning and value of the (five?) sacraments.

Sethianism has sometimes been called "classic Gnosticism," taken to be the starting point of other gnostic movements.[157] A non-Christian origin, perhaps in alienated Jewish circles, is likely; several texts seem to have been taken over and adapted by Christians. Whether there were actual Sethian communities is controversial; it may be safer to regard Sethianism as an interpretive tradition that could crop up in various contexts at different times.[158] For Sethian circles, Seth, the third son of Adam, rivaled Christ in importance; some even identified the two as manifestations of the same divine entity. Sethians placed exceptional importance on their spiritual ancestry as offspring of Seth and elaborated this theme with mythological speculation.[159] The Deity is generally portrayed as a trinity of Father, Mother, and Son.

The *Apocryphon of John* (from the latter half of the second century, in Egypt?), once quite an important text,[160] consists of the Savior's revelatory speeches to the apostle John. It describes the eternal realm of the true God, the making of the material world by the arrogant creator Yaldabaoth, and the possibility of salvation. Biblical creation narratives are radically reinterpreted. Related traditions are found in the *Hypostasis of* the *Archons* (likewise from the second century?). The *Trimorphic Protennoia* (The Three-formed [Divine] First Thought) is a multilayered document; during a last revision, specifically Johannine Christian materials seem to have been incorporated and interpreted in a consciously docetic fashion.[161] A writing not included in the Nag Hammadi library that displays Sethian features is the recently published *Gospel of Judas*. This is a revelation dialogue in which Judas is the star disciple, who even agrees to fulfill Jesus' stunning last request—to free him from the shackles of his body by handing him over.[162]

Other gnostic writings from the Nag Hammadi library that cannot be classified either as Valentinian or Sethian include the following. The *Sophia of Jesus Christ* is a dialogue between the risen Jesus and his disciples. Its mythology is of a simple sort and the writing contains no polemic between gnostic and nongnostic Christians, which indicates a relatively early date (before 150?).[163] The *Letter of Peter to Philip* (late second century?) is important in that it clearly shows that even gnostic Christians could regard Jesus' suffering as real and as having some positive significance. A different point is made in the Nag Hammadi *Apocalypse of Peter* (which has nothing to do with the writing with the same name mentioned earlier, p. 71): a substitute is crucified, while the living Jesus laughs above the cross at the stupidity of the executioners. The *Second Treatise of the Great Seth* shares this notion and also mocks the minions of the Old Testament God as laughingstocks. The *Apocalypse of Paul* tells of the ascension of Paul through the heavens during which he passes an old man on a throne in the seventh heaven (cf. Dan. 7:13). This man tries to prevent him from reaching the higher heavens—a hostile reference to the Jewish God. The *Testimony of Truth* is an ascetically ori-ented polemical tractate with strictures not only against the nascent orthodoxy but even against the followers of Valentinus and Basilides.

The Marginalization of Gnostic Christians

Irenaeus became bishop of Lyon in 177, yet having grown up in Asia Minor he belonged to the tradition of Pauline churches and also knew the tradition of the Johannine circle. He wrote a comprehensive work *Against Heresies* (c. 180), intended to rebut gnostic interpretations of Christianity; another work that has survived is the *Proof of the Apostolic Preaching*. Irenaeus is often called the first "catholic theologian,"[164] and his work may well be regarded as a synthesis of proto-orthodox Christian teaching at the end of the second century. A stern defender of tradition, he appealed to scripture (being the first known author to consistently refer to a canon of the New Testament), to the rule of faith, and to the succession of bishops.

Tertullian of Carthage stands on the borderline of early Christianity as here conceived. He was the most learned Christian writer of the day and the first great Latin Christian author in the West. Some thirty of his eloquent and fiercely polemical works, written at the end of the second and at the beginning of the third century and concerned with the proper conduct for a Christian in a pagan society, have been preserved. He held to the tradition of the proto-orthodox church, but eventually turned to Montanism, whose eschatology and ethical rigorism appealed to him better than the more conventional life of mainstream Christianity.

The boundary line between gnostic and (proto-) orthodox Christianity remained fluid for quite some time. Two important third-century church fathers put great emphasis on

3.5   Marble portrait head of the emperor Constantine I. c. 325–370 C.E. Metropolitan Museum of Art, New York. Photo: © The Metropolitan Museum of Art/Art Resource, NY.

of the Christian as the true gnostic. Clement was followed as an intellectual leader by Origen (c. 185–254), who was defeated in a conflict with the bishop in Alexandria and had to move to Palestine. He reestablished his philosophical school in Caesarea, where he produced a huge amount of important controversial writings.

In the second century, Christian congregations were still small groups that assembled mainly in private homes. In Rome, for instance, different groups and different Christians showed a relatively tolerant attitude to one another, and gnostic Christians could participate in the common worship without problems. With the growth and institutionalization of the church, however, suspicions toward gnostic interpretations of the faith increased, and they finally came to be regarded as heresies. When Christianity strengthened its grip on the empire, the position of gnostic Christians weakened, especially after Christianity became favored by the state in the fourth century. Gnostic Christians were not counted among the adherents to officially accepted Christianity; their orthodox opponents gained the support of the emperor, which rendered it possible for them to use even violent means. Gnostic Christianity as a serious alternative way of interpreting the faith thereby received a deadly blow; remnants of it found a foothold in Mandaeism and Manicheism.

knowledge (as opposed to "simple" faith), made ample use of Platonic philosophy, and often came close to the views of gnostics. Clement of Alexandria (c. 200) established a school and "became the voice of a lively, acculturated expression of Christian philosophy."[165] Although he argued against gnostics, he himself maintained the ideal

PART II

BASIC PROBLEMS & SOLUTIONS

4

Last Things First
God, History, and Beyond

"Being a Hindu, I am not a victim of the notion that history is going anywhere," an Indian once remarked to a Christian friend.[1] No doubt he hit on a crucial difference between two great traditions. The classic Christian (and Jewish) view used to be that history *is* moving, or rather is moved by God, toward a goal. This vision has had an effect even on secular views of history in the West. "It could be argued that the Bible, with its tale of human history stretching from a long-ago beginning to a final culmination in glory yet to come and its presentation of the historical process as the primary arena of the activity of God, has been the single most important source of the West's historicizing orientation."[2]

A vivid expectation of a great and decisive *turn of history*, brought about by God, was basic to the genesis of the new movement from which Christianity was to develop. This expectation had its roots in Jewish hopes that had evolved during the exile, in the disappointing postexilic conditions, and amid the Maccabean crisis. In critical situations, when Israelite identity was

under threat, the (highly idealized) memories of bygone days, when Yahweh had helped his people "with his mighty hand and his outstretched arm," were actualized, and his promises to intervene again one day became the source of great hopes.

Israelite and Jewish Hopes

The God Who Acts: From Exodus to Exile

The common ancient Near Eastern belief that each people is aided in its fortunes by its Gods is shared by the authors of the historical and prophetic books of the Hebrew Bible;[3] Yahweh is experienced and portrayed as the "God who acts" in Israel's history. The exodus, the deliverance from Egyptian bondage, came to be portrayed as the classic divine act. Albeit historically at best a very minor incident (if it ever happened at all), it

80   became the celebrated archetype of battles won through divine intervention, along with the sensational conquest of Canaan, imagined to have taken place under Joshua. Yahweh was envisaged as providing help in local battles in the time of the judges and of the early monarchy. The idealized memories of such incidents from the golden times, combined with the royal propaganda of court theologians who equated Yahweh's cause with that of the state (for example in Ps. 2), fostered the faith that in the future, too, this God would protect his people and make it victorious on the crucial Day of Yahweh. Tales about the warrior God, painted with colors adapted from old Near Eastern combat myths that celebrated the victory of a God over the monsters of primeval chaos, were combined with hoary Canaanite traditions about Zion, the primeval dwelling place of the Deity. As a result, many were convinced that Jerusalem was inviolable. From this site of cosmic importance a Davidic heir would rule forever.[4]

The dream was shattered by the Babylonian troops. Independence was lost, Jerusalem sacked, upper-class people exiled. "For those who had believed that Yahweh would protect his own people it must have been a time of serious loss of faith after the holocaust."[5] Yet it did not take very long until the belief that Yahweh and his people would eventually be victorious asserted itself once more. In the prophetic visions collected in Isa. 40-55, the expansion of Persia is welcomed as the prelude to a new age. Israel had, through suffering, atoned for her sins. The exiles would return to their land, the tribes of Israel would be regathered. God's mighty act of deliverance would replicate the past: Yahweh would enact a new exodus, explicitly paralleled with his victory over the chaos monsters to conjure up the idea of a new creation. A tremendous

material and spiritual renewal awaited both Israel and the nations, to whom Israel would be a light so that they too would turn to Yahweh.[6] And all this was happening, now! The future had broken into the present. Second Isaiah took "the radical step of identifying God's decisive act with a historical event," the rise of Cyrus, king of Persia (Isa. 45:1-6, 13-14).[7] This is nothing short of inaugurated eschatology—a phenomenon that is by no means limited to early Christianity alone.

The exiles did get permission to return, though few of the new generation took advantage of it. For those who did, the hopes for peace and prosperity were bitterly disappointed. Judah remained a vassal to foreign powers; the dynasty of David was extinguished; the living conditions were poor. The only hopes that were realized were the survival of a community centered on Jerusalem, and a rebuilt—but modest—temple, which was its focus.

The historical experience clashed with expectations. But the optimistic promises were not forgotten. The oracles were gathered and edited into written collections, reinterpreted and reapplied. Other parts of what was to become Israel's scripture, too, were considered to contain divine promises that awaited fulfillment: the promises of great progeny to the patriarchs, the blessings listed at the end of Deuteronomy, the psalms (sung from year to year in public worship) that praised God's mighty reign in Zion.

Not that this expectation of divine deliverance in the future was ever shared by all. The notion of the history of the people and the nations as the scene of God's activity is fairly foreign to wisdom literature before Ben Sira (Proverbs, Job, Ecclesiastes). "For the wise men Yahweh may have been present in the world in many subtle ways but he was not a manipulator of empires in relation to Israel, nor was he known by specific actions in the nation's past."[8] The history-oriented view is *one* important Israelite way of perceiving reality.

For a long time, the would-be turn of history remained this-worldly. On this earth, in the center of which stands Jerusalem with its gloriously renewed temple, a quite new order would be established. Israel would be vindicated. The dispersed tribes would return. Piety and purity would flourish in individual lives and in the cult. About the destiny of other nations various views are found: some predict world peace (to be sure, on the condition that Yahweh's sovereignty is confessed by all nations), but others await the destruction of the Gentiles.[9] Some oracles envisage cosmic upheavals: the skies are wrapped together, the stars fall down from the firmament.[10] This may have originally been metaphoric speech that emphasized the severity of the judgment of the enemies.[11] Later the expectation of cosmic signs became an established belief, and the images were probably understood more literally. Sometimes even the creation of a new cosmos—heaven and earth—is envisaged (Isa. 65:17-18; 66:22; 60:19-20; cf. Zech. 14). Here a novel dualistic vision is about to emerge that emphasizes the contrast and the gap between old and new. The hoped-for new beginning is conceived to be so spectacular that it belongs beyond the world as humans have known it. Still, even the new creation bears evident characteristics of earthly life, though in transformed conditions. The center of Third Isaiah's new earth is still Jerusalem, and while people will there reach an extremely old age—no one dies young—they will still die. But the circumstances are those of an earthly paradise:

> For I am about to create new heavens and a new earth; and the former things shall not be remembered or come to mind. But be glad and rejoice forever in what I am creating; for I am about to create Jerusalem as a joy, and its people as a delight. . . . No more shall the sound of weeping be heard in it, or the cry of distress. No more shall there be in it an infant that lives but a few days, or an old person who does not live out a lifetime; for the one who dies at a hundred years old will be considered a youth. . . . They shall build houses and inhabit them; they shall plant vineyards and eat their fruit. . . . The wolf and the lamb shall feed together, the lion shall eat straw like the ox; but the serpent—its food shall be dust. They shall not hurt or destroy on all my holy mountain. (Isa. 65:17-25)

Apocalypticism

Most of the expectation even in the Persian period seems to have been due to an intra-Israelite development. In the turmoils of Greco-Roman times the expectation received international coloring from the apocalyptic world of ideas then generally in vogue.[12] As the Egyptians[13] and Babylonians[14] had lost their kings, too, "the Hellenistic age was marked by widespread nostalgia for the past and alienation from the present."[15] Now as before, old hopes were sustained, but they were reinterpreted; old prophecies were reapplied in new situations, of which the crisis under Antiochus Epiphanes, with the defilement of the temple, stood out.

The classic view, expressed in the prophetic books, had been that either salvation or destruction could ensue, depending on whether the people mended their ways. Apocalyptic revelations, from *1 Enoch* and Daniel on, seem to imply instead that Yahweh has an immutable plan for the course of events. Events that have already happened in heaven will take place on earth as well. This may be seen as a reaffirmation of the old

82 conviction that eventually Yahweh will save his people; what is new is the notion that the stages on the road to final salvation are predetermined and can, with heavenly aid, be discovered by the sage.[16] This determinism is largely a side effect of the *ex eventu* technique: of the fiction that events of the time of the real author had been revealed to the ancient seer (the alleged author) many centuries ago, which would guarantee that he was able to predict the future of the (real) readers as well. Sometimes the determinism is, as in Zoroastrian theology and in Greek political propaganda, also connected with the idea of world periods; four successive world powers on the stage of history are depicted in drastic imagery in the book of Daniel.[17] But in the end the determinism is mitigated (or contradicted, if you like) by the rival notion, more at home in the ideology of the prophetic books, that the course of events can be affected and the end brought about, for example, by the prayers of the righteous, by conversion to the Torah, or by the deaths of the martyrs.

Largely due to external (above all, Persian) influences, dualistic notions gained in intensity. Sharp distinctions could be drawn between this age and a coming new aeon (temporal dualism), between the wicked and the righteous even in Israel (social dualism),[18] and between this earth and a transcendent heavenly sphere (cosmic dualism). Much of this is palpable in the book of Daniel, composed during the time of Antiochus. After the present time of tribulation, perceived as the worst catastrophe ever in world history, God will prepare deliverance for his people (Dan. 12). In a cosmic battle in which angelic hosts fight infernal beasts,[19] he will break the hostile kingdom into pieces (with his own sovereign might, with no help from "a human hand": 2:45) and establish his own reign: "In the days of those kings the God of heaven will set up a kingdom that shall never be destroyed, nor shall this kingdom be left to another people. It shall crush all these kingdoms and bring them to an end, and it shall stand forever" (2:44). This everlasting dominion is given to "one like a son of man," a mysterious figure whom Daniel sees in a "vision by night" coming "with the clouds of heaven" to God ("the Ancient of Days," 7:13-14). The interpretation of the vision given to the seer apparently identifies him collectively with the saints of Israel, as they are singled out as the possessors of the eternal kingdom: "The kingship and dominion and the greatness of the kingdoms under the whole heaven shall be given to the people of the holy ones of the Most High; their kingdom shall be an everlasting kingdom, and all dominions shall serve and obey them" (7:27).

A great judgment (depicted in more detail in *1 Enoch*, a composition largely from the same period) will take place (Dan. 7:9-14).[20] "Many of those who sleep in the dust of the earth shall awake, some to everlasting life, and some to shame and everlasting contempt" (Dan. 12:2).

Indeed, the Maccabean crisis helped notions of postmortem retribution and life after death gain ground in Judaism. Life after death seems "a kind of appendix to the eschatology of the Old Testament. It doesn't quite fit and the logic of most Old Testament thought doesn't require it, but there are historical reasons here that transcend logic."[21] Daniel 12:2 is the first (and last) unambiguous reference to the idea of resurrection in the Hebrew Bible.[22] The idea, like many other apocalyptic ideas, is clearly Zoroastrian in origin.[23] As is often the case in religious history, encounter with a foreign tradition helped one to come to terms with a dilemma in one's own; it "produced the necessary stimulus for the full development of ideas that were slowly under way in Judaism."[24] The idea of resurrection provides a radical resolution to the problem of innocent suffering; even though it was not caused by the Seleucid oppression,[25] it must have been strengthened in the ordeal. In a situation where those faithful to Yahweh were persecuted and killed, a solution that defied death was, it seemed, capable of saving God's righteousness and sustaining the people's hope. The martyrs would be vindicated and the oppressors punished; the faithful would be resurrected to eternal life.

In the book of Daniel the righteous martyrs are a special case. "Many, not all, will rise; presumably the very good and very bad."[26] The reference to resurrection life is abstract and vague; yet if the author of Daniel 12 saw any connection at all between his vision and that implied in the earlier chapters of the book, especially in chapters 2 and 7,[27] the resurrection life was probably to be lived in a theocracy on this earth.[28] This is clearly the case in the *Animal Apocalypse* (*1 En.* 90), which likewise reflects the Maccabean crisis,[29] and in the (later) *Similitudes of Enoch* (*1 En.* 51.5;[30] 45.5-6; 63) according to which the righteous will lead a happy life on earth, from which sinners have been expelled.

Still, the wording of Dan. 12:2-3 is also "open to the idea of transformation into heavenly existence, glory and light."[31] It could be taken to mean that the "wise men," the righteous leaders of the community, will be raised to the realm of the stars (and thus become like angels); yet this reading, though adopted by many, is hardly the most probable one. If "the wise" are the righteous leaders of the community,[32] it is natural to take their "shining" as referring to their eminence among their companions in the earthly kingdom of God.[33] The destiny of those wicked ones who are called back to life is "shame" and "contempt"; such expressions are easier to connect with a pitiful existence on the earth than with a pun-

ishment in hell. But later the *Testament of Moses*, likewise having the Maccabean crisis in view, does envisage a heavenly future for the whole people after cosmic upheaval and the destruction of its enemies: "God will raise you [Israel] to the heights. Yea, he will fix you firmly in the heaven of the stars. . . . And you will behold from on high. Yea, you will see your enemies on the earth" (*T. Mos.* 10.9-10). Here "the notion of a new creation of heaven and earth is replaced by a division between earth, turned into the place of punishment, and heaven, the realm of salvation."[34]

Expectations at the Time of Jesus

The Maccabean uprising was successful. Yet paradise did not materialize nor did the martyrs wake up. The national heroes began to pursue very mundane power politics. A century later Rome arrived in Palestine, and the land was once more under the thumb of foreign overlords. In these circumstances the predictions of the great reversal stayed alive and were, time and again, reinterpreted. Calculations were revised, disappointments were overcome, and cognitive dissonance reduced by ever new contemporizations. A rich diversity of expectations was the rule.

Nonetheless, with due caution some main features, which must have been shared by a large number of people, can be singled out for the time of Jesus.[35] A central hope (clearly visible in the Gospels) was still that of *collective national restoration*, fostered by reading scripture: God would maintain his covenant loyalty to Israel, or to the faithful among the people. The restoration would entail the deliverance of Israel from its foes, a general resurrection (though this was controversial), a judgment and destruction of the wicked, the reestablishment of the twelve tribes, the subjugation or conversion of Gentiles, possibly a renewed temple, and purity and righteousness in

84 worship and morals.[36] For some in the Diaspora, the notion of a dramatic reversal was replaced by the demythologized notion that the superiority of the Jewish religion would gradually win through universally, although the collective-national eschatology (found, for example, in *Sib. Or. 3*) was dominant even there.[37]

The present was often assessed in pessimistic terms, so much so that a cosmic adversary of the true God—a fallen angel, variously called Mastema, Belial, or Satan—was thought to rule the earth with the aid of a host of demons.[38] The perceived political and/or moral chaos could also be interpreted as divine punishment for the sins of the people. In many scenarios, the coming turn was to be preceded by tribulations, sometimes called "woes," the depiction of which was colored by horrible experiences from Maccabean times (the "desolating sacrilege" had become a stock figure of speech). A variety of eschatological mediator figures existed, too; yet the expectation of a Messiah was not the rule. But various historical events and persons could easily kindle the flames of hope of imminent fulfillment of the great predictions.

Different visions—earthly and transcendent—of the restoration lived side by side. Common to them is the conviction that there will be a point in history after which life will no longer continue its (hitherto) normal course on earth. There will be a great, dramatic reversal of fortunes. There will be a new start for one group of people and an enormous catastrophe for others. The reversal is conceived of in collective terms. One may conceive of the restoration as a fulfillment of paradisal-utopian hopes on this earth, on which a complete reversal will take place, a restructuring of the political and social order. The collective fulfillment can also take place on a new earth, or on the earth created anew, a vision that places less emphasis on historical continuity. Or again, the fulfillment may take place in a transcendent heavenly realm, but it will still have the form of communal life, lived in some continuity with previous communal life on earth.

It is of lesser importance just how soon the reversal is thought to take place—in any case it is expected to happen soon enough, surely in the lifetime of the generation in question. For the Essenes whose views are reflected in the Qumran texts, the crucial events had already begun; the consummation was anticipated in their worship, in which angels participated.

In *4 Ezra* (end of first century C.E.), different expectations are eventually arranged in a sequence of events: first tribulations and battles; then a peaceful kingdom on earth; finally a cosmic reversal, the resurrection, the judgment, and a transcendent kingdom (7.26-44). This attempt at systematization is, however, an exception. As a rule, different notions are not consciously harmonized.

The expectation of the great turn has its roots in experiences of political frustration or alienation (which need not, however, mean intolerable oppression)[39] that are interpreted in the light of the traditions of God acting in history. "Eschatological hopes arise both to compensate for the powerlessness of Israel among the nations and to console groups that were alienated from the power structures within Jewish society."[40] But once they have established themselves as part of a widespread worldview, they are capable of stirring the emotions and actions of people even apart from situations of deprivation (real or perceived).[41] There is, of course, a moral side to the problem: the lack of justice in the world and, often enough, the perceived moral chaos in one's own community. The belief that God's justice will eventually be realized in Israel is based on the covenant relationship thought to exist between Yahweh and the people. The expectation thus also contains the answer to the problem of theodicy: right now few signs of God's loyalty may be visible, but without the slightest doubt the future will show that he *is* faithful to his promises.

Different roads to the great turn were conceived. Some people were guided by a militant view, others (probably the majority) by a more quietistic conviction. The militant tradition looked back to the stories about the conquest of Canaan, to Phinehas (Num. 25), to Gideon (Judg. 6–8), and to the more recent events of the Maccabean times. In this vein, some were ready to take up arms; the Enochic *Animal Apocalypse* encourages support for the Maccabean revolt. The book of Daniel, however, does not. Many were indeed ready to die rather than transgress the law. This conviction, which relied on a direct intervention of God, independently of the doings of humans, could lean on the book of Isaiah and the bulk of apocalyptic literature. Intermediate expectations also existed: God would play the crucial part, but the faithful too would bear arms.[42] Of course, there were those who, due to their social position and welfare (notably the aristocratic priests in Jerusalem), were more or less content with the status quo and did not wish for upheavals.

No doubt there were substantial socioeconomic factors that led to unrest, and finally to rebellion, in Roman Palestine. But the religious tradition itself contributed a great deal to that end. The memories of independence and the promises of a glorious future, both held alive through reading and interpretation of scripture, were themselves a reason for the disdain felt by many toward the Roman reign.[43]

However, the expectation of a concrete, dramatic, collective reversal was never a central concern for all pious Jews. Individual hopes took more individualistic and personal forms. This holds true even for the apocalyptic literature, where we do find "hope for a glorious kingdom, but the hope of the individual even in many apocalyptic texts is for eternal glory with the angels."[44] In a more Platonic vein, some authors in the Diaspora express a view of immortality that is largely disconnected from the historical orientation of the mainstream hopes and more attuned to the Greco-Roman world of thought. We shall return to it in the next chapter, but it is appropriate to mention some examples here. In 4 Maccabees, "immortality is conferred at the moment of death, which is the eschaton for individuals. There is no need for a future consummation."[45] "The idea of an 'end time,' a 'last day,' is replaced by the death of the individual, as the most decisive change."[46] Likewise, the *Testament of Abraham* contains "a consistent teaching of the immortality of each soul, implying immediate judgment after death."[47] Philo gives a spiritualized account of the Jewish tradition, regarding "death as the moment of change, the soul's liberation from the prison of the body."[48] Still, the individual afterlife is often simply juxtaposed with the thought of collective restoration. In the *Book of Watchers*, the souls' expectation of angelic glory (*1 En.* 22) is found alongside a depiction of paradisal conditions on the earth, where the righteous will live a long and happy (yet not eternal!) life (*1 En.* 10; 25). The Alexandrian book of the Wisdom of Solomon holds the view that "the immortal life of the righteous is begun in the temporal life and is not broken by physical death" so that their death "is no real death after all,"[49] as their souls are preserved in God's hand (Wis. 3:1-9); yet the work also contains "clear references to the basic ideas of the Jewish apocalyptic traditions"[50] (especially in a section that depicts

86 the final battle, Wis. 5:17-23).[51] Even in the writings of Philo, who goes perhaps furthest in a spiritualizing direction, there are traces also of a national-utopian scenario.[52] In terms of function, the different hopes boil down to the same effect: justice will ultimately prevail. The meaning of life is not lost in the midst of adversities.

One may distinguish between two ideal types of future hope: a collective earthly expectation on one hand, and an individual transcendent expectation on the other. The former would involve an eternal kingdom of peace and prosperity on this earth into which the righteous dead would rise to share it with the righteous of the last generation. For the latter, events on this earth would be of little or no interest; the righteous would receive their reward, a spiritual eternal life in the transcendent heaven, immediately after death. But while one of these types generally predominates in a given source, features from the other type are more often than not present as well. The symbolic worlds reflected in the sources are a more colorful mixture than a simple logic of ideal types would dictate.

Not surprisingly, much of the diversity found in Jewish sources reappears in the thought world of nascent Christianity.

JESUS AND GOD'S KINGDOM

Eschatological?

Jesus announced the coming of the "kingdom of God." Though direct proof is not abundant, "kingdom of God" can hardly have been a rare term in his environment, for, apart from terminology, the *notion* of God's visible end-time reign was prominent.[53] The Gospel of Mark self-evidently assumes that pious Jews were "waiting for the kingdom of God" (Mark 15:43).[54] All the Gospels presuppose that Jesus did not have to explain the term itself, though he did describe the nature of the *basileia* ("kingdom") in suggestive parabolic language.

The notion of God's reign was familiar, but its meaning for Jesus is open to many interpretations. The "Jesus quest" is split: an eschatological figure and a noneschatological ("sapiential") figure are in hard competition with each other. The former proclaimed God's kingdom as the imminent great turn of history. The latter taught only "subversive wisdom," criticizing the values of this world with witty aphorisms and parables, urging people to live under God's rule in the here and now. Despite the eloquence with which the latter picture is presented,[55] general considerations support the former alternative—a dramatic, eschatological interpretation of Jesus' message.[56] On this view, Jesus proclaimed a dramatic turn that would concern all humans in the near future and involve the restoration of Israel.

To begin with, there is the ideological continuity from John the Baptist to Paul (and beyond). Jesus was baptized by John, who probably announced an imminent turn;[57] though Jesus later went his own way, he always held his mentor in high esteem. Paul still wrote that the turn was so close that few Christians would die before it (1 Thess. 1:9-10; 4:1-18; 1 Cor. 7; 15); in his writings at least vestiges of an earthly fulfillment are found (Rom. 8:19-21). His hope had its roots in that of the early Christian community that lived in vivid expectation of Jesus' return, praying *maranatha*—"Our Lord, come!" (1 Cor. 16:22; *Did.* 10.6). It was thought that the fulfillment of God's promises had begun. The post-Easter visions of Jesus' followers were interpreted in accordance with the eschatological thought world. God had, it was believed, raised Jesus, and this must have been an end-time event, for it anticipated Jesus' return to hold the judgment. In the next generation(s) after Paul, the Synoptic Gospels came into circulation—replete with references to a more or less imminent reversal. If only a couple of such Synoptic sayings (to be mentioned below) were established as authentic words of Jesus, the issue would be settled. But even if one (with a somewhat extreme skepticism) ascribes all of them to Christian prophets or teachers, one still has to explain why *they* interpreted Jesus' message in such a manner.

A plausible reconstruction must find a place for Jesus in this trajectory from the Baptist through the Jerusalem community to Paul and to the Synoptics. A person whose message is concerned simply with living in this world, whether he preaches religious or social reform or just aphoristic wisdom, simply does not fit.

"Postponement sayings" such as Mark 9:1 (*some* of Jesus' hearers will live to see the reversal) and 13:30, 32 (this generation will not pass away, though no one knows the exact hour) defer the expected turn somewhat further to the future: the end is not yet, but it will come during "this generation." They may not be authentic words of Jesus,[58] but then all the more there must be a good reason for their existence. Why did they have to be created? Obviously Jesus' followers had to cope with the delay of what had been hoped for. A different solution to a similar problem finds expression in some noneschatological materials, for example, in the *Gospel of Thomas*. Sayings that depict in noneschatological terms what the kingdom is *not* (Gos. Thom. 3, 113) are best understood as cases of secondary de-eschatologization.[59] In this case too one is reacting to something that was there first. The author of the *Gospel of Thomas* knew of the eschatological understanding of the kingdom taught by Jesus, and he disparaged it.

The eschatological interpretation receives strong support from the fact that Jesus died on a Roman cross. Jesus was arrested by Jewish authorities and executed by the Romans as "the king of the Jews." It is hard to see how preaching love, or pragmatic wisdom, could have brought such a death upon him.[60] It is much easier to understand why Jesus was condemned to death if he spoke of God's kingdom as an imminent reversal. The talk of the kingdom must have evoked in the minds of many hearers, in accordance with (say) the second chapter of Daniel, associations of the end of Roman rule.

Still, it does not seem that Jesus was pronouncedly anti-Roman. His message of a reversal of things was directed to people who were afflicted by hunger, illness, and poverty rather than foreign troops (which were not present in Galilee).[61] Jesus did not envisage a black-and-white contrast between Israel and Rome.[62] He claimed on the contrary that Israel would be divided; only the poor and penitent who accepted his message would enter the kingdom. The envisaged restoration did not concern the whole of Israel. In this, Jesus continued the tradition of social dualism, well established in Jewish apocalypticism, which distinguished between the righteous and the wicked, though the criteria for the dichotomy may have differed somewhat. The divisions in the families of the followers of Jesus (Q 12:51-53) and between himself and his own family (Mark 3:21-35) may have suggested the messianic woes, "the painful eschatological necessity as a present experience."[63]

Prominent features in the Jesus tradition that point in the direction of an imminent reversal and that may well go back to Jesus himself are the notions of *judgment* and *resurrection*.

88 Jesus seems to have pronounced judgment over Galilean towns that did not accept his message. One's relation to Jesus would decide one's fate at the judgment. The imminence of the judgment is such a permeating feature in the tradition (looming large even in the letters of Paul) that it is impossible to exclude it from the message of Jesus.

The references to (a general) resurrection in the Synoptic tradition are more disputed. Q 13:28-29 implies the resurrection of Israel's patriarchs, Q 11:31-32 that of well-known ancient Gentiles (and by implication of all humanity); Mark 12:18-27 and parallels discuss the ("angelic") resurrection life in a controversy with the Sadducees.[64] The authenticity of these texts is controversial.[65] More weight can be put on the general point that principal followers of Jesus interpreted their Easter experiences with the aid of resurrection language: God had *raised* Jesus *from the dead*. Other ways of interpreting the visions would have been available (cf. chapter 5 below). The choice of this particular idiom suggests that the resurrection of the dead had intrigued Jesus' followers already before his death. It is a plausible inference that Jesus himself had turned their thought in this direction (or rather shared the hope they would have held anyway) by telling them that the imminent drama would involve the resurrection of the dead. The cognitive dissonance caused by his fate was then overcome with the aid of the explanation, propelled by the Easter visions, that Jesus had indeed been raised. He was a special case, though: he had been raised before the others and translated to heaven to await the carrying out of his special task.

I have left the Son of Man sayings out of discussion here. Of course, if only a single saying that refers to the expectation of the coming of the Son of Man (for example, Q 17:24) can be established as authentic—and be plausibly interpreted as identifying this Son of Man with Jesus—that would settle the issue and confirm the eschatological interpretation of Jesus' message.[66] Yet the questions of authenticity and meaning of these sayings are highly controversial. Suffice it to say that in any eschatological picture of Jesus' message, Jesus is seen as having envisaged a role for himself in the end-time process. At its most modest, the role is that of an eschatological prophet (comparable to John the Baptist) who simply proclaims the kingdom. But Jesus can also be seen as a Messiah of sorts, God's viceroy ruling over the restored Israel (see below, p. 197).[67]

Proponents of a noneschatological Jesus deny the authenticity of the sayings that refer to an eschatological turn. They rely greatly on the *Gospel of Thomas*, which, however, presupposes (and opposes) an eschatological interpretation of the kingdom. Another source favored by these scholars is the hypothetically reconstructed earliest layer of the Sayings Gospel, Q. It is held that the message of Jesus in this alleged early layer was of a purely sapiential nature, lacking an eschatological dimension.[68] One may question the wisdom of building so much on a controversial reconstruction based on a rather small amount of material;[69] it might be more prudent to view the (reconstructed) text of Q as a whole. It is also far from clear that one can play off sapiential and eschatological concerns against each other. In itself (that is, if we had no weighty eschatological sayings of Jesus in hand), the bulk of wisdom material in the Jesus tradition could well be taken in a noneschatological sense. Q 6:27-35, elaborated in Matt 5:43-48, is a case in point: here the benevolence of the Creator toward his creation, rather than a coming reversal, seems central. However, sapiential and eschatological passages are often found in one and the same Jewish writing.[70] Concern with the affairs of the present world and admiration of the works of creation on one hand, and expectation of a new world on the other, contradictory as they may seem to us, need not exclude each other in apocalyptic thought.[71]

One saying that looms large in noneschatological interpretations of Jesus' message is Q 11:20: "If I cast out demons by the finger of God, then the kingdom of God has come upon you." The authenticity of the saying can be doubted, since it is inseparable from its literary context in Q.[72] But even if one regards it as authentic, it is still open to doubt whether it can support the idea that Jesus did not expect a future kingdom. The saying states that the kingdom has come "upon" the hearers;[73] but is this so decisive an event that nothing else should be expected? Obviously not, since there still are demons to be exorcised. The context (Q 11:15-23) shows that the kingdom of Satan still stands; at best, then, a decisive battle for the kingdom of God is in the process of being fought (on Jesus as an exorcist, see below).

Proponents of a noneschatological picture of Jesus can with some justification refer to a number of parables.[74] It is not immediately clear how the parables of the sower (Mark 4:1-8 par.), the mustard seed (Mark 4:30-32 par.), the leaven (Q 13:20-21), or the seed growing secretly (Mark 4:26-29) fit together with the expectation of a sudden cataclysmic event, comparable to the flood in Noah's days. Yet these parables may be fitted into an eschatological framework, if the modern notions of gradual development and slow organic growth are discarded[75] and the parables in question are taken, following Joachim Jeremias, as contrast stories.[76] They then emphasize the difference between small signs in the present and a wonderful outcome in the future. They could be intended as an antidote against the skepticism of such hearers as may have maintained (reasonably enough) that a few exorcisms, though helpful for the individuals concerned, have not brought the kingdom any nearer.[77] Again, various "parables of crisis" (for example, the unjust steward, Luke 16:1-8) "serve as warnings that one must decide in favor of Jesus' message immediately, for any moment may be too late."[78]

Still, one has to admit the presence of a fair amount of material that can in itself be interpreted without reference to eschatological expectation, and it is easy to see why some interpreters take that as their starting point. Indeed, the presence of this material has made it easier for subsequent Christian tradition to relegate the expectation of the turn of history to the margins. Yet a noneschatological reconstruction leaves too many riddles and does not satisfactorily account for the development from the Baptist onward. Even if Jesus—against all odds—had been a Cynic-like teacher who focused his teaching on living cleverly in this world, then he would have remained an isolated figure, whose real impact on his devotees was short-lived indeed. For in their transmitted form, neither Q nor the *Gospel of Thomas* portrays a this-worldly Jesus. In Q he speaks emphatically of the coming judgment and the parousia of the Son of Man; in the *Gospel of Thomas*, too, he looks forward to a consummation (for insightful individuals) beyond this world (see below). Jesus, as he was remembered, had more to say than, "See how it's done? You can do it also."[79] To understand the rise and early development of Christianity one cannot just dispense with an eschatological Jesus.

On Earth or in Heaven?

If one accepts an eschatological overall view, one is still faced with the problem of conflicting elements: some signs point in the direction of an

90 *earthly* expectation, while others suggest fulfillment in the *beyond*.

1. Indications of a concrete change in the affairs of this world (in such texts as have some claim to authenticity) include the following.

a. During his last meal Jesus says that he will not drink wine until he drinks it "new" in the kingdom of God (Mark 14:25). Irenaeus for one was, sensibly, of the opinion that one does not drink wine in heaven (*Haer.* 5.33.1).

b. The singling out of *twelve* followers as a specific group (which must have been an act of the historical Jesus, as the subsequent "traitor" Judas is included in the number) clearly alludes to the restoration of the tribes of Israel, commonly expected in Jesus' time. The Twelve will sit on thrones and judge those tribes (Q 22:30—but the authenticity of this saying is controversial).[80] The ranking order in the kingdom causes a controversy, which may suggest earthly circumstances (Mark 10:35-45). More importantly, the restoration of the circle of the Twelve after Easter

4.1   Abraham, Isaac, and Jacob in the kingdom of God, here conceived of as a celestial city. Fresco, church of the Virgin Mary's Nativity, Rila Monastery, Bulgaria. Photo by W. Buss. Photo: © DeA Picture Library/Art Resource, NY.

(cf. Acts 1:15-26: Judas had to be replaced in order to preserve the number twelve) was meaningful only if the twelve tribes were expected to be fully represented at the breakthrough of God's reign, conceived of as a kingdom for the purified and restored Israel (cf. Acts 1:6).

c. This hope accounts for the position that *Jerusalem* came to have for Christian Jews, and for their reservations toward the Gentile mission. The coming of the kingdom would take place in the Holy City—where else? The settling in Jerusalem of the leading (Galilean) members of the movement, and their persistence in staying there, is an unmistakable sign that something special was expected to happen there. This connection with a place suggests that the expectation kindled by Jesus was of a concrete kind; the kingdom would come onto the earth.

d. People "arrive" at the banquet of the kingdom "from east and west" (Q 13:29), an expression not well suited to a journey to heaven.[81] The authenticity of the verse, which in its present context envisages a pilgrimage of Gentiles to the kingdom, is not beyond doubt, but whoever phrased it seems to have thought of an actual dinner together with the (resurrected) patriarchs of Israel.

e. The prayer "your kingdom come" (Q 11:2) also suggests an event on the earth. How would the kingdom "come" to heaven, where it had always been present? The demand of the sanctification of God's name (found in the same connection) is in Jewish tradition associated with the eschatological restoration of the dispersed people in the land of Israel.[82] Moreover, the kingdom will bring *material* benefits to the needy, for it belongs to the poor and to those who hunger and weep.[83] "Blessed are you, the poor, for yours is the kingdom of God. Blessed are you who hunger now, for you will be *fed*. Blessed are you who now weep, for you will laugh" (Q 6:20-21).

f. Jesus' healings are understood (by him and his followers) to be a foretaste of the kingdom—a concrete corporeal sign.[84] Through his striking exorcisms,[85] Jesus is struggling for the kingdom by fighting Satan and his demons, thus "binding" and defeating the "strong man" (Mark 3:22-26; cf. Q 11:15-23).[86] In good apocalyptic fashion, the battle has already been decided—God has won the victory over Satan in heaven (Luke 10:18)[87]—but the battle is still to be waged on earth. Yet Jesus is fighting not enemy armies, but Beelzebul's demons in the lives of some Galilean individuals.[88] The combat myth has been moved to a microcosmic level. Interpreting exorcisms and healings as end-time events seems to be Jesus' original invention, unprecedented in his environment.[89]

g. Jesus predicts that the temple will be destroyed (Mark 13:2; 14:58) and replaced with a new one (implying that sacrifices would not cease?). Whatever his attitude to the present temple and its priesthood—a difficult issue that hinges on the interpretation of his rather opaque "temple act"—the expectation of a new, God-built sanctuary would seem to assume (improved) earthly conditions. Why pay special attention to the fate of the temple, if one expects the whole earth to perish anyway?

h. The expectation of an earthly kingdom does not imply that it is built by humans; Jesus does not preach a social gospel. His thought world is probably close to that of the book of Daniel: the kingdom is the work of God alone. It is like weather: the only thing humans can do about it is to get ready for it.[90] Indeed, the radical sayings found in the Jesus tradition about breaking human relations, even hating one's kin, are best explained by the expectation

92 of an imminent turn that demands radical action. One has to prepare for the coming of the kingdom by totally dedicating oneself to living according to God's will, even at the cost of one's life (Mark 8:34 par.). Two decades later Paul still counsels his converts not to marry (if possible), as the end of the present order of things is so near (1 Cor. 7).

2. On the other hand, there are also elements that seem to point to, or are at least compatible with, the expectation of a transcendent fulfillment.

a. According to Q 17:26-37, the coming turn will be a cataclysmic event, comparable to the flood in Noah's days, which will put an end to the present order and bring God's judgment over the impenitent.[91]

b. In this connection it is stated that some people will be "taken," while others are "left" (apparently to perish; Q 17:34-35). It is easier to think here of people being gathered up to heaven[92] than of events on the earth. The same is true of sayings that speak of (the conditions of) "entering life" (Mark 9:43-48; cf. 10:17-27). Here it is not the kingdom that comes but people who "enter" it; "kingdom" (9: 47) is paralleled with "life" (9:43, 45), and the semantic opposite of both is "hell" (Gehenna).[93] The embarrassing harshness of the conditions may be taken as a sign of authenticity.

c. There is an individualizing touch as well: the destiny of a person depends on how he or she succeeds in conquering the temptations caused by his or her "limbs." The "treasure in heaven" (Q 12:33-34; Mark 10:21) refers to the reward awaiting the righteous in the beyond.[94]

d. The debate with the Sadducees (Mark 12:18-27 par.) also reckons with a heavenly fulfillment: the sarcastic question of the opponents presupposes a thoroughly material view of the consummation (which they are mocking), but Jesus' answer envisages asexual resurrection life similar to that of the angels in heaven, and to God's heavenly world such life most naturally belongs.[95] The problem here is the authenticity of the story—an open question at best.

Reconstructions of the thought world of the historical Jesus and of the early tradition-historical trajectories will remain conjectural. Too much depends on the respective judgments on authenticity on one hand and on the different ways of putting together the elements deemed authentic on the other. It remains likely that Jesus reckons with an earthly kingdom; this possibility is supported by the occurrence of such expectation in the thought world of the early post-Easter community—and (in vestiges) still in Paul, whose own thought moves rather in the opposite direction. Yet Jesus himself may have been less than clear as regards the setting of the consummation. His thought world (like that of many authors of Jewish texts from this time) may have contained elements of both earthly and transcendent eschatology, so that he may not have made a clear distinction "between a millennial kingdom and the eternal world to come."[96] We stand on firmer ground with respect to the elements themselves. Kingdom of God, reversal, cataclysmic disaster, judgment, resurrection, eternal life, hell, the age to come, restoration of Israel, angelic glory—all these pieces are there in the early tradition, but how are they to be (or can they be) connected to form anything like a coherent, total picture? In the long run it may be the elements as such that deserve closest attention, independently of any particular synthesizing reconstruction. Their having become part of a sacred tradition has enabled them to live lives of their own. Different pieces of early Jewish or Christian eschatology have been actualized in different historical situations.

Soon enough the expectations develop in different directions in any case. The earthly expectation has left traces in Paul and the Synoptics (though these authors themselves seem to entertain a more transcendent notion); palpably terrestrial conceptions are found in Revelation and in a large stream of subsequent millenarian interpretations. But quite early the earthly expectation has to compete with spiritualizing transcendent visions, some radical, some more modest; these visions do not look forward to a great new future for the world. Some writings combine a vision of transcendent salvation with the expectation of a series of last things on the earth; but as these can take place even in a distant future, they are on their way to being an appendix to world history. This time, too, it is a question of ideal types; in practice it is impossible to draw clear-cut boundaries.

Millenarian Expectation

The concrete expectation of the early community lives on and is elaborated in what may be called a millenarian type of eschatology. One hopes for a gloriously transformed material existence *on the earth*. What is new is that, as in some Jewish writings, the *eschaton* is expected to take place in two stages. One might have thought this to mean that a first stage, during which the reign of Christ or God is established on the earth, would be followed by the final consummation in the beyond (as is the case in *4 Ezra* and *2 Baruch*). This is indeed sometimes the case, but quite often it is not. For it can happen that *both* stages of fulfillment are conceived to take place on the earth (which

may be transformed or re-created), or the two phases will fuse without a clear demarcation line. Apparently the treasure of eschatological tradition is becoming too rich to allow much rational control.

Before we discuss more familiar sources of millenarian eschatology, one lesser-known witness deserves attention. If concrete earthly expectation was a central feature of the thought world of (Jesus and) the early Jerusalem community, one would expect it to live on in the hopes of those who are the most likely heirs of the early community: the Jewish Christian circles proper, often called Ebionites. Yet Jewish Christian witnesses to such a conviction have been ambiguous at best.[97] However, F. Stanley Jones calls attention to a Jewish Christian source in the *Pseudo-Clementine Recognitions* 1.27-71, which I call the *Ebionite History*.[98] Here the land of Israel is of particular importance. The present occupation of (some of) the land of Judea by Christians is seen to be in continuity with God's promise to Abraham for return of the land (*Rec.* 1.37.2; 1.39.3). This present occupation would lead to an earthly kingdom: Jesus "called the poor blessed and promised earthly rewards so that they, the virtuous, would inherit the earth and would be filled with foods and drink and things similar to these" (1.61.2, according to the Syriac text).[99]

This terrestrial kingdom would in turn be followed by the resurrection of the dead (in *Rec.* 1.55.4, "the kingdom of heaven"[100] and the "resurrection of the dead" appear as successive stages in the future). The earthly expectation has thus developed to entail two successive stages of fulfillment.

The earliest surviving document to present a two-stage-fulfillment scenario, however, is a century older than the one just mentioned. The book of Revelation illustrates the anomalies

94 faced by anyone inclined to systematize the end events. For in Revelation (chs. 21–22), even the final consummation is located on the *earth*, albeit on a re-created earth. Before this final stage is reached, however, a lot of things will have happened. An intense period of plagues and tribulations, the escalation of evil, will introduce the final battle between Christ and his enemies, the worst of whom is the Roman emperor, represented through the Danielic image of a mighty beast (Rev. 13 and 17 in particular).[101] The enemies will, of course, be slain—a christianized version of the age-old myth of the battle with the monster (which is directly reflected in Rev. 12). Then there will be a resurrection to life. Satan will be bound, and the faithful—or, more likely, the martyrs—will, after the "first resurrection," reign with Christ[102] for one thousand years in Jerusalem:[103]

> I also saw the souls of those who had been beheaded for their testimony to Jesus and for the word of God. They had not worshiped the beast or its image and had not received its mark on their foreheads or their hands. They came to life and reigned with Christ for a thousand years. The rest of the dead did not come to life until the thousand years were ended. (Rev. 20:4-5)

The passage conveys a strong exhortatory emphasis: if the cost for confessing Christ is high (impending martyrdom), then so is the reward. This is the point of the whole book, as is clear from the letters to the seven churches in its beginning (Rev. 2–3): in them, the author tries to persuade the adressees to remain steadfast in their faith among the coming tribulations. The mention of the reign, however, remains quite

4.2 Apocalyptic scene: the flood and corpses of men, women, children and animals. From the manuscript of Beatus of Saint-Sever, eleventh century c.e. Ms. Lat. 8878, f. 85, Bibliotheque Nationale, Paris. Photo: © Snark/Art Resource, NY.

abstract. It is not even made clear over whom the saints will reign.[104]

Anyway, this paradisal state will not last. When the predetermined time is finished, Satan is let loose to deceive the nations to mount a last attack. A new period of tribulation will ensue, eventually followed by the final bliss (now enjoyed by *all* faithful of all generations) on a new earth, under a new heaven, after a new creation. God dwells with humanity on earth (Rev. 21:3) and can be seen face-to-face (22:4). The new Jerusalem comes down (21:2, 10); eternal life will be life on a new earth. The twelve tribes have been reassembled in the resurrection (21:12). Strikingly enough, even "the kings of the earth shall bring their glory" (21:24, 26) to this new Jerusalem; the leaves of the tree of life there are "for the healing of the nations" (22:2). Such a pilgrimage ill fits the fate of the nations described a little earlier, but precisely therefore it is important: it serves to underline that mundane history has not quite dropped out of view. The vision of the consummation in Revelation preserves some continuity with the vicissitudes of history that have now been healed. God can be claimed to be in control *on earth*.

There is no actual vision of the disappearance of heaven and earth and of the re-creation; its mention in 21:1 (cf. v. 5) is very brief and bleak (likewise in 20:12).[105] By contrast, the depiction of the new Jerusalem is colorful and detailed.[106] Clearly this is where the emphasis lies.

Some have claimed that a realistic understanding of Revelation 21 contradicts the view set forth in Revelation 1–20 of the world as God's creation: why should God first see to it that he takes over the reign on the earth, and then destroy this very earth? But if this is a problem, it is not peculiar to Revelation. It underlies apocalyptic eschatology as a whole, including the preaching of Jesus: if God is the benevolent creator, why the cataclysm? Has the earth been spoiled to such a degree that it cannot be purged (cf. 19:2)? Remembering that systematization of different eschatological notions is rare in Jewish tradition, it is wise not to overvalue the juxtaposition of different expectations in Revelation, as if it were a conscious theological accomplishment. Like other eschatologists, the author presents discrepant scenarios, the main concern being that there *will be a dramatic change* in the future. The borderline between destroying the earth and transforming it is slender; the emphasis may well lie on the latter.

The book of Revelation is flooded with ominous signs of the end. The "woes" are birth pangs of the new things that will happen on the earth. The notion that a series of historical events (such as the escalation of a war) and natural disasters (earthquakes, famines) will lead up to the final culmination had come alive in many circles during the horrors of the Jewish War; it is reflected in Mark 13 and parallels[107] and in the Q apocalypse (Q 17). Behind the Markan apocalypse stands a group of Christians who had interpreted the war as the beginning of the *eschaton* and had apparently been disappointed, as the great turn of history did not take place. Mark encourages his readers, postponing the turn somewhat. The observation of eschatological signs can thus serve opposite ends. Some people infer from signs that the turn must now be very close; this view, earlier set forth by the Christian prophets criticized in Mark 13, becomes central in Revelation.[108] Others, by contrast, try to master the situation by underlining that since the decisive signs are not to be seen, the turn cannot be at hand as yet; therefore, one has to remain calm (Mark, 2 Thessalonians). The author of 2 Thessalonians in particular relies on a clear-cut timetable in the spirit

96 of eschatological determinism: the end cannot be at hand (which some have claimed), for the mysterious "son of lawlessness" (an antichrist figure reminiscent of the beast of Revelation) must appear first, put himself in God's place, and seduce people. This, however, cannot happen until "that which restrains" (2 Thess. 2:6-7, whatever that perpetual *crux interpretum* means)[109] has been removed. As nothing like this is in sight, there is no reason to abandon daily routines.

In subsequent tradition, depictions of the millennium abound, especially in Asia. Papias tells that he has learned from "the unwritten tradition" (notably not from the book of Revelation) that "after the resurrection there will be a period of one thousand years, when the kingdom of Christ will be here on the earth in a bodily shape" (Eusebius, *Hist. eccl.* 3.39.11-12). Similar ideas are held by Christians as different as the editor of the *Ascension of Isaiah* (4.14-17), Cerinthus,[110] Melito of Sardis, and Methodius of Olympus.[111] However, earthly expectation was also well established in Africa, as is shown by Eusebius's account of the view of Bishop Nepos in Egypt,[112] as well as by the writings of Tertullian, Commodianus, and Lactantius.

For Justin, belief in the millennium is a criterion of perfect orthodoxy, though he admits that not all "pious and pure Christians" think in this way: "I and all other entirely orthodox Christians know that there will be a resurrection of the flesh for a period of one thousand years in a Jerusalem rebuilt, adorned and enlarged, as the prophets Ezekiel and Isaiah and others affirm" (*Dial.* 80.5).

In this millenarian tradition, the vague hints of Revelation yield to graphic descriptions of a most concrete kind. The resurrection will introduce a new bodily life on earth. A rebuilt (or descended) Jerusalem is often thought of as the stage. Enormous material blessings are made possible through the incredible abundance of nature. According to Irenaeus, there will be a time

> when the righteous shall bear rule upon their rising from the dead; when also the creation, having been renovated and set free, shall bring forth an abundance of all kinds of food (simply) from the dew of heaven, and from the fertility of earth . . . the Lord used to teach, saying: The days will come in which vines shall grow each having 10,000 branches, and in each branch 10,000 twigs, and in each twig 10,000 shoots, an in each shoot 10,000 clusters, and on every cluster 10,000 grapes, and every grape when pressed will give 25 measures of wine. And when any one of the saints shall lay hold of a cluster, another shall cry out: I am a better cluster, take me; bless the Lord through me. . . . All the animals, feeding only on the produce of the earth, shall in those days live in peaceful harmony together, and be in perfect subjection to man. (*Haer.* 5.33.3)

The millennium is thus painted with colors supplied by Old Testament prophecies, in particular Isaiah 65. There will be an abundance of crops, splendid food and drink;[113] some even think of special sexual pleasure and numerous descendants.[114]

Earthly expectation is often, especially in the beginning, connected with experiences of oppression and persecution. This is palpable in the book of Daniel, of course. In Revelation, in Justin (who suffered a martyr's death himself), and still in Irenaeus the hope is also connected with the idea of recompense. Irenaeus—the bishop of a persecuted community during widespread social unrest—claims that *God's justice requires a material kingdom*: it is necessary that those who were killed for their faith may awake to life and reign in the very same world where they suffered wrong (*Haer.* 5.32.1). The same point is made by Tertullian: the blessings of the millennium are awarded "in compensation for those which in this world we have either refused or been denied. For it is both just, and worthy of God, that his servants should also have joy in that place where they have suffered affliction in his name" (*Marc.* 3.24.5). God's righteousness is at stake, as it was when the hope for resurrection first entered the biblical world of thought.

Something of the original connection with a crisis is thus preserved in millenarian Christian eschatology. Yet this way of thinking can also contribute to the interpretation of a situation as an unbearable crisis as happened in connection with the events leading up to the Jewish War in Palestine. Recent research favors the view that the book of Revelation was not written during a severe persecution; rather, the symbolic world of the seer has a strong influence on how he experiences the world around himself.[115] He carries his religious and social critique of the Roman Empire so far as to demonize the present.

Irenaeus also raises the question of God's promises in more general terms. The righteous must, before attaining the final transcendent salvation, first gain the inheritance that God promised to the fathers. They must be allowed to reign on the earth, for only in this way can the promises concerning the land be fulfilled (*Haer.* 5.32.2).[116] It is a question of God's loyalty to his covenant; it is likewise a question of the dependability of scripture. To be sure, the people of Israel have now been replaced by Christians as the beneficiaries of God's covenant. The promises of scripture have been denationalized, but their full spiritualization or transcendentalization would render them null and void. For several reasons, then, God's trustworthiness requires an eschatological verification in the form of a material kingdom on earth.

Another important point is the positive emphasis on God's creation. Irenaeus truly appreciates material blessings.[117] He makes use of millenarian visions especially in his battle against gnostic Christians, and Lactantius later dwells on the analogy between the days of creation in the beginning and in the millennium. The earthly expectation emphasizes that the creation that has been spoiled through sin gets a new chance. Irenaeus finds yet an additional reason for the millennium: it is needed as pedagogical preparation for the final bliss (for example, *Haer.* 5.32.1; likewise Methodius).

In most scenarios the earthly millennium is followed by a final fulfillment in a different transcendent sphere. Tertullian for one is positive that the "kingdom of heaven" is quite different from the millennium; in it, humans will be transformed into the "substance of angels" (*Marc.* 3.24). The *Elenchus* of Hippolytus anticipates much more clearly than any previous work "the hope of ultimate participation in God himself that will be characteristic of the eschatology of later Greek fathers."[118] The final stage can, however, also be located on a transformed earth, or the two reigns can fuse without any unambiguous demarcation (as seems to be the case with Justin).[119] Sometimes the focus of the millennialists was "so closely fixed on the first resurrection that the second often received no attention."[120] The emphasis has thoroughly changed: whereas in Revelation the millennium is mentioned briefly and the final consummation depicted in vivid detail, it is now the other way round.

One might expect that millenarian hope belongs to the atmosphere of imminent expectation, but this is not always the case. Sometimes the millennium is, on the contrary, deferred into

98 a remote future. This happens when it is embedded in speculation about world periods (so already in the *Epistle of Barnabas*, which, however, stresses that one has to be always awake "in these last days"). Hippolytus (*Dan.* 4.23) reckons with a cosmic week, each of the seven days covering one thousand years. The millennium will begin in the year 6000. As Christ's first coming is calculated to have happened 5,500 years after the creation, one obviously still has to wait for a few centuries.[121] Irenaeus, commenting on scriptural passages, gives the impression that it will take quite some time until all the prophesied events can take place.[122] The millennium is thus on its way to becoming a doctrinal topos; one of its basic functions is now to guarantee the dependability of scripture. The millennium will come to be, since so many biblical passages point to it, and its appearance will solve many problems concerning promises not yet fulfilled.

Indeed, concrete expectation faded in the fourth century. When the position of the church had radically changed, there was no political need for a vision that hinted at a change of rulership in this world. A little later Augustine's rejection of the millennium became hugely influential.

Toward a Kingdom in Heaven

As the great reversal was delayed, in many circles the notion of Jesus as a heavenly ruler on his throne (for example, Phil. 2:9) facilitated the transfer of the kingdom of God to heaven. Jesus had proclaimed that God would establish his kingdom in which he, Jesus, would hold a key position. This had not happened (yet), but God had vindicated Jesus' message by raising him—therefore Jesus had to return for the expectation to be realized. Any cognitive dissonance that may have resulted from the fact that no outward signs of the kingdom were to be seen was overcome through the belief in Jesus' invisible enthronement in heaven. In the long run, this move came to pave the way for a thoroughgoing spiritualization of the hope. "It seems quite likely that the exclusive concentration on the redemption as taking place in another sphere, not on this world at all, may indeed be the result of the resurrection experiences." While in Jesus' time his followers expected "his kingdom to be on a renewed earth, in a transformed situation," the hope was later shifted to heaven (cf. 1 Thess. 4) by the resurrection.[123]

Paul

The process of spiritualization and the concomitant individualization is visible already in Paul's letters, which nevertheless still display traces of the expectation of an earthly kingdom. These letters provide glimpses of a community life in which present experience receives an enhanced positive significance (as it also does, for example, in the texts from Qumran). It goes with this that the notion of the kingdom of God is partly spiritualized (and that the term occurs rarely in Paul): *basileia tou theou* can mean life "in Christ" here and now (for example, Rom. 14:17; 1 Cor. 4:20), though it also refers to a sphere that one may (or may not) "enter" in the future (1 Cor. 6:9-10; Gal. 5:21; cf. 1 Cor. 15:50; 1 Thess. 2:12). Present experience anticipates and points to future consummation.

Paul still looks forward to shattering events in the near future (see especially 1 Thess. 4; 1 Cor. 15). Christ will return to judge the world, the faithful will be saved, the unrighteous apparently destroyed. One singular passage, Rom. 8:18-21, adds that the whole creation will be affected. The final outcome is that "all things are subjected to God," who will be "all in all" (1 Cor. 15:28).

But does Paul still expect that a transformed earth will be the stage for the final consummation? The hints he gives to this effect are, at best, vague.

In his earliest letter, 1 Thessalonians, Paul consoles the recipients who have experienced cases of death among them. Apparently at least some of them had believed the return to be so close that everybody would participate in it. Making use of a piece of tradition, Paul affirms that the deceased are at no disadvantage compared to the living:

> For this we declare to you by the word of the Lord, that we who are alive, who are left until the coming of the Lord, will by no means precede those who have died. For the Lord himself . . . will descend from heaven, and the dead in Christ will rise first. Then we who are alive, who are left, will be caught up in the clouds together with them to meet the Lord in the air, and so we will be with the Lord forever. (1 Thess. 4:15-17)

Does Paul think that those "caught up" will accompany Jesus to the earth? This would accord with earlier terrestrial expectation, and the word *apantesis* ("meeting") has connotations of escorting that might support such an interpretation. Yet for Paul the only really important thing is that the believers will now *always* be *in the presence of Christ*; everything else fades. In the following passage (1 Thess. 5:10), Paul underlines that whether we are now alive or dead, what matters is "to live *with him*" when he returns.

First Corinthians 15:20-28 (a digression in which Paul draws on earlier traditions in his ef-

fort to refute people who deny bodily resurrection) has led some interpreters to think that Paul expects a transitional messianic kingdom on the earth (and he does say in v. 25 that "Christ must reign"). However, a different reading is plausible. Paul is drawing a contrast between Christ and Adam: death came to the world through the first man, but "as all die in Adam, so all will be made alive in Christ" (v. 22). For Christ is the "first fruits" of resurrection, and at his coming "those who belong to Christ" will be resurrected as well (v. 23). Then Christ hands over the kingdom to God, having destroyed every inimical power (v. 24). This is elaborated in verses 25-26: "For he must reign until he has put all his enemies under his feet. The last enemy to be destroyed is death." Should verse 25 refer to an earthly reign, death would be destroyed only *after* this reign, meaning that even those made alive in the parousia could die once more. It is much more natural to equate the destruction of death with the resurrection of the Christ-believers at the parousia (v. 23), and this is confirmed by verse 54: "death has been swallowed up in victory" precisely "when this perishable body puts on perishability," that is, in the resurrection (of the believers).

The subjugation of enemies is already in the process of being realized and will be completed in the parousia. The mention of Christ's reign (v. 25) must thus refer to his *heavenly* rule in the *present*; indeed, the statement "he must reign" (an inference from Ps. 110) is far too colorless to be an allusion to an earthly kingdom. However, it could well be a vestige of a concrete expectation, transmitted to Paul by tradition[124] but grown pale in his own mind. In 1 Cor. 7:31, Paul founds his exhortation to the unmarried on the conviction that "the form of this world is passing away," without giving any hint whatsoever that, say, a new form of life would be introduced

100   on a transformed earth. The only statement by Paul that could be conceived of as an allusion to an actual event on the earth after the parousia is the sentence that the saints will participate in the judgment, pronouncing a verdict even on (fallen) angels (1 Cor. 6:2-3). This reminds one of the notion of the Twelve as judges over Israel, though the idea has been democratized (*all* believers appear as judges; cf. Dan. 7:28-29). But even in this case there is no hint at life (and even less at a reign) on the earth after the judgment. It is hardly a coincidence that, unlike the Synoptic tradition, Paul never states that the kingdom "comes."[125]

At the end of 1 Corinthians 15, Paul claims that the bodies of the resurrected, and of those alive at the Lord's coming, will be transformed into a "spiritual" form (on the anthropological issue see the next chapter). The kingdom of God is now equated with "imperishability" (v. 50). No interest in any events on the earth is detectable.

Paul can eventually even juxtapose to the participation in the parousia a different road to salvation. In the admittedly difficult passage 2 Cor. 5:1-10,[126] he speaks as if one could reach the state of being "with the Lord" immediately at death, when the "earthly tent we live in is destroyed" and we may "put on our heavenly dwelling" (vv. 1-2). The parousia is mentioned in the context (2 Cor. 4:14),[127] but only the first half of the passage (vv. 1-5) contains a possible allusion to it,[128] whereas verses 6-10 seem to have the individual's death in view. But, apart from the "putting on" of the new body, even verses 1-5 reveal no interest in any *events* expected to take place on the earth. Paul's gaze is fixed on the invisible heavenly world (cf. 4:18).[129] He has the desire to leave his earthly body, to change it for a heavenly dwelling or garment (vv. 1-2), for he knows that "while we are at home in the body

we are away from the Lord" (v. 6) and he "would rather be away from the body and at home with the Lord" (v. 8). The contrast is between "being away" (from the Lord) and "being at home" (with the Lord), bodily existence belonging to the former phase. If Paul still has the parousia also in mind, he must be thinking even more of the invisible things to be gained after it. However, the drama of the parousia seems to have lost its interest. Not only is death before it reckoned a possibility; it is even desirable.[130] Paul seems to be moving toward an individualized transcendent hope. What remains constant in his expectation is the affirmation of a final judgment, which for the faithful opens the door to being with the Lord forever.[131]

This reading is confirmed by Phil. 1:20-26, where Paul ponders whether he would rather like to die than continue his labors in the world. "My desire is to depart and be with Christ, for that is far better; but to remain in the flesh is more necessary for you" (vv. 23-24). "Dying is gain" (v. 21), because it is a direct route to being "with the Lord." The parousia fades from sight, though it reappears in Phil. 3:20-21: the "commonwealth" of the Christians is "in heaven," from where Christ will come "to transform the body of our humiliation that it may be conformed to the body of his glory." But if the home of the Christians is in heaven, it is natural to think that *that* is where the transformed believers will go after the parousia.

Paul never ceased to wait for the parousia (cf. Rom. 13:11-14), but its significance diminished. The parousia is important, since it brings the faithful to "be with the Lord"; yet this goal can be reached simply through death as well. The experience that the present time continues longer than originally expected, the awareness that many Christians had actually died, and

Paul's own situation (waiting in custody for the outcome of his trial, which could be a sentence of death) certainly contributed to this development.

To be sure, Rom. 8:18-22 confuses the picture. Here the old expectation of a transformed earth makes itself felt. The creation is "groaning" in its "bondage to decay," but it will "obtain the freedom of the glory of the children of God." A cosmic change leading to paradisal harmony within the creation seems to be in view. Paul is probably taking up traditions of the wolf and the sheep sharing the pasture and the lion converting to a vegetarian (Isa. 65), but he uses rather abstract language; his point in the passage seems to be to encourage the "groaning" believers who will soon be "revealed" in glory.

If one simply added up Paul's eschatological passages, one would have to conclude that the kingdom must be on earth;[132] this would be the only way to accommodate Rom. 8:18-22. Philippians 1 and 2 Corinthians 5 would then have to be adjusted, for example, by positing an intermediate state for the naked selves before their return to earth in the resurrection. As such a harmonization is implausible, the view is preferable that in Romans 8 Paul is exploiting a piece of traditional eschatology that no longer belongs to the core of his own convictions. Paul's future hopes do not add up to a consistent picture.[133] The constant features of his expectation—the certainty of judgment and the hope of eternally being with the Lord—can be placed into different frameworks. But if there is a trend, it is toward heaven, away from the earth.

Now one may, very properly, ask: what is the point of the resurrection, if nothing of importance happens on the earth (apart from the parousia itself)? From the early days of the Maccabean crisis on, resurrection faith in Israel had been conceived of as the ultimate solution to the problems of oppression and unjust suffering on this earth. For Paul, however, the parousia seems to be the *end* of history rather than a decisive turn within history. His notion of resurrection and parousia does reflect (and conceptually presupposes) the inherited view that the new life will be lived on (a transformed) earth, but Paul does not seem to share (or to give weight to) this presupposition any more. Paul does not seem overly concerned with problems of oppression or unjust regimes in this world. Unlike the seer of Revelation, Paul, a middle-class cosmopolitan of sorts, apparently does not experience Roman rule as something from which he specifically needs to be redeemed. Not unlike Philo, he may even have deliberately defused or neutralized Israel's (earthly) messianic hope.[134] No social unrest is desirable (Rom. 13:1-7!); no social or political alienation makes itself felt. Theodicy is not his problem (except on another level, in connection with the election of Israel: Rom. 9–11).[135] Unlike the Jesus tradition, for Paul even liberation from illness or poverty does not seem very important.

Paul is still strongly oriented toward the future, but he combines his imminent expectation with a tendency toward spiritualizing and individualizing. He lives his life "in Christ" in the firm hope that he will one day be "with Christ"—forever. Indeed, one may wonder whether someone who had once been raptured to the third heaven and there heard divine secrets (2 Cor. 12:2-4) could have conceived of the final consummation as being located on a lower plane. But Paul walks a tightrope: going in a spiritual direction himself, he simultaneously wants to tone down some even more radical spiritualizing tendencies in his congregations (see below).

One thing is missing from Paul's agenda altogether: the observation of signs of the end.[136]

102 "The day of the Lord will come like a thief in the night," all of a sudden. Therefore, while on earth, Christians have to "keep awake," to be prepared to meet the Lord at any time (1 Thess. 5:1-11).

Developments after Paul

In the Synoptic Gospels we find a peculiar combination: a cataclysmic end of the world and its history, preceded by an utterly dramatic series of eschatological events on the earth is awaited, but the fulfillment is apparently located in a transcendent heaven

In Mark's materials, the "kingdom" sometimes seems (as in Paul) to be anticipated in the present life of Jesus' followers. It is like the leaven in the dough (Mark 4:30-32);[137] an uncharacteristically perceptive scribe is "not far from the kingdom of God" (12:34). Other passages suggest transcendent fulfillment (with an individualistic flavor) in the future.[138] In 9:43-48 the kingdom (v. 47) is equated with "life" (vv. 43, 45), and "hell" (*geenna*) is its semantic opposition. In 10:17-27 the kingdom, mentioned in v. 25, is equated with "eternal life" (v. 17), with the "age to come" (v. 30), with having one's treasure in heaven (v. 21) and with being "saved" (v. 27). Statements about humans "entering" the kingdom (9:43, 45, 47; 10:15) probably envisage the kingdom in the beyond. As we saw, the tension between this notion and the expectation of an earthly kingdom may well go back to an unclarity in Jesus' own conviction.

The author of the Gospel finds himself in a precarious situation, caused by the disastrous Jewish War. The horrors of the war, culminating in the destruction of the temple (which has probably happened, or at least it is impending, in the time of Mark), had evoked a fervid expectation of the parousia. Some people had interpreted the (actual or anticipated) fate of the temple as the signal that the final events had begun. In chapter 13, Mark makes a delicate effort to reach a balance between an eagerly imminent and a somewhat tempered expectation. Adapting traditional materials, he creates a great apocalyptic speech in which Jesus instructs his followers about coming events. As an answer to the question, "what will be the sign that all these things are to be accomplished?" (v. 4), Mark's Jesus "provides a virtual apocalyptic timetable."[139] Those who connect the destruction of the temple directly with the eschatological fulfillment are, for Mark, false prophets who misguide the believers and cause them to be disappointed (vv. 1-6, 21-23). Wars and tribulations "must take place," yet they are "but the beginning of the birth-pangs." "The end is still to come" (13:7-8). Therefore, the readers should not be alarmed. No one, not even Jesus in heaven, knows the exact time of the end (v. 32), but in more general terms it can be known: "this generation will not pass away until all these things have taken place" (v. 30). The saying according to which some (but not many) of Jesus' original hearers will still be alive when the kingdom comes in glory (9:1) is diluted through the Markan composition, where it is immediately followed by Jesus' transfiguration, which thus comes to be seen as its fulfillment. Like Paul, Mark strongly stresses the importance of "staying awake" (13:33-37).

The present is a time of suffering and persecution (Mark 13:9-13), but also a time for witnessing (13:10-11). Soon the Son of Man will come in his glory, and the elect will be gathered by angels from all over the earth, presumably to heaven, as in 1 Thessalonians 4 (Mark 13:24-27).[140] Cosmic disasters (the sun will be darkened, the stars fall down from heaven, 13:24-25) indicate that this world will perish; "heaven and earth will pass away" (v. 31). We hear nothing of a new earth and a new heaven; it would take a lot of special pleading to make verses 24-27 refer simply to the restoration of Israel.[141] Apparently the consummation is conceived as angelic life in the beyond (cf. 12:25).

In the Sayings Gospel, Q, the kingdom has present features in the Pauline vein: it is an effective power within the Jesus movement (Q 11:20). Both in Q and in 1 Cor. 4:20, the kingdom of God involves a threat to its opponents. On the other hand, the expectation of an imminent end is strongly present. This duality has given rise to redaction theories; either the sapiential or (more often) the eschatological layer has been deemed as secondary. It is questionable, however, whether such a dichotomy can be convincingly carried through. An anticipation of the consummation in the present is fully compatible with future expectation, and it is simply not the case that sayings like Q 11:20 imply a full and definitive arrival of the kingdom of God. But, strikingly enough, the parousia passages of Q disparage all observation of signs of the end. The Son of Man will come when people are amid their everyday affairs, suspecting nothing (Q 17:23-37); in this, Q contrasts markedly with Mark. As in Mark, bitter experiences from wartime seem to loom in the background,[142] but Q goes much further in its criticism of signs. Apparently disappointments have made the Q editors very cautious concerning signs: none (except those of repentance and judgment) will be given. In addition, whereas Mark "expressly notes the positive side of the events" (the angels will gather the elect), "Q represents the parousia as a disaster which overwhelms the world." Whereas Mark is concerned with exhortation within the community of the elect, Q seems to represent preaching to the unconverted.[143] The rapture saying Q 17:34-35 seems to imply that those who are saved will enjoy the fulfillment in heaven, not on earth.

Matthew reckons with a prolonged waiting time, setting forth several parables that deal with the delay of the parousia (Matt. 24:32—25:46). But when the last day finally does arrive (Matthew preserves in 24:34 the saying that it will happen during "this generation"), it will be of paramount significance. In some sense the kingdom is undoubtedly present in the life of the congregation right now, but the parousia will make a real difference: a final judgment will take place, and it will bring great surprises. "All causes of sin and all evildoers" will be thrown "into the furnace of fire," but the righteous "will shine like the sun in the kingdom of their Father" (13:42-43). Undoubtedly they find themselves in the glory of the heavenly realm. Indeed, the kingdom has been prepared for the righteous ever since the creation of the world (25:34). It is not said that it will "come" or "descend" (as in Rev. 21), so that the righteous must probably be moved beyond this earth; in his depiction of the parousia Matthew repeats Mark's statement that the elect will be gathered from the four winds, probably to some other place (Matt. 24:31). The kingdom is equated with eternal life (25:46); its opposition is eternal fire (v. 41, also prepared in the beginning and thus already in existence somewhere) or punishment (v. 46). All these traits indicate that we should think of the kingdom in transcendent terms: it will be in heaven.[144]

Nevertheless, some sayings might be taken as references to an earthly consummation.[145] The "rebirth" (*palingenesia*), which is the setting of the Twelve judging the tribes of Israel (Matt. 19:28), could suggest a renewal of this earth, but probably envisages the resurrection of the dead. Matthew is unlikely to put much emphasis on the activity of the Twelve as judges;[146] the point of

104 the passage is the vast compensation promised for their sacrifices. One wonders how literally Matthew conceives of the meal with the patriarchs "in the kingdom of heaven" to which many (Gentiles) come "from east and west" (8:11), or of the drinking of wine there (26:29)—but he does add "with you" to the last-mentioned verse (cf. Mark 14:25), indicating that the rendezvous in the Father's kingdom would be a happy social event. Perhaps Matthew feels no need to make a clear distinction between earthly and heavenly restoration—an ambiguity that he then shares with a great many Jewish writers (and perhaps with Jesus himself). The point is that there will be a great day of judgment, when the sheep and the goats, or the wheat and the tares, will be separated, and everybody will be repaid for what he or she has done (Matt. 16:27). The actual delay notwithstanding, God's justice will prevail.

Luke vigorously emphasizes the present, the time of the church. He plays down the imminent expectation found in his sources. The claim that "the time is near," which Mark (no doubt correctly) presents as the conviction of Jesus (Mark 1:15), is put into the mouth of false prophets by Luke (Luke 21:8). Mark 1:15 is, in its context, replaced by the statement, "today this scripture has been fulfilled" (Luke 4:21). One day the parousia will take place, but only long after the destruction of the temple ("the end will not follow soon," Luke 21:9), and one is left wondering how much difference it will really make. The "last" things are not denied, but they make the impression of an appendix. The individual seems to attain his or her future state right after death, as is the case with Lazarus in the example story (Luke 16:19-31) or with the robber on the cross (Luke 23:43)—or even Jesus and Stephen, both of whom commend their "spirit" into God's hands in death (Luke 23:46; Acts 7:55-56, 59).[147] On

the very day of his death, the robber will be with Jesus in paradise—just as the aging Paul hopes to be with the Lord immediately after death. The parousia and resurrection on one hand, and the private road to Jesus' kingdom on the other, stand side by side in an unresolved tension, which reminds one of a similar tension in many Jewish texts.[148] Apparently the private-road option comes to the fore almost by itself, as soon as the death of an *individual* is considered.

On the other hand, Luke is one of the few early Christian authors to take up explicitly the question of "restoring the kingdom to Israel" (Acts 1:6), which we assume to have been a central part of the earliest hope. He lets the question surface several times, starting with the prophecy of Zechariah that God is about to fulfill "the oath that he swore to our ancestor Abraham, to grant us that we, being *rescued from the hands of our enemies*, might serve him without fear, in holiness and righteousness before him all our days" (Luke 1:75). But gradually it must dawn on the reader that there will be no such kingdom,[149] for the promises about the concrete redemption of Israel have been fulfilled in the resurrection of Christ. Time and again, statements that at first seem to suggest a special hope of redemption for the Jewish people tacitly fuse with or yield to a more individualized and spiritualized view of salvation, even though Luke never admits this in so many words. He lets the national-political promises meld with a spiritual fulfillment.[150] The redemption as Israel's liberation from foreign oppressors (Luke 1:68-75) is tacitly identified with forgiveness of sins (1:77); the risen Jesus' answer to the question regarding the restoration of the kingdom (Acts 1:7-8) suggests that this should be identified with the spread of the Christian mission, and so on.[151] Such spiritualization parallels the neutralization of national messianism by Philo—or by Paul. Spiritualizing and denationalizing were part of intra-Jewish wrestling with the political promises of the Bible.

Spiritual Reinterpretations

We met with tendencies to move the fulfillment from the earth to heaven in our investigation of Paul and others. Here we are concerned with more radical spiritualizing, some of which goes back to very early times. Like the more modest spiritualizing tendencies in Paul and the Gospels (and already in Jewish eschatology), it is influenced by popular Platonic-Stoic notions. It is, however, still visibly connected with notions of a great turn; but terms and expressions traditionally connected with such an event are now being thoroughly reinterpreted. Above all, there is even less interest in possible future events on earth than we have met so far.

Many Gentiles in particular who were drawn toward the early Jesus movement may not have longed for the re-creation of the world, much less for the restoration of Israel. More likely what they hoped for was a meaning for life, liberation from anxiety, and personal happiness. Many a believer was not primarily attracted by concrete visions of the future, but could more easily conceive of the significance of Jesus in vertical categories: Jesus had overcome death and made it possible that *heavenly realities could also be experienced on earth.* The religious experience itself, the anticipation of the final consummation in the joyful, often ecstatic gatherings of the elect, where angels were thought to be invisibly present (cf. 1 Cor. 11:10), paved the way for

more radical spiritualization of the hope. The experience of the presence of God's spirit or of Christ himself could serve to de-emphasize the expectation of a visible turn of history. When the expected outward fulfillment was delayed and little sign of it was to be seen, compensation could be found in the present communion with the indwelling Christ. "Thus the temporary relationship with the exalted Christ, while the Parousia was awaited, readily became of central importance itself. What was sought was that reward which was laid up in heaven: freedom from this world and union with Christ in his presence and that of the Father for ever."[152] A terrestrial kingdom was no longer in the range of vision of many Christians.

Yet a spiritualized eschatology predates the problem of delay. Its earliest representatives in our sources were some members of Paul's congregation in Corinth. Some of those who "say that there is no resurrection" were criticized by Paul in 1 Corinthians 15. Since they belonged to the congregation, they can hardly have denied all postmortem hope for Christ-believers.[153] The sense of fulfillment presently experienced by the believers would, they may have held, continue in another form of existence after death. It may have been the same people who felt that they were already "filled," "rich," and "kings" (as Paul polemically exclaims in 1 Cor. 4:8). This is apparently a spiritualized interpretation of the blessings of the kingdom promised by Jesus to the hungry and the poor, cross-fertilized by the Stoic notion of the wise man as "king" in his independence of external matters.

A consistently spiritual interpretation of the great turn may have been represented by Hymenaeus and Philetus, who are mentioned as Paul's contemporaries in 2 Tim. 2:17-18 and blamed by the author for scandalously claiming

106   that "the resurrection has already happened."[154] The names may be fictive,[155] but they probably stand for some persons who downplayed the significance of death, reckoning with spiritual postmortem life without bodily resurrection. If so, their position was not far from that of such disciples of Paul as the authors of Colossians and Ephesians.[156] Colossians proclaims that Christ has conquered the inimical powers that have barred human access to the divine realm and thus brought harmony back to the cosmos (Col. 2:15, 20). The author goes beyond Paul in claiming that the believers have already been raised with Christ from the dead into life in baptism (Col. 2:12; 3:1; contrast Paul's more reserved formulation in Rom. 6:3-4). Therefore, their life is already now, albeit in a hidden way, life in God (Col. 3:3), and they are to seek "the things that are above," where Christ is (Col. 3:1-2). The earthly pilgrimage has its goal in the heavenly realm. What is expected of the future is the public revelation of the present secret (Col. 3:4). Traditional parousia language[157] is transformed to refer to something that does not take place on earth; no interest in the destiny of the earth is visible. In Ephesians, eschatology has almost[158] been replaced with "a kind of heavenly ecclesiology."[159] Ephesians emphasizes that God has raised us up together with Christ, "and seated us with him [namely, on thrones] in the heavenly places in Christ Jesus" (Eph. 2:5-6)—a statement that reinterprets the notion of the reign of the saints with Christ and might have stemmed from a "Hymenaeus" or a "Philetus" as well. The last word of the epistle summarizes it all: what matters is "imperishability" (Eph. 6:24).

In 1 Peter the earthly pilgrimage of the "aliens and exiles" (1 Pet. 2:11) in this world is contrasted with their heavenly destination. Such language "immediately transfers the focus of interest of the believer from his or her present world to the joys of heaven."[160] "An inheritance that is imperishable . . . [is] kept in heaven for you," who will attain "a salvation ready to be revealed in the last time" (1:4), but this will be "the salvation of your souls" (1:9). This is "the living hope" to which the Christians have been born anew through the resurrection of Christ (1:3). There are references to the "end" (1:4; 4:7: "the end of all things is at hand; therefore keep sane and sober for your prayers") and the judgment (1:17; 2:12; 4:17-18), but the emphasis lies on the vertical dimension.

In the Epistle to the Hebrews the crucial contrast is not between "now" and "later," but between "down here" and "above in heaven."[161] The blessings of this world are a pale shadow of that which has always existed in heaven. While believers still look forward to future consummation,[162] the world is for them only a place of transition during their pilgrimage. The wandering people of God seek for a "heavenly homeland" (Heb. 11:13-16), a "heavenly city" founded by God himself (11:10; 12:22-24); there God's "rest" (*katapausis*) has from all eternity been ready to receive the pious (4:3, 10-11). Now believers may be certain that salvation awaits them in heaven since the exaltation of Christ. A century later, the apologist Athenagoras makes the nonworldly goal of the Christians absolutely clear: "when we depart this present life we shall live another life better than that here, a heavenly one, not earthly, so that we may then abide with God" (*Leg.* 31).

A prominent representative of a spiritual, nonterrestrial type of expectation is the Fourth Gospel. To be sure, references to a future resurrection of the dead and to the judgment are found in this work.[163] But even in these references no renewal of the cosmos is envisaged. The Gospel of

John devotes no attention to the future destiny of the world. "The coming of Christ is not intended to change *the world*; that is merely an arena where the shepherd seeks to gather all his sheep into the fold."[164] The "hour," "when the dead will hear the voice of the Son of God, and those who hear will live," is *now* (John 5:25). The judgment has already taken place (3:18). Jesus is "resurrection and life"; whoever believes in him already has eternal life and will never die—or lives even if he or she dies (11:25-26). All that is decisive has already taken place when the believer "has passed from death to life" in the present (5:24); the decision that has taken place in the life of the believer will be confirmed on the last day.

Physical death is unimportant. Still, eternal life before death is not identical with eternal life as it will be lived in fullness after death, or after the parousia; it is simply a foretaste of the latter. The notion of Jesus' return is still there: not only will Jesus go away to "prepare a place" for the believers; he also says that "I will come again and will take you (*paralambano*)[165] to myself" (John 14:2-3; cf. Paul's talk of being "with the Lord").[166] Yet this is a rather pale allusion to the parousia, entailing an echo of the traditional notion of rapture, but wholly stripped of such apocalyptic language as is found in 1 Thessalonians 4.[167] Jesus will take his own up to the heavenly dwelling places. No reader of John 14 could possibly think of an earthly kingdom after the parousia, nor is any concern for public vindication visible. Verse 23 shows that even a foretaste of the eternal dwellings is available, now, to those who love Jesus: "Those who love me will keep my word, and my Father will love them, and we will come to them and make our home with them."[168]

Ignatius of Antioch, addressing a number of congregations during his enthusiastic and determined path to martyrdom, repeatedly speaks of "attaining God." Clearly he has in mind a transport to heaven immediately upon death. For him, dying is living (Ign. *Rom.* 6.2); "to be near the sword is to be near God" (*Smyrn.* 4.2); "death into Christ" will bring this willing martyr "into the pure light" (*Rom.* 6.1-2; cf. 2.2). But Ignatius also indicates that this lot will not be his alone, but belongs to other Christians as well (*Magn.* 1.2; *Eph.* 11.2). He does mention the impending "last times" (*Eph.* 11.1), but this occasional expression sounds like a faint echo of eschatological urgency. While Ignatius undoubtedly retains the notion of the believers' bodily resurrection at the parousia, this expectation has grown quite pale in comparison with the hope of immediately attaining God's presence.

In the Gospel of John, the certainty of future fulfillment in the dwellings of the Father is surely intended to strengthen the community in its troubles. By contrast, an overwhelmingly joyful atmosphere of present fulfillment dominates in the *Odes of Solomon*, a collection of liturgical poems from the eastern Syrian church in the first half of the second century. Eternal life has been given to all who trust in Christ: "Death has been destroyed before my face, and Sheol has been vanquished by my word. And eternal life has arisen in the Lord's land, and it has become known to his faithful ones, and been given without limit to all that trust him. Hallelujah!" (*Odes Sol.* 15.9-10). "Because the Lord is my salvation, I will not fear . . . if everything visible should perish, I shall not die, because the Lord is with me and I am with him. Hallelujah!" (*Odes Sol.* 5.11-15).

The sense of the present salvation is so dominant that the end of the world, the judgment, and even the resurrection are not at all mentioned as future realities; many lines read as if the believers were already immortal and incorruptible. The "temporary boundary between

108 present and future has been obliterated within the context of charismatic worship, where the glories of the future eschatological salvation are experienced and actualized."[169]

There are close affinities between the Gospel of John and the *Gospel of Thomas*,[170] whose perspective also has partial analogies in Q and in Paul. There is a heightened stress on present fulfillment. The disciples ask, "When will the rest for the dead take place, and when will the new world come?" They receive the answer: "What you look for has come, but you do not recognize it" (*Gos. Thom.* 51). A similar question about the kingdom is answered by Jesus in words reminiscent of Luke 17:20: "it will not come by watching for it. It will not be said, 'Look, here it is,' or 'Look, there it is.' Rather, the Father's kingdom is spread out upon the earth, and people do not see it" (*Gos. Thom.* 113). If it is claimed that "'the kingdom is in heaven,' then the birds of heaven will precede you";[171] "rather, the kingdom is inside you,[172] and it is outside you" (*Gos. Thom.* 3).[173] In the *Dialogue of the Savior* (77-78), the Lord likewise states, in reply to his disciples' question as to where they will go after departing this earth, that they are already standing in that place.[174] In the *Apocryphon of James*, the risen Lord says that the disciples have received life through faith and knowledge; "whoever will receive life and believe in the kingdom will never leave it" (*Apoc. Jas.* 14.8-17).

Thomas criticizes the eschatological tradition "in a programmatic and polemical way," stripping the message of Jesus of all traces of collective, national, or earthly hope, and ridiculing "those who teach that the kingdom will be some concrete reality within the visible world" (*Gos. Thom.* 3).[175] The kingdom of God is an invisible reality that permeates everything. *Thomas* does not speak of its "coming";[176] enlightened individuals are said to find (27, 49), enter (22, 99) or know it (46). Salvation has become "an individual project of seeking true human existence."[177] Yet the tension between present and future is not completely eliminated. "The present situation of Thomas' audience can be characterized as a state of being 'in-between' rather than one of final consummation."[178] The world is "a threat which tries to deprive a Thomasine Christian of the salvation already actualised in the present life (*Gos. Thom.* 51) and of the profit expected in the future consummation (21; 49)."[179] *Thomas* reveals no interest in the affairs of this world, but hints at the destruction of heaven and earth (11, 111). The material cosmos will perish, but this is of no consequence for one who is "living."

A radical elimination of terrestrial eschatology is found in such writings as display more pronounced gnostic inclinations.[180] Menander is said to have promised his disciples actual immortality (they "are able to receive resurrection through their baptism into him [Menander]; they can no longer die but remain ageless and immortal"[181]), though it is impossible to say whether this was his authentic teaching or a malevolent travesty of his teaching by his opponents.[182] Elsewhere such claims should surely be taken in a metaphorical sense (just as in John or in *Thomas*): physical death has lost all significance; it is a question of a way of life in which death and the corruptible world do not master the person. It is through their reception of saving knowledge that persons come to full realization of their divine nature in the present. The spiritual person has already been transferred to the realm of light: "We suffered with him, and we arose with him, and we went to heaven with him" (*Treat. Res.* 45.24-28).[183] "Flee from divisions and bonds, and then you already have the resurrection" (*Treat. Res.* 49.9-16). The believer "who knows of death's inevitability should consider himself as dead already and thus as already participating in the resurrected state" (49.22-25), realizing "the mystical union" between the experience of the Savior and that of himself or herself.[184]

In the *Gospel of Philip* 73.3-5 it is said: "People who say they will first die and then arise are wrong. If they do not receive the resurrection first, when they are alive, they will receive nothing when they die." The context contains a reference to baptism. *Apocryphon of John* 31.22-25 connects the metaphorical immortality explicitly with baptism: "I raised and sealed the person in luminous water with five seals, that death might not prevail over the person from that moment on."

Yet even gnostically inclined Christian teachers share the notion of a *future* spiritual fulfillment: what can be, by way of anticipation, experienced already now will be completely realized when the soul or the *pneuma* is, in death, released from the prison of the body and begins its ascent to the heavenly realm. Nor can it be claimed in a generalizing way that salvation is, for a pneumatic, a merely individual event. For when the naked souls of the enlightened ascend, the particles of light will be gathered together back to their good origin. According to the Valentinian *Tripartite Tractate*, redemption is "an entry into that which is silent, where there is no need of voice, nor of understanding, comprehension, or illumination, but (where) all things are light which does not need to be illumined" (*Tri. Trac.* 124.18-25). The souls, then, have a common, collective goal, the "restoration" (*apokatastasis*) of "all the members of the body of the church" into the Fullness (123.16-21). All who have come forth from the Father will return to him (*Gos. Truth* 38.2-3). It is a question of an escha-tological process that transcends the individual, a teleological plan that must have rendered the experience of the present meaningful for those who knew about it. Still, it should be noted that in quite a few gnostic Christian texts there seems reflected a desire to retain also some kind of personal identity in the postmortem state (see chapter 5 below).

Perhaps unexpectedly, some gnostic texts combine the spiritual eschatology of the soul with a cosmic disaster. One waits, after a series of portents in traditional apocalyptic style, for a cosmic conflagration (originally a Stoic notion) that puts an end to the material world; see, for example, the tractate *On the Origin of the World* (125.33-127.14).[185] But unlike the more orthodox combinations, this one is consistent: no parousia is expected, and no new heaven or new earth will be created.[186] The world will perish, but there will be no new beginning. Everything will be restored to its original good state when the work of the demiurge is annihilated.

In the gnostic perspective, the most profound reality is to be sought within the human beings themselves. This internalized vision is the view of intellectuals concerned with reinterpreting their religious tradition. That traditional expectation is indeed being reinterpreted is suggested by the fact that the "variety of images used to describe the 'End time'" includes a number that stem from standard eschatological usage: restoration, harvest, consummation of the aeon, end of days, the hour, rest in the consummation—along with more peculiar ones like the completion of the Fullness, the entry of the spiritual *syzygoi* into the heavenly bridal chamber, or the time of dissolution.[187]

Despite significant dissimilarities in the notions about creation and humanity, the difference between spiritualizing interpretations of

110 the Christian hope by gnostic Christians on one hand and by many proto-orthodox teachers on the other does not seem overly great. Some non-gnostic theologians even distinguish between enlightened gnostics (like themselves) and simple believers. According to Clement of Alexandria, for the true gnostics death means liberation to be with the Lord in a heavenly home, and their final goal is the eternal vision of God. One receives a foretaste of this consummation already in the present life. But, typically, this spiritual view of the consummation appears mainly in Clement's private notes and esoteric writings.[188] Origen goes even further in presenting a "constructive, respectful and pastorally fruitful way of demythologizing" eschatology for those who are capable of profound thought.[189] A second (allegorical and, for Origen, "truer") parousia is "the coming of Christ in perfected men and women."[190] "The kingdom of God is within you" (Luke 17:21) is a favorite verse with Origen. For him, too, the vision of God is the ultimate goal, and he emphasizes that the "spiritual body" of the resurrected is something quite different from the present body. Although no one has adopted Origen's internalized interpretation of eschatology in its whole radicalness, his influence on the Eastern church has been great. For later fathers it was a commonplace that God's kingdom amounted to his reign in human hearts. The kingdom had changed its nature: it had become an inner reality in the present and a transcendent entity in the future hopes. In the radically changed situation of the church in the fourth century, a revolutionary vision of the earthly future was not desirable anyway.

OUTCOME AND IMPACT

Sometimes the different types of expectation directly compete with one another.[191] Second Peter is involved in a heated conflict with a group that criticizes the expectation of the parousia on the score that everything is as it has always been; no great turn of history is to be seen. Against this, the author insists that a spectacular end is on its way: "the heavens and earth that now exist have been stored up for fire"; the heavens will be kindled and dissolved (cf. 2 Clem. 16.3); "we wait for new heavens and a new earth in which righteousness dwells" (2 Pet. 3:7, 12). The author defends the certainty of this grand finale with miscellaneous arguments: as the deluge once destroyed the earth, so will fire; with the Lord a thousand years are like one day; the delay is also an act of patience, giving all people time to repent—despite the recommendation that the Christians are to *hasten* the coming of the day through holy living.[192]

On the other side of the debate, visible fulfillment is polemically denied in the *Gospel of Thomas* and in writings with gnostic inclinations. Earthly expectation is also criticized by representatives of a spiritual view such as the Roman bishop Gaius,[193] Clement of Alexandria, and Origen. Origen plays down all material expectation and puts forward the idea of *apokatastasis*, the restoration of all, as an impressive version of theodicy.

Obviously, then, the nonoccurrence of the parousia did cause problems. Many passages in the Gospels (for example, Mark 9:1 or the Matthean parousia parables, which emphasize the importance of being "awake") already testify to this, and so does *1 Clement*. Clement presents a kind of apology of traditional expectation in view of the delay of the end (especially chs. 23–28).

Traditional eschatological themes are presented, yet not as connected with a crisis, but (in sharp contrast to 2 Peter) as the culmination of the *orderly* course of world history. Where the stability of the cosmos—the fact that "the heavens, revolving under God's government, are subject to him in peace" (*1 Clem.* 20.1)—is to prove that resurrection too will take place in its time, as day and night follow their rhythm, and growth follows from sowing (ch. 24), cosmic reversals and disasters surely seem out of place.

It would be exaggerated to speak of a profound crisis, but undeniably a thoroughgoing (if tacit) process of reinterpretation did take place. While the more radical spiritualizers dropped concrete expectation altogether, even mainstream theologians adapted themselves surprisingly easily to the "time of the church," which provided the present—the existence under Christ's invisible rule—with meaning and let the future grow pale. Toward the end of the second century, Christians could already *pray for the delay* of the final fulfillment (Tertullian, *Apol.* 39.2).

Eventually it came to be of great importance that Augustine polemically rejected millenarianism and put forward a compromise solution.[194] The millennium of Revelation was identified with the church, in which Christ and the saints already reign—spiritually, by conquering their vices. Augustine's combination of spiritualized soteriology (the individual finds bliss in a transcendent realm) and a postponed expectation of "last things," including the traditional "signs of the end" in a possibly distant future,[195] came to be established as the orthodox doctrine. The last things were to be awaited, since they were foretold in scripture, but inevitably they were "tamed" and turned (in a way already anticipated by Luke) into a kind of appendix.

Terrestrial expectation was banned from mainstream theology, and the great churches have throughout their history been officially quite reserved toward it. Still, the expectation lived on in popular religion, surfacing with significant social consequences, for instance, in medieval movements that culminated in the Anabaptists.[196] Indeed, the vision of an ideal end-time kingdom has played a significant role in Western civilization as a whole. In instigating people to work actively toward that goal themselves, it has inspired various ecclesial and imperial reform programs.[197] In a new guise, millenarian expectation has even fuelled optimistic secular ideologies of progress.[198] It is "becoming increasingly clear that vast numbers of Enlightenment and post-Enlightenment thinkers were influenced by apocalyptic religious traditions, and that through some of these persons, elements of these traditions have been mediated to and reconstituted in important modern political movements such as National Socialism and Communism."[199]

The expectation of a concrete great turn of history has helped people maintain their hope in difficult times. For countless Christians down to the present, it has invested history with meaning and hope.[200] But it has also been dangerous because of the innate power of end-time beliefs "to foster self-righteousness among the elect and at times violent opposition to, even persecution of, those identified as belonging to Satan's party. Apocalypticism has been the source of hope and courage for the oppressed, and—not *too* paradoxically—intransigence and savagery on the part of some oppressors."[201]

The expectation has proved dangerous, when, from the Crusades on,[202] people began to aid God's cause by taking it upon themselves to embark on what was taken to be the eschatological battle. Thereby many came to give up

112 the part of the original hope that stressed that the turn will be wholly God's work. Yet one could appeal to another feature of the biblical (Deuteronomistic) theology of history: God will help his people in its wars against its enemies.[203] The ideologies both of the former Soviet Union[204] (based on Marx's theory, the similarity of which to Judeo-Christian millennialism is striking),[205] and of the United States[206] (which has come to conceive of itself as the "redeemer nation") can in part be traced back to biblical roots, to the battle of the children of light against the children of darkness in order to realize the supernatural goal of history.[207] History exists, as it were, to fulfill prophecies.[208] The view that the course of history is predetermined has led to "foolhardy optimism" on the part of those who thought that God is on their side. "No matter how destructive the battles become, it is the saints who will prevail both in this world and in the next."[209] Something like this is true even of the Third Reich.[210] "Hitler did not reject Christianity entirely, but he worshipped the avenging God of the apocalyptic books, which are often overlooked as sources for the Nazi cult of the glorification of war."[211] Millenarian hope has been a truly mixed blessing in Western history.

Mainstream Christian theology has emphasized the spiritualized expectation of transcendent fulfillment in heaven. Only quite recently have theological conceptions been developed in which this-worldly eschatology is once more in a key position, aided by the "recovery of a psychosomatic understanding of ourselves as unitary beings" and "our fresh appreciation of the importance of the natural environment."[212] This in turn easily leads to the assessment of transcendent expectation as degeneration, especially in theologies of liberation. Heaven can be reinterpreted altogether, so much so that Jürgen Moltmann

can rhetorically ask, "Is there any way of talking about the heaven of glory except in terms of a visionary future of a new earth?"[213]

But undoubtedly earthly expectation is burdened with tremendous problems. That Jesus was mistaken in his crucial expectation is only the beginning of the troubles. More aggravating is the history of Christendom ever since. In its light it is very difficult—some would say frivolous—to believe in a divine will that steers the course of events toward its good and righteous goal. It is easy to sympathize with the nonconformist rabbi Richard Rubenstein when he refuses to accept an omnipotent God, who could have saved Jews from the Holocaust but chose not to intervene.[214] Theodicy asserts that there are hidden reasons for God's allowance of (even this) evil: God is bringing good (it is implied: using a Hitler as his chosen instrument), although its full design is hidden from our eyes. For the likes of Rubenstein,[215] no theodicy can rationalize the enormity of unjust suffering of the Holocaust or vindicate divine justice in the light of innocent Jewish victims.[216] After Auschwitz, at the latest, it has become difficult to believe in a God of history.[217]

Even independently of the theodicy problem, modern theologians have increasingly turned away from a teleological theology of history, which is simply seen to be part of an antiquated worldview. Not only is this the case with Protestant existentialism (made famous by Rudolf Bultmann), in which the significance of "eschatology" consists only in its underlining the importance of the decision required of the individuals in their present encounter with the preaching ("kerygma"). Even an important current of Catholic dogmatics, represented for example by the Rahnerian theologian Medard Kehl, holds that nothing spectacular whatsoever should be expected to happen on the earth. The hope of Christians is oriented to the future and is fulfilled at their death. The parousia of Jesus has taken place in his resurrection, and it also happens continually in the celebration of the Eucharist; in another sense, "Jesus Christ returns when each person arrives to him" (Karl Rahner).[218] These modern solutions come close to the Hindu view—or to the gnostic Christian alternative, for that matter—of taking leave of the "historical process" ideology that has been so characteristic of Western thought: history is after all *not* "going anywhere."[219] Yet traditional earthly expectation has left a trace in the form of a "real-symbolic" aspect: as social justice within bodily reality was of utmost importance in the tradition of terrestrial expectation, during their earthly life Christians are called to struggle for this-wordly justice.

Obviously, both earthly and spiritualized expectation can with some justification appeal to *part* of the early Christian evidence.[220] "Eschatology" is rooted in a dialectical hermeneutical process: present experiences are interpreted in the light of traditions; traditions are reinterpreted in the light of new experiences. In times of crisis one leans on memories of a glorious past on which promises of a bright future can be based. Both the negative experience of the nonarrival of the turn of history, and the positive experiences of the renewal of life here and now, may lead to spiritualizing the hope; new crises can again actualize a more concrete expectation. It is a never-ending story.

5

After Death

The Destiny of the Individual

The previous chapter was concerned with the notion of God's guiding history toward its climax or end, and the reinterpretation of that notion in a more spiritual vein. Here the "last things" will be considered more from the perspective of the individual. Faced with the prospect of death, what could a person hope and what had he or she to fear? In the latter part of the chapter I will examine the mode of the post-mortem existence: was life in the beyond to be lived in a body or not?

JEWISH AND
GRECO-ROMAN VISIONS

From the World of Shadows to Different Destinies

Few Israelites ever thought that death would be the definite end of everything. In Israel, as elsewhere, care was devoted to dead ancestors and relatives.[1] Food and drink were offered to them at their graves. Obviously, a distinction between the perishable body and something that might be called soul or spirit (but was never defined) was current in Israel, as well as elsewhere. The care for the dead presupposed a belief in some kind of afterlife. Occasionally the dead could even be summoned to show themselves to the living, as Samuel appeared to Saul. But when exclusive monotheism broke with Israel's religious past, not only the worship of other Gods and Goddesses but also the veneration of ancestors was banned as inherently pagan; "orthodox Israelites no longer defined themselves in relation to their ancestors but exclusively in relation to their national God."[2]

The existence of the dead in Sheol, the netherworld, was conceived of as an existence of shades, void of vitality and joy, perhaps even void of consciousness. Indeed, "existence" seems too strong a word; "nonlife" might be better. The only worthwhile life was this life. Sheol was a place where Yahweh could no longer be praised.[3]

A "state of equal wretchedness"[4] awaited all who died.

Besides being analogous to Mesopotamian notions of the "land of no return," these Israelite ideas of Sheol were fairly close to old Greek conceptions of the afterlife.[5] According to Homer, the dead did not cease to exist, but spent their time in Hades as feeble shades without strength or pleasure. A common destiny awaited all, apart from a few notorious cases.[6] Yet from early on there are traces of a differentiated view as well, and when time went on, the view (enhanced by mystery cults)[7] spread that different postmortem destinies awaited normal mortals as well. In death, souls separate from bodies and are transferred to Hades. We shall discuss the nature of the body-soul dichotomy later and focus first on the destinies of the deceased.

In Hades, the souls face judgment; the good are rewarded, the bad punished. Such notions are reflected in Plato's varied depictions of the beyond.[8] In the *Republic* he tells the tale of Er, who returns from the netherworld to report the judgment of the dead and the gruesome punishments of evildoers. The souls pass through an interim period of reward or punishment, after which they return to the earth and are reincarnated in new bodies.[9] The souls retain their individuality—they are recognizable—but they become "someone else" in the next life. Greco-Roman sources from the Hellenistic and Roman period also attest "a strong strand of belief in differentiated fates for different souls after death."[10] Notably, Plutarch vividly describes the horrible punishments, which vary according to the severity of the deeds (*Sera* 567b-d). But in *On Superstition* he refutes not so much the reality of the punishments as the immoderate fear of these punishments and their eternity. For him the punishments are a kind of therapy, meant to purge the wicked souls (and to

prevent them from doing evil); only the totally incurable will sink into oblivion.[11]

Apart from the reincarnation, the tale of Er might have struck a familiar chord in many Jewish minds in the Greco-Roman period. In Israel, too, there had by this time been a development toward differentiation with regard to the ultimate destinies of different people. In the books of Isaiah (Isa. 14) and Ezekiel (Ezek. 32) the hope is expressed that in the somber realm of Sheol "the Gentile oppressors of Israel would suffer more than the common lot." Here hatred of national enemies has "given the impetus to imagining She'ol as a place for the retribution of the wicked,"[12] though nothing is as yet said of a judgment, and punishment falls on armies, not on individuals.

It is in the apocalyptic literature from the *Book of Watchers* that we meet the vision of a differentiated afterlife as regards individuals. *First Enoch* 22 contains a famous (if confused) description of the different postmortem destinies for the sinners and the righteous, whose souls are allocated to different places "in the west," though it is never told how they came to this separation in the first place.[13] The destiny of each soul seems to be taken for granted on the basis of the person's earthly life; no special act of judgment is singled out. There will, however, be a great judgment in the future; Enoch is shown the mountain that will serve as the throne of the Lord, when he comes down to hold the judgment.[14] The righteous will then enjoy a long life in the "blessed land" (*1 En.* 25.6). In the midst of this land the seer sees an "accursed valley," which is for "those who will be accursed forever," those who speak "unbecoming words against the Lord" (27.2). A similar differentiation between the good who are rescued to a transformed earthly life and the wicked who are condemned

116   to a fiery hell is envisaged in the *Animal Apocalypse* (*1 En.* 90).

The traditional conception of Sheol has here undergone a remarkable change: Sheol has become a waiting place, where the dead are assembled until their fate is decided (or rather confirmed) at the final judgment. Eventually the former postmortem residence for all and sundry becomes the place of punishment for the wicked. It was always a joyless place, but now it is a place of torment and pain. The visualizations of the place of punishment are enriched with the image of fire, partly derived from depictions of the Greek Tartarus, but mostly from the notorious Valley of Hinnom (Ge-hinnom, hence "Gehenna") where offerings had once been burned to foreign Gods.[15]

But if the souls that now find themselves in the waiting chambers are to participate in the last judgment, a resurrection that involves the reunion of soul and (some kind of) body must take place in between. The *Animal Apocalypse* gives a clearer hint of this: all those who had been "destroyed and dispersed" reassemble (*1 En.* 90.33). The redeemed will enjoy a new life on earth, but, in the parabolic language of the writing, the sheep are transformed into white bulls (90.38). The elect are not merely resuscitated, but are transformed to a different mode of life.

The vision of the souls waiting in different places for the final judgment, the good separated from the bad, has as its consequence that *two* judgments seem to be envisaged: an immediate one at the death of each individual, and the great collective event on the last day. An interim waiting period makes sense in the Platonic scenario, in which the souls return to the earth for reincarnation in *another* body. In a Jewish context it seems less appropriate, as the same verdict will apparently be imposed twice. Since the

retribution suffered by the wicked in Sheol is described as continuing forever, it would seem to eliminate the raison d'être of yet another, final judgment; and, as we shall see, such a judgment is actually missing from many Jewish visions of afterlife.

In some cases there may be a point: the judgment and punishment of the mighty oppressors (such as Antiochus Epiphanes and his minions) must take place publicly, before the world; this is why individual retribution in the beyond may not seem to be enough. At least this seems to apply to Daniel 12, where a resurrection of particular individuals—the righteous martyrs and their wicked persecutors—seems envisaged, and to the (somewhat later) *Similitudes of Enoch*: the faces of "the kings and the mighty and all who possess the earth" shall be "filled with shame," and they will be delivered "to the angels of punishment, to execute vengeance on them because they have oppressed his children and his elect"; the latter "shall rejoice over them" (*1 En.* 62). Here the prospect of a day of judgment is not a cause of terror for ordinary people. For the righteous, the judgment brings joy: "On that day, they shall raise one voice, blessing, glorifying, and extolling in the spirit of faith" (*1 En.* 61.11).

On the whole, however, it would be very difficult to make sense of the postmortem visions of many writings as harmonious wholes. This results simply from the fact that different eschatologies have been combined. That is why *4 Ezra* in particular "struggles with the question whether the otherworldly retribution takes place immediately after death or only after the judgment on the last day" (cf. *4 Ezra* 7.75). "The answer is: both."[16] The soul separates from the body at death and immediately experiences its future fate, the righteous rejoicing and the wicked grieving (*4 Ezra* 7.78-99). When the world has come to its end (after a messianic age that confuses the picture even more), the dead will rise; the soul and body of each will reunite to face the judgment (which will not, however, bring any surprises). *Second Baruch* shows a similar picture. The bodily resurrection therefore "seems somewhat superfluous; it is only needed for the judgment and the recognition of the dead while the ultimate goal is angelic life."[17] The main point is, however, clear: different fates await different people after death.

The texts just mentioned presuppose a *general* resurrection at the turn of history. However, others (for example, *Pss. Sol.* 3.10-12) posit a *resurrection of the righteous* only, taking extinction (in Hades)[18] or annihilation (on the earth)[19] to

be the destiny of the impious. This latter version of the punishment theme continues the earlier tradition of divine destruction of the people's enemies on the crucial "Day of Yahweh," envisaged in popular expectation,[20] but now even "wicked" Israelites have come to be included among those punished. What matters is to belong to the right group. Typically (in contrast to the usual Greek view) only two groups—the righteous and the wicked—and two kinds of eternal fate, which can never be changed, are envisaged. Sometimes the judgment can become fearful even for those to whom it had hitherto been a cause of comfort, as in *4 Ezra* (chs. 7–8, for example, 7.119; *2 Bar.* 48.11-18) or in the famous (though untypical) story (from the second century C.E.?) of Rabbi

5.1   The vision of Ezekiel (ch. 37) of the revivification of dry bones, originally an image for national restoration, was later taken as a depiction of bodily resurrection. Fresco. c. 239 C.E. Synagogue, Dura Europos, Syria. Photo: © Art Resource, NY.

118   Yohanan ben Zakkai's anxiety on his deathbed (*b. Ber.* 28b).[21]

We also hear of attempts to mitigate the harshness of the judgment. The *Apocalypse of Zephaniah* (11) narrates how the patriarchs and "all the righteous" daily pray on behalf of the souls in torments, and the seer himself does the same (2.8-9).[22] In the *Testament of Abraham* (A 12.18) and in rabbinic thought a middle group of people is introduced whose good and bad actions are in balance. Their postmortem destiny can be affected by intercessory prayer, or they can, while in Gehenna, go through a kind of purgatory and finally be saved. Intercession of the righteous is thought to move God to mercy, and to Rabbi Aqiba is ascribed the view (based on an adventurous exegesis of Isa. 66:23-24) that the punishment of hell will last twelve months only (*m. Ed.* 2.10).

Bodily Resurrection and Immortality of the Soul

The earliest references to bodily resurrection seem to connect it with new life on the earth. In the case of the Enochic *Animal Apocalypse* this is clear. In Daniel 12 the reference to resurrection life is ambiguous, but it would seem that it will be lived on this earth (see chapter 4 above). Surely this is where bodily resurrection conceptually (and, in its Iranian setting, originally) belongs, even though precisely the corporeal character of the resurrection mentioned in Daniel 12 is controversial.[23]

The physical nature of resurrection is emphasized without the slightest doubt in the account of the martyrdoms in 2 Maccabees. In 2 Macc. 7:10-11, a martyr expresses the hope to receive his hands and tongue back from God; 14:46 tells how another Jew, preferring suicide to capture by the Seleucid governor, tore his entrails from his dying body "and hurled them at the crowd, calling upon the Lord of life and spirit to give them back to him again." The picture is equally clear in the *Fourth Sibyl*: history ends with a fire, but then God "will again fashion the bones and ashes of men, and he will raise up mortals again as they were before" (*Sib. Or.* 4.181-82). The resurrection is physical and earthly, and this very combination makes sense. *Second Baruch* raises the issue of personal identity and recognition in resurrection: the deceased will rise in the form in which they departed. After the judgment, however, "the appearance of the evildoers will go from bad to worse," while the righteous "will assume a luminous beauty so that they may be able to attend and enter the world that does not die" (*2 Bar.* 51.3). What is envisioned is "a bodily resurrection, to facilitate recognition of the dead. Ultimately, however, the emphasis is on transformation, as the body is then made luminous in an angelic state."[24] In Jesus' time, the Pharisees confess belief in bodily resurrection,[25] but the issue remains open to different interpretations.

But restoration of the present body is never the sole, perhaps not even the dominant, concept. While the *Animal Apocalypse* (from Maccabean times) has a renewed earthly life in view, the somewhat later *Epistle of Enoch* (*1 En.* 91–105) moves the vindication of the righteous from earth to heaven: they "will shine like the lights of heaven"; "the gate of heaven will be opened" to them; they "will have great joy like the angels of heaven" (104.2–6). Here the reward is eternal spiritual life with the host of heaven. This is not the Greek idea of immortality of the soul, though it accords with the idea that had become popular in the Hellenistic era, that good souls ascend to the sky to join the Gods. But neither is it the resurrection of the body. "Rather, it is the resurrection, or exaltation, of the spirit from

Sheol to heaven. The bodies of the righteous will presumably continue to rest in the earth."[26]

The Greek way of thinking inevitably had an even deeper influence on Jewish conceptions of afterlife. Greek philosophical thought could not accommodate anything like a resurrection of the body; yet neither was the soul in general conceived of as being wholly immaterial. "The *psyche* in archaic Greece was conceived of as a material substance, very fine and akin to air and aether, but *material* nonetheless."[27] To be sure, by the time of Plato new suppositions about human nature had emerged:[28] the derivation of the soul from the divine world, and the opposition of body to soul. The soul came to be viewed as superior to the body; the body became a distraction for the soul. It is worth pointing out that "modern beneficiaries of medical care may overlook how troublesome life in the body was for the ancients."[29] Plato was persuaded that the soul was uncreated, immortal, immaterial, and the true vehicle for human identity. The body can corrupt the soul; therefore the soul must separate itself from the body as far as possible.

In the Greco-Roman period even philosophers spoke of the soul "as if it were composed of some substance that we would consider 'stuff'"[30]—a fine, fire-like substance, very different from the fleshly material of human bodies. Separated from their bodies, Greco-Roman dead nevertheless kept their recognizable form and appearance, for the surviving soul bore the "image" of the body. In stories, the disembodied souls of the dead even bore the marks of the death wounds of the persons.[31] The categories spiritual and physical were not mutually exclusive: *the soul itself was a kind of material "body."*

In many Jewish circles, too, the resurrection was understood as the immortality of the soul. Philo does not mention bodily resurrection (or judgment for that matter); instead, one finds the influence of Plato and the doctrine of the immortality (and preexistence) of the soul. Of the souls Philo says, "To them the heavenly region, where their citizenship lies, is their native land; the earthly region in which they become sojourners is a foreign country" (*Conf.* 78). All the references to resurrection found in the traditional literature of his time are understood by him as being only a figurative way of referring to immortality.[32] One also finds in Philo a strong emphasis on the superiority of soul to body, which dissolves with death. Yet the soul is, even for Philo, not immaterial, but "composed of small particles, as was aether or fire in ancient conceptions."[33]

Fourth Maccabees for its part conceives of the immortality of souls as a prize conferred by God for victory in the conflict endured by the pious. The writing shows no evidence for a belief in corporeal resurrection—in marked contrast to its literary source, 2 Maccabees. The violent death of the martyrs "transforms them into incorruptibility and transports them into the presence of the patriarchs."[34] Nevertheless, in this writing (for example, 4 Macc. 9:9) the tyrant is threatened with torment by fire in the afterlife; the author does not pause to ask how this could be effective without a body. The Wisdom of Solomon holds that rewards and punishments are received at the time of one's death, and they relate to one's soul. Different from Platonic thought, however, the soul is not inherently immortal; immortality is the reward of a righteous life (Wis. 5:15-16).

In the *Testament of Job* the children of Job are raptured to heaven immediately after death, and the soul of Job himself ascends in a shining chariot driven by angels, while his body lies in the grave (*T. Job* 52). But even writings that do not resort to this conception (for example, 2 *En-*

120 *och*) can speak of a postmortem heavenly ascent, paying attention to the reward and the punishment of the dead, but being silent about a general resurrection. The focus on individual afterlife is compatible with the Greek belief in the immortality of the soul, even if it is expressed in a different idiom.

Visions of Judgment in the Jesus Movement

The notion of an imminent and final judgment plays a larger role in early Christian communities than in other religious groups of the time.[35] The threat of God's impending judgment has a conspicuous place in the gospel tradition and probably stems from Jesus himself, anticipated by John the Baptist, who called people to repent in the face of the unquenchable fire. While the coming of the kingdom is the focus of Jesus' message, the necessity of judgment, proclaimed regarding certain Galilean towns (Q 10:13-15) and the leaders of the people (Q 11:39-44), is the other side of the coin. The threatening character of much of Jesus' proclamation is routinely explained away by modern interpreters, but its harshness should not be denied.[36] It is better to lose a member, Jesus asserts, than to have the whole body thrown into hell (Mark 9:43-48 par.).[37] That threats of hell are addressed as warning exhortations to the in-group,[38] sometimes in drastically hyperbolic language, is a feature that cannot easily be traced back to earlier Jewish tradition.

Annihilation
In Christian thought various Jewish visions were taken over and reapplied. Some texts suggest that the unrighteous will not survive at all. If they are alive when the end comes, they will perish in the drama. If they are dead, they may not be resurrected, or they will rise only to be judged and punished with extinction: they will disappear forever.

Thus, in two passages that graphically depict glimpses of the parousia, Paul seems to assume the resurrection of the righteous only: the "dead in Christ" (1 Thess. 4:16) or "those of Christ" (1 Cor. 15:23)[39] will rise, when Jesus returns; it is the resurrection of Jesus that makes possible the resurrection of those who have lived in communion with him in the first place. This would seem to imply that dead nonbelievers will not be resurrected at all,[40] though it is not clear how such an idea fits with the notion of judgment of all and sundry according to their deeds that Paul puts forward elsewhere.[41] Those unbelievers, again, who are alive on the last day will conceivably be judged and condemned, probably to annihilation.[42] The assertion that eventually God will be "all in all" (1 Cor. 15:28) speaks for this option: nothing that opposes God will remain in existence.[43] Paul's fragmentary allusions to the eschatological events cannot be combined into a consistent whole; his interest is focused on the salvation of believers.

In many hortatory passages, Paul supports his parenesis by underlining the accountability of even Christians on the day of judgment,[44] but the event of judgment is not present in his actual visualizations of the Day of the Lord (1 Thess. 4; 1 Cor. 15), nor is there much room for it in them. God's victory over the evil spirits/powers (including personified Death) and the transformation of believers into incorruptible existence is what the parousia is all about. In Rom. 14:10-12 and 2 Cor. 5:10, Paul mentions the necessity of all Christians to appear before the judgment seat of Christ. Here he seems to have an individual scrutiny of each Christian in view—everybody stands or falls before his or her Lord; the building constructed by each person either stands or falls (1 Cor. 3:15). Still, a fall does not mean a final collapse; Paul seems to reckon with temporary sanctions that do not exclude Christians from final salvation. The decisive criterion is whether one is "in Christ." A total eschatological condemnation or annihilation of a Christian is, in Paul's view, unlikely (in contrast to Matthew's view), though he knows of that possibility, too.[45]

Luke 20:35 suggests that only those who are "worthy" may gain the "resurrection of the dead," meaning that Luke thinks of a resurrection of the just only—a view confirmed by Luke 14:14 but contradicted by Acts 24:15, where Luke's Paul assures that there will be a "resurrection of the just *and the* unjust."[46]

Some later writings are more explicit. The *Didache* (16.7) states plainly that "there will be the resurrection of the dead, but not of all." Clement of Rome seems to share this view (*1 Clem.* 26.1 mentions the resurrection of the pious).[47] *Hermas* consistently speaks of an irreversible death as the punishment of sinners, whether non-Christians or lapsed Christians. All those who surrender themselves to evil desires will definitively die (*Mand.* 12.2).[48] A Christian interpolation into the *Ascension of Isaiah* (*Ascen. Isa.* 4.14-18) states that Christ will drag Beliar's hosts into Gehenna, but then fire will consume the impious, "and they will become as if they had not been created"—a phrase that suggests annihilation after a time in hell.

The Gospel of John mentions a future judgment but lacks the notion of eternal torment. Those who do not believe are "condemned already" (John 3:18); without faith in Jesus one can

only "perish" (3:16). The evildoers will rise to the "resurrection of condemnation" (5:25-29), but as God's wrath is expressed as a denial of life, they are probably annihilated. The judgment "will yield eternal life for those who believe but judgment, wrath, death for those who do not. This is not a theory of eternal punishment. . . .The excluded die, are destroyed or annihilated."[49]

Hell

A more common notion is, however, that of a judgment that will divide humankind into two permanent groups, whose destinies are sealed forever at the judgment: the saved will enjoy eternal life, but the lot of the others will be eternal torment.[50] Such a universal judgment is widely presupposed, though it is often in tension with other notions of human destiny found in the very same writings.[51] Hebrews 6:2 mentions "the resurrection of the dead and the eternal judgment" among the basic articles of faith. In Rev. 20:11-15, all the dead are resurrected and judged according to their deeds.

Matthew is most explicit about the eternal torment.[52] In his famous portrayal of the last judgment (Matt. 25:31-46), "all nations" are brought before the judgment seat of the Son of Man. Yet it is not nations as nations that are being judged, but groups of individuals; they are rewarded or punished according to what they have (or have not) done to the "least brothers" of Jesus. The decision comes as a surprise to these people, who have not been aware that they have served, or failed to serve, the coming Judge. In disregarding the needs of the little ones, they have offended the divine majesty of the King (v. 34), who will now take vengeance. The identity of the "least brothers" will be discussed in chapter 7. Here it is sufficient to note that all humanity will be judged (cf. Matt. 16:27) and

122   divided into "sheep" and "goats." The verdict is final and the punishment in the fire of hell of those condemned will be very painful: the "wailing and gnashing of teeth" of the damned is a favorite phrase of Matthew, who repeats it ad nauseam.[53]

In Q, the judgment falls in general on Israel, who has rejected Jesus, but Matthew partly changes the emphasis, addressing many warning words also to Christians themselves. The references to judgment and punishment that recur throughout the Gospel make clear that even Christians have reason to fear, for no one can be certain of his or her fate before the great day, which will bring bitter surprises. Matthew is very concerned to emphasize that disciples of Jesus must bear "good fruit" in their lives. Mere words of adoration do not help (7:21-23). Those who correspond to the "weeds" or to the "bad fish" in the Matthean parables are thrown into the furnace of fire (13:41-42, 49-50). The prospect is terrifying: though many are called, few will be saved (22:14).[54] The parable of the ten virgins (25:1-13) suggests that half of the members of the congregation may fail the test of being "awake," when the Son of Man comes, and may be excluded from the kingdom. The *Didache* (16) states in the same vein that the whole time one has lived in faith is useless if one is not "made perfect" in the end time, when lawlessness will increase and many will fall away and perish.

Luke's story of the rich man and Lazarus provides some details of the postmortem punishment,[55] which in this case is put into practice immediately after death. The rich man finds himself tormented in Hades in great pain. He is in agony in flames and cannot get help for his terrible thirst (Luke 16:24). As in some Jewish texts, the torments begin right after death in a place to which the soul is carried by angels; there is no need to regard this just as an interim state.[56]

A special feature is that the wretched man can see the blessed (Lazarus in the "bosom of Abraham"), who, however, can do nothing to help him.

Revelation 20:14-15 predicts that Death and Hades, conceived of as demonic beings, are thrown into the fiery pit.[57] Also everyone whose name is not found in the book of life will be cast there—any number of ordinary "inhabitants of the earth" who are not adherents of the Lamb. Some commentators take this to mean their annihilation, but Rev. 20:10 refers to an eternal torment of the beast and the pseudoprophet in the pit, and undoubtedly this is the lot of those damned as well. Indeed, 14:9-11 mentions that "they will be tormented with fire and sulfur in the presence of the holy angels and in the presence of the Lamb. And the smoke of their torment goes up forever and ever. There is no rest day or night for those who worship the beast."

The terrible threat of the fire is underlined in many other texts as well, for example, Heb. 10:26-27 for apostates,[58] and Ignatius (*Eph.* 16.2) for both those who teach bad doctrines and those who listen to them.[59]

Polycarp (*Mart. Pol.* 11.2) addresses his executioner: "You threaten me with fire that burns for an hour, and after a little is extinguished; you are ignorant of the fire of the coming judgment and of eternal punishment, reserved for the ungodly." As for Christians, the fire of their executioners "appeared cool to them, for they kept before their view escape from that fire which is eternal and never shall be quenched" (2.3). With reference to persecutions, the *Epistle to Diognetus* also states that a Christian who subjects himself to an earthly punishment will "fear what is truly death, which is reserved for those who shall be condemned to the eternal fire" (*Diogn.* 10.7, alluding to Matt. 10:28). Justin Martyr returns to the punishment in fire over and over again. If all people were aware of it, "no one would choose wickedness even for a little, knowing that he goes to the everlasting punishment of fire" (*1 Apol.* 12.1-2).[60] To hostile critics he says that "you can do no more . . . than kill us; which indeed does no harm to us, but to you . . . brings eternal punishment by fire" (45.5). In *1 Apol.* 8.4, Justin notes that Plato too knows of postmortem punishments, even though he mistakenly thinks them to last one thousand years only. The punishments inflicted by Christ are, however, eternal.

If the Gospels and Revelation are still relatively reserved in their visualizations of hell, the *Apocalypse of Peter* from the early second century (long regarded as canonical by many) has no scruples, but revels in lengthy descriptions of the horrendous punishments of the sinners in unquenchable fire; it is hardly too much to speak of sadistic fantasies.[61] The punishments correspond to the transgressions: the blasphemers will be hung up by their tongues, and so forth. This kind of literature, which took much of its descriptions of torture from Greek mythology, but omitted the Greek idea that in general the punishments were thought to be temporary and therapeutic, has had an immense influence on Christian exhortation in sermons, church paintings, psalms, and tractates. To some extent this influence continues, though in our days it is probably kept alive more by horror movies than by religious education.

This history is not without irony. At an early stage, the notion of a final judgment was apparently meant to encourage ordinary people, who could expect their oppressors to get their due in the end. But eventually the judgment comes increasingly to be the source of fear for just such ordinary people—even for the "righteous."[62]

What may have been the relation of joyful trust to the fear of punishments? The relative weight or diffusion of each aspect is probably impossible to assess. There must have been great differences. But the "fearful" aspect is not negligible, and it remained so through centuries. Christians did not invent hell. Postmortem punishments were known, and even feared, in their environment, in particular apparently in the Greco-Roman tradition. But fear of hell seems to have taken on a new intensity among Christians, some of whom also use it effectively as a means of persuasion—that is, as a means of power.[63] In Revelation 14 the Lamb seems pleased with the sight of the pain of the unrighteous. *Second Clement* 17.7 suggests that when the righteous see the terrible torment in the unquenchable fire inflicted on those who have denied Jesus, they give glory to God, saying that "there is hope for him who serves God wholeheartedly."[64] Tertullian explicitly expresses joy over the prospect of watching the persecutors and unbelieving philosophers and, even better, the Jews, march into the fire (*Spect.* 30).

Yet hell could become an emotional and moral problem for Christians. The apologist Aristides (*Apol.* 15) displays some compassion in stating that Christians weep bitterly at the death of a sinner, knowing that he will be punished.[65] For some Christians, the current notions of hell were incompatible with God's nature. Following philosophical traditions, Clement of Alexandria and Origen could conceive of the punishments only as pedagogical and therapeutic and thus as temporary; hell thereby became a kind of purgatory.[66] Some gnostic Christians developed similar thoughts. *The Concept of Our Great Power* (46.23—47.8) suggests that impure souls will be chastised during a limited period of time until they become pure. Only the "children of matter" will be totally destroyed.

God does not revenge, Origen held; that would mean repaying evil for evil. While the

124 deterrent value of the biblical description of eternal penalties was to be appreciated, Origen makes clear when addressing the "advanced" that the fire of hell is really a metaphor. Its pain is mental, caused by an uneasy conscience, and the punishments are corrective, serving the eventual well-being of those punished. For why should God's mercy come to an end when a person dies? The final goal is *apokatastasis*, the restoration of all and everything.[67]

While Origen had important followers in the East (for example, Gregory of Nyssa), his view faced furious opposition from the eremites and monks. As so often, it was Augustine who came to represent a decisive milestone. Taking his cue from passages like Matthew 25, he was determined to postulate eternal destinies in heaven or hell. For a millennium and a half, the view of Origen was the loser, but it has resurged in recent centuries. "Humanitarian feelings steadily rendered Christians uncomfortable about the apparent contradiction between the idea of a God of love and a vengeful Judge, who finally condemns the majority of his creatures to eternal torment."[68] Today the majority of mainstream theologians[69] take a more or less metaphorical view of hell to the extent of explaining it away altogether. It is stated, for example, that while hell is according to Christian tradition "a real possibility of human freedom," it is very much the question "whether this possibility has ever been or will ever be realized," and we can "hope that it will not become a reality for anybody."[70]

Another development in a milder direction in the speculation concerning punishments was due to the feeling that a mere dichotomy was simply too rigid. Greek visions of afterlife had indeed divided humans into more groups than just two, and the black-and-white scheme of earlier Jewish texts came later to be loosened. For similar reasons (along with the intellectual need to account for the condition of the dead between death and last judgment), Christians gradually developed the morally less offensive belief in purgatorial punishment.

RESURRECTION OR IMMORTALITY?

Resurrection of the Flesh?

The phrase "resurrection of the *flesh*" in the third-century Roman creed (from which the phrase was carried over to the Apostles' Creed, still used in many churches) reminds us of the Maccabean martyrs. Second-century Christian spokesmen for the idea, such as Tertullian, were likewise deeply concerned with the bodies of martyrs. That persecutors sometimes scattered and burned the remains of martyrs caused some anxiety to Christians (cf. Eusebius, *Hist. eccl.* 5.1). Believing that one will be resurrected in the very same body could make the fear of violent death more bearable—though others would have found better consolation in the idea that the destruction of the body (even in a martyr's death) brings life to the incorporeal soul or spirit.[71]

The exact formulation "resurrection of the flesh" is first found in Justin (*Dial.* 80.5),[72] but the notion that "this very flesh" will be resurrected occurs in several second-century writings.[73] Tertullian for one was adamant: what is raised is "this flesh, suffused with blood, built up with bones, interwoven with nerves, entwined with veins" (*Carn. Chr.* 5). Indeed, the belief came to gain ground that God would in the resurrection bring back and put in place again even the tiniest bit of each person's body, down to the last hair or fingernail. Tertullian also stated that the resurrection of all the dead is necessary in order that all can be judged, since "the soul alone, without solid substance, cannot suffer anything" (*Apol.* 48).[74] And, since body and soul are so intimately united in all their activities, divine justice requires that both must come together for judgment (*Res.* 14–16, with Jewish precedents).

Not only in Zoroastrian eschatology,[75] but also in many early Jewish conceptions, bodily resurrection was connected with an *earthly* expectation. This was possibly the case also with Jesus. It is hardly accidental that Justin, Irenaeus, and Tertullian, the stern defenders of the resurrection of the fleshly body, were all enthusiastic millenarians. "For Justin, the prospect of a coming millennium of earthly peace for the just seems to be indispensable to a realistic understanding of a bodily resurrection."[76] For Irenaeus, too, the two beliefs go together; neither of them can be taken as an allegory (*Haer.* 5.35). At this stage, even the emerging doctrine of incarnation was invoked: since the Word assumed *flesh*, he must have done so in order to save it (Irenaeus, *Haer.* 5.14; Tertullian, *Res.* 5). The final argument to clinch the matter was the appeal to divine omnipotence.

The Risen Jesus as a Model

Tertullian and the Roman creed, however, stand at the end of the development—or rather at the end of one line of development. For a long time, the nature of the postmortem existence was a bone of contention among Christians. Debates concerning the resurrection were closely connected with debates concerning the nature of the appearances of the risen Jesus, who was conceived as the model, the "firstfruit" of the resurrection to be followed by others in due time. Some accounts of these appearances (Luke 24; John 21) stress their bodily character: Jesus has

flesh and bones (Luke 24:39), he eats food, he presents his arms and feet for touching.[77] In Acts 2:31 the corruption of his "flesh" in the grave is denied. The stories of the empty tomb (Mark 16:1-8 par.) also presuppose that the very body that was buried rose from the dead (even if it may have undergone changes in the event). Yet both Luke and John also narrate scenes in which the disciples do *not* recognize Jesus, implying that his resurrected body is different from his previous body (Luke 24:13-35;[78] John 21:4-12).

The appearance stories as we have them are relatively late, and so are the stories about the empty tomb. How the early witnesses would have described and interpreted what they saw is a matter of educated guessing, but valuable hints are dropped by our earliest witness, Paul. From the way Paul imagines the resurrection body of Christians, one can infer what his vision of Jesus had been like and in what form he believed Jesus to have risen. For Paul expected that Jesus would, at the parousia, "change our lowly body to be *like his glorious body*" (Phil. 3:21). Consequently, Jesus must have appeared to Paul in a transformed "spiritual body" (1 Cor. 15:44) that he could even call a spirit (1 Cor.15:45; cf. 2 Cor. 3:17-18);[79] indeed, "flesh and blood cannot inherit the kingdom of God" (1 Cor. 15:50). In light of Paul's testimony, which is supported by the visions of Stephen (Acts 7:55-56) and John of Patmos (Rev. 1:13-16), a development from the intangible toward the tangible seems much more likely than the other way round.

Luke seems to react against such a luminous visualization, emphasizing the flesh and bones of the resurrection. He is anxious to distinguish Paul's vision of Christ from the appearances to the apostles as being different in kind: a light not seen by the others who were present, though they heard the voice speaking to Paul (Acts 9:3-8;

125

126 22:6-9; cf. 26:13-14). Luke presents the ascension as the milestone that separates the real Easter appearances from later experiences. Paul, however, makes no such distinction; he quite naturally connects his own experience with the earlier ones listed in 1 Cor. 15:3-8.[80]

Many gnostic Christian writings, on the other hand, develop this notion of the risen Jesus: he emerges as a luminous presence who speaks out of the light and does *not* appear in the ordinary human form that the disciples would recognize. The *Letter of Peter to Philip* states: "Then a great light appeared, and the mountain shone from the sight of him who appeared" (134.9-13). This took place on the mountain "where they used to gather with the blessed Christ when he was in the body" (133.13-17), the implication being that the bodily existence of Jesus belonged to the past.[81] According to the *Sophia of Jesus Christ*, "the Savior appeared, not in his previous form but in invisible spirit. And his likeness resembled a great angel of light" (91.10-13). Or Jesus transforms himself into multiple forms, as in the *Apocryphon of John*: "I saw in the light [a youth who stood] by me. While I looked [at him he became] like an old man. And he [changed his] likeness (again), becoming like a servant . . . the [likenesses] appeared through each other, [and] the [likenesses] had three forms" (1.30—2.9).[82]

Whatever the visions themselves may have been like, many of those who heard the preaching of the resurrection, and accepted it, did not conceive of it in "fleshly" terms. Unlike Tertullian, many people did not, and could not, equate that which would rise (or, in the case of Jesus, had risen) with the earthly body of flesh, blood, and bones. In this, they were guided by the popular philosophy of the time.

Paul and the Corinthians: Spiritual Resurrection?

As we have seen, even Greek philosophical thought held that the soul itself was a kind of material "body." Consequently, some of the physical activities claimed for the post-Easter Jesus were common religious inheritance for the postmortem soul. Any soul could appear to the living, still bearing the recognizable form of the body and the death wounds of the person, pass through closed doors, give preternatural advice, and vanish. That Jesus was "real" after death followed naturally from speculation about the soul as the "real" person.[83] To Christians trained in such ideas, including even many Christians with a Jewish background, "resurrection" would have meant "that the soul was raised, without the flesh."[84]

Some Corinthian Christians held a conviction of the resurrection that evoked a lengthy digression from Paul in 1 Corinthians 15. Paul's wording in verse 12, and especially his polemic from verse 29 on (if there is no resurrection, let us eat and drink; there is no point in responsible life, if death is the end of everything), seems to indicate that those criticized by him denied all postmortem life.[85] Yet it is difficult to understand why people with such an attitude would have joined the congregation in the first place; verse 29 (a reference to the baptism for the dead) shows that Paul knew about postmortem hope among them. His subsequent discussion in verses 35-49 is indeed an attack on a position for which the problem was not the survival of the human self, but the notion of *bodily* resurrection. So it seems safe to assume that the Corinthian Christians attacked by Paul did not wish to deny eternal life, but interpreted it differently from him—or differently from Paul as they had (mis)understood him, taking his talk "to refer to the crass resuscitation of a corpse."[86] It is plausible to assume that they held the standard educated Greco-Roman view of the immortality of the soul.[87] But before we trace the further course of this trajectory, it is appropriate to discuss Paul's relation to it—for his view differs less from that of the Corinthians than one might think on the basis of the vigor of his polemics.

In the previous chapter I described a formidable tension in Paul's eschatological thought. On one hand, the parousia of the Lord, connected with the resurrection of the believers and the judgment, is quite central to him. On the other hand, he glides away from the notion of a concrete kingdom on the earth, which would have been a logical context of resurrection, toward a fulfillment "with the Lord" in heaven. Second Corinthians 5:1-10 and even more clearly Phil. 1:20-26 express the hope that a Christian— notably, Paul himself—can meet the Lord right away at death, apparently thereby undergoing an immediate private judgment. This idea stands in unresolved tension with the expectation of bodily resurrection in the parousia, and also with the idea that the deceased Thessalonian Christians are fully and totally dead until their resurrection on the day of the Lord (thus 1 Thess. 4).[88]

In 1 Cor. 15:35-57, Paul speaks of the parousia and of bodily resurrection, but instead of showing interest in any alleged post-parousia events (such as the continuation of bodily life) on the earth, he is concerned with the *change* that he expects humans to experience. His point is that "flesh and blood," or "perishability," cannot inherit the kingdom of God (v. 50). Heavenly existence requires that the bodies of those who are alive at the parousia will be decisively transformed into an imperishable pneumatic form; surely the body of "flesh and bones" of the risen

Jesus according to Luke 24 would not have qualified. What Paul is really concerned with in the parousia is the "putting on" of imperishability (1 Cor. 15:49). The bodies of those alive at the parousia will be transformed "in the twinkling of an eye" into "spiritual" bodies. Paul also uses the image of putting on new clothes: what is perishable and mortal must "put on" imperishability and immortality (vv. 53-54).

Correspondingly, those Christians who have died before the parousia will rise in a *different* body. The earthly body they once had was mortal, perishing, and "soulish"; what will rise is a "*spiritual* [or *pneumatic*] *body*" (v. 44).[89] The earthly mortal body that we have "borne" or carried is the image of the "man of dust," whereas the glorious resurrection body amounts to the image of the "man of heaven" (v. 49).[90]

In setting forth all this, Paul is anxious to refute those who deny bodily resurrection. But while he intends to emphasize the true corporeality of the resurrection body, in fact his "stress is all on the *difference* of the new 'spiritual' body from the old, perishable mortal body."[91] A. J. M. Wedderburn notes that "Paul's characterization of the resurrection body in 1 Cor 15.35ff is more notable for the *absence* of those qualities which we normally associate with bodies than with any positive description of the spiritual body,"[92] and asks, "*why this resurrection existence should be described as bodily* at all."[93] An answer may be found when one realizes that at that time even philosophers did not think in terms of a matter/spirit dichotomy. Paul is speaking in terms that resemble the educated Greco-Roman view of the immortal, but material, *soul*. His language also reminds one of those Jewish visions that are characterized as "resurrection of the spirit from Sheol" by modern scholars.

128   Daniel Boyarin observes that what Paul provides in 1 Corinthians 15 is an "absolutely astonishing combination . . . of a biblical 'positive' sensibility towards the body, combined with a hellenistic/platonistic devaluation of the physical," so that "body itself becomes for him a dualistic term": there is a physical body and a spiritual body.[94] Ultimately, the division is less between body and soul than between "flesh" and "body" or, more precisely, between "flesh *and blood*" on one hand and *some kind of* body on the other. In this light, Paul's battle for the resurrection of spiritual bodies against the survival of souls (with somatic qualities!) seems largely a battle about words. The ex-Pharisee might have looked more kindly on the Corinthians he opposed, "had not his upbringing made the resurrection of the body a shibboleth for him."[95] Conversely, quite possibly the wayward Corinthians might have been able to accept the kind of resurrected body suggested by Paul in 1 Corinthians 15.[96]

In a later letter to the Corinthians (2 Cor. 5:1-10), Paul resumes some of the language he used in 1 Corinthians 15, such as the image of putting on new clothes. The passage does not make the nature of his eschatological hope any clearer. Paul's thought fluctuates between traditional and novel notions—between the public event of the parousia and the ascent of the individual self—without relating these notions to each other in any way. The emphasis, however, now clearly lies on individual eschatology. It very much seems as if one could reach the state of being "with the Lord" in heaven immediately at death, when the "earthly tent we live in is destroyed" and we may "put on our heavenly dwelling" (vv. 1-2). While Paul, in his clothing metaphor, uses language familiar from 1 Corinthians 15, hoping that "what is mortal may be swallowed up by life" (v. 4), little in this passage would suggest a transformation of the earthly body.[97] *Discontinuity* between the earthly and heavenly forms of existence is in focus:[98] Paul has the desire to leave his earthly body (the wretched appearance of which has been criticized in Corinth!), to change it for a heavenly "dwelling" or "garment"; he even suggests that this "dwelling" is preexistent in heaven, waiting for the believer to gain it (5:1). There is a decisive contrast between "being away" from the Lord and "being at home" with him (v. 8), and bodily existence belongs to the phase of being away (v. 6); however, Paul "would rather be away from the body and at home with the Lord."[99] Very properly, Paul abstains here altogether from using the "somatic" language of 1 Corinthians 15 of his hoped-for state in the presence of the Lord. Having left their earthly bodies behind, individual Christians[100] may appear before the judgment seat of Christ (v. 10); an immediate private judgment (of the deeds done "in the body"—the body now clearly belongs to the past) seems envisaged.[101] Having stood the test, they will then stay with the Lord. It is hard to see any real difference between this description and the idea that the soul continues its existence in the beyond.

Paul's reflections in Phil. 1:20-26 go in the same direction. "Dying is gain" (v. 21), because it is a direct way of gaining union with the Lord. Broadly speaking, the man who dictated this passage would seem to agree with those "deniers of resurrection" he had previously attacked; yet, despite dropping the "body" language with regard to believers' heavenly existence, he could not bring himself to use the current Greco-Roman idiom about the "soul" either. Attentive readers of Paul were (and are) left in a state of confusion.[102] But then many Jewish notions of postmortem existence were never very clear either.

The Spiritual Trajectory after Paul

Mark, followed by Matthew and Luke, lets Jesus silence the skeptical Sadducees with an astonishing demonstration of the reality of the resurrection: God calls himself the God of Abraham, Isaac, and Jacob, and he is not the God of the dead but of the living (Mark 12:25-27). The view that the patriarchs live with God is found in Jewish writings as well (for example, 4 Macc. 7:19; 16:25), but it is unusual to extrapolate from it a general view that applies to all others in the manner of Mark 12. Luke makes the point even clearer by adding the clause "for all live to him [God]." Taken literally, such statements presuppose an immediate resurrection at death. In connection with the statement on the angelic existence of the risen (Mark 12:25 par.), this results in a strongly spiritualized conception of resurrection. Luke, at least, leaves no doubt that this is his own view as well.

Luke speaks of resurrection in the traditional way in some places, but his own emphasis lies clearly on the idea of immediate postmortem retribution. He suggests that the deceased find themselves right away in a sort of bodily form in the beyond, though this is not identical with their earthly body. The rich man (Luke 16) can see and recognize both Abraham and Lazarus, and takes for granted that Lazarus can dip his finger in water. Hades is for him a "place of torment": he is in pain in fire, his tongue yearns for water. In Luke 23:42-43, the kingdom of Jesus is also called paradise; Jesus will "arrive" there on the very day of the crucifixion, and the robber hanging on the cross next to him will join him there at once—certainly not in a resurrected body. As in the story of Dives and Lazarus, there seems to exist a direct route to the beyond. In neither case is an act of judgment envisaged; people just self-evidently get to the right place (as in *1 En.* 22,

too). Stephen, too, seeing the heaven open and Jesus standing at the right hand of God, asks the Lord to "receive his spirit";[103] his body remains in the earth, as the emphatic mention of the burial in Acts 8:2 makes clear.[104]

In a similar vein, Clement of Rome assumes that, having been martyred, Peter and Paul went directly to a place of glory (*1 Clem.* 5.7), where they found a multitude of other martyrs and saints: *all* righteous people from the time of Adam have gone to the "place of the righteous" from which they will be revealed when the reign of Christ appears (50.3-4). Polycarp, too, was known to have already received his "crown of imperishability" while his body was being burned (*Mart. Pol.* 17–18).

The *Gospel of Thomas* refutes the conception of an eschatological resurrection (saying 51; see above). The desired state of the individual, both in the present and in the future, is the "rest" of the soul. The present possession of rest is the "sign" of the Father in the disciple (*Gos. Thom.* 50), available to one who has come to Jesus (*Gos. Thom.* 90). Saying 21 presents an allegory: the disciples "undress" in death, which releases them from the "field" of the material world. This would seem to mean the removal of the body at death and the ascent of the soul to the heavenly realm. According to saying 22,[105] entering the kingdom entails, among other things, putting on a new body or "image."[106] The author is here speaking of "the new state of being in which old anthropological differences, such as the sexes or the body/soul (inside/outside) dichotomy, have disappeared." While some of this is probably thought to be realized in the present situation of the Thomasine Christian, the reference seems to be to a future consummation that "still involves *some kind of (pneumatic?) body*."[107] Here Thomas comes close to the Pauline view of the resurrection body.[108]

130   Some writings in the platonizing trajectory even use Pauline language. If the apostle went a long way in the direction of the Corinthians he tried to correct, it comes as no surprise that some of his more radical admirers took advantage of his way of expressing himself concerning the spiritual body. The *Dialogue of the Savior* (1) holds that "rest" is something the Christians have reached, but it will be definitely realized only when they are liberated from the burden of their bodies and put on the promised *heavenly clothes*. "You will clothe yourself in light and enter the bridal chamber" (*Dial. Sav.* 50-52). The disciples "want to understand what sort of garments we are to be clothed with when we leave the corruption of the [flesh]"; the Lord answers that these are not temporary, transitory garments, but "you will be blessed when you strip off your clothing" (84-85).[109] Such statements sound rather similar to what Paul had said about putting on the heavenly garment, or what John wrote about the heavenly dwellings (John 14:2-4). What is different is the notion of the heavenly *origin* of the soul (also found, for example, in *Gos. Thom.* 49, 50), so that its journey to its heavenly home is actually a return.

The Valentinian *Treatise on Resurrection* suggests (if Malcolm Peel's reading is on the right track) that, in the ascension after death, "the living parts" within the person will arise, covered by a new, spiritual "flesh" (*Treat. Res.* 47.1-8; 47.38—48.3).[110] The resurrection is spiritual (45.40); it is spoken of by means of symbols and images (49.6-7). But it is not an illusion, as the postmortem appearance of Elijah and Moses in the transfiguration episode proves (48.3-11); the author conceives of the pneumatic "as retaining the identifiable characteristics of his earthly *sarx* despite its transformed nature." There is, then, between the earthly and the risen person, conti-

nuity "furnished by the inner, spiritual man and a spiritual flesh which retains personally identifiable characteristics."[111] This might be considered a more faithful interpretation of Paul's conception of the resurrection body than is the interpretation of many "orthodox" church fathers, who affirm a literal identity between the physical body and the resurrection body.[112]

According to the *Gospel of Philip* (see esp. 56.26–57.8), it is a false belief that one needs the earthly flesh ("this which is on us," 57.1) at the resurrection. On the other hand one cannot go naked to meet the King either (58.15-17); the necessary true clothing is the flesh and blood of Christ, received in the Eucharist (cf. John 6:53-58) and identified with the Logos and the holy spirit (57.6-7). Through this identification the author "gives a spiritual interpretation to the Eucharist—and to the resurrection body. The flesh that rises is a 'spiritual flesh'—an idea that the author no doubt found in line with Paul's teaching on the 'spiritual body.'"[113] In another passage (68.31-37) he seems to use the word "flesh" even in connection with the Lord's rising from the dead; this was, however, "true flesh" as distinct from our flesh, which is nothing, for we possess "only an image of the true." This Valentinian writing could thus use language even more orthodox than Paul's, and yet emphasize the otherness of the new "body."

Even more obvious is the Pauline basis of the language of those Valentinians whom Epiphanius derides as saying something ridiculous: "that it is not this body that rises, but another rises from it, which they call spiritual" (*Pan.* 31.7.10). It is a bit difficult to see what is ridiculous in such a statement, if one starts from the premise that Paul's view should make some sense, or keeps in mind the oscillation and diversity of Jewish views of resurrection. The Ophites for their part could appeal to 1 Cor. 15:50 to prove that the resurrection body was formed of soul and spirit.[114] In these and numerous other gnostic Christian texts, "there seems reflected some desire to retain a sense of personal identity in the postmortem state as opposed to a mystical yearning to be absorbed into the impersonal All."[115]

The denial of fleshly resurrection was not limited to Christians with Platonic leanings. Polycarp (*Phil.* 7) referred to the claim of "the firstborn of Satan" (Marcion?) that there is "neither a resurrection nor a judgment" as the vanity of the *majority*. Tertullian admitted not only that "almost all heretics" accept the "salvation of the soul" (*Res.* 2), but also that "a great many" Christians claim that resurrection means going out of the body itself, that is, the ascent of the disembodied soul (*Res.* 17). He also assailed the habit of some to call the new soul the "soulish body" (*corpus animale, Res.* 53). Those who held this view identified Paul's *soma psychikon* (1 Cor. 15:44) as the soul alone and held that this "body" was raised, while the physical body remained in the grave. As it was assumed (with the Stoics, also by Tertullian himself) that the soul is a material substance, his opponents would argue: the soul is a "body" and can be termed a "soulish body." When it is raised and receives the fullness of the spirit, it becomes a "spiritual body." In Tertullian's words, meant sarcastically, these Christians were advocating "the resurrection of the *soul*." For them, Paul's *soma pneumatikon* was identical with the Greco-Roman material soul.

To the exasperation of orthodox theologians, the idea of the resurrection of the flesh was to generate puzzlement among the faithful for centuries. Nor were all theologians happy with it either. Origen developed a sophisticated reinterpretation of "resurrection body," designed to steer a middle course: the bodies in which the saints rise will be identical with their earthly bodies as regards their "form" (identical with the Stoic principle of energy that maintains the body's identity), but their "material substratum" will be different, "spiritual" rather than fleshly. This distinction was severely criticized by orthodox opponents, in whose eyes this was no real resurrection at all. Our resurrection bodies (they held) will have heightened qualities, but they will be materially identical with our earthly bodies. Yet surely Origen's was a reasonable attempt to make sense of Paul's account in 1 Corinthians 15.

A Basic Tension and Its Consequences

In summary, the idea that the actual flesh should survive the grave was new in the empire and, to many, abhorrent. Christians in Corinth in the mid-50s, Christians of the Thomas tradition, and many others both within and without the orthodox church during many centuries denied it. They were only interpreting "resurrection" in categories that their own culture had developed.[116] Even Paul's stance seems to be much closer to this view than to the doctrine of the resurrection of the flesh that came to be established as Christian orthodoxy.

The boundary between spiritual and material is very imprecise in any case. The soul as imagined by the Greeks can probably do all the things that the spiritual body as envisaged by Paul can do (sex and defecating being out of the question anyway). If Paul's view serves to maintain the identity of the person in the afterlife[117] (the common opinion), it is hard to see why the Valentinian view in the *Treatise on Resurrection* would not. The situation is the same when the specific value of Paul's position is found to consist in its alleged emphasis on the goodness of creation and the significance of interpersonal relationships and social communication. It is difficult to see why the

132

idea of the immortality of the soul (which, in the Greek view, did have somatic characteristics, too) would be any less compatible with these goods than is Paul's vague notion of corporeality (which goes together with his otherworldly vision of eternal life).[118] It is actually the crude view of the resurrection of the flesh in an earthly kingdom (whatever its problems!) that would safeguard best the values commonly connected with corporeality. Again, if the point of bodily resurrection is found in the idea that only so can the actual restoration of God's people take place, then it would be logical to posit the (renewed) *earth* as the place of this resurrection life. But precisely at this point Paul is, at best, quite vague.

5.2 Figure of a resurrected woman. Detail of a window from the church of St. Vivien, Rouen, fifteenth century C.E. Stained glass, 30 x 24 cm. Inv. Cl.23637. Photo: © Réunion des Musées Nationaux/Art Resource, NY.

In short, the notions of resurrection and immortality are conceptually different, having their logical places in different eschatologies. The resurrection logically belongs to the collective hope for an earthly kingdom, the survival of souls to the expectation of a direct transfer of individuals to heaven. The natural location for resurrected bodies is a space-time world. On the other hand, it would seem natural that the souls that have reached heaven would stay there, no longer needing to return to the earth. The only natural reason for souls to return would be their transmigration into a new body, and in fact this Orphic-Platonic idea was taken up by some gnostic Christians: an impious soul is punished by casting it down to be imprisoned in a new body (possibly even in an animal body).[119]

An attempt to remove the inconsistency is to postulate, in accordance with many Jewish writings, an interim state, in which the souls find themselves between death and resurrection, waiting for the last day. The writings of Paul and Luke (the latter in particular) were open to interpretations that later went in this direction. In the theology of the church, the notion of the judgment of the individual soul at death became crucial, and a conception of an active interim existence of the souls emerged. Speculations concerning the interim state helped to create the notion of purgatory, which supplies the interim with a meaning (and mitigates the moral problem of eternal hell).

The notion of an interim was coherent if the waiting place was located in the netherworld (a common view in the second and third centuries, especially in the West), in which case the last day would actually bring about a clear improvement in the existence of the saints.[120] But when it is assumed that the souls of the righteous go to *heaven* immediately at death, an awkward scenario results, as we already saw in connection with some Jewish apocalypses. Now the soul ascends, if not to the very throne of God, at least to a very pleasant waiting chamber. When the last things start on earth, it will go back, unite with the body, and get the reward it had already enjoyed[121]—in order to return eventually to heaven. If set in the overarching framework of immortality, resurrection of the body inevitably becomes a dispensable appendix to individual eschatology.

A somewhat less artificial picture emerges if the eternal life after the interim is lived in a re-created space-time world, in which case the return to the earth has something of a point. Such a scenario may be implied in the book of Revelation. John sees the souls of the martyrs under the heavenly altar (Rev. 6:9-10) anxiously waiting for the revenge on their oppressors. When this takes place, they will participate in the "first resurrection" (Rev. 20) and live a new earthly life in the millennium. But the pertinent passages in Paul and Luke do not give the impression that being with the Lord right after death would be just temporary.

In modern theology the notion of an interim has not fared well. Protestants have quite often resorted to the notion of "total death": resurrection amounts to a *creatio ex nihilo*. This view is largely based on the mistaken idea that "total death" is the original "biblical" idea.[122] In recent Catholic theology, by contrast, a consensus (based on the thought of Karl Rahner) is said to be emerging: one speaks of a "resurrection at death," which concerns the whole person (soul and some kind of transformed "body," defined in the vaguest of terms;[123] the fleshly body will rest in the grave). This is the only "resurrection" envisaged.[124]

This seems a complete victory of one early Christian line of thought (in a modernized version) over another. But the tables are now turned, and the result amounts to nothing less than a full turn in the history of the doctrine of resurrection: it is a tacit vindication of the Valentinian interpretation of Paul.[125] Nor does the paradox end there. For if we have interpreted at all correctly the position of those Corinthians who claimed that "there is no resurrection of the dead" (1 Cor. 15:12), then this modern view, disseminated in books with papal imprimaturs,[126] serves to rehabilitate their position as well.

6

Sold under Sin?
The Human Condition

In the preceding chapter, I treated the issue of different postmortem destinies: some will be saved, others perish. I shall deal with the preconditions and means of reaching salvation and avoiding perdition in the next chapter. Before that, a closer look at an interrelated question is in order here: what exactly ought one to be saved from? What kinds of obstacles were thought to exist in the relation of humans to God and how grave were they?

The notion of salvation itself presupposes an unsatisfactory situation, a plight from which one should be liberated and transferred to a wholesome condition. Those in the Western Christian tradition generally see this plight as tragic,[1] as enslavement either to the power of sin, or to hostile external forces, or to both. The Lutheran Augsburg Confession states that "our churches" teach that "since the fall of Adam all humans begotten in the natural way are born with sin, that is, without the fear of God, without trust in God, and with concupiscence; and that this disease, or vice of origin, is truly sin, even now condemning and

bringing eternal death upon those not born again through baptism and the Holy Ghost" (article 2). This is the traditional view of the Western church, mainly based on the ideas of Augustine, who held that this original sin alone suffices to damn even unbaptized infants.

ISRAELITE AND JEWISH NOTIONS OF SIN

This is rather different from the dominant worldview of old Israelite religion. Here one generally reckoned with a given state of well-being. This could be disturbed through transgressions (some willful, others due to ignorance of the divine will). Cultic sins, no less than moral ones, were considered offenses against God and incurred similar punishments. But a healthy state was restored or regained by way of pertinent (mostly cultic) expiatory measures.[2]

Universal Sinfulness

To be sure, the idea that all humans are sinful was widespread in the ancient Near East.[3] A Mesopotamian worshiper addresses his God Marduk by saying: "Who has not transgressed, and who has not committed sin? Which one understands the way of the God?" Psalm 51 is a powerful Hebrew example of the same notion, especially verse 5: "Behold, I was brought forth in iniquity, and in sin did my mother conceive me." Sin was regarded as "a universal moral flaw, pandemic in the human race";[4] therefore, Gods should not expect too much of humans. Psalm singers could appeal to the universality of sinfulness in petitions for leniency, as in Ps. 143:2: "Enter not into judgment with your servant; for no person living is righteous before you."[5]

It is important to note that this sinfulness of all is "related merely to creatureliness."[6] Despite Psalm 51, it cannot be taken as a carefully thought out, pessimistic theological principle. For, as James Barr points out, it "lay alongside other ideas which pointed in a very different direction," the striking thing in many psalms being just "the poet's insistence that he (or the worshipper for whom he speaks) is free from blame and guilt. There are sinners and evildoers everywhere, of course, but the poet himself is not one of them, nor is the worshipper who uses the poem."[7] It is one thing to belong to the frail human race; it is quite another to willfully and persistently transgress God's will. In other words, there is a difference between individual transgression, which no one can avoid in the long run, and the way of life of "sinners" who choose to disregard God. Barr goes on to note that "the whole atmosphere of the Hebrew Bible works against the idea that sin and evil were taken, as a matter of theological principle, as something that belonged of necessity to all human life. Vio-lent outbreaks of evil, yes, but a steady unchanging subjection to sin, no."[8]

Of course the scripture "has page after page of evil deeds, and disasters that follow failure to pursue the will of God are practically normal within it. But these are *actual* evils, not evils that are necessitated by a given inheritance, a propensity towards evil which humans cannot of themselves overcome."[9] Even the extreme case of the generation of the flood, which God decided to destroy because of its sinfulness, makes clear that sin was avoidable: in that very generation, Noah found mercy before God precisely because of his blamelessness.

The story of the fall of the first humans in Genesis 3 did not have anything like the weight it later came to have in post-Augustine Christianity.[10] The atmosphere of tragedy is lacking.[11] "There is nothing here about lusting for superhuman status and power."[12] The origin of sin is not reflected on; "in itself the passage only tells us that the labour of man and woman will get more difficult (Gen. 3:16-19), not that any predisposition to evil on the part of their children would also follow."[13] In the totality of the Hebrew Bible this story is not at all central. It is never referred to anywhere else—neither in creeds nor in prayers nor in those narratives that dwell on the sins of Israel or its kings. No other texts are interpreted with its aid.[14]

Judaism, then, inherited from the biblical tradition a relatively optimistic view of the human condition in God's world. Transgressions and evil were obvious and serious facts and had to be dealt with, but the world as a whole was *not* conceived to be in bondage to sin; "universal sinfulness is related to common sinful activity, rather than to hopeless sinful status."[15] Humans were far from perfect, simply due to their *creatureliness*. That was often a problem, but it was

136   not a deep tragedy. Mikael Winninge coined the term "the sinfully righteous" to denote those who, despite their actual transgressions, wanted to stay faithful to God's covenant.[16] In the jargon of the Reformation, one could well call a loyal member of Israel's covenant *simul iustus et peccator*.

Since blamelessness did not mean perfection, it was not regarded as impossible to fulfill God's commandments. It was worth the effort to stress their importance from generation to generation. True, humans are weak, and an evil inclination fights within them against a good inclination, for God provided humans with the impulse to do evil as well as with the impulse to do good. Basically, sin stems from the human beings themselves; one is responsible for the wrongs one commits. But one who sincerely repents can definitely gain forgiveness.[17]

If, however, people persist in sinning, the effects of their evil acts would bring harm and eventually disaster upon them. A causal connection was posited between sin and calamity. It was possible even for the whole people to go astray, and, according to the Deuteronomistic History, it had. Theological reflection on the exile from the sixth century on inevitably led to the conclusion that the people must have been guilty of heinous sins, subject to God's wrath and punishment. Why should God otherwise have withdrawn his protection, leaving his people at the mercy of its enemies? If Yahweh was all-powerful and in control of history (the axiom), then *he* was responsible for everything that happened. And as the exile could not possibly testify to weakness, let alone injustice, on his part, the only option was to explain it as a punishment. One inferred the cause from the result: because they had incurred punishment, the people must have sinned—and sinned gravely. By thinking backward one came to establish widespread sin as the cause of a dis-

aster that had actually happened.[18] The need to justify the present plight in terms of God's control over history led to the result that quite ordinary (tolerant) cultic practices were, in retrospect, branded in the Deuteronomistic History as fateful apostasy. This coping with the problem of theodicy led to cultic confessions of collective sins of the nation (for example, Isa. 59:12-13; 64:4-5; Ezra 9:6-15; Dan. 9:4-11).

The same logic was later applied to the destruction of the Holy City by the Romans in 70 C.E.[19] The author of *4 Ezra* tries to cope with the disaster, finding no other explanation than that the elect people must be full of sin in the eyes of God. Thus his thoughts are led in the direction of a radical view of human sinfulness. "We are all full of ungodliness" (*4 Ezra* 4.38). There is "none of the earth-born who has not dealt wickedly" (8.35); the seer asks that God have compassion on those who lack good works. "Ezra's" views are, however, corrected by the angel who points out that there *are* some righteous people left, including Ezra himself (6.32). Those who perish have transgressed willfully and are without excuse (7.72). All the more there is reason to be thankful for those few who will be saved (7.60); "they have striven much and painfully to overcome the innate evil thought, that it might not lead them astray from life into death" (7.92). The author repeats mutatis mutandis the steps that the Deuteronomist authors had taken centuries ago: he concludes in retrospect that normal observance of God's law (in which Israel was certainly not worse than the thriving "Babylon"!) had not been enough.[20] Greater perfection was expected.

Apart from *4 Ezra*, the most radical Jewish statements on human sinfulness stem from Qumran. In the hymns of 1QH and 1QS, confessions of sin by the singers reveal a profound sense of insufficiency, probably reached in part at least through introspection.[21] But "the frequent statements to the effect that man is worthless and incapable of doing good are always said in the context of comparing man and *God*."[22] They stand in the age-old tradition that highlights the human plight as creatureliness. "As for me,"[23] the psalmist states, "I belong to wicked humankind, to the company of unjust flesh. My iniquities, rebellions, and sins, together with the perversity of my heart, belong to the company of worms and to those who walk in darkness" (1QS 11.9-10). But this is not a lament over one's inability to fulfill the law; as the context shows, it is "an expression of human inadequacy in the face of the mystery of God." "These confessions are not made with a view to seeking forgiveness. . . . Awareness of personal sin is more than matched by an awareness of the sufficiency of God's mercy," being "firmly located within the context of the psalmist's ultimate security in the membership of the covenant."[24] The pessimistic view does not "become a basic element to be overcome in the *path* to salvation, since nothing can be done about it until God destroys wickedness itself at the end. For practical purposes of the sect's life, sin remains *avoidable* transgression."[25] Creatureliness is not something that incurs damnation. Members of the Essene movement definitely belong to the "sinfully righteous."

The Origin of Sin

Subjection to oppression continued even after the Babylonian exile. This may explain why interest in the origin of sin and evil increases strongly in the Hellenistic and Roman periods: the plight of permanent foreign occupation must have a reason. As individuals and nations are obviously driven by forces outside their own control, evil comes often to be attributed to supernatural powers. In some writings the reason for the presence of evil in the world is found in the fall of rebellious angels, "sons of God" or "Watchers." Not only did they marry human women with disastrous consequences, as demonic giants were born from these unions; they also taught humanity reprehensible skills, such as the making of weapons for the shedding of blood. This myth surfaces in Genesis 6; an elaborate version is found in the *Book of Watchers* (*1 En.* 6–11).[26] Here the giants of old can perhaps be taken as prototypes of the rulers who claimed divine parentage and waged disastrous wars in the author's own time; their sexual transgression may have been associated in the minds of some with the life of the Jerusalem priesthood, unduly secularized in the eyes of pious critics.[27] The evils of the author's own time are derived from a primordial act of rebellion in a superhuman realm; a myth set in primal times explains the present plight and promises its end.

A corollary of this myth is the idea of evil spirits as causes of sin: demons came out of the corpses of the giants when they were killed (*1 En.* 10.15; 15.8—16.1; cf. Justin, *2 Apol.* 5). According to *Jub.* 10.1-14, humans were incited to sin by these demons, who were led by a spirit called Mastema or Satan. In the *Testaments of the Twelve Patriarchs*, the spirit of darkness, now called Belial (well known from Qumran as well) or Satan, is a recurring figure, who not only causes humans to sin but can also be seen as the cause of death in the world.[28] Outside influence is unmistakable here. In the Hebrew Bible, Satan still has a relatively innocent investigative role; even evil things come from Yahweh himself. Satan (or however he is called) as a major adversary of God is probably "at once the result of the 'splitting' of the archaic image of Yahweh" and "of the influence of Iranian dualistic doctrines."[29] Now, however, Belial is the master of the spirits of error; the present age is under his control. Chief among his works is sexual promiscuity. But even

138 though Belial may be the ruler of the world, the righteous can resist him. *Testament of Dan* (5.1) is typical in its exhortation, "Observe the Lord's commandments . . . that Belial may flee from you."

Instead of focusing on the demonic realm when looking for the origin of evil, others turned their attention to the action of the first humans in the garden of Eden. It is in *4 Ezra*, "among the biblical and near-biblical books, that we come closest to the idea of universal and 'original' sin."[30] The author complains, "O Adam, what have you done! For though it was you that sinned, the fall was not yours alone, but ours also who are your descendants!" (*4 Ezra* 7.118). Adam, "*burdened with an evil heart*, transgressed and was over-

6.1   Adam and Eve after the Fall (Genesis 3). Fresco from the catacombs of Saints Marcellinus and Peter (c. 306–337 C.E.).

come, as were also all who were descended from him" (3.21). The author also complains that God did not take away from humans their evil hearts (3.20).[31] On the other hand, he seems also to suggest that all humans are themselves responsible for their sins (7.119-26, immediately after the "Adam" passage). The angel's reply to Ezra's complaint (7.127-31) indeed emphasizes the *freedom and guilt* of humans. The author vacillates: was Adam only the first sinner, or did he bring an inevitable sinfulness upon his descendants?

Fourth Ezra's tracing human sinfulness back to Adam is challenged in *2 Baruch*: "For though Adam first sinned, and brought untimely death upon all, yet of those who were born of him, *each one* of them has prepared for his *own* soul torment to come. And, again, each one of them has chosen for himself glories to come" (*2 Bar.* 54.15). "Adam is therefore not the cause, save only of his own soul, *but each one of us has been the Adam of his own soul*" (54.19).

Sin as a Way of Life: "Sinners" as a Social Category

While the righteous were generally not considered perfect,[32] a clear boundary tended to be drawn between them and the real sinners. Whereas the righteous acknowledge their sins and atone for them by means of prescribed rituals (*Pss. Sol.* 3), the sinner "allows sins to pile up without dealing with their consequences."[33] There is, then, all the difference in the world between the occasional sins of the righteous and the "utterly lawless orientation to life which characterizes sinners without conscience."[34] Sometimes the division may depend on a moral judgment, based on some sort of empirical evidence. Often enough, however, the boundary between the righteous and the wicked is identical with that between different social groups.[35] Gentiles can be lumped together as a mass of sinners by some Jewish groups.[36] In other cases, "sinner" is a "factional" term in an inner-Jewish context:[37] those "others," who do not belong to a given group or do not accept its specific rules or interpretations, are branded as wicked both in the Hebrew Bible and in postexilic tradition.[38] The slander need not be (and certainly often was not) affected by facts. In this, it was not much different from the customary polemics between philosophical schools in antiquity.[39]

Sin and the Human Condition in the Jesus Movement

Sin as Transgression

The relatively optimistic view of the Hebrew Bible lives on both in Jewish tradition in general[40] and in the early Jesus movement.[41] All people sin, no doubt—the common notion of universal sinfulness remains unshaken—but that can be handled; it is not a tragedy.[42] All humans are "evil" when they are compared to God, the generous Giver (Q 11:13), but then again there is a vast difference between the "good person" who "out of the good treasure of the heart produces good" and the "evil person" who "out of evil treasure produces evil" (Q 6:43-45). John the Baptist preached a baptism of *repentance* for the remission of sins. Jesus himself went to be baptized by John, indubitably in order to repent and to receive forgiveness for his sins.[43] When a man asks how he can inherit eternal life, Jesus refers him to the commandments of the Decalogue. When the man says that he has observed "all these" from his youth, Jesus does not object; instead, he adds one more commandment (Mark 10:17-20).[44] The

moral claims imposed by Jesus on his adherents (for example, in Mark 8:34—10:45) likewise presuppose capability: Jesus' followers are supposed to be able to follow the harshest requirements of an ascetic ethic. Jesus' mission is to seek "sinners"; he does not deny the existence of those who are "well" and not in need of a physician (Mark 2:17; cf. Luke 15:7).

"Sins" are spoken of in the plural: individual wrong deeds or thoughts that can be forgiven, if

6.2   John the Baptist in the wilderness. S. Marco, Venice.
Photo: © Cameraphoto Arte, Venice/Art Resource, NY.

140 one repents, are in view. The Lord's Prayer reckons with individual "debts" or "sins"; Matt. 6:14-15 speaks of "trespasses." This understanding continues in early Christianity (Matt. 1:21; Luke 1:77; Acts 2:38; Col. 2:13; and elsewhere). Generally, it was not denied that even church members sinned; they could therefore be exhorted to confess their sins to one another (Jas. 5:16; cf. 1 John 1:9).

To be sure, in his exorcist actions, which he interprets as a sign of the breakthrough of God's rule, Jesus assumes that the world is under an alien, demonic power (Mark 3:23-27; the head of the demons is called Beelzebul). Luke 10:18 likewise refers to a battle against Satan. Yet the rule of Satan, which brings about sickness, does not seem to be directly connected with human sin in the Jesus tradition; no tyrannical rule of an external power in any way comparable to that set forth by Paul in Romans 7 (see below) is in evidence.[45] For sinning, people are themselves responsible, even if Satan may be active in leading them to temptation, as he tried to do with Jesus (Q 4:1-13). No direct connection is established between the liberation from unclean spirits and liberation from sin in the Gospels.

In Matthew, nothing suggests that humans are generally unable to fulfill the commandments, which are radicalized by Jesus' interpretation in the Sermon on the Mount (programmatically in Matt. 5:20).[46] The disciples are called to let their light shine—people are to see their good works and praise God (5:16);[47] at the core of all ethical behavior lies a "good heart" (Matt 12:33-35 and elsewhere), "an essential inner goodness, without which there can be no truly good living."[48] Luke, for his part, portrays both the Christians and their pious Jewish predecessors as wholly fulfilling the law. There are righteous people who do not need repentance (Luke 15:7). The parents

of John the Baptist were "righteous before God, living blamelessly according to all the commandments and regulations of the Lord" (Luke 1:6; cf. old Simeon in 2:25). The piety of the Christian community in Jerusalem is painted in the same colors. So is the life of the devout and God-fearing Gentile Cornelius (Acts 10:2, 5), who, when he heard of Jesus, needed only to be baptized and did not need to repent, because "in every nation anyone who fears him [God] and does what is right is acceptable to him" (an inference by Luke's Peter in Acts 10:35).

According to Hermas, little children "do not even know what evil is"; no evil thought enters their mind. Sinfulness is, then, "not innate but acquired"[49] and clearly avoidable, for some believers have "defiled in nothing the commandments of God" but have "remained like children all the days of their life in the same mind" (*Sim.* 9.29.1-2).[50] The devil tempts humans to sin but he has no power, and humans can therefore gain mastery over him (*Mand.* 7.1.2).

It is commonly held that Paul put forward a most profound diagnosis of the hopelessness of the human condition, but the apostle himself indicates that he was not conscious of any personal sin (1 Cor. 4:4),[51] apparently not even in his pre-Christian life (Phil. 3:6), save the one grand error of persecuting the church (1 Cor. 15:9). He put forth effort to ensure that his congregations, too, remain blameless and without fault until the Lord comes (Phil. 2:15; 1 Thess. 5:23). (On his statements on humans' slavery to sin, see below.)

"Sinners" as a Social Category in the Jesus Tradition

It is generally thought that Jesus had a special mission to "toll collectors and sinners,"[52] often taken to be people at the fringe of or outsiders to the larger society, and that consorting with these people was central to his activity, perhaps even a cause of his fate.[53] The picture of Jesus as a great friend of sinners is, however, largely due to Luke's literary activity;[54] the non-Lukan material on sinners only comprises Mark 2:15-17 and parallels (toll collectors and sinners at dinner in Levi's house) and Q 7:34 (the Son of Man is vilified as "a glutton and a drunkard, a friend of tax collectors and sinners"). Perhaps the historical Jesus had only a few associates who were suspect in the eyes of pious people;[55] Luke had his own reasons to inflate the memories of this into a large-scale mission to the "lost."[56]

Jesus' followers generally regarded all those who did not accept their message as wicked sinners, cut off from God. In Q and the Synoptic Gospels, "this generation" (which rejects the messengers of Jesus) is branded as "evil," "adulterous," and "sinful" (Q 11:29; Mark 8:38 par.; Matt. 16:4). Galatians 2:15 takes up the common notion of a distinction between those born Jews and "Gentile sinners"[57] upheld by the conservative Jewish Christians whom Paul criticized in Galatians.[58] In Rom. 5:8, the phrase "while we were yet sinners" refers to the pre-Christian existence both of Paul (cf. 1 Tim. 1:15) and of his readers. Drawing a clear line of division, often in the vein of customary factional polemics, between the old way of life in paganism (or even in Judaism!) and the new life became a Christian commonplace (for example, Col. 3:5-8; Eph. 2:1-3; 1 Pet. 1:14; 4:2-4). A particularly gross caricature of pagan life is found in Rev. 9:20-21: those who were not killed by the plagues described in Revelation 9 did not repent of their idolatry nor "of their murders or their sorceries or their fornication or their thefts."[59]

In an extreme case, the rejection of the message of Jesus or of the Christians could be branded as an unforgivable "blasphemy against the spirit." For Mark and Matthew, this means the attribution of Jesus' exorcisms to demonic powers by his adversaries and, by implication, the refusal to acknowledge the divine power at work in his charismatic followers: "whoever blasphemes against the holy spirit can never have forgiveness" (Mark 3:29; Matt. 12:32). In the Lukan context, instead, the unforgivable sin consists in the denial of the Son of Man in a situation of persecution by followers of Jesus, rather than in the rejection of the message by outsiders (Luke 12:9-12). The author of Hebrews continues in this vein, stating in harsh words that those who persist in sin after conversion cannot be forgiven (Heb. 6:4-6; 10:26-27).[60] The boundary between the pious and the sinners now runs through the in-group, which results in a very bitter tone in drawing the line: those who have "spurned the Son of God," "profaned the blood of the covenant," and "outraged the spirit of grace" certainly deserve the worst possible punishment (Heb. 10:28-29).

With time, such a rigorous ethics had to be adapted to reality. Hermas first receives in a vision confirmation for the stern view that there is no forgiveness for sins done after baptism (*Mand.* 4.3.1-2); yet soon enough it becomes clear that the Lord has granted one more opportunity for repentance (4.3.4-5). But after that there will be no more chances (*Vis.* 2.2.5).

For the Gospel of John, the whole world (*kosmos*) is under the power of darkness and lies, indeed, under the "ruler of this world" (12:31; 14:30; 16:11). People love darkness, because their deeds are evil (3:19), so much so that everyone who commits sin is a slave to sin (8:34). This may sound like a profound existential analysis (and was famously elaborated in such terms by Rudolf Bultmann).[61] A closer look reveals that John is engaged in harsh factional polemics. Only

142   one "deed" *could* qualify as not being "evil," and that is a believing response to Jesus (in practice, to the christological claims of John's community). Sin is explicitly identified with not believing in Jesus (John 8:21-24; 16:8-9), and it is "the Jews" in particular who are guilty of this. Unless the Jews believe that Jesus is who he is, they will die in their sin (8:21-24). It is this unbelief that makes them slaves to sin (8:34).[62] John's Jesus also attributes to "the Jews" (all lumped together)[63] the will to kill him (7:19; 8:37), which leads him to make the extreme statement that the devil, the murderer par excellence, is their father (8:44). If Jesus had not come and spoken to them, they would not have sin, but now they have no excuse for their sin (15:22). "Sin" is defined in retrospect, from the point of view of the "revelation" brought by Jesus—a "revelation" that for those outside (including the well-disposed Nicodemus: John 3) is always mysterious and incomprehensible. John reckons with more or less closed groups and often (though not consistently) resorts to deterministic statements that suggest that one cannot really choose or change the group one belongs to (see ch. 10 below).

The ultimate aim of the denigration of the "others" as slaves of sin and children of the devil is to encourage the faithful to bear the hatred shown toward them by the "world": "If the world hates you, be aware that it hated me before it hated you" (15:18). This very hatred shows that the world is hopelessly entangled with sin and darkness, and at the heart of it all is the "dogmatic" sin[64] of not believing in Jesus—that is, in not accepting the message of those who do believe in him.

The "others" are "proved" to be grave sinners in light of Jesus' esoteric revelation. So John, too, argues backward. Indeed,

the sharp dualism in John may reflect bitter disappointment caused by a growing realization of how a great majority of the Jews in Johannine surroundings refused to accept Jesus as the fulfilment of Jewish tradition. Dualistic polemic in John is not written with the outsiders in mind but tries to confirm the insiders who are faced with the world's rejection; this polemic aims at justifying the decision to turn their backs on central aspects of Jewish traditions.[65]

Behind the polemic thus looms a social conflict: drifting away from the synagogue, a process apparently connected to the alienation of John's community from Jewish practices on one hand and its increasingly high Christology on the other. We are faced with a clear case of factional polemics.

First John (5:19) repeats the idea that the whole world lies in the power of the evil one. Everyone who sins is a child of the devil (1 John 3:8). By contrast, those born of God and abiding in Christ cannot sin. Sin is, as in traditional polemics, used as a social boundary marker. But unlike the Gospel of John, 1 John focuses on a split *within* the congregation, rather than on one between the congregation and "the Jews." The criterion, which shows whether one belongs to the children of God or to those of the devil, is defined as love: does one love one's brothers and sisters or not (3:10; cf. 1:9-11; 3:17; 4:20-21)? But lack of this love is apparently thought to come to expression simply in the fact that some have left the inside group and turned to heresy (2:19-29).

The use of different types of discourse in different contexts may solve the old problem of bluntly contradictory statements on sin in 1 John. For the author also affirms that "we" are all sinners, that sins must be confessed, and that "if we say that we have not sinned, we make him [God] a liar" (1:7-10). Here he avails himself of the traditional notion of universal sinfulness, which is due to the gap between humans and God. But when he boldly claims that those born of God do not and even cannot sin (cf. also Ign. *Eph.* 14.2), and that those who do sin are of the devil (3:4-10), he relies on the equally traditional way of underlining the contrast between the righteous and the wicked, using "sinners" as an established social category.[66]

In both categories treated above (sin as transgression, sin as a way of life), sin is viewed as avoidable.[67] "Do not sin any more," John's Jesus says to a healed man (John 5:14).[68] If sin is an individual trespass, it is possible not to sin, even though all humans, being weak, inevitably do sin at some time or other.[69] This is not a tragedy; a repentant sinner can rely on God's mercy. Even those for whom sin has been a way of life can repent and start a new life. In most forms of Judaism and Christianity, it is not doubted that God wishes to save sinners, ready to welcome the lost sheep back to the fold. Atonement and repentance are at hand as practical means. According to some who take a rigorous point of view (such as the author of Hebrews), apostates are an exception to the rule, but then their terrible fate is the consequence of a false decision on their own part.

Under Cosmic Powers

Even authors who share the view, inherited from certain Jewish traditions, that the universe is subjected to hostile cosmic powers consider sins as individual transgressions and do not speak of "sin" in the singular, let alone as an overwhelming enslaving power. In Hellenistic tradition, planets and stars were commonly taken to affect people's lives, which made astrology an important area of even religious life; the heavenly bodies could be regarded as Gods. In some Jewish circles it was held that certain stars (which were, of course, creations of the one and only God) had "transgressed the commandments of the Lord" (*1 En.* 21.6; cf. Jude 13); astrological notions were amalgamated with the tradition of the fallen angels. Many early Christians draw on the tradition about the rebellion of some angels (explicitly mentioned in Jude 6; 2 Pet. 2:4). This Jewish tradition is extended, so that the "rulers and authorities" of the cosmos (Col. 2:15; cf. 1:16), a Hellenistic conception, "are considered in the same light; they are essentially hostile to God and seek to reign over the earthly realm."[70] These powers bring about that humans are not in control of their own lives—a situation from which Christ has delivered his adherents. Ephesians explicitly connects the cosmic rulers with the "evil one" (Eph. 6:11-12, 16); Hebrews notes that the devil has "the power of death," and he can therefore hold humans "in slavery by the fear of death" (Heb. 2:14-15; cf. Wis. 2:24). A drastic picture of the activities of the devil is given in Revelation: he is thrown out from heaven to the earth, where he pursues the church of Christ "with great wrath" through the beasts who symbolize the Roman Empire (Rev. 12–13). Humans are not, however, doomed to serve the devil (the beast); when the majority of them nevertheless do so, this is their own choice.

Even if the picture of humanity living in the fear of death, the devil, and the cosmic powers may seem dark, the point to be made here is that human beings are not regarded as helpless victims in face of these powers. It is simply the case that under this "dominion of darkness" (Col. 1:13), "sins," "evil deeds," and "trespasses" are committed (Col. 1:14, 21; 2:13). As a consequence of Christ's salvific act, they can be forgiven; the wiles of the devil are to be resisted (Eph. 6:11-12;

144   1 Pet. 5:8-9). In Colossians and Ephesians "there is no concept of 'sin' as a power of bondage. . . .The bondage from which humanity must be redeemed (or liberated) is of a cosmic order, redemption from the reign of the 'principalities and powers.'"[71] The author of the Pastorals "thinks of sins essentially as vices, of which he gives a long list (2 Tim. 3:2-5). . . . Vices are due essentially to serving self and the passions which arise from selfish desires (2 Tim. 2:22; Titus 2:12; 3:3)."[72]

Sin as Enslaving Power in Paul

A darker view of sin and consequently of the human plight is found in Paul's letters. Especially in a dense section in Romans (5:12—8:3), Paul depicts sin as an active power almost as potent as God (hence the capital *S* in what follows). It is easy to get the following impression, which reflects a standard scholarly view: "Paul sees sin as a universal human condition. Flesh qua flesh is inhabited by Sin . . . God solves the problem by sending his Son 'in the likeness of sinful flesh.' . . . For Paul, sin has so infected the human race that the problem can be solved only through the appearance of a new Adam."[73] A more extreme view even states that Paul rejected his mother religion just because of this pessimistic anthropology, finding the more optimistic Jewish view untenable.[74]

The active character of Sin emerges in Rom. 5:12, which states that Sin "entered the world" at a particular moment—due to Adam's trespass. Thereafter "Sin *reigned* in death" (5:21). Sin may "reign" in a person's body (6:12) or "have dominion" over people (6:14). Sin as a power may be served (6:16), and thus it enslaves (6:20). But humans present themselves voluntarily as slaves to Sin, therefore bearing responsibility for the matter (6:13, 16).

The point of contact or door of entry for Sin in humans is "flesh." The word *sarx* denotes the bodily character of humans on one hand, but it carries strong overtones of weakness, selfishness, and even hostility to God on the other. "Flesh" incites to sin. In Gal. 5:13-21, the "flesh" is equipped with features that almost seem to turn it into an independent sphere of power ("what the flesh desires is opposed to the spirit, and what the spirit desires is opposed to the flesh," v. 17); still, flesh is here a possibility within the person him- or herself. Romans 7:14-25 goes further and suggests that, being fleshly, humans are helplessly in bondage to Sin, which dwells in them as an external power.

"Flesh" is thus something in humans that causes them to be under the power of Sin. This may be seen as a radicalization of the Jewish notion of the evil inclination, or evil heart, as the source of sin. Yet on the other hand it is difficult not to see in this dark picture of the "flesh" some influence from the depreciation of the body in Hellenistic popular philosophy that, continuing the legacy of Platonic dualism, largely regarded human involvement with matter as a misfortune, sometimes of cosmic dimensions.[75] The passions that rise out of the bodily nature conquer the spirit. In Rom. 7:22-24, there are clear hints that corporeality brings miserable consequences with it: "I delight in the law of God in my *inmost self*, but I see in my *members* another law at war with the law of my *mind*, making me captive to the law of sin that dwells in my *members*. Wretched man that I am! Who will rescue me from this *body* of death?"

Moral philosophers and tragedians alike noted that a constant battle is going on between ethical insight and condemnable passion. Humans do what is wrong, even though they know what is right. This experiential wisdom is epitomized in Medea's[76] lines in Ovid: "some strange power (*nova vis*) holds me down against my will. Desire persuades me one way, reason another. I see the better and approve it, but follow the worse."[77] A discrepancy was felt to exist between intention and achievement (for example, Epictetus, *Diatr.* 2.26.1, 4). But characteristically, according to Epictetus, wrong behavior can be corrected through right knowledge. This ultimately optimistic view went back to Socrates and Plato; doing wrong was largely regarded as a matter of ignorance about what is truly good. Others, like Cicero and Seneca, presented more pessimistic judgments of the human condition. People do not use the divine gift of rational thought to do good; they use it to deceive one another (Cicero). Seneca wrote the sentence *peccavimus omnes* (we have all failed), some more gravely, some less (*Clem.* 1.6.3); no one is free from guilt. Still, this condition was not felt to be a hopeless tragedy. The dualism "always maintains an underlying faith in the capacity of the mind to overcome the passions and choose the right path."[78] It was still maintained that good or bad behavior can be freely chosen; lists of virtues and vices were an integral part of moral exhortation. Humans had always the chance to turn from material encumbrances to the philosophical life.[79]

Long ago, Paul Wernle observed on Paul: "Sin clings to man's bodily nature. Man is sold under sin because he is flesh. Nothing good dwells in him, that is, in his flesh. So closely are the body and sin connected that St. Paul creates the expression 'body of sin.' This theory is neither Jewish nor Greek, but an original creation of the apostle's. . . . Sin does not originate in the flesh—it takes up its abode therein as a visitor from outside, just as the Spirit."[80]

Romans 7 describes an "I" who finds himself in a sad plight—a corrupt "fleshly" person who is "sold under Sin" (7:14). The interpretation of

this chapter has been controversial since patristic times; but, especially in the light of the adjacent chapters 6 and 8,[81] it is plausible to take it as a depiction of the situation of a person outside the sphere of salvation in Christ. The "I" is definitely not a Christian and was seldom regarded as one, until Augustine brought about something like a volte-face in the interpretation of the passage.[82] Paul describes a person who is outside the union with Christ. By using the rhetorical "I," he probably includes himself among those who, before encountering Christ, lived under the power of Sin—which does not mean that he would have felt Sin as a heavy burden upon his neck. Paul contemplates the plight of non-Christians from the vista of his life in Christ. His point of departure resembles that of John: whoever does not believe in the message of Christ lives under the power of Sin.

Sin is, in Romans 7, a "law" (an order, a state of things) that lurks in the person's members: in one's "body of death" (v. 24). In principle, one's "inmost self" or "inward man" takes delight in the law of God (7:22-23). Yet the indwelling Sin prevents one from doing what one would like to do; one is under the compulsion to do what is bad: "I do not understand my own actions. For I do not what I want, but I do the very thing I hate" (v.15; cf. v. 19). Paul is taking up the above-mentioned notion, well-known in Greco-Roman tradition, of a moral conflict within humans: one often (but not always!) does what is wrong, even though one knows what is right. This everyday observation is, however, radicalized to the extreme by Paul, so that a completely wretched picture of the ego ensues.

In the next section (Rom. 8:5-11), the picture of the non-Christian is even darker. There is nothing left to correspond to his "delight in the law of God" as far as his "inward man" is

146 concerned (so 7:22); no "mind" (*nous*) with positive intentions is singled out as an antipode to the "flesh," as in chapter 7. The comparison set forth in chapter 8 is absolutely black-and-white. The "fleshly" non-Christians display a fleshly way of thinking, which amounts to enmity with God (8:5-7), in sharp distinction to the Christians, who fulfill the law and live according to the spirit.[83]

If Paul's depiction of "flesh" can still be seen to be in some continuity with the idea of "evil inclination," in another respect he departs much further from normal Jewish notions in Rom. 7:5-13. This section sets the stage for the description of the person sold under sin in 7:14-25. Paul brings together flesh, Sin—and the Torah: "While we were living in the *flesh*, our *sinful passions, aroused by the law*, were at work in our members to bear fruit for death." This peculiar view of the law will be dealt with later;[84] here we may note the increasingly active power attributed to Sin (instigated by the law). Sin found opportunity in the commandment (of the law) and "produced in me all kinds of covetousness" (7:8).[85] Sin "revived" (7:9) and, "seizing an opportunity in the commandment, deceived me and through it [the commandment] killed me" (7:11). Sin "worked death in me through what is good" (7:13). This is how the situation depicted in 7:14-25 came about.

Sin is here treated as a power, a mighty rival to God. Before the sending of Christ it often had the upper hand, cleverly appropriating even God's best weapon—the law—for its own use. This boosting of Sin partly explains why Paul makes little use of the standard Jewish (and Christian) idea of repentance; one does not manage to escape bondage to an alien power by such a human effort. Something much stronger is needed. The rule of Sin can be escaped only through death

(6:2-11). Christians have died with Christ to Sin (6:6, 11), and they have thereby got rid not only of Sin but also of the law.

Romans 5–8 teaches that where Christ is not acknowledged as the Lord, Sin rules and humans live in hopeless bondage to it. Such a conception is a far cry from the classic Jewish view that God created the world, declared it good, and put humans in charge of it. Indeed, that biblical doctrine is not easily reconcilable with the view that Sin is a power strong enough to usurp the law from God's control and to render humans absolutely powerless to do what is good.[86] A look at the early chapters of Romans reveals internal problems as well in this Pauline conception.

Paul first introduces the notion of Sin as a power in Rom. 3:9. There he states that "all, both Jews and Greeks, are under the power of Sin." He suggests that he has shown this in the previous sections (obviously, 1:18—2:29 is in view) and clinches the argument with a catena of psalm quotations in 3:10-18. Paul's reasoning seems indeed to be that, since the human situation is hopeless, everybody being under the power of Sin, God sent Christ as the solution to this problem (3:9-12, 23-24). This argument is, however, undermined by 2:6-16, a passage with a forceful emphasis on judgment according to deeds. Verses 9-10 stand in stark contrast to the conception of Sin as a cosmic power in control of all people: "There will be anguish and distress for everyone who does evil, the Jew first and also the Greek, but *glory and honor and peace for everyone who does good*, the Jew first and also the Greek." Romans 2 holds out the definite possibility of acting properly in God's eyes. Even good Gentiles are in the position to obey God's will: "When Gentiles, who do not possess the law, *do instinctively what the law requires*, these . . . are a law to themselves" (2:14; cf. 2:26-27).[87] In Romans 1–3, sin appears simply "as the accumulation of evil actions which people freely, and even enthusiastically (Rom 1.18ff!) commit."[88]

What sort of actions? In Rom. 1:18-32, Paul paints a desolate picture of the Gentile world, drawing on standard Jewish polemics. All Gentiles are lumped together as idolaters and homosexuals[89] to whom the vice list in 1:29-31 applies. In 2:17-24 Paul in turn attacks Jews to whom he attributes stealing, adultery, and sacrilege. Obviously the charges are exaggerated to the extreme.[90] Even if one accepted their veracity, Paul's argument would prove no more than that *many* Gentiles and *some* Jews are guilty of heinous transgressions[91] and are therefore exposed to God's wrath. "The conclusion in 3:9 does not correspond to what leads up to it in any respect: the charges in chaps. 1–2 overstate the case and the conclusion is contradicted by 2:13-14. What this means is that Paul's conclusion, that all are under Sin, was not derived from the line of observation and reasoning he had presented in the previous chapters."[92] In fact, Paul has resorted to the well-worn strategy of factional polemics (though he replaces the Jewish polemic against Gentiles with a Christian attack on Gentiles *and Jews*).

The second passage that argues for the universality of Sin's dominion, Rom. 5:12-19, also has its problems. Adam sinned, and this introduced Sin and its corollary, death, into the world (vv. 12-13), so that all humans stand condemned (v. 18). There is an internal tension in 5:12: on one hand, Sin entered through Adam; on the other hand, each person sinned ("so death spread to all people because[93] *all* sinned," 5:12d). The latter statement approximates the idea found somewhat later in *2 Bar.* 54.19 that each person is his own Adam.[94] Sin seems to be both an action within the compass of personal responsibil-

ity and also a power that surpasses human will. Paul balances on the edge between his two portrayals of sin: "all sinned" connects to Romans 1–2, where sin is the accumulation of humanity's evil deeds "freely committed and uninfluenced by the coercive effects of any sort of supernatural power"; by contrast, "Sin entered to reign, death spread," points to Romans 6–7, where Sin is a mighty power in its own right. "These conceptions are not compatible, yet 5:12 looks toward them both."[95]

Paul admits that not everybody has transgressed like Adam, for he states that "death reigned from Adam to Moses, *even over* those whose sins were not like the transgression of Adam" (Rom. 5:14). Why Sin (and death) nevertheless has dominion over them is not explained, apart from the implied statement that these humans were ruled by Sin because they sinned.[96] Paul just asserts the conclusion that "by the one man's disobedience the many were made sinners" (5:19). "His anthropology did not include the conception of inherited sin, and thus he had no logical way of proving universal condemnation by appeal to Adam. He simply asserted it, while himself citing points which count against it."[97]

In both cases (Rom. 1–3 and Rom. 5), then, Paul's conclusion is independent of the arguments that were meant to lead up to it. This suggests that Paul held the conclusion in advance and tried to glean arguments in favor of it, though without logical success. These observations support the thesis that in Romans 7, too, Paul has taken an empirical observation as his starting point but has jumped to a theological non sequitur: he infers from the well-known discrepancy between intentions and actions that no one (outside the dominion of Christ) does any good at all. "What was difficult in classical dualism has become utterly impossible in Paul."[98]

148   How could Paul hold so strong a view of Sin?[99] How had the world become so estranged from God? A possible (partial) explanation might be that Paul had adopted aspects of the worldview, influenced by Iranian dualism, according to which the creation is at least partly under the control of dark powers. There are echoes of this in Paul: Satan can do tricks (2 Cor. 11:14); "this age" is ruled by "another God" (2 Cor. 4:4) or by other "rulers" (1 Cor. 2:6); it can be called an "evil age" from which Jesus has set the believers free (Gal. 1:4). Paul believed in the reality of evil spiritual forces, "so-called Gods" (1 Cor. 8:5; cf. Gal. 4:8) or demons (1 Cor. 10:20). These beings are able to enslave humans (Gal. 4:8), as is Sin (Rom. 6:6). Sin may be seen as the functional equivalent of the evil spirit (Belial,[100] Satan) of some postexilic literature, yet Romans 7 goes beyond these dualistic texts in emphasizing humanity's complete helplessness. But even though Paul was surely influenced by some form of dualism, he did not put Satan and Sin together to form a dualistic theology. Paul did not conceive of Sin ontologically in demonic terms. Satan is never referred to in the "Sin" passages. Similarly, Satan and fallen angels are absent from the Adam section (Rom. 5) and also from Romans 7, a passage with echoes of the paradise story. It is also worth noting that Paul does not start his reflections from the problem of suffering, let alone from the issue of structural sin (for example, in the form of violence), as a modern version of the doctrine of original sin might do.

Eventually Paul takes the bold step of integrating even sin in *God's* purposes. God controls what happens, both in nature and in history. This means, applied to the issue of sin, that God intended human disobedience! Paul comes to suggest that "God intended universal sin so that he could subsequently save everyone by grace"[101] (Gal. 3:22; Rom. 11:32). Whether Paul really meant this, or whether he was simply carried away by the train of his argument, is another matter.

It is hard to avoid the impression that Paul is forced to create a bleak picture of the world in bondage to Sin for the reason that otherwise God's radical act in delivering Christ to death would seem futile. Rather like the Deuteronomists before him, or *4 Ezra* after him, Paul thinks backward. Yet unlike these writers, Paul's problem is not that of theodicy and the sufferings of the people, but rather the dogmatic need to confirm the absolute truth that he has found "in Christ": outside life in Christ there can be no life worth the name at all. Paul's statements on Sin are a reflection of his conviction that God has prepared salvation for all humans in Jesus Christ, and in him alone.

That Paul reasons "from the solution to the plight," not the other way round, has been strongly emphasized by E. P. Sanders,[102] but the point was made long ago, for example, by Paul Wernle:

> St. Paul's pessimism is intended to serve his apologetic. It is because Jesus alone is the Redeemer, that the world has to be presented as irredeemably wicked, and every other road to salvation closed to men. It is not the actual recognition of the greatness of sin and the impotence of man which is at the root of this theory, but faith in Christ necessitates these pessimistic postulates as presuppositions. . . . [Paul] first violently extinguished every other light in the world so that Jesus might then shine in it alone.[103]

To be more precise: Paul extinguishes the light of the *Torah*. In making this move, Paul exploits in passing as an auxiliary notion even the Greek idea of the body being inferior to the "inner person."[104]

When Paul is not reflecting on the plight of humans from the perspective of his Christ-centered conviction, he finds it quite natural that they can fulfill the demands of the law. Such "anthropological slips" (above all Rom. 2) reveal that Paul's commonsense view of humankind differs from his theological interpretation of the human condition. "At the level of common sense he believed that in the eyes of an impartial God there are similarly moral people among Jews, Gentiles and Christians."[105] This commonsense view yields, however, to Paul's forced theological analysis, which requires that everyone outside Christ *must* be a corrupt sinner, imprisoned by evil powers. Paul exploits the traditional notion of universal sinfulness, but he radicalizes it to the extreme, combining the traditional concept with his new idea about Sin as a power.[106] From the notion of universal sinfulness, he alone draws soteriological conclusions: a new divine action is necessary to save humans from such a plight. "In a surprising way Paul denies the possibility of being 'sinfully righteous.' . . . Paul's application of universal sinfulness involved the denial of fundamental Jewish convictions."[107]

The commonsense view reappears, however (one might say, with a vengeance), in Paul's thoroughly "optimistic theory of Christian conduct enabled by participatory union with Christ."[108] Whereas non-Christian Jews are incapable of coping with the law, Christians fulfill in the spirit all that is required by it (Rom. 8:4, 9-11; 13:8-10; cf. Gal. 5:14-16).

In Romans (6:14), a letter sent from Corinth, Paul states with joyous assurance that Sin will not reign over Christians. Yet precisely the story of the Corinthian congregation puts this optimism in a dubious light.[109] Paul compares Christian life at its best (if not an ideal picture

of it) with Jewish life at its worst (if not a pure caricature), thus using different standards for "us" and "them," respectively. All this shows the strained character of his effort to show that humans under the law are hopeless victims of Sin, whereas those in Christ have overcome Sin. More realistic is his exhortation that Christians should live up to their calling—the so-called tension between the "indicative" and the" imperative": "If we live by the spirit, let us also walk in the spirit!" (Gal. 5:25; cf. Rom. 6:13).[110]

Paul's theological analysis, then, boils down to a restatement of the factional "us/them" division—as does John's! Paul opposes those "under the law"; John attacks "the Jews." "We" bear fruit of the Spirit; those "under the law" are under Sin. But Paul redraws the group boundaries with regard to his all-important concern for the full inclusion of Gentile believers into the people of God.[111] It is no longer one's relationship to the Torah that dictates whether one is righteous or a sinner. In Gal. 2:17-18, Paul goes so far as to admit that he and his like have actually made themselves "sinners" in disregarding some stipulations of the Torah. This cannot mean that Christ is a "servant of Sin" (probably a conclusion drawn by conservative critics); therefore, the Torah cannot be a fully reliable guide in matters of sin and righteousness. But it is plausible to speculate that if a sufficiently large number of Paul's compatriots had accepted his law-critical gospel, he would not have developed the vision of humans "sold under Sin" at all—for the simple reason that such a view would then have been unnecessary for his theology.[112]

Paul's dark line of thought is not taken up by others with anything like this radicalness until Augustine draws his own conclusions.[113] Before Augustine, it is the gnostic Christians who come closest in presenting their own pessimistic analysis of the human condition.

150 *Blinded by Ignorance*

The Platonist Christians participate in their way in the philosophical discourse of antiquity, taking for granted the Platonic notion of the imprisonment of the soul in the body.

In the *Gospel of Thomas*, Jesus complains that the sons of men are intoxicated and blind (*Gos. Thom.* 28); not knowing themselves that they "dwell in poverty" (3). Yet this Gospel is not overly pessimistic about the world and, unlike works that can properly be classified as gnostic, it never suggests that the material world was created by an evil demiurge.[114] The *Authoritative Teaching* states that those who are ignorant and do not seek after God live in "bestiality" (*Auth. Teach.* 33.4-9), due to the fall "into bestiality" of the soul, metaphorically depicted as a prostitute who fell "into drinking much wine in debauchery" (24.1-23). The *Gospel of Mary* claims that "there is no such thing as sin; rather, you yourselves are what produces sin when you act in accordance with the nature of adultery, which is called 'sin'" (*Gos. Mary* 7.12-16). Karen King comments that "the sinfulness of the human condition, the estrangement of God, is caused by mixing together the spiritual and material natures." No sin exists as such, but "people do produce sin when they wrongly follow the desires of their material nature instead of nurturing their spiritual selves."[115]

Christians with more distinctly gnostic inclinations draw darker conclusions from the entanglement of the spiritual substance with matter: it has made humans prisoners of demonic powers. They are "cast down to live, not only in a body, but also in a cosmos dominated by hostile, clever forces continually seeking their destruction."[116] This picture bears some resemblance to the notion of humanity in bondage to cosmic powers as presented in Colossians and Ephesians, though the reason for the bondage is different and the situation is regarded in more pessimistic terms in the gnostic writings. A fundamental disorder reigns; suffering is built into the structure of the universe itself. This disorder is mostly traced back to the fact that the whole material cosmos has been created because of a basic error, which is often described with the aid of complicated cosmogonic myths.[117] The unenlightened human condition is characterized by such metaphors as darkness, error, sleep, or drunkenness. But unlike the philosophers (and in accordance with other Christians), the gnostic Christians hold that true knowledge cannot be reached through rational thought alone; it can be gained only through revelation. Humans have forgotten their spiritual origin and goal and have to be reminded of it.

For example, the Valentinian *Gospel of Truth* (17) describes the reasons for the human plight as follows: As the "totality" searched for the Father in vain, ignorance emerged and caused "anguish and terror." Anguish then gave rise to Error, which worked at matter and created "a substitute for truth." "Error" is here spoken of as an independent figure, rather like Paul at times speaks of Sin (and Death) as demonic powers. People are "in darkness because of forgetfulness," until Jesus reveals the gospel to them (*Gos. Truth* 18.12-17). Even for gnostic Christians, the miserable nature of the human condition becomes clear only when it is seen in retrospect from the perspective of one who has found enlightenment. As long as one is unsaved, one is asleep, unconscious of one's situation.

Sethian myths emphasize the active malevolence of evil more than does Valentinian theology.[118] The *Hypostasis of the Archons* tells that Adam was a victim. "Betrayed and deceived by the forces of evil, created as a by-product of their desires and jealousies, Adam was helplessly caught within a battle of spiritual forces and could only hope that the powers above would defeat his tormentors and release their human prisoner from his cosmic confinement."[119] The work "proclaims, as its title indicates, the reality of the archontic rulers." "These rulers indeed exist. This is a grim reality for the Christian Gnostics, who define their own spiritual nature in opposition to that of the ruling and enslaving authorities" (but in the end the rulers will perish).[120] Having expelled Adam and his wife from paradise, the rulers "threw mankind into great distraction and into a life of toil, so that their mankind might be occupied by worldly affairs, and might not have the opportunity of being devoted to the holy spirit" (*Hyp. Arch.* 91.7-11).

While Paul presses the concept of universal sinfulness into the service of his notion of Sin as enslaving power, gnostic Christians resort to the notion of universal ignorance, due to oblivion, which likewise makes humans subject to hostile powers. But whereas Paul's notion stands in palpable tension with other notions of his, suggesting that there is something strained in his theology of sin within the framework of his *own* thought, the gnostic view seems more consistent in its pessimism.

However, suffering because of ignorance is not the only trouble. Ignorance leads to *sin*;[121] sin is a relevant concept and plays a major role in Valentinian thought.[122] It refers to "a human act or thought not in harmony with the supreme God or Father." On this score the Nag Hammadi writings provide a major correction to older views concerning these Christians: patristic heresiologists had claimed that the Valentinians were prepared for all kinds of evil, ascribing to them a libertinist attitude, for which sin was of no concern. But in Nag Hammadi texts Valentinian Christians are constantly exhorted to "do the Father's will" and "the ethical directives of the Sermon on the Mount are often noted explicitly."[123] "Valentinians were extremely concerned about acting and thinking correctly."[124] The *Gospel of Philip* exhorts them to examine themselves: "Let each of us dig down after the root of evil within us and pull it out of our hearts from the root. It will be uprooted if we recognize it. But if we are ignorant of it, it takes root in us and produces fruit in our hearts; it dominates us." The author continues in a Pauline vein: "We are its slaves, and it takes us captive so that we do what we do [not] want and do [not] do what we want.... The word says, 'If you know the truth, the truth will make you free.' Ignorance is a slave, knowledge is freedom" (*Gos. Phil.* 83.18—84.11).

In the Valentinian view, sin does concern all people,[125] though in different ways. Some are dominated by their fleshly nature and cannot refrain from sinning. By contrast, those who have become aware of their spiritual nature recognize the Father's will and are inclined to act accordingly, though they do not always succeed in practice. Without knowledge of who the Father is and what he wants, it is impossible to act correctly. Yet even this knowledge is no guarantee of a sinless existence. For instance, James, in the *Second Apocalypse of James*, is a righteous individual who still admits to having sinned, and when faced with death is terrified by the consequences of his sinful acts.[126] The human condition "includes sinning, either constantly, repeatedly, or infrequently."[127] The standard notion of universal sinfulness has not been abandoned. People are faced with a powerful force that instigates them to act improperly. This external power, which is given various names (for example, the Devil, Error, Evil),[128] has settled in people's "hylic" (material) part.[129] It poses a constant threat. "People sin, then, because they are strongly urged to do

152 so by an evil power residing within them, and ignorance of the Father for some makes the situation hopeless."[130]

Idealization of the in-group occurs often enough, but, in comparison to Paul or John, there generally seems to be less wholesale denigration of those outside their own fold. The Valentinians' attitude to the "psychics" (a term that could denote average "Catholics") was remark-ably open.[131] Their vision of sin seems less black-and-white than Paul's theological theory (as in Rom. 8), but it appears to be fairly close to Paul's commonsense parenesis: even the pneumatic has to fight against sin.

A HISTORICAL EPILOGUE

In the fourth century, the two visions of the human condition came to a famous head-on clash. The more optimistic vision was maintained by Pelagius; Augustine seized on Paul's pessimistic line of thought and developed it in a new direction.[132]

Augustine found proof for "original sin" in Psalm 51, Job, and Eph. 2:3, yet above all in Rom. 5:12 (where he read "*in whom* [= in Adam] all sinned") and John 3:3-5.[133] The general wretchedness of humanity's lot and their enslavement to their desires seemed to clinch the matter. Unlike Paul, Augustine resorted to a psychological and empirical explanation, obviously stimulated by his stormy personal experience. By far the most violent, persistent, and widespread of the evil inclinations, he held, was sexual desire.[134] Augustine believed that the taint of original sin was propagated in the semen as the result of carnal excitement, which accompanied the act of generation and was present in the sexual behavior even of baptized persons. The essence of original sin consists in our participation in, and coresponsibility for, Adam's perverse choice. We were one with him when he made this choice. Augustine could speak of "a cruel necessity of sinning."[135] The whole of humanity would be destined to everlasting damnation, were it not for the grace of Christ.

6.3   Augustine. Painting by Joos van Ghent, c. 1475. Louvre, Paris. Photo: Erich Lessing/Art Resource, NY.

Augustine confronted Christians with his conception of humankind as a *massa perditionis*, in themselves unable to make any move whatsoever toward salvation. Pelagius, seriously concerned for right conduct in view of the coming judgment, was shocked by what he considered a demoralizing view. The assumption that humans could not help sinning seemed an insult to their Creator.[136] Pelagius's eminent disciple, Julian of Eclanum, even wrote that Augustine's "impious" doctrine of original sin "makes it seem as if the devil were the maker of men." Pelagius maintained that God set life and death before humans, bidding them to choose life (Deut. 30:19), but leaving the final decision to their free will. The power comes from God, but the will and the realization belong to us; that is the human response to the gospel.[137] Adam's trespass did have harmful consequences: it introduced death and began a habit of disobedience. But this is propagated not by physical descent but by custom and example. Deeply stirred by the stern radicalism

of the Sermon of the Mount, Pelagius did not shrink from the conviction that "a man can, if he will, observe God's commandments without sinning" (cf. Lev. 19:2; Matt. 5:48); it is impious to suggest that God enjoins what he knows to be impossible. Scripture points to many examples of blameless lives. He is a Christian who can justly say, "I have injured no one, I have lived righteously with all."[138]

For all the "icy puritanism"[139] that his position may involve, it is Pelagius who stood in continuity with the bulk of biblical tradition and early Christianity. It is indeed quite astonishing that Augustine's radical novel views came to prevail in Western Christianity.[140] Augustine leaned on Paul's radical, artificial line of thought, though for reasons quite other than Paul's; the Reformation followed suit. Apart from the radical side of Paul, early Christianity before Augustine is much closer to Judaism (and Islam!) than to mainstream Protestantism with regard to the issue of the human condition.

7

What Must I Do to Be Saved?

Different Paths to Salvation

Christianity is regarded as a religion of salvation. It is not self-evident that humans should long for salvation from their present condition.[1] In the ancient Egyptian worldview, for instance, the existing order of things was regarded as sound, being in harmony with an eternal order. What was desired was not liberation (neither in a this-worldly nor in a transcendent sense) from the present state, but the reassurance of the existing order and avoidance of disturbances.

COVENANTAL NOMISM

In the same vein, the old Israelite religion did not look forward to liberation from the present world either. This religion valued a happy, mundane life: health, family, peace, and prosperity were conceived of as divine blessings. God's grace or goodness (*hesed*) was experienced in the gifts of nature and in his providential care in the life of the people.

However, the vicissitudes of history did not always allow for peaceful thriving. Israel was repeatedly exposed to external threat. In times of calamity and danger, rescue from the troops of the changing enemies—be it the Philistines in the eleventh or the Babylonians in the sixth century B.C.E., or the Greeks, Syrians, or Romans in the time of the Second Temple—was a constant object of hope. The source of this hope was, of course, the God of Israel. Salvation was conceived to be wholly based on his redemptive action.[2]

Yahweh was trusted to be able to rescue his people from the situation of opposition and danger to one of peace and well-being. Salvation or redemption meant collective, national survival. The term *salvation* itself (Hebrew *yeshua*, Greek *soteria*) is frequently used in a military sense (victory, aid)—first in particular situations, then in a final drama of history (on which see chapter 4).

In order to participate in this salvation, one obviously had to belong to the right group—to the elect for whom Yahweh cared. If salvation equals collective survival, what counts is to be on the right side when God intervenes. With time, however, a differentiated vision emerged. God would eventually deliver his faithful from their enemies—just the faithful, not the whole people. Its individual members would be put on trial and judged. The faithful would be acquitted and saved into a life beyond death, but the wicked would perish either in this world or in the next; for them, God would be a terrible enemy who poured his wrath on them.

The differentiated notion of salvation evokes fundamental questions. What would guarantee one a place among the righteous? Who is in and who is out? How does one enter the sphere of salvation or, once in, stay there securely? In what relationship does human effort stand to divine initiative? If a judgment is envisioned, what are its criteria?

Postexilic Jews knew the criteria. God had given Israel his Torah—his guidance or law—which expressed his will. When the life of each person was assessed individually in the judgment, their obedience to the Torah would be scrutinized. The judgment would take place according to one's deeds. In the more rigorous perceptions—most conspicuously in Qumran, but emphatically exclusivist views of salvation were not limited to that group[3]—only a small remnant of the people would be found to be on the right side.[4] The majority, however, seem to have taken a more optimistic view of the nature of the judgment, so much so that at the other end of the spectrum the notion is found that (practically) "all Israel" will be saved in the end.[5]

For a long time, early Jewish attitudes to obeying the law were distorted in Christian scholarship. Obedience to the Torah was portrayed as bondage and as a burden, which led either to mental misery or else to bigotry. Jews were depicted "either as living in terror that at the last judgment their sins would outweigh their good deeds, or as self-righteous boasters in the good deeds by which they earned their salvation."[6] During the last generation this caricature has largely been laid to rest. Broadly speaking, the common denominator of Jewish attitudes can be characterized as "covenantal nomism," an expression coined by E. P. Sanders.[7] In the biblical narrative the lawgiving came to be integrated in the story of Yahweh's saving action on behalf of his people; the lawgiving at Sinai followed the liberation from the Egyptian slavery. By redeeming the people from their plight, God elected Israel, showing himself to be its benefactor and king, who could justly expect loyalty and obedience to his stipulations from those redeemed. The Torah was conceived of as the terms of the benevolent covenant, which the heavenly king made with his elect; the people, on their part, voluntarily consented to these terms. The covenant was based on God's mercy and grace, but this did not mean that no human contribution was involved. Unlike later Protestant theology, Judaism had no need to claim *absolute* divine gratuity, that is, to claim that humans can contribute *nothing* to their election.

Stephen Westerholm provides a judicious discussion of the debate on grace and works in Judaism that has followed Sanders's work.[8] Sanders is often taken to have argued (rightly or wrongly, depending on the reviewer) that the Judaism of "covenantal nomism" preached "good Protestant doctrine: that grace is always prior; that human effort is ever the response to divine initiative; that good works are the fruit and not the root of salvation."[9] Westerholm grants Sanders "that Judaism did not generally believe that salvation was earned from scratch by human deeds of righteousness" but notes that this "by no

156 means differentiates Judaism from the classical opponents of 'Lutheran' thought. Each acknowledged human need of divine grace." For in fact,

> the position of Judaism on the relation between grace and works *as Sanders himself portrays it* seems to differ little from that of Pelagius, against whom Augustine railed, or that of the sixteenth-century church, upon which Luther called down heaven's thunder. . . . What the opponents of "Lutheranism" emphatically did *not* do, however . . . was to suggest that humans can contribute *nothing* to their salvation. *That* insistence is . . . the very essence of "Lutheranism." It seems fair to say that it is not to be found in Judaism as depicted by Sanders.[10]

Westerholm's point is well taken. We need only to add that (as we shall see) such insistence hardly conforms to any early Christian view either.

The human response to God's beneficial action was obedience to his stipulations, expressed as orthopraxy rather than orthodoxy. Identity markers that distinguished Jews from other peoples gained special importance: monotheism, circumcision, Sabbath, and food laws in particular.

Given human frailty (see chapter 6), perfection was not expected nor total obedience required. What was crucial was the will and intention to obey the law. In his mercy, God had provided means for coping with transgressions so that unwelcome consequences could be removed: there were sacrifices, the annual Day of Atonement (*yom kippur*), and, not least, the chance to repent. In various ways the sacrificial system was expected to restore a broken relationship with God, to set right what had gone wrong. "Sacrifice may purify uncleanness, or it may make reparation for guilt that has been incurred through wrong action. In both cases it brings equilibrium and wholeness between the divine and human partners of the covenant. The Day of Atonement ritual epitomizes these functions."[11]

However, already the prophetic books had made it clear that a ritual without a right attitude was null and void (for example, Isa. 1:11-17; Am. 5:21-24). The will to *repent*, to return to God, was all-important. Philo is representative of Jewish sentiments in general in stating that those who bring sacrifices should "ask for pardon and forgiveness for their sins" (*Spec.* 1.67), or that Moses "holds the sacrifice to consist not in the victims but in the offerer's intention and his zeal" (1.290).[12] Even Ben Sira, a strong advocate of the temple and its priesthood, maintains that pious deeds stand alongside the sacrificial system as a means of atonement.[13] Repentance has rightly been called the Jewish way to salvation. God would show mercy to a repentant sinner; sincere prayer could ward off his anger.[14] The centrality of repentance and sacrifices goes together with the prevailing understanding of *sin*: the view of the human condition in God's world was relatively optimistic.

On the other hand, God could employ suffering to "discipline" the covenant people so that they would turn from their sins (for example, 2 Macc. 6:12-17). The innocent acts of martyrs are acts of obedience that deliver Israel from the curse and restore the blessing of God (cf. especially 4 Macc. 17:20-22).

The relation between God's grace and human effort can be studied in the texts of Qumran with special profit. In the lives of those who could not avail themselves of the temple cult in Jerusalem, the proper inner attitude before God came to be stressed all the more. Members of the Essene movement thought that there were, at present at least, few persons who still belonged to God's elect. The majority of the Jewish people were outside, not to mention the mass of the Gentiles. The members of the movement were the tiny remnant, the real people of the covenant.[15] They believed that they were God's elect, destined to attain salvation, but not because of any merits of their own. The priority of God's grace was emphasized, just as it had been emphasized in the traditional doctrine of election. The significant difference is, however, that it was not the people as a collective that had been elected, but rather the individual sectarian (1QS 11.11-15):

> As for me, if I stumble, the mercies of God shall be my salvation always, and if I fall in the sin of the flesh, in the justice of God, which endures eternally, shall my judgment be. If my grief commences, he will free my soul from the pit and make my steps steady on the path; he will draw me near in his mercies, and by kindnesses set in motion my judgment; he will judge me in the justice of his truth, and in his plentiful goodness always atone for my sins; in his justice he will cleanse me from the uncleanness of the human being and from the sins of the sons of man.

God has given wisdom, righteousness, and glory to his elect "as everlasting possession, until they inherit them in the lot of the holy ones" (1QS 11.7). The poet feels his sinfulness; as such he belongs to those who walk in darkness (11.9-10). A stark contrast is thus established between sinful human beings and the righteous God (see chapter 6). The view of life is theocentric. Salvation, one's lot in the holy community, depends on God's grace alone. "*Only* by your goodness is man acquitted [or: justified]" (1QH 5.23). The acknowledgment of grace leads to loyalty shown through obedience to the Torah or, in practice, to the distinctive *halakah* (tradition of law-observance) of the movement.[16] Still, even

correct obedience is conceived of as an act of divine grace.[17] Humans themselves are unable to establish their steps, so everything is established by God, which for the psalmist is a cause of delightful confidence: "As for me, in God is my judgment; in his hand is the perfection of my path" (1QS 11.2). "For to man [does not belong] his path, nor to a human being the steadying of his step; since judgment belongs to God, and from his hand is the perfection of the path" (11.10-11).

The emphasis on grace is overwhelming, but this grace benefits only those who follow the strict interpretation of the Torah of the movement, which one could do only with some effort. But we will see that this synergism (if that is what one wishes to call it), the combination of divine grace and human effort, is something that unites the Qumran in-group and other Jews with early Christians. This is not surprising in light of the fact that both aspects, "gift" and "demand," are combined in the all-important notion of covenant from the start in a way that is bound to engender tensions. The tension between those who stress the "gift" aspect and those who emphasize the "demand" reappears in early Christianity.

THE PATH OF REPENTANCE AND OBEDIENCE

John and Jesus

In the prophetic vein, but with Qumranic severity, John the Baptist preached repentance. If some Israelites wished to count just on the fact that they belonged to the chosen people (that is, if they wished to count—whether seriously or smugly—on God's mercy and faithfulness!), they were completely wrong. Belonging to the

158 offspring of Abraham was of no help at all, if "fruits worthy of repentance" were missing. God was coming to settle the accounts; radical repentance was in order (Q 3:7-9). John was searching for individuals from among the nation to be rescued from the judgment, ominously called "the coming wrath."[18] Repentance was sealed by a bath that was undertaken for the remission of sins. Having its religious background in Jewish purificatory rites, yet being distinct from the usual repeated ablutions because of its once-and-for-all character,[19] John's baptism was an effective visible sign of serious repentance. The necessity of such a rite confirms that, for the Baptist, the collective ethnic covenant was no longer effective. A new start was needed. Thus John's preaching amounted to a new version of the not-so-new idea that only a faithful remnant of the people was to gain salvation from the expected disaster.

Jesus accepted John's challenge, underwent the baptism of repentance, and joined the Baptist's circle, apparently himself conducting baptisms for a while (cf. John 3:22—4:2). He later gave up this activity and went his own way, but he always held the Baptist in high esteem (Q 7:24-28), and the demand of repentance remained in focus in his own mission. In the Synoptic Gospels, sin is conceived of as concrete transgression, and the path to salvation is marked by repentance, the remission of sins, and the production of "good fruit." A radical renewal of life in view of the approaching reign of God, of which signs were seen in Jesus' activity, was needed. The Gospels give a somewhat inconsistent picture of Jesus' attitude to standard Jewish piety, but apparently he did not renounce in so many words the usual means of keeping or staying in the covenant. "Staying in" continued to be based on obedience to the Torah (Q is quite firm on this),

even though some particulars of Jesus' interpretation of its commandments (for example, of the Sabbath) were controversial.

For those who transgress, repentance is the remedy: "The time is fulfilled and the kingdom of God has come near—repent!" (Mark 1:15).[20] God's forgiveness is readily available to those who ask for it and are in turn prepared to forgive their neighbors (Q 11:4; 17:3-4; Mark 11:25). The rich man who claims to have obeyed the commandments all along (Mark 10:17-27) is on the right path. But he is also right in surmising that he still lacks something, and Jesus points this out to him: he should *leave everything* and follow him, Jesus, whatever the cost.

Jesus' attitude to his audience seems ambiguous in the Gospels. On one hand he seems very open-minded, willing to accept "sinners" who do not meet standard requirements of piety. Meals with publicans brought him the censure of the pious (Q 7:34; Mark 2:16).[21] Jesus is known as a great healer and helper of people in need. He sets forth the salvific significance of the kingdom of God in positive, life-affirming images: a treasure, a precious pearl, a festive meal, a wedding. On the other hand, Jesus presents rigorous, even ascetic requirements both to his followers and to people in general: one should leave one's possessions, give up familial relationships, "amputate" tempting members of the body. Was Jesus' mind divided, or do our sources mislead us? In fact, the portrait of Jesus as the gentle friend of sinners is largely due to Luke. Apparently Jesus' "love for sinners" has been exaggerated, first by Luke and in his wake by modern scholars as well.[22]

It is indeed the trademark of Jesus' vision of salvation that the commandments of the law are interpreted (mostly) in a more rigorous way than usual. The prohibition of murder is taken to forbid anger and insulting words (Matt.

5:21-22); when a man casts a lustful glance on a woman, the prohibition of adultery is already being transgressed (Matt. 5:27-28). Divorce and remarriage are absolutely against God's will, even for the abandoned party (Mark 10:2-9 par.). Jesus, like the Baptist, stands in the apocalyptic tradition: the righteous will be saved from the coming disaster, the others—even within Israel—will perish. The envisaged restoration of Israel thus amounts to the restoration of the repentant *remnant*. The meaning of "repentance" shifts, however: the choice for or against repentance merges with a choice for or against *Jesus*. Galilean towns that have failed to acknowledge Jesus' mighty deeds will be condemned (Q 10:13-15);[23] "this generation" ought to perceive that in the ministry of Jesus something greater is encountered than in that of Jonah, the great preacher of repentance, or Solomon, the wise king (Q 11:31-32; cf. Q 10:23-24).[24] More than that, at the judgment one has to account for one's relationship to Jesus' person: "Everyone who acknowledges me before others, the Son of Man will acknowledge before the angels of God; but whoever denies me will be denied before the angels of God" (Q 12:8-9).[25] Whoever rejects Jesus or his itinerant envoys rejects God, who sent Jesus (Q 10:16).[26]

The same combination of a pious way of life, defined by loyalty to God's commandments, *and* a commitment to the charismatic leader subsequently characterizes the different paths to salvation in the minds of the early Christians, who mostly cannot imagine genuine repentance apart from faith in Jesus. The future exclusivity of Christian soteriology is thus found *in nuce* in the message of Jesus himself, even though "faith" here lacks any doctrinal significance, denoting trust in the power of the healer ("your faith has made you well": Mark 5:34; 10:52; and elsewhere).

References to a saving significance of Jesus' death (Mark 10:45; 14:22-25 par.) remain isolated. The ransom saying is probably post-Easter.[27] The issue of Jesus' last meal is very complicated; what exactly he may have said in that connection seems impossible to trace.[28] It is even controversial whether Jesus anticipated his imminent death. His disciples experienced it as a shock, for which they had hardly been prepared. In Q, Jesus' death is interpreted as the typical fate of a prophet; this would be hard to understand if Jesus had spoken to his followers of its extraordinary saving significance.

Early Christianity

The combination of loyalty to the commandments *and* commitment to Jesus is not an easy one.[29] Good deeds and a devout life persist in the Jesus movement in the traditional way as the crucial criterion of the last judgment, more or less in tension with the criterion of having acknowledged Jesus. Even Paul, who in general emphatically represents a (very partial) Christ-centered soteriology, can at times insist that at the judgment God will show "no partiality," but "will repay according to every one's *deeds*: to those who by patiently *doing good* seek for glory and honor and immortality, he will give eternal life; while for those who are self-seeking and who obey not the truth but wickedness, there will be wrath and fury." There will be "glory and honor and peace for everyone who does good," whether Jew or Greek (Rom. 2:6-11; cf. 2 Cor. 5:10). In 1 Thess. 1:9-10, the human act of turning to God from idols is singled out as the gateway to salvation. In Gal. 5:16—6:10, Paul, employing the established Jewish form of two-ways instruction, describes human deeds in terms of vices and virtues, underscoring their respective eternal consequences, either corruption or eternal life.[30]

160 In the gospel tradition, a strong emphasis on proper conduct dominates. It is stressed in Q that a tree is known by its fruit, and the point is taken over by Matthew and Luke (Q 6:43-45). To call Jesus "Lord, Lord," is of no avail, if one does not do what Jesus tells one to do (Q 6:46). The community that now experiences hatred and vilification looks forward to a reward in heaven (Q 6:23). Altogether, Q presents a serious call to repentance for the people of Israel. On the other hand, the acknowledgment of Jesus is also demanded (Q 12:8-9, quoted above).

Mark and Matthew contain glimpses of another path to salvation, as they occasionally allow the idea of a salvific significance of Jesus' *death* (on which see below), but the real emphasis in these writings lies elsewhere. Mark mentions Jesus' giving "his life as ransom for many" (Mark 10:45) but refrains from elaborating the idea; as we saw, he puts a lot of emphasis on right action as outlined in the commandments of the Torah (10:17-31; 12:28-34). This is connected with a commitment to Jesus. Above all, following Jesus' path of suffering is the way to salvation. "If any want to become my followers, let them deny themselves and take up their cross and follow me" (8:34); "you will be hated by all because of my name, but the one who endures to the end will be saved" (13:13). A disciple is asked to be faithful all the way to a martyr's death; he or she is to be able to drink with Jesus the cup he drinks, or to be baptized with the baptism he is baptized with (10:38).

The passion of Jesus is indeed strongly underlined in the Gospel of Mark, which has often been called, with slight exaggeration, a passion narrative with a long introduction. But Jesus' suffering is seen as a divine necessity, foretold in the scriptures, on one hand and the predictable destiny of a righteous man and a prophet on the other. Suffering (followed by vindication in the resurrection) is a crucial part of Jesus' ministry and is not to remain in the shadow of his magnificent miracles; yet apart from the isolated clause in 10:45 and the liturgical reference to a covenant sacrifice in 14:24, Mark does not suggest that Jesus died for the sins of others. In Mark's narrative, forgiveness of sins is mentioned several times (1:4; 2:5, 10-12; 3:28), but in none of these cases is it connected with Jesus' death.

Somewhat similar ideas about martyrdom are later presented in the *Apocryphon of James* (sometimes misleadingly referred to as gnostic): the Savior exhorts his disciples, "Scorn death. . . . Remember my cross and my death, and you will live!" (*Apoc. Jas.* 5.31-35); "none will be saved unless they believe in my cross. But those who have believed in my cross, theirs is the kingdom of God. Therefore, become seekers of death . . . the kingdom belongs to those who put themselves to death" (6.4-9, 15-18). The disciples are to emulate Jesus' martyrdom; indeed, they should become better than he in this regard (6.19). The cross has no atoning significance, but it does have a salvific meaning in that it helps the believers "cease loving the flesh" (5.7-8) and turn toward life.

In Matthew, the bearing of good fruit is all-important. Matthew develops Q's radical ethics into a strictly Jewish-sounding program of observing the law. One has to fulfill the Torah as interpreted by Jesus to meet the demands of righteousness (Matt. 5:17-20). Verses 18-19 stress that not one stroke of a letter will pass from the law; verse 20 states that more is required of the disciples of Jesus than of others: "unless your righteousness exceeds that of the scribes and Pharisees, you will never enter the kingdom of heaven." The section 5:21-48 and indeed the whole Sermon on the Mount (chs. 5–7) describe this greater righteousness as nothing short of perfection; the high points include the commandment to love even one's enemies (5:44) and the Golden Rule: "In everything do to others as you would have them do to you; for this is the law and the prophets" (7:12). Matthew 5:48 is explicit about the goal: "Be perfect, therefore, as your heavenly Father is perfect." A heavenly reward is often mentioned in this Gospel to encourage the faithful in their efforts (5:12; 19:21; and elsewhere).

To be sure, Matthew does present Jesus as the one who saves his people from their sins (without telling how) in 1:21, and in the Eucharist liturgy forgiveness is connected with the blood of Jesus (26:29). In the bulk of the Gospel this kind of soteriology fades, however. The idea that forgiveness is connected with Jesus' death is not integrated with Matthew's action-oriented perspective. Isaiah 53:4 ("he took [upon himself] our weaknesses, he carried [away] our diseases") is quoted in Matt. 8:17 as a prophecy not of Jesus' death, but of his healing mission. In Jesus' instruction on prayer (6:14-15), God's forgiveness is said to depend on whether people themselves forgive others (cf. 18:21-35), not on the shedding of Jesus' blood. When, in the final scene of the Gospel, the disciples are sent out to evangelize "all nations," their task is to teach those baptized to keep the commandments laid down by Jesus (28:19-20). His death is not mentioned.

The crucial importance of right action is clear in the great judgment scene (Matt. 25:31-46), which has had an immense influence on subsequent Christianity. Here performing deeds of mercy—feeding the hungry, clothing the naked, visiting the sick and the imprisoned—is the sole criterion at the judgment; nothing is said about the death of Christ or of faith in him as the means of salvation.

Deeds of mercy—toward whom? Who are the "least brothers" of the Son of Man (Matt. 25:40, 45)? On the face of it, the phrase would seem to refer to all the needy in the world. A comparison with 10:40-42, however, suggests that Christian missionaries may be in view.[31] Perhaps one can distinguish between the perspective of the traditional parable and that of Matthew himself.[32] In the tradition, the objects of the required charity seem indeed to be Christian missionaries. But in the Matthean context (in the light of such central Matthean tenets as the Golden Rule or the love of enemies), the object could be all those who are needy. Above all, in chapters 24–25 the way is paved for a judgment scene, in which even Christians will be judged on such a basis; *their* actions will be scrutinized quite rigorously.

Matthew, then, envisages "salvation through action."[33] People will be judged according to their deeds (Matt. 16:27). Nevertheless, obedience to the Torah is not enough, as 19:16-30 shows—the rich man, who does not quite qualify for the kingdom of heaven, has followed even the love command![34] The tension between the centrality of Jesus' message and the centrality of the commitment to him makes itself felt. Both losing one's life for Jesus' sake (16:25, a verse taken over from Mark) and acknowledging Jesus (10:32-33, from Q) are necessary.

Here something of a gap opens between Matthew's theory and his practice.[35] In theory, Jewish covenantal nomism with its emphasis on repentance and obedience is in force. But in that case a Jew who kept all the commandments, especially the double commandment of love, should surely be on the side of the saved. In practice, Matthew does not think in such terms. The story of the rich young man shows that what is actually at stake is the commitment to Jesus' person. "Good fruit" is necessary, but Matthew

162 is—at least when confronted with non-Christian Jews—not prepared to acknowledge the existence of such fruit, if the decision to follow Jesus is lacking. This decision becomes concrete in baptism (Matt. 28:19).

On the whole, then, the Gospel of Matthew leaves an ambiguous impression. On one hand, commitment to Jesus and willingness to follow him on the narrow road is imperative. On the other hand, the main function of Jesus seems to be "to make possible a life in obedience to God";[36] any other salvific significance of Jesus fades when the last judgment is envisaged. A similar Matthean picture is painted by the *Didache*, which lacks any notion of atonement brought about by Jesus (but takes baptism for granted: *Did.* 7.1-4). Jesus is God's servant who has brought the knowledge of life (9.3). The way of life consists, in a nutshell, of the double commandment of love and the (negative) Golden Rule (1.2). These basic commandments are illustrated through a series of sayings from the Sermon on the Mount (1.3-5), a paraphrase of the second tablet of the Decalogue, and a long series of miscellaneous other commandments. The perfectionism of the Sermon is, however, toned down in a reassuring way: "If you are able to bear the entire yoke of the Lord, you will be perfect; but if you are not able to do this, do what you are able" (6.2).

Later Jewish Christians held fast to the Torah, honoring Jesus as teacher and prophet. According to Hippolytus, the Ebionites "live in everything according to the law of Moses,[37] claiming that they become righteous in that manner."[38]

In the depiction of the judgment in Revelation 20, the mass of humankind are judged "according to their works, as recorded in the books" (v. 12).[39] Salvation or damnation depend entirely on their own merits or the lack of them; nothing is said of a vicarious significance of Jesus' death in this connection—although it is stressed elsewhere in the same writing that Christ "freed [or washed] us from our sins by his blood" (Rev. 1:5) and praise is given to the slaughtered Lamb, who by his blood "bought for God [humans] from every tribe and language and people and nation" (5:9; cf. 14:3-4). The martyrs have "washed their robes and made them white (!) in the blood of the Lamb" (7:14), and they "cry out in a loud voice" that "salvation belongs to our God . . . and to the Lamb!" (7:10). The two preconditions of salvation stand side by side; the works according to which one is judged include commitment to the cause of Christ (as in Mark or Matthew), meaning in this context fidelity to the Lamb in the middle of persecutions. Any compromise with the Roman Empire will be severely punished.

Luke elaborates the requirement of right conduct in an impressive series of memorable stories. The desired action is exemplified by the Good Samaritan (10:25-37). In this example story, Jesus counters the initial question, "What must I do to inherit eternal life?" with a new question, "What is written in the law?" The Jewish discussion partner cites the dual commandment of love: you shall love God with all your heart, and your neighbor as yourself. Jesus accepts the answer and adds: "*Do this* and you will live" (v. 28). The story of the Samaritan, who helped his neighbor, follows. It ends on an exhortatory note: "go and do likewise" (v. 37).

Right action is indeed what is needed, and the proper instructions are found in the Torah. It is implied in the story of Dives and Lazarus that the rich man would not have landed in Hades had he heeded what "Moses and the prophets" had written (Luke 16:29, 31).[40] The Torah is there for anyone to obey; that is the way to life.

It is no surprise, then, that in his infancy stories Luke paints a very positive picture of the pious Israelites around Jesus who, like old Simeon, "look forward to the consolation of Israel" (Luke 2:25). On Simeon the holy spirit rests long before the Pentecost miracle (Acts 2); Zechariah and Elizabeth, too, are filled with the spirit (Luke 1:41, 67). Biblical figures such as David (Acts 4:25) and Isaiah (Acts 28:25) spoke in the holy spirit. One can hardly think that these people would have found themselves, in Luke's view, outside the sphere of salvation. Devout life along the guidelines found in the Torah is what counts.

One may wonder what Jesus is then needed for.[41] Luke evades this dilemma by in effect assimilating devout life with acceptance of Jesus (and, after Easter, with joining his community): the pious figures of the infancy stories immediately recognize Jesus as the (future) Messiah of Israel. One can indeed argue that Luke thinks of one covenant only, made with Abraham, continuing in the church.[42] God has acted all the time in an unbroken continuum of salvific events (for example, Acts 7:2-53); this is why any single event (even the death of Christ) cannot be made crucial in an exclusive sense.[43] The standard Jewish combination of living devoutly while rejecting Christian claims is unthinkable for Luke. A pious Gentile, too, can be acceptable to God even before he knows of Jesus. When the devout centurion Cornelius, following an angelophany, sent for Peter and asked him to preach, the spirit suddenly fell upon all who heard the sermon (Acts 10:44-48); as a consequence they were baptized. Like the truly pious Jew, a devout Gentile will (in Luke's view) almost automatically accept the message about Jesus when he or she encounters it. The case of Cornelius is said to show that "in every nation anyone who fears God and does what is right is acceptable to him" (10:35), but

the real proof is that such a person willingly accepts the message. Godly lifestyle and acknowledgment of Jesus fuse together.

More often, however, those confronted with Jesus or with the Christian message need to *repent*.[44] This is indeed Luke's key word in connection with salvation. Examples of effective repentance are plenty. John the Baptist gives practical advice about the "fruits worthy of repentance": one should share goods and refrain from fraud (Luke 3:10-14).[45] Luke paints an impressive picture of Jesus as the great friend of sinners—but these are always repentant sinners. The "many" sins of the woman with a doubtful reputation "are forgiven, for she loved much" (7:47 RSV).[46] The prodigal son in Jesus' best-known parable (largely created by Luke himself)[47] is joyously received by his father when he finally returns home (15:11-32). The toll collector Zacchaeus promises to give half of his possessions to the poor and to pay back "four times as much," if he has "defrauded anyone of anything."[48] He elicits from Jesus the praise "today salvation has come to this house," for "the Son of Man came to seek out and to save the lost" (19:8-9). The penitent robber crucified with Jesus is promised that he will be "today" in paradise with Jesus (23:42-43).[49] Repentance "is not only a necessary but also a sufficient precondition for salvation."[50]

Jesus' whole ministry stands in the service of the good news that God is always ready to show mercy to the repentant sinner. By contrast, any salvific significance of Jesus' death fades out of sight—much more clearly than in Mark or Matthew.[51] What corresponds in Luke's story to Mark's (and Matthew's) ransom saying (Mark 10:45; Matt. 20:28) is the statement, "I am among you as one who serves" (Luke 22:27). Jesus' death is simply the judicial murder of an

164   innocent righteous man (cf. Luke 23:47), and his resurrection demonstrates his vindication by God.

When in Acts Peter's Pentecost sermon "cuts to the heart" of his hearers and they ask what they should do, the answer is this: "Repent, and be baptized in the name of Jesus Christ so that your sins may be forgiven; and you will receive the gift of the holy spirit" (Acts 2:38); that is the means of getting saved "from this corrupt generation" (v. 40). The sin to be forgiven is, in light of the sermon, the assumed participation of the audience in the crucifixion of Jesus. Repentance is the medicine; but now, after Easter, allegiance to the group of Jesus' followers, actualized in the reception of baptism, is also required. In fact, a "remarkable assimilation" takes place, as contrition and conversion to the new movement are molded.[52] Repentance now includes the recognition that the Jesus crucified by the Jews[53] is their Messiah, whom God has raised from the dead. Later Luke lets Peter proclaim that there is "no other name in which salvation is to be found" than the name of Jesus (Acts 4:12). Why this is so is not really explained. But the forgiveness of sins is in Luke–Acts connected with Jesus' resurrection rather than with his death (Luke 24:46-47; Acts 3:26; 5:31; 13:38-39); on the basis of the resurrection, repentance is somehow made accessible to all people (including Gentiles: Acts 11:18).

The importance of repentance as the way to salvation also emerges in the famous Areopagus speech (Acts 17). There Luke's Paul closes his all-but-Stoic treatise on natural knowledge of God with an abrupt demand to repentance (vv. 30-31)—which in this context apparently means abandoning idol worship in pagan temples.

In Acts, Luke sets forth a kind of order of salvation (*ordo salutis*). The process starts with repentance, which is followed by baptism, for-giveness of sins, and reception of the spirit. The first part, repentance, depends on the human; if it is lacking, nothing happens. The rest, however, is a gracious gift of God.

In Acts, Luke also has some Christian Jews raise the claim that circumcision is another precondition of salvation for all male Christians, even for Gentiles: "Unless you are circumcised according to the custom of Moses, you cannot be saved" (Acts 15:1; cf. 15:5). Luke then has Peter answer by referring to the events in the house of Cornelius: God, who knows the human heart, had given the holy spirit even to Gentiles, "cleansing their hearts by faith" (15:9); both Jewish and Gentile Christians, with no distinction between them, "will be saved through the *grace of the Lord Jesus*." Still, the claim of the conservative brothers is taken into consideration by issuing the Apostolic Decree proposed by James: "we should not trouble those Gentiles who are turning to God, but we should write them to abstain from things polluted by idols and from fornication and from *pnikton*[54] and from blood" (15:20; cf. v. 29). The final motivation given by Luke's James in verse 21 leaves, however, the impression that the decree is understood to be an adaptation to Mosaic custom rather than a real condition of Gentile salvation: "For in every city, for generations past, Moses has had those who proclaim him. . . ."[55]

The Epistle of James polemically argues that "justification" is by works, not by (mere) faith. "What does it profit . . . if a man says he has faith but has not works? Can his faith save him?" (Jas. 2:14). "Was not Abraham our father justified by works, when he offered his son Isaac upon the altar? You see that faith was active along with his works" (2:21-22). Such words are to be taken as self-conscious polemic against Paul as the author had understood him (see below).[56] "James" does emphasize the importance of faith, understood as trust (1:6), but he is appalled by the thought that "faith" may be used as an excuse to avoid social responsibility. It seems that "the works that keep faith alive (v. 26) . . . are especially such works that benefit the poor."[57] The author's "plea in behalf of the poor, the widow, the orphan, and the laborer resonates with overtones from the Hebrew Bible."[58] Right conduct is crucial for his Christianity, but it would be quite wrong to brand it as human-centered legalism (just as it is quite wrong to speak of normal Jewish religion in such terms). The "indicative" is clearly stated in Jas. 1:17-18: "Every good endowment and every perfect gift is from above, coming down from the Father of lights. . . . Of his own will he brought us forth by the word of truth that we should be a kind of first fruits of his creatures." Paul's formula of "faith active in love" (Gal. 5:6) could be used as an epitome of the ethics of the Epistle of James,[59] even though the author himself prefers to articulate the idea of a "perfect work" (Jas. 1:4). But inevitably the question arises: How or why is Jesus, who is barely mentioned in the epistle, really needed?

The Epistle to the Hebrews emphasizes in a great treatise of ancient religious heroes that faith in God naturally leads to daring deeds and that God always rewards obedient faith (Heb. 11:1—12:2). Since the "cloud of witnesses" consists wholly of men and women who lived before Christ, a reader is here too confronted with the question of how Jesus can then really be said to be the "author of faith."[60] The author adduces his great gallery of witnesses in order to admonish the readers to perseverance in view even of persecution. The necessity of strong effort is taken very seriously. Confronted with the possibility of apostasy, the author claims that there will be no forgiveness and no chance to repent again for those who turn away (10:26-31).

A strong emphasis on repentance is found in *1 Clement*: God "gave those who wanted to turn to him, from generation to generation, opportunity for repentance" (*1 Clem.* 7.5; the reference is to Noah's generation and to the Ninevites).[61] It is God's will that people should repent (8.5); when a person turns to God, he or she does so out of obedience to the merciful One (9.1). God has always granted humans the possibility of repentance—and he has also always "justified" everyone through faith: We "do not become righteous through ourselves . . . or through the works we have performed in the purity of heart, but through faith, through which Almighty God has justified everyone from eternity" (32.3-4). Clement here uses language familiar from Paul (see below), but there seems to be no difference in substance between repentance on one hand and justification by faith on the other. "Faith" means for Clement such unconditional trust in God as some have shown in all ages. Evidently Christ could be removed from this theocentric soteriology without changing its structure, even though Clement also (inconsistently) states that it was the shedding of Christ's blood that brought the grace of repentance to the world (7.4).[62] But repentance is not regarded as a meritorious "work."[63]

For Hermas, salvation consists "not least in proclaiming the law and in teaching the ways of life."[64] Baptism frees from previous sins; as for sins done after baptism, the new revelation accorded to Hermas promises one more possibility of forgiveness (*Vis.* 2.2.4-8; *Mand.* 4.3; *Sim.* 9.26.6). Repentance is the greatest insight (*Mand.* 4.2.2); one who walks according to God's commandments will live (*Mand.* 4.2.4).[65] At first, Hermas finds God's commandments exceedingly difficult, but the heavenly messenger corrects him: the commandments are easy. If

166 a person only desires to do so from his or her heart, he or she can keep them; since humans received from the Creator lordship over the world, why shouldn't they also have the strength to keep his commandments? (*Mand.* 12.3.4–.4.7). Hermas does suggest (in the course of a tortured allegory) that the Son of God has cleansed God's people from their sins with much work and toil (*Sim.* 5.2.3-4; 5.6.2-3), but this is not atonement theology. The choice of words "has nothing to suggest that Hermas might be thinking of crucifixion. . . . It is a question of the labour of building up the Church," of sanctifying and cleansing an already existing community, of removing from its midst sin (conceived of as a "weed" that hinders faith from producing fruit).[66]

It is a thoroughgoing conviction of early Christians that repentance and grateful obedience toward God (shown in good deeds), who has shown us his mercy, is a precondition of salvation. The notion of sin as transgression that can be avoided is the other side of the coin. The judgment will be according to deeds. Statements on salvation or judgment are often made without any reference to Jesus. The question of the real significance of Jesus is thereby raised, since salvation seems to be, or has been in the past, available even without him.

7.1 The embarrassment caused by a crucified savior is illustrated in this mocking graffito from the Palatine in Rome with a donkey on the cross. The text reads "Alexamenos worships his God."

SALVATION THROUGH JESUS

Jesus' death was a terrible shock to his followers, and its nature, a typical execution of lower-class criminals, did not make the matter any easier. The Easter experiences cast the matter in a different light. One early response was to subordinate the death to the resurrection: in that all-important event Jesus had overcome death. Belief in God's act in raising Jesus gave the believer a share in the salvation that God had thus prepared for humans: "If you confess with your lips that Jesus is the Lord and believe in your heart that God raised him from the dead, you will be saved" (Rom. 10:9). The resurrection began the process of a final victory over hostile powers that was to be completed at the parousia (1 Cor. 15:25; Rom. 8:34-38); the perspective of resurrection included the prospect of the risen Jesus' imminent return (1 Thess. 1:9-10; 4:14).[67] Jesus brought hope to his devotees *despite* his death, not because of it. Luke still presents in Acts a theology of resurrection (rather than of death), creating a stark contrast between the killing of Jesus by the Jerusalemites and his raising by God to be the "Author of life" (Acts 3:15; cf. 2:23-24; 5:30-31).[68]

Yet many still felt the need to account for

the scandal of the cross. Several explanations (which cannot be arranged into a straightforward chronological sequence) emerged. Some of these do not imply that Jesus' death had salvific significance. Often it is seen as a necessity, long ago planned by divine providence (though the "why" is thereby not really explained). "The Son of Man *must* undergo great suffering . . . and be killed, and after three days rise again" (Mark 8:31). What had happened, had happened according to the scriptures (Mark 14:49 par.). Luke makes ample use of this motif (Luke 24:27, 46; cf. Acts 17:3); the passion was the inevitable gateway to glory. Strikingly, though, no actual scriptural passage is mentioned; it is simply postulated that Jesus' fate must have been foreseen in the scriptures.

In other connections some actual passages do play a part. In shaping the passion narrative, biblical language from psalms concerned with the innocent suffering of the righteous (Pss. 22 and 69 in particular) was used to depict Jesus' last hours: the division of his clothing (Mark 15:24) alludes to Ps. 22:19; the mockers' shaking their heads (Mark 15:29) to Ps. 22:8; the soldiers' giving Jesus sour wine (Mark 15:36) apparently to Ps. 69:22.[69] Jesus' last words were, according to Mark 15:34, the opening words of Psalm 22: "My God, my God, why have you forsaken me?" Jesus had to suffer, as all righteous people have to.[70]

Jesus' death came also to be regarded as a recent, if extreme, instance of the allegedly customary fate of a prophet[71] (for example, 1 Thess. 2:15; Q 11:49-51; Mark 12:1-9; Acts 7:52). This understanding is prominent in Q, where no other explanation is offered. It occurs in polemical contexts and is less an explanation of the fate of Jesus than a fierce accusation against the enemies of Jesus or of his followers.

Jesus' Death as Saving Event

A different line of thought emerged in other branches of early Christianity, a line to which I have referred a few times already. Here the death of Jesus is singled out as a salvific event, from which one may benefit in order to prevail at the judgment. For a long time, there was probably little awareness of the tension or even contradiction that exists between this and other paths to salvation.

Especially in the altered circumstances, when the gospel was proclaimed among people who previously knew nothing about Jesus, an explanation had to be given for his death. Despite the resurrection, it was unthinkable, given the ignominious nature of the death, that he would have "died for nothing" (Gal. 2:21). A positive explanation that went beyond those mentioned above stated that Jesus' death was, in some sense, vicarious: it had happened "for us" (1 Thess. 5:10) or "for our sins" (1 Cor. 15:3). Those who first interpreted Jesus' death in such terms probably thought backward, from the event to its cause. That is, the problem to be solved was not the plight of humans, but the fate of Jesus. This accounts for the striking fact that the usual Jewish paths to salvation fade. Questions such as, "Why does sincere repentance no longer suffice to restore our relation to God?" were not pondered, because they were not the burning issue at hand.

Later religious history provides illuminating examples, parallel to the early Christian case, of a profound positive significance afterward ascribed to a shocking event. Husayn ibn Ali, a grandson of the prophet Muhammad, was killed in the battle of Kerbela (680 c.e.).[72] Although the Qur'an stresses that no soul can carry the burden of another, Shia thought ascribed redemptive significance to Husayn's death: it gave

168 him (and his mother, Fatima) the right to speak for all Shiites on the day of judgment. If God intends to punish Shiites for their sins, Husayn and Fatima intervene with intercessory prayers; one single tear that a person has shed because of Husayn's death will protect him or her from the fire of hell.[73]

The seventeenth-century messianic claimant Sabbatai Zevi first aroused great hopes of redemption among his fellow Jews and then caused an immense scandal by converting to Islam (in captivity, given the choice of conversion or death). Astonishingly, many remained loyal to their Messiah despite the stumbling block of his apostasy. The experience of redemption had been so profound that they could not believe that it had been an illusion, and an explanation was soon found: by the seemingly impious act of apostasy, the Messiah had continued his lifelong battle with the forces of evil. Some believers held that he had become one of the Gentiles in order to save them from utter destruction, others that he had descended into the realm of darkness in order to destroy it from within.[74] Gershom Scholem points to striking analogies with early Christian thought. "The disciples of Jesus were dumbfounded by the crucifixion, since the death of the messiah was not provided for in their eschatological traditions. In due course the Old Testament Scriptures were made to yield what they never contained: a profound doctrine accounting for the paradox of the savior's atoning death. The Sabbatian believers were under even greater pressure, since the mass of the people and not merely a small band of disciples had followed the messiah."[75] In both cases, the disciples proclaimed the birth of a new form of Judaism, heretical in the eyes of others. "Both movements gave rise to a mystical faith centered on a definite historical event, and drawing its strength from the paradoxical character of this event."[76]

The interpretation of Jesus' death as vicarious must be old, for it is widespread in early Christianity.[77] It is found in pre-Pauline formulas (1 Cor. 15:3; 2 Cor. 5:14-15; Rom. 3:25-26; 4:25), in Johannine tradition (especially John 1:29), and in a number of passages formulated by Paul himself (Rom. 5:8; 8:32; 2 Cor. 5:21; Gal. 3:13; and elsewhere). It is conspicuous in Hebrews. It was part of most Eucharist liturgies (1 Cor. 11:24; Mark 14:24 par.).[78] Yet this interpretation probably did not emerge immediately after the Easter experiences. If it were part of an archaic tradition, common to all branches of the movement, it would be strange that it is nevertheless missing from several versions of early Christian faith.

When the death of Jesus is interpreted as a saving event, a variety of pictures and terms from different areas of life are used. The very variety of images and models itself suggests that theories about the nature of the event were of secondary importance; the point was finding ways of coping with it. One possibility was to understand Jesus' death with the aid of concepts connected with the temple cult as a sacrifice for the sake of humans; the function of Jesus then corresponds to that of animals sacrificed in the temple. Sacrificial language is prominent in some writings from the end of the first century. Christians have been ransomed from futile ways "with the precious blood of Christ, like that of a lamb without defect or blemish" (1 Pet. 1:18-19; cf. 1:2). Similar imagery is used in John, even though the emphasis of the Fourth Gospel lies elsewhere.[79] The Baptist's word, "Here is the Lamb of God" (John 1:29), probably refers to Jesus as the Passover lamb;[80] the following phrase, "who takes away the sin of the world," introduces the notion of sin offering (the Passover sacrifice itself was not thought of as expiatory).[81] The sacrificial understanding is assumed and stressed in 1 John: the blood of Jesus purifies from all sin (1 John 1:7); Jesus is the expiation (*hilasmos*) for our sins (2:2; 4:10). In Eph. 5:2, sacrificial terminology ("a fragrant offering and sacrifice to God") is used, but the emphasis falls on the lovely fragrance to which the author refers with an exhortatory purpose.[82]

Sacrificial language dominates in Hebrews. The author sees Jesus' death in terms of the great sacrifice of the Jewish Day of Atonement (especially Heb. 9–10). He never gives a rationale for the sacrificial system, but assumes without question that "without the shedding of blood there is no forgiveness" (Heb. 9:22). The rite is considered to be definitely fulfilled in Jesus death, but the application becomes strained: Jesus offers himself as sacrifice, thereby fulfilling both the role of the priest and that of the victim. But then the author exploits cultic language primarily in order to show that the Jewish sacrificial cult has now been superseded through Jesus, and warns his readers not to lapse into Judaism. He is involved in another logical inconsistency as well: if salvation awaits the righteous in heaven from all eternity, how can it depend on a contingent event (Jesus' death and exaltation) on the earth? How could Jesus' access to the heavenly priesthood bring about something "new" in heavenly affairs?[83]

Some interpreters assume that the sacrifices in the temple of Jerusalem would have led early Christians self-evidently to conceive of the death of Jesus as a sacrifice in general and as a sin offering in particular. This, however, is unlikely. To begin with, not all sacrifices had to do with *sins*. There were thank offerings, the Passover sacrifice commemorating the exodus (Paul calls Christ "our Passover lamb" in 1 Cor. 5:7), and the sacri-fice connected with the making of the covenant. The meaning of the sin offering in the Israelite cult is controversial, and the precise way in which an expiatory sacrifice was thought to be effective is not clarified in the Hebrew Bible. "Judaism provided no explicit rationale for sacrifice: it was simply the God-given way of dealing with sin, and as such was to be accepted gratefully and humbly."[84] It is unlikely that a first-century Jew who performed the offering in the temple would have identified himself with the victim, contemplating that *he* should have died, not the animal.[85] It is therefore improbable that the sin offerings would have incited the early Christians to think that Jesus had suffered the punishment that others had deserved. It seems rather that the notion of this death as vicarious came first and was afterward connected with the idea of a sacrifice.[86] This point is strengthened by the observation that a sacrificial understanding in itself ill suits the all-important conviction of resurrection: "the whole notion of sacrifice becomes a farce, if the victim rises again."[87]

Alternatively, it is often thought that the Servant Song of Isaiah 53 is the source of vicarious interpretations of Jesus' death,[88] but this too is far from obvious. The idea that an individual person suffers and dies for the sins of God's people (if that is what the song has in view; the question of his identity—whether he is an individual or symbolizes the people of Israel—is not settled) is unique in the Hebrew Bible and remained without influence on subsequent developments of Jewish thought.[89] As the song had not been regarded as messianic in Jewish tradition, it was not a self-evident source to turn to for early Christians; it took some scribal skill (and some time, one would think) to discover this proof text. Followers of Jesus did seize on it at some point, to be sure, and they gave it a quite

170 new application.[90] But Isaiah 53 is quoted less often than one might expect, and even then— apart from the late 1 Peter (2:24)—without paying attention to any vicarious suffering of the Servant (for example, Matt. 8:17; Luke 22:37).[91] Romans 4:25 may be influenced by Isaiah 53, but the formula "he was handed over because of our trangressions" seems to be the product of more advanced reflection and not to represent an archaic layer of tradition.[92]

A more likely background to the notion of the offering of a human life for others is the vicarious effects ascribed to deaths of outstanding Jewish martyrs, which in turn are influenced by Greek ideas of a noble death for others; among the numerous examples are Alcestis and Iphigeneia.[93] According to 2 Macc. 7:37-38, the martyr dies for (*peri*) the paternal laws and hopes that God therefore becomes merciful (*hileos*) to the people and that his wrath ceases. Even closer to Christian ideas is 4 Macc. 6:27-29: old Eleazar dies not just because of the law; he also bears with his death the punishment for his people. He prays: "Be merciful to your people . . . satisfied by our punishment for (*hyper*) them. Let my blood serve for their purification (*katharsion*) and accept my life as a ransom (*antipsykhon*) for them." The death of the martyr has a vicarious significance for the people, and cultic terminology ("purification") is also used. In 4 Macc. 17:20-22, the act of the martyrs is commented on in the following way: "because of them . . . the homeland [was] purified—they having become, as it were, a ransom (*antipsykhon*) for the sin of our nation. And through the blood of those devout ones and their death as an atoning sacrifice (*hilasterios*),[94] divine Providence preserved Israel that previously had been mistreated." The author uses metaphorical language associated with the Day of Atonement (blood, expiation), but the temple background does not account for the notion of a *human* sacrifice.

In the martyr ideology of 2 and 4 Maccabees, Jewish and Greek traditions merge. The notion of a judgment on the people because of its sins is Jewish; the appreciation of the vicarious dying for others is of Greek origin.[95] Early Christians—the Antiochene community may have taken the first initiative, though we cannot be sure—took up this notion, but applied it in a somewhat different way: Jesus died not just for his people, but for other humans too.[96] It is sometimes emphasized, in accordance with the martyr traditions, that Jesus, the victim, took the initiative (Gal. 1:4; 2:20; Titus 2:14); more often, however, God is said to be the subject (Rom. 4:25; 8:32).

An early instance of an interpretation that leans on martyrological and, in the last analysis, on Greek models, is found in the traditional substratum[97] of Rom. 3:25-26: God "put [Christ Jesus] forward as a sacrifice of atonement [or: *means of expiation* (*hilasterion*)] by his blood. . . . He did this to show his righteousness, because in his divine forbearance he had passed over the sins previously committed; it was to prove at the present time that he himself is righteous." In this view, Jesus' death apparently resulted in forgiveness for earlier sins, possibly of the collective sins of the people in breaking God's covenant.[98] In making use of this tradition, Paul does not linger on the idea of expiation; he interprets the formula in terms of his specific notion of justification by faith in Jesus (v. 26b). Romans 5:9 ("now that we have been justified by his blood, we will be saved through him from the wrath of God") apparently harks back to 3:25-26; here too Paul connects the different images of justification and blood, the result being that "we" are saved from God's wrath.

This is the closest Paul comes to sacrificial categories in interpreting Jesus' death. He does hold that Jesus' death was vicarious: it had good effects for others. It is important, however, to Paul to consistently stress God's initiative in the matter, a fact that does not fit well with an understanding in strictly sacrificial (or martyrological) categories. Romans 8:3 is a case in point. In an overloaded sentence that omits parts of what is clearly intended, Paul states that what the law was unable to do, God did by sending his Son "in the likeness of sinful flesh."[99] This happened "because of sin" (*peri hamartias*).[100] If a vicarious sacrifice were in view, one might now expect a statement on the condemnation of sinful humans whose punishment Jesus bore. What Paul aims at, however, is the condemnation or abolishment of *sin*: God "condemned sin in the flesh," no doubt in the crucified body of Jesus. This happened in order that those in Christ would now be able to fulfill the law in the spirit (8:4). What is decisive for Paul is that Jesus' death (and resurrection) have made possible the liberation of humans from sin's sphere of power and their transfer to the realm of the spirit in Christ; here we come close to the understanding of Jesus' death as redemption (see below).

A related thought is developed in 2 Cor. 5:14-21 in the framework of the overarching notion of *reconciliation* between God and humans (again, see below). Here too God is the acting subject who takes the initiative to remove humanity's alienation from God or the enmity that has grown between them. Jesus "knew no sin," but "for our sake he [God] made him to be sin," that is, he put him into the position of a sinful human being.[101] This happened in order that "we" would become "the righteousness of God in him": reconciled with God, "we" may now live as "a new creation" (v. 17) in union with Christ. The passage

as a whole shows how Paul combines a number of different concepts and images to describe the new situation in which those "in Christ" now live. What matters is this new life; the various models used to describe the transfer that has taken place are in themselves of less significance.

The initiative of God in nullifying sin and its effects is thus strongly emphasized in early Christianity. Nevertheless, one should not forget that what humans are thereby saved from is *God's* own wrath (for example, Rom. 5:9). There is, then, a sense in which the idea of appeasing an angry God does lurk in the background, even if it is not expressed in so many words (and is routinely denied by modern interpreters).

The nature of the death of Jesus can be, and often is, described also with the aid of models or images, which neither draw on sacrificial language nor seem readily compatible with it. Thus Jesus' death can be described as *redemption*. "Whereas the interpretation in terms of expiation is about liberation from a danger which threatens from God himself, the notion of *ransom* suggests, rather, liberation from an alien power."[102] *Lytron* and cognates (especially *apolytrosis*) have overtones of the practice of redeeming slaves or prisoners of war by paying a suitable ransom price for their liberation. In a Jewish context, however, this vocabulary recalls first of all God's great act of liberation in the exodus, whereby the idea of a price paid drops out of sight. God's "redeeming" of Israel simply refers to his rescuing it, including his hoped-for eschatological intervention (cf. Luke 1:71; 24:21). It is unlikely that early Christians ever thought of Jesus' death concretely as a price to be paid for the liberation of humanity, even though the idea became popular in later patristic thought, with great discussions about whether the price was paid to God or to the devil (Origen, for example,

172 opted for the latter). In stating "you were bought with a price" (1 Cor. 6:20; 7:23), Paul is probably simply using the language of the slave market in order to stress that Christians are no longer under their old master, Sin, but under a new master, God. In Rom. 6:18 and 22, he speaks of the same event of changing masters as being "set free" from Sin.

In Gal. 3:13 and 4:5, Paul states that the Christians are liberated from the curse of the law, or from an existence "under the law" (cf. Rom. 7:3), called "the yoke of slavery" in Gal. 5:1. Strangely enough, the Torah is here conceived of as an inimical alien power, comparable to the "ele-ments of the world" that rule tyrannically over the heathen world. The death of Jesus liberates believers both from the power of sin and from the power of the law, and there is not much difference between the two. The precise sense of the "ransom for many" in Mark 10:45 is difficult to define—but then "redemption" and related words can, in the end, refer to any plight from which humans need or have received liberation: sins or transgressions (Rev. 1:5), Sin as power (Rom. 6; John 8:32, 36), the law (Gal. 3:13—5:1), lawlessness (Titus 2:14), "futile" old ways (1 Pet. 1:18), spiritual powers, ignorance, decay (Rom. 8:21), the devil. . . . Whatever the problem, the Christ event is the solution. In a sense the solution was there first, and the problem(s) came to be defined in light of the existing solution: Christ had died, certainly not in vain (cf. Gal. 2:21)!

Neither in the case of expiation nor in that of ransom is resurrection logically needed, but the notion has been adapted to the "fact," and Paul can even state that death alone does not bring forgiveness (1 Cor. 15:17). Then the resurrection becomes a *victory* over the hostile cosmic and/or demonic powers (cf. 1 Cor. 15:24-25; Phil. 2:10; Rom. 8:35-38). But even Jesus' death is seen as a victory in Col. 2:14-15, where the striking image of a military parade over disarmed hostile (spirit) powers is used; the author also states that a "promissory note"

7.2   *Christ Descending into Hell* by Giovanni Canavesio and Giovanni Baleison, 1492. Chapelle Notre Dame des Fontaines, La Brigue, Alpes Maritimes, France. Photo: © François Guenet/Art Resource, NY.

(*kheirographon*) that was "against us" (a veiled reference to the Torah?) was thereby nailed to the cross (!). Elsewhere the powers opposed to God are conceived of as concentrated in a single devil figure, and Jesus' death is seen as his final overthrow (cf. John 12:31; 1 John 3:8).

It is at first not explained just how the devil or the powers were defeated, but later a widespread tradition recounts Jesus' descent on Good Friday into Hades, where he opens the gates for those who put their trust in him (for example, *Odes Sol.* 42.11-20;[103] *Acts Thom.* 10; 156).[104] In patristic thought the notion of *Christus victor* became very important; it has left strong traces in the Greek Orthodox tradition, but has largely dropped out of theological reflection in the West.

The understanding of Jesus' death as *reconciliation* (*katallage*) is confined to the Pauline tradition and uses language from the area of diplomacy and peacemaking.[105] It is probably rooted in Paul's personal experience: he was once an enemy of the Jesus movement, but God reconciled him with himself "in Jesus" (in Paul's call vision). In 2 Corinthians 5, the notion is connected with Paul's specific apostolic task of reconciling opposed groups of people with each other. Here too God is the subject of the action, which is seen in a cosmic dimension: in Christ, God was reconciling "the world" to himself (v. 19). This dimension is in a marked way developed in Colossians. Following certain lines of thought in Hellenistic philosophy, Col. 1:15-20 speaks of the achievement of cosmic harmony on the basis of the death and resurrection of Christ; the author connects this with the notion of reconciling alienated people to God (1:21-23). The author of Ephesians, for his part, utilizes Colossians, but develops the notion of reconciliation in an ecclesiological direction: the blood of Jesus has effected reconciliation between Jews and Gentiles in somehow removing the barrier of the "law of the commandments and stipulations" that had stood between them. Peace between the two groups has been established, as the enmity between them has been "killed" at the cross (Eph. 2:14-18).

Justification, or the passing of a liberating verdict in court, is yet another model used to interpret the significance of Jesus' death. The judgment that God was about to pronounce on humanity has been passed on the crucified Jesus. However, the language of justification (words from the root *dikaio-*) is used by Paul mainly in the context of his battle concerning the conditions of the inclusion of Gentiles in the people of God (especially Gal. 2:15-21; 3:6-14; Rom. 3:21—4:25). It serves to give a biblical slant to Paul's argument.[106] Paul's proof is Abraham, who believed (in what God had promised him); God reckoned his faith to him as righteousness (*dikaiosyne*; Gal. 3:6; Rom. 4:3, 9). Paul reads this as proving that Gentiles need not be circumcised when they join the new people of God. For Abraham just *believed* (Paul's argument implies: in Jesus Christ!), and did not do the works required by the law (in this context: such works as circumcision and food regulations). We have already seen that more than once Paul has introduced the language of justification into contexts where other models of interpreting the saving character of Jesus' death are used (see above on Rom. 3:25-26 and 5:9; cf. 2 Cor. 5:21).

In his confrontation with Corinthian enthusiasm, Paul comes to emphasize the "scandalous" side of Jesus' death, the "cross" (especially 1 Cor. 1:18-31). Paul's "theology of the cross" is not really another soteriological interpretation of Jesus' death. It can be seen as part of a theology of election in which standard values are reversed. God elects what is low and despised in the world.[107]

174

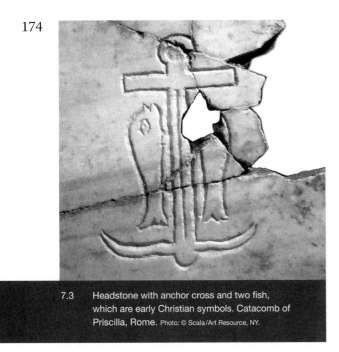

7.3 Headstone with anchor cross and two fish, which are early Christian symbols. Catacomb of Priscilla, Rome. Photo: © Scala/Art Resource, NY.

New Life in Union with Christ

Paul takes up and employs most of the images used in his traditions to explain Jesus' death and resurrection. That Paul can mix imageries indicates that the individual images and the particular interpretations suggested by them are not of central importance to him. What is crucial is the experience of new life,[109] of which Paul is an enthusiastic proclaimer.

"Forgiveness" is not one of Paul's great themes,[110] nor do even "redemption" or "expiation" stand in the inmost center of his own vocabulary of salvation. The new life involves much more: it means a new union or participation "in Christ"; an almost physical identification[111] of the believer with Christ seems to take place.[112] "If anyone is in Christ, there is a new creation" (2 Cor. 5:17). "There is no condemnation for those who are in Christ" (Rom. 8:1). Paul has "suffered the loss of all things" that he previously valued in order to "gain Christ and be found in him" (Phil. 3:8-9). The believer will share in Christ's destiny, visualized in baptism: those who have been "baptized into Christ Jesus" (thus also Gal. 3:26) were baptized "into his death"; having been "united with him in a death like his," they will also be "united with him in a resurrection like his"; for the moment they must consider themselves "dead to sin and alive to God in Christ Jesus" (Rom. 6:3-11). Conversely, "it is no longer I who live, but it is Christ who lives in me" (Gal. 2:20), for "I have been crucified with Christ" (v. 19). The closest analogy to this is found in mystery religions, where the initiates participated in the destiny of the Deity. A difference is that Jesus died once and for all (and baptism too was a once-and-for-all event), whereas in mystery cults participation in the death of the God/ess could be experienced repeatedly.[113] Participation in the death and resurrection of

In view of the significance that a soteriological interpretation of Jesus' death has received in later Christian thought, especially in Protestantism, it is worth underlining that it is either missing from or is only of minor significance in many first- and even second-century writings. It is missing from Q, Luke, and James, and barely mentioned in Mark and Matthew. Although convinced that Christ died for us (often the repetition of the formula has a conventional ring—as in Luke), the Apostolic Fathers, too, assign a relatively minor place to the atoning value of his death. What looms much larger in their imagination is the picture of Christ as the lawgiver, the bestower of knowledge, immortality, and fellowship with God.[108] No soteriological significance of Jesus' death is mentioned in the later Apostles' Creed either.

Jesus joins believers into the "body of Christ" (1 Cor. 12:12-31, especially v. 27; cf. Rom. 12:5). One enters this new union when one receives God's spirit (for example, Rom. 8:9-17; 1 Cor. 3:16; 12:13; 2 Cor. 1:22; Gal. 3:2-5); if one is "in Christ," the spirit dwells in the person. Christ himself is the source of the new life: he can be identified with the "life-giving spirit" (1 Cor. 15:45) that enables human beings to obtain the "spiritual body," which is necessary to enjoy the resurrection life.

The "in Christ" theme continues in a somewhat weakened form in the Pauline tradition. In Colossians the claim that the fullness of the Deity dwells in Christ "bodily" (*somatikos*) may be a reference to the church as the body of Christ.[114] The expression "in Christ" occurs frequently in Ephesians, yet as often as not it seems to lack the strong idea of incorporation; the emphasis is on Christ being *head over* the church.[115] Ignatius of Antioch uses phrases suggesting a mystical relationship with Christ ("in Christ" occurs some twenty times, for example, *Eph.* inscr.; 1.1; 11.1) or even with God ("in God," for example, in *Eph.* 1.1; 6.2; *Magn.* 1.2), but he "does not exploit the mystical possibilities of such language"; the expressions seem to have become stereotypical and mean little more than "godly."[116]

176   In some sense participation in Christ is also present in the Johannine tradition. One has to abide in Jesus, even after he is gone; when he returns in the form of the Paraclete-Spirit (see below, chapter 9), the disciples "will know that I am in my Father, and you are in me, and I in you" (John 14:20). Mutual love connects Jesus and those who keep his commandments (v. 21); Jesus promises that "we [my Father and I] will come to them and dwell in them" (v. 23). The relationship is then described with the aid of the metaphor of the vine and the branches (15:1-11), which brings home the lesson, "Abide in me as I abide in you" (v. 4). John's conception is more individualistic than Paul's: "there is mutual belonging to Christ, but not a mutual interdependence in that belonging: each sheep hears the shepherd's voice for himself or herself (John 10:3-4, 16); each branch is rooted directly in the vine (15:4-7)."[117] First John, too, shows traces of mystical participation, but the believer dwells not "in Christ" but "in God." "God is love, and those who abide in love abide in God, and God abides in them" (1 John 4:16); the condition for this loving relationship is that one "confesses that Jesus is the Son of God" (4:15) who has "come in the flesh" (4:2-3).

In the *Odes of Solomon* the union with Christ is provided with an erotic touch: "I have been united (to him), because the lover has found the Beloved; because I love him that is the Son, I shall become a son" (*Odes Sol.* 3.7); "you who are loved in the Beloved; and you who are kept in him who lives; and you who are saved in him who was saved" (8.21). "This pervasive tone of oneness becomes so developed in the Odes that frequently the Odist ceases speaking as himself and speaks of Christ."[118] In a similar individualistic vein, Jesus states in the *Gospel of Thomas:* "Whoever drinks from my mouth will become like me.

I myself shall *become he*, and the hidden things will be revealed to him" (*Gos. Thom.* 108).[119] The *Treatise on Resurrection* suggests a "mystical unity between the experience of the Savior and that of the believer"[120]: the Savior "swallowed death" and "granted us the way to our immortality"; "we are embraced by him" until death, "we are drawn upward by him, like rays by the sun" (*Treat. Res.* 45.14—46.1).

The notion of participating in Christ's destiny or of a union with him presupposes a high level of emotional experience in order to be compelling. If the excitement is reduced, it is natural to emphasize less emotion-laden soteriological aspects, such as Christ's vicarious death or his role as lawgiver or revealer.

Faith and Works: A Pauline Contrast

For God's gracious act to become effective for humans, a proper response is required. While God is for Paul the subject of reconciliation, the apostle can nevertheless summarize his evangelical task with an appeal to the will of the addressees: "Let yourselves be reconciled to God" (2 Cor. 5:20). Very often the appropriate response is characterized as *faith*. One has to *believe* that God has resurrected Jesus and made him the Lord of all: "If you confess with your lips that Jesus is Lord and believe in your hearts that God raised him from the dead, you will be saved" (Rom. 10:9). This faith is the result of preaching (Rom. 10:17), which is acknowledged and accepted by the addressees. It should be followed by baptism and reception of the spirit (in either order) and lead to a new life in Christ. Believing acceptance of the message is so characteristic that "faith" comes to function as an umbrella term for the whole process of conversion and for new life—and not just in Pauline tradition.

Therefore in Acts, the words "faith" and

"believe(r)" recur over and over again, so much so that "believers" becomes an overall designation for members of the Jesus movement (Acts 2:44; 4:32; 11:21; 19:18).[121] "Faith" was an important term already in Jewish tradition, where it signified trust in God. Christians took up the term, but gave it a lot more prominence.[122] More importantly, the object of faith changed in the process. Scripture said that Abraham believed, that is, put his trust, in God and his promise (Gen. 15:6). Jewish tradition emphasizes Abraham's obedience to God's will and commands.[123] Paul quotes the passage as if Abraham had believed in Christ.[124]

The enhanced importance that "faith" gains probably hangs together with the fact that Christian preaching contained something that was not easy to believe. To accept that God had raised this executed man to life and made him the cornerstone of salvation for all and sundry (Acts 4:12) involved an intellectual challenge. Indeed, when Paul sets forth Abraham as the great example of faith, he dwells at some length on the almost heroic trust shown by the one-hundred-year-old ancestor in the divine promise that he would still have descendants; Abraham believed "in hope against all hope" that he would become the father of many peoples (Rom. 4:18-21). A comparable act of irrational trust was expected of those who put their allegiance in Christ and his resurrection.[125]

Unlike most other early Christians, Paul is keen to emphasize "faith" at the cost of "works." He states in Rom. 3:24 that the believers "are justified by [God's] grace as a gift." Members of the Qumran movement emphasized God's grace in rather similar phrases. But in contrast to Qumran, justification by grace implies for Paul that "works of the law" are not required of the believers. There is only one way to salvation,

which God has graciously opened and revealed in the end time: faith in Jesus Christ. Surprisingly, the Torah, God's great gift according to the Jewish vision, sides with sin, against grace, the spirit, faith, and God's promises. In a number of texts in Galatians and Romans (listed below), Paul attacks the Torah as a rival principle of salvation; as God's act in Christ is the only true basis of righteousness, the way of the law is a dead end.

The interpretation of Paul's view continues to be a scholarly battlefield; in particular, a heated contest continues between what is often called the "Lutheran" view and the "New Perspective on Paul."[126] For the former, Bultmann's description of nomistic Jewish piety in existential terms was particularly influential during the latter half of the twentieth century. Bultmann understood it as an expression of the general desire to show off (in Pauline terminology, to "boast") that drives humans to accomplish works, whether beneficial or absurd. The Jews tried, on this view, to earn God's acceptance; grace is something that the pious person did not need at all. Such an attempt to become righteous by obeying the law is sin, for it is an expression of the human need to boast. Reading Bultmann, one even gets the impression that zeal for the law is more damaging than transgression.[127]

A more traditional Lutheran view[128] likewise starts from the notion that "the operative principle of the law, for Paul, was its demand for works"; Paul's primary objection to submission to Torah-obedience lay "in his insistence that human beings are sinners who do not, and cannot, do the good that the law demands of its subjects."[129] Zeal for the law is not sinful, but it is useless, due to the human plight under the power of Sin. By contrast, the "New Perspective," which is primarily connected with the names of Krister

178   Stendahl, E. P. Sanders, and James Dunn, finds that the main problem with the law is, for Paul, that it separates Jew from Gentile.[130]

No doubt all sides are able to score some points—not least because Paul himself takes different, even mutually incompatible approaches to the question. Paul does argue in Romans 1–3 as if the universal sinfulness of human beings had so infected the human race that God had to send his Son "in the likeness of sinful flesh" (see above, pp. 146–47), and apparently he does suggest in Gal. 3:10 that the law imposes a curse on anyone who fails to fulfill all of it, a hundred percent. The problem is that he argues in other ways and suggests other things about the law as well. My understanding is that, while the Lutheran interpretations can appeal to the wording of several passages, close attention to the contexts tips the scales in favor of the New Perspective. It is striking how often the polemics against law are found in a context where the question of the inclusion of the Gentiles in the people of God is the most important issue (Gal. 2–3; Rom. 3–4; 9–10), a point forcefully made by proponents of the New Perspective. The contrast "by faith—by works (of the law)" originally probably belongs to this context, the "works" meaning above all "identity markers," which Jews took for granted but which would have made the life of Gentile converts cumbersome: dietary regulations and, in particular, the demand for circumcision. While more conservative Christian Jews emphasize that humans have no right to abandon God's decrees and that the requirements of the Torah therefore also apply to Gentile Christians, let alone to Jewish Christians in their dealings with Gentiles, Paul insists that "works of the law" must not be required: "A person is not justified by works of the law but through faith in Jesus Christ" (Gal. 2:16);[131] "Were righteousness available through

the law, then Christ would in fact have died in vain and God's grace would be null and void" (Gal. 2:21); both statements are made in the context of the Antiochian incident when food and table fellowship were the issue. The claim that "you who want to be justified by the law have cut yourself off from Christ; you have fallen away from grace" (Gal. 5:4) is made by Paul in reply to the demand that Gentile converts be circumcised. The Christian is under grace, not under the law (Rom. 6:14).

In Galatians, Paul defends the right of his new converts to lead a life in Christ free from circumcision and food laws, but in chapters 3 and 4 he turns to a fierce polemic against the Torah and nomistic piety as a whole. In Gal. 3:6, Paul states that Abraham gained righteousness, because he had faith in God. In the next verses he speaks of "those who believe" as blessed and as the true progeny of Abraham (vv. 7-9); by contrast, those "who rely on the works of the law" are cursed (v. 10). In verse 10, the reason seems to be the inability of those under the law to fulfill *all* of its demands, but in what follows the inferiority of the law seems to be assumed as a matter of principle.[132] "Law" and "faith" are contrasted sharply in verse 11: according to scripture, the righteous person will have life by faith (Hab. 2:4).[133] Paul here assumes that faith and law exclude each other: "the law does not rest on faith" (Gal. 3:12). The law is also the opposite of God's promises (Gal. 3:18, 21-22). Similar contrasts reappear in Romans (Rom. 3:27-28; 4:2-5, 14; 10:5-6); compare also the contrast between the righteousness of faith and one's own righteousness in Phil. 3:6 (cf. Rom. 10:3). It seems that the heat of the battle with more conservative Christian Jews (and probably with non-Christian Jews as well) has caused Paul to resort to gathering all kinds of critical points that could possibly be made against the Torah. Many of these are ad hoc, but it is also possible that Paul actually adopted some of these polemical discoveries: the conflict situation caused him to go much further in a negative direction than would have been necessary in light of his basic convictions "in Christ," and he may well have added these new ideas to his existing tenets without smoothing over the ensuing discrepancies.

Even in Romans 3 and 4 Paul puts forward a harsh polemic against the works of the law—and in these chapters, too, the right of uncircumcised Gentile Christians to belong to the congregation is in focus. As in Galatians 3, Abraham functions in Romans 4 as the great precedent, Paul's "star witness":[134] God reckoned his faith to him as righteousness even before he was circumcised. Even for the Gentiles, who cannot produce the works required by the law, the way to salvation has been opened by God: faith in Christ is enough. Abraham did not "work" (but believed); the work in view in Rom. 4:4 is his circumcision (Rom. 4:9-12).

Nevertheless, Paul does make clear that Christ is the way to salvation even for those who are born Jews. Non-Christian Jews err in imagining that they can be saved by clinging to the law rather than by believing in Christ. Indeed, some of Paul's statements engender the impression that he does regard Judaism as a legalistic religion, which teaches that a person is saved because of his or her own merits ("works"), a point underlined by proponents of the Lutheran interpretation. This is true of Rom. 4:4, if considered in isolation; yet the context indicates that even this verse can readily be taken to support the New Perspective.[135] In the section Romans 9–11, Paul twice uses the expression "not by works" in a new context, where the problem is not the inclusion of Gentiles but the rejection of the message by most Jews (9:11-12; 11:5-6). However, Paul's intention here is not to establish a doctrine of grace and works, but to solve the problem of Israel's unbelief, which he attributes to divine hardening. Paul states that God decides to show his grace to (some) humans quite independently of their "works," but the reference is not to "works of the law." The works that God does not take account of are here any deeds at all: God chose Jacob and rejected Esau even before they had been born. If maintained consistently, this notion would lead to a terrifying doctrine of double predestination, but Paul does not elaborate on it and soon drops it altogether (see below).

In Rom. 10:3 Paul accuses non-Christian Jews of establishing their "own righteousness," but in light of the context this is identical with their *rejection of Christ*. God has made Christ the only true way to salvation, but Israel stubbornly insists on an antiquated (or simply wrong?) system, that of the law. There is no talk of relying on one's own merits, still less of boasting of one's works. Israel just does not understand that a new age has begun.

The verses Rom. 9:30-33 are likewise best understood from this point of view. Israel has not fulfilled or "attained" the law (v. 31), that is, understood what the law is all about; therefore they have not received the blessing promised in it, although they have been pursuing "the law of righteousness." The reason is that they pursued it "not on the basis of faith but as on the basis of works" (v. 32a). This statement (which, to be sure, may sound as if the Jews tried to earn their salvation by works) is explained by what follows (vv. 32b-33): the main reason for the Jewish failure is a christological one. *Christ* rather than, say, "boasting" is their "stumbling stone." Paul is simply stating his basic axiom: "faith" (in Christ) and "works" are contrary principles of salvation.

180   If one rejects the scriptural testimony to Christ and the apostolic preaching about him, one rejects the salvation offered in Christ and thus, by definition, clings to the system of "works" (of the law). Neither the character of these works nor humans' attitude to them is the point.

To be sure, Paul was soon deemed by many to have dismissed any role for obedient works in answering the question of how a human being can be found acceptable to God. Thus the pseudonymous Letter to the Ephesians uses Pauline language, but the question of the Torah is no longer a live issue for the author. He stresses that the readers have been saved by grace through faith (Eph. 2:5, 8), "not by works" (v. 9). Here the works declined are not works *of the law*, but humans' own accomplishments in general. Ephesians represents indeed to some degree the idea ascribed to Paul in the Lutheran perspective: humans are not saved "by works" "so that no one may boast" (v. 9). Salvation is God's gift, it is not "from you" (v. 8).[136] But it is to be noted that the context speaks in dark colors of the heathen past of the readers (2:1-5; cf. 4:17-24). It is not suggested that even though they had done a lot of good works, they were not saved by them; the idea is rather that they had done no good works at all, but have nevertheless been saved by God's grace. There is no attack on "Jewish legalism" or the like.[137]

For Paul, to opt for grace means to opt for Christ and against the law. From a standard Jewish point of view the contrast between grace and law is strange. The Torah was to be observed out of gratitude to its Giver; obedient observance served the sanctification of everyday life. In the theological jargon of New Testament scholars, one might say that the law had the status of the "imperative," which was based on the "indicative" of God's prevenient gracious acting. Paul drives

a wedge between law and grace, limiting grace to the Christ event (except in Rom. 11, on which see below). Outside life in Christ, there is no salvation. This means that grace is understood in Pauline Christianity more *narrowly* than in those forms of Judaism that allowed (and allow) for the salvation of righteous Gentiles.[138]

Some interpreters hold that Paul believed in two equally valid covenants, one for those born Jews, another for Gentiles, the law-free gospel of Christ being meant only for the latter. Romans 11:25-27 is taken to show that Israel will be saved independently of Christ's work, simply on the basis of God's covenant with Abraham.[139] This theory is often connected with the idea that Paul remained a practicing "good Jew," fully loyal to his old tradition. The theory is admirable in its ecumenical scope, but there is very little exegetical evidence for it. Paul states in 1 Cor. 9:20 that even Jews must be "won," that is, converted. If Jews were not expected to believe in Jesus, why should Paul complain about their unbelief (Rom. 11:20, 23) or disobedience (11:31)? What is supposed to arouse the "jealousy" of Israel, if the Gentiles have not gained anything that Israel would not possess already?[140] The "mystery" of Romans 11 is a tenuous basis for an assertion that would nullify everything Paul writes elsewhere (including Rom. 10!) about the crucial significance of Jesus for all humanity, for the Jew first (!) and also for the Greek.

In the context of his polemics, Paul presents "faith" as something simple and easy as compared to "works." This is why James could not but attack Paul's doctrine as he (mis)understood it:[141] the case of Abraham, who had been prepared to carry out the most difficult sacrifice one could imagine, showed that "a person is justified by works and not by faith alone" (Jas. 2:21, 24).[142] Devoted interpreters of Paul to this day emphasize the gratuity implied in his "by faith alone." But Paul did not devalue human effort, the way of life that was according to God's revealed will, though he regarded good deeds as the proper "fruit," not as a precondition. To accept the faith preached by Paul required a lot more effort on the part of the addressee than did most religions in antiquity. Gentile believers had to give up their traditional cult and often cut family ties. Entering the community that promised salvation to its members presupposed a profound change of life (as it did in Qumran). Faith denotes a strong commitment; grace and human effort go together.[143]

In his polemics against conservative Christian Jews, Paul insists that law-free Christians walk by the spirit automatically as it were, simply due to the fact that they live in the spirit. But in other connections, he too speaks of right behavior as necessary for salvation. The judgment will still be according to deeds (2 Cor. 5:10; cf. Rom. 2:1-16). Salvation has to be "worked out" (katergazesthai!) by Christians with fear and trembling (Phil. 2:12); the correspondence between sowing and reaping (Gal. 6:7) would seem to imply that God will reject disobedient Christians.[144] God is severe toward those who fall away from his kindness (Rom. 11:20-22). Even Paul's understanding of salvation can be called "synergistic"[145] in the sense that a human contribution (of whatever size) to the process is assumed.

A combination of grace *and* effort is, indeed, all-pervasive in early Christianity (though in different ways).[146] No dramatic difference from average Judaism (nor from "Pelagianism" for that matter) is to be seen. Indeed, one hundred percent gratuity would be possible only within the framework of double predestination (God decrees with sovereign freedom some to be saved and others to be destroyed) or else in the framework of a doctrine of *apokatastasis* (uni-

versal salvation in the end). In Romans 9–11, Paul seems to go in both these (mutually exclusive) directions, but both times he stops short of drawing the conclusion that seems to follow from his argument.

Predestination—or Universal Salvation?

In the passage that precedes Romans 9–11, Paul puts forward the idea of a "positive" predestination to salvation: "those whom he [God] foreknew he also predestined to be conformed to the image of his Son. . . . And those whom he predestined he also called; and those whom he called he also justified; and those whom he justified he also glorified" (Rom. 8:29-30). In Romans 8 the ancient tradition of Israel's election is reinterpreted and applied to Christians. The passage has a pragmatic consolatory function: "if God is for us, who is against us?" (8:31). "The sufferings of the present time" are not to disturb Christians (8:18-25). But while the emphasis is on grace within God's overarching purpose, the notion of election is here connected with the concomitant notion of a loving response by humans: "We know that everything works together for good for *those who love God, who are called* according to his purpose" (8:28). The elect are those who actively love God.

Romans 9 takes a different tack.[147] Here the notion of a *negative* predestination (divine hardening) without regard to a person's deeds is brought into the picture. The chapter was long read as a doctrinal treatise on predestination, but recent research has established that Romans 9–11 deals with a different question altogether: the problem of the unwillingness of the majority of Israel to accept Christian preaching. Paul tries to account for this opposition, resorting along the way to arguments that later served to fuel doctrines of predestination. He first explains the

182   Jewish lack of faith with the aid of the idea of a divine election that takes place even before the person is born, paying no attention whatsoever to his or her deeds (Rom. 9:11; obviously Christians who are justified without doing works of the law are in this happy situation). But such an emphasis on God's sovereign grace has unwelcome consequences. One of the peculiarities of this section is that faith is not mentioned in it at all.[148] The opposite of "works" is here not "faith" (as usually) but "his call" (v. 12). Nor would a mention of faith fit into this passage; it would damage it. Where any human activity is excluded, even faith inevitably disappears from the picture. Paul speaks here as if humans were saved simply by God's arbitrary action: their destinies are decreed by God before they are born.[149]

Moreover, in order to make sense of the unwillingness of the majority of Israel to accept his preaching, Paul correlates this emphasis on prevenient grace with its mirror image, the notion of a predestined hardening that leads to damnation. God "hardens the heart of whomever he wills" (Rom. 9:18); as the great Potter he has also produced "vessels of wrath" that are destined for destruction "in order to make known the riches of his glory for the vessels of mercy, which he has prepared beforehand for glory" (9:22-23). This sounds very much like a doctrine of double predestination,[150] but Paul does not leave it there. Having apparently arrived in a cul-de-sac (perhaps realizing that if one's salvation is predestined by an eternal decree, no function will be left either for faith or for Christ), he moves in 9:30-33 to emphasize his standard notion of faith commitment, ascribes Israel's hardening to their own stubbornness (Rom. 10), and eventually assures that God will see to it that the elect Israel, though as yet hardened, will finally find faith after all (11:25-30).

All this will be treated in more detail in chapter 10 on identity. Paul is wrestling with the problem of (dis)continuity between Israel and the church, which for him is nothing less than the problem of the reliability of God's promises. The idea of double predestination emerges as a side product. For Paul it is an interpretive device that he tries and then drops. But this trial-and-error argument amounted to playing with fire: Paul's experiment was to have tremendous effects on Christendom. Greek fathers explained the notion of predestination away, but it was taken up in different variations by interpreters of the rank of Augustine, Luther, and, not least, Calvin.

In Calvinism, a strict doctrine of election was built on Romans 9: each person is predestined either to heaven or to hell. Predictably, the haunting question "Am I predestined to hell?" presented itself. The peculiar existential importance of the notion of "calling" in Calvinism is said to be linked with anxieties occasioned by the doctrine of predestination derived from Romans 9. To overcome such anxiety, there was a "psychological pressure to demonstrate one's election by exhibiting the signs of election,"[151] among other things through active involvement in the affairs of this world—a matter that according to Max Weber's famous theory led to the emergence of capitalism on Protestant soil. If so, there is a good amount of irony in the effective history of the text, as the statements on predestination were originally meant to produce consolation, not anxiety.

Paul is confronted with a social problem, to which he applies different tentative solutions, among them the idea of predestination. Traces of a related situation are found in the Gospel of John.[152] Here, however, the actual struggle seems to belong to the past; a remaining result of it is a discrepancy between a decision of faith and election in the ideological world of the text. There are statements with a predestinarian ring, in particular John 6:44, where Jesus states: "no one can come to me unless drawn by the Father." Alongside them, others stress the necessity and possibility of decision as well as the human responsibility: whoever believes in the Son of God is not condemned; one who does not believe is condemned already. The light came into the world, but "people loved darkness rather than light because their deeds were evil" (3:16-21); anyone prepared to do God's will shall know whether Jesus' teaching is from God (7:17). John's polarized way of speaking in contrasts may suggest a dualism, where everything is fixed from the beginning. Yet the context of the dualistic statements sometimes lets the polemical-apologetical background shine through, most clearly in 12:37-40: despite Jesus' many signs, his audience did not believe in him, because Isaiah had prophesied that God would blind their eyes and harden their hearts "lest they should see or hear or understand" (Isa. 6:9-10).[153] In the background looms a bitter confrontation of John's group with the Jewish community.

A comparable tension is found in Revelation: there are those whose names have not been written in the book of life "before the foundation of the world" (Rev. 13:8; 17:8)—they have been ordained to worship the beast and to incur eternal punishment. The other side of the coin is the election of the faithful, and this is the point: the "endurance and the faith of the saints" (13:10) will be tested in the coming affliction, and the idea of predestination gives them courage. On the other hand, exhortatory passages in the book appeal strongly to the hearers' will and call vigorously to repentance (chs. 2–3), and it is implied in 3:5 that a name written in the book of life can also be blotted out of it.

If Romans 9 suggests that some are predestined to damnation, two chapters later Paul goes to the other extreme.[154] Having put forward the argument that God, being true to his promises to the patriarchs, will see to it that all Israel eventually finds salvation, Paul clinches the matter with the statement, "God has imprisoned all in disobedience so that he may be merciful to all" (Rom. 11:32). Such a phrase hints at the possibility of universal salvation[155]—a conclusion from God's omnipotence that contradicts the exclusivist view to which Paul usually (even in Rom. 10 and 11:17-24) gives expression. In Romans 5, too, the logic of his argument seems to lead to a universalist conclusion, although Paul stops short of drawing it: the typological comparison of Christ with Adam leads him to state that "just as one man's trespass led to condemnation for all, so one man's act of righteousness leads to justification and life *for all*" (Rom. 5:18).[156] In this scheme Christ does have a decisive function (his act has undone the harm caused by Adam's disobedience), whereas his role in the vision of Romans 11 is unclear, the basis of Israel's assumed salvation being God's promise made long before Christ. Yet it is likely that in both cases the train of the argument used by Paul (almost) carries him away rather than that he would have had the salvation of all in view.

In any case, on the basis of the Pauline hints, Origen constructed his well-known doctrine of *apokatastasis*: the final paradisiac restoration of everything, the salvation of all and sundry. To a degree, he was anticipated by gnostic Christians. Independently of Paul, the Sethian *Apocryphon of John* argues for the salvation of most of humanity, excluding only apostates (*Apoc. John* 25.16—27.30).[157] Even one who has remained ignorant has hope: after death, his or her soul will be "handed over to the authorities" who

184 "bind her with chains and throw her into prison and go around with her[158] until she is liberated from forgetfulness and acquires knowledge. This is how she attains perfection and is saved" (27.5-11). The Valentinian *Gospel of Truth*, for its part, states that all who have come forth from the Father will return to him (*Gos. Truth* 38). In consonance with its "tendency toward radical monism in which there is only one ultimate principle of existence," this Gospel appears to presume that all of humanity will be saved.[159]

Probably independently of Paul, some passages in the *Testaments of the Twelve Patriarchs* (in their christianized versions) testify to a "rare breadth of vision."[160] "All Israel will be gathered to the Lord" (*T. Benj.* 10.11; 10.5 states as a precondition: "If you live in holiness, in accordance with the Lord's commands"). "The Lord will raise up from Levi someone as a high priest and from Judah someone as a king, God and man. He will save all (!) the Gentiles[161] and the tribe of Israel" (*T. Sim.* 7.2). Whether "all Israel" is expected to convert to Jesus before its "gathering" remains unclear, but Stephen Wilson's suggestion seems plausible: "Perhaps the author believed that Christians, Jewish or Gentile, would be saved by Christ and the bulk of the Jews through God's original promise."[162] Christ does have here the role of a Savior, but its precise nature remains unclear.

SAVING KNOWLEDGE

The significance of salvific revelation of divine secrets is emphasized in apocalypticism, most explicitly in *1 Enoch*. Humans live in ignorance of certain facts that cut them off from the possibility of divine blessing. The revealer, who has traveled to the heavens, provides revealed law, for example, about the calendar. He also encourages the faithful by assuring them of the certainty of the eschatological judgments. Enoch's revelation rivals the Mosaic Torah; its life-giving power is limited to the few in Israel who follow its law.[163] At many points in the Qumran scrolls, too, salvation is construed as knowledge and revelation.[164]

A similar point is made in many branches of early Christianity. While there is very little teaching by Jesus in Paul,[165] Q embodies the notion of Jesus as teacher and revealer. The "Johannine bolt" (Q 10:21-22), taken over by Matthew and Luke, indicates that it is a question not of ordinary wisdom, but of a heavenly revelation from the Father. The Jewish Christians for whom the *Pseudo-Clementines* speak maintain that the True Prophet alone is able to enlighten human souls, so that they may be able to see the way of eternal salvation (*Hom.* 1.19.1; *Rec.* 1.16.1).[166] The Fourth Gospel essentially "construes salvation in terms of an eschatological revelation that is the property of the elect community."[167] The coming of Jesus reveals the glory of God (John 1:14); the only begotten Son is uniquely in a position to make God known (1:18). He is sent to be the Light of the world (3:16-21). He can speak of "knowing" as crucial for the disciples (17:3, 6-8). The cross is less a sacrificial or redemptive event than the moment when the full glory of God is revealed.[168] Jan van der Watt correctly observes: "If the question were asked, 'From what must a person be saved according to John?', the answer would be, 'From a lack of spiritual knowledge and blindness in order to be able to see and know the Father in the Son.'"[169]

First Clement states that through Christ we taste immortal knowledge (*1 Clem.* 36.2); through him God has called us from ignorance to knowledge of the glory of his name (59.2).

The *Epistle of Barnabas* concurs: Christ has rescued us from the darkness of error (*Barn.* 14.5). *Second Clement* (1.6-8) affirms that, because of the enlightenment received from him, those who are now Christians abandoned idolatry. The *Didache*, too, emphasizes that knowledge, faith, and immortality are disclosed by God through his servant Jesus (*Did.* 9.3; 10.2). *Hermas* states that Christ makes God's law known to us and even identifies the law with "the Son of God" (*Sim.* 5.5.3; 8.3.2-3).

In the *Gospel of Thomas*, Jesus is the teacher who invites people to seek saving knowledge.[170] Those who become enlightened are promised by Jesus that they will "find the kingdom. For you have come from it, and you will return there again" (*Gos. Thom.* 49). The enlightenment consists in the recognition of one's origin in the light and one's destiny in the "rest" (50); salvation means returning to one's origin by stripping off the fleshly garment (37) and "passing by" (42) the present corruptible existence. Jesus' death and resurrection play no role. The true meaning and the goal of life can be understood only by means of discovering the beginning of all things (*Gos. Thom.* 18). "There is light within a person of light, and he [or: it] lights up the whole world. If he [it] does not shine, he [it] is darkness" (24). It is crucial that the disciples discover this light within them: "What you have will save you if you bring it forth from yourselves" (70). Christ's role is exhausted in making this insight available, so much so that he can say, "I am not your master; because you [Thomas] have drunk, you have become intoxicated from the bubbling spring which I have measured out" (13); Jesus himself becomes the person who drinks from his mouth (108).[171] The same point is made in the *Gospel of Philip*: one who has seen Christ has become Christ him/herself (61.30-

31); one who has received the proper unction "is no longer a Christian but is Christ" (*Gos. Phil.* 67.23-27). But the saving insight also includes an act of *repentance*: when the "intoxicated," blind humans "shake off their wine, then they will repent" (*Gos. Thom.* 28).

The gnostic Christians in particular regard Jesus as the bringer of salvific knowledge. Those will be saved who receive this knowledge and become enlightened; they will be redeemed from the hold of evil powers. In the famous words of Theodotus (*Exc. Theod.* 78.2), "It is not only baptism that liberates, but also the knowledge (*gnosis*) of who we were; what we have become; where we were, or where we have fallen into; where we hasten to; from what we have been redeemed, what is birth; what is rebirth."[172]

The precondition of salvation is coming to know one's true origin—recovering one's spiritual substance that has fallen into matter—and orientating one's life on that insight. Salvation thus depends on something that a human being has in himself or herself. Nevertheless, salvation for a Christian gnostic is not one's own "achievement"; the help of a revealer from outside is necessary for humans to find the saving knowledge (even if it is to be found within them). The gnostic texts "regularly portray the necessity of a savior (often Christ),[173] and they portray the plight of humanity in terms of ignorance that must be enlightened with true teaching, impurity that must be cleansed, and evil that must be resisted and overcome."[174] The *Gospel of Truth* (35-36) tells how the saving knowledge springs from the compassionate heart of the Father. Because of his mercy he sent Christ "so that those who were troubled might be restored. . . . The doctor rushes to where there is sickness."[175] The focus is entirely on enlightenment, on bringing the elect out of ignorance into the knowledge of the Father

186 (*Gos. Truth* 18.9-11; 24.30-32). The redeeming knowledge enables the elect to know that "the Father is in them and they are in the Father, being perfect" (42.26-29). Through his teaching[176] and resurrection, the Son reveals the Father and restores the souls to restful unity with him, as they are refreshed by the spirit and attracted to him like a sweet fragrance (34), participating in his nature "by means of kisses" (41.34).[177] Here the notion of salvation as revelation merges with the notion of salvation as union with the Redeemer, which comes close to Paul's conviction of participation in Christ.

Scholars used to think, following the early heresiological polemicists, that for gnostics salvation is "by nature."[178] The texts from Nag Hammadi now show that this view is very one-sided: "It is quite clear that belief in the divine nature of the soul or spirit does not necessarily imply that no moral effort is required on the part of the individual."[179] "The 'pneuma-nature' of the gnostic can on the one hand be understood also as the grace of God, while on the other hand salvation is not automatically assured, but must be accompanied by a corresponding way of life."[180] The pneumatic seed needs a certain "training," beginning with its awakening; the gnostic must prove him- or herself in the conflict with the passions of the bodily and psychic nature and the temptations of the archons.[181] The Valentinians "emphasize the need for the psychics to lead perfect lives if they are to share in some way the final 'marriage feast,'" and even the "pneumatics" are expected to reflect their spiritual nature in their actions.[182] They are time and again exhorted to obey "the will of the Father." "Steady the feet of those who stumble and extend your hands to the sick. Feed the hungry and give rest to the weary. . . . Do not be a place for the devil, for you have already destroyed him . . . do the Father's will, for you are from him" (*Gos. Truth* 33). This position approximates the scheme of "indicative and imperative" in Pauline soteriology.

SALVATION OUTSIDE THE CHURCH?

The fate of those who died before Christ had come should not be a problem, if the judgment will be strictly according to the deeds. But the uneasy combination of this postulate with the other central idea that acknowledging Christ (or living in union with him) is an indispensable precondition of salvation makes it a serious issue, though it is at first seldom reflected on.[183] In particular, what about those who lived a pious, God-fearing life? For most early Christians this would mean pious characters of scripture.

Many authors handle the issue (more or less unconsciously?) by assimilating trust in God with faith in Christ (cf. *1 Clement*, above); implicitly even Paul favors this view when he sets up Abraham as the great example of faith that brings righteousness. Others have, however, felt that something new must take place to make salvation available to those who could not yet benefit from Christ's work (however understood). An obscure section in 1 Peter (3:19-22) states that Christ spoke after his death to "the spirits in prison" who had been disobedient "in the days of Noah."[184] This may refer to an occasion during the ascension to heaven, on which Christ preached (with whatever outcome) to the generation of the flood, regarded as the worst sinners ever, showing that the preaching of the gospel knows no limits.[185] More influential was the idea that Christ spent the time between his death and resurrection preaching the good news to the dead.[186] In the *Gospel of Peter* (41-42), a heavenly voice asks Jesus, who is coming forth from the tomb, "Have you preached to those who sleep?" whereby "from the cross there was heard the answer, 'Yes.'" Ignatius states that Jesus went to Hades and raised from the dead the Old Testament prophets, who expected him "as their teacher" (*Magn.* 9.2).[187] Hermas holds that deceased apostles and elders preached to the righteous dead and even baptized them so that they could now be saved (*Sim.* 9.16).[188] In the *Epistle of the Apostles* (26-27), it is Christ himself who baptizes the patriarchs and prophets.

What about the Gentiles? In Jewish perspective, the Torah defined God's will for Israel, but not for the Gentiles. Insofar as the destiny of Gentiles was reflected on, quite different views existed: Gentiles may be annihilated as a *massa perditionis* or they might join Israel and convert at the end of days; or they may be saved at the judgment (or in the beyond after death) apart from the Torah, if they have lived a decent life. Naturally, thoughtful Christians also realized that all Gentiles were not wicked sinners. Matthew indicates in his great judgment scene (Matt. 25:31-46) that Gentiles may be judged according to their deeds, the criterion being whether they have done deeds of mercy (possibly toward Christians); even so, their attitude to Christ is decisive, but only in the rather indirect sense that in the "least brothers" and sisters whom they have helped they have, without knowing it, encountered Christ incognito.[189] Clement of Rome noted that the ancient Ninevites, who repented when Jonah preached to them, received salvation (*1 Clem.* 7.7), implying that the opportunity to repentance, which God has always granted to willing humans (v. 5), has also concerned foreign peoples. Clement of Alexandria (*Strom.* 2.43.5) refers to the passage of Hermas quoted in the previous paragraph, but makes the apostles baptize even Gentiles who have been pleasing to God. Sensitive Christians, who could not tolerate the idea that all the great poets and philosophers of antiquity were doomed to everlasting torment, later postulated a special compartment in hell called limbo. It would accommodate those who had lived good lives but had not known of Christ. They suffered no torment, but could not enjoy the bliss of salvation either. The related problem of the destiny of unbaptized children was solved by inventing another limbo for them.

SALVIFIC RITES

Rituals make adherents of a religion tick more often than its doctrines. For early Christians, too, salvation was concretized in salvific rites. Baptism in particular came to be closely connected with the attainment of salvation, albeit in different ways.

In our sources, baptism occurs self-evidently as the rite of entrance that needs no legitimation (and does not seem to invite antagonism either). The practice was presumably rooted in the end-time baptism ministered by John (though some uncertainty remains), yet why it was taken over remains something of a mystery.[190] Apparently the legacy of the Baptist had a more significant role in shaping the new movement than is immediately visible (cf. Acts 18–19). Jesus once belonged to the circle of John and probably himself conducted baptisms for a while (John 3:22; 4:1).[191] His followers took up this activity again after Easter, when the great eschatological turn seemed to be just around the corner.

188   John's baptism was closely linked to the demand of repentance and confession of sins. Connected with the baptisand's serious will to repentance, the baptism would cleanse and liberate them from God's impending judgment. No doubt the bath was connected with the rich Jewish tradition of purificatory rites, though unlike other washings it was a once-for-all event and was not performed by the baptisands themselves.[192]

If Acts is any guide, the strong link with repentance was preserved in the early Jesus movement, but now the rite was conducted "in(to) the name of Jesus" (Acts 2:38), indicating that those baptized had given their allegiance to the risen Jesus as their Lord.[193] Peter states that repentance and baptism are the condition for the remission of sins,[194] for the reception of the spirit, and for being saved "from this crooked generation." Later a close connection is also established with baptism and faith (Acts 16:30-34);[195] the order of the two may vary.

Baptism played a great role in the Gentile mission. The acceptance of the Christian message meant for a Gentile a turn away from the ancestral Gods and from many inherited values. As a public act,[196] baptism amounted to a dramatic change, a death to one's past and a rebirth to a new life—and a transfer to a new community. Galatians 3:28 is probably a baptismal formula that gives expression to a vivid experience of the removal of ethnic and other barriers: there is no longer Jew or Greek, slave or free, male or female, "for all of you are one in Christ Jesus." Paul's "in Christ" language as a whole is to be seen in this context: baptism initiates the new life in union with Christ.[197]

To be sure, for Paul the critical turning point in the life of believers was their reception of the spirit; baptism is linked to it, but it is the less emphasized of the two events.[198] Paul did not conduct many baptisms himself and warned about the false security that could result from trusting in the mere performance of the rite (1 Cor. 10:1-13). But he also gave a powerful theological interpretation of baptism in Rom. 6:3-4: it is seen, like a burial, as participation in the beneficial death of Christ, as a death to the power of sin, and a rebirth to new life in the spirit. Later on, baptism is explicitly connected with "rebirth" (Titus 3:5; John 3:5; Justin, *1 Apol.* 61.3-10; 66.1). The formulation "bath of rebirth" recalls the language of mystery religions, but the mention of the "renewal through the holy spirit" introduces a new feature.[199]

In the beginning, baptism followed the decision to convert and to join the new community. Thus an active human effort was involved,[200] even if the rite itself was understood to represent the "objective," divine side of salvation. In fact, baptism as the expression of faith commitment correlates with the understanding of John's baptism as the expression of repentance.[201] In 1 Pet. 3:21, "the nearest thing we have to a definition of baptism in the NT,"[202] baptism is said to save "as an appeal to God for a good conscience." But inevitably the rite came to gain independent salvific value. It became an indispensable means of rebirth (John 3:5), so much so that, according to Hermas, the righteous dead who have died before Christ must be baptized in Hades to be able to partake in salvation (Herm. *Sim.* 9.16). Faith alone (or even along with repentance) no longer suffices. With time, all the attributes and images used of the salvation process are gathered together in baptism. Baptism is said to effect regeneration, illumination, and remission of sins (Justin, *1 Apol.* 61; *Barn.* 11.1; 16.7-8).

It cleanses the soul and bestows the spirit (Irenaeus); it imparts regeneration, enlightenment, divine sonship, immortality, and remissions of sins (Clement of Alexandria). Origen states that baptism is the unique means of obtaining remission of sins; it frees us from the power of the devil. Even little children, defiled as they are with sin, must be baptized. For Augustine, every child born into the world is polluted with sin, and baptism is the indispensable means to its abolition.[203]

Almost from the beginning, baptism was such a self-evident link in the process of salvation that even many of those Christians who held a pointedly "spiritual" view could hardly conceive of salvation without it (or without some other comparable rite).[204] Symptomatically, the idea of the necessity of baptism for salvation surfaced early on in Corinth: some of those spiritual-minded fellow Christians, whom Paul criticizes, practiced vicarious baptisms for dead relatives or ancestors (1 Cor. 15:29). Clearly they held that the rite had powerful salvific efficacy, and it was not on this score that Paul tried to refute them.

For gnostic Christians, the Son's descent brings the saving enlightenment to those able to receive it. Equally important, though, are the salvific rites instituted by the Son, notably baptism (or baptisms).[205] Theodotus (Exc. 78.2) implies that it is not only knowledge that makes us free, but also the "bath."[206] Baptism in the spirit gives people the power to counter the evil force present in their hylic nature.[207] Irenaeus reports that Valentinians regard baptism as an act that imparts to the baptisand the spirit of immortality, redemption, and resurrection and thereby makes him or her a pneumatic; one obtains in baptism one's "immortal garment" or the "perfect man." This notion is confirmed by the *Gospel of Philip* (75.21-25; 61.12-20).[208] The Sethians, according to Hippolytus (*Haer.* 5.19.21), also practiced baptism as the means whereby one partook of immortality.[209] This conception has evidently become characteristic of the gnostic interpretation of baptism,[210] yet the same conception is conspicuous in the proto-orthodox ideology of baptism as well (though it is there coupled with the idea of the remission of sins).

In some branches of gnostic Christianity, anointing with oil (chrism) is regarded as even more significant.[211] "Chrism is superior to baptism, for it is from the word 'chrism' that we have been called 'Christians' . . . Christ also has his name from chrism, for the Father anointed the Son, the Son anointed the apostles, and the apostles anointed us. Whoever is anointed has everything: resurrection, light, cross, holy spirit" (*Gos. Phil.* 74.12-21).

By anointing, the gift of immortality or redemption is transmitted. Redemption by unction is closely bound up with the paradisiac tree of life, conceived of as an olive tree (*Gos. Phil.* 73.15-19). One who has received the unction "is no longer a Christian but is Christ" (67.23-27).

A similar ritual is undertaken on behalf of the dying.[212] The Marcosian deathbed ritual called redemption (*apolytrosis*) involved an unction and supplied answers that one should give to the hostile powers one was expected to meet in the hereafter during one's ascent: "I am a child of Father, of preexistent Father, I am a child in (?) the preexistent one . . . I am returning to my own, whence I came . . . I know myself, and I know from whence I am, and I call upon incorruptible Wisdom who is in Father and who is the Mother of your Mother who had no Father, no male consort" (Irenaeus, *Haer.* 1.21.5; cf. *1 Apoc. Jas.* 33-34). This invocation shows that the Valentinian

190   tale of Wisdom was not only a speculative myth; there were groups in which the knowledge of this myth was considered necessary for salvation, and a special ritual practice was developed to achieve it.[213] Irenaeus (*Haer.* 1.21) describes different ways that Valentinians performed the redemption: in addition to the Marcosian deathbed ritual, the redemption could consist in the bridal chamber ritual or in a baptism involving special Hebrew invocations and anointing, or anointing without baptism.

The *Gospel of Philip* apparently presupposes the practice of the bridal chamber ritual, but does not describe how it was performed. The spiritual meaning of the rite is, however, explained: the "separation," that is, the division of humankind into two sexes, considered a consequence of the fall, is removed (*Gos. Phil.* 70-71, 73). The ceremony that, as the "Holy of Holies," ranks above other rituals has probably become "even a kind of sacrament for the dying accompanied by unction and recitations. . . . The object in view was evidently to anticipate the final union with the pleroma (represented as a bridal chamber) at the end of time and realizing it in

7.5   Basket of bread and fish. Glass of red wine in basket symbolizes Eucharistic meal prefigured by the Miracle of the Loaves and Fishes. Early Christian fresco, third century c.e. Catacomb of S. Callisto, Rome.
Photo: © Scala/Art Resource, NY.

the sacrament, although not by a sexual act or a kissing ceremony, as was frequently assumed."[214] This "marriage" is of a strictly spiritual kind. "The pneumatics or gnostics are understood as brides of the angels, and their entrance into the world beyond as a wedding-feast," at the end of which they "enter the bridal chamber within the (Pleroma) border (*horos*) and attain to a vision of the Father, and become spiritual aeons, (entering) into the spiritual and eternal marriage of the union (syzygy). . . . The Gospel of Philip understands this eschatological state very clearly as dependent upon the earthly consummation of the 'bridal chamber' which manifestly served the purpose of a safe ascent."[215]

It stands to reason that rites of passage, such as baptism or the bridal chamber ceremony, which were bound up with a person's transfer from one state of existence to another, were attributed salvific power. However, similar interpretations were sometimes connected also with repeated rites, such as the sacred meal. In the Gospel of John (probably in a late layer), eating "the flesh of the Son of Man" and drinking his blood are said to grant eternal life, for which they are preconditions (John 6:53-58). Ignatius agrees: the Eucharist is "a medicine which procures immortality (*pharmakon athanasias*), an antidote against death, which enables one to live forever in Jesus Christ" (Ign. *Eph.* 20.2). The bread is Jesus' flesh and the cup his blood (Ign. *Rom.* 7.3); no doubt Ignatius already "intends this realism to be taken strictly,"[216] for in *Smyrnaeans* 7 "he makes it the basis of his argument against the docetists' denial of the reality of Christ's body."[217] He also suggests that partaking of this flesh of Christ is a precondition of resurrection: it would be better for the docetist opponents "to have meals of love that they also might rise again" (*Smyrn.* 7.1) In an analogous way, the

Gospel of Philip states concerning the Valentinian Eucharist: "When we drink this (cup), we shall take to ourselves the perfect man" (75.14-21). "The eucharist anticipates the union of the gnostic with his 'angel image'; it effects a realization of the original oneness of the Pleroma. . . . The recipient is in the possession of perfection and eternal life."[218]

The prominence of ritual even among gnostic Christians suggests that the mental act alone seemed too intangible, perhaps not certain enough. Salvation had to be guaranteed by a ritual action that could be experienced.[219]

PROSPECTS

Different paths to salvation can be discerned in the mental world of early Christians. One main route can be called the path of obedience and repentance: the deeds of persons are scrutinized at the judgment on which their salvation depends. Another route focuses on an act of Jesus that is thought to have beneficial effects. The decisive event can consist in his resurrection or in his death, but also in the revelation brought by him. The routes seem distinct, but they do intersect: the authors who stress obedience and good deeds generally do not acknowledge that a person could bear the required good fruit without a special commitment to Jesus. Conversely, those who underline the significance of an act of Jesus do not cease to expect a pious life of the believers.

Two problems stand out: What is the relation between human effort and divine grace?

What is the real significance of Jesus? Apart from Paul's more polemical statements, made in conflict settings, the all-but-unanimous answer to the first question is that God's mercy and grace are the indispensable basis of salvation, but without the consent and cooperation of humans this grace remains ineffective. What Rosemary Ruether wrote about "ordinary Christianity" in general applies fully to early Christianity: it "assumes the view that we are already loved by God, and yet must also *do* something to become what we are supposed to be. . . . In practice, Christianity constantly tends to boil down to a religion of grace and good deeds structurally identical to Judaism."[220] But then the question arises, "For such an ethic, does one need a Messiah? It would seem that Creation, covenant, and commandments would be sufficient."[221]

The Messiah does seem indispensable, when something Jesus did or effected is construed as part of the "indicative." A corollary then is that relying on God's previous salvific acts—the covenant and the gift of the Torah—does not save one who does not accept Jesus. Yet an author's confession to the indispensability of Jesus often appears to stand in contradiction to other convictions of the very same author (for example, Luke or Clement of Rome). This adds force to critical questions, which a non-Christian, especially a Jew, might have asked anyway: Was God's grace not available all along to those who put their trust in him? Why would God have ceased to be merciful? For what exactly was Jesus needed? The putative indispensability of (faith in) Jesus remains a problem for Christian theology, not least in the context of interreligious dialogue.

8

True Man or True God?

The Mediator of Salvation

The position of Jesus and the understanding of his nature are the most crucial features that distinguish Christian doctrine from Judaism and Islam. To begin with, Jesus of Nazareth is claimed to be the Messiah (the "Anointed One," in Greek, "the Christ"), that is, the promised eschatological redeemer allegedly predicted all over the Bible. But that, of course, is only the beginning of the story. True man, Jesus is in the end taught to be true God as well, the coequal Second Person of the Trinity; "perfect in deity and perfect in humanity" in the words of the Council of Chalcedon (451 C.E.). Yet the road from Capernaum to Chalcedon was long and arduous, rutted with controversy and confusion.

DELIVERERS AND MEDIATORS IN JEWISH TRADITION

Royal Figures

The introduction of the monarchy to Israel brought in some central Near Eastern conceptions about the king.[1] When a righteous monarch—worthy of the legendary model king, David—sat on the throne, there were certain expectations, projections into the future about what would occur: peace, fertility, and justice in the land (cf. Isa. 9:2-7; 11:1-9).

Although the emphasis in eschatological traditions is on Yahweh as king, there is, on occasion, a place for a righteous Davidide as well. The roots of such expectation lie in Nathan's oracle (2 Sam. 7:12-14; originally a prophecy about Solomon): the Davidic line will not die out; God will establish a successor on David's throne who will be to him as his son. Some texts attest to the hope of a radically good Davidic ruler (for example, Ps. 18:50; Ezek. 37:23-24). Yahweh remains, however, the ruler par excellence. Thus Second Isaiah refers frequently to Yahweh as king, but does not seem to expect a restoration of the Davidic dynasty; for him, the anointed one is Cyrus, the Persian ruler (Isa. 45:1)! Similarly, Third Isaiah has no place for a Davidic king in Israel's future.[2] We are left without any *eschatological* Messiah at all in the Hebrew Bible.[3]

The king is often called "son of God," as in 2 Sam. 7:14: "I will be his father, and he will be my son," or in Ps. 2:7: "You are my son; today I have begotten you." The title indicates that the king has his kingship from God; the saying belongs to the coronation day or its anniversary. There is no question of deification; the designation "son of God" does not express anything more than a special relationship to God.[4] In continuation of this usage, the Davidic Messiah ("the Branch of David") is occasionally called God's son in the texts of Qumran (4Q174 = 4QFlor 1.10-11),[5] as is the Messiah in *4 Ezra* (7.28-29; 13.32, 37, 52; 14.9).[6]

Even in other extant Jewish literature, the expectation of an individual figure who effects deliverance from foreign oppression and brings in God's kingdom is less common than one might expect; instead, God himself often appears as the sole bringer of the kingdom (for example, in the *Testament of Moses*). The Qumran scrolls reflect the expectation of two messianic figures, a priestly one and a kingly one (1QS 9.9-11; CD 14.19; 1QSa 2.17-22), in obvious opposition to the Hasmonean usurpation of priesthood and kingship.[7] The *Psalms of Solomon* depict a Davidic king who overthrows the Romans (and probably the corrupt Hasmoneans too) and ushers in an era of peace, ruling over a holy and righteous kingdom (especially *Ps. Sol.* 17–18).

Deliverer figures appear in only a minority of texts, but then again the extant texts may not be representative of the general sentiments. Serious attention has to be paid to popular movements with messianic[8] or prophetic[9] leaders, and a large peasant following, in Palestine from 4 B.C.E. to 70 C.E. and beyond—Bar Kokhba was recognized as a messianic general by a large proportion of the Judean peasantry and even by the revered Rabbi Aqiba (though not by many of his colleagues).[10] These movements were oriented toward bringing about liberation from alien rule, whether by force or by relying on a divine miracle. Messianic expectations with a this-worldly social and political emphasis were, then, not uncommon in Palestine after all. This picture is confirmed both by the synagogue prayer *Shemoneh Esreh*[11] and by the Gospels. Nor was the situation very different in the Diaspora either, as the Jewish books of the Sibyl (for example, *Sib. Or.* 3.266-67, 652-56; 5.108-9, 414-27) and, most concretely, the revolts against Rome in 115–117 C.E. in Egypt and elsewhere show. Messianism is connected to discontent with present rulers; therefore it is lacking in writings like 1 Maccabees or Ben Sira. "Those who placed their hopes in the institutions and leaders of their day, whether the High Priests, the Ptolemies, or the Maccabees, had little interest in messianism."[12]

Transcendent Figures

In apocalyptic texts, messianic expectations develop in a somewhat different direction. There we meet the mysterious "son of man." In Dan. 7:13-14, this is simply a figure that looks like a human being (in contrast to the beasts in Daniel's visions); a representative of the oppressed Jewish people (7:27),[13] he is figuratively elevated to the presence of God ("the Ancient of Days") and given everlasting dominion over all peoples. This passage caught the imagination of later

194 readers, and the figure of "one like a son of man" seems to have taken on a life of its own. In the *Similitudes of Enoch*, the seer sees a scene rather like Daniel 7, involving a figure "whose face was like that of a human being" (*1 En.* 46.1); thereafter (v. 2) Enoch refers to this figure as "that son of man." He has a role to play in the final judgment, and eventually Enoch himself seems to be identified with him (71.14). The *Similitudes* may not be pre-Christian, but in any case they hint at the existence of a tradition in which the human-like figure of Daniel 7 was interpreted in individualistic terms as one who would play a role in the coming judgment.[14] In this connection a fusion takes place, so that "Messiah" (the term occurs in 48.10 and 52.4) is identified with the "chosen one," "(that) son of man," and "servant." Consequently, "Messiah" here becomes the designation of a heavenly figure; he is no longer Davidic, nor does he bring an earthly kingdom. The author "believed that the biblical promises about the future king and the traditional messianic function of the judgment had to be fulfilled by a transcendent savior—one he found described in other traditions" (which he conflated).[15]

In *4 Ezra* the Messiah has a limited but important role, here too fused with the figure from Daniel 7; the Messiah is, however, not the ultimate focal point for hopes of vindication.[16] In *2 Baruch*, the Messiah is a transcendent, probably preexistent figure who comes to earth; in contrast to *4 Ezra*, however, he is a victorious warrior who overthrows Rome and brings in the divine kingdom, finally returning to heaven.[17]

Though direct evidence is lacking, one may surmise that the increasing tendency to emphasize the role of transcendent, heavenly figures in the eschatological events reflects a certain disillusionment with human Messiahs and consequently a desire to *diminish politically dangerous*

messianism,[18] even if there is no intrinsic reason why a transcendent deliverer should necessarily be incompatible with a this-worldly time of peace. A transcendent emphasis underlines that the hoped-for great turn is not expected to develop directly out of existing trends or movements, and thus serves to emphasize that the community in question is politically harmless.

The texts just mentioned are roughly contemporary with later New Testament writings and thus somewhat late to shed direct light on the roots of the Jesus movement; one should probably rather see them as parallel attempts to adapt messianic traditions to a new situation. In Qumran, however, we do find earlier examples of heavenly (angelic) figures who are expected to play a part in the hoped-for turn. Thus the Prince of Light(s) (Angel of Truth) in 1QS (3.20) and 1QM (13.10) is portrayed as a heavenly being set in dualistic opposition to Belial. In 1QM, the Prince of Light is apparently identical with Michael, who aids the children of light to a victory (17.6-8), and Melchizedek in 11QMelch is possibly to be identified with him as well. Melchizedek (especially in 11QMelch 9-16) is associated with the deliverance of divine judgment, with a day of atonement, with a Jubilee Year, and with a role that exalts him high above the assembly of other heavenly beings; he is a quasi-divine figure (passages of scripture that speak about God are applied to him), who also has messianic traits. "Thus an earthly figure is given an extraordinarily exalted position, and apparently accorded divine status and function." It seems that the way in which a figure like the Qumranic Melchizedek is portrayed "can be used to shift the emphasis of messianic hope away from the present age (or society)."[19]

In the case of Philo we can observe a concern for defusing messianic hopes (see above), or spiritualizing or "transcendentalizing" them, connected with highly developed intermediary concepts (see below).

Such developments are significant for any attempt to understand christological developments in the Jesus movement. Equally if not more significant is the now commonplace observation that it was not only in relation to eschatological activity that Jews could conceive of God having some kind of agent alongside him to assist him. God could use various mediators in his regular dealings with the world (and it is to be noted that, originally at least, the Messiah was *not* such a mediating figure). The mediator could be an angel. He could also be an originally human celebrity of the past, such as Enoch, Elijah, or Moses. In a more Platonic vein, attributes of God could be personified or even hypostatized. Divine features or functions were often ascribed to these mediators.

Thus angelic figures can be described in extraordinary terms. In the (probably Palestinian first-century C.E.) *Apocalypse of Abraham*, the angel Iaoel is portrayed in terms usually reserved for God; he even shares God's name.[20] From here the step is not very great to the characterization of the angel Metatron, apparently identified with Enoch, as "the lesser Yahweh" "because my name is in him" in 3 *En.* 12.5 (a much later writing, to be sure).

We also hear of the exaltation of some humans to heaven. Enoch has already been mentioned. Adam and Abel are given an extraordinarily high status as eschatological judges in the *Testament of Abraham* (late first century C.E., from Egypt).[21] In some texts from Qumran, passages of scripture that speak about God are applied to Melchizedek. The fragmentary text 4Q491 also seems to speak of a human figure enthroned in heaven (on "a mighty throne in the congregation of the Gods"); he has taken his seat in heavens and "shall be reckoned with Gods." The speaker claims "to have undergone a virtual apotheosis."[22] According to Ezekiel the Tragedian (cited by Eusebius, *Praep. ev.* 9.29.4-5), God gave Moses his own scepter and asked him to mount his throne.[23] John Collins notes that such "divinization" never impinges "on the supremacy of the Most High, the God of Israel," but that "it clearly involves the exaltation of some human figures to a status that is envisaged as divine and heavenly rather than human and mortal. The sharp distinction between heaven and earth that was characteristic of the Deuteronomic tradition and much of the Hebrew Bible was not so strongly maintained in the Hellenistic age."[24]

Other texts even hint at the preexistence of the human hero. The *Testament of Moses* (1.14) states that Moses "was prepared from the beginning of the world to be the mediator of the covenant." A *Prayer of Joseph*, of which brief fragments have been preserved in patristic citations, portrays Jacob as an angel called Israel who is "the firstborn of every living thing to whom God gives life," "the archangel of the power of the Lord and the chief captain among the sons of God" who apparently "had descended to earth" and "tabernacled among men" (frg. A, quoted by Origen, *Comm. Jo.* 2.3). Here "the human progenitor of the nation Israel is seen as an incarnation of a superangelic being."[25]

Personified concepts, or attributes of God, occur in wisdom literature, starting with Job 28, Proverbs 8, and Sirach 24. Philo's writings are replete with them. Philo refers to Wisdom as a personified, mediatorial figure whose designations include "beginning," "image," and "vision of God"; she is portrayed as active and instrumental in creation (*Virt.* 62; *Her.* 199; *Fug.* 109), being both the mother of the world and the daughter of

196   God. A more central position, however, belongs to the Logos (identified with Wisdom in *All.* 1.65), to whom Philo applies designations developed in the wisdom tradition, such as "firstborn" and "beginning." Angelological traditions are also applied: the firstborn Logos is "chief elder among the angels," the archangel with many names (the beginning, the name of God, the man after his image, "he that sees," that is, Israel; *Conf.* 146). To this archangel and Logos the Father has "given the special prerogative to stand on the border and separate the creature from the Creator. This Logos is both the one who supplicates constantly to the Immortal for afflicted mortality and also he who acts as the ambassador of the ruler to the subject" (*Her.* 205). The Logos is divine (for example, *Migr.* 67) and eternal (*QE* 2.117), God's "firstborn son" (*Agr.* 51), and is even called a "second God" (*QG* 2.62). But while the Logos thus seems, in some respects at least, to be on a par with God, he is not identical with God, but is clearly subordinated to him (for example, *All.* 2.86: God is the primary being, the Logos is second to him). Somewhat inconsistently, the Logos is both the aspect of God's activity vis-à-vis the world and also separate from God, existing alongside God in the heavenly world.[26]

The Wisdom of Solomon goes even beyond Philo, portraying Wisdom seated on the throne of God (Wis. 9:4, 10), from where God may send her to the world, and supplying her with very high attributes: "She is an exhalation from the power of God, and a pure effluence from the glory of the Almighty . . . an effulgence (*apaugasma*) of everlasting light, an unblemished mirror of the active power of God, and an image (*eikon*) of his goodness" (7:25-26). Wisdom brought Israel out of Egypt (10:15-21); Wisdom holds all things together (1:7).

The precise significance of divine attributes as "beings" alongside God is hard to assess, but at least such formulations leave open the possibility that a separate being may be thought to exist. Behind this tendency toward hypostatization one may surmise Platonic influence: a God conceived of as the "Ground of Being" cannot easily be thought to intervene directly in the affairs of the world. An intermediary is welcome to build a bridge—however fragile or artificial—to the "God who acts."

The three categories of intermediaries overlap and are bound together. The point is that several exalted humans and angelic beings, and also some personified divine attributes, are elevated into positions very close to God himself. Indeed, they are close enough to cause some embarrassment from the point of view of strict monotheism.[27] Worshiping angels is prohibited in apocalyptic works, and rabbis later sounded warnings against positing "two powers in heaven,"[28] a heresy associated especially with Rabbi Elisha ben Abuya. But monotheism is a flexible thing, in the last analysis a matter of perception;[29] the very existence of prohibitions and warnings shows that not all Jewish monotheists were of the strict sort. New problems arose when the hypostasis theology was applied to a person who had lived and died recently.

JESUS' SELF-UNDERSTANDING

In Jesus' career different social roles are combined. He is conscious of a calling, connected with a particular experience—possibly in his baptism (Mark 1:9-11 par.), though the ecstatic vision to which Luke 10:18 refers in the first person in connection with Jesus' ability to heal may be a more likely candidate: "I watched Satan fall from heaven like a flash of lightning."[30] He carries out symbolic acts in the manner of a prophet (election of twelve representatives of a restored Israel, threatening the temple). Like a rabbi, he gives sapiential teaching.[31] He performs healings like other charismatics.[32] But all of these activities serve his all-important proclamation of and preparation for the kingdom of God.

The kingdom will come as a miracle of God, without any military power, though Jesus himself would probably play a part (which is not specified) in its establishment. His role may well be called "messianic," whether or not Jesus applied the title "Messiah" to himself (he may not have, but some of his adherents may have). Strikingly, Jesus did not include himself among the Twelve; this suggests that he reserved for himself a place above them (cf. Mark 10:35-45).[33] The statement that one's destiny on the day of judgment will depend on one's attitude to Jesus (and not just to his message, Q 12:8-9) also points to a special eschatological role. It also fits with the challenge that Jesus presented to his followers, whom he bound to himself even at the price of their life (Mark 8:35 par.). An atmosphere of authority surrounded him, as various memories of the impact of his speech (Mark 1:22, 27 par.; 11:28 par.) suggest.[34] That his followers concluded from their Easter visions that Jesus had been enthroned and vindicated precisely as the *Messiah* is easiest to explain on the basis of indications in this direction in the mission of Jesus himself.[35]

The designation "Son of Man" occurs in the Gospels on the lips of Jesus only (differently in Acts 7:56); it is not used in the confessions of early Christians, and it soon all but disappears.[36] This strongly suggests that Jesus himself used the expression.[37] Its meaning for him is, however, impossible to pinpoint with any certainty.[38] The

Synoptic tradition also connects the term with the manlike figure from Daniel 7 (for example, Mark 14:62 par.), but the notion that Jesus, as the Son of Man, will appear from heaven presupposes the conception of Jesus' exaltation. It is dubious that Jesus himself would have maintained such a notion. Some sayings that may be traced back to Jesus either distinguish between "Son of Man" and "I" (Q 12:8-9) or do not demand (or even suggest) an identification of the Son of Man with Jesus (Q 12:39-40; 17:24-30; Mark 13:26-27 detached from its Markan context).[39] If the hypothesis is on the right track that a tradition, based on Daniel 7, which expected an individual Son of Man with a judicial task to appear at the end, was evolving in Jesus' time, the old view that Jesus expected such an eschatological figure but did not identify himself with it is still plausible.[40] In the final analysis, a decision on this issue is not crucial, since Jesus seems, on the basis the evidence presented above, to have thought that he would have a special role in the end events anyway, apart from the question of titles.

Like some other Galilean healers,[41] Jesus must have felt himself to be in a close personal, even filial communion with God, whom he called Father (*abba*).[42] It seems safe to assume that Jesus' conviction of a special calling or sending (Matt. 10:40) in view of the coming of the kingdom is also linked to his discovery of his ability to heal and to exorcise (cf. Luke 10:18). But on the whole only very hypothetical answers can be given to the question of Jesus' self-understanding. What *is* clear is that Jesus must have made a tremendous impact on his first followers. Probably a great deal of the christological speculation during the first hundred years or so can be traced back to the memory of his electrifying person, actualized and enhanced in the worship of the early Christians.

What Difference Did Easter Make?

The Easter event seems to have made little impact on the transmitters of Q. In this document, no weight is put on the resurrection of Jesus, which is not even mentioned in so many words; the emphasis lies entirely on Jesus' mission and teaching and the more or less imminent coming of the Son of Man. A comparable lack of interest is later found in the reports on the views of the conservative Jewish Christian Ebionites, who regarded Jesus as a righteous man who received a special task and a spiritual equipment in his baptism. Resurrection here seems to be more like an appendix to the career of a teacher and a prophet.

On the whole, however, the Easter experiences started a far-reaching process of interpretation among the followers of Jesus. These visions, in which Jesus was apparently seen or felt as a luminous presence, gave rise to the conviction that he had been exalted to a heavenly throne next to God. Various existing traditions may have facilitated such an interpretation, for example the notion of exaltation ("rapture") of humans (for example, Enoch) to heaven or the conviction that righteous martyrs would be vindicated.[43] Psalm 110:1, a promise by Yahweh to the Israelite king believed to be recorded by David ("The Lord said to my Lord, 'Sit at my right hand until I put your enemies under your feet'") was repeatedly cited to explain what had happened.[44] The hymn quoted by Paul in Phil. 2:6-11 praises the exalted Jesus by saying that God gave him his own name "Lord," *kyrios* (v. 9); this entails the highest possible position of honor and power. A depiction of the enthronement in the heavenly court is given in Rev. 5:6-13.[45] Thus Jesus was in a

hidden manner already reigning over the world and ready to return soon in order to subject the world to God's rule in a definitive way.

A creedal formula, probably from Antioch, quoted (and adapted) by Paul in Rom. 1:3-4, indicates that the man Jesus, of Davidic descent, was installed into a new status of power on the basis of the resurrection, the twofold structure of the statement suggesting some kind of contrast between the two halves:[46] "(Paul is a servant of) the gospel of his Son, who was descended from the seed of David in terms of the flesh (*kata sarka*) and was appointed (*horisthentos*) Son of God in power in terms of the spirit of holiness (*kata pneuma hagiosynes*) as from the resurrection of the dead (*ex anastaseos nekron*), Jesus Christ our Lord."[47]

"The originally exchangeable expressions Son of David and Son of God are here conferred on the earthly Jesus and the risen Lord, it being presupposed that before his death Jesus was Messiah-designate, and that the resurrection implied a new position."[48] A similar point is made in sermons attributed to Peter and Paul by the author of Acts. The resurrection vindicated Jesus' message about the imminent kingdom of God (cf. Acts 17:31). Jesus, the righteous one, had been killed by lawless men, but God had raised him up from among the dead and exalted him to a place of lordship at his own right hand (Acts 2:22-36; Ps. 110 is quoted). God *made* Jesus, who had been crucified, Lord and Christ (Messiah), according to Peter (Acts 2:36). Luke's Paul for his part quotes Ps. 2:7 and applies it to Jesus' resurrection: what God had promised to the ancestors, he fulfilled "by raising Jesus, as also it is written in the second psalm, 'You are my Son, today I have begotten you'" (Acts 13:32-33). As in Rom. 1:4, Jesus' divine sonship is connected precisely with his resurrection.

Even though Acts is a relatively late literary document, this christological conception must be old. If a Christology "from below" did not exist at a very early stage, one wonders how it could have come into existence at all, given the increasing tendency to venerate Jesus in very exalted ways.[49] Presumably the author had access to archaic traditions through contacts with Jewish Christian groups.[50] His own Christology combines different approaches that are in mutual tension, but the dominant impression still is that "the Lukan Jesus is a figure who is very much subordinate to God, . . . supremely a *man* chosen by God to do God's will (Acts 2:22; 17:31)."[51]

In accordance with this theocentric Christology, Luke has preserved an archaic designation of Jesus that is rarely used elsewhere, the term (God's) *servant* (*pais*): the enemies had "gathered together against your holy servant Jesus whom you anointed" (Acts 4:27), but God "has glorified his servant Jesus whom you [the Jerusalemites] handed over and rejected" (3:13); "God raised up his servant" (3:26). This usage is influenced by biblical references to David as God's servant (for example, Ps. 18:1; cf. Luke 1:69; Acts 4:25) and carries a "royal-messianic connotation."[52] The antiquity of this notion, which clearly subordinates Jesus to God, is indicated by the fact that, apart from Septuagint quotations, *pais* is used as a title of Jesus almost exclusively in liturgical material of the first and early second centuries (*1 Clem.* 59.2-4; *Mart. Pol.* 14.1, 3; 20.2; *Did.* 9.2-3; 10.2-3).[53]

Support for the subordination Christology of Acts comes from the Epistle to the Hebrews. There too the point is made that Jesus has *become* what he is by virtue of an act of *appointment*. This idea recurs prominently throughout Hebrews (though there is also a different line of thought, on which see below). Jesus has *become*

superior to the angels (Heb. 1:4); he has been begotten by God to *become* his Son (1:5; 5:5, both verses citing Ps. 2:7); Heb. 5:5 makes clear that this happened on the basis of Jesus' death. He has been anointed by God above his fellows (1:9), crowned with glory and made perfect because of his suffering, through which he learned obedience (2:9-10; 5:7-8). This is why he is able to help those who suffer (4:15). He was appointed by God and reckoned to be more worthy than Moses (3:2-3).

A peculiar later variant of the view that the man Jesus was elevated to heavenly company is offered by Hermas in the course of a rather diffuse exposition of the parable of the vineyard. Jesus was God's servant; God had caused "the holy preexistent spirit" to indwell "in the flesh that he [God] wished." Since Jesus' flesh cooperated so willingly with this divine spirit, "walking in holiness and purity," God promoted him to be "a partner with the Holy Spirit" (*Sim.* 5.5-6). Thus in the beginning there were apparently *two* divine beings, God the Father and the Spirit (whom Hermas also calls the "Son"). The Savior, or Lord, was elevated to be their companion as a reward for his merits.[54] This notion of God may be characterized as "an amalgam of binitarianism and adoptianism,"[55] "binitarianism" here denoting a dyad of which Christ is not a part!

JESUS' FUTURE TASK

Somewhat like the Son of Man in the *Similitudes of Enoch*, Jesus was expected soon to return from his exalted position in heaven as redeemer and judge. The believers wait for the Son of God, "who rescues us from the wrath that is coming" (1 Thess. 1:10; cf. Phil. 3:20). Once again, an

200 ancient idea is preserved by the author of Acts when he lets Peter preach repentance to the Israelites "so that times of refreshing may come from the presence of the Lord, and that he may send the Messiah appointed for you, that is, Jesus, who must remain in heaven until the time of universal restoration that God announced long ago through his holy prophets" (Acts 3:20-21).[56] The joyful petition "Our Lord, come!" of the early community has even been preserved in its original Aramaic diction (*maranatha*, 1 Cor. 16:22; *Did.* 10.6; in Greek in Rev. 22:20). Paul describes the return of Jesus to gather the faithful in a colorful passage that draws on traditional material in 1 Thessalonians 4. In this passage, the word *parousia* is used of Jesus' "coming" (1 Thess. 4:15). This word, which was to become in Christian vocabulary a technical term for Jesus' return, carries imperial overtones, being routinely used of a ruler's visit in a town, as well as of epiphanies of Gods.[57]

An early hymn cited by Paul extols the awaited ultimate victory of Jesus when "every knee in heaven and on earth and under the earth" will bow to him and "every tongue" will confess his lordship (Phil. 2:10-11). Christ will destroy "every ruler and every authority and power," including superhuman powers such as Death, the "last enemy" (1 Cor. 15:24-26).

In the pseudo-Pauline 2 Thessalonians, the adversary to be defeated by the Lord Jesus "with the breath of his mouth" is the "man of lawlessness," who will, in the spirit of Antiochus Epiphanes or Caligula, take his seat in the temple and declare himself to be God (2 Thess. 2:3-12). In the book of Revelation the returning Jesus appears as a terrifying warrior, "King of kings and Lord of lords," clothed in a robe dipped in blood, followed by the armies of heaven. "From his mouth comes a sharp sword with which to strike down the nations, and he will rule them with a rod of iron; he will tread the winepress of the fury of the wrath of God the Almighty" (Rev. 19:11-16). The slaughter of the kings of the earth and their armies is followed by a judgment and the millennial reign of the resurrected martyrs with Christ (Rev. 19:17—20:6). In episodes like this the coming Jesus does carry out a function that is, by way of exception, characteristic of the Messiah in politically attuned Jewish traditions, though in a more gruesome way than in any known Jewish source.[58]

In the Synoptic tradition, Jesus' future task as judge is often closely connected with his characterization as the Son of Man, that mysterious figure from the book of Daniel. This emphasis is crucial in Q (Q 12:8-9; 17:27-35). Even apart from that title, Jesus has a grand eschatological role in Q: Jerusalem will still see him (Q 13:34-35), and the parable of the nobleman (Q 19:12-26) shows Jesus as "the unique mediator of the kingdom"[59] who will return with royal power (v. 15). In Mark, Jesus' eschatological speech in chapter 13 has a central place (more so than in Matthew or Luke, who have to pay increasing attention to the problem of the delay of the parousia); it culminates in the promise that the Son of Man, here clearly identified with Jesus, will come "in clouds with great power and glory" (v. 26). In the post-Pauline Pastoral Epistles, epiphany language commonly associated with rulers and their cult is used with reference to Jesus' return, even though the word *parousia* does not occur (1 Tim. 6:14; 2 Tim. 4:1, 8; Titus 2:13). The talk of the "epiphany of the Savior" is probably intended as a Christian response to the claims of the ruler cult (in which the emperor was widely acknowledged as a "savior," bringing "salvation" to the world by his achievements).[60] The connection is hardly surprising: both the Hellenistic ruler cult and the Jewish messianic idea, of which the Christian notion is a modification, go back to the same source, the kingship ideology of the ancient Near East. No wonder that the two later merge in the Byzantine Empire.

But no matter how high Jesus' new name (Phil. 2:9), in the end the Son will surrender all power to the Father, who then is "all in all" (1 Cor. 15:28).[61] Indeed, for Paul, Jesus is the Son of God supremely as one who is *obedient.* Paul thinks, at least most of the time, within a clearly monotheistic framework. The status of Jesus as the one to whom every knee shall bow almost seems to elevate Jesus to take the place of Yahweh himself, for in the Bible (Isa. 45:23) "every knee" is said to bow to God. Yet it is explicitly stated that the purpose of all this homage to Jesus is to bring glory to God the Father (Phil. 2:11). Jesus' lordship is a way of distinguishing Jesus from God.[62] Even as the Lord of his devotees, the Son remains subordinate to the Father.

Jesus' Present Function

From the beginning, believers venerated the risen Jesus as their Lord whose return to take over power in the world they awaited—and anticipated in their worship. Early on the cultic acclamation *kyrios Iesous* (Jesus is the Lord)[63] is attested; Paul already knows it as a traditional formula (1 Cor. 12:3; Rom. 10:9; Phil. 2:11). The notion of heavenly enthronement, to be followed by a victorious return, implies the claim that the whole world is to be subjected to Jesus. The designation *kyrios* is better suited than "Christ," with its national associations, to express the universal claim of the Risen One. As *the* Lord he is more than just "our" Lord.[64]

Jesus quickly became the object of devotion in Christian cult. Prayers could be addressed to him. The early Aramaic exclamation *maranatha* ("our Lord, come!") addresses him directly, asking him to return soon. Paul mentions his own repeated (vain!) requests to the Lord (Jesus) to take off his "thorn in the flesh" and thus act as a personal helper and healer (2 Cor. 12:8-9). Baptism is undertaken "in the name" of Jesus; the exalted Jesus is believed to preside at the "Lord's Supper," a cultic meal. Paul routinely places Jesus alongside God in his letter openings: the grace and peace which he wishes his addressees will come from God the Father and from Jesus Christ (for example, 1 Thess. 1:1; 1 Cor. 1:3).

Such devotion to someone other than God is unprecedented in the context of Jewish monotheism,[65] but it does not equate Jesus with God. Thanksgiving is, in Paul's letters, never addressed to Christ, but always to God (1 Thess. 1:2; 1 Cor. 1:4; 2 Cor. 1:3; Phil. 1:3), though it is sometimes mediated "through Christ" (Rom. 1:8; 7:25). The scholarly debate whether one should speak of worship (Hurtado) or only of veneration of Jesus (Dunn) appears to be a battle over words: both sides acknowledge both that Lord Jesus enjoys an extraordinary status in the cult, and that the boundary line between the Father and him has not been crossed. We may say that Jesus was worshiped, but this still means "something short of the adoration reserved for God alone" (Dunn); cultic worship is offered to Jesus "in obedience to the one God, and God 'the Father' is given primacy" (Hurtado).[66] The difference is clearest in the context of eschatology. When Paul speaks of the last things in 1 Corinthians 15, the distinction between the Son and the Father, to whom the Son eventually surrenders authority, could not be clearer, whereas in the hymns and prayers of the cultic gatherings, it tends to get blurred.

202   Still, in the Pastoral Epistles, Jesus, the mediator between God and humans, is explicitly called a *man* (1 Tim. 2:5). In light of this passage, Titus 2:13 should hardly be read as implying that Jesus is in some sense "God";[67] it is feasible to translate (with the NRSV footnote): "we wait for the blessed hope and the manifestation of the glory of the great God and our Savior Jesus Christ," the reference being to two different persons.[68]

The much-discussed issue whether monotheism remains intact in this worship also seems a moot question. Monotheism is a flexible (modern!) category. Yet the more one emphasizes the actual devotion to Jesus (rather than the honorific words used about him), the more plausible it is (against the intentions of scholars such as Hurtado) to see in it a latent tendency toward *ditheism*, a doctrine of two Gods. Celsus for one was of the view that Christians acted inconsistently in that they rejected the worship of the Gods, claiming to revere only the one true God, and yet they "worshiped to an extravagant degree" the man Jesus (Origen, *Cels.* 8.12). The two Deities are not equal, however. Jesus appears as a sort of deified hero whose place is below the supreme God, but who is a Godlike being himself.[69] Cultic enthusiasm, sometimes extravagant, did for Jesus what popular devotion was later to do for his mother.

As angels were rarely given such high honors in Jewish piety, the closest contemporary point of comparison remains the cult of personal helpers, such as Heracles or Asclepius, and of foreign savior deities, notably Isis and Serapis; they too were thought of as *kosmokrators*[70] to whom their devotees developed a personal relationship. The main differences are that Christians expected final salvation in the future and that their world ruler was a figure from recent history.[71]

As time passed, the emphasis laid on the present glory and reign of Jesus as the heavenly Lord increased. Paul already betrays a shift from the future toward the present. In his depiction of the parousia in 1 Corinthians 15, the statement "he must reign," a conclusion from two biblical verses, in all likelihood refers to Christ's present reign before the parousia (see above, p. 99), though his final overthrow of the hostile powers still lies in the future. A few decades later the author of Ephesians, a disciple and imitator of Paul, even relates the biblical verses that refer to this victory (Pss. 110:1; 8:6) to the *present* status of Christ (Eph. 1:20-22). The Pastoral Epistles (for example, Titus 2:13) and Luke (for example, Luke 2:11) apply to Jesus the term *Savior* (*soter*), which was associated in Greek ears with honoring rulers.

The author of Revelation applies to Jesus expressions that are elsewhere used of an angel (Rev. 1:13-16; 14:14).[72] What is startling is that Jesus is worshiped without embarrassment (while the angel who appears to John forbids worship of himself; the object of worship can be God alone: 19:10; 22:9). John implicitly makes some extraordinarily high claims for Jesus by virtually placing him in a divine category while still maintaining a monotheistic framework,[73] but he is well aware that God and Jesus are separate. God is Jesus' "Father" (1:6; 2:27; 3:5, 21; 14:1); Jesus is never called either *pantokrator* ("Almighty," the oft-repeated epithet of God in this writing, a rendering of Hebrew *sebaot*) or *theos*.

The believed reign of Christ entailed a powerful missionary impulse: the imminent and inaugurated lordship of Jesus was to be proclaimed to the world. In the old hymnic fragment 1 Tim. 3:16, his victory is claimed as a fact already realized: "revealed in flesh, vindicated in spirit, seen by angels, proclaimed among Gentiles, believed in throughout the world, taken up in glory." Paul was driven by this conviction to ever new efforts to bring about "obedience of faith" (Rom. 1:5) toward the Lord. A generation later, the grand finale of the Gospel of Matthew (Matt. 28:18-20) portrays the risen Jesus as a heavenly figure to whom "all power" has been given both in heaven and on earth. He will be present with his followers throughout their time on earth, and his presence means (or mediates) the presence of God (28:20; cf. 18:20); he bears the title Immanuel, "God with us" (1:23).[74] Here Jesus' actions and those of God overlap significantly. While this is still a far cry from Chalcedonian orthodoxy, a uniquely exalted status is already being claimed for Jesus.[75]

Paul, however, also envisages a more intimate presence of Jesus among the believers. He seems to assume that the person of Christ is some kind of "macro-entity," enveloping and encompassing all Christians so that they are "in" him (see also above, pp. 174–75) or "clothed with" him (Gal. 3:26-27). One characteristic context relates to the way in which the Christians have somehow been joined to the death of Jesus (for example, Rom. 6:3, 11; 8:1). In a key passage, the expression "in Christ" parallels "in Adam" (1 Cor. 15:22). As a new Adam, Jesus is the source and origin of a new humanity, so that all who are "in him" can share in the new life that is his by virtue of his resurrection.[76] His resurrection is the firstfruits, the guarantee that others will be raised to postmortem life as well.

The corporate "in Christ" language may have been derived from Jewish ideas of national solidarity and the way in which Jews could identify themselves as a group with their ancestors,[77] but then Paul has developed the usage far beyond this. The "ancestor" in whose destiny one can participate is now a figure of the recent past, and the devotee's union with him has intimate personal overtones. This is what really makes Paul tick. Jesus is, to change the image, the firstborn within a large family (Rom. 8:29). His divine sonship is a status to be *shared* with others. But therefore Jesus' full humanity is crucial. Much of Paul's view of salvation *demands that Jesus be fully human*: as the new Adam (see also Rom. 5:12-19), he is the one who, for the first time, related to God in the way human beings should.[78] But we will see that a strong tension arises in Paul's thought at this point, as he also indicates that Jesus was sent to the world in the "likeness" (only?) of humans.

In Hebrews, too, Jesus is the supreme representative of (other) humans. Hebrews 2:6-8 (Ps. 8:4-6) makes very clear that Jesus is above all seen as a human figure.[79] His exalted position is one to be shared by others in the future, his role being to "bring *many* children to glory" (2:10). Therefore he is called the "pioneer" (*archegos*) of their salvation (2:10; 12:2), and a forerunner (6:20). This is similar in some ways to Paul's Adam Christology, though lacking any notion of corporate personality. On the other hand, Jesus' present significance is interpreted in priestly terms. Christ is imagined as dwelling in heaven as the priestly mediator between God and humans; he is depicted as continuously employed in the office of the Jewish high priest (rather than as eschatological ruler or judge; 5:14-16; 7:24-25). Having made his once-for-all sacrifice, Jesus continually pleads the cause of other humans before God.

Luke tends to play down somewhat the significance of the return of Jesus at the end of time, placing more stress on the *present lordship* of Jesus in the church.[80] The ascension story (Luke 24; Acts 1; anticipated in Luke 9:31, 51) is pivotal for Luke. Yet Luke is different both from Paul and from Matthew in that he presents Jesus as

204 for the most part *absent* in the post-Easter period (the ascension is an exaltation to heaven, a final removal). Any mediation between the heavenly world of God and the world of everyday events is principally through the holy spirit, not the risen Jesus.[81]

JESUS' PAST MINISTRY

Death

The early followers of Jesus wrestled in many ways with the offense caused by his death on the cross. He was seen as a rejected prophet and an envoy of Wisdom (Q 11:49-51; cf. 1 Thess. 2:15), as an innocent sufferer given into the hands of men (the Synoptic passion narratives, using biblical language: Pss. 22 and 69; cf. Isa. 53). His fate was planned by divine providence; this is why he was delivered into the hands of wicked humans (for example, Mark 9:31 par.; Acts 3:15). Jesus was obedient to death (Phil. 2:8). The obedience shown by him in his agonizing prayer (the Gethsemane tradition, Mark 14:32-42 par.; Heb. 5:5-10) was highlighted: "Although he was a Son, he learned obedience through what he suffered; and having been made perfect, he became the source of eternal salvation for all who obey him" (Heb. 5:8-9). Others found a causal connection between Jesus' death and the salvation of humans. Christ bore the curse that rested on humans, effecting reconciliation or expiation.

This wrestling of early Christians with the death of Jesus was discussed in chapter 7 above, but one central additional point is to be noted here. The scandalous fact of the cross came to have a strong effect on the way in which the nature of Jesus' (axiomatic) messiahship was conceived: the category of the *suffering Messiah* emerged. The term *Christ* thus rapidly lost its original, nationally oriented, royal-eschatological significance; Paul already uses it almost as a surname of Jesus. But Paul, too, often connects, paradoxically and provocatively, the title with Jesus' death on the cross; he speaks of "Christ crucified" and never, say, of the "crucified Lord." The outcome was that the nature of Jesus' putative messiahship was changed, being now associated with weakness and death (though the eschatological passage 1 Cor. 15:23-28 is still reminiscent of royal messianism).[82] Something similar happened to the designation "Son of Man," originally connected with exaltation and glory, which came to be associated with suffering and death in some strands of the Synoptic tradition ("the Son of Man must undergo great suffering," Mark 8:31 par.).[83]

Luke in particular promotes this development of a Christian doctrine of the Messiah. It is precisely in his capacity of "Christ" that Jesus has suffered. "The Christ *must* suffer," the risen Jesus instructs his followers, going through the whole scripture from Moses to all the prophets to prove his case (Luke 24:26-27). Luke wisely refrains from specifying the alleged predictions. He simply assumes that so central a fact must have been announced by the holy writers; the suffering of the Messiah emerges (ex post facto, of course) as a necessity imposed by the divine order of salvation history. This claim that the "Messiah must suffer" (as prophesied) seems to be a Lukan innovation.[84]

Luke also tacitly does away with a political doctrine of the Messiah. He effectively deletes almost all the ideas and expectations associated with the term *Messiah* in Jewish thought. Jesus is a royal, even Davidic, figure, but his throne is in heaven, not on earth. Luke pays lip service to the expectation of a this-worldly kingdom in, for example, the hymn of Zechariah (Luke 1:68-75), but already there he insinuates that the political prediction finds its fulfillment in the spiritual phenomenon of the forgiveness of sins. Gradually the "kingdom for Israel" (Acts 1:6) drops out of sight altogether. Jesus is a Davidic king, but one who is quite unlike any Davidide who has reigned in the past, and his activities also differ from those expected of the Davidic Messiah. The Gospel of John connects Jesus' death with his exaltation, in its own manner getting rid of the offense (see below, p. 219).[85]

Actions

Paul pays practically no attention to Jesus' life, apart from the events of death and resurrection. However, this life was of interest to some branches of tradition, especially of course to such circles as had had contact with the historical Nazarene. Naturally Jesus' career was reinterpreted, as it was in retrospect seen in light of his subsequent exaltation and in light of the experiences of the communities that cherished the traditions about him.

Jesus was often regarded as a *prophet* (Mark 8:27-28 par.; Luke 7:16; 24:19), and he is remembered to have used the title as a self-designation (Mark 6:4 par.; Luke 13:33). The category of "prophet" is somewhat vague. One so designated may be regarded as a recipient of divine revelation (in the tradition of the biblical "book" prophets), a sage, or one who does marvelous deeds with the help of God's power (like Elijah or even Moses in the biblical tradition, or the "sign prophets" reported by Josephus). It is the last aspect that is prominent in the case of Jesus, "a prophet mighty in deed and word before God and all the people" (Luke 24:19). But there was also a tradition about a particular eschatological prophet who was to appear to fulfill the promise given by God to Moses: "I will raise up for them a prophet like you from among their own people" (Deut. 18:18). Jesus is set forth as the fulfillment of this promise in speeches attributed to Peter (Acts 3:22-23) and Stephen (Acts 7:37).[86] The notion of Jesus as the promised prophet from among the people is of a piece with the archaic Jewish Christian picture of Jesus as a man chosen by God for a special task, of which we have seen other glimpses in Acts 2–4. Among the proto-orthodox, this category declined, but it was long retained in Jewish Christian circles, especially in those responsible for the Jewish Christian layer of the *Pseudo-Clementines*.[87] In the "*Ebionite History*" (*Rec.* 1.27-71), Jesus appears as the prophet predicted by Moses, who has come to abolish the sacrifices (1.37.2-3; 1.54.1), but also as the Christ who has come and who will come again (1.49.4; 1.69.4).[88]

Those who had known Jesus in person could hardly forget that he was prominent as a healer, exorcist, and miracle worker. These memories are strongly present in Q and the Synoptic Gospels.[89] In Q, Jesus' healing activity is described in terms that suggest that the new age promised by Isaiah (Isa. 61:1; 29:18-19; 35:5-6) is being inaugurated: "the blind receive their sight, the lame walk, the lepers are cleansed, the deaf hear, the dead are raised, the poor have good news brought to them" (Q 7:22).[90] Jesus' healings and exorcisms serve the breakthrough of God's rule (Q 11:20). Loyalty to old tradition may be detected in that neither in connection with healing nor anywhere else in Q is the term *Christ* used; it seems as if the bearers and molders of the Q tradition felt that the term does not fit the facts. Jesus acts as the envoy and authoritative teacher of Wisdom, healing the sick and authorizing others to do that too.

Mark, too, portrays Jesus as a powerful and colorful exorcist (for example, Mark 1:23-28; 5:1-20); yet his Jesus is much mightier than this. Mark's picture is colored by the post-Easter conviction of Jesus' close communion with God: he "transfers back into Jesus' life the divine dignity of Jesus which is in substance grounded in the Easter appearances."[91] The winds and waves of the sea obey his commands (4:35-41), as they obey Yahweh's commands in biblical psalms (see Ps. 106:9); Jesus walks freely on water (Mark 6:45-52) and miraculously transforms tiny elements of food into a meal for thousands (6:35-44; 8:1-9). Such marvels raise the question, "Who is this?" (4:41), and apparently they eventually evoke from Peter the confession that Jesus is the Christ (8:29). The Messiah/Christ is, for Mark, a being with supernatural powers,[92] and the transfiguration scene (9:2-10) shows in an anticipatory way that Jesus really belongs to the heavenly realm into which he will one day be exalted.[93]

Mark's Jesus shares in heavenly powers, but that does not make him equal to God. God alone, not Jesus (or any other human), is to be called "good" (Mark 10:18); precisely as the "Son" Jesus has to subject himself to the will of the Father, which is not an easy task at all (14:36). The Father also possesses knowledge that is inaccessible to the Son (13:32). Jesus owes his dignity wholly to the power of God that overcomes death. Nevertheless, a divine splendor also lies over his life, though shrouded in mystery. Mark has taken steps on the road that eventually leads to the deification of Jesus.[94]

This, however, is not the whole story. Mark also makes much of Jesus' destiny as the suffering Son of Man. This necessary suffering is the other side of the coin, and it may have something to do with the veil of secrecy that Mark at times[95]

spreads over Jesus (for example, Mark 3:7-12; 8:30; 9:9).[96] Jesus' glory cannot be understood apart from his suffering—and vice versa. For Mark, the title "Christ" is not sufficient, if one wants to understand Jesus properly. The reason for this may be that "Christ" still has for Mark (differently, for example, from the usage in Paul) connotations of glory, even if the splendor of national restoration has been replaced by the glory of miraculous power. To get the full picture, the designations "Christ" and "Son of God" (used as synonyms in 14:62) must be taken together with the title "Son of Man," whose mission it is to suffer. That the suffering of the Messiah is difficult to accept is shown by Peter's desperate reaction to Jesus' announcement of his passion, a reaction that Jesus refutes with the strongest of words (8:32-33).

For Matthew, Jesus' healings can fittingly be called "works of *the Christ*" (Matt. 11:2);[97] the intrinsically messianic title "Son of David" often occurs, surprisingly enough, precisely in connection with healing (9:27; 12:33; 15:32; 20:30-31). Perhaps Matthew consciously seeks to alter other conceptions of what Davidic messiahship is all about: it is not a question of political leadership but of merciful healing activity.[98] Even a quotation from the Suffering Servant passage, Isaiah 53, much belabored in earliest Christianity, is applied by Matthew to Jesus' miracles rather than to his passion: the phrase "he bore our diseases" (Isa. 53:4, quoted in Matt. 8:17) is taken to imply simply that he removed the diseases, not that he vicariously bore our sins. Although Matthew, possibly responding to hostile remarks by nonbelieving Jews, emphasizes the traditional qualifications that should prove that Jesus is indeed the Messiah of Israel (Davidic descent, birth in Bethlehem), he interprets the role of the Messiah without reference to the liberation of the people from foreign domination, with a view to spiritual qualities only.

Luke gives a stylized picture of Jesus as the loving savior who was a friend of sinners, compassionately inviting "the lost" to repent and to gain salvation (for example, Luke 15:1-32; 19:1-10; 7:36-50; 23:42-43). His miracles breathe the same spirit; when the Lord saw the widow who had lost her only son, "he had compassion for her and said to her, 'Do not weep,'" and called the dead young man to rise up (Luke 7:13-14). Acts summarizes: "God anointed Jesus of Nazareth with the holy spirit and with power" so that "he went about doing good and healing all who were oppressed by the devil, for God was with him" (Acts 10:38). Even more than the Synoptic stories, miracle stories in John draw attention to the person of Jesus himself. For John, Jesus' miracles are *signs* that reveal Jesus as the promised deliverer to those with eyes to see (for example, John 2:11, 4:54, 20:30).

The Peter of Acts locates the "anointing" mentioned in Acts 10:38 with Jesus' baptism (v. 37). In this he follows a strong tradition that contends that Jesus' ability to work wonders is to be traced back to that very event. At the time of the baptism, the spirit descends on him (Matt. 3:16; Luke 3:22) or enters *into* him (Mark 1:10)[99] "like a dove," and a heavenly voice declares him to be God's Son. Jesus' divine sonship is thus dated back from the resurrection to the beginning of his public career.[100] It is based on Jesus' permanent endowment with God's spirit, which takes possession of him; indwelling in him, it makes him capable of marvelous deeds (cf. also Matt. 12:18-21; Luke 4:14-22). Isaiah 42:1, a verse speaking of God's elected Prophet-Servant, is alluded to in the words "with you I am well pleased" (Mark 1:11 par.). The Markan story implies that "Jesus was an ordinary man—not divine—before he

was filled with the Spirit at his baptism."[101] One stream of the tradition, preserved in some manuscripts in Luke 3:22, lets the divine voice speak with the words of Ps. 2:7 (elsewhere applied to the resurrection): "You are my Son, *today I have begotten you.*"[102] Matthew and Luke (according to the majority of manuscripts) differ somewhat from Mark; their versions suggest that the baptism confirms Jesus' already existing sonship.[103]

The notion that Jesus, an ordinary righteous man, was endowed with special powers since his baptism lives on in the thought world of the

8.1   Christ and John the Baptist, detail from the Baptism mosaic of the Dome of the Baptistery of the Arians. Sixth century C.E. Baptistery of the Arians, Ravenna, Italy. Photo: © Scala/Ministero per i Beni e le Attività culturali/Art Resource, NY.

208   Ebionites. Jesus became acceptable to God, since he did everything according to the law, being the most pious of all humans (Hippolytus, *Haer.* 7.34-35). He is "a prophet, man, Son of God, and Christ—and yet a mere man . . . though owing to virtue of life he has come to be called the Son of God" (Epiphanius, *Pan.* 30.18.6; cf. Eusebius, *Hist. eccl.* 3.27). Baptism is the turning point: "They mean that Jesus is really a man . . . but that Christ, who descended in the form of a dove, has entered him . . . and been united with him" (*Pan.* 30.14.4; cf. 30.16.3; 30.18.5). In this report by Epiphanius, the "spirit" of Mark's baptism story has been replaced by "Christ," and the latter term has come to denote in a rather un-Jewish way a divine element that can enter a human being. But otherwise the notion is in keeping with the earliest (Markan) account, and the *Gospel of the Ebionites*, quoted by Epiphanius in the same connection (*Pan.* 30.13.7-8), follows the Markan wording: "he saw the *holy spirit* in the form of a dove coming down and entering him." The spirit is also mentioned in a fragment of the *Gospel of the Hebrews*. Having come down on Jesus, the spirit speaks to him: "My Son, I was waiting for you in all the prophets, waiting for you to come so I could rest in you. For you are my rest; you are my first-begotten Son who rules forever."[104] The passage reflects the Jewish idea of "God's eternal and personified Wisdom that is wandering and looking for a place to rest" (cf. Sir. 24:6-7); this is finally found in Jesus, who becomes God's Son at his baptism.[105]

The old view, which may be called "possessionist," was that Jesus worked wonders with the help of God's spirit, which indwelt him since his baptism. This view persevered even outside Jewish Christianity in what came to be called "dynamic monarchianism," represented, for example, at the end of the second century by the shoemaker Theodotus of Byzantium (see Hippolytus, *Haer.* 7.35)[106] and still in the third century by Paul of Samosata, who distinguished between the "Word" and Jesus.[107] Behind such a view was clearly a concern to save monotheism, due to the (not quite unfounded) "suspicion that orthodoxy was virtually committed to ditheism."[108] The special twist given to this possessionist notion in what can be called *separationist* Christology (the spirit becomes an active agent that works through the man Jesus but is finally separated from him when Jesus is going to die), represented by Cerinthus and many gnostic Christians,[109] is discussed below (pp. 222–23).

It is not just Jesus' power to work miracles that sets him apart. Jesus possesses a special *authority* from God (Mark 1:22, 27) that legitimizes and makes possible other extraordinary actions, such as the "cleansing" of the temple (Mark 11:28-33 par.).[110] The Synoptic Gospels emphasize that Jesus was authorized by God to heal even on the Sabbath ("the Son of Man is Lord even of the sabbath," Mark 2:28 par.)[111] and to forgive sins, an act that Jesus' adversaries in the story world take to interfere with God's exclusive right to forgive (Mark 2:5-12 par.) and that in the minds of believing hearers of the story no doubt puts Jesus on a level close to God.[112]

Teaching

A number of traditions make much of Jesus' teaching—of his role as an envoy of Wisdom, a sovereign interpreter of the law, or the bringer of enlightenment to the ignorant. Much of this was discussed in the section on "Saving Knowledge" (in chapter 7), so that a few general points may suffice here. Paul, who focuses on Jesus' saving work, supplies little of his teaching. Q portrays Jesus as the messenger of divine Wisdom; he possesses an intimate knowledge of God that he is also able to communicate to his followers (Q 10:22).[113] In Matthew (for example, Matt. 11:28-30), the figure of Jesus approaches that of Wisdom, with whom Jesus even seems to be more or less identified.[114] For Matthew, Jesus is also a new Moses figure who fulfills the mission of Moses, the great legislator, providing an even more profound, authoritative interpretation of the law. Matthew collects the teachings of Jesus into five long speeches, the best known of which is the first one, the programmatic Sermon on the Mount; throughout, Jesus speaks "in a majestic, powerful, and completely authoritative stature."[115]

The *Gospel of Thomas* consists wholly of a string of "secret words" spoken by "the living Jesus" to his inner circle. Jesus' "redemptive role" is "that of a teacher who shows the way to others";[116] eventually his person is to yield to his message altogether (*Gos. Thom.* 13; 108). The salvation-historical bond to Israel is broken (for example, 52); Jesus is the mediator of timeless esoteric wisdom. The *Gospel of Thomas* contains a number of old traditions (many sayings and parables are arguably independent of the Synoptic tradition, and a few may well have preserved a more ancient form) to which later layers of sayings with a more Platonic or mystical orientation have been added. Jesus reveals and underlines the true origin of the soul and its path back to the supreme God.

In a somewhat similar vein, John also has a number of revelation speeches. John ascribes them all to the earthly (rather than the risen) Jesus, but they are thoroughly permeated by insights gathered during many decades after Easter. The promise of the sending of the Paraclete (the Advocate), the holy spirit, who will not only remind the disciples of what Jesus has said but also teach them everything (John 14:26; cf.

15:26), sounds rather like an admission that the Gospel contains revelations that were not yet accessible to the followers of Jesus during his time on the earth. The spirit will guide them into "all the truth" and "glorify" Jesus (16:13-14), and indeed the Fourth Gospel is full of such glorification. Unlike the Synoptic tradition, and also unlike *Thomas* and the gnostics, John's speeches focus almost totally on the person of Jesus himself. As Rudolf Bultmann put it, "Jesus as the Revealer of God reveals nothing but that he is the Revealer."[117]

The perspective of *Thomas* is shared by a large number of gnostic Christian writings. Christ is portrayed as a (school) teacher in Valentinian texts; *Gos. Truth* 19.19-20 explicitly states that he went to "schools" and "spoke the word as a teacher," and *Interp. Know.* 9 calls him the church's "teacher of immortality." "Jesus Christ enlightened those who were in darkness because of forgetfulness. He showed (them) the way, and that way is the truth he taught them" (*Gos. Truth* 18.16-21).

JESUS' BIRTH

The beginning of Jesus' special relationship to God and the heavenly world continued to be dated further back from resurrection and baptism; soon it came to be connected with his conception in his mother's womb.[118]

Paul states that Jesus was, as a true human, "born of a woman" (Gal. 4:4), but he shows no interest in the circumstances of the birth. Mark has no birth narrative (nor has John).[119] By contrast, Matthew and Luke have stories connected with Jesus' birth.[120] The two sets of stories are quite different, yet some sort of common substratum

210 shines through. It consists of a Hellenistic Jewish Christian tradition concerning the miraculous nature of Jesus' birth. His mother, Mary, betrothed but not yet formally married, became pregnant without sexual intercourse "from the holy spirit" (Matt 1:20; Luke 1:35 resorts to more circumspect language); the matter was explained either to Mary (Luke) or to her fiancé (Matthew) by an angel.[121]

For Matthew, however, the virgin birth is something of an embarrassment, since it seems to jeopardize Jesus' Davidic ancestry.[122] To Matthew, it is all-important that the Messiah be a descendant of David.[123] Thus he puts together an artful genealogy in which three series of fourteen generations (a sign of God's providential planning) lead from Abraham through David and his royal descendants to Joseph (Matt. 1:1-17). If, however, Jesus was not Joseph's son, the genealogy seems pointless. Matthew is concerned to show that this is not so; he emphasizes that Joseph, encouraged by the angel, adopts Jesus as his legal son and thus includes him in David's family (1:18-25). Jesus is the Davidic Messiah, not because, but almost in spite, of the circumstances of his birth.[124]

If the Matthean genealogy presents an attempt to interpret Jesus in messianic categories, the quite different Lukan one, which traces Jesus' origin through seventy-seven generations back to Adam and finally to God (Luke 3:23-38), reveals a universalistic picture, an Adam typology of sorts. But the historical interest of the genealogies is outstripped by the metahistorical concern of the birth stories.

The notion of a miraculous conception was well known in the Hellenistic world, ultimately going back to the birth myth of the pharaohs, who were thought to have a divine father (although it was not denied that a pharaoh had a human father, too) and a human mother. This myth was applied to kings (for example, Romulus, Alexander), heroes (Heracles), and philosophers (Pythagoras, Plato). On Jewish and Christian soil it came to be cross-fertilized by the biblical notion of miraculous pregnancies of barren women. In the biblical stories the husband is normally not excluded. Later, however, God's part could be emphasized to such a degree that the normal way seemed out of the question. Philo states that the literal meaning of the story of the barrenness of Sarah, who at the age 90 finally bore a son to 100-year-old Abraham, is this: "it is not owing to the faculty of conception that a barren woman should bear a son, but rather to the operation of divine power" (QG 3.18; cf. 3.56). The story of the birth of Melchizedek in *Slavonic Enoch* is explicit about the exclusion of the male human element.[125]

Hellenistic Jews seem to have prepared the way for those Christians who resorted to the idea of a virginal conception. It was surely neither a question of conscious borrowing nor an attempt to advertise Jesus to people accustomed to the divine births of their heroes. But the idea was in the air in the Greco-Roman world.[126] Scriptural support was found in the Septuagint rendering of "young woman" (Hebrew *'almah*) with "virgin" (Greek *parthenos*) in Isa. 7:14, quoted in Matt. 1:23.

Of course, the begetting is ascribed not to God but to his spirit. This is different from the more sensual Greek tales—though one should note the sublimation already implied in the notion that Danae was impregnated by Zeus from a distance, in a shower of gold, or in the Egyptian idea that Apis was conceived from a ray of moonlight. The begetting by the spirit converges with attempts of educated pagan authors, such as Plutarch, to reinterpret the mythology,[127] and the idea of copulation with a Deity is avoided in some accounts of the birth of Plato or of Apollonius, which mention only a vision of Apollo or of Proteus.[128] Educated Christians from Justin on saw the connection clearly, though they explained it in their own way. Justin (*Dial.* 67) claimed that the Greek myths had been invented by Satan to counterfeit the subsequent and true miraculous birth of Jesus.

While Matthew mentions the virginal conception more in passing, concerned to solve the emerging problem, Luke seems to connect it with Jesus' divine sonship (Luke 1:26-38).[129] Luke interweaves the birth and early childhood of Jesus with related stories about John the Baptist. John is great, and his birth to old parents is nothing short of a miracle (Luke 1:5-25). But Jesus excels his precursor in everything; his birth too is even more miraculous than John's. In reply to Mary's question, how she—a virgin—can bear a son, the angel states: "The holy spirit will come upon you, and the power of the Most High will overshadow you; therefore the child to be born will be holy; he will be called Son of God . . . for nothing is impossible for God" (vv. 35, 37).

Strikingly, however, Luke's birth Christology apparently makes no significant difference to his unfolding narrative.[130] Jesus is proclaimed God's Son by the divine voice at his baptism (Luke 3:22); and in Acts, God's raising of Jesus from the dead is singled out as the beginning of his divine sonship. Luke makes no effort to harmonize different notions of Jesus' relation to his Father,[131] but on a general level Luke 1:35 can well be integrated into his overall theocentric view. Jesus is destined to be the Savior before he is born. The verse anticipates what is to come: the spirit guides the ministry of Jesus and gives it its stamp (Luke 3:22; 4:1, 14; 10:21; Acts 10:38; cf. also Luke 4:36; 5:17). Luke 1:35 shows that the roots of Jesus' spirit power are to be traced even further back in time than to his baptism. The annunciation story serves to remind that nothing is impossible for God's creative power (Luke 1:37, quoting Gen. 18:14, where the plight of barren Sarah is in view).[132]

The idea of a virginal conception is not found in those first-century writings that presuppose preexistence (such as the letters of Paul and the Gospel of John). This is so for good reasons: *if* the manner of Jesus' birth is understood to *make* Jesus the Son of God in an ontological sense, this seems conceptually incompatible with

8.2   Fragment of a fresco with Madonna, a prophet, and a star. Catacomb of Priscilla, Rome. Photo: © Scala/Art Resource, NY.

212 the notion of incarnation, which regards Jesus as a preexistent being, who was always the Son of God in a heavenly existence. Ignatius of Antioch is the first author to combine both traditions.[133]

The poetic passage Ign. *Eph.* 7.2 already contains the kernel of the later two-nature Christology: Jesus is "both fleshly and spiritual, begotten and unbegotten, God come in the flesh . . . *both of Mary and of God*." For the first time a causal connection is unequivocally established between Jesus' divinity and his conception. Ignatius *Eph.* 18.2 speaks of "Jesus the Christ, our God, who was carried in the womb by Mary according to God's plan—of the seed of David and of the holy spirit." Ignatius stands in the tradition of Rom. 1:3-4, but instead of the two-stage Christology of Romans we have here practically a two-nature Christology. Unlike Rom. 1:4 or Luke 1:35, this statement describes what the preexistent Jesus always was. Yet the mention of the mother is even here primarily intended to emphasize Jesus' true humanity, not the supernatural birth. This becomes clear in *Trall.* 9.1: Jesus was "of the family of David, of Mary"; he was "truly born, both ate and drank, was truly persecuted . . . was truly crucified and died." Even after Ignatius, the virgin birth had to safeguard the reality of the incarnation in the battle of the proto-orthodox church against more docetically inclined views.[134]

The virgin birth gained more significance in the second century.[135] The presence of this notion in Matthew and Luke established it in due time as a basic Christian truth, which came to underline the divinity of Jesus. For centuries, however, it was sternly denied by the Ebionites, who held fast to the view that Jesus was a "mere man," "engendered from sexual intercourse and the seed of a man, namely Joseph."[136] The Valentinian *Gospel of Philip* (55.23-27) also seems to polemicize

against the virginal conception,[137] and Origen refers to some Gentile Christians who still in his time denied it (*Comm. Matt.* 16.12).

In most layers of early Christian tradition there is little interest in the mother of Jesus.[138] Mark portrays her and her other sons in an almost hostile tension with Jesus, who, they think, has gone mad (Mark 3:21, a comment understandably dropped by both Matthew and Luke). By contrast, Luke sketches a sympathetic picture of Mary as an exemplary Christian woman—a humble listener to the divine word spoken to her (cf. Luke 2:18, 51; 8:19-21).[139] John introduces the mother in key scenes at the beginning and end of Jesus' career (John 2:1-11; 19:26-27), but her role remains somewhat vague.[140] Still, one gets the impression that she has been regarded as a person of rank in John's circle. The second-century *Protevangelium of James* goes further in the veneration of Mary. In this novelistic work, Jesus is totally eclipsed by his mother; "a reader who knew only the Protevangelium might reasonably conclude that Mary is the holy figure and that Jesus' holiness derives from hers."[141] "James" tells stories about the life of young Mary in "sacred purity" (spent in priestly custody in the temple, which is described with paradisal overtones), of her engagement to the old widower Joseph, and of the seemingly scandalous but in truth miraculous circumstances of her pregnancy. It is here that the notion of virginal conception first receives ascetic overtones. The delivery itself is miraculous too. A midwife testifies that it has not affected Mary's virginity (*virginitas in partu*).[142] The birth is painless as well, thus proleptically undoing the curse on Eve (Gen. 3:16). Mary appears as a new Eve, the prototype of a redeemed woman.[143] The combination of this kind of popular storytelling with the hoary tradition of mother Goddesses (in Ephesus in particular) later produced a doctrinal Mariology and a multifaceted cult of the Virgin.

Jesus' Preexistence

Already during the first two decades or so,[144] another rapid christological development, different from those so far discussed, took place: an otherworldly prologue came to be added to the story of Jesus. This development had diverse tradition-historical roots (not necessarily mutually exclusive),[145] and tracing it remains largely guesswork. Apologetic reflection played a part: it must have seemed unthinkable to many that God had just happened, as it were, to find a man worthy of becoming the Messiah or the Savior. God must have had a plan, and that from all eternity—God does not change his mind or invent improved schemes along the way. Thus "the eschatological awareness of the earliest community was matched by a certain interest in protology. . . . Ultimately the idea of pre-existence was a favourite means of bringing out the special significance of particular phenomena for salvation" in Jewish tradition.[146] Remember the Jewish notion of the preexistence of Moses or of Jacob/Israel. In this perspective it is plausible to assume that "the assertion of preexistence was at first an assertion about the context or background of Jesus' human existence," which was still, in itself, a normal human existence.[147] This context was found in God's eternal wisdom; Jewish wisdom traditions soon came to be used in relation to Jesus.

In 1 Cor. 8:6, an older creedal formula quoted by Paul, the role of Wisdom as the mediator of creation is transferred to "Lord Jesus Christ, *through* whom[148] everything [is] and we through him." This notion is further developed in Colossians, Hebrews, and in the Logos hymn of John 1.[149] The very exalted view of the preexistent Christ in the pseudo-Pauline Colossians goes well beyond Paul's notion. The author emphasizes the innate superiority of the person of Jesus over all other, potentially rival, powers (angels). In Col. 1:15-20, what had been said about Wisdom in Hellenistic Judaism is applied to Jesus.[150] He is the "*image*" of God (*eikon*; cf. Wis. 7:26), an agent of creation, existing before the creation of the world (the *firstborn* of all creation) and providing the goal of creation.[151] It is he who, like Wisdom, or the Stoic or Philonic Logos, holds all things together. He is the head of the body—an image that underlines his extraordinarily high position;[152] in him, God in his fullness was pleased to dwell (Col. 1:19; cf. 2:9).[153] Altogether, in this passage Jesus is "being put up into the realm of the divine in a way that exceeds much of the rest of the New Testament."[154] Still, the Wisdom parallel suggests an element of dependence of Jesus on God, perhaps even as one created by God, albeit before other created beings. However exalted his role, there is also a sense in which Christians share in that role: "you have come to fullness in him" (2:10).[155]

In Islam, the views about the Qur'an went through a similar development (it was understood to be written by God in heaven before time). More strikingly, even the prophet Muhammad came to be regarded in mystical circles as early as the ninth century (at the latest) "as the pre-existent light of God's light, created as primal creation before all creation. . . . Muhammad is the foundation and goal of creation, through whom the world came into being and who mediated the grace of God to human beings. It is from Muhammad's pre-existent body that the world was created"![156] To be sure, it took a couple of centuries to reach such a point—not a couple of

214 decades as in the case of Jesus—but then again the initial obstacles against such a development were far more pronounced: the Qur'an makes extremely clear that Muhammad is "only a human being" (41:5) and nothing but "a clear warner" (46:9). Nor did he cease to be that: "even when most idealized, Muhammad always remains a creature."[157]

The talk of Jesus' role in creation remains fairly abstract (and it is indeed rather difficult to imagine how it could have been expressed in concrete terms). This gives some plausibility to readings that deny that those who resorted to this kind of language would have thought of Jesus

8.3 Moses bringing forth water from the rock. Christians frequently took the rock to symbolize the preexistent Christ. Chamber of the Four Seasons, Early Christian fresco, late third century. Catacomb of SS. Marcellino e Pietro, Rome. Photo: © Scala/Art Resource, NY.

literally as a preexistent being in heaven. For instance, James Dunn claims that in 1 Cor. 8:6, "the thought is not of Christ as pre-existent but of the creative act and power of God now embodied in a final and complete way in Christ."[158] But talk of mediating in creation was not the only way to assert Jesus' preexistence.

Hellenized Jews could speak of God's sending his Wisdom onto earth; some early Christians speak of God's sending his Son (Gal. 4:4; Rom. 8:3), here apparently conceived of as a heavenly being. This may have involved a polemical nuance: it is in Jesus, not in the Torah (as non-Christian Jews would have it), that the divine Wisdom dwells. Paul takes over this sending Christology.[159] In 1 Cor. 10:4, Paul (in this case, too, resorting to existing Christian exegesis of scripture) presupposes that Christ was in a real, not just in a symbolic, sense present during the desert wandering of the people of Israel, nurturing them in the form of the rock from which they could miraculously drink.[160] This line of thought is taken much further by later theologians, starting with Justin, who finds Christ acting as the Logos in several events in the history of Israel "as a man and an angel" and even as fire in the burning bush seen by Moses (*Dial.* 128.1-3). Justin is following Jewish models: many accounts of angels acting in human guise on earth were in circulation. Philo could speak of an angel who appeared to Moses in a beautiful "form" in the bush (*Mos.* 1.66); the story of God's visit to Abraham (Gen. 18) is taken to describe a visit of angels (for example, *Abr.* 118).[161] Since it was believed that Jesus had been exalted into heaven, it is no great surprise that traditions about angels came to be applied to him also.[162]

However, neither Wisdom theology nor traditions about visiting angels can fully account for the presentation of the career of a historical person in divine terms. To achieve this, Greek notions of Gods coming (temporarily) to earth were needed[163] (indeed, such traditions had already influenced Philo's depictions of angelophanies).[164] It is not, of course, a question of conscious borrowing, but rather (as in the parallel case of miraculous births) of nonreflective adaptation of one's ideas to ideas that were in the air. Gods could manifest themselves (one could say "incarnate") in humans, for example, in rulers, sages, or propagators of civilization.[165] Empedocles "journeyed around as an immortal God." Plutarch (*Romulus* 28.2) lets Romulus say after his transportation to the Gods: "It was the will of the Gods . . . that I should dwell so long among men, build a city destined to the greatest power and praise, and then again inhabit the heaven whence I came." Luke reports that Simon Magus had a significant group of followers who were devoted to him, calling him "the power of God that is called Great" (Acts 8:10); this implies that Simon's adherents worshiped him as God.[166] Luke's description a few chapters later of the reception of Paul and Barnabas by the Lycaonians shows how naturally the thought of an epiphany or incarnation of Gods could come to people's minds. Because of a miraculous healing, the apostles are taken to be Gods: "The gods have come down to us in the likeness (*homoiothentes*) of men" (Acts 14:11 RSV). This story, which continues by telling how the local priest of Zeus wanted to sacrifice oxen (!) and garlands to the putative Gods, also proves that divinity could be applied to *contemporary* persons who worked wonders; it was not just the privilege of remote figures from the ancient past.

In this vein, the celebrated pre-Pauline "Christ hymn" (Phil. 2:6-11; see especially vv. 7-8) makes use of Greek terminology, which was related to the temporary appearance of Gods in the world in a lowly human guise: "form" (*morphe*),[167] "likeness" (*homoioma*), "figure" (*schema*).[168] Christ Jesus, "though he was in the form of God, did not regard equality with God as something to be exploited, but emptied himself, taking the form of a slave, being born in human likeness. . . . being found in a human form" (*schema*; the KJV renders "in fashion as a man"). The exaltation in resurrection now becomes the return of the divine being to his place of origin. Nevertheless, the focus in the hymn is not on glory, but on the self-humiliation of the Son of God, which is set forth as an example to the Christians who should have "the same mind that was in Christ Jesus" (Phil. 2:5). The model of epiphany had to be adapted to a man who had suffered death. In Rom. 8:3 Paul quotes and adapts another traditional formula that resorts to similar language: Jesus was sent "in the *likeness* (*homoioma*) of sinful flesh."

John Knox senses that Paul's use of such words as *fashion* (*schema*) and *likeness* (*homoioma*), which emphasize appearance, points to a contradiction in Paul's thought. It signals the presence of a "reservation, or misgiving, as to the full genuineness of the humanity of Jesus, which is essentially incompatible with Paul's basic conception of its function in God's saving act."[169] Paul introduces, "perhaps without intending to or even knowing that he was doing so, a hint of the flesh's unreality," apparently because he was not able to attribute anything like sin to Jesus.[170] Paul leaves open the possibility that Jesus did not completely identify with sinful humans.[171] Docetic or docetically inclined Christologies could later seize on this point.[172] Yet, as we saw, much in Paul's view of salvation (insofar as Jesus' obedience as the new, different Adam is emphasized, as in Rom. 5:20) demands Jesus' full humanity.

216 A problem related to Paul's appears in Hebrews. In the opening passage (1:2b-3), Wisdom language is lavishly used: God has spoken in his Son "through whom he created the worlds. He is the reflection (*apaugasma*; cf. Wis. 7:26) of God's glory and the imprint of God's very being (*character tes hypostaseos*), and he sustains all things by his powerful word." Later on, the author compares Jesus to the mysterious Melchizedek, imagined to be "without father, without mother, without genealogy" (7:3), and stresses the unchanging nature of Jesus Christ, who "is the same yesterday and today and forever" (13:8).[173]

Nevertheless, the idea of preexistence is not central in Hebrews. Alongside the language of preexistence, "appointment" language is found in abundance (see above). The Wisdom Christology remains something of an erratic block, while the appointment language seems more typical of the writer's thought.[174] Even in the Wisdom section itself, there is a tension between the Son's eternal being and his *becoming* greater than the angels through his enthronement in the resurrection (Heb. 1:3-4). This awkward tension in Hebrews' presentation of the Christ seems to result from the author's merging of two worldviews, biblical and Platonic. He blends together the eschatological mediator of the new covenant on one hand and the ideal heavenly being on the other.

This bipolarity indicates a basic problem of early Christology that is crystallized in Hebrews: the author can evidently think of Jesus as a preexistent, heavenly being, but he also presents him as a thoroughly and genuinely human figure, a forerunner (Heb. 6:20) who was *similar in every respect* to other human beings—as indeed he had to be, if he was to be their true helper.[175] But how could he be both? This dilemma was to accompany Christian thought down to the present. Take Irenaeus: for him Jesus' full humanity (along with his divinity) was crucial, because otherwise Jesus, the Second Adam, could not have reconciled humanity's sinful nature to God. The Adam/Christ parallel would not have been valid "if His flesh had differed in any respect (*sinlessness excepted*) from ordinary human flesh."[176] Unfortunately, the exception (which is explicitly stated already in Heb. 4:15) makes all the difference.

The *Gospel of Thomas* also presents the Savior-Jesus as the manifestation of the primordial Light who was the agent of creation—and even refers to this activity himself:[177] "I am the light that is over all things. I am all: from me all has come forth, and to me all has reached" (*Gos. Thom.* 77); "I am the one who comes from what is whole [the undivided].[178] I was given from the things of my Father" (61). Such statements indicate "that Jesus shares some of the divine qualities with his Father."[179] As in Philippians 2 or in John, Jesus is a preexistent heavenly figure manifested in a human body. But what is different in the cosmic drama as described in the *Gospel of Thomas* is "the emphasis on the divine origin of all humanity, not only on the divinity of Jesus." "Jesus is the prototype of all those who realize their true selves and find their way back to their original home."[180] In this anthropological perspective (though not in his role as an agent in the creation!), Jesus is similar to other humans. The Syrian Christians for whom the Gospel speaks have applied to Jesus the standard Hellenistic "belief in the divinity of the self and its return to the heavenly home."[181] The difference between Jesus and his true followers is that Jesus is aware of his heavenly origin: "I took my stand in the midst of the world, and in flesh I appeared to them" (28). Nor does it seem as if Jesus would, even "in the flesh," have shared the ignorance that is the plight of humans, and needed an awakening experience himself. But as the role of Jesus is that of the Revealer of the saving insight, and not one of acting on behalf of humanity, *Thomas*'s theology does not really need a Savior who is similar to other humans in *every* respect either.

From Kenosis to Epiphany

It is one thing to confess the preexistence of the human Savior in worship or meditation,[182] especially if one has not known the historical Jesus in person. It is another thing to try to give a consistent account of the life of a flesh-and-blood man as an epiphany of a preexistent angelic or divine being. K.-J. Kuschel's description of the situation is apt: until John wrote his Gospel,

> Christians either told of the appearance of the man Jesus as the Messiah and Son in time or reflected on the significance of his career in hymns, reflections and meditations, and praised him as the one exalted by God over time, who had now also been recognized as the Son "before" all time. The two did not seem to go together. The Synoptic confessions of the Messiah do not know any statements about pre-existence[183] and the universal christology of Paul and the Deutero-Paulines do not know any material directly relating to Jesus.[184] These two things hardly seem to fit together. . . . However, a remarkable thing happened. Towards the end of the first century, a single Christian community, John's community, dared to attempt to square the circle.[185]

In Paul, the sending of the Son entails *kenosis* (emptying oneself): when the heavenly being becomes man, he identifies with the human condition of slaves (Phil. 2:7); the glory shines only on the face of the Risen One. The "Lord of glory" came incognito into the world, and that is why the inimical powers did not recognize him (1 Cor. 2:7-8). By contrast, John depicts Jesus' sending and mission in the world as an epiphany of divine glory. In John we can see what happened when the "prologue" to the story of Jesus "insisted on becoming the first act": the original "first act" that had depicted the earthly life had to be completely rewritten (by someone who very probably had not known the historical person).[186]

To be sure, the depiction of Jesus' life in the Synoptic Gospels had already become permeated by the sovereignty of the Exalted One, though without any clear indication of his preexistence. The stories of Jesus walking on water and multiplying loaves as told by Mark provided a good starting point for John's story of a heavenly figure striding through the world. But the reservations still shown by Mark's paradoxical aim to describe hidden epiphanies are now gone. The messiahship and divine sonship of Jesus are no secret at all in John; it is obvious to the disciples from the start (John 1:34, 41, 49) and openly proclaimed by Jesus even to the crowds (see, for example, 5:19-47 and the numerous "I am" sayings).

In itself, the idea of sending need not imply a very high Christology. The language of sending is rooted in the prophetic tradition and shows Jesus as a true prophet. Prophets are sent (Isa. 6:8-9), and so is John the Baptist (John 1:6). The idea of sending is in John's Gospel frequently coupled with the idea of Jesus as "Son (of God)." The sonship language on its own need not imply a very high Christology either (as is clear from the Synoptics and Acts). Sonship may imply an element of unity with the parent, but it is a unity based on total obedience and dependence. Thus alongside, say, John 10:30—"I and the Father are one"—must be placed statements that underline the Son's total dependence, for example, 14:28—"the Father is greater than I."[187]

218   But John goes much further. Wisdom traditions are applied to Jesus in the prologue. He is the Logos who existed in the beginning, before the creation of the world, in which he participated (John 1:1-3). No doubt John thinks of Jesus as a genuine human being; after all, the Word became *flesh* (1:14). But Jesus' humanity is in the process of being thoroughly qualified. John presents Jesus explicitly in far more exalted terms than anything we find in the Synoptic Gospels, let alone in Paul. In the story as rewritten by John, Jesus' humanity is all but swallowed by his divinity. "When John opens the floodgates of his christology of pre-existent sonship it sweeps all

before it and leaves no room at all for the earlier stress on Jesus' sonship as an eschatological status and power that opens the way for others to share in."[188] "The more fully the logic of pre-existence is permitted to work itself out in the story, the less important the resurrection is bound to become there."[189] "We have beheld his glory," says this writer, speaking of the man Jesus, "glory as of the only Son of the Father" (1:14).

The baptism of Jesus "drops from sight as unsuitable for one of his dignity, and even the possibility of a temptation is denied."[190] A specific transfiguration scene is not needed; the constant glory of Jesus' earthly life leaves no room

8.4   Resurrection of Lazarus. Early Christian fresco, late third century C.E. Catacomb of the Giordani, Rome.
Photo: Scala/Art Resource, NY.

for it.[191] Jesus lets Lazarus lie dead several days before setting out to awaken him (John 11:4-6) and prays only for the sake of the people who watch him (11:41-42). There are indications that Jesus was omniscient[192] and hints, at least, that there were no limits to his power. He was always in complete control of what happened to him. His dying was a deliberate act, and he was able to rise back to life by himself: "No one takes [my life] from me, but I lay it down of my own accord. I have power to lay it down, and I have power to take it up again" (10:18). John totally rewrites the story of Jesus' arrest. In the new scene, Jesus controls everything in a sovereign way. The master of his own fate, he actually arranges the arrest: the soldiers and their helpers fall to the ground before him and are able to catch Jesus only after he has voluntarily offered himself to them (18:1-12). The crucifixion scene hardly testifies to any real suffering;[193] "in the case of the Fourth Gospel 'passion' is a misnomer."[194] Jesus is in full control of the events. From the cross, he takes care of his family affairs (19:26-27). He does say "I am thirsty," yet not because of any real inconvenience, but "in order to fulfill the scripture" (19:28). And instead of the agonized cry, "my God, my God why have you forsaken me?" (Mark 15:34; Matt. 27:46), John has Jesus say as his last words, "It is fulfilled" (19:30). The crucifixion already means Jesus' exaltation.

This exaltation is, however, really a return—and Jesus knows it. Jesus has come from heaven and tells humans what he has seen and heard there (John 3:32; 8:26, 38; 12:49). Jesus knows that he has come from God and is going to God (13:3; 16:5). He can speak of God's love for him before "the foundation of the world" (17:24) and of the "glory that I had in your [God] presence before the world existed" (17:5);[195] he can also say, "Before Abraham was, I am" (8:58).[196] God

has given Jesus his "name" (17:11-12); Jesus embodies God's own glory (1:14).[197] Jesus *is* the revelation of God (1:18): whoever has seen Jesus has seen the Father (14:9). What he reveals is—almost tautologically—that *he* is the revealer: the Way, the Truth, the Life, the Light of the world, the Vine, and so on.[198] Jesus is also able to dispense the spirit (John 7:37, 39; 14:16; 20:23), which (again) means that he has "a role otherwise uniquely God's in biblical/Jewish tradition."[199]

The portrait of a Jesus who is fully aware of his heavenly preexistence and possesses superhuman knowledge and a power so unlimited that he can himself take back the life that he has first surrendered certainly raises the question "whether one who enjoyed that sort of consciousness can be said to have been fully or genuinely human." But Dennis Nineham, who raises the issue, goes on: if such a question "was not one which greatly troubled John, that would not be surprising, for the genuineness of Jesus' humanity was something about which many early Christians were much less concerned than later churchmen were to be."[200] Ernst Käsemann's talk of "naive" (that is, nonreflective or unintended) docetism has much to commend itself.[201] Jesus' earthly life is "only the foil to the Son of God who strides through the world of men."[202] Michael Goulder makes the same point: "John is almost, if not quite, a docetist. His Jesus weeps and is weary, but that is the limit of his humanity."[203] And Maurice Wiles states that if John's depiction is taken at face value, we have here "on the one hand a conscious pre-existent being alongside God the father" and "on the other hand a self-consciously incarnate Jesus who is *not in any proper sense of the word human*."[204]

No wonder the Jews of John's story are scandalized, finding that Jesus has blasphemously made himself equal to God (John 5:18; 10:33). In

220 the former passage Jesus parallels his "work" with that of the Father (5:17); in the latter he bluntly asserts: "The Father and I are one" (10:30).[205] The narrator opens the book by stating that, in some sense at least, the Logos also "was God" (1:1), and toward the end the previously doubting disciple Thomas confesses that Jesus is his "God" (20:28). While this Christology has vague counterparts in Jewish speculations about "two powers in heaven" and even closer points of comparison in the Logos theology of Philo, it moves further "toward a definition of Jesus' divinity that is well on the way to ditheism. Father and Son . . . are separate but so intimately related that the Son shares essentially in the divine being."[206] Once more, the seventeenth-century "Messiah" Sabbatai Zevi provides an analogy. His figure "was recast by the passage of time, becoming entirely mythical: gradually the element of historical truth was diminished until nothing was left but a legendary hero who had inaugurated a new epoch of world history." The process started in his lifetime. "Like the early Christians, in fact, the 'radicals' [among the Sabbatian believers] eventually came to believe that the Messiah had not been a mere superior human being, but an incarnation of God Himself in human form."[207]

John's Jesus is like other humans in that he has a body of flesh (and blood); there is little doubt about that.[208] But as regards his mental qualities (omniscience, awareness of having descended from heaven) and miraculous abilities (turning water into wine, raising even himself from the dead), he is vastly *different* from all other human beings. Whether one calls this "docetism" or uses some other term is merely a question of definition. John's Jesus may be a "true God," even in a genuine human body, but he is definitely not a "true man." But then again Jesus' role in the Fourth Gospel is mainly that of revealer, and

disclosing the way and the truth to humans does *not* necessarily require that the teacher be fully human (as Paul's soteriology does); John comes here quite close to ideas represented by Platonist Christians.[209]

From John's portrayal of the divine Jesus there is a short step to the idea that the human body of Jesus was just an appearance—the view traditionally called "docetic" (and attributed to "heretics" only). It is hardly a coincidence that the earliest battle on the issue of Jesus' humanity of which we have traces of evidence is connected with a split just in the *Johannine* community, documented in 1 John (2:18-24; 4:1-3).[210] Conceivably the "antichrists" who, according to the epistle, denied that Jesus was the Christ come in the flesh (4:2), held that the divine Christ was separate from the man Jesus; they may, in a Cerinthian vein (see below), have thought that this divine element left Jesus at his death.[211] Stories about a vastly superhuman Jesus, told in a language reminiscent of John's Gospel, still circulated in the late second century and found their way into the *Acts of John*. There Jesus frequently changes shapes (his body is sometimes soft or immaterial, at other times hard as rock), leaves no footprints, and seems to be of vastly different ages (being sometimes seen as a boy, sometimes a beautiful man, sometimes a bald-headed man with a long beard; see chs. 87–93). It would seem that this Jesus is "not a human being at all," but "a spiritual being who adapted himself to human perception."[212]

In its own way, the Sethian *Trimorphic Protennoia* also reflects the struggle over the interpretation of the Christology of the Fourth Gospel. There the Protennoia, the divine "First Thought," descends into the world of mortals as the Word, assuming a human appearance: "I put on Jesus. I bore him from the cursed wood and established him in the dwelling places of his Father" (*Trim. Prot.* 50.12-14). Traditional titles (Christ, Beloved, Son of God, Son of Man: 49.6-20) "are polemically interpreted in a consciously docetic fashion so as to suggest that these titles were inappropriately applied to the human Jesus by the apostolic church"; the Jesus of the proto-orthodox is shown to be the Christ of the evil spiritual powers.[213]

The idea that there are no limits to the power of Jesus reaches its peak in the second-century infancy gospels. In the *Infancy Gospel of Thomas* (2.1-7), the playing child Jesus displays the power of the Creator in separating some of the flowing water into ponds (cf. the Genesis creation account, Gen. 1:6-10) and purifies it with a single command, and by shaping twelve sparrows out of soft clay and bringing life to them through a command (cf. Gen. 2:19). Jesus also miraculously lengthens a beam of wood for Joseph. In a long story of a Jewish teacher instructing him, Jesus displays his own superior knowledge.[214] Clearly, in this *Infancy Gospel*, "what appears to be a young boy is actually a divine being in thin disguise." This writing "represents a sincere (but very unsophisticated) religious inference that, as the Son of God from his birth onward, Jesus should (or can) be portrayed as already manifesting his divine powers, which include his knowledge of all that Christian faith came to claim about his transcendent status and origins. Of course, this also involves portraying him as not really subject to normal human limitations or development."[215] But the difference of this naive docetism from that found in the Gospel of John is one of degree only.

"Docetic" or "Real" Incarnation?

Distinguishing between "docetic" and "non-docetic" views of Jesus' humanity often resembles

drawing a line in the water. If a boundary line can be drawn at all, it certainly does not run neatly between what are traditionally regarded as "orthodox" and "heretical" writings. Thus the *Epistle of Barnabas* (5.10) states that the Son of God "came in the flesh" in order to save humans from having to face the divine glory directly, as this would have destroyed them. Here, in a writing that is generally not considered heretical, Jesus' "flesh" is just a protective cover for superhuman divinity.

A recurrent emphasis in the *Ascension of Isaiah*, thought to have "emanated from proto-orthodox hands,"[216] is the descent of the "Beloved One" from heaven, where he has been the object of glorious worship (9.27-32), and his subsequent ascent back to glory. The descent involves his transformation into "the likeness of a man" (3.13). Descending through all seven heavens, he successively transforms himself to resemble the angelic inhabitants of each level; in the third and second heaven he supplies the password required by the angels who guard the gates. The purpose of all this secrecy is that the heavenly powers might not recognize him until after he has completed his redemptive work (cf. 1 Cor. 2:7-8); then God will openly announce his exaltation (*Ascen. Isa.* 10). Jesus arrives in the world of humans in a miraculous way, the infant who had been in her womb suddenly appearing to Mary, born without an ordinary delivery process.[217] This too is hidden from the spiritual powers, and the infant Jesus will suckle Mary's breast as does any ordinary infant in order not to be recognized (ch. 11). One is fully justified to speak of "naive" (that is, nonreflective) docetism here.[218] Both before his descent and after his exaltation, the Beloved receives massive worship along with God—and with "the angel of the holy spirit." The *Ascension of Isaiah* may be taken to reflect "a primitive

222 effort at what later became trinitarian doctrine," but whether the author really managed "to avoid the idea that there are three gods"[219] is doubtful. Clearly the text suggests that there are three divine beings who are not "one" in any sense, two of them being subordinated to the "Great Glory" (9.37) and the "Most High," whom "Isaiah" calls "the Father of my Lord" (10.7).

Platonizing Christians with gnostic inclinations were able to adopt the "body language" and to interpret the Savior's connection with "flesh" (John 1:14) to mean simply his making himself a visible man. In the Valentinian *Gospel of Truth* (31.4-5), for example, the Savior (who brought the knowledge of the Father) "came in the likeness of flesh, and nothing blocked his way, for incorruptibility cannot be grasped." If this sounds docetic, it is good to note that Jesus granted humans "to taste him and smell him and to touch the beloved Son" (*Gos. Truth* 30.27-31; cf. 1 John 1:1). Even more importantly, the *Gospel of Truth* definitely does not deny Jesus' death; on the contrary, it includes a positive evaluation of his suffering: "the merciful, faithful Jesus was patient and accepted his sufferings . . . since he knew that his death would be life for many"; "he humbled himself even unto death, though clothed in eternal life. He stripped off the perishable rags (that is, the body) and clothed himself in incorruptibility, which no one can take from him" (20.6-34). It is hard to see why this Valentinian Jesus should be deemed either less or more genuinely human than the Jesus of John's Gospel.[220] How open the fronts were is further shown by the fact that the proto-orthodox *Epistle of the Apostles* (21) lets Christ speak of himself as "I who am without flesh and yet have borne flesh."[221]

In order to safeguard the full divinity of the Savior, some Christians brought about a *division* of the redeemer into two separate beings (two natures, if you like): the earthly, transitory Jesus on one hand and the heavenly, eternal Christ on the other. An early representative of this view is Cerinthus at the turn of the first century: after the baptism, the divine element "Christ" descended onto Jesus in the form of a dove, "and then he worked miracles; finally, however, Christ flew away from Jesus, and Jesus suffered and rose from the dead."[222] The resurrection is mentioned almost as an afterthought.[223] Whether Cerinthus's view should be deemed as truly docetic is questionable, for, unlike "Christ," *Jesus* is here a real human being who dies (and is subsequently raised). The defectors against whom the author of 1 John polemicizes (1 John 4:1-3) may have shared this view, and similar thoughts may have been present in Antioch in Ignatius's time: Ignatius warned of wandering heretics, according to whom Christ only seemed to suffer (*Trall.* 10; *Smyrn.* 2).

The separationist Christology was exploited to the full by some gnostic Christians: the higher Christ, who brought liberating knowledge, left the human Jesus in the end. Jesus "died when the spirit that had come upon him at the Jordan departed," but when the body had died, "the Savior sent forth the ray of power which had come upon him, and destroyed death, while he scattered the passions and raised the mortal body" (*Exc. Theod.* 61.6-7). Again, it would be problematic to brand this view simply as docetic, as a bodily being undeniably dies.[224] In the Nag Hammadi *Apocalypse of Peter* (81.4—82.3), Peter sees Jesus "apparently being arrested"; he also sees someone else "smiling and laughing above the cross." The Savior confirms: "The one you see smiling and laughing above the cross is the *living Jesus*. The one into whose hands and feet they are driving nails is his *fleshly part*, the *substitute* for him. They are putting to shame the one who came into being in his likeness."[225] The fleshly part of Jesus does suffer, yet the spiritual eye sees deeper: the suffering does not reach the inmost spiritual reality of the Savior.[226] In *1 Apoc. Jas.* 31.15-22, Christ states: "I am the one who was within me. Never did I suffer at all, and I was not distressed. These people did not harm me." The point of this "sham of a crucifixion" was "to expose the impotence and arrogance of the world rulers," whom Jesus reproves by his resurrection (30.1-6).[227] Irenaeus ascribes to *Basilides* the view that Christ caused Simon of Cyrene to look like Jesus, so that Simon was crucified while Christ was laughing (*Haer.* 1.24.4); a similar idea has been found in *Treat. Seth* 55.30—56.19: "The death they think I suffered they suffered in their error and blindness. They nailed their man to their death . . . I was laughing at their ignorance." Yet the correctness of Irenaeus's report is in doubt,[228] and the text in *Treatise of Seth* does not actually claim that Simon was crucified instead of Jesus.[229] Its point seems to be that the crucifixion was not suffered by the real Jesus, "but only by the body which he inhabited."[230] Is this a "docetic" idea or not? At least the man Jesus does suffer bodily pain.[231]

In any case, it is misleading to build on such texts generalizations about "the" gnostic view of Jesus' death. The Nag Hammadi library has brought to light several gnostically oriented writings (for example, the *Gospel of Truth*; the *Letter of Peter to Philip*), in which Jesus does really suffer and die.[232] Some writings can even *criticize* docetic views, as does the Sethian *Melchizedek*. While the writing displays some clearly gnostic features,[233] the author nevertheless "predicts" the rise of a docetic heresy and condemns it (*Melch.* 5.1-11).[234] On the other hand, the Christ of the *Odes of Solomon* (a writing generally no longer classified as gnostic) states in clearly "docetic"

terms that neither his coming into the world nor his leaving it was like that of normal humans: "I did not perish, because I was not their brother, nor was my birth like theirs. And they sought my death but were unsuccessful, because I was older than their memory" (*Odes Sol.* 28.17-18).

A Jesus whose body was certainly not like that of all other humans was presented by those who did not accept his physical birth. Irenaeus ascribed to Ptolemy the view that Jesus passed through Mary as water passes through a tube (*Haer.* 1.7.2), for his body was not material. Cerdo taught that Jesus did not really suffer nor was he really born; his body was a mere phantom (Ps.-Tert. 6.1). Saturninus regarded the Savior as a being who was not born, had no body and no form, but who manifested himself in an apparently human form (Irenaeus, *Haer.* 1.24.2). That Jesus was not born was also the view of Marcion (Hippolytus, *Haer.* 7.31), although his thought as a whole cannot be characterized as gnostic.[235]

Another difference from ordinary mortals was suggested by Valentinus (frg. 3), who undergirded Jesus' divine essence with a peculiar theory on Christ's digestion: unlike other people, he did not defecate.[236] The idea may seem distasteful to modern sensitivities, but the issue was a serious one in the second and third centuries. That Christ ate and drank was considered crucial evidence for his true humanity (it was a common argument against docetism since Ignatius, *Trall.* 9), but it was felt difficult to reconcile this with his divinity.[237] Clement of Alexandria even put forward the suggestion that Christ ate food not because his body would have needed it (he was sustained by the holy spirit), but because he wanted to reject the docetic heresy in advance (*Strom.* 6.71.2)! No doubt "Clement's quip at the docetic position is in itself one step closer to full-blown docetism than Valentinus' teaching";

224 unlike Clement, Valentinus did *not* assume that Christ's body did not need nourishment.[238]

Proto-orthodox teachers engaged in a battle against what they regarded as docetism, but in doing so they emphasized the divinity of the man Jesus in confusing ways. In this battle, the author of 1 John provided the traditional confessions to Jesus as the Christ (1 John 2:22; 5:1) or as the Son of God (1 John 4:15; 5:5) with a new significance, taking his cue from the Fourth Gospel (John 1:1; 20.28): Jesus is assimilated to God in a way unheard-of in a Jewish context;[239] "he is *the true God* and eternal life" (1 John 5:20). It was considered crucial that Jesus had "come"

in a genuinely human body; it did not bother proto-orthodox Christians if he seemed very different from normal humans in other respects.

Ignatius shows how Christology is well underway toward the creedal statements of the councils. "There is one physician, who is both flesh and spirit, born and yet not born, who is God come in flesh, true life in death, born of Mary and of God, first passible and then impassible, Jesus Christ our Lord" (*Eph.* 7.2). "Our God Jesus Christ was conceived by Mary" (18.2). Ignatius even speaks of the "blood of God" (*Eph.* 1.1) and of "the suffering of my God" (*Rom.* 6.3) and seems to suggest that Jesus himself brought

8.5   Christ Pantocrator. Byzantine mosaic. Duomo, Cefalu, Sicily, Italy. Photo: © Scala/Art Resource, NY.

about his resurrection from the dead (*Smyrn.* 2.1, in an antidocetic context!). His polemics against those who hold "docetic" views are grounded in an existential concern: how could his own impending death have any meaning if the Lord did not really die?[240] Ignatius fights for the humanity of Jesus (he was Son of Man and Son of God, *Eph.* 20.2)[241] by in effect distinguishing him clearly from other humans. Interestingly, the Valentinian *Tripartite Tractate* speaks of Christ in terms that seem very similar to those of Ignatius: Jesus was the "unbegotten, impassible one" who "came to be in the flesh" (*Tri. Trac.* 113.37-38) and "out of willing compassion" became for the humans' sake "manifest in an involuntary suffering" (114.31-35). "Not only did he take upon (himself) the death of those whom he thought to save, but he also accepted their smallness, . . . let himself be conceived and born as an infant with body and soul" (115.3-11), having "let himself be conceived without sin, pollution, or defilement" (115.15-17).[242] Thus Jesus was born, suffered, and died, and yet he, in his incarnation, "transcended human nature so that he could prevail over death by divine power."[243]

The assimilation of Jesus with God soon becomes the rule among the proto-orthodox. *Second Clement* (1.1) states that we are to think of Jesus as of God. In *Ep. Apos.* 17 (28), Jesus refers to the parousia as "the coming of *my Father*"; as this causes confusion in the minds of the apostles, he explains in an (exaggerated) Johannine vein: "I am completely in my Father and my Father is in me." Toward the end of the second century, Melito of Sardis can even claim that the Creator of heaven and earth was nailed to the cross (*Homil.* 96).

The farther one moves from the Jewish-messianic roots of Christology, the more the humanity of Jesus fades. While some Jewish Christians consistently emphasized Jesus' full humanity and some gnostic Christians equally consistently his full divinity, the proto-orthodox and many gnostic Christians tried to have it both ways. On the orthodox side this led to a complicated doctrine of Christ's two natures; one tried to work out a view of God that "maintained a monotheistic stance while also doing justice to the divinity of Jesus."[244] For a modern perception, neither the proto-orthodox nor the gnostics assume a fully human being who is truly similar to all others (but then they might not have cared too much about that either).[245] For ancient perception the matter was somewhat different. The gnostic view at least avoided distinguishing the Savior radically from humans—for at heart humans too were potentially divine, due to the divine spark hidden within them, and those who came to recognize their true selves were to become no less divine than Jesus was.

Epilogue

The patristic writers had to take for granted John's fictional story of the all but docetic Jesus—a Jesus with a genuinely human body but with a superhuman consciousness. To harmonize it with such evidence as pointed to his full and normal humanity was an impossible task from the start. As John Knox puts it, could anyone imagine a true man speaking in the fashion of John's Jesus: "Father, glorify me in your own presence with the glory that I had in your presence before the world existed" (John 17:5)?[246] The problem was insoluble, hence the bitter controversies: different christological positions "were upheld by inadequate arguments and distorting exegesis

226 of scripture; and compromise formulae were devised which did nothing more than restate the impossible paradox and leave it unresolved."[247] In this "distressingly human story," "deep emotions and profound intolerance stirred up councils, churches and armies of monks into horrific attacks upon one another, and to the excommunication and exile of upright and sincere church leaders."[248]

The result was a compromise formula devised by the Council of Chalcedon (451 C.E.). This council affirmed the Nicene Creed of 325 C.E., which had stated that Jesus is "God from God, Light from Light, True God from True God, begotten not made, of one substance with the Father." It also confessed to "one and the same Christ, Son, Lord, Only-begotten . . . in two natures, inconfusedly, unchangeably, indivisibly, inseparably." It is universally recognized that this was no real definition, but simply "a setting up of a number of parameters, or boundary conditions, within which it was decided that all future Christian discussion about Jesus should remain."[249] The council "in effect merely asserted that Jesus was 'truly God and truly man' without attempting to say how such a paradox is possible"; the formula is "a philosophical artefact having whatever meaning it is defined to have."[250]

One last time, let us listen to John Knox: "Whatever 'one Person'—in, say, the Chalcedonian statement—is taken to mean, how can two 'natures' (each presumably involving consciousness and will) belong to it 'inconfusedly, unchangeably, indivisibly, inseparably'? I cannot pretend to understand how this could be. . . . What I do venture to assert . . . with great conviction, is this: of no normal human being could such things be truly said. . . .[251] We can have the humanity without the pre-existence and we can have the pre-existence without the humanity.

There is absolutely no way of having both."[252] Maurice Wiles concurs, concluding that "the church has never succeeded in offering a consistent or convincing picture" of Jesus as *both* fully human *and* fully divine. "Most commonly it has been the humanity of Christ that has suffered."[253]

What started as an effort to solve the problem of Jesus' relation to God had slowly developed into the problem of the Trinity: three persons within one and the same God. This was "a very complicated and partly self-contradictory, protracted process of thought" in which the three Cappadocian fathers (Basil the Great, Gregory of Nazianzus, Gregory of Nyssa) eventually played a key part.[254] In fact, trinitarian speculations were long felt to be a threat for monotheistic faith. Theologians such as Tertullian, who first began to speak of the Logos as "God" or even used trinitarian formulations, met with bitter opposition from many simple believers who charged them with ditheism or tritheism. "The beginnings of the ecclesiastical trinitarian theology were felt to be polytheism and were rejected as heresy in the name of the biblical God."[255] Hans Küng points out that if pre-Nicene Christians were to be gauged with the statements of this council, not only the Jewish Christians but almost all Greek fathers of the three first centuries would also be heretics, for they taught in a self-evident fashion that the Son was subordinated to the Father.[256]

The Christian theologian of the first centuries faced two key questions: How is the Lord Jesus related to the one and only God? How is God related to the world?[257] The philosophical framework of patristic theology was popular Platonism with Stoic and Pythagorean influences.[258] God, the Ultimate One, the Ground of Being, was perfect, therefore impassive, unaffected by anything external. He could have no history and no involvement. It was hard to relate this God with the world. The solutions to this problem implied some kind of system of mediators or a "hierarchy of Being"; one finds schemes of emanation and mediation in both philosophical and in gnostic systems. Educated Christians shared this outlook. For theologians like Clement of Alexandria or Origen, "the quasi-divine Logos filled the role of the one and only mediator who was both One and Many, sharing in some sense the nature of both and bridging the gulf between them."[259] But the scheme was illogical in itself, and the Arian controversy showed this up.

The Platonic scheme was based upon a contrast between the transcendent God and the world, but it avoided drawing a line between the divine realm and the created order. Arius (or the circle of early Arians)[260] raised the implicit question about where the line should be drawn (and the Bible insisted on the contrast between God and his creation!). But drawing the line meant that the mediator fell on one side or the other, putting in doubt his ability to mediate (the Nicene line being no better than the Arian on this score). The Arians conceded that the Logos existed before all creation, but termed him too a created being, stressing "the creaturely commonality of Christ with those he was to redeem and, hence, Christ's importance as representative creature and model."[261] By contrast, the Council of Nicea stated that Jesus the Son is "of the same substance" (homoousios) as the Father.[262] Arius came to sever the mediator from God, but he could accept all traditional creeds and was able to give a realistic exposition of those New Testament passages that assume that, when tempted by Satan, Jesus had the same moral experience as we have, so that the possibility of his sinning was open. Athanasius (the most prominent de-

fender of the Nicene Creed), on the other hand, argued that the Logos became man in order that we might become "God"; therefore he must have been God himself, or he could not have accomplished such a task. If Arius severed the mediator from God, Athanasius severed him from the world and was consequently led to read such Gospel passages as the temptation stories in ways that were "inevitably docetic in tendency, though not in intent."[263]

While many (most?) theologians continue to regard the doctrine of the Trinity and a realistic understanding of the incarnation as indispensable,[264] ordinary Christians are often perplexed. One experienced teacher had to write a book on Christology based on the assumption that "believers today are not convinced that Christology is essential to their faith."[265] No wonder, then, that a reorientation has been taking place in many quarters. For example, the contributors to The Myth of God Incarnate, a volume edited by John Hick in 1977, emphatically sided with the early "recognition that Jesus was . . . 'a man approved by God' for a special role within the divine purpose" (Acts 2:22).[266] Sharing the thoughts of "a growing number of Christians, both professional theologians and lay people," they stated that the conception of Jesus as the Second Person of the Trinity living a human life is a "poetic way of expressing his significance for us." And they went on: "This recognition is called for in the interests of truth; but it also has increasingly important practical implications for our relationship to the peoples of the other great world religions."[267] During the past quarter of a century, similar metaphoric[268] approaches to Christology have increasingly been taken, not least in the context of interfaith dialogue.

9

The Empowering Presence
Experiences and Doctrines of the Spirit

Early Christians were convinced that they had been granted the special gift of possessing God's spirit (Greek *pneuma*), which often manifested itself in conspicuous ecstatic phenomena. In this chapter, I review their convictions concerning the spirit on one hand, and the spectrum of extraordinary religious phenomena, whether or not they are explicitly ascribed to the activity of the spirit, on the other. Finally, we must consider the development of the spirit from a divine power to a person of the divine Trinity.

THE DIVINE SPIRIT IN JEWISH AND GREEK TRADITION

Various extraordinary abilities and skills are traced back to a divine power in the Hebrew Bible. This power is often called the spirit of Yahweh.[1] The term *ruah* conjures up the notion of God's "breath." It is a life-giving force (cf. Gen.

2:4b-25) that is at a later stage given a role in the creation of the world (Gen. 1:2; cf. Ps. 33:6).

In stories from early times, the spirit of Yahweh empowers prominent individuals to astonishing deeds, above all as charismatic, courage-infusing leaders in battle (Judg. 6:34; 11:29; 1 Sam. 11:6-7). It also provides a Samson with the physical strength that enables him to kill a lion (Judg. 14:6; cf. 13:25)—and a group of thirty Philistine men as well (14:19).[2]

Among the experiences ascribed to the mysterious and awesome action of the spirit are also raptures that drive people to ecstatic speech and behavior. As in other parts of the ancient Near East, in Israel groups of prophets wandered around and produced oracles in trancelike states, dancing to the accompaniment of music, sometimes speaking in intelligible words, sometimes uttering meaningless sounds that had to be interpreted. Their enthusiasm (like that of the charismatic war heroes) could be contagious: when Saul met a band of such prophets, "the spirit of God came mightily upon him, and he prophesied among them" (1 Sam. 10:6-11; cf. 19:19-24).

Religious rapture was known in Greek tradition, too: on one hand in the frenzied cults of Dionysus and later of Cybele, on the other hand in what is known as mantic prophecy.[3] At some point the activities of the Pythia in Delphi came to be characterized by ecstatic features: she was able to deliver prophetic oracles, because she was possessed by the spirit of Apollo that suffused her from below, when she sat on her tripod.[4] Plato refers several times to prophecy, which he calls a kind of madness, yet beneficial;[5] the reason of those who prophesy is "turned off" during their inspired speech, which is in need of interpretation (by qualified cultic personnel or, according to Plato, by the philosopher), as they do not know at all what they are speaking.[6] The God(dess) himself (herself) speaks through such a person. In a similar way, Philo explains that a prophet does not at all proclaim something that is his "own," being in a state of enthusiastic unknowingness; "his own reasoning powers . . . have quitted the citadel of his soul, while the divine spirit has entered and taken up its abode there" (Spec. 4.49).

To be sure, divine causation can be assumed and expressed even without reference to the spirit. In the writings ascribed to preexilic prophets, the prophetic gift or vocation is generally not attributed to the action of the spirit;[7] some prophets even dissociate themselves from the ecstatic raptures connected with prophets (for example, Hos. 9:7; Amos 7:14). Later on the spirit is, however, given a crucial role in all prophecy. The spirit enters Ezekiel and speaks to him (Ezek. 3:24), and transports him from one place to another (Ezek. 8:3). Zechariah 7:12 generalizes: Yahweh has sent the law and his words "by his spirit through the former [preexilic] proph-

ets." Other people, too, can prophesy in ecstasy, when the spirit given by Yahweh rests on them (Num. 11:25; 24:2). In rabbinic Judaism, the holy spirit is specifically the spirit of prophecy.[8] Some streams of rabbinic tradition hold that prophecy had ceased after Ezra and would return only in the eschatological age (for example, m. Abot 1; b. Yoma 9b). This view, however, forms after the destruction of the Second Temple; in the works of Josephus alone there is abundant evidence for first-century Jewish prophecy.[9]

Reports on communications with the heavenly world abound in apocalyptic works that reflect "a belief in direct revelation of the things of God which are mediated through dream, vision or divine intermediary."[10] As a rule, the intermediary is an angel; the spirit is not mentioned—except in 4 Ezra 14, a vivid description of an ecstatic experience.[11] Despite the pseudonymity and other literary conventions used in the apocalypses, there is no reason to doubt that genuine experiences often underlie the accounts. "The use of the vision as the form of pseudepigraphic writing in the apocalypses presupposed, for its plausibility, the prevalence of actual visionary activities within the society."[12]

Traces of other ecstatic phenomena are attested in the fringes of Judaism. In his account of the ascetic sect of Therapeutae in Egypt, Philo hints at their enthusiastic worship, which can resemble drunkenness (Contempl. 89); aspiring after a mystical vision of God, they "are carried away by a certain heavenly love, give way to enthusiasm, behaving like so many revellers in bacchanalian or corybantian mysteries" (Contempl. 12). The Testament of Job (48–50) narrates how the three daughters of Job praise God in an altered state of consciousness, in the language of angels.[13] The Qumranic Songs of Sabbath Sacrifice (4QShirShab) with their "repetitious, almost

230 hypnotic quality," would seem to have "increased the possibility of ecstatic experience among some worshippers"[14] in a group that believed that they were worshiping together with angels (for example, 1QH 11.21-22). Some have also assumed that the mention of a "vision of knowledge" (1QH 12.18) or the characterization of the people of the covenant as "seers of the holy angels, with open ears, hearing profound things"(1QM 10.10-11), presupposes actual ecstatic experiences of visionary or auditory nature.[15]

Philo himself held a refined notion, reminiscent of Plato, of the ecstasy-inducing spirit. He thought, on the basis of Genesis 2, that a breath of the divine spirit lived in all humans from birth as their higher reason, but he also expressed a longing for the extraordinary gift of ecstasy. Such a gift was available, though only to exceptional individuals who had engaged in an arduous process of self-examination. Eventually they might, through God's grace, receive a fresh gift of his spirit that would "drive out" reason and bring them into the state of divine ecstasy, "a sort of sober intoxication like the zealots engaged in the corybantian [Dionysian] festivals" (*Opif.* 71). Philo himself had sometimes experienced such a "heightened vision into supranormal reality"[16] in the course of his studies on scripture: when coming empty to his work he had "suddenly become full, ideas being, in an invisible manner, showered upon me, and implanted in me from on high"; through divine inspiration he had lost consciousness of place, persons, or himself, of words spoken or lines written (*Migr.* 34-35).[17]

The spirit, then, can be understood as a power that seizes a person in particular situations. On the other hand, it is also seen as a power permanently allotted to a person, in which case it often serves to establish that person's position in the community. Leadership in particular

was connected with empowering by the spirit (Moses: Num. 11; Joshua: Num. 27:18; Deut. 34:9). When David was anointed by Samuel, "the spirit of Yahweh came mightily upon him from that day forward" (1 Sam. 16:13). The stress on the permanent resting of Yahweh's spirit upon the king legitimized his position. Isaiah 11:1-5 combines the whole spectrum of virtues in the person of the king: wisdom, power, and righteousness are his traits as the bearer of the spirit.[18] In another stratum of the Hebrew Bible a permanent possession of the spirit (in the form of ecstasy!) is attributed to a group of seventy elders, who receive their share of the spirit that was originally bestowed on Moses (Num. 11); a "succession" of the spirit thus legitimizes a body of lay leaders in the postexilic community.[19] The spirit also helps some to gain learning (as in Philo), wisdom, knowledge of God, and even craftmanship.[20] One may surmise some rivalry between various appeals to the spirit: wisdom as a permanent divine gift was probably emphasized in circles other than those who marveled at abnormal phenomena.[21]

While possession by the spirit was seen as the privilege of some individuals who had special prestige, the hope of a democratization of this divine gift came also to be voiced. The bestowal of the spirit that causes prophecies and visions on all and sundry is singled out as a distinctive mark of the messianic era in Joel 3:1: "I will pour out my spirit on all flesh; your sons and your daughters shall prophesy, your old men shall dream dreams, and your young men shall see visions. Even upon the menservants and maidservants in those days, I will pour out my spirit."

But even virtuous everyday life in obedience to God's commands came to be ascribed to empowerment by the spirit. Full observance of God's decrees was expected in the future as a miraculous gift of the spirit. In Ezekiel's great vision of the valley of dry bones (Ezek. 37), God's spirit appears as a power that can breathe life into dead bones, which here represent the "house of Israel." When God puts his spirit within people, they will be able to walk in his statutes (Ezek. 36:27; cf. 39:29). Other prophets, too, could look forward to a general outpouring of God's spirit to effect a renewal of his people (Isa. 32:15).[22] The *Community Rule* of Qumran states that a man is cleansed of all his sins "by the spirit of the true counsel," "by the spirit of holiness," "by the spirit of uprightness and of humility" (1QS 3.6-8); in the end time God will cleanse humanity "with the spirit of holiness from every irreverent deed" and "sprinkle over him the spirit of truth like lustral water" (1QS 4.20-21). Actually the Essenes claim the presence of the spirit in their midst; several Qumran hymns mention "the spirit which you gave me" (1QH 20.11, adding "and I have listened loyally to your wonderful secret through your holy spirit"; 5.25; 8.19-20: "I have appeased your face by the spirit which you have given me . . . to purify me with your holy spirit"). The eschatological expectation of a general outpouring of the spirit attested by ecstatic phenomena (Joel) is thus coupled with a form of expectation where the work of the spirit is manifested in a religious and moral renewal of the people (or of a group)—with or without tangible, outward proofs.[23]

The Spirit and Extraordinary Phenomena

Jesus acted as a charismatic healer and exorcist whose fame as a miracle worker attracted crowds. No doubt he traced back his healing ability (which he connected with the approaching of God's kingdom) to divine power, whether or not he spoke specifically about God's spirit; it is Matthew who makes him ascribe his exorcisms explicitly to the spirit (Matt. 12:28).[24] The Synoptic authors describe Jesus as filled with the spirit since his baptism (in the case of Luke, even since his conception: Luke 1:35) and emphasize the role of the spirit in his work throughout. John, too, states that the spirit remains upon Jesus since his encounter with the Baptist (John 1:32-33). The accounts of the baptism do not seem to be based on a firsthand description by Jesus, however.[25] It is more likely that a crucial visionary experience underlies the saying in Luke 10:18. To what extent Jesus displayed erratic behavior is difficult to tell. In any case, his exorcistic activity evoked insinuations of black magic (of acting with the power of the archdemon Beelzebul and therefore perhaps being himself demon-possessed: Mark 3:22; Q 11:15) from adversaries, and even his family is reported to have thought that he was out of his mind (Mark 3:21).

The Synoptic Gospels also report that Jesus sent his disciples out to heal (and to proclaim the kingdom), giving them "authority" (Luke 9:1 adds: "and power") over demons and diseases (Mark 6:7 par.; cf. Mark 3:15 par.). Whether or not the account of a once-and-for-all sending reflects an actual event, it is likely that at least some of Jesus' disciples took part in his healing and exorcistic activity (with whatever success). The gift of healing connects Jesus with early Christianity; by contrast, his mission does *not* seem to anticipate the importance attributed to ecstatic speech among his followers.

Acts reports a great number of extraordinary phenomena in the earliest community. The

232 appearances of the risen Jesus were visionary experiences (see above, pp. 57–59), and visions continued to have a significant role in the life of the believers. The assumption has some plausibility that the appearance to "over more than five hundred" (1 Cor. 15:6) is identical with the "outpouring of the spirit" at Pentecost that Luke depicts in Acts 2:1-13.[26] In any case, "Luke's idea that at the beginning of the Christian church there was some sort of group experience involving a large group of people is probably correct."[27] But Luke has evidently changed the nature of the experience, turning it to a "language miracle":

the recipients of the spirit proclaim in numerous foreign (known) languages "the great acts of God."[28] The tradition underlying Luke's account must have envisaged a case of ecstatic glossolalia, as the ending of the story makes clear: outsiders conclude that the speakers are drunk (2:13)—an inference that fits incomprehensible speech much better than preaching in foreign languages.

The ecstatic outburst is interpreted as the fulfillment of the prophetic promise of a general outpouring of the spirit,[29] even though that prediction (Luke's Peter refers to Joel 3:1) singled out prophecy, dreams, and visions rather than

9.1   Christ breathes the Holy Spirit on the disciples, an illustration of John 20:22. Mosaic, sixth century. S. Apollinare Nuovo, Ravenna, Italy. Photo: © Erich Lessing/Art Resource, NY.

speaking in tongues.[30] Luke has preserved an old conviction, for Paul already takes for granted that possession of the spirit is the distinctive mark of all Christians, and that the gift of the spirit is the divine guarantee that the new era is at hand.[31] The experiences of the spirit are taken to be the "down payment" or the "seal" of the coming fulfillment (2 Cor. 1:22; 5:5; cf. Eph. 1:13; 4:30), or the "first fruits" of the harvest (Rom. 8:23).

In Peter's Pentecost speech, the gift of the spirit is tied to the rite of baptism (Acts 2:38). Whether or not this corresponds to the earliest understanding of baptism,[32] the connection is old enough for Paul also to take it for granted (1 Cor. 12:13; cf. 2 Cor. 1:22; also John 3:3, 5). At least some Christian circles evidently expected that baptism would bestow visible gifts, such as glossolalia and prophecy, on those who underwent the rite; the stories in Acts 8:15-17 and 19:1-6 suggest that, for some, a baptism without accompanying tangible signs was not a true baptism at all.[33] It is clear, however, that baptisms were not always connected with such "signs" and were nevertheless regarded as fully valid.[34] Otherwise it would have been difficult to uphold the notion that the gift of the spirit belonged to every Christian rather than just to a charismatic elite. The spirit is the possession of the congregation and consequently its members have their part of it—by definition, as it were. The analogy to the Essenes is evident.[35]

That ecstatic phenomena were not foreign to the early Jerusalem community is confirmed by the fact that *prophets*—immediately inspired spokespersons for God who received intelligible oracles that they felt impelled to deliver[36]—traveling from Jerusalem to Antioch are mentioned as a matter of course in Acts 11:27.[37] One of these prophets, Agabus, "predicted by the spirit" a great famine (11:28). He later appeared in Caesarea, this time too arriving from Judea; quoting the very words of the holy spirit, he predicted the arrest of Paul in Jerusalem

9.2   Pentecost, illustrated in a twelfth century service book. The scene differs from the account in Acts 2 in interesting ways: the Spirit is poured on the twelve apostles, not on the whole congregation; standing to the right of Peter (who is holding a key), is Paul, who was in reality an enemy of the congregation at this early stage. From "Ottenbeueren Collectarius," a service book. Y.T.2 Folio No: 27b-28. British Library, London. Photo: © HIP/Art Resource, NY.

234 (21:10-11). Miracle-working Philip is said to have four virgin daughters who had the gift of prophecy (Acts 21:9; these women were later famous in Asia Minor).[38] In the midst of the Q community, prophets appeared who, in the vision of this writing, represent unbroken continuity to the prophets of old Israel (Q 11:47-51); their legacy is visible in the community of Matthew, who values prophets (Matt. 10:41; cf. 5:12), even though he also has to come to terms with the ambiguity of the phenomenon (Matt. 7:15-23; see below).[39]

Even John of Patmos, the author of Revelation, was a visionary prophet,[40] apparently with a Palestinian background, rooted in the tradition of the wandering charismatics who had followed Jesus.[41] The book of Revelation assumes that it is the Lord himself who addresses his church through his inspired spokesman, expressly in the letters to the seven congregations in chapters 2–3, but also throughout the apocalypse (Rev. 1:1). Revelation 2–3 provides a vivid illustration of the fact that a Christian prophet could present his topical message as an utterance by the risen Jesus; it is a plausible inference that quite a few such utterances may have found their way to the Gospels as well.[42] In the *Odes of Solomon*, too, Christ often speaks through the mouth of the singer in the first person, which may be taken to express a "claim to prophetic inspiration."[43] The great significance of prophets in Jewish Christian tradition is finally testified to by the *Didache*, a work that comes from a community that both honors prophecy and has come to experience it as a problem (see below, p. 244). In Montanism, prophecy experienced a new period of flourishing but was eventually subdued for reasons that had more to do with established doctrine and practice than with the spiritual enthusiasm itself. Finally, Irenaeus (*Haer.* 1.13) gives us a glimpse of the activities of Marcus the "magician," a wandering prophet[44] of Valentinian persuasion, "a charismatic figure who attracts female followers in particular, teaching them to prophesy by inviting them to partake of his 'grace' and thereby become united with their own angels."[45] Not surprisingly, this ecstatic union receives a malicious sexual interpretation from Irenaeus.[46]

Visions and glossolalia are given a crucial role in the transfer of the faith to the Gentile world; they legitimize this major change in the understanding of sacred tradition. In Luke's narrative, the holy spirit suddenly falls upon the audience of Peter's sermon in the house of the uncircumcised Roman centurion, Cornelius: "The circumcised believers who had come with Peter were astounded that the gift of the holy spirit had been poured out even on the Gentiles, for they heard them speaking in tongues and extolling God" (Acts 10:45-46). The reception of the spirit by these Gentiles in the form of ecstatic glossolalia justifies Peter's spontaneous decision to baptize them: "Can anyone withhold the water for baptizing these people who have received the holy spirit just as we have?" (10:47) Refusing baptism would have been equivalent to hindering God, who had given the Gentiles the same gift as the circumcised believers (Acts 11:17). To be sure, weighty grounds speak against the historicity of the Cornelius story as Luke presents it,[47] and yet it does not lack plausibility: it is quite probable that incidents like this made some early Christians (though the historical Peter was certainly not the pioneer!)[48] opt for accepting uncircumcised converts who had "received the spirit." In reminding his Galatian converts of their recent past, Paul emphatically refers to their great experience: God had supplied them with the spirit and worked miracles among them (Gal. 3:2-5).[49] In 1 Thess. 1:5, Paul also underlines the importance of the spirit experience in the mission situation, which had made the former pagans convert: the message came to them "not in word only, but also in power and in the holy spirit and with full conviction" (cf. also 1 Cor. 2:4).

In Luke's report, Peter's encounter with Cornelius is prepared by a vision that Peter sees in a trance (Acts 10:9-16). In it, a heavenly voice instructs him that the old purity regulations concerning food are no longer in force; "what God has made clean, you must not call profane" (v. 15). In the rest of the story the food issue does not come up, however; evidently Peter's vision is an insertion to the Cornelius narrative. Nevertheless, the story seems to contain oblique historical information: some Jewish Christian probably had a vision of this sort (its ascription to Peter seems a Lukan idea), which once legitimized the relaxation of food laws in some circles.[50] Paul speaks of his vision(s) and presupposes that his rivals in Corinth appealed to visions (2 Cor. 12:1-7).[51] His mention of a "revelation" that caused him to go to Jerusalem (Gal. 2:2) probably refers to a dream or to a vision.[52] Matthew refers to dreams as reliable disclosures of God's will (Matt. 1:20; 2:13, 19, 22; 27:19). Visions abound, of course, in the book of Revelation; the ultimate source of these revelations is the exalted Christ (Rev. 1:1), and the seer refers to a trancelike state, in which he found himself when receiving auditions and visions (Rev. 1:10; 4:2; 17:3; 21:10).[53] Another man of many visions was the prolific Hermas. The visions in his *Shepherd* are commonly devalued as tedious and uninspiring,[54] but one can also be moved by the sincere ethos, in which they advise Hermas, a simple Roman Christian, both in his personal problems and in issues that seem to threaten his by now somewhat institutionalized church.[55]

The Valentinian "magician" Marcus told that he saw the "Supreme Tetrad" descend in female form upon him to reveal him things "which it had never before revealed to any one either of gods or men" (Irenaeus, *Haer.* 1.14.1; cf. Hippolytus, *Haer.* 6.37).[56] Some take Valentinus himself to hint at a "fundamental visionary experience": he is claimed to have mentioned that he had seen the Logos in the form of an infant who spoke to him.[57] The Valentinian *Interpretation of Knowledge* (15–17) shows a community split in two parties that are engaged in a debate over charismatic gifts, rather like the Corinthian community in Paul's time.[58]

A rich treasure of "spiritual gifts" (1 Cor. 12:1) was indeed on display in the gatherings of the Christian community in Corinth (12:4-11; 14:1-33): frequent outbursts of glossolalia, understood as the language of angels (13:1); ecstatic prophecy (notably performed also—perhaps even primarily—by women, 11:5-16); cases of healing and other miracles (12:9-10). Since the glossolalia did not consist of intelligible words, even the speaker did not understand it; an interpreter was required[59] on whom the spirit had bestowed the ability to give "interpretation of tongues" (12:10)—a skill that obviously gave the interpreter a lot of power, as no one else could know what was actually said.[60] Much as Paul appreciated the situation—he claims to speak more in tongues than any of the Corinthians (14:18) and may well have been responsible for introducing glossolalia to the community in the first place (cf. 2:4)[61]—it caused him quite some embarrassment. Deep down, the conduct of the "pneumatic élite" reminded him in an uneasy way of "the frenzied worship of the devotees of Dionysos (12:2)."[62] The women who prophesied without wearing veils, perhaps letting their hair flow free,[63] may even have been associated in his

236   mind with the Pythia, whose ecstatic oracles had obvious sexual connotations.[64] It can be said that the apostle "sexualizes women's unveiled ecstatic speech" by alluding to the lust of angels (11:10) that it is supposed to stimulate.[65] We shall return to Paul's handling of the situation shortly.

While it is true that "it is impossible to determine how widespread glossolalia was in earliest Christianity"[66]—apart from 1 Corinthians and Acts "there is no hint of the practice of glossolalia in any other Christian writing before the middle of the second century"[67]—it can hardly be doubted that it was of significance during the first formative decades; otherwise it is hard to understand how Luke could have given the phenomenon (which he may indeed not have experienced in his own environment any more) so prominent a position in his praising account of earliest Christianity. It may be that the shortage of documentation depends on the fragmentary and selective character of our extant sources.[68] A noteworthy new outburst came in the mid-second century with the Montanists, who thought that Jesus' promise of the Paraclete in the Gospel of John was realized in the activity of their prophets.[69] Montanus regarded himself as a passive instrument of the holy spirit, "like a lyre struck with a plecton" (Epiphanius, *Pan.* 48.4.1). He understood his "strange speech" as a form of prophecy; it was "accompanied by the frenzy associated with mantic prophecy."[70] Tertullian, who went over to Montanism, cites the occurrence of ecstatic speech in his community as a proof of its authenticity, against Marcion (*Marc.* 5.8). Irenaeus also claims to have heard "many brethren in the church having prophetic gifts and speaking through the spirit in all tongues," a phrase that indicates that he understood tongues to mean "other languages" in the vein of Acts 2; but his report on the Valentinian "magician" Marcus mentions women whose manner of speech "suggests glossolalia or mantic prophecy."[71] Then, however, glossolalia seems to have moved to the fringes of Christianity[72] until its latter-day resurgence in Pentecostalism and the charismatic movement.

A number of miraculous *cures* are ascribed to the apostles: they are reported to have healed lameness, blindness, and paralysis (Acts 3:1-10; 8:7; 9:18, 33-34; and elsewhere), expelled demons (19:11), and even to have brought dead people back to life (9:36-41; cf. 20:9-12). Conversely, they also have the power to cause illness and even death as punishment for opposing the Lord (13:8-12) or lying to the spirit (5:1-11). Stephen, the leader of the Seven, "full of faith and the holy spirit" and of "grace and power," does "great wonders and signs" (6:5, 8); his work is carried on by Philip, who heals many demon-possessed, paralyzed, and lame (8:5-8). Even the shadow of Peter and some handkerchiefs touched by Paul possess healing power (5:15-16; 19:11-12).

All wonders listed in the preceding paragraph are narrated in the book of Acts, whose author can with good reason be suspected of credulity and exaggeration. Sometimes his account seems to be miles away from what may reasonably be assumed to have been the case: for Luke, Paul's handkerchiefs have a magical power, but Paul himself says that he was not able to heal himself from his "thorn in the flesh," despite his repeated efforts of intense prayer (2 Cor. 12:8-9). On the other hand, Paul admits in the very same context that "signs and wonders and mighty works" belong to "the signs of a true apostle"; charismatic "superapostles" (as Paul ironically calls these rivals of his) may have performed such signs in abundance, but then Paul is not at all inferior to them, having done the same among the Corinthians (2 Cor. 12:11-12). In a somewhat less polemical context (though here too Paul feels a pressing need to recommend himself to a more or less reserved audience), the apostle appeals to what Christ has accomplished through him "by the power of signs and wonders, by the power of the spirit of God" (Rom. 15:19). So clearly "signs and wonders" (a phrase that primarily suggests miracles of healing) were expected of a religious leader, and Paul assures his readers that he has met the requirement.[73] It is equally clear that the power to work signs was connected to power over souls and could easily lead to rivalry and conflict. This is what happened in Corinth, where Paul had constantly to defend his authority. Second Corinthians shows him engaged in a battle with rival preachers who, even on Paul's testimony, had excelled him in spectacular feats. In countering them, Paul appeals to his own pneumatic ability on one hand but plays down the significance of charismatic display on the other; almost making a virtue out of a vice, he sets out to fight the power displayed by the others by praising his own weakness—"for power is made perfect in weakness" (2 Cor. 12:9-10; cf. 4:7).

Paul established a connection between his weakness, which relativized the significance of miracle-working power, and his emphasis on the sufferings of Christ, in which his followers were expected to share (on this "theology of the cross," see, for example, 2 Cor. 13:3-4).[74] As Acts shows, however, miracles continued to be valued increasingly highly; even though Luke, too, stresses the suffering of Christ, it is hardly exaggerated to speak of a "theology of glory" in connection with his story of early Christianity. The development of the gospel tradition points in the same direction, as ever more impressive feats are attributed to Jesus in the Synoptic Gospels (stilling a storm, walking on the water), in John (raising Lazarus, who is in the process of putrefaction),

and in the infancy gospels. Irenaeus writes that miracles are frequent among Christians, even claiming that often "the spirit of a dead man has returned at the prayers of brethren"—a feat that the heretics, according to Irenaeus, are unable to perform (*Haer.* 2.31.2). The apostolic novels of the second century know of no limits to the power of the Christian heroes to work miracles with God's aid. A case in point is the showdown between Simon Peter and Simon Magus in the *Acts of Peter*: Simon demonstrates his power by flying around above the city of Rome, but Peter makes him fall down, whereby Simon breaks his leg and is stoned to death by the crowds.[75]

THE SPIRIT AND EVERYDAY CHRISTIAN LIFE

Above I noted a current in the Hebrew Bible that singles out wisdom, practical skills, and God-fearing life as manifestations of the spirit of God, implicitly playing down the significance of extraordinary accomplishments. The tension between the two notions of spirit-possession carries over to early Christianity.[76] Paul makes a concerted effort to raise normal workaday abilities to the same level with ecstatic gifts, if not above them.

In dealing with the tumultuous situation in Corinth, Paul sets forth a ranking order of the ecstatic gifts: prophecy is to be valued over glossolalia,[77] because it contains a comprehensible message from God that *edifies the community*. By contrast, speaking in tongues, even though inspired by the spirit, is human speech addressed to God (thus also Rom. 8:26); if it is not interpreted, it serves only to edify the indi-

238 vidual in her or his private relationship with God (1 Cor. 14:1-5 and the whole chapter). Prophecy is clearly a much more valuable gift—and even it should not cause disorder in the gatherings (14:33).

Paul thus tries to domesticate the ecstatic behavior of the pneumatic élite by subordinating glossolalia to prophecy (and in effect both to decent order!). But he goes further. He starts his instruction on the "spiritual gifts" (1 Cor. 12:1) by emphasizing that the same spirit endows different people with rather different gifts: "to each is given the manifestation of the spirit for the common good" (12:7). In the list of the gifts that follows, the tongues and their interpretation are mentioned last, and prophecy just before them.

Strikingly, the spiritual gifts are said to include the "discernment of spirits" (*diakriseis pneumaton*, v. 10), which seems to mean that it is necessary to distinguish between genuine and false ecstatic utterances. The implication (which Paul carefully avoids stating in so many words) is that spirits other than God's may be involved on the charismatic scene![78] Paul makes a similar point at the end of his instructions for the gatherings: when prophets speak, the others[79] are "to weigh (*diakrinein*) what is said" (14:29). The same concern had already appeared in Paul's first extant letter, where he admonished the Thessalonians not to "quench the spirit" nor "despise the words of prophets," yet to "test everything" and "hold fast to what is good"[80] (1 Thess. 5:19-21).[81] Unfor-

9.3   Ancient Corinth. Photo: Marshall Johnson.

tunately, this is easier said than done; letting the spirit reign and at the same time calmly weighing its manifestations in a rational vein is a very difficult combination. One of the two very different orientations is likely to carry the day, at the cost of the other. The delicacy of Paul's situation becomes clear when one thinks of the early Christian warnings of blaspheming the spirit (Mark 3:29 par.): the insinuation that the power displayed by early Christian healers may stem from a source other than God is branded as an unforgivable sin. Paul is indeed walking a tightrope.

At the beginning of the list of gifts in 1 Corinthians stand some that evidently do not require anything like an altered state of consciousness: wisdom and knowledge (1 Cor. 12:8-9).[82] The subsequent comparison of the community with a body underlines the necessity of all members and even reverses standard evaluations, claiming that God has given "the greater honor to the inferior member, that there may be no dissension within the body, but the members may have the same care for one another" (12:24-25). Paul is clearly trying to play down the value of ecstatic phenomena: no special prestige in the community should be connected with them! Paul clinches the matter by inserting an almost lyrical passage (1 Cor. 13) that praises love as the "more excellent way," far superior to tongues or prophecy (or even to knowledge); in Gal. 5:22, too, Paul singles out love as the prime fruit of the spirit (cf. also Rom. 5:5).

The process of what might be called demystifying the manifestations of the spirit culminates when Paul returns to the comparison with the body in Romans (Rom. 12:4-8). The list of the different gifts now starts with prophecy (glossolalia is not mentioned at all), but it continues with such gifts of grace (charisms) as ministering, teaching, exhortation, generous giving, and

leadership. Even good administration is counted as a spiritual gift. What started as enthusiastic, extraordinary experiences are here domesticated, or adapted to the requirements of normal everyday life.

Not only are various common-life skills attributed to the power of the spirit. The (pre-Pauline) notion that everybody receives the spirit in baptism leads to the conviction that in Christian communities *everything* (except, of course, wrong behavior, which should not occur at all) is caused by the spirit. This is a tenet strongly emphasized by Paul, and it too serves to turn attention away from the more spectacular manifestations of the spirit. God has given Christians the spirit (1 Thess. 4:8; 1 Cor. 2:12; 2 Cor. 1:22; 5:5; Rom. 5:5); indeed, its possession is a necessary condition for being a Christ-believer (Rom. 8:9). Unlike non-Christian Jews, Christians have been born from the spirit (Gal. 4:29) and have received the "spirit of adoption" that makes them cry, "*Abba!* Father!" (Rom. 8:14-15). The spirit is the liberating power of the new life that frees from the power of sin, death, and flesh (cf. Rom. 8:1-11; 2 Cor. 3:17), starting with the resurrection of Jesus by the power of the spirit (Rom. 1:4). The participation in (the body of) Christ that stands in the center of Paul's view of salvation takes place in the realm of the spirit. "In Christ" and "in the spirit" can be used interchangeably (cf. Rom. 8:1, 9); consequently the presence of the spirit is equivalent to the presence of Christ. The spirit is the driving force behind the believer's morality; "in the spirit" comes to mean "Christian life." The spirit is "no longer conceived of as a force that comes and goes, but as a Christian's permanent and abiding possession."[83]

Here, however, a gap opens between theory and reality.[84] As a great number of passages (for example, 1 Thess. 4:3-8;[85] Gal. 5:13-15;

240 and 1 Cor. 5:1-6, 20) show, the spirit certainly did not guide the Christians automatically (as it were) to holy life in Paul's congregations. In 1 Corinthians, Paul even criticizes the self-styled pneumatics by verbally denying them the status of "spiritual people" (1 Cor. 3:1-4). They are still "fleshly" and should correct their conduct, so that Paul can treat them as adults rather than as spiritual infants.[86] In this light, the great eulogy (Rom. 8:1-17) that paints a wonderful picture of life in the spirit (in contrast to life in the flesh) actually turns out to be a piece of *group polemics*, which idealizes those who believe in (Paul's gospel of) Christ and denigrates those who (like the majority of the Jews) reject it (cf. above, p. 149). But Paul does his best to instigate his converts to live up to their calling: "If we live by the spirit, let us also be guided by the spirit!" (Gal. 5:25).

For gnostically inclined Christians, *pneuma* is the divine spark that is found inside *all* humans,[87] even though it must be discovered and activated through a special illumination. Anyone who gains this insight and realizes his or her potentiality is a spiritual person, a pneumatic. In this case, too, the crucial impulse to fulfilled life comes from outside, from the divine world of light. The fountain of the spirit is the true God, the ineffable Father, who also bears the name (invisible) spirit in cosmogonic accounts, for example, in the extended doxology in *Apoc. John* 2.26—4.26. But although the spirit is thought to reside within the person, waiting to be discovered, the event of salvation can also be in more conventional Christian style described as the "descending" of the spirit on the enlightened:

> Those on whom the spirit of life will descend and whom the spirit will empower will be saved, and will become perfect . . . and be cleansed of all evil and the anxieties of wickedness, since they are no longer anxious for anything except the incorruptible alone, and concerned with that from this moment on, without anger, envy, jealousy, desire, or greed of anything. They are affected by nothing but being in the flesh alone, and they wear the flesh as they look forward to a time when they will be met by those who receive them. Such people are worthy of the incorruptible, eternal life and calling. They endure everything and bear everything so as to finish the contest and receive eternal life. (*Apoc. John* 25.23—26.7; see the whole passage 25.16—27.30)[88]

This description of the cleansed pneumatics resembles Paul's praise of the fruit of the spirit in Galatians 5 and Romans 8. And the gap between proto-orthodox and Valentinian Christians continues to narrow down when one realizes that Theodotus, the Valentinian, ascribes fundamental significance to baptism as the locus of the bestowal of the spirit.[89] The invisible presence of the spirit transforms the water (*Exc. Theod.* 81.2), leads to sanctification (82.2), and makes possible the removal of evil from the person. The baptismal seal "holds the promise of a sinless existence for the psychics (!) and, consequently, entry into the joyful marriage feast in the Ogdoad at the end of this Age."[90] The *Gospel of Philip* stresses the "dual baptism" (baptism and chrism): one who has been anointed possesses everything, including the holy spirit (*Gos. Phil.* 74.18-21). Its possession provides the Christian with life and escape from death and the clutches of the evil powers (68.22—69.8; 59.19). Unclean spirits will not cleave to one who possesses the holy spirit (66.2-3).[91] Michel Desjardins convincingly shows that the traditional view (based on polemical patristic accounts) of Valentinian Christians as an elite, highly restricted group of pneumatics, predetermined to salvation regardless of how they live, is proved wrong by the Nag Hammadi library.[92]

The Spirit Guides the Church

According to the Acts of the Apostles, the spirit is effectively present at every important turn in the life of the church. Everything happens according to a divine plan that is disclosed to the apostles or to the congregation when needed, whether through prophetic utterances or through visions.[93] In such connections, the spirit can be referred to in personal terms: it speaks in direct words and makes concrete moves. But Acts 21:4 states explicitly that the spirit speaks through other Christians (cf. 20:23), and that is probably Luke's actual view in most cases. The spirit's orders to Peter to follow the envoys of Cornelius without hesitation (10:19) lead in Luke's scheme of events to the baptism of the first Gentiles. The spirit tells, probably through a prophet, the congregation of Antioch to set apart Barnabas and Saul for missionary work (13:2). It guides the two on their travels very specifically by forbidding them to work in certain places (16:6-7), while a nocturnal vision makes them understand where they *are* needed (16:9-10). Having listened to Peter's testimony and James's exegetical reflections, the congregation of Jerusalem decides to issue the Apostolic Decree (15:22); what seems to be a democratic decision by the community (or its elders) is, however, solemnly introduced with the words "it has seemed good *to the holy spirit and to us*" (15:28). Likewise, it

is the spirit that has made certain persons overseers of a community (20:28).

Luke's narrative reveals a clear apologetic tendency: the whole history of the church, as Luke sees it, has been guided by the spirit. This appeal to the spirit amounts to a powerful legitimization of what has actually happened. The decisions of the (leaders of) the congregations are depicted as decisions of the spirit. The emphasis on providence leads Luke to play down the many actual conflicts in the early history of the church, as a comparison of Acts with Galatians soon makes clear. The guidance of the spirit is impressively portrayed in stories that on examination prove fictional (the story of Peter as the initiator of the Gentile mission being a case in point).

A more inward view of guidance emphasizes the necessity of the work of the spirit in the discovery of religious truth within the congregation. Paul of course counts himself among those spirit-filled teachers (1 Cor. 12:28) who are "not taught by human wisdom but taught by the spirit, interpreting spiritual things by the spirit's means" (1 Cor. 2:13).[94] Undoubtedly Paul thought that God had revealed to him through the spirit (1 Cor. 2:10) the mysteries that he had discovered (1 Cor. 15:51; Rom. 11:25; at least in the latter case in the course of combing the scripture with his present problems in mind).[95] In the scripture the spirit speaks,[96] but precisely therefore only those who possess it can understand the scripture correctly (cf. 1 Cor. 2:14).[97] In 2 Corinthians 3, Paul argues the case at length against some critics, who apparently put weight on the law of Moses, with the aid of a curious allegory about the veil on Moses' face (Exod. 34:29-30). The "letter"—a literal understanding of the scripture—kills, but the spirit gives life (2 Cor. 3:6). When non-Christian Jews interpret the scripture, a veil lies over it (or on the hearts

242 of the readers); it is only removed when one converts to the dominion of the spirit (3:17). Time and again, Paul's exegesis in the spirit produces truly astonishing results; he is capable of squeezing from a text a meaning that is just the opposite of the original meaning (a case in point is Rom. 10:8).[98] Subsequently, the scripture comes increasingly to be seen as words spoken by the prophetic spirit that has foretold Christian truths in a more or less enigmatic manner.

The Johannine tradition presupposes that the spirit is experienced in the congregation (cf. John 3:5-8; 1 John 2:20, 27; 3:24; 4:13). But it is not presented primarily as a power that works miracles and causes striking psychic phenomena,[99] not even as the power and norm of Christian life in the Pauline vein. The spirit has more to do with right knowledge.[100] The risen Jesus breathes the spirit on his disciples in order to enable them to lead and control the community (John 20:22-23). In a late stratum of the Gospel, in Jesus' farewell speech to his disciples, the author introduces the figure of the Paraclete (Counselor or Advocate), in whom the holy spirit (14:26) and the ascended Jesus (14:16; cf. 1 John 2:1) merge in a peculiar way; the Paraclete is, as it were, "the presence of Jesus while Jesus is absent."[101] One of the functions of the Paraclete is to lead the community to "all the truth" (16:13), to teach it everything; this involves "reminding" it of all that Jesus has said (14:26). This is a hermeneutical task that amounts to seeing incidents in Jesus' earthly life in a new light and giving them new meanings, as indicated by repeated remarks on how the disciples "remembered" what Jesus had said or what had happened to him (2:21-22; 12:16; and elsewhere). Evidently the bold reinterpretation of Jesus' teachings throughout the Gospel that actually amounts to a critique of the tradition[102] was understood by the author(s)

as the true interpretation, to which the Paraclete had guided him (or them). "The whole Gospel of John is nothing but an exposition of the Christ-event through the Paraclete, in whom again the glorified Christ speaks and legitimizes the Johannine tradition."[103] The introduction of the Paraclete serves to legitimize the work and status of those who were responsible for shaping this tradition.[104] This reinterpretation of the person and message of Jesus means also a reinterpretation of the role of the spirit in a cognitive, almost doctrinal vein.[105]

In exercising his office as bishop, Ignatius could appeal to the spirit. Among the Philadelphians, he once "spoke with a loud voice, the voice of God: give heed to the bishop, and to the presbytery and deacons." Ignatius assures that he had not been informed of the divisions among the community beforehand; it was the spirit that proclaimed: "Do nothing without the bishop!" (Ign. *Phld.* 7.1-2). The charisma is there, but it serves to "reinforce church order through the developing regular channels."[106]

In the Pastoral Epistles, the officeholder is clearly the primary bearer of the spirit. The general possession of the spirit by all the baptized is naturally assumed (Titus 3:5), but it sounds like a faint echo from the past, so closely is the gift of the spirit tied to the office. "Timothy" has received this gift through the laying on of hands by "Paul" (2 Tim. 1:6-7) and by the council of elders (1 Tim. 4:14). One has moved a long step back toward the archaic notion of extraordinary individuals as spirit-bearers—but this time the possession of the spirit does not manifest itself in extraordinary phenomena (as Ignatius still claims, trying to connect the extraordinary with the orderly) but on the contrary in the sober, rational management of the household of the *ekklesia*. The help of the spirit is most of all needed in guarding the treasure of tradition that is entrusted to the officeholder (2 Tim. 1:14). "The author of the Pastorals can properly be regarded as the first churchman to deal with enthusiasm by rejecting it totally and shutting it out wholly from the life of the Church."[107]

Conflicts
around the Spirit

Manifestations of the spirit are notoriously ambiguous. The problem of conflicting prophecies is age-old and richly documented in the Hebrew Bible.[108] Any criteria for distinguishing true prophets from false ones were too vague to be truly helpful. Lamentations complains of the false and deceptive visions and oracles by which prophets have misled the people (Lam. 2:14), and the problem is not made easier by the notion that Yahweh himself may have sent deceitful messages through prophets (for example, 1 Kgs. 22:19-23).[109]

While it was generally not denied that Jesus and some of his followers performed miraculous cures, the source of their power was not obvious to all. Outsiders could trace their exorcisms back to Satan and his demons, an explanation that was seen by many Christians as an unforgivable sin against the holy spirit (Mark 3:22-30; Matt. 12:32). But even among the Jesus-believers themselves, the gifts of the spirit caused confusion and conflict, despite the fact that Ephesians stresses the work of the spirit in creating unity in the church (Eph. 4:3-7). Manifestations of the spirit among Gentiles may have persuaded some to accept them into the congregation without circumcision (Acts 10:44-48), but this was not acceptable to others, as the actions of Paul's critics in Galatia and Luke's Christian Pharisees in Acts 15 show. Paul found it necessary not only to subordinate glossolalia to prophecy, but also to exhort his congregations to test and weigh even the utterances of the prophets (1 Cor. 14:29). Paul's bottom line is that a prophet who disagrees with the command of the Lord will not be recognized—and what the command of Lord is, is evident from what he, Paul, stipulates![110] In his subsequent attacks on his critics in 2 Corinthians, Paul displays a reserved attitude to "visions and revelations of the Lord" (2 Cor. 12:1) and gives a seemingly humble report on a visionary experience of his own (12:2-4). Yet, for all his reservations regarding the visions of others, Paul places an enormous amount of emphasis on his *own* visionary encounter with the risen Christ (1 Cor. 9:1; 15:8-10; Gal. 1:11-17). That is the only source of the tremendous authority that he claims for himself (at the expense of those who had actually known Jesus). Throughout his correspondence, Paul makes clear (though this often happens indirectly) that he is unquestionably a bearer of the spirit and that questioning his authority or his motives amounts to opposing the spirit and thus opposing God (for example, 1 Cor. 2:13-16; 2 Cor. 1:20-22).[111]

In the narrative of Acts, the spirit gives Paul contradictory advice. The Christians in Tyre tell him "through the spirit" not to go to Jerusalem (Acts 21:4), but the very same spirit has already taken Paul "captive" and is taking him toward "imprisonments and persecution" in the Holy City (Acts 20:22-23). Luke does not seem to be bothered by the discrepancy; he accepts without question that all inspired utterances within the Christian community are given by the holy spirit.[112] Others are more critical.[113] For all his emphasis on charismatic healing,[114]

244   the phenomenon of prophecy seems suspect to Mark; he seems to know only *false* prophets in his own environment (13:22).[115] Matthew does value Christian prophets of his own time (Matt. 10:41; cf. 5:12). However, he also directs harsh criticisms against "ravenous wolves" in sheep's clothing who (he says) prophesy and do deeds of power but do not do the will of God (Matt. 7:15-23).[116] Whom he is thinking of is anybody's guess.[117] First John 4:1-3 expressly warns the community not to "believe every spirit"; the spirits are to be tested "to see whether they are from God, for many false prophets have gone out into the world." The criterion given by the author is agreement with Johannine Christology.

The *Didache* is deeply aware of the ambiguous nature of prophets. The instructions given for handling the problem are somewhat incongruous, which may indicate different hands over an extended period of time (but the discrepancies would also be understandable as arising from the delicate nature of the phenomenon itself). It is an unforgivable sin to question a prophet when he speaks in the spirit (*Did.* 11.7), and yet some things are not to be tolerated even if said "in the spirit" (11.12). More than that: "not everyone who speaks in the spirit is a prophet, but only if he has the ways of the Lord" (11.8). The criterion of true prophecy is whether the person teaches according to the truth (11.1), but even so he is a deceiver if he does not practice what he teaches (11.10). Hermas, too, receives the advice to examine the person's life (*Mand.* 11.7-17). A true prophet, who has the divine spirit, does not answer questions; that is, he does not act in the way of heathen oracles (*Mand.* 11.4), nor does he take payment. He speaks only when God makes him speak (that is, in the gathering of the congregation). In all this, the false prophet, whom the devil fills with *his* spirit (!), is different. Still, Her-

mas has to admit that at some points even the false prophet speaks the truth (*Mand.* 11.3). The issue was, then, anything but straightforward.

In the last analysis, *any* differences and conflicts between different Christian groups can be described in terms of conflicting appeals to the guidance of the spirit, often connected with a flat denial to such guidance on the part of the other side. "The concept of the gift of the Spirit provides an easy way of disposing of criticism: the gift has not been given."[118] When the author of 1 Timothy asserts that "the spirit expressly says" that some "liars" will demand asceticism and abstinence from certain foods (1 Tim. 4:1-3), he at least implicitly challenges the Apostolic Decree. The decree does demand such abstinence and is presented by Luke as a decision made with the express guidance of the holy spirit (Acts 15:28). Revelation testifies to a battle of prophets: John of Patmos fiercely attacks the Thyatiran woman leader "who calls herself a prophet" but, in John's opinion, leads Christ's servants badly astray (Rev. 2:20); here too the Apostolic Decree seems to be an issue (see p. 287). What Christ tells John to write (Rev. 2:1, 8, and elsewhere) is at the same time "what the spirit says to the congregations" (2:7, 11, and elsewhere). John provides his message with utmost authority (which he may, however, have lacked in his social circumstances).[119] Ironically, for centuries large parts of the church had great reservations about his message.

There were also early Christian circles that could speak of Christian life *without* recourse to "spirit" language. For Matthew, the inner source of moral actions and attitudes is not the divine spirit but the human heart; therein lie the roots of both good and evil (Matt. 12:33-35, and elsewhere).[120] The disciple is not alone in his moral quest, for Jesus will always be present in the church (Matt. 18:20; 28:20; cf. 1:23), but there is no identification of Jesus' presence with the spirit,[121] and the responsibility of the individual for his or her conduct (and its consequences) is emphasized. The Epistle of James, standing in the wisdom traditions of the Hebrew Bible, speaks of "the wisdom from above" (Jas. 3:17) in a way that parallels Paul's talk of the fruits of the spirit (Jas. 3:13-18; cf. 1:5, 17 on divine gifts); the author does not speak of the spirit as an eschatological gift (but presupposes that healings can be performed in the congregation with the aid of "prayer in faith" and of unction with oil).[122]

PERSONIFYING THE SPIRIT

Originally, the spirit (*pneuma*) is clearly an impersonal force, occasionally even understood as a kind of fluid stuff (for example, as regards the "spirit body" of 1 Cor. 15:44, 46).[123] Consequently, the spirit can be "poured" upon humans, or they can be "filled" with it, or the spirit may "indwell" them. Yet in other connections the spirit tends to get hypostatized (rather like the divine attributes Wisdom and Logos in Jewish tradition), or it receives personal traits. It can be referred to as if it were an acting subject: it has spoken (in the scripture) and continues to speak in the present, giving orders and advice, or providing harassed Christians with courage in courtrooms, where it speaks through their mouths (Q 12:12; Mark 13:11 par.). Paul mentions the intercession of the spirit in prayer (Rom. 8:26-27). The spirit also functions in the manner of an active subject when it distributes gifts (1 Cor. 12:11).[124]

It is one (small) step further in a personal direction when Paul speaks of the "sending" of the spirit (Gal. 4:6), which he parallels with the sending of Christ (Gal. 4:4). The spirit and the risen Christ have largely similar functions in his thought world: the spirit of Christ or of God lives in the believers, and so does Christ (Rom. 8:9-11; cf. Gal. 2:20). The risen Christ acts as a life-giving spirit (1 Cor. 15:45). Such statements that equate, to some extent at least, the functions of the risen Christ and the spirit serve to give the spirit a more personal, independent role and can even raise the question of their mutual relationship (and, in the thought of subsequent patristic thinkers, the question of the relationship of each to God the Father).[125] The spirit certainly receives a personal character, with far-reaching consequences, in the Gospel of John, which portrays the Paraclete, the spirit of truth, in personal terms and virtually identifies him with the ascended Christ.

Others thought of the spirit in personal terms without identifying him (or her!) with Christ. In Acts and in Revelation, the spirit alternates with an angel or angels as the provider of revelations, but in some other circles the spirit itself is understood as an angel. Hermas, for whom the spirit is above Jesus in rank (see below), seems to equate the spirit with the archangel Michael.[126] The prophet Elchasai was reported to have received his heavenly book from two huge angels: one was the Son of God, the other, a female one, the holy spirit (Hippolytus, *Haer.* 9.13.2-3). In the *Ascension of Isaiah*, "the angel of the holy spirit" is worshiped along with Christ and sits on the left hand of the "Great Glory" (*Ascen. Isa.* 11.33).

The notion of the spirit as an angelic being comes close to the notion of a hypostasis, a personified attribute of God, such as Wisdom or Logos. In the *Gospel of the Hebrews* (frg. 2), the spirit comes down on Jesus at his baptism and

246 speaks: "My Son, I was waiting for you in all the prophets, waiting for you to come so that I could rest in you. For you are my rest; you are my first-begotten Son who rules forever" (Jerome, *Comm. Isa.* 11.1-3). The spirit has here taken the role of God's Wisdom, which in some Jewish traditions wanders around, looking for a place to rest (Sir. 24:7). In another fragment of the same Gospel (3), this spirit seizes Jesus by his hair and carries him away to Mount Tabor (cf. Mark 1:12; Matt. 4:1), thus combining its Wisdom character with the nature of a numinous power that raptures charismatic persons. Jesus calls the spirit his mother, which reflects the fact that in Hebrew the noun "spirit" (*ruah*) is feminine (not neuter as *pneuma* is in Greek).

Given that both christological and pneumatological ideas were nourished by the same source, the world of ideas connected with God's Wisdom and his Word, it comes as no great surprise that the roles of Christ and the spirit were easily blurred. Hermas may not have a unified view of the matter,[127] but it seems that it is the holy spirit (rather than Jesus) who is the beloved Son; he is above Jesus in rank (*Sim.* 9.1.1). Originally there were apparently two divine powers, the Father and the spirit; only later was Jesus, the Savior, elevated to be their companion (*Sim.* 5.6.5-7). Justin, for his part, seems to equate the spirit with the Logos (*1 Apol.* 33.1);[128] both are worshiped by Christians, but Justin makes clear that the "prophetic spirit" is lower in rank than Christ (and the Creator God is, of course, above both, *1 Apol.* 13).[129] Theophilus of Antioch identified the spirit with Wisdom and was the first to apply the term *triad* to the Godhead, stating that the three days that preceded the creation of sun and moon were "types of the Triad, that is, of God and of His Word and of His Wisdom" (*Autol.* 2.15).[130] J. N. D. Kelly notes, however, that "the Apologists appear to have been extremely vague as to the exact status and role of the Spirit," whose essential function still seems to have been to provide the inspiration for the prophets.[131]

By contrast, in what came to be called "modalistic Monarchianism," distinctions between Father, Son, and Spirit tended to blur. For Sabellius in the third century, the Son and the Spirit were the Father's modes of self-expression; the same Godhead that was called Father when regarded as Creator, and Son when regarded as Redeemer, "operated as Spirit to inspire and bestow grace."[132] Modalistic ideas of a slightly different sort were presented by gnostic Christians in "a more mythologically elaborate" version.[133] In the Sethian *Apocryphon of John*, the Savior reveals himself to John as the Father, the Mother, and the Son, that is, as the one God who is without form but can manifest itself in different forms. The divine Mother has taken the place occupied by the Spirit in proto-orthodox triads.[134] The title "Spirit" is reserved in this writing for the true God, who is beyond description.

"Orthodox" patristic writers long alternated between the ideas of the holy spirit being a good gift of God through Christ on one hand and (as the Spirit) a part of the eternal Godhead on the other. Eventually, in the fourth century, the doctrine of the Trinity came to be established, in which the Spirit is a person of the Godhead, being of the same substance with the Father and the Son. Although the doctrine is constantly invoked in liturgical formulas, it has always remained unclear to ordinary Christians.[135] In popular imagination, the Trinity of the theologians has found a formidable rival in the veneration of the Virgin Mary;[136] in many forms of Catholic piety, the Virgin has for all practical purposes usurped the third place in the divine triad.[137]

10

True Israel?

From Jewish to Christian Identity

What became Christianity started as a Jewish movement. Most important to the self-understanding of the early Christian communities was their allegiance to Jesus, but the problem that most plagued them was their relation to other manifestations of Judaism. With reference to the Jewish scripture they could establish a respectably ancient past for themselves in a world that did not appreciate innovation. Jewish tradition supplied them with resources for reflection about identity. However, liberties taken with regard to the practical observance of the Torah caused the movement to drift gradually away from Judaism. The parting of the ways is a fact in the second century: by the time of Pliny it is clear that Christians are not Jews.[1] But this change is hard to understand if a process of separation was not already going on in the first century. Nero's persecution in the 60s shows that the Christians in Rome were a group distinct from Jews at the social level, no matter whether they saw themselves as the true Israel or how much they drew on Jewish traditions. We will see that the process is at work even earlier, *pace* a trend in current biblical scholarship that one-sidedly emphasizes the Jewishness of all early Christianity.

JEWISH IDENTITY

As was set forth in chapter 1, Israelite religious ideology was radically reconstructed in terms of exclusive monotheism in and after the exile, above all by the Deuteronomist movement.[2] As a consequence, Jewish identity[3] in the time of the Second Temple was based on the notion of common ancestry and shared religious and cultural practice. The putative ethnic bond was supported by the twin concepts of election and covenant. The one God of the universe had chosen Israel to do his will; he had made a covenant with the people and set forth its terms in the Torah. Israel was to serve and obey him alone; worship of the Gods of other people in any form was strictly forbidden as idolatry. This basic

248 obligation was poignantly expressed in the first lines of the Shema ("Hear!"), the centerpiece of Jewish liturgy: "Hear, O Israel, the Lord is our God, the Lord alone" (Deut. 6:4).[4] Monotheism and observance of the Torah bound Jews together and set them apart. In Jewish perception, the world consisted of Jews and non-Jews (Gentiles, "the nations"); the boundary between the two was also the boundary between the holy and the profane.[5]

The classic formulation of the doctrine of election is found in the book of Deuteronomy: "For you are a people holy to Yahweh your God; Yahweh your God has chosen you to be a people for his own possession, out of all the peoples that are on the face of the earth" (Deut. 7:6). The reason given is Yahweh's incomprehensible love for this people,[6] along with the "oath" he had sworn to their ancestors (Deut. 7:7-8), namely, the promise given to Abraham and later repeated to Isaac and Jacob: Israel's very existence would mediate a blessing to all nations of the earth (Gen. 12:1-3). Yahweh's election of Abraham and his descendants manifested itself in his great deeds for them, especially in the exodus from Egypt and also in the subsequent conquest of the land of Canaan.[7] The notion of election goes together with the gradual formation of an authoritative scripture around a Deuteronomic core, which legitimizes and undergirds this notion. This scripture remained the unquestioned authority for early Christians as well.

Election is closely bound up with covenant. Israel's unique status entails the obligation to obey Yahweh's will in a holy life; this will is enunciated in the commandments of the Torah that were delivered to the people as part of the act of covenant making.[8] Being Jewish was understood to consist in responding to God's call by faithfully obeying these commandments—a pattern of religion labeled "covenantal nomism" by E. P. Sanders (see chapter 7).[9] The notion of the divine origin of some laws, or of the principles of legislation, was not uncommon in antiquity; what was peculiar to the Jewish religion was, however, that *all* of its law came to be derived from Yahweh's revelation, either directly or indirectly through Moses.[10] Even the (originally non-Israelite) worldly wisdom came to be identified with the law in Sirach 24, where the Torah is portrayed as the repository of heavenly Wisdom (cf. also Bar. 4). *First Enoch*, however, speaks of heavenly wisdom without any reference to the Mosaic law. God's will was revealed to Enoch, and it came to expression in the order of creation rather than in a historical covenant. In any case, here too God's gift precedes his demands.

Obedience to the Torah was a very practical matter that affected the everyday life of all Jews. But while the Torah was the ideological center of the Jewish symbolic universe, its application varied. A great deal of freedom was displayed toward its wording in many circles: commands could be replaced or complemented with others that made the observance of the law either easier (when fighting on the Sabbath was allowed) or more difficult (when extra restrictions with regard to marriage partners were set up).[11] New interpretations could be assimilated with the Torah as if they had always been part of it;[12] novelties could be presented as God-given revelation from Sinai. Both *Jubilees* and the *Temple Scroll* of Qumran follow the example of Deuteronomy in having God reveal their own new commandments to Moses in the first person.

Though all Jews had the Torah in common, different groups could castigate one another quite heatedly for having forsaken the covenant.[13] The Essene movement in particular raised the issue of "true Israel," claiming that others had gone astray. The status of the new halakah reflected in the texts from Qumran is somewhat unclear. Was it understood as something new, only recently revealed to the in-group, so that one had to take a *new* step by joining the righteous remnant, the true Israel? Or did one think that the majority had gone astray and that the Essenes alone had *remained* faithful, so that the right thing to do was to *return* to the Mosaic Torah that they interpreted? Both views are present in the texts; indeed, both can be found within one single passage in 1QS (which has parallels in other versions of the *Community Rule*). There it is stated that whoever joins the council of the community, "*enters the covenant* of God in the presence of all who freely volunteer. He shall swear with a binding oath to *revert* to the Law of Moses with all that it decrees, with whole heart and whole soul, in compliance with all that *has been revealed* concerning it *to the sons of Zadok* . . . and to the multitude of men of their covenant" (1QS 5.7-10). We shall find a similar ambiguity within early Christianity.

While much of the Torah, especially the bulk of the moral law, conformed to general notions of antiquity, special emphasis came to be placed on what was distinctive. Jews, both in Palestine and in the Diaspora, held divergent beliefs, but different groups were united on a social level, because they held to distinct convictions and practices that marked the Jews off from other people, especially in the eyes of outsiders. The most prominent identity markers were the abstention from idolatry (ceremonies and acts connected with Gentile religion), circumcision, food laws (*kashrut*), and the observance of the Sabbath (and other festivals). These were traits that caught the attention of Gentile critics such as Tacitus, who attacked Jewish isolation and regarded Jews as enemies of humankind. One may

justly speak even of anti-Semitism in antiquity; apparently "Jews were hated and feared to an extent that is not comparable with the attitude felt towards other ethnic and religious groups."[14] But on the other hand Jewish monotheism, ethics, and charitable activities were often appreciated, and the Jewish communities attracted a number of sympathizers—often called "God-fearers" by scholars—to attend the synagogues.[15] At times, even the habit of adopting various Jewish customs seems to have been fairly widespread, causing Seneca to react against the influence of "this accursed race" on Roman life (quoted by Augustine in *Civ.* 6.11). The few who took the full step of converting to Judaism "underwent such a thorough resocialization as to acquire in effect a new 'ethnicity' in kinship and custom"; proselytes were, practically speaking, transferred into the Jewish nation.[16]

First and foremost, Judaism rejected the "alien, pluralist, and iconic cult"[17] that was branded as "idolatry."[18] The idolatry of the Gentiles was considered the basic error that provokes all other sins (*L.A.B.* 27; 44). Even someone like Philo could not regard what went on in the cults of the nations as proper worship.[19] To be sure, it was possible to find a parallel to Jewish monotheism in the worship of Zeus as the supreme God by philosophically minded Gentiles, but since what really mattered was cultic practice and "since it was rare for non-Jews to restrict their worship to one cult, all could be castigated as 'polytheists' whatever they understood their worship to mean. The counter charges of 'atheism' and 'impiety' are only what should be expected from Gentiles who found their multiform religiosity categorically rejected."[20]

In contrast to Greek and Roman practice, in Judaism the view prevailed that there should be only one temple. The temple service had been

250   ordained by God in scripture. The "overwhelming impression from ancient literature is that most first-century Jews . . . respected the temple and the priesthood and willingly made the required gifts and offerings."[21] Nevertheless, for Diaspora Jews the temple seems to have been of greater symbolic than practical significance; after all, Diaspora Judaism survived its destruction and continued in most respects unchanged.[22]

Circumcision was once common among many ethnic groups in the eastern Mediterranean. By Roman times, however, it was mostly regarded as a distinctively Jewish practice, derided by non-Jews as a mutilating, barbarian rite on a par with castration. Therefore for Jews to maintain this custom (based on God's command to Abraham, Gen. 17:10, 14) under such circumstances was in itself a strong affirmation of their distinct ethnic identity. The collective memory of the Maccabean martyrs strongly enhanced the symbolic value of this sign of Jewishness.[23] It was indeed considered the mark of the covenant par excellence, "the covenant of the flesh."

The biblical food laws were conducive to "separatism at meals."[24] The Torah prohibits the consumption of certain foodstuffs (Lev. 11; Deut. 14), of which pork is the most conspicuous. More generally, biblical narratives (for example, Exod. 32; Num. 25) "reflect uneasiness about the association between food and 'idolatry,' and, given the frequency of meals in the temples and the common association between food and sacrifice (even in private homes) it was natural that the Jewish stance against 'alien cult' should spill over into rejection of 'tarnished' foodstuffs." This wariness could include Gentile wine (commonly offered in libations). To be sure, Jews could eat with Gentiles without transgressing their laws, "if, for instance, Jews were the hosts, or brought their own food to Gentile homes, or ate only certain foods from the fare provided by Gentiles, or if the normal libations were dispensed with." But it would have been difficult to comply with the requirement of *reciprocity* with regard to hospitality and simultaneously to remain fully faithful to one's Jewish tradition. Still, it seems that in general at least the most important dietary laws were kept even in the Diaspora and that this "did create an habitual distinction between Jews and non-Jews." As a result, Jews could be considered unsociable and even misanthropic for eating at separate tables (Tacitus, *Hist.* 5.5.2).[25]

No doubt there were differences. Some may have considered all table fellowship with Gentiles abominable, while others took a more open attitude. Educated Diaspora Jews did their best to rationalize the food laws through allegorical explanations, but avoided transgressing them. "Even if not every Jew maintained this demarcation, it typically served to bind the Jewish community together and thus to solidify Jewish ethnic identity on a daily basis."[26] This symbol of Jewishness, too, was nurtured by memories from the Maccabean times, when heroes of faith preferred sacrificing their lives to eating pork.

Jews universally observed the Sabbath (though they could differ in their interpretations of what this demanded), resting from work on the seventh day of the week. This observance, too, set them apart, as it was "so regular, so noticeable and so socially problematic," suggesting to hostile Gentile minds "stupidity or laziness or both."[27]

One effect of the notion of election was, then, exclusivism to a degree. Jews did maintain various kinds of relations with Gentiles, but "exclusivism was part and parcel of Judaism. Breaking down all the barriers would have finally meant accepting idolatry, and this was strongly resisted."[28] To forgo too much contact, most Jews even in the Diaspora opposed intermarriage.[29] Separation did not necessarily mean that they thought (though many did) that Gentiles were condemned by God. Some Jews thought that there were "righteous Gentiles" who could have a share in the world to come. The rabbis later seized on the biblical notion of a covenant made by God with Noah that comprised all humanity, and they consequently debated on the number and content of the Noahide commandments that Gentiles had to keep in order to be acceptable to God (first and foremost the prohibition of idolatry).[30]

Many rabbis allowed for the salvation of "righteous Gentiles," and so did apparently the author of *2 Baruch*. By contrast, such a possibility would seem to be excluded in *Jubilees*[31] and in the Qumran texts, and there is very little evidence from Hellenistic Judaism[32] that the salvation of Gentiles who did not convert was seen as a possibility. It is explicitly excluded in *Joseph and Aseneth*, and probably not really allowed even by Philo.[33] Indeed, "it would seem that, in this sense, Hellenistic Judaism was more consistently exclusivist than Palestinian Judaism," and one can understand why membership within the covenant would be more stringently insisted upon in an alien environment than in Palestine.[34]

Yet the plight of the Gentiles outside God's covenant must have been a real issue for many sensitive Jews. One may speak of a tension within Judaism itself between "ethnocentrism and universalist monotheism."[35] Daniel Boyarin puts it sharply: many Jews of the first century sensed that "something was not right." "Why would a universal God desire and command that one people should circumcise the male members of the tribe and command food taboos that make it impossible for one people to join in table fellowship with all the rest of his children?"[36] One

solution may be seen in the expectation that in the end the Gentile nations will stream to Zion in an "eschatological pilgrimage" (for example, *1 En.* 90.33; *2 Bar.* 72–73; *Sib. Or.* 3.716-20), based on the oracle in Isa. 2:2-4; they will probably then be saved as Gentiles, that is, without circumcision, but they will have turned from idolatry to worship the God of Israel alone.[37]

Philo seems to have been worried about the division of humankind. He was perplexed by the apparent arbitrariness of the law (*Spec.* 1.212-14; 4.100-123), for example, the listing of some animals as unclean; it is only in allegory that he found an explanation. His Platonist leanings produced an "inevitable tendency to universalize the text," to read the Bible "as a philosophical analysis of the human condition" in general. "Thus in Philonic allegory there is neither Jew nor Greek. In principle, any lover of wisdom could read the Pentateuch as his 'story.'" Philo's philosophy leads away from Jewish particularity, and yet his universalism is held in check; his allegory becomes in effect "an effort to make Greek culture Jewish."[38]

That Philo remained "a philosopher in and for the Jewish community"[39] is made clear in a famous passage in which he criticizes some Alexandrian "allegorists" (*Migr.* 89-93). Like him, they too ascribed symbolic meaning to the "irrational" precepts, but unlike Philo they had given up the practical observance of those precepts. In view of the relative mildness of Philo's criticism, it is impossible to see in them militant champions for the abrogation of the Torah; they seem to have been individualists who were rather harmless from the Jewish community's point of view.[40] Philo's critique shows where he draws the line—as well as the fact that he himself is very close to stepping over it. Philo shares the symbolic interpretation of the Torah; yet when the

252 allegorists draw practical conclusions and give up full observance of the law, Philo turns against them. His main argument is, however, a social consideration: the allegorists fail to appreciate that they live in a community, endangering their reputation. Circumcision does have a concealed symbolic meaning, "but let us not on this account repeal the law laid down for circumcising"; in so doing "we shall not incur the censure of the many and the charges they are sure to bring against us" (*Migr.* 93). The nature of his reasoning suggests that "in combating these allegorists, Philo combats a large part of himself and thereby lays bare the tensions inherent in his own life."[41] Yet in the end Philo shows steadfast loyalty to his tradition—to the point of expressing heightened zeal against apostates.[42]

There were also Jewish critics of the Torah, who lamented the isolation from Gentile neighbors caused by it;[43] full-fledged criticism would, however, move a person outside the pale of Judaism. A singular account of the views about the law of a Jewish renegade is given by Josephus (*Ant.* 4.145-47) in a speech of the sinner Zambrias, who has taken a Gentile wife and sacrifices to many Gods. He ascribes the whole legislation to Moses, seen as an impostor who duped the simple-minded Hebrews. Moses' orders are those of a tyrant. Zambrias wishes to make his own decisions and follow the ideas of the majority of people rather than to live in seclusion. Here the voice is heard of a man who "says that the law is not from Heaven" (*m. Sanh.* 10.1).[44]

Jesus and Jewish Identity

Jesus aimed at the restoration of Israel. But since only a small group accepted his message, it seemed more like establishing a faithful remnant. Though Jesus probably did not use the term, those few who accepted Jesus' message constituted the "true Israel" that would receive God's kingdom (Luke 12:32).[45] The Gospels give a contradictory picture of Jesus' relation to central Jewish symbols: his attitude to the law ranges from extreme conservatism to quite radical statements.[46] On one hand, according to Q, "it is easier for heaven and earth to pass away than for one stroke of a letter in the law to be dropped" (Q 16:17). On the other hand, the Gospel of Mark states that "there is nothing outside a person that by going in can defile" (Mark 7:15). Historically, the truth may lie somewhere in between. Considering the uncertainty of Jesus' followers during the subsequent decades precisely regarding the practical application of the Torah, one may infer that Jesus made no pronounced statements in either direction. He can hardly have been as scrupulous a conservative as Q presupposes, but had he simply rejected the food laws in the manner Mark 7:15 suggests, it would be hard to understand why table fellowship[47] later became so controversial an issue (Gal. 2:11-13).[48] Either Mark 7:15 is not a word of Jesus,[49] or at least it was not intended to declare "all foods clean" (thus Mark 7:19).[50]

It seems that Jesus did not challenge the authority of the law, but he may not have scrupulously subscribed to all its individual points either; like other Jewish sages, he summarized its contents in the dual commandment of love (Mark 12:29-31 par.). His humane interpretation of the Sabbath laws aroused objections among the Pharisees, but need not have transcended the limits of what was possible in some Jewish circles at the time.[51] Jesus' followers did not possess in the words of the Master clear directives to guide them in the midst of subsequent developments. And whatever the nature and meaning of Jesus' rather opaque act in the temple just before his arrest (Mark 11:15-16 par.),[52] he can hardly have attacked the temple cult as such. The object of his (possible) attack might rather have been the putative misuse of the cult (for financial gain?) by the priesthood.[53] Had Jesus been known for a thoroughly negative attitude to the temple, his followers would not have continued to participate in its cult (Acts 2:46; 3:1; Matt. 5:23-24).

Regarding Gentiles, too, we may "understand the debates in early Christianity best if we attribute to Jesus no explicit viewpoint at all."[54] He, and most early Christians in his wake, may have shared the common Jewish notion that, at the end, some Gentiles would be admitted to the people of God. Yet the conditions on which this would happen remain vague—would such Gentiles become proselytes? It is not clear whether and how their admission might affect the identity of God's people.

Preserving Jewish Identity

The earliest Jesus-believers understood themselves as a special group within Judaism. They continued to participate in the temple cult (Acts 2:46; 3:1) and observe the Torah. The circle of the Twelve was reestablished in expectation of the restoration of Israel. After some turmoil in connection with the appearance of the Hellenists (see below, p. 256), the congregation in Jerusalem maintained a distinctly Jewish identity until its disappearance after the Jewish War. While Luke greatly exaggerates the numbers, he gives a fair impression of the piety of this church a generation after Jesus, in letting James inform Paul that

there are "many thousands of believers" among the Jews in Jerusalem, "all zealous for the law" (Acts 21:20). James, the brother of the Lord, was since the 40s the leader of the community and the most prominent representative of conservative Christians. His devotion to the Torah was admired even by non-Christian Jews, including some Pharisees who protested against the high priest who executed him in 62 c.e. (Josephus, *Ant.* 20.197-203; cf. Eusebius, *Hist. eccl.* 2.23.4-18, reporting Hegesippus).

Even if many of the details transmitted by Hegesippus are questionable,[55] the Nazirite image of James was hardly created without any historical basis at all. His special concern for sanctity probably led him to demand the separation between Jewish and Gentile believers, at least in the situation of table fellowship.[56] While there is no evidence that he opposed the mission to Gentiles or even the admission of uncircumcised believers, he seems to have allowed them only a second-rate position in the church: they could be accepted as a people of God "in addition" to Israel, but (not being part of Israel itself) they could not be permitted to endanger the sanctity of Israel, for instance by mixing without restrictions with those born Jews at the table.[57]

In this spirit, some visitors from Jerusalem (Paul calls them "false brethren") were offended by the table fellowship practiced in Antioch and demanded that Gentile believers be circumcised (Gal. 2:4). No doubt they were able to produce very good biblical arguments for the necessity of circumcision for the "children of Abraham" (who had, after all, himself been circumcised: Gen. 17).[58] Nevertheless, at the Jerusalem conference that followed, a compromise was worked out and Paul was given the right to accept uncircumcised converts, but it seems that the conditions of the common life were not clearly defined. The table

254 fellowship in Antioch later again proved unacceptable to visiting "men from James," who, to the consternation of Paul, persuaded Jewish Christians (including Peter and Barnabas) to give it up (Gal. 2:11-14). Presumably they acted in accordance with James's point of view. Paul regards this incident as a precedent for what happened later in Galatia, and there is probably a connection between those who appealed to James and the Judaizers who encouraged Gentile Christians in Galatia to be circumcised. Presumably these Jewish Christians, who became the target of Paul's fierce attack in Galatians, had been sent from Jerusalem to amend Paul's missionary work, felt to be incomplete in not fully integrating Gentile converts into "God's Israel." Matthew 5:19 may have preserved a glimpse of the Jerusalem view about the likes of Paul: "Whoever breaks one of the least commandments and teaches others to do the same, will be called least in the kingdom of heaven."[59]

Still, James seems to have sought some kind of a compromise with Paul whom he (according to Acts 21) met when Paul came to bring his collection to Jerusalem. Tragically, James's association with the notorious apostate (that Paul was in Jewish eyes) may have cost him his life; a historical connection is plausible between Paul's arrest in Jerusalem as a lawbreaker in the late 50s and the execution of James and some others as putative transgressors of the law a few years later.[60]

The execution of James, the Jewish War, and the Bar Kokhba rebellion greatly diminished the significance of the Jerusalem community in the development of Christianity. In the following centuries some of its spiritual descendants known as "Ebionites" continued to attend synagogue, observe the Torah (including circumcision and food laws), and hate Paul. They did not think that following Jesus demanded anything like a break with Jewish piety. The *Circuits of Peter*, a source reconstructed from the *Pseudo-Clementine* novel, presents to us Jewish Christians from early third-century Syria who practiced circumcision, observed menstrual separation, avoided the "table of demons," and displayed an aggressive anti-Paulinism.[61] Nevertheless, these Jewish Christians were able to find a place for Gentile believers in the Christian community.[62] According to the *Circuits*, believing in teachers of truth is something that comes from God. The "Hebrews" have it from God to believe in Moses, the Gentiles to believe in Jesus. But in addition to believing, which comes from God, some individual human action is necessary for salvation: "the recognition of the other teacher."[63] Whereas Jewish Christians must (by definition) acknowledge Jesus, Gentile believers must acknowledge Moses. Moreover, the "Hebrews" must be baptized to be saved, which naturally means that non-Christian Jews are outside salvation. Gentile believers for their part must observe regulations that concern purity.[64] The *Circuits* sets its own group apart as a tertium quid "between Hebrews and believing Gentiles."[65]

If the *Pseudo-Clementines* are any guide, the followers of Jesus who carefully observed the Mosaic Law and preserved theological traditions of Jewish origin had notable communities in Syria down to the fourth century.[66] Yet the Jewish identity even of the most conservative branch of Jewish Christians is less than perfect, and in retrospect it seems clear that a centrifugal tendency had been there from the start. The relation between Jewish Christians and other Jews was asymmetric. For while the likes of James the Just could count on being recognized by their average compatriots (though not by the high priests) as good Jews, despite their ideas about the Messiah that many must have found eccentric, they themselves may not have regarded the nonbelieving majority as full members of God's people any more. To be a true Israelite required covenantal nomism *plus something more*—a confession of Jesus. Whether this was initially more than an implication, not spelled out in so many words, we do not know, but the *Circuits* at the latest makes it explicit: even in *Jewish* Christian perspective, Jews must be baptized into the Christian community to be saved. Even conservative Jewish Christians thus found themselves "between the fronts."[67]

A modified Jewish identity meets us in the *Ebionite History* (*Ps.-Clem. Rec.* 1.27-71); its author perceives Christianity as "a Judaism purified of the sacrifices (and temple) that acknowledges Jesus as Messiah."[68] The author regards Christianity as the religion intended by Moses. The Ten Commandments are recognized as the law that Moses originally received (*Rec.* 1.35.2); all later legislation (the sacrificial laws are singled out) was given to the Israelites only because they had become incurably accustomed to the evil ways of the Egyptians. Moses himself had indicated that another prophet would come to correct this provisional legislation (*Rec.* 1.36.1-2). The author feels the discontinuity with respect to race to be a problem, but he has a solution to it: "Gentiles *had* to be called [into "Judaism"] in the place of those Jews who had not believed in order that the number that had been shown to Abraham might be filled" (*Rec.* 1.42.1).

A related line of tradition was cherished among those early followers of Jesus, possibly in Galilean communities, to whom we owe the Sayings Gospel, Q. Its editor(s) coined the statement of the inviolability of the Torah (Q 16:17), apparently with the intention of guarding against possible liberal (mis)interpretations of the pre-

ceding saying that states that "the law and the prophets were (only) until John" (Q 16:16).[69] "The horizons of Q Christians" are "firmly fixed within the bounds of Torah-observance."[70] Although the Pharisees are blamed for forgetting the practice of justice and love, even the followers of Jesus are not to neglect the purifications and tithes with which the Pharisees are concerned: even their scrupulous tithing of "mint and dill and cumin" is affirmed (Q 11:42c).

The group reflected in Q, then, seems to be a "'reform movement' working within Israel"; there is "little evidence of a specifically Christian community consciousness or of social self-awareness."[71] Sayings like Q 6:32-33 and 12:30 display at best a reserved attitude to Gentiles— even though Q is certainly aware of the early Christian mission to Gentiles and of the fact that many of them have responded positively (cf. 7:1-10; 13:28-29)—and imply a "national self-consciousness": "the way in which the 'out-group' . . . can be referred to quite casually as Gentiles . . . suggests that the Q Christians regarded themselves primarily as Jewish and (at least part of) Israel."[72] Yet the community has distanced itself from the great majority of Israel, hurling words of doom at "this generation" that has rejected its message (for example, 11:30-32).[73] The response had sometimes been outright hostile,[74] and this was interpreted as persecution comparable to that allegedly suffered by the prophets (according to the Deuteronomistic pattern). Undoubtedly there has been some antagonism—"taunts, verbal abuse, social ostracism. But there is no direct evidence of sustained physical attacks, nor of any deaths. . . . What seems to have provoked the strongest language in Q is simply the refusal of the audience to respond positively."[75]

The Jewish identity of the community, then, resembles that of the Essene movement: it

256 regards itself as the true Israel (though the designation does not occur), implicitly at least denying this status to other Jews. The temple of Jerusalem is called "your" house, and its destruction is proclaimed (Q 13:35a, a *vaticinium ex eventu?*). Still, the ominous prophecy ends on what seems to be a hopeful note: "you will not see me until the time comes when you say, 'Blessed is the one who comes in the name of the Lord'" (13:35b). It seems that the conversion of at least some of the unbelieving compatriots is expected in connection with the parousia (cf. Rom. 11:25-26). But the seeds of separation are clearly there in this case as well: in order to have any hope, other Jews have to convert to the beliefs of the Q community. Jesus has a unique position as the final revealer of the Father's will (Q 10:22) and as the Son of Man, who will return to hold judgment.

Even Gentile Christians could be drawn to adopt marks of Jewish identity. The author of the *Epistle of Barnabas* warns his Christian readers "that we might not shipwreck ourselves by becoming, as it were, proselytes to their [the Jews'] law" (*Barn.* 3.6) in believing those who claim that "the covenant is both theirs and ours" (4.6). These proponents of a shared covenant seem to have been Gentile Christians willing to adopt Jewish practices.[76]

CROSSING BOUNDARIES, REMOLDING IDENTITY

A rather different line of tradition also started early on in Jerusalem with Stephen and the Hellenists (Acts 6–8), Greek-speaking Diaspora Jews who had joined the new movement (see above, pp. 59–60). Some tension occurred between them and the Aramaic-speaking "Hebrews." Their relation to non-Christian Jews worsened to the extent that Stephen was stoned to death. Luke attributes this to his free attitude to the Torah and criticism of the temple. It is very difficult to trace the actual situation beneath Luke's narrative, but both the fate of Stephen and the hints we get of the later activities of his companions suggest that they offended others by showing, in one way or another, a liberal attitude to standard Jewish practice. The Hellenists, or some of them, had to (or decided to) leave Jerusalem, while the "Hebrews" could stay; apparently the latter were not felt to be a threat to the identity of other Jews.

Acts 11 reports that some of the Hellenists addressed even Gentiles in Antioch, where the Jesus movement gained its first uncircumcised male members. The Jesus-believing Hellenists may have been active in local synagogues (or a synagogue) that already had a positive attitude toward Gentiles.[77] New experiences, such as Gentiles displaying what was taken to be gifts of the spirit (Gal. 3:2-5; Acts 10:44-48), seem to have inspired a bold reinterpretation of Jewish tradition: the observance of some of God's commands became optional. Requirements of the Torah could be sidestepped when table fellowship with Gentile believers demanded it. Breaking social barriers was characteristic of the charismatic atmosphere of the movement. In a famous statement in Galatians (3:28), Paul may be quoting a slogan from the congregation of Antioch. "There is neither Jew nor Greek . . . for you are all one in Christ Jesus." If it was the Hellenists who first adopted the self-designation "*ekklesia* [congregation or gathering] of God"[78] instead of referring to themselves as this or that synagogue, this signals a new self-understanding, though it does not mean that a conscious separation from Judaism was intended.[79]

Paul's account of his call indicates that it must somehow be connected with the Gentile mission and, consequently, with the struggle over the legacy of Israel. Paul suggests that his vision of Christ immediately made clear to him that he had been called to work as an "apostle" to the Gentiles (Gal. 1:15-16). The implication is that precisely the (law-free) mission to Gentiles had been controversial between Paul and those his zeal had led him to "persecute." When the vision changed his life, his conclusion was clear: the Jesus-believers were right after all, even in their convictions about the Torah and the Gentiles. They were right about what it meant to be heir to the promises of the God of Israel in the present. In his earliest letter, Paul applies the biblical key word *election*, central to Jewish identity, without further ado to the Gentile Jesus-believers who had accepted his "gospel" (1 Thess. 1:4); the God of the patriarchs has become the God in Christ.[80] One can speculate that in some sense the law had been a (suppressed) problem for Paul all along, perhaps as an entity that separated Jews from other nations.[81] The Christian Paul and his Hellenist predecessors resemble a Philo who has given in to the allegorists!

Paul's Practice

Having adopted the Hellenists' point of view, Paul strongly encouraged Jewish and Gentile believers to live together, sharing meals without regard to dietary laws.[82] He was convinced that God had made this coexistence possible by making faith in Jesus the only condition of entrance to God's people; the significance of obeying the law was thereby reduced. The matter did not rest there, however. Paul ended up by drastically reinterpreting his Jewish symbolic world in the light of his new experiences, including his ongoing missionary experience. This was filled with

social and ideological conflicts with conservative Christians who were devoted to keeping the old symbolic world intact. In trying to do justice both to his tradition and to his new experience "in Christ," Paul landed in a situation of conflicting convictions.[83]

Paul selected from the Torah what he had to observe. He recommended, especially through the model of his own behavior, that the dietary code of the Torah could be relaxed when table fellowship between Jewish and Gentile believers was at stake. A passage in which Paul describes his mission is revealing:

> To the Jews I became *as a Jew*, in order to win Jews. To those under law I became as one under the law (though *I myself am not under the law*) so that I might win those under the law. To those outside the law I became as one outside the law (though I am not free from God's law but am under Christ's law) so that I might win those outside the law. . . . I have become *all things to all people*, that I might by all means save some. (1 Cor. 9:20-22)

Paul here discloses that he acts among his kinsfolk *as if* he were committed to the Torah, implying that deep down he was not. Although he had by no means broken all continuity with his Jewish heritage, he had become internally alienated from central parts of it: he felt free to be selective. Daniel Boyarin rightly points out that Paul's flexibility regarding food laws "thoroughly undermines any argument that Paul intended Jews to remain Jewish, although Paul . . . would probably argue that he was redefining Jewishness in such a way that everyone could be Jewish."[84] As a consequence, Paul faced grave opposition both from the synagogue and from more traditional Jewish Christ-believers.

258 Paul's mission strategy entailed that even Jews had to *enter a new* community, they had to be "won" (1 Cor. 9:20). That is, Paul applied the entrance requirement "faith in Jesus Christ" to Jews as well as to Gentiles. In Pauline theory, Jews who entered the new movement renounced nothing, but in practice "Christian Jews would have to give up aspects of the law if they were to associate with Gentile Christians." In other words, they had to reshape their identity.[85] In social reality, Paul's congregations were distinct from the synagogues.[86] They cherished an additional cult of their own, and even the Jewish members underwent the new initiation rite of baptism that signaled the beginning of a quite new life. In 1 Cor. 10:32 ("give no offense to Jews or to Greeks or to the church of God"), he implies that "the church (*ekklesia*) of God" "is wholly distinguished from both Jews and Greeks, a third entity within the human race."[87] Paul's activity involves something of a break with Judaism, even if he did not acknowledge or perhaps even perceive it.[88]

Some scholars claim the opposite: Paul was a practicing "good Jew," so much so that one should speak of his "law-respectful" gospel.[89] But to maintain this view one has to resort to tortuous interpretations of a number of passages, including the one just mentioned about "all things to all people" (1 Cor. 9:20-22) and the Antiochian incident (Gal. 2:11-14).[90]

In Galatians 2, Paul relates what had happened in Antioch in order to support his strong opposition to the demand, or wish, that Gentile Christians in Galatia be circumcised. Fearing the envoys of James, Peter had given up table fellowship with Gentile Christians and the others had followed his example. Paul accused him of hypocrisy: "If you, though a Jew, live like a Gentile and not like a Jew, how can you compel the

Gentiles to live like Jews?" (Gal. 2:14). Since Paul uses this conflict as a springboard to his negative discussion of circumcision in the Galatian context, he apparently regards the situations as comparable: he probably felt that Peter's action implied that Gentiles had to become Jews in order to fully enjoy the benefits of the fellowship in Christ. It is hardly possible to find out exactly what the problem was for the men of James, apart from the general point that it had to do with eating together. But in Paul's view (and probably in the view of the conservatives, too) the Torah was involved (perhaps the food was not beyond suspicion), for in what follows (Gal. 2:15-21) Paul proceeds to justify the fact that he has actually "died *to the law*" (v. 19), apparently by "tearing it down" (v. 18). God himself had seen to it[91] that Paul and others had died to the law in order to die for God. "Law" and "God" here become opposites—an impossible statement from a normal Jewish point of view!

Paul's position on "idol meat" (on which more in chapter 11) is also relevant. A devout Jew wanted to know the origin of the meat on the table before eating in order to ascertain that it had not been involved in a sacrifice to a pagan God, but in 1 Cor. 10:25 Paul recommends to "eat whatever is sold in the market without raising any question on the ground of conscience."[92] In another treatment of the scruples of some in view of foods, he declares that "nothing is unclean in itself" (Rom. 14:14) and that "everything is clean" (v. 20). In neither case is the question directly one of the law, but Paul could hardly have made such sweeping statements about the cleanness of *everything* or about eating *any* kind of meat, had he in his personal life been keen on observing the kosher laws.[93] The view that Paul remained perfectly loyal to the Torah also leaves wholly unexplained why, then, he gained the reputation of teaching Jews "to forsake Moses" and "not to circumcise their children" (Acts 21:21) and why the Ebionites considered him an enemy, in fact, *the* enemy.

In light of such evidence, most scholars agree that Paul did not observe *all* of the law all the time, but many do not take seriously the significance of this point.[94] Thus, according to James Dunn, Paul wrote Galatians "as a Jew anxious to fulfil the covenant obligations of his people."[95] Dunn emphatically denies any break, explicit or implicit, with Judaism on Paul's part, and he has a considerable following among scholars today.

It is true that Paul's debate with other Jews was an inner-Jewish controversy, but it does not automatically follow that Paul therefore truly maintains continuity with Judaism. John Barclay helpfully distinguishes between different kinds of hellenization. Compared to other Diaspora Jews, Paul does not rank high in terms of acculturation (use of the Greek language and literary heritage); regarding accommodation, he even stands near the bottom of the scale, as his moral values were thoroughly Jewish. But Paul must be placed high up on the assimilation scale, which has to do with social integration, and this is decisive. Paul would not have been judged on the basis of theological niceties;[96] what counted was how other Jews regarded his practice. "In most of the Diaspora it mattered a thousand times more if a Jewish man was Hellenized in respect of his genitals than if he was Hellenized in respect of his speech."[97] Donald Riddle long ago found a proper formulation: "Always regarding himself as a faithful and loyal Jew, his [Paul's] definitions of values were so different from those of his contemporaries that, notwithstanding his own position within Judaism, he was, from any point of view other than his own, at best a poor Jew and at worst a renegade."[98] The thirty-nine lashes that Paul received five times (2 Cor. 11:24-25) show that he kept returning to the synagogue and that he was not considered an outsider: had he been one, he would not have been punished. On the other hand, someone thus treated was certainly not regarded as a "good Jew" either. "There were limits to the diversity of Judaism and Paul encountered them in the form of the synagogue lash."[99]

Paul's Theory

Paul's practice thus militates against the view that he had remained a "good Jew," but even his theory is ambiguous, to say the least: at points it too comes "painfully close to apostasy."[100] At times, Paul can simply allegorize the Torah. He speaks of circumcision of the heart, possibly following a tradition of interpretation developed in the congregation of Antioch. "A person is a Jew who is one inwardly, and real circumcision is a matter of the heart—it is spiritual and not literal" (Rom. 2:29); "we are the [true] circumcision, who worship in the spirit of God and boast in Christ Jesus and have no confidence in the flesh" (Phil. 3:3). But in the course of his debates Paul could go much further in a negative direction. This is especially the case in Galatians.

For Paul, Gen. 15:6 proves that "men of faith" (rather than those who rely on the Torah) are the true "sons of Abraham" (Gal. 3:7 RSV), even if they be uncircumcised Gentiles. He thus redefines in Gal. 3:6-9 the descendants of Abraham as those who believe (in Jesus). Observant Jews, by contrast, are under a curse (3:10-14).[101] The law is an "addition" to God's promise ("will") to Abraham and therefore not valid (3:15-18). Paul even suggests in an ad hoc argument that the law may not stem directly from God at all, but has been "ordained through angels by a mediator" (3:19).[102] In the following verses (3:22-25)

260 Paul does attempt to find some positive purpose for the law after all, but the positive connection suggested between the law and salvation gives the "impression of an afterthought."[103] Paul quickly abandons this line of thought and proceeds to construct a stunning analogy between the law and the demonic "elements of the world," drawing a parallel between law-observance and Gentile idolatry. He asks, "how can you [former pagans] turn back again to the weak and beggarly elemental spirits? How can you want to be enslaved to them again? You are observing special days, and months, and seasons, and years" (4:9-10). As if this were not enough, Paul later sarcastically compares the holy rite of circumcision to castration (5:12).[104]

Paul does not seem to think of Abraham as an ancestor of the covenant people at all, but "as an exemplary *individual* who received promises that aimed far into the future."[105] The history of Israel as God's chosen people is ignored. In Gal. 4:21-31, Paul does draw a historical line, but it is a line of slavery: the covenant of Sinai gives birth to slaves (4:24-25). Abraham and Sarah have nothing to do with the history of empirical Israel! Non-Christian Jews are descendants of the slave woman Hagar; the Jesus-believers alone are "children of the promise, like Isaac." In Galatians, the Jews have been "allegorized out of real historical existence."[106] In such a context the expression "God's Israel" (Gal. 6:16) can only refer to the Christian community.[107] The nascent church is the true Israel; traditional Jewish terms, motives, and approaches "are reinterpreted in such a manner that the continuity remains only nominal."[108]

Many claim that Paul merely extends Israel's covenant to embrace even Gentiles.[109] Yet, in Galatians, no previously established salvific covenant exists into which Gentiles could be included

in the first place. Paul may once have started by demanding that Gentiles be included within the covenant, but by the time of dictating Galatians he has left this position behind. In effect, apart from Romans 9–11 (on which see below), Paul's letters convey the clear impression that Israel as God's people has been *replaced* by a new community that Paul variously calls the "*ekklesia* of God" or the "body of Christ" that one joins through the rite of baptism; the members of this community find themselves "in Christ." In 1 Cor. 10:32, he clearly shows that they are a new entity, beyond the usual dichotomy of Jews and Greeks. The adoption of the term "*ekklesia* of God" to signify both the local community and the ideal total "church" instead of "synagogue" suggests both continuity with Jewish tradition[110] and an attempt to draw a boundary against it. Paul uses traditional epithets connected with the "people of God" (the "holy,"[111] the "elect") and applies the notion of election to the Christians (in 1 Thess. 1:4 and 1 Cor. 1:26-31 specifically to *Gentile* believers). Both in 1 Thessalonians and in the Corinthian correspondence continuity seems in effect to be superseded by discontinuity.[112]

Paul belabors the case of Abraham to obliterate circumcision as an identity marker of God's people. He asks in Romans 4 whether the patriarch was circumcised at the time when faith was reckoned to him as righteousness (Gen. 15:6). No, he was not (yet) circumcised, and therefore he is "the ancestor of all who believe without being circumcised" (Rom. 4:10-11). Embarrassingly, though, two chapters later in Genesis (Gen. 17) Abraham does receive the commandment of circumcision as an "everlasting covenant." In Galatians, Paul had chosen not to mention this at all. By the time of Romans he has discovered an explanation: Abraham "received the sign of circumcision as a seal of the righteousness that he had by faith while he was still uncircumcised" (Rom. 4:11). (One would have thought this argument to be a first-class weapon in the hands of his pro-circumcision opponents!) To be sure, Paul admits that Abraham is "the ancestor of the circumcised" as well—insofar as they share Abraham's faith, which, for Paul, means faith in Jesus as the Christ (4:12).

Despite all this polemic, quite a few interpreters argue that Paul did not, after all, regard the Torah as abolished; what he attacked was only a legalistic or nationalistic misunderstanding of it.[113] An increasing number find in two verses in Romans proof that Paul wanted, in spite of his many criticisms, to keep the Torah in force: this is why he uses such expressions as "the law (*nomos*) of faith" (Rom. 3:27) and "the law (*nomos*) of the spirit of life" (8:2). These are taken as references to the Torah "insofar as one responds to it in faith"[114] or to "the right attitude to the will of God as this finds its expression in the Torah."[115] However, neither sentence makes a statement on what has happened *to* the Torah (so that a true understanding of the Torah would have put it in its proper place); Paul speaks of the *nomos* as an active subject that has made an end to "boasting" (3:27) and has liberated Christians from "the law of sin and death" (8:2). Paul seems to have exploited the polyvalency of the Greek word *nomos* that had preserved its old broad meaning "principle," "rule," "order";[116] this enables him to make a polemical wordplay. He seems to suggest that a new order has replaced the Torah, but that this order has something to do with the Torah as well. As Mikael Sundkvist concludes, these mentions of *nomos* "are ambiguous allusions to the Mosaic Law, both confirming and rejecting this law." "Paul is following roughly the same procedure as he does when he says that Christians are the true circumcision (Phil. 3), or that they belong to the Jerusalem above."[117]

Paul's most radical move was to connect the law with sin, curse, and death. He could speak of the "sinful passions *aroused* by the law" (Rom. 7:5),[118] associate the law with the demonic forces from which Christians had been freed (Rom. 7:13—8:8), and write that "the letter kills, but the spirit gives life" (2 Cor. 3:6). "Letter" here refers to the "stone tablets" of the Decalogue (v. 3), and indeed the work of Moses is characterized as "the ministry of death" and of "condemnation" (vv. 7, 9). The law, "letter" by nature, is a thing of the past. Christians are no longer under it; they have died to it (Gal. 2:19). Paul himself had

10.1   Paul preaching to the Jews in the synagogue at Damascus. Byzantine mosaic from near the end of the twelfth century. Duomo, Monreale, Italy. Photo: © Bridgeman-Giraudon/Art Resource, NY.

262 been "blameless" as to "righteousness under the law," but he had come to regard his many "gains" as "loss" and even as "rubbish" (Phil. 3:4-9).[119] Christ is the end, that is, the termination, of the law (Rom. 10:4).[120]

Yet Paul can exhort his readers to Christian lifestyle by emphasizing that love is the fulfillment of that very law (Gal. 5:14; Rom. 13:8-10). He can also, occasionally at least, motivate various moral or practical instructions by appealing to words of the law (1 Cor. 9:9). "The law is holy, and the commandment is holy, just, and good" (Rom. 7:12). Now as before the law is justified in putting a claim on humans, even on Christians; the special thing with Christians is that they alone fulfill that just requirement (Rom. 8:4). Paul claims that, far from annulling the law, he actually establishes it. It is he, rather than his opponents, who really does justice to the law (3:31: "we uphold the law"). Paul's legitimizing techniques include appeals to biblical texts and figures as witnesses for his stance (for example, 4:1-15: Abraham, David; 10:5-8: Moses), whereby he often freely changes even the wording of these texts.[121] Paul is, in Romans at least, quite reluctant to admit how far he has gone in his rejection of the law. His sometimes baffling statements on the law "defy a consistent interpretation";[122] clearly they are "an attempt to clarify the *rationale for his revolutionary praxis.*"[123]

Contradictions in Paul's thought point to a theology in process. In Galatians 3–4, he had gone a long way toward virtually denying any significant continuity between the people of Israel and his own faith communities. Yet he could not just leave the matter there. In Romans 9, he raises the worrisome question, how the gospel can be taken to represent a triumph for God, even though most Jews have rejected it. What gain will Israelites have for all their salvation-historical ad-

vantages (the long list of which comes as a total surprise to a reader of Galatians), if they remain outside the salvation in Christ? Paul testifies with an oath to his "great sorrow and unceasing anguish": "For I could wish that I myself were accursed and cut off from Christ for the sake of my own people, my kindred according to the flesh. They are Israelites, and to them belong the adoption, the glory, the covenants, the giving of the law, the worship, and the promises; to them belong the patriarchs, and from them, according to the flesh, is the Christ" (Rom. 9:3-5).

The warm personal tone of the passage is striking, especially in comparison with the earlier angry exclamation in 1 Thess. 2:14-16. There "the Jews," as a people, were declared guilty of killing Jesus, and God's wrath had, according to Paul, definitively reached them;[124] here he shows himself deeply concerned about their destiny. And there is more. God's integrity is at stake: has his word failed, as Israel stays outside? Paul answers by redefining "Israel"—or, in Hans Hübner's words, by "juggling" with the concept of Israel:[125] all those who are "of Israel" (the historical people) do not really belong to Israel. Who belongs to it and who does not is freely decreed by God, and always was. God has always *freely* called some, such as Jacob, and not others, such as Esau, without any regard to their character or ancestry. God is wholly sovereign in his decisions, so much so that he loved Jacob and hated Esau even before they were born (Rom. 9:6-13). It follows that the gospel is after all not being rejected by the elect of God, for the majority of ethnic Israel never belonged to the elect![126] The gospel is being rejected by the nonelect and accepted by the true "Israel." Everything is as God meant it to be.

Paul goes to great lengths to undergird the thesis of God's free election. That God can show unexpected mercy is in line with the surprising experience that he has lately called Gentiles to join his people.[127] But to make this point, the positive verse 15 would suffice: "I will have mercy on whom I have mercy, and I will have compassion on whom I have compassion." Such a concern alone does not, however, account for the negative side of God's action (vv. 17-18).[128] Since Paul's problem is the rejection of his message by most Jews, he is led to develop this other side of God's sovereignty as well. Not only does God freely choose whom he will to be saved; just as freely he also "hardens whom he wills" (9:18).[129]

Paul senses that a moral problem is involved (v. 19), but he asserts that the Great Potter has the right to produce whatever he wants, even "vessels of wrath" prepared (!) for destruction (9:22). The unbelieving Jews of Paul's time are to be seen as such predestined objects of God's wrath. Paul then shows from scripture that God always intended to also call Gentiles to be his children. Of Israel only a remnant will be saved (9:24-29).

Undoubtedly Paul has Jewish *Christians* in mind all the time when he speaks of God's merciful election; the status of Israel belongs to Christians. The shape of Paul's argument prevents him, however, from spelling this out; otherwise the point about God's sovereignty would be destroyed. Paul omits to mention "faith" altogether in Rom. 9:6-23 and speaks as if humans are saved simply by God's arbitrary action; their destinies are decreed by God before they are born. In saying this, however, he is not developing a doctrine.[130] He is wrestling with a burning practical problem: why does Israel not accept the message?

The next section (Rom. 9:30—10:21) introduces a quite different point of view. Paul explains why Israel, now seen as an ethnic entity after all, has failed to attain righteousness, whereas Gentiles have found it (9:30-33). We now hear nothing about sovereign hardening. On the contrary, God has held out his hands toward Israel "all day long," patiently inviting them to salvation, but Israel remains "a disobedient and contrary people" (10:21). Clinging to works, they have refused to obey God and to accept his action in Christ with faith. Thus they have stumbled over the stumbling stone, Christ (9:32-33).

Then, however, Paul suddenly asserts that God cannot have rejected his people, ethnic Israel (Rom. 11:1-2). This is rather surprising after chapter 9,[131] but it continues the argument about the remnant. Ethnic Israel has split into the elect remnant and the hardened rest (11:7). Paul goes on to suggest that the hardening of Israel has a positive purpose in God's plans: somehow it serves to bring salvation to the Gentiles (vv. 11-12). He then compares Israel to a cultivated olive tree from which some "unbelieving" branches have been broken off and onto which branches of a wild tree have been grafted (vv. 17-24). This would mean that (ethnic) Israel has remained God's people; only some apostates have been excluded, and some believing Gentiles have been included as proselytes. The present state of things is caused by the unbelief of "some" (vv. 17, 20): by human failure, not by a divine decree. Gentiles are admonished to remain in faith so that they will not be "broken off" as well (v. 22). But God has the power to graft back again even those Israelites who have fallen, "if they do not persist in their unbelief" (v. 23). And indeed a miracle will happen. Paul discloses a "mystery": the hardening will not be final. When the "full number of the Gentiles" has "come in," *all Israel*—not just a remnant[132]—will be saved (vv. 25-26), for "the gifts and the call of God are irrevocable" (v. 29).

264   Much is made of the olive tree parable by those who emphasize Paul's alleged continuity with Judaism. But this parable does not reflect Paul's usual ecclesiology, which is that of the body of Christ. Paul's all-important "in Christ" language is missing from Romans 9–11 altogether. His normal position is most clearly stated in 1 Cor. 10:32, where the *ekklesia* is something different from both Jews and Greeks. Again, the idea of the salvation of "all Israel"—in whatever way this is conceived to happen—is at odds with Paul's other soteriological statements and has rightly been called a "desperate theory."[133] From a Jewish viewpoint, the idea of the salvation of all Israel is less generous than many Christians think, for it implies that Jews will be saved since they will eventually become Christians.[134] "If the only value and promise afforded the Jews, even in Romans 11, is that in the end they will see the error of their ways, one cannot claim that there is a role for Jewish existence in Paul."[135]

Paul's arguments go back and forth, as if he is searching for a solution to the problem of continuity and discontinuity that is, however, too difficult to be solved.[136] The section shows him struggling to legitimate his mission and to assert his and his little group's identity in terms of traditional values. For Paul, "two loyalties were absolute and both were constitutive of his identity: to Jewishness and to Christ. Neither was negotiable, intellectually or emotionally."[137] In the olive tree parable Paul talks as if his church were a mainstream synagogue, with some new proselytes, from which a few apostates have been expelled. The social reality is, of course, quite different. Paul is involved in the usual strategy of new religious movements, which tend to justify novel practices and ideas by claiming that they are in full agreement with the tradition, if only the tradition is understood properly. His strug-

gle exposes problems inherent in any attempt to relate the new to the old in the nascent Christian symbolic universe.

Ambiguous Continuity

Ambiguity with regard to the issue of continuity is not at all just a Pauline peculiarity. The Gospel of Mark is rooted in Jewish traditions. The narratives about Jesus reflect Galilean local color; scripture is quoted as the supreme authority that interprets Jesus' story (starting with a quotation from "Isaiah" at the very beginning: Mark 1:2-3).[138] Several editorial touches show, however, that the evangelist himself views Jewish traditions from a distance.[139] In an aside, he makes a sweeping generalization, claiming that "the Pharisees and all the Jews" always wash their hands before eating, "thus observing the tradition of the elders" (7:3), and adds a derogatory comment about the "many other traditions that they observe, the washing of cups, pots, and bronze kettles" (v. 4).[140] These statements introduce a debate in which the Pharisees and scribes complain that the disciples of Jesus eat with unwashed hands. Jesus replies by castigating his opponents for replacing God's commandment with "human traditions" (7:6-13), but in the same breath he himself in effect does away with any commandments concerning food: "Whatever goes into a person from outside cannot defile" (7:15). Mark's editorial comment in verse 19 leaves no doubt of how the evangelist understands this saying: "Thus he declared all foods clean." One gets the impression that Mark regards the biblical kosher rules merely as human traditions of the Pharisees. Such traditions can be crudely ridiculed: food will in any case end up in the sewer (7:19).[141]

While the Markan Jesus thus strikes at a Jewish identity marker that had a firm foundation in the Pentateuch, Mark never presents either his own comments or the critical remarks of his Jesus on Jewish customs as a critique of the Torah.[142] It is as if he assumed that God's old revelation must have been based on the same principle of inwardness as Jesus' proclamation of God's will. For in some sections he even greatly emphasizes the continuity between the best Jewish tradition and the teaching of Jesus. Jesus cites the ethical commandments of the Decalogue as authoritative (10:19) and answers a scribe's question about "the first commandment" by quoting the Shema and the dual commandment of love (12:28-31). The scribe agrees: to love God and one's neighbor is "much more important than all whole burnt offerings and sacrifices" (v. 33).[143]

Mark wants to maintain a certain continuity to Jewish tradition (as his repeated appeal to scripture also shows), but he subjects this tradition to critical rational or even rationalistic (Mark 7:19) scrutiny. His Jesus advocates a humane and rational interpretation of the law, of which he himself is the authoritative interpreter,[144] rejecting the (for Mark) superstitious-looking traditions of "the Jews" and devaluing the nonrational sacrifices. The role of the Mosaic legislation remains unclear.[145] Appealing to God's original purpose in creation, Jesus prohibits divorce (10:2-9); the fact that Moses did permit it (Deut. 24:1) is explained as follows: "because of your hardness of heart he wrote this commandment for you" (Mark 10:5). The double reference to "you" suggests distance and alienation from those to whom Moses had written.[146] On the other hand, in 7:10 the same Moses is appealed to against the Pharisaic traditions as one who spoke God's word. What matters for Christians, then, is that Jesus has given them the right interpretation of God's commandments. Mark comes close to dividing the law into two parts of different value, distinguishing between moral and other commandments, but he stops short of making the division explicit. Still, the covenantal Torah is tacitly replaced with ethical-rational rules. Mark never uses the word *law* (*nomos*) at all, thus disclosing that the question of Jewish identity that caused Paul such anguish is no longer a burning issue for him.

Mark presents "no developed theory of the relationship between Jews and Christians," yet he does give "a hint of supersession" in Jesus' parable of the vineyard (Mark 12:1-12).[147] In the vein of Paul's outburst in 1 Thess. 2:14-16, Mark blames the killing of Jesus on the malicious Jewish leaders (the "tenants" in the parable).[148] The step to identifying them with the whole Jewish people is not long; in any case, as the consequence of their murderous action, the "vineyard" will be given to "others" (Mark 12:9)—no doubt to Jesus-believers (from Mark's perspective, largely Gentile Christians).[149] And while Mark generally describes the relation of the crowds to Jesus as sympathetic,[150] he also puts forward an astonishing theory of hardening, "the cruelty of which vies with its oddity and pointlessness."[151] Jesus speaks to the crowds in parables in order that they would *not* understand, repent, and be forgiven (Mark 4:11-12, quoting Isa 6:9-10, a biblical passage henceforth often appealed to in the early church). The statement on hardening makes sense only as an attempt to account for the fact that the great majority of Jews had, by Mark's time, not accepted the message of the Jesus-believers.[152] Mark and his community find consolation in the idea that this has been God's will from the start (rather like Paul in Rom. 9,

266 but lacking a counterpart to Paul's more optimistic idea in Rom. 11). While he appreciates continuity, Mark has taken steps on the road that would lead Jesus-believers away from Judaism and Jewish identity.

The Gospel of Matthew has a distinctly Jewish flavor. Unlike Mark, Matthew shows a keen interest in the law. At first glance, there is a strong emphasis on continuity with Judaism and the Torah. The section 5:17-20 sets forth a program: Jesus did not come to abolish the law, but to fulfill it (Matt. 5:17); "not one stroke of a letter" will pass from it (5:18). Breaking commandments is out of the question (5:19); the "righteousness" of the followers of Jesus must exceed that of the scribes and Pharisees (5:20). The program sounds strictly Jewish, but its ap-

plication in the antitheses that follow (5:21-48) raises questions. The prohibition of divorce (5:31-32) and of oaths (5:33-34) contradicts the Torah, but Matthew may have thought that Jesus was simply giving a new, stricter interpretation. Yet "the discrepancy between the law and Jesus' teaching becomes sharper with every new antithesis, so that what initially could be understood as the radicalization of the old law eventually appears to be a total rejection of the transmitted law."[153] Thus the fifth antithesis (5:38-42) cites the *lex talionis* "rather malevolently" as if it were a summary of the law, suggesting that the spirit of the law is at odds with Jesus' ethic. Finally, in the sixth antithesis the author artificially creates a contrast to Jesus' teaching by distorting the wording of a Mosaic commandment: "You have

10.2   Adoration of the Magi. In the thought world of the Gospel of Matthew, the sages from the East (Matt. 2) anticipate the reception of the Christian message by Gentiles and its rejection by Jesus' own people. Early Christian relief. Catacomb of Priscilla, Rome. Photo: © Scala/Art Resource, NY.

heard that it was said, 'You shall love your neighbor and *hate your enemy*'" (5:43). "Here, indeed, we find Matthew 'falsifying the torah to praise the gospel.'"[154]

The programmatic passage Matt. 5:17-20 aims "at the impression that nothing new has come into existence."[155] Nevertheless, the words of Jesus possess a higher authority than the law, and in the climactic end of the Gospel the disciples are sent to broadcast the commandments of Jesus, not those of the law (28:20). The Jewish program has turned into the teaching of Jesus' commandments.[156]

Throughout the Gospel an ambiguity about the status of the Torah prevails. The reader does not learn how the law should be observed in practical life; he or she "will not even know whether or not it is the Mosaic law that one should obey."[157] Even though Matthew avoids in 15:1-20 the impression (given by the Markan account he uses) that Jesus explicitly denounced the food laws,[158] the offensive character of Jesus' words is retained.[159] When Jesus defends his eating with sinners and taking liberties not allowed by his adversaries on the Sabbath, Matthew cites biblical evidence (Hos. 6:6) to demonstrate that God desires "mercy, not sacrifice," apparently putting moral demands above other obligations (Matt. 9:13; 12:7). But Matthew also preserves the Q saying that tithes are to be scrupulously paid (23:23). Jesus even tells the audience to follow the teaching (though not the practice) of the scribes and Pharisees (23:2-3). His attitude to the Sabbath seems both lenient (12:1-8) and strict (24:20 prohibits flight on a Sabbath).

In any case, Matthew is very much concerned to show that the followers of Jesus are called to fulfill the *essence* of the law. In addition to the prophetic maxim "mercy, not sacrifice," the "weightier matters of the law" can be expressed by the triad "justice and mercy and faith" (Matt. 23:23) and in particular by the two commandments of love on which "hang all the law and the prophets" (22:40, an addition to the Markan version of the discussion about the commandments), as well as by the Golden Rule ("in everything do to others as you would have them do to you") that likewise "is the law and the prophets" (7:12). By appealing to such selective principles, Matthew wants to prove that Jesus was true to the real intent of the law even when he was accused of violating its letter. Kari Syreeni astutely notes that "an intense hermeneutical quest for the essence of a phenomenon is often called forth by a progressive distancing of that phenomenon," and this is the case here: what is to be taught and obeyed is ultimately not the Torah, but the words of Jesus. But Matthew cannot admit that Jesus' ethic has, in many respects at least, actually replaced the Torah in his symbolic world; that is why he resorts to an ambivalent fulfillment theology.[160] The flexible term *fulfill* (5:17) proves useful indeed: in whatever way Jesus relates to different aspects of the law, he "fulfills" it—whether by observing or by (neglecting and) reinterpreting it. Apparently Matthew starts from the conviction that whatever Jesus teaches *must* fulfill God's law in a way that does justice to the necessary continuity. The true intentions of the Torah are fulfilled in his church, which is the true upholder of the heritage of "the law and the prophets." Matthew thus assimilates the old with the new without making it clear that there is a difference. The result is a christianization of the Torah.

The striving for continuity also finds expression in Matthew's manner of explaining even seemingly random details of Jesus' life in his formula quotations from scripture as the fulfillment of specific predictions (for example, Matt. 1:22-23; 2:15; 4:14-16; 8:17).[161] Such a thorough

268 exploitation of scripture hints at the existence of a group of Jewish Christian "scribes" in Matthew's community (cf. 13:52). Jesus the Messiah emerges "as the ultimate fulfillment of centuries of accumulated hope," allegedly being "the culmination and completion of an ancient Israelite tradition."[162]

Indeed, the church is the only true upholder of that ancient tradition. Jesus threatens the leaders of Israel: "The kingdom of God will be taken away from you and given to a people that produces the fruits of the kingdom" (Matt. 21:43). The loosely appended verse 21:44 compares Jesus to a stone that crushes the Jewish leaders (and implicitly the people as well) who rejected him.[163] Ulrich Luz notes that Matthew must be regarded as one of the fathers of the later supersessionist theory; the roots of Christian (theological) anti-Judaism are found already in this biblical text.[164] Matthew's community seems to have recently been separated from the synagogue; its distancing itself from the old community finds expression in the repeated formulation "*their* synagogues" (4:23; 9:35; 12:9; 13:54).[165] The counterpart of "their synagogues" is now the *ekklesia*—indeed, "*my* ekklesia," as the Matthean Jesus puts it—which Jesus founded and whose iconic leader is Peter (16:17-19).

Recent traumatic experiences (the break with the synagogue)[166] are undoubtedly reflected in the harsh polemics against Jewish leaders throughout the Gospel, but in particular in chapter 23, which does not exactly breathe the spirit of loving one's enemy, demanded by Jesus of his followers in 5:44-48. The scribes and the Pharisees, a "brood of vipers" (23:33) show that they are "descendants of those who murdered the prophets" (v. 31); upon them will come "all the righteous blood shed on earth" (v. 35). And it is not just the leaders who are accused: "all

this will come upon *this generation*" (v. 36). Jesus complains of the hard-heartedness of Jerusalem, "the city that kills the prophets and stones those who are sent to it. How often have I desired to gather your children together as a hen gathers her brood under her wings, and you were not willing!" (vv. 37-38). Matthew's polemic against his kin according to the flesh reaches its peak in the scene, equally impressive as it is horrendous, that he has inserted into his passion narrative. Pilate washes his hands, declaring himself innocent of Jesus' blood, and the crowd takes responsibility; the whole people shout: "His blood be on us and on our children!" (27:25). No doubt Matthew thought that the punishment had been realized in the recent sack of Jerusalem (70 C.E.), to which he also refers in an insertion to the parable of the wedding of a king's son: when those invited turned the invitation down and some of them even killed the envoys, the enraged king "sent his troops, destroyed those murderers, and burned their city" (22:7). Tragically, many of his readers have inferred that ever new Jewish generations should suffer the punishment for their alleged murder of Jesus.

The Epistle of James assimilates the new, "perfect law of liberty" (Jas. 1:25; cf. 2:12) with the old law in a way reminiscent of Matthew. Everything the author says about the *nomos* is absolutely positive. The "royal" law (2:8) leads one to true freedom. Contrary to Paul's insinuations, there was never anything wrong with God's law: it has precisely the life-giving and liberating power that Paul had denied it.[167] The author is, however, at a greater distance from Judaism than either Paul or Matthew: the law is for him fully christianized. The Jewish-Gentile problem is not a burning issue; the battle of the significance of the Torah has become a matter of the past.[168] In view of verses like 4:11-12, where God is referred to as the lawgiver, "*nomos* clearly means the 'old' law." However, the author simply passes over the distinctively Jewish obligations in silence; even when he speaks of the "whole law," he ignores their existence.[169] Nothing suggests that the author considers circumcision and all food and purity laws to be in force.[170] The biblical Torah tacitly fuses together with the norms of Christian life.[171] The author even fuses the law with the "word of truth" that is effective in baptism.[172] His theology can be taken as a christianized version of covenantal nomism, the basic difference being that "election pertains to the individual through conversion (through baptism)."[173]

The *Didache* is deeply rooted in Jewish traditions and takes the observance of the law seriously (see *Did.* 13.3-7).[174] However, Jewish influence goes "hand in hand with a conscious distancing from, or even hostility toward, Judaism."[175] Thus the community has taken over from Judaism the practice of fasting twice a week, but the author is anxious to create a difference and exhorts his readers: "Let not your fastings be with the hypocrites, for they fast on Mondays and Thursdays, but do you fast on Wednesdays and Fridays" (*Did.* 8.1). And he continues in the same vein: "Do not pray as the hypocrites, but as the Lord commanded in his Gospel" (8.2; the Lord's Prayer follows). The community applies to itself a biblical image for Israel, the "vine of David" (9.2); this holy vine has been "revealed to us through your servant Jesus," that is, Jesus has caused the author's community "to appear as the real and true Church of God."[176]

The book of Revelation views Christians as the true Israel. They have been made "a kingdom" and "priests" by the God and Father of Jesus Christ (Rev. 1:6, echoing the words that God commanded Moses to tell the people of Israel according to Exod. 19:6). Those saved are "called and chosen" (Rev. 17:14) and represent the twelve tribes of Israel (7:4-8). The church, a "woman clothed with the sun," is symbolically presented as the mother of the Messiah (Rev. 12); the vision of the new Jerusalem whose gates bear the names of the twelve tribes (21:12) likewise implies (if somewhat vaguely) "Christian inheritance of the promises to Israel."[177] Eating meat offered to idols is considered a grave sin (2:20); the mention of just a single "burden" (*baros*) put on the faithful in 2:24-25 would seem to refer to the Apostolic Decree,[178] in which case the implication is that the Torah remains valid for Jewish Christians. Quite radically, local Jews are twice referred to as "those who say they are Jews but are not" and are labeled "the synagogue of Satan" (2:9; 3:9);[179] a bitter reaction to some harassment on their part is combined with the desire to convince the outside world that the Christians, and they alone, are the true Jews.

The *Testaments of the Patriarchs*, in their final christianized version, maintain that the Messiah renews the law (*T. Levi* 16.3).[180] While Jesus is thus presented as a figure congenial to Judaism, Jewish identity markers such as circumcision and food laws are not mentioned at all. The Torah-piety of the *Testaments* is connected to a universal, natural law: the ethical ideals appeal "to universal moral virtues shared by Jew and Gentile alike."[181] Here too the Torah has been assimilated to Christian ethical principles that are no longer distinctly Jewish.

"Levi" also predicts, in the vein of Matt. 27:25, that a curse will lie on Jews because they will in their wickedness take innocent blood on their heads. Consequently, "your holy places shall be razed to the ground. You shall have no place that is clean, but you will be as a curse and a dispersion among the nations." There is a limit to the suffering, however: the curse will be in force

270 "until he will again have regard for you, and will take you back in compassion" (*T. Levi* 16.3-5).

In a more positive vein, some passages in the *Testaments* affirm the future salvation of both Israel and the Gentiles (*T. Benj.* 10.11; *T. Sim.* 7.2; see above, chapter 7), even if it is not clear how this will take place. "Such breadth of vision is rare in the early Christian world. . . . Israel is neither rejected nor replaced by a 'new people' or a 'third race.'"[182]

In Luke's view, the law and the prophets point to Christ, and true obedience to the law is in accordance with listening to Jesus (Luke 16:29-31).[183] Luke's portrait of Jesus is that of a pious Jew (he alone mentions the circumcision of Jesus, 2:21), whose attitude to the law was unproblematic. Mark's law-critical chapter 7 is dropped altogether. The supreme value of living according to the law is highlighted in Jesus' discussion with a lawyer (Luke 10:25-28), followed by the story about the exemplary Samaritan (10:29-37).

The validity of the law is important to Luke, who is concerned to legitimate the Christian claim of being God's people: he needs to show that an unbroken continuity exists between God's covenant with Abraham and the Jesus movement. Luke seems to imply that only this *one* covenant has ever been made. No new covenant is needed. God acts on the basis of that made with Abraham (Luke 1:72-73; Acts 3:25; 7:8); the church has inherited the promises once given to Israel. But while maintaining the role of the covenant, Luke tacitly changes its contents. The covenant points to the future: "ideal Jews are those who wait for the future redemption."[184] Symptomatically, the good Jew Zechariah (the father of the Baptist) extols God's great acts by suggesting that God's covenant with Abraham and his oath to him (Luke 1:72-73) will be realized in the remission of sins, to which John and Jesus will lead the people (v. 77). As a powerful illustration of the continuity between the old and the new, Luke presents in his infancy narratives (Luke 1–2) "those devout Jews who meticulously observed the law while knowing from scripture that salvation would come through faith in Christ. . . . For a pious Jew the law was all he needed, for the law told him that he needed to convert to Christianity."[185]

Luke also stresses continuity at the cost of producing a rather unhistorical portrait of Paul and other Christian figures of the recent past. Even Paul becomes a pious Jew, more conservative than the Jerusalem pillars ever were; it is Peter and James (of all people) who make all the critical decisions needed for the Gentile mission to flourish (Acts 10–11, 15).[186] In his apologetic speeches, Luke's Paul asserts his loyalty to the law (24:14; 26:4-5; cf. 22:3; 23:1-6), which he has impressively proved by circumcising his half-Jewish fellow worker, Timothy (16:3). Yet Luke also assumes without explanation that the law, being impossible to observe, had been a heavy burden even for the most faithful Jewish Christians (13:39; 15:10). "These novel ideas are introduced quite suddenly and briefly without further comments, and one may wonder if Luke really had reflected upon their compatibility with his other assertions about the law."[187] Luke views the law from the distant vantage point of a Gentile Christian. It is important to his legitimating concern to ascertain that his religion is based on a glorious, ancient tradition. But it is equally important to him to point out that the venerable Jewish customs are not binding on the Gentile Christians of his time, although they do observe the Apostolic Decree.

In Acts, Luke has some Christian Jews from Judea claim that circumcision is a precondition of salvation even for Gentile Christians (Acts 15:1; cf. 15:5). The claim is rejected, but the concern of the conservative brothers is taken into consideration in the form of the Apostolic Decree: the Jerusalem congregation accepts the proposal by James "that we should not trouble those Gentiles who are turning to God, but we should write them to abstain from things polluted by idols and from fornication and from *pnikton*[188] and from blood" (15:20; cf. v. 29). Luke's presentation of the decree is none too clear (we do not learn what is meant by *pnikton*, and even the significance of the other three restrictions is open to debate). It seems that he is taking up a tradition that was in use at least in some places in his time. The final clause in James's statement leaves the impression that the decree is meant to be a gesture of respectful adaptation to Mosaic custom: "For in every city, for generations past, Moses has had those who proclaim him, for he has been read aloud every Sabbath in the synagogues" (15:21). The decree means, in Luke's view, that a permanent place in the people of God has now been established for Gentile believers.

The law is valid for Jewish Christians, but its main significance lies in its prophetic quality. The law and the prophets testify to Christ "in a double way by prophesying his advent as saviour and by proclaiming repentance, faith in Christ and a life compatible with that faith."[189] Luke manages to do some justice to the law as the lasting characteristic of the Jewish faith without christianizing it like Matthew or demonizing it like Paul precisely because the law is not a burning personal issue for him.[190] It is "treated with an outsider's unconcerned piety. The law was a respectable symbol from the past just as the Jerusalem temple was. But thanks to the guidance of the Holy Spirit—and to the great relief of the Gentile Christians—there was concretely as much of the law left to be obeyed as remained of the temple."[191]

Luke often refers to the hardening of the people of Israel. The sympathetic picture of

ancient biblical characters and of the pious Israelites who appear in the infancy stories (and immediately acknowledge Jesus as the Messiah) contrasts starkly with the depiction of the Jews or Paul's (and, implicitly, Luke's own) time. The strange story of Jesus' encounter with the people in his hometown who are all of a sudden filled with irrational rage and try to kill Jesus (Luke 4:16-30) may well be taken "as a miniature overview of the narrative to come."[192] In Acts, the

10.3   This caricature from the Winchester Psalter, twelfth century, shows Jews, presented as crude stereotypes, participating in the betrayal and flagellation of Christ. The process of attributing collective guilt for the killing of Jesus to "the Jews" and minimizing the role of the Romans begins in the Gospels and has played a part in the persecution of Jews in Christendom. © The British Library Board. All Rights Reserved. Cotton Nero C. IV.

272 nonconverted Jews are insulters and persecutors who always oppose the apostles and disturb their work (for example, Acts 13:45, 50; 14:2, 5). In his last words in Acts, Paul applies the well-known biblical saying about hardening (Isa. 6) to the Jews: "this people's heart has grown dull . . . so that they might not look with their eyes, and listen with their ears, and understand with their heart and turn—and I would heal them" (Acts 28:27).

The book of Acts thus ends with a programmatic vision of hardened Jews and Gentiles receptive to the gospel. No clear sign of hope (in the manner of Rom. 11:25-32) is in sight. Altogether, Luke's tension-filled references to Jewish values and actual Jews would seem to justify Lloyd Gaston's dictum (only seemingly paradoxical): "Luke–Acts is one of the most pro-Jewish and one of the most anti-Jewish writings in the New Testament."[193]

In Peter's speeches in Acts, Jews (either the people or their leaders) are addressed as those who killed Jesus (Acts 2:23; 3:14-15; 4:10; 5:30). Luke's changes to the passion narrative produce the impression that Jesus was taken away to the cross by the Jewish crowd and their leaders (Luke 23:25)! What could be the result of editorial carelessness in Luke is developed with full seriousness in the *Gospel of Peter*. Pilate is completely exonerated. Herod presides over the trials and orders (!) Pilate to carry out the death sentence; Pilate then gives Jesus over to the people (*Gos. Pet.* 5). The executioners are Jews; the Romans disappear from the picture.[194] "They fulfilled all things and accomplished their sins upon their own heads" (*Gos. Pet.* 17; cf. 1 Thess. 2:16). The people have drawn upon themselves a final, unavoidable punishment and the elders and priests acknowledge it themselves: "Woe, because of our sins, the judgment and the end of Jerusalem is at hand" (*Gos. Pet.* 25). The *Gospel of Peter* "shows a sharp alienation from Judaism and its leaders, to the point of extreme hostility." Six times it speaks in a generalizing manner of "the Jews" (cf. John; it refers to "their feast" (*Gos. Pet.* 5); it "portrays a malevolent and unrepentant deicide, executed by those who chose to be guilty of the greatest sin."[195]

First Peter refers to the Christians as "chosen" (1 Pet. 1:2) and applies to them the divine words once spoken through Moses to Israel (Exod. 19:6; cf. Rev. 1:6): "you are a chosen race, a royal priesthood, a holy nation, God's own people" (1 Pet. 2:9). The church is the ideal and true Israel. The history of the ancient Israel plays no part: neither the promise to Abraham nor the Torah (the word *nomos* is totally lacking) is mentioned in the epistle.[196] *First Clement* likewise speaks of the Christians as the elect people and quotes "Israel" passages from the scripture without further ado as references to the church (chs. 29–31). Abraham was the father of the Christians (*1 Clem.* 31.2), and the main task of the prophets was to give predictions about Jesus (17.1). Jesus himself speaks already in the scripture through the holy spirit (22.1-8). Judaism is simply bypassed by Clement.

TOWARD NON-JEWISH IDENTITY

The Gospel of John signals a breaking away from practices and beliefs that were integral to Jewish identity. The Johannine community, though consisting predominantly of those born Jews, "already seems to be living physically and mentally at a greater distance from Judaism than, say, the Matthean churches."[197] John's portrayal of Jewishness is much more ambivalent than is often claimed today. It cannot be understood simply as a response to the—alleged—violent policy of Jewish leaders in John's environment. No doubt the Gospel reflects a conflict between the synagogue and John's community, but it was not external pressure[198] that made the Johannine Christians view some basics of Jewishness as outsiders; they themselves saw their faith in Jesus not only in continuity with earlier Jewish tradition but also in contrast with it.

To be sure, Jesus is pictured as "a loyal cherisher of the best Jewish traditions"[199] who fights for the sanctity of the temple (John 2:13-22) and even states that "salvation is from the Jews" (4:22). Moses has written about him (5:46-47) and Abraham has "seen his day" (8:56). Jesus is the fulfillment of old promises. John's community probably saw itself as part of the Jewish tradition and its faith in Jesus as its culmination. Yet the very same passages that suggest continuity "also suggest that the Johannine Christians had become alienated from their Jewish heritage in real life."[200]

First, in John 2, Jesus' strivings for the purity of the cult soon fade out of the picture, and his body is presented as the replacement of the material temple (2:21-22). In John 4, he is really speaking from the point of view of a new group whose "true worship" supersedes earlier forms (4:23-24). Salvation originates from the Jews, but it is moving away from them.[201] Second, Jesus violates Sabbath regulations—or "abolishes the Sabbath," depending on the rendering—on purpose, in order to show that he is equal to God

10.4　"Salvation is from the Jews, but true worshippers will worship the father in spirit and truth": Jesus teaching the Samaritan woman at the well (John 4). Early Christian fresco, fourth century. Catacomb of Via Latina, Rome. Photo: © Scala/Art Resource, NY.

274 (5:17-18). He deliberately provokes a clash over the Sabbath.[202] His liberal attitude to the Sabbath is taken for granted and developed into a christological argument (5:19-47). Jesus does not attempt to show that what he did on the Sabbath was legal, but points out that the Jews themselves do not always keep the law. He finds a discrepancy between two central obligations of the law, circumcision on the eighth day and the Sabbath, and exploits it to undermine his opponents' appeal to the law and thus the authority of the law itself (7:19-24). Basic aspects of Jewish identity are here viewed from the standpoint of an outsider.

Finally, the revelation at Sinai is of no significance unless one believes in Jesus (5:37). Jesus even claims that "you have never heard his voice" (v. 37)—a "cavalier denial of a central Jewish belief."[203] In John 6, Jesus contrasts himself, the true bread of life, with the manna given by Moses (6:32-51). The manna, associated with the law, is unable to give life, and Jesus even connects it with death.[204] Moses and Abraham have positive functions as witnesses to Jesus, but Jesus' superiority over them is clear.[205] The law was given through Moses, but it was superseded by the revelation of grace and truth in Christ (1:17).[206] On the whole, the scriptures bear witness to Jesus, yet no traces of a salvation-historical dimension of the church are visible. The birth of the church is a consequence of the eschatological sending of the Son and of the Paraclete and thus something novel.[207] Here is "a point of departure for a later Christian belief that saw the Hebrew Bible exclusively in the light of christology. This belief denies the Jews the legitimacy of their scriptural heritage and also interprets the content of the Hebrew Bible very narrowly."[208]

Jesus' ambivalent attitude to Jewish basics in John no doubt reflects the ambivalence of the Johannine group itself. It suggests that the Johannine Christians assessed central symbols of Jewishness exclusively in light of their faith in Jesus, thereby obliterating the relevance of these matters as fundamentals of Jewish identity. They no longer regarded such practices as Sabbath observance or circumcision as integral to their identity. They had their roots deep in Jewish traditions, but they interpreted their faith in Jesus in such a way that they eventually became alienated from these roots. John's Jesus distances himself by repeatedly speaking to his audience of "*your* law" (John 8:17; 10:34; cf. 7:19; 15:25), and John's striking use of *Ioudaioi* ("Jews," some 70 occurrences)[209] leaves the impression that Jesus and his disciples are not "Jews" at all. All this suggests that Johannine Christians were adopting a non-Jewish identity and that the author was aware of his drift away from Jewishness.[210] Quarrels over dietary regulations, so central in Galatians, are not at all in view; such battles seem to lie in the past. Nonobservance does not need justification any more.

The polemical relation to the synagogue leads to the harsh statement that the Jews are children of the devil (John 8:44). "They epitomize everything that is dark and diabolical, that belongs to the unbelieving and antagonistic world. Hostility toward the Jews is thus lifted to a new and more insidious plane."[211] Curiously, though, Jesus denounces the Jews who *believe* in him (8:31-33) and portrays *them* as children of devil. This suggests, according to Raimo Hakola, that the break with Jewish identity may not have been as complete as the author would have hoped for.[212] Jesus' shocking words "destroy any illusion the reader might have concerning the capability of the Jews to believe."[213] The evangelist does away with a clear distinction between different Jewish groups, which no doubt intensifies the separation of those who acknowledge his authority from other Jewish groups. Therefore, John's sharp dualism may be taken as both a result of the growing alienation of the Johannine group from its surrounding society and as an attempt to intensify this alienation.

Another example of this estrangement can be seen in the Epistle to the Hebrews, which clearly differentiates between old and new. To be sure, Moses was a faithful servant in God's house (Heb. 3:2-5), Abraham obtained the promised blessing because of his patient endurance,[214] and the great cloud of (biblical) witnesses presented in chapter 11 suggests a sense of continuity.[215] The continuity is, however, definitely broken when the author states brusquely that the law of the "old covenant" has been abolished—and that this law, crystallized as the cultic law concerning sacrifices, was "weak" and "useless" from the start, not being able to make anything perfect (7:12, 18-19). Being concerned with external matters, the old law was "fleshly" (7:16); this view is in sharp contrast to Paul's view, who, for all his criticisms of the Torah, nevertheless stated in Romans 7 that the law was spiritual (whereas sinful humans were "fleshly").[216] For the author of Hebrews, the first covenant was not "faultless" (8:7) and in any case it had grown old; through the "new covenant" God has made it "obsolete" (8:13). The logic of the argument runs backward, from the solution to the problem. Evidently the first covenant never had any real relevance, for "it is impossible for the blood of bulls and goats to take away sins" (10:4). From the outset it was designed to be just a pale shadow of the good things to come (8:10; 10:1); no wonder, then, that Christ has replaced it.

A nagging question will not go away: just why should all this prefiguration of Christ's deed of salvation, which no one in the time before Christ could understand, have been instituted at all?[217] Like John's, this author's roots lie deep in Jewish tradition, but he views it wholly from the viewpoint of an outsider, undertaking "a strong attack on the Jewish sacrificial system and the law."[218] Readers would have gotten the impression: "Judaism is defunct, because it has been surpassed."[219] The actual Jewish people are not at all in the purview of the author.

Even among the followers of Paul, one can see a distancing from Paul's struggle concerning continuity and discontinuity. According to Colossians, "Judaism perhaps had some importance in the past; certainly it has none in the present and in the future" (cf. Col. 3:11).[220] Baptism is interpreted as the spiritual circumcision of Gentile Christians, but nothing in the context implies that they have thus become true Jews or part of Israel (Col. 2:11-13). Ephesians 2:12 reminds Gentile Christians of their pagan past, picturing their deficiencies then in the light of Israel's privileges. They were at that time "without Christ, being aliens from the commonwealth of Israel, and strangers to the covenants of promise, having no hope and without God in the world."[221] After the coming of Christ, however, the commonwealth of Israel has been changed into the church of Jewish and Gentile believers. For this author, "Israel as God's privileged people seems to be only an entity of the past; in the present it has been replaced by the church, and this church has entirely lost sight of the unbelieving Israel."[222] And he even emphasizes that the election of the Christ-believers has taken place in an absolute act of God's will before the foundation of the world (Eph. 1:4-5, 11; cf. 2:10; 3:11).

In the Pastoral Epistles, too, the Christian community seems to have usurped the place of Israel and its scriptures (cf. 2 Tim. 3:15-16);[223] the expression "a people of his own," linked to

276 Israel's self-understanding in the Hebrew Bible, is used for the church (Titus 2:14). At the same time, Jews are ridiculed: "those of the circumcision" are "idle talkers and deceivers"; one is not to pay attention "to Jewish myths or to commandments of men who reject the truth" (Titus 1:10, 14); for "everything is pure to the pure" (Titus 1:15, echoing Rom. 14:20). "Here speak Gentile Christians who have taken up Israel's scriptures and Israel's place as God's chosen people. But it is to be doubted whether they are aware of those acts of usurpation, since for them Jews are just ridiculous."[224]

Jewish Identity Denied

Many subsequent authors distance themselves even more clearly from the Jewish heritage.[225] The *Epistle of Barnabas*, apparently written by a Gentile for Gentile Christian readers, reminds one in many ways of the Epistle to the Hebrews but goes further in suggesting that the Jews never had a valid covenant in the first place. The author has "filled his little book with the dichotomizing language of 'us and them'"[226] and explicitly warns of an "inclusivist" stance: "be not made like some, heaping up your sins and saying that the covenant is both theirs and ours. It is ours" (*Barn.* 4.6). To be sure, God once offered the covenant to the Jews, but they lost it forever, when they turned to idolatry. Moses' breaking the tablets of the law demonstrates that their covenant was shattered "in order that the covenant of dear Jesus be sealed in our hearts" (4.7-8).

The author does not reject the law (as he understands it). It belongs to Christians, who understand its meaning. It was always a mistake to take all of the law literally; the author even attributes the literal understanding of circumcision to an evil angel (*Barn.* 9.4).[227] God's moral law remains in force, as is shown by the detailed description of the "way of light," which follows without reservations the moral teaching of the Diaspora synagogue (ch. 19). It is assimilated with "the new law of our Lord Jesus Christ," which is "without the yoke of compulsion," that is, without "irrational" precepts (2.6); otherwise, the "new" law is by no means new in content. The author interprets its embarrassing parts by way of fanciful allegorizing (see, for example, ch. 10 on dietary laws), squeezing moral lessons from everything; the Jews have misunderstood Moses "owing to the lust of their flesh" (10.9). Another device is to find allegorical predictions of Jesus (cf. 9.8) or of Christians.[228] The author declines Jewish customs, but he is keen on finding support for his view in scripture (for example, chs. 2–3, 15–16). The question of Christianity's relation to Judaism is answered from the enlightened viewpoint of an outsider.

It is noteworthy that *Barnabas* provides us with one of the earliest indications[229] that some Christians replaced the Jewish Sabbath with a communal celebration on Sunday (the day of Jesus' resurrection). The author engages in a frontal attack against a literal observance of the Sabbath. He quotes Isaiah (Isa. 1:13): God says that "the present Sabbaths are not acceptable to me." The true Sabbath will be a future event, the eschatological beginning of another world— "wherefore we also celebrate with gladness the eighth day in which Jesus also rose from the dead" (*Barn.* 15.8-9).

How the transition from Sabbath to Sunday took place is unknown. No doubt Jewish Christians originally observed the Sabbath.

References to an additional or alternative day of worship begin to crop up around the turn of the first century; in addition to *Barnabas*, a passage in Ignatius (*Magn.* 9.1), which likewise sets up a polemical contrast between Sabbath and Sunday, is instructive (more neutral references are found in Rev. 1:10 and *Did.* 14.1).[230] The need to establish such a day reflects a desire "to dissociate from Judaism and to assert the superiority of Christian practice."[231] A similar development is visible somewhat later in the gradual replacement of the Jewish Passover by the Christian Pasch culminating in Easter Sunday.[232]

Ignatius understands Judaism to be something clearly different from the new faith. In his letters we meet for the first time the designation *christianismos*, properly translated "Christianity," in semantic opposition to *ioudaismos*: if we continue to live "according to Judaism," characterized as "useless old fables," "we confess that we have not received grace" (Ign. *Magn.* 8.1); "Let us learn to live according to Christianity, as we have become disciples" (*Magn.* 10.1); and "It is monstrous to talk of Jesus Christ and to practice Judaism; for Christianity did not believe in Judaism, but Judaism in Christianity" (*Magn.* 10.3).[233]

Ignatius "radically Christianizes the 'prophets,'" who, as true followers of Christ already within the seemingly Jewish tradition (*Magn.* 8.1-2), did not feel obliged to observe the Torah, but ceased to observe the Sabbath and "lived according to the day of the Lord" (9.1). Christianity seems to be the true manifestation of the divine revelation at Sinai; Judaism, including the Judaism of Jewish Christians, represents a misconception.[234] Ignatius argues from a position outside Judaism, even though he is perhaps involved in a conflict with *Jesus-believing* Jews in particular.[235] Christians should withdraw from Judaism, which is identified with "tombstones and sepulchers of the dead" and with "wicked arts and snares of the prince of this world" (*Phld.* 6.1-2). "In Ignatius' version of the Jesus movement, Jewishness had to give way to a common Gentile identity—Christianity as we know it was about to be born, and the end result . . . seems to have become the complete contradiction of the beginning."[236]

In the *Preaching of Peter*, the apostle is depicted as preaching in the name of pure monotheism against the dangers of paganism, but also against the falsity of Jewish worship. The Jews do not really know God, "serving angels and archangels, the month and the moon."[237] The Christians, by contrast, worship "God through Christ in a new way," different both from the way of the Greeks and from that of the Jews, having found in the scriptures the promise of the new covenant (Clement of Alexandria, *Strom.* 6.5.39-41).[238]

The anonymous *Epistle to Diognetus*, possibly from around 200 c.e., speaks unabashedly about the "superstition of the Jews" that finds expression in their "superstitious" observance of the Sabbath, their "boast" of circumcision, and their "hypocritical" observance of fasting rules and the phases of the moon (*Diogn.* 4.1). The author stands completely outside Judaism, which he ridicules in a crude manner.

In the *Gospel of Thomas*, Jesus teaches that there is no need to pray, fast, give alms, or obey any dietary or purity regulations (*Gos. Thom.* 6; 14; 27; 104); the author thus rejects the Jewish legacy altogether. Through vocabulary, he may give a positive connotation to fasting, Sabbath observance, and circumcision, but the practices undergo such a radical reinterpretation that nothing is left of their original concrete meaning.[239] Necessary "fasting" means fasting "from the world" (27.1), that is, the ascetic, world-denying lifestyle recommended in the *Gospel*; "observing the Sabbath as a Sabbath" is also necessary in order to

278   see the Father (27.2), and this too probably symbolizes abstinence from worldly values.[240] "True circumcision in spirit" is "profitable" (53); whatever this may mean for the author, he certainly repudiates the bodily operation (if it were beneficial, "their fathers would beget them already circumcised from their mothers"). Some practices (including prayer!) can even be seen as harmful for one's spiritual existence. "If you fast, you will bring sin upon yourselves; and if you pray, you will be condemned; and if you give alms, you will harm your spirits" (14). Thus it is not surprising that the *Gospel* is critical of the scriptures as well (52).[241] "In the same way as the Jewish religious practices are dead institutions, so also the Jewish scriptures seem to be incapable of providing life to their readers."[242] Jesus alone brings divine revelation; any previous salvation history disappears. Even the standard Christian claim that the scriptures contain prophecies about Jesus is sternly rejected; the author's community is instead connected "to a mythological past that dates to a time before Adam."[243] However, the amount of space devoted to the discussion of elements of Jewish faith suggests that some readers of *Thomas* were still attached to their Jewish heritage, from which the author wishes to liberate them.[244] In saying 43 the Thomasine Jesus blames the disciples for having "begun to resemble the Jews" in that they do not understand. In this respect, however, the Jews are no different from other "worldly" people who have not adopted the values of the Thomas circle. They are not being demonized.

A full rejection of the Jewish scriptures was carried out by some gnostically oriented Christians. Many texts pay no attention whatsoever to the Jewish matrix of Christianity; it is simply ignored. The *Gospel of Truth*, for instance, makes use of the early Christian "revelation pattern" (for example, Rom. 16:25-26): God's mystery—Jesus Christ—was hidden to previous generations, but has been revealed at the present moment through the mercy of the Father (*Gos. Truth* 18.11-21). History is here replaced with protology.[245] Other authors, however, engage in a frontal attack against Jewish tradition. *The Second Treatise of the Great Seth* presents Moses, the patriarchs, and the twelve prophets as "laughingstocks," and the same is true of the Old Testament God, "Archon," who claimed, "I am God, and there is none greater than I" (*Treat. Seth* 62.27—65.1). Sethian documents, such as the *Apocryphon of John* and the *Hypostasis of the Archons*, retell stories of scripture with novel twists, for example, letting Adam and Eve perceive that the creator of the world was not the true Deity. A very polemical stance toward Jewish tradition is adopted, and yet the very need for denigration indicates that the roots of these enlightened authors lie in Jewish soil. Michael Williams rightly points out that, in presenting "radical" reinterpretations, these authors are mostly concerned with such texts as had seemed problematic to a great number of other Jewish and Christian interpreters as well.[246] Their "reversal" of biblical texts can therefore be seen as exegetical attempts to solve genuine problems by removing embarrassing features from the texts.[247]

Marcion tackled the same problem in a partly similar and yet different way.[248] He assessed the scriptures critically—we might say, by way of ethical criticism—without explaining the problems away with the aid of allegorical interpretation, as his "orthodox" contemporaries tended to do. As a result, he downgraded scripture as the book of an inferior God. This God, the creator, could not be identical with the Father of Jesus, for the scripture speaks of him as a harsh ruler with a passion for war and a thirst for blood. Marcion pointed out one contrast after another between the two Gods or their representatives.[249] He replaced the scripture of the creator with the writings that he considered to be the genuine founding documents of Christianity: ten letters of Paul and Luke's Gospel. The key to the contrast between the old and the new order he derived from Galatians. Paul had struggled to find a solution to his salvation-historical dilemma, but Marcion coolly concluded that an order that loses its validity (the Torah, according to a straightforward reading of Galatians) cannot have been ordained by the true God. Marcion thus adopted an extreme position, believing that there was no connection at all between Judaism and Christianity. He picked one side of Paul's ambivalent legacy and brought it to a head. His proto-orthodox opponents cultivated the other side of this legacy.

For Marcion's star pupil, Apelles, the Jewish scripture was full of fairy tales and lies, so much so that it was not worthy to be attributed even to the demiurge. It was the work of another angel, a spirit of deceit who spoke to Moses from the burning bush. This evil angel was the God of Israel (and of those Christians who believed in this God). In Apelles's interpretation, then, the God of the scriptures became an almost satanic figure (in contrast to Marcion, who regarded this God as stern but just).[250]

Marcion's concept of two Gods was, of course, offensive from a monotheistic point of view, but the theology of Paul and others could be taken to imply a no less scandalous idea: that the one God had, despite his own repeated affirmations to the contrary, changed his mind.[251] It was clear to Marcion that God could not display such instability. His critics agreed, but put forward different solutions. A moderate solution from a position outside Judaism was proposed by the Valentinian teacher Ptolemy in his *Letter to Flora*. Unlike Marcion, he did not reject all of Jewish scripture out of hand,[252] but unlike orthodox Christians he did not resort to tortuous reinterpretations of scripture either (in order to be able to accept it as a whole). Ptolemy was the first to make explicit critical distinctions within the scriptural law itself, taking his cue from the words of Jesus (as set forth in the Gospel of Matthew). Scripture contains human additions to the law (Jesus had distinguished between the traditions of the elders and the commandment of God), but even after they have been removed, the law is not uniform. Jesus abolished such parts of it as are righteous but not consonant with the goodness of the true God (they take human weakness into account). Another obsolete part is the cultic law, which is to be interpreted allegorically (cultic stipulations are given an ethical interpretation). The highest part of the law is that which Jesus accepted, the Decalogue in particular. But even that part is imperfect, for Jesus had to fulfill it through his interpretation in the Sermon on the Mount. For Ptolemy this proves that even the highest part of the law did not come from the perfect Father but from the demiurge (3.7).[253] It is hardly far-fetched to regard Ptolemy's differentiated, rational view of the law as a foreshadowing of modern biblical study.

Marcion's more orthodox critics, too, recognized the problem, but they resorted to a different solution, reinterpreting scripture for their own ends. Parts of the law had indeed been abolished, but not because God had changed his plans; people had just misunderstood those plans. Justin held, like *Barnabas*, that God's moral law is permanently valid, whereas the "irrational" part of the law had only a temporal purpose.[254] It was given in order to discipline the Jews, who, as an exceptionally sinful people, needed special chastisement (*Dial.* 19.6—20.1).[255]

280

Justin explained as many texts from scripture as possible as predictions about Jesus and interpreted the law in completely Christian terms. Consequently he construed the Jews, who could not accept this usurpation of their tradition, as an extremely stubborn people who had always opposed the will of God.[256] Like most Christian authors, he picked up the scriptural passages that declare the people stubborn and hardened (for example, Deut. 32:20; Ps. 106:37). The Jews have always killed the prophets sent by God (*Dial.* 73.6; 95.2); following their nature, they have killed Jesus and persecute Christians (*Dial.* 133.6). By contrast, those passages in which God approaches the elect people in a positive way are explained to speak of Christians (or of such Jews as can be regarded as their predecessors). All of God's promises belong to Christians: "*For the true spiritual Israel*, the family of Judah, Jacob, Isaac, and Abraham, whom God accepted as uncircumcised and whom he blessed and called the father of many nations, *are we*" (*Dial.* 11.5).

Marcion is often portrayed as an enemy of the Jews, and certainly Judaism was, for him, an inferior religion. Yet, unlike so many orthodox church fathers, Marcion does not blame the Jews for killing Jesus. The death of Jesus was to be blamed on the imprudent creator. Tertullian indeed complains that Marcion had formed "an alliance with the Jewish error" (*Marc.* 3.6.2), "borrowing poison from the Jew" (3.8.1). Marcion conceded to the Jews that Jesus could not be their long-awaited Messiah. He believed that the Jewish Warrior-Messiah would still come to establish a temporary earthly kingdom for his people (3.6.1-2), regathering them out of dispersion (3.21.1).[257] Marcion may not have liked the Jews, but he was definitely much less anti-Jewish than were his orthodox opponents.[258]

Marcion came to act as a catalyst, however, in that he forced others to pose the question of continuity with new seriousness. If, as many Christians agreed, parts of the law were to be abandoned, how could one take seriously the God who made such an inferior arrangement in the first place? Tertullian's answer in his attempt to refute Marcion is representative: since the giver of the law cannot (by definition) be criticized, the blame is transferred to the people who cling to this law. The scriptural law was deficient and had to be replaced, yet this was the fault not of God, but of the Jews. For example, the law of retaliation ("eye for an eye") had to be given, because "that stiff-necked people" was unable to expect vengeance from God. Dietary laws were imposed on the Jews because of their gluttony. By that rationale, the law is nothing more than a burden, given for discipline; its individual parts (such as sacrifices) are comparable to superstitious practices in the Gentile world.

If God visited the fathers' sins upon the children, "it was Israel's hardness that demanded remedies of that sort, to cause them to obey the divine law at least through consideration for their posterity" (*Marc.* 2.15.1). Tertullian ominously finds here a preview of Matthew's passion narrative, which makes the Jewish people cry, "His blood be on our heads and on our children" (Matt. 27:25): "so then God's foresight . . . passed censure upon this which he heard long before it was spoken" (*Marc.* 2.15.3).

The future development of Jewish-Christian relations is ominously anticipated in the Easter sermon by Melito, bishop of Sardis (in the latter half of the second century), which makes it "painfully evident that those who celebrated Easter on the same day as the Jewish Passover were not motivated by special friendliness towards Judaism."[259] Israel has committed an unheard-of crime: it has murdered its God! Melito is the first Christian author who unambiguously accuses the Jews of deicide. Israel—the term is used by Melito without differentiation with reference to all Jews—should have recognized in Jesus the God who created the world and guided the chosen people throughout its history (*Homil.* 81-86). "He who hung the earth is hanging; he who fixed the heavens has been fixed; he who fastened the universe has been fastened to a tree; the Sovereign has been insulted; the God has been murdered; the King of Israel has been put to death by an Israelite right hand" (96). The road to the Holocaust had been marked out.

Orthodox Christianity wrenched the scriptures from the Jews. Ethical teachings of the Bible were lavishly used and assimilated to the new law of Jesus. Orthodox Christianity comes structurally close to covenantal nomism, except that the covenant is established in Jesus, and the nomism is stripped of "irrational" commandments. Covenantal symbols were appropriated by way of spiritualizing interpretation. Circumcision of the flesh was replaced with circumcision of the heart, observance of the law with obedience to moral commands. The notion of Christian ethics as the "law of Christ," largely characteristic of second-century Christian thought, reflects a relative end point in the legitimating process: central and suggestive vocabulary from the old symbolic universe is retained, but it is given a new interpretation and a new place in the new whole. The actual discontinuity is camouflaged with the use of language suggesting continuity.

Precisely because it was asserted that the scriptures spoke of Jesus, the continuing existence of Judaism as a religion with rival claims to the same authority was felt to be a threat to Christian identity; for, as Kari Syreeni notes, unlike old Simeon in the Lukan infancy narrative,

Judaism refused to be dismissed in peace when Jesus had entered the scene.[260] In the course of time, the threat was repressed with violent means. Rosemary Ruether's thesis about anti-Judaism as the left hand of Christology was not spun out of thin air.[261]

By contrast, the identity of neither Marcion nor of gnostic Christians was threatened by the continued existence of Judaism. For all his contempt for Jewish scripture, Marcion did grant the Jews the right to expect their own Messiah and his earthly kingdom. He conceded to them their rites and symbols, as long as Christians did not observe them. Where Catholic Christianity took the symbols and attacked the people, Marcion "attacked the symbols but left the people alone."[262] Stephen Wilson writes:

> It is clear that both the Marcionite and the Catholic position involve a denigration of Judaism. . . . I would not like to be found defending either view of Judaism. However, it might be argued that the one which more obviously belittles Jewish symbols was, ironically, in practice the lesser of two evils . . . Judaism is the loser in either case. Whether the Marcionite position, had it prevailed, would have led to the same sad consequences as the view of its opponents is hard to say. But it is worth a moment's reflection.[263]

Consider a nineteenth-century parallel. It has been noted that "the same Harnack who frankly denied any importance of the Old Testament to the Christian faith" also stated that "to write anti-semitism on the banners of Evangelical Christianity is a sad scandal." On the other hand, Adolf Stöcker, the Berlin court preacher who delivered anti-Semitic speeches to large audiences, was a conservative theologian who saw

282 the importance of the Old Testament "in the traditional scheme of prediction and fulfillment." This is no paradox at all. Henning Graf Reventlow, who pointed out the parallel, rightly notes: "The apparent contradiction disappears with the insight that reading the Old Testament as part of the Christian canon . . . denies the claim of current Judaism to any right of its own to the text."[264]

A SHORT EPILOGUE

Looking back, one is tempted to think that history has repeated itself, not without some irony: the Jewish architects of the intolerant Deuteronomistic innovation had appropriated the past, claimed to cherish ancient traditions, and condemned as idolaters the adherents to old practices. Proto-orthodox Christians, too, laid claim to Israel's history. They reinterpreted Jewish values, abandoned many central symbols of identity, and asserted that it was they who fulfilled God's law. Jews who clung to the old symbols had, they claimed, gone astray. Most Jews, of course, opposed Christian innovation as wrongheaded and impious.[265] From a Jewish point of view, Christians can be seen as Gentiles who claim for themselves the Jewish idea of being God's chosen people and, in the process, deny this claim to Jews. Christian anti-Semitism is thus the underside of a Christian competitive relationship to Jewish claims of divine chosenness. Today, some Jewish thinkers believe that Jews should abandon the idea of special election; Jews are special in the same way that each people claim their own uniqueness.[266] This brings a new kind of irony onto the scene: liberal Jewish thinkers may disavow chosenness, but many Christian theologians reaffirm the continuing election of the Jews.[267]

11

Strangers in a Transitory World
Christians and Pagans

Some early Christians broke the barrier between Jews and Gentiles, allowing Gentile converts to join their community without circumcision and full observance of the Torah. But while they thus gave up some crucial Jewish identity markers, they were just as adamant as Jews had ever been with regard to the Gentile polytheistic cult, which they too branded as "idolatry." Christianity, like Judaism, "demanded renunciation and a new start."[1] It was the Christians' refusal to participate in the civic religious activities of their day that most markedly set them apart in Gentile society and served to create clear boundaries of identity. Thus a barrier came to be raised between converted Gentiles and their pagan past. Conversion to Christ could mean cutting one's old social ties (including family ties) and rejecting old commitments.

Christians came increasingly to present themselves as a new people who identified with neither Jews nor Gentiles. The phrase "third race" first occurs in Aristides (*Apol.* 2), but the idea is found in a nutshell already in 1 Cor. 10:32, where Paul distinguishes between Jews, Greeks, and "the church of God." Many felt that they lived as strangers and "sojourners" in the midst of an alien, sometimes hostile, world (Phil. 3:20; 1 Pet. 1:1, 17; 2:11; *Diogn.* 5.5; and elsewhere). Still, early Christian attitudes to social interaction, which could involve some contact with pagan cults, present a striking variety, ranging from strict rejection to remarkable flexibility. Attitudes to pagan philosophy and culture develop from outright rejection or cautious appreciation to unacknowledged borrowing or even to generous use.

IDOLATRY

Worshiping idols

Pagan religiosity was basically tolerant. The religious landscape in the Greco-Roman world was governed by flourishing traditional cults, and adherence to a particular God did not exclude

284   participation in the worship of another. The festivals of the Gods were great joyful events that supported a city's identity (see above, p. 41). But for most early Christians, the adherents to these cults were condemnable idolaters and their festivals acts of idolatry.

Inevitably, Jewish and Christian polemicists (from Deutero-Isaiah on: Isa. 44:9-20) misrepresent the cults in which images are used. The connection that was perceived to exist between statue and God varied. It could be very close, but in general no full identity should be assumed: it is not the material object itself that is worshiped.[2] To be sure, Christian contempt for image-worship converged with that of many philosophers, who nevertheless in general did not abandon the conventional practice. But Christians, like Jews, connected—in contradiction to their own idea that pagan Gods were just pieces of wood or stone[3]—sinister notions with idolatry: it brought its practitioners into contact with demons and led, automatically as it were, to all kinds of depravity.

Paul praises his Greek converts for having turned "from idols" to serve the living and true God (1 Thess. 1:9). In Romans, he presents (drawing on Hellenistic Jewish traditions; see especially Wis. 13–15) an utterly dark picture of the "idolaters": those who have changed God's glory for human or animal images are the victims of "degrading passions," "filled with every kind of wickedness" (a vice list of some twenty items follows, Rom. 1:26-31). Many commentators take Paul's tirades at face value, speaking of the gross immorality of the pagan world.[4] But Robin Lane Fox points out that "it is quite untrue that pagans lived in unfettered sexuality before Christianity came" (although Christians did create a different code in this area). Even in the pagan Greek world, sexuality was "governed by the profound restraints of honour and shame."[5] Paul's attack on Gentiles is part of his artificial argumentative strategy that aims at the conclusion that the whole world is "under sin" and needs Jesus as its redeemer. When he is not arguing for this theological conclusion, Paul shows a greater sense of nuances in his picture of the Gentile world. In Phil. 4:8, he summarizes the ideals of a Christian life in terms of Greek popular moral philosophy: one is to contemplate whatever is true, honorable, just, pure, pleasing, commendable. . . .

First Corinthians reveals that the relation of Paul's Greek converts to the traditional cults was a practical problem that the Corinthian believers had debated. Paul makes clear that participation in a pagan cult is impossible for a Christian (1 Cor. 10:14-22). The intensity of the argument suggests that some people in the Christian community had actually been involved in pagan religious occasions. Paul warns them severely: Do not become idolaters! "You cannot drink the cup of the Lord and the cup of demons. You cannot partake of the table of the Lord and the table of demons" (1 Cor. 10:21). The worship of pagan Gods involves the frightening world of evil spirits. But we will see below that the matter was, for Paul, less straightforward than this, as polytheistic cults were connected with social events that the apostle was not prepared to condemn right away.

Luke narrates how Paul, visiting Athens, "was deeply distressed to see that the city was full of idols" (Acts 17:16). In his Areopagus speech that follows, the Lukan Paul criticizes handmade shrines where pagan Gods are "served with human hands" (v. 25). "Paul" aligns himself with the philosophers' critique of popular religion, yet unlike the philosophers he does not accept their compliance with its customs, but goes on to demand "repentance" of such ignorant practice. The intellectual tensions inherent in the speech are discussed below.

A blanket condemnation of the "idolaters," lumped together as murderers, sorcerers, fornicators, and thieves, which goes even a long step beyond Romans 1, is given by the seer of Revelation (Rev. 9:20-21). Second-century apologists polemicized against pagan religion, attacking the foolish worship of images and the wretched human weakness of the Greek Gods in the old myths.[6]

It is not clear that the attitude of gnostic Christians to polytheistic cults was much different from that of other Christians. Valentinus (frg. 1) takes up traditional Jewish polemic against "handmade" images of Gods.[7] To be sure, there are hints that some gnostic Christians themselves fostered a cult of images, even owning statues of Gods; if so, they may have reinterpreted the significance of these statues. According to Irenaeus, the Carpocratian disciples of Marcellina in Rome had, along with busts of philosophers, even images of Jesus that they crowned and observed "like the heathen" (*Haer.* 1.25.6). This practice surely points, at the very least, to tolerance with regard to the standard use of cultic images. On the other hand, some Valentinians seem to have made a strict separation between Christian truth and pagan religion. Heracleon (frg. 21: Origen, *Comm. Jo.* 13.17) states, referring to the *Preaching of Peter*, that "one is not allowed to pray as the Greeks, who believe in material things and worship wood and stone."

Idol Meat

More controversial than idolatry pure and simple was the issue of eating or not eating sacrificial food (in Christian vocabulary: "idol meat," *eidolothyta*)—food that had been offered to a pagan God/dess and was then to be eaten in the temple precincts (say, in the gathering of a guild) or to be sold in the public market. Some Corinthian Christians had scruples about eating such food, while others saw no problem in the matter, and Paul was asked for advice. Paul makes a broadminded move by dissociating idol meat from idolatry proper: under certain conditions it is perfectly possible for Christians to eat meat that has been sacrificed to a pagan God. True, such meat cannot be eaten at the God's table, but when it is later sold in the marketplace, it is allowed (1 Cor. 10:25-26). It is even permitted to accept a pagan host's invitation to a dinner and to "eat whatever is set before you," including sacrificial meat. If, however, a dinner companion points to the origin of the meat and thus makes the eating a matter of conscience, one should abstain from eating it (10:27—11:1).

This seems clear enough, but 1 Corinthians 8 shows that Paul's position is ambiguous. Here the case is that of a Christian causing offense to his "weaker" brothers and sisters by eating in the "idol's house" (v. 10)—something we would not expect to happen at all if we read only chapter 10. Paul is answering a question raised by the enlightened party of the "strong" in the Corinthian church. He concedes to them that pagan Gods do not really exist (v. 4; not a word on demons here). Sacrificial meat is just ordinary food and could in itself be freely eaten, just as the strong had thought. Yet other Christians whose conscience is "weak" regard the pagan Gods as somehow real; for them the temptation to eat "idol meat" means enticement to apostasy. Therefore the strong should abstain from eating it if there is a risk than they might be observed by the weak.

So in principle Paul agrees with the strong: there is nothing wrong in eating even in a temple—when one is not watched by "weak" fellow

286 Christians. But since two chapters later Paul is so adamant about the "table of demons," he probably has something other than religious festivals proper in mind here. He may think of meals with a predominantly social character, such as dinners of trade guilds or some family events. A Christian may eat with unbelieving companions, but not participate in idolatrous ritual. The problem is, of course, that drawing a line between religious and social occasions must have seemed like drawing a line in water. When social events took place in "the idol's house," sacrifices and libations were an inevitable part of the program.

Paul's position therefore seems ambiguous. Intellectually he sides with the strong, making it easy for subsequent liberal interpreters to appeal to his authority. But he also shares some of the sentiments of the weak, even some of their fear of demons, so much so that Oda Wischmeyer concludes: Paul's attitude toward Gentile religion, of which his knowledge is "rudimentary and superficial," is "anxious and defensive."[8] Like Jewish thought in general, Paul wavers on the issue of the nature of the pagan Gods: are they mere figments of imagination or are they real evil spirits?[9]

The issue of eating meat is connected with social stratification.[10] Meat was seldom available to common people in antiquity. The situation was different for those with a higher social standing, and some such people were in the Corinthian congregation. Invitations to meals with religious overtones were part of their routine communication with their peers. Professional and social associations in the cities had a patron Deity, to whom sacrifice was made in the meetings; the meat from such a sacrifice was then shared by members as part of a common dinner. Restrictions on the eating of sacrificial meat were therefore restrictions on social relations. Some-

one like Erastus, the city treasurer of Corinth (Rom. 16:23), would surely have been forced to give up his public office right away had he turned down all invitations that implied eating sacrificial meat;[11] yet this man joins Paul in sending the Roman Christians greetings from Corinth. But in the end the internal cohesion of the Christian group was more important to Paul than the contacts with outsiders; the latter were to be set aside in the name of inner-Christian love if they jeopardized the unity of the congregation.[12]

Ironically, given his basic flexibility on the issue, Paul came to appear as coauthor of the so-called Apostolic Decree in the work of his great admirer, Luke. Luke claims that a decree that, among other things, flatly forbids the consumption of "idol meat" (along with the consumption of blood and *pnikton*, and with fornication) was promulgated at the "apostolic conference" in Jerusalem (Acts 15:20, 28-29). Paul's account of the meeting (Gal. 2) does not mention such a decision, and his emphatic assertion that the Jerusalem pillars "added nothing to" him (Gal. 2:6 RSV) seems to exclude it categorically. Such an agreement would indeed be very difficult to combine with the fact that in principle Paul had sympathy with those who did eat sacrificial meat in certain circumstances. The tortuous discussion of idol meat in 1 Corinthians 8–10 would have been unnecessary had Paul been aware of (and committed to) a decree that prohibited it. It is likely that the decree was issued after Paul's time and that its basic intention was precisely to prevent Christians from participating in the cults of pagan Gods, understood as demons. The decree became very influential, but we also hear dissenting voices: Colossians 2, which attacks those who forbid "tasting and touching" (v. 21), goes implicitly against it, and so do Mark 7 (the Markan Jesus declares *all* foods clean: Mark 7:15, 19) and

1 Tim. 4:3 (polemic against those who "demand abstinence from foods").[13]

Long ago, classical scholar Eduard Meyer pointed out that the decree brought about a rupture in the relations between Christians and pagans. In everyday life, this rupture was more acute than the one caused by Jewish food laws, since families and close personal relations were often involved. "Christians would have been spared a great many persecutions, if Paul's more liberal view had prevailed."[14]

We may detect some influence of the decree in Revelation. The author pronounces a fierce judgment on the "idolaters": they are classed together with "dogs, sorcerers, fornicators, murderers, everyone who loves and practices falsehood" (Rev. 22:15; cf. 9:20-21; 21:8). But he also attacks some fellow Christians in Pergamum called "Nicolaitans," followers of someone called Nicolaus,[15] whom he charges with eating idol meat (2:14). Similar criticisms in an even more fierce tone are addressed to the followers of a prophetess in the congregation of Thyatira whom John calls "Jezebel" after the pagan queen known for favoring the cult of Baal in the time of Israelite monarchy (2:20-23).[16]

The backdrop of John's criticism of the Nicolaitans is apparently constituted by the Apostolic Decree that he takes as a norm (Rev. 2:24).[17] In view of the social circumstances in Thyatira, a prosperous trade center, commentators recognize the relevance of guild membership to the issue. Some socially better-off Christians seem to have been members of trade guilds.[18] They were therefore likely to be involved in social events that took place in pagan temples and included meals. The parallelism with the situation in Corinth in Paul's time is obvious. The Nicolaitans are also said to practice fornication. Since "fornication" is a standing scriptural meta-

phor to describe Israel's apostasy from Yahweh, the word is probably used in this sense even here, in a context that bristles with scriptural allusions: it is simply another name for eating idol meat. John could hardly have praised the Thyatirans for their love, faith, service, and endurance (2:19) if the congregation had tolerated actual promiscuity.

Paul, for whom the issue of sacrificial meat was first and foremost a problem of personal counseling, might have cautiously approved of the practice of the Nicolaitans. Nor do the congregations in Pergamum and Thyatira seem to have been disturbed by some members' eating "idol meat." For John, by contrast, eating or not eating is a question of life and death in the ideological battle between Christ and the beast,[19] so much so that he constructs a subtle connection between the "fornicating" Christian leader (Rev. 2:20) and the great harlot "Babylon," who symbolizes Rome and its culture (ch. 17). His counsel to the congregations is that of social separation: "Come out of her [Babylon], my people, lest you take part in her sins, lest you share in her plagues" (18:4). Adela Yarbro Collins points out that the Christian lifestyle as John understood it was "incompatible with ordinary participation in the economic and social life of the cities"; John's strict position on idol meat does not seem "compatible with continued membership in a guild."[20] Paul Duff generalizes this insight: "While 'Jezebel' advocated engagement with the larger society (probably with an eye to reforming it from within), John recommended withdrawal into the ghetto."[21] "Babylon" was "the dwelling place of demons" (18:2). "'Jezebel's' assimilationist strategy threatened the boundaries between John's 'us' and 'them.'"[22] What John here demands of Christians is roughly what Paul had rejected as a *mis*understanding in 1 Cor. 5:9-10:

288 Christians were, according to Paul, definitely *not* to "go out of the world." Eating "idol meat" has become for John a symbol for idol worship (that includes the cult of the emperor). Paul had held the two apart. In Paul's time, Christians had not yet found themselves in situations where they were required to sacrifice in front of the image of the emperor, as had apparently happened to some Christians in John's time.

John and the Nicolaitans represent two different types of Christians, coupled with different social situations. In the words of Leonard Thompson, John's group "sets up high boundaries between itself and the rest of the world" and "holds to a concomitant 'separatist' definition of the church," seeing "Greco-Roman society as demonic." The group of the Nicolaitans is "less concerned with sharp boundaries and exclusive self-definition and seems to have little conflict with . . . Greco-Roman urban institutions."[23] The conflict with the pagan world thus goes hand in hand with an inner-Christian conflict over lifestyle.

The conflict continued in the second century. The Apostolic Decree was observed within proto-orthodox Christianity (idol meat is prohibited, for example, in *Did.* 6.3), but possibly ignored in gnostic Christian circles. The refusal to eat blood is repeatedly mentioned in apologetic contexts: how could Christians eat children (as the rumor had it), when they do not even consume the blood of animals?[24] But Justin Martyr complains that many who in his view are only nominal Christians (he mentions the followers of Marcion, Valentinus, Basilides, and Saturninus) do eat food offered to idols and claim that they have no harm from it (*Dial.* 35.1-6). True Christians, by contrast, suffer a martyr's death rather than eat such food (34.8). Irenaeus (*Haer.* 1.6.3) likewise states that some gnostics (apparently

Valentinians) eat idol meat without scruples, "thinking that they are in no way defiled by these foods," and are even the first to arrive at pagan festival parties held in honor of idols; some even enjoy the spectacle of fights in the circus. The followers of Valentinus and Basilides included Christians of a relatively high social standing; a liberal attitude to sacrificial meat—and to pagan feasts—would have been a sign of a greater integration into society.[25] Unfortunately we depend here on polemical secondhand sources. The Nag Hammadi texts are silent on both sacrificial meat and on festivals. It should also be noted that some gnostic Christians were persecuted by state officials, which speaks against generalizations about great integration.

CONFLICT AND APOLOGY

Harassment and Persecution

Pagan authors agree that "hatred for humankind" was a general reason for pagan distrust of Christians.[26] Exclusivity and isolation were likely to cause suspicion and misunderstanding, as Jewish communities in the Diaspora had already often experienced. First Peter reflects a climate in which Christians are maligned by their neighbors as evildoers; astonishingly, they have acquired the reputation of being murderers, thieves, criminals, and mischief makers (1 Pet. 4:15). The author hopes that through the honorable conduct of the Christians the neighbors may eventually glorify God (2:12; cf. 3:16), but his attempt at peaceful coexistence is compromised by his lumping together the pagans themselves as evildoers who live "in licentiousness, passions, drunkenness, revels, carousing, and lawless idolatry," and are "surprised that you no longer join them in the same excesses of dissipation, and so they blaspheme" (4:3-4).[27] Christians have withdrawn from their previous social contacts (one can think of organized feasts and guild meals). This has created suspicion, and the result is mutual vilification.

Traditional rituals gave people a sense of security and identity; they would feel threatened and hurt if a new cult failed to pay respect to the customary forms of worship. This failure branded the Christians also as enemies of the state (cf. Tertullian, *Apol.* 35). They were dan-

gerous "because they put the advancement of their beliefs above the common good and the welfare of the state."[28] Moreover, there was always the danger that the Gods might show their anger by bringing natural disasters and diseases on whole areas, if they were not content with the worship given to them. It was the fear of this anger that "impelled people to persecute Christian 'atheists,' dangerous groups who refused to honour the gods."[29] Rumors spread that the Christians attacked temples and practiced incest and that their clandestine nocturnal rites involved

11.1   The ruins of the Colosseum. Photo: Robert Farlee.

290   cannibalism (a misunderstanding of the Eucharist?).[30] Tertullian sums up the atmosphere in observing that "if the Tiber rises to the walls, if the Nile does not rise to the fields; if the sky stands still, if the earth moves, if there is famine, if there is pestilence, the cry goes up, 'Christians to the lion!'" (*Apol.* 40.5).

Somehow the Christians must have made a negative impression on people in the city of Rome. Nero was able to make them scapegoats for the fire that destroyed the city in 64 C.E. only because they already had the reputation of being "a deadly superstition," "hated for their abominations" (Tacitus).[31] Perhaps the trial of Paul had made clear to the emperor that there was a differ-

ence between Jews and Christians.[32] Jewish synagogues were tolerated by the state, as they could be regarded as funerary collegia permitted by the law, and because they had been granted special permission for assembly by Julius Caesar.[33] As long as the authorities did not distinguish between Jews and Christians, the Christian groups seem to have enjoyed this same permission. But when the magistrates became aware of the differences between the two, Christians lost this protective cover. The Neronian persecution increased the negative publicity, branding the Christians as dangerous outsiders.[34] In addition, Christians (unlike Jews) were active in trying to make others convert, which may well have inflated the tension between them and the rest of the society.[35] Nevertheless, when sporadic persecutions broke out toward the end of the century, it was not the Roman authorities who were responsible for the trials of Christians, but the local population—the suspicious neighbors.[36] The authorities became active, often reluctantly, only after a denunciation from the people's side; governors probably felt that they had more important tasks than dealing with the Christians. This is confirmed by the correspondence of Pliny, governor of Pontus and Bithynia, with the emperor Trajan around 112 C.E.

Pliny wanted to know whether the mere fact of being a Christian was punishable, or whether a Christian should be punished only if demonstrably guilty of criminal acts. He had found out that the Christians brought to him were harmless, even though he executed as insolent those who refused his order to sacrifice to "our Gods." For though no other crime could be established, the practice of the Christian faith was in itself illegal, as private associations were prohibited.[37] Nevertheless, the emperor proposed a relatively lenient procedure, possibly in order to prevent

11.2   Colossal head of Nero. Roman marble, 65 C.E. Staatliche Antikensammlung, Munich, Germany.
Photo: © Bildarchiv Preussischer Kulturbesitz/Art Resource, NY.

mass executions: Pliny was not to actively track down Christians nor should he take anonymous denunciations into account.

Contrary to a common view, the imperial cult seems *not* to have been a central issue in either official or unofficial attitudes toward Christians. There are no indications in Paul's letters that the cult would have been a problem for Christians under Claudius or the young Nero.[38] Hans-Josef Klauck warns against exaggerating its significance, noting that in the case of the persecutions of Christians, it "does not appear in isolation, but as part of the entire polytheistic system."[39] "Most imperial sacrifices were offered to the gods *on behalf of* the emperor";[40] "the cult attached itself to the lively, traditional religiousness."[41] The primary problem was that Christians could not sacrifice to *any* God, be it on behalf of the emperor or otherwise. That put them on a collision course with local religious activity. The common people in the provinces did not denounce Christians because of their refusal to pay cultic homage to the emperors.[42] The issue of sacrificing before the image of the emperor arose in the courtroom *after* a person had been arrested as a suspect Christian: during the legal process he or she could be tested by being ordered to sacrifice. "The issue is only aired in the courtroom by governors themselves, and at times they air it as an easier way out for the people on trial."[43] The persecutions of Christians were a tragic consequence of their strained relations with their pagan neighbors, the adherents to traditional cults.

To be sure, the book of Revelation has traditionally been connected with a severe persecution during Domitian; this persecution for its part has been connected with the boosting of the imperial cult by this ruler. However, several scholars have persuasively argued that the situation under Domitian was rather different from the seer's perception of it.[44] "Some persecution had been experienced, more was expected; a disparity of wealth existed and economic survival was a problem," but "there is no need to posit a widespread or recent outbreak of persecution by Roman authorities against Christians."[45] Indeed, John knows only one martyr (Antipas of Pergamum: Rev. 2:13). To be sure, something had happened. Antipas had been killed and John himself banned (1:9). One can assume that some local actions (not always bloody—John had not been killed) had taken place. In addition, there was the memory of Nero's persecution a generation ago.[46] The letters to the seven churches in Asia Minor (chs. 2–3) point to an internal crisis in the communities as the seer's main problem. In the visions that make up the bulk of the book, however, worship of the "beast," the Roman emperor, emerges as a horrible threat: the servants of this cult, portrayed as a second beast "that rose out of the earth," see to it that "those who would not worship the image of the beast" are to be killed; every person willing to worship the beast is to be marked on the right hand or the forehead, "so that no one can buy or sell who does not have the mark, that is, the name of the beast or the number of its name" (13:11-17).[47] Domitian undoubtedly promoted the cult of the emperor, but it is questionable whether he demanded any greater divine honors than either his predecessors or successors.[48] Klauck notes that it is "a gross anachronism to suppose that Christians were always and everywhere at risk of being dragged in front of an image of the emperor to be tested to see if they would sacrifice, with martyrdom as the necessary result of their failure to do so." He distinguishes between "hard" and "soft" forms of the emperor cult. The hard version requires one to sacrifice before the image and to curse Christ, but this was rare and occurred, as

292   stated above, mostly only after denunciations. What John probably had to deal with in his social environment was the "soft" form of the cult, which was much more common, being based on social ties: gestures of respect in connection with association meals, legal processes, taking oaths, and making contracts.[49]

What Revelation testifies to is a *perceived* crisis rather than one that would have been noted also by an outside observer. John's expectation of a worldwide persecution is due to the tremendous impact of his apocalyptic thought world. In early Christian expectations predictions of persecutions, modeled on the war of the end-time enemy against the saints (Dan. 7:21, 25, and so on), are a fixed topic. John's symbolic world makes him see other signals of the end as well, such as the beginning apostasy of the congregation. He saw in the world around some small signs that were capable of an apocalyptic reading and magnified them vastly in his interpretation: limited local pressure anticipated huge massacres; a broadminded attitude to social communication with outsiders on the part of people like the Nicolaitans was the starting signal to a mass apostasy.

John's animosity cannot be explained, in the vein of liberation theology, on the basis of the difficult situation of the oppressed.[50] Duff points out that "although there is evidence for significant tension between rich and poor in the late first and early second centuries, there is *virtually nothing to support the notion of resentment of Rome by the poor anywhere in the empire*," whereas there is "a mountain of indirect proof of the popularity of the empire among the lower classes." No doubt, "the lower classes resented the elite, but not because they viewed the elite as collaborators with Rome in their oppression," but because they "saw the elite lining their own pockets at their expense. They did not see the wealth passing from the hands of the native elite on to Rome."[51] John thirsts for vengeance on all "those who dwell upon the earth" (Rev. 6:10), for slaves no less than for kings and generals (6:15; cf. 8:13; 9:4-6, 13-21; 11:10; 13:8; and so on). All non-Christians, and quite a few fellow Christians, too, are demonized; John does not mount a social justice argument. Rome is not blamed for oppressing the conquered peoples. On the contrary, the peoples are attracted to the beast and have voluntarily "given over their royal power" (17:17) to him; their kings have willingly fornicated with the harlot Rome.[52] John's hatred of Rome stems from religious reasons. He has made the emperor cult as he experienced it (mainly in its "soft" form) in Asia Minor "the occasion for a fundamental declaration of war on this world. The Roman empire did not declare war on the Christians; a Christian prophet declared war on the Roman empire."[53]

Persecutions occurred now and then in the second century. They could be cruel and fierce, like the one that fell upon Irenaeus's congregation in Lyon in 177, but they were local actions, directed against Christian individuals or small groups. Not until the mid-third century did large-scale persecution take place. Before that, the emperors from Trajan on "did more to protect Christians than to stamp them out."[54] When a wave of persecutions did occur, usually only bishops and other leaders were targeted. For rank-and-file Christians, the threat of martyrdom was slight.[55]

Estimations of the number of Christians that died in persecutions before Constantine's time differ vastly, from "hundreds rather than thousands"[56] to fifty thousand and more. In any case, Origen could still in the late 240s insist that only "few" Christians who could be "easily numbered" had died for their faith (*Cels.* 3.8).[57] The importance of the persecutions to the propagation of the Christian cause is likewise debated. Tertullian coined the slogan: "the blood of Christians is a seed" (*Apol.* 50.13), and historians have tended to follow him. In recent times, doubts have arisen. For instance, Lane Fox claims that "despite the rhetoric, martyrs were not a very prolific 'seed of the Church'"; in any case, in Christianity's greatest age of growth "martyrdom was no longer an option."[58]

It is generally thought that the phenomenon of martyrdom served to strengthen the internal coherence of the church. However, martyrdoms occurred in very different branches of Christianity, not just in (proto-) orthodox circles, and persecution experienced by "heretic" Christians was not appreciated by others.[59] The *Apocryphon of James* encourages believers who face persecution to choose suffering and death just as Christ did: "Make yourselves like the son of the holy spirit!" (*Apoc. Jas.* 6.19-20).[60] Marcionites were known for having a large number of martyrs, and if the Ptolemy who wrote the letter to Flora is identical with the Ptolemy who was executed as a Christian, we have here a case of a Valentinian martyr. While the customary claim that gnostic Christians tried to avoid persecution is not without some foundation (see below), the Valentinian *Tripartite Tractate* shows that it is too vast a generalization; this writing leans upon the idea of a persecuted church and employs myth to account for the existence of violent power that Christians (even Valentinians) confronted from time to time.[61] The *Second Treatise of the Great Seth* even suggests that true Christians are persecuted not only by "ignorant" outsiders, but also by other ("orthodox") Christians who "think that they are advancing the name of Christ" (*Treat. Seth* 59.19—60.1) and who yet proclaim "the

doctrine of a dead man" (60.22), that is, who establish their theology on Jesus' death.[62] The *Letter of Peter to Philip* (138.17-28) also seems to refer to the impending threat of a persecution.

The assessment of martyrdom also caused tensions. On one hand martyrs were highly respected, even adored. Christians could adopt and adapt the veneration of martyrs developed in Jewish piety and literature in the aftermath of the Maccabean revolt and of the Jewish War. Imprisoned, Paul had contemplated the possibility of his death as a "libation" (Phil. 2:17; cf. 2 Tim. 4:6), and the author of Colossians had interpreted Paul's sufferings as "completing what was lacking in Christ's afflictions" (Col. 1:24). Later martyrs were regarded as examples and their sufferings were ever more closely connected with the sacrifice of Christ himself; in facing the authorities a Christian might feel that he or she was reenacting Christ's passion. Polycarp (*Phil.* 8) appeals to the example of Christ; martyrs were loved because they were "disciples and imitators of the Lord" (*Mart. Pol.* 17.3). Stories about them, such as the famous *Martyrdom of Polycarp*, were written "as a training and preparation for those who will follow suit" (*Mart. Pol.* 18.3), and the cult of martyrs came to play an important role.[63] The rewards reserved for the martyrs exceeded those of other Christians. According to Tertullian, their blood was the key to paradise (*Anim.* 55.4-5). Many Christians could display a longing for martyrdom. Some deliberately attracted the attention of the authorities in order to be able to suffer for the faith. Ignatius, for his part, turned off the offers of fellow Christians to buy his freedom and eloquently described his lust for death and his hopes of being ground by the teeth of wild beasts in the arena into the "pure bread" of Christ—a grim kind of Eucharist offering (Ign. *Rom.* 4.1).[64] Polycarp, too, offers

294

himself in a prayer that carries eucharistic overtones as a sacrifice and gives thanks for the gift of martyrdom (*Mart. Pol.* 14.2-3).

On the other hand, it is clear that most Christians never suffered martyrdom, and many did their best to avoid it. Ignatius knew that Christians tried to ransom prisoners and had to ask the churches not to intervene in his favor (Ign. *Rom.* 1; 4). Tales of voluntary martyrdom represent "the ideals of extremists, exceeding sensible leaders' opinion."[65] The question whether a Christian had to confess his or her faith publicly at all costs was debated, and the overwhelming veneration of martyrs came to be criticized in some circles. Followers of Valenti-

nus[66] and Basilides are reported to have avoided persecution, and Basilides himself claimed that the Christians who died in persecutions had suffered because of their own secret sins[67] (Clement of Alexandria, *Strom.* 4.81.1–83.1; Löhr's frg. 7). The Elchasaites are said to have taught that "it is not a sin if someone happens to have worshiped idols in the face of imminent persecution, if only he does not do so from conviction" (Epiphanius, *Pan.* 19.1.8; cf. Eusebius, *Hist. eccl.* 6.38).[68] Clement of Alexandria criticized other Christians for excessive eagerness for martyrdom, as some have "rushed to death" and "given themselves in vain to death" (*Strom.* 4.4). Those who voluntarily announced themselves to the

11.3   Two martyrs-to-be, Ignatius and Polycarp, are portrayed in this painting, *Meeting of Saint Ignatius and Saint Polycarp at Smyrna* by Giacomo Triga (d. 1746). S. Clemente, Rome. Photo: © Alinari/Art Resource, NY.

authorities were in his opinion even accomplices of the persecutors (*Strom.* 10).[69]

Political Apology

From the beginning, a rather different tendency toward accommodation to the world and the powers-that-be in order to secure a modus vivendi in a hostile world had also existed in the church. Whatever criticism of the present powers Jesus' proclamation of the coming kingdom may have implied, he did not attack Rome directly, and he even said that one should "give to the emperor the things that are the emperor's" (that is, taxes: Mark 12:13-17 par.), in agreement with the standard Jewish strategy of accommodation (see above, p. 26). Paul's advice of complying with the government that has a divine right to use the sword might be taken as an anticipatory counterposition to the stance later taken by John the Seer: "whoever resists authority resists what God has appointed," for "rulers are not a terror to good conduct, but to bad" (Rom. 13:1-7). Klauck correctly points out that "Paul could scarcely have spoken of the God-given authority of rulers as he does in Romans 13:1-7 if he had seen the emperor as posing a problem that dominated every other concern."[70] Politically engaged readings that claim the opposite founder on this text (if not before).[71] Paul seems to accept the empire as ordained by God.[72] Many Christians toward the end of the first century took a similar line. First Peter urges readers to hold firmly to their faith, but the author also advises them "for the Lord's sake" to accept the authority of governors and to honor the emperor (1 Pet. 2:13-17). The Epistle to Titus reminds the readers that they are to be "subject to rulers and authorities" (Titus 3:1). Clement of Rome, who stresses the importance of order in the church, likewise emphasizes that it is God who has given the rulers their authority (*1 Clem.* 60–61).

Above all, Luke presents with great skill a picture of Jesus' and Paul's encounters with Roman officials that amounts to a political apology: from the point of view of the state, this movement is harmless. Both its initiator and his greatest apostle are proved innocent of any crimes before Roman governors. Pilate finds Jesus not guilty of any capital offense; Luke tries to whitewash the governor and even implies (though perhaps unintentionally) that it was actually the Jews who executed Jesus.[73] In the early chapters of Acts, the apostles are flogged by Jewish leaders, but when Paul and his co-missionaries move out into the Gentile world, they receive fairer treatment (Acts 13:7, 12; 16:22-24, 35-39; 17:6-9; 18:12-16; 19:23-41). In Acts 24–26, Paul defends himself on three occasions, two of them being formal proceedings before the Roman governors in Judea. Luke makes clear that Paul is innocent of any breach of Roman law. The followers of Jesus are no threat whatsoever to the empire, though ill-disposed Jewish authorities repeatedly try to prove the opposite. The positive picture painted of several Roman officials and soldiers, in particular of the centurion Cornelius (Acts 10–11), is noteworthy. Luke's stress on Christianity as an ancestral faith not only serves the theological purpose of demonstrating continuity with God's covenant people, but has also a vital political purpose: to attest that Christianity "was not a new religion and therefore not liable to contribute to political instability, but was the inevitable development of ancient Jewish tradition."[74]

Justin, too, underlines that Christians, following the teaching of Christ, take efforts to pay all taxes. "We worship God alone, but in all other things we are happy to be your servants,

296 acknowledge you as the kings and rulers of men, and pray that your royal power will prove to be in accordance with sound reason" (*1 Apol.* 17.3). The prayer for the emperor and the state compensates, as it were, for the Christians' refusal to sacrifice, as it demonstrates the loyalty of Christians as citizens against the accusations of enmity to the state. In Christian apologetics from the second century on, the demonization of the political power as expressed in Revelation yields increasingly to the Pauline theory of the God-given state. Tertullian's statement is typical: "It is our duty to respect the emperor, for our Lord has elected him" (*Apol.* 33.1).[75]

Pagan Philosophy and Culture

While early Christians generally took a totally negative attitude toward pagan cults, attitudes toward pagan philosophy and moral value systems were more ambiguous.[76] Paul was suspicious of the wisdom of the Greeks and contrasted it with his own message of the cross of Christ (1 Cor. 1:18-25).[77] He made some use of popular philosophy (1 Cor. 7:29-31 has points of contact with the Stoic ideal of *ataraxia*, being imperturbable), leaning on its lists of vices and virtues (a habit that continued in his "school");[78] but he often gave philosophical topics a peculiar twist (see chapter 6 on his treatment of the human condition in Rom. 7). In criticizing pagan religion, Paul admitted that humans were capable to reach at least an approximate conception of God's nature by contemplating creation, but he used this natural theology to demonstrate that the Greeks are "without excuse" (Rom. 1:20; 2:1) for having (by turning to idolatry) forsaken this knowledge of God that would have been available to all.

In a more positive vein, the author of Luke–Acts tries to establish a positive contact with Hellenistic moral-philosophical traditions. When his Paul addresses Gentiles, the argument from prophecy and from the history of Israel, which is used in sermons to those born Jews in Acts, yields to an argument from natural theology. God can still be perceived in the natural order of the cosmos: he has left himself a witness in "giving you rains from heaven and fruitful seasons, and filling you with food and your hearts with joy" (Acts 14:17).

Luke narrates how Paul, visiting Athens, had the chance to give a great speech on the Areopagus (Acts 17).[79] The speech is rhetorically impressive, but ambiguous in content. Using an altar with the inscription "to an unknown God"[80] as his starting point, Paul claims that the Athenians already worship the true God without knowing him. Paul makes clear that this God who created everything does not live in "shrines made with human hands, nor is he served by human hands, as though he needed anything." God is not far from any of us, for "in him we live and move and have our being" (v. 28). Paul here cites a Stoic maxim, and he confirms his statement by quoting "one of your own poets" (the valued and widely read *Phainomena* of Aratus) to the effect that mortals are God's offspring. Therefore, one ought not to think that the Deity is like an image formed by human art (v. 29). This is a point with which philosophers would have agreed; Luke's Paul is criticizing popular Greek religion in terms that contemporary philosophers accepted. But then he suddenly moves to an attack: God has overlooked the times of ignorance, but now he commands all people to repent, having fixed a day for judgment and giving assurance of this by raising the coming judge from the dead (vv. 30-31).

Luke tries to be inclusive, to treat the men of Athens almost as anonymous Christians, but the attempt miscarries. As Martin Dibelius recognized, apart from its abrupt ending the speech is a Stoic creation, in its basic ideas alien to most of the New Testament.[81] But the claim that the period before Christ was a time of ignorance contradicts the argument just presented that Gentiles possess a natural knowledge of God before Christ, and that God saw to it that people might "grope for him and find him" (Acts 17:27). Luke first appeals to general human experience, but finally he "crushes that appeal under the weight of his system."[82] The final impression is that the reference to the spiritual life of the Athenians is used just as a point of contact with the missionary purpose of freeing them from their actual ignorance. Nevertheless, the ambiguity of the speech suggests that somehow Luke may have felt that there is a problem with his Christian exclusivism. He is not able simply to brush aside the considerations dictated by universal morality, but wrestles with the issue of pluralism and exclusivism, without being able to solve it except through a deus ex machina in Paul's final call to repentance. For all their tentativeness, Acts 14 and 17 anticipate some of the main lines of second-century Christian apologetics.

By comparison with the Jews, who had an acknowledged position as a people with ancient laws and literature, the Christians seemed a bunch of newcomers who lacked roots and cultural weight. Pagan critics could claim, as Celsus was to do, that Christianity was a novel doctrine, and this fact was sufficient to render it irrelevant (if not dangerous); what was not new in it had been better stated by philosophers. Educated Christians had good reasons to try to defend their religion before pagan audiences, and the second century saw several such attempts, sometimes addressed to (though scarcely read by) the emperor himself. Christians replied to the accusation of novelty by appealing to the Jewish scriptures (which they had appropriated).[83] The Christian teaching was derived from Moses, who was (as Jewish apologists, for example Philo, had claimed) the most ancient of authors. Therefore the Christian teaching was older and truer than that of all poets and authors.[84] Some apologists, such as Justin, were audacious enough to appropriate even the best of pagan tradition: the philosophers had received their glimpses of truth precisely from Moses.[85]

It was crucial to the proto-orthodox, however, to establish a clear difference between Christian truth and the philosophers' intimations. Some went to a violent counterattack. Tatian and Tertullian ended up with a wholesale rejection of Greco-Roman culture (though themselves fully exploiting the resources of its rhetoric in their polemics). For Tatian, everything Greek was foolish, vain, and immoral. Tertullian asked provocatively, "What has Jerusalem to do with Athens?" (*Praescr.* 7.9). Thoroughly negative assessments of classical culture could be found on different sides of the Christian ideological map. For the Jewish Christian homilist, the philosophers are vainglorious and "the whole learning of the Greeks is a most dreadful fabrication of a wicked demon" (*Ps.-Clem. Hom.* 4.9, 12); but the Valentinian author of the *Tripartite Tractate* draws a no less negative view of the philosophers and their views (Judaism fares a lot better): the sages "speak in a vague, arrogant, and imaginary way concerning the things that they thought of as wisdom . . . they thought that they had attained the truth, when they had attained error" (*Tri. Trac.* 109.32—110.1). Evil powers hinder them from seeing the truth. The author proceeds to condemn the entire culture of the polytheists—their medicine, rhetoric,

298 performing arts, and logic—thus taking an unusually rigorous position even among early Christians.[86]

Most apologists, however, display a more positive attitude to philosophy and literature. They could not deny that pagan philosophy had sometimes come close to the truth, but such similarities could be treated positively under the rubric of natural theology or *praeparatio evangelica*, God's way of preparing the soil for the gospel. Humankind was at first not capable of comprehending the full truth; it had to be gradually prepared for it by God, and in this process Greek philosophy and education were a helpful tool.[87] John's use of the philosophical key concept *Logos* in his prologue provided a fitting starting point, introducing (following the example of Hellenistic Judaism) a mediating figure between humans and the transcendent God. Christianity thereby came to be situated in a strong Middle Platonic current. Justin builds the bridge to philosophy with a theory of the divine Logos as "sower" (*logos spermatikos*), who, before his incarnation, has scattered "seeds" of truth in human minds. Some humans possess more of the truth than others; this applies not only to the prophets but even to philosophers like Heraclitus or Socrates.[88] Yet it is only in the incarnation of the Logos in Christ that the full truth has become accessible. Jesus fulfilled not only the predictions of scripture, but the anticipations of the philosophers as well. This view of pre-Christian philosophy parallels the notion of the Epistle to the Hebrews that the Torah is "a shadow of the good things to come"; indeed, it may have been inspired by this approach to the scriptures.[89] Thus similarities between Christianity and paganism were accommodated, "but only under the guise of pre-eminence."[90] Any borrowing on the part of the Christians was denied. Parallels between pagan and Christian rites could be accounted for by explaining (as Justin also does) that demons had imitated Christian rites in order to discredit Christian practice.

Christians with gnostic inclinations made ample use of Greek philosophy. Basilides, whom Birger Pearson regards as "the very first Christian philosopher known to us,"[91] was a precursor to other great Alexandrian teachers, Clement and Origen. Valentinus, who like Justin led a "school" in philosophical style in Rome (in itself a clear token of Christian inculturation),[92] took over the Platonic distinction between the eternal-model world of ideas and the sense world dependent upon it (frg. 5), and his eloquent poem *Harvest* gives expression to the Stoic notion of the all-pervasive spirit that keeps all things together (frg. 8). The extant fragments witness to a poetic, rhythmic style, which even his opponents could not but praise.[93] Valentinus's pupils Ptolemy and Heracleon likewise made skillful use of classical education.[94] Ismo Dunderberg shows that "Valentinians contextualized their faith in Christ by expressing it in terms that made it seem more understandable, and more readily acceptable, to those having received philosophical education" in that they offered "a distinctly Christian theory of how desire can be cured" (presenting Christ as the healer who "came to restore the emotions of the soul": Hippolytus, *Haer.* 6.36.3).[95] Indeed, one can say that several gnostic Christian authors attempted in various ways "to reduce the distance between on the one hand elements of the inherited Jewish and/or Jesus-movement traditions, and on the other hand key presuppositions from the wider culture, including Platonic philosophy."[96] The same is true of the elusive but influential Bardaisan of Edessa, who combined

Stoic philosophy with some Christian convictions in the "spiritualizing" trajectory.[97]

SOME EFFECTS

Apologetics paved the way for a developing Christian dogmatics in a philosophical vein. It is a result of the confrontation with and accommodation to pagan culture that Christian faith came to be presented as a philosophy that exploits terms and categories developed by Middle Platonism and Stoicism. By opting for the Logos theory (instead of just arguing from scripture), Christian philosophers from Justin on laid the foundation for theology as rational reflection on the faith, even though their way of philosophizing, at bottom based on the idea of divine revelation and seasoned with Paul's tirade against the wisdom of this world, differed from the usual way of perceiving philosophy. With time, though, the harmonization of revelation with the dictates of reason became an acute problem; "the new 'good tidings' would have to accommodate themselves to the demands of rational thinking if they would take hold in the Classical world."[98] By the early third century the need to harmonize faith and reason had gone so far that it produced Origen's *De principiis* as "the first manual of dogma."[99] The influence of Plato came to loom large in Christian theology, so much so that one might be tempted to view (some versions of) Christian doctrine as forms of modified Platonism, which has, along the way, absorbed into itself a certain amount of Jewish traditions.[100]

Despite all platonizing, the iconoclastic attitude to idolatry, so different from the essentially tolerant pagan religion, persisted. The intolerance with regard to polytheistic cult backfired on the Christians in the form of persecutions that were at bottom a tragic consequence of their strained relations with their pagan neighbors. This tragedy bore in itself the seeds of victory, but it was a victory for a price. In the words of Bishop R. C. P. Hanson, "it must not be denied that one of the great reasons for Christianity prevailing over its rivals was its intolerance. . . . It paid the price for this strength by the intolerance which it continued to show when it had won."[101] Despite its eagerness to break barriers, mainstream Christianity proved to be far more exclusive than Judaism, for Jews did not necessarily expect Gentiles to become Jews in order to be saved (though some Jews did think so). Christians maintained that Gentiles need not (indeed, should not) become Jews, but they needed to become Christians (and to break with their past).[102]

This intolerance was to remain a constant feature of mainstream Christianity. Wilfred Cantwell Smith deplores the "Christian (and Jewish)[103] failure to understand . . . what is going on in the spiritual life of communities served by images," a failure that "has done untold damage on the human scene through centuries."[104] This damage is highlighted by the Indian New Testament scholar George Soares-Prabhu, who points to a "distinct anti-gentile bias" in important parts of the Hebrew Bible, in some ways parallel to the anti-Jewish bias in Matthew and John that "also emerged from a situation of a desperate struggle for self-definition." This anti-Gentile bias was adopted by early Christians, and it has been "no less catastrophic in human history" than has the anti-Judaism of the New Testament: it has resulted (due to its appropriation by powerful Christian nations) "in a destruction of peoples and cultures

300 even more devastating than the Holocaust." Soares-Prabhu notes that the "massive destruction" of temples and "cherished religious texts" in South America and in Asia was the work not of the "barbarous" conquistadores but of the pious friars accompanying them, fired with zeal for the only God of the Bible and a paranoid hatred of idolatry. The history of Christianity has been extraordinarily destructive of peoples and cultures, and this is surely at least partly because of the fanatical iconoclasm of the Bible, which is the dark side of monotheism.[105]

12

Toward Christian Orthodoxy

Christianity emerged out of Judaism, but Judaism was a religion focused on practice. Apart from the confession that God is one (Shema), and the tenets that Israel is his people and the Torah is the symbol of God's covenant with the people, doctrinal issues were not regarded as very important. Christianity came to be different. The original doctrinal diversity was increasingly regarded as a problem, and by the second century various groups asserted themselves as the only bearer of the true faith (conceived of as the right doctrine), to the exclusion of others. In the course of these debates one could appeal to three main authorities: scripture, tradition, and persons. All three were closely interconnected: tradition was based on scripture, but it also dictated how to interpret scripture; the trustworthiness of the tradition again depended on that of the persons who had transmitted it, and of those who now guarded it.

AUTHORITATIVE SCRIPTURE

Christianity inherited from Judaism a rich treasure of authoritative writings, a collection of sacred writings or scripture(s) (*graphe, graphai*), even if one should not speak of a "canon" in this connection, for Judaism had not formally defined the boundaries of its scripture.[1] But formative Christianity was not a scriptural religion in the sense that Judaism was. Faith was evoked by and centered on the person of Jesus; it was his words (authentic or not), orally transmitted in the communities, that possessed the greatest authority.[2] Only secondarily was Jewish scripture (by and large, the Septuagint) invoked for the exposition and defense of the new faith; its use was selective and often arbitrary in content and method, stressing prophetic and messianic elements. Christian writings began to be composed by the mid-first century C.E. and gradually increased in number and variety, but none of them was composed or originally conceived of as "scripture," let alone as "canonical" works.[3] Only very gradually,

302 through their use in worship and teaching alongside the Jewish scriptures, did some Christian writings acquire an authority that surpassed that of other writings produced within the church. The history of the New Testament canon—the process that led to a (more or less) closed list of authoritative writings—extended to the fourth and fifth centuries. This process was far from deliberate or self-conscious.[4]

The New Testament canon is a collection of collections, each of which has its own history. Paul's letters were in themselves unlikely candidates for scriptural regard because of their situation-bound character (most of them owe their existence to the countermission against Paul). Still, by the early second century they had perhaps been gathered up by a group of Paul's associates and admirers.[5] In the beginning there seem to have been smaller local collections (for example, a collection of the four "main letters"),[6] but the earliest known collection consisted of ten letters and lacked the Pastoral Epistles. It was superseded still during the second century by a larger collection of thirteen letters that included the Pastorals. But all through the first century, congregations (such as the Matthean or the Johannine communities) existed that seem not to have possessed a single Pauline letter.

Paul's letters had thus been collected and were widely (though not universally) valued in the church already before Marcion, which is why Marcion was able to build so much on "the apostle" in the first place. Still, Marcion does signify an important chapter in the battle for identity, for he alone is known to have made a deliberate attempt to *create* a new canon; at the same time it was an attempt to cut Christians loose from their Jewish past and thus to establish a quite new Christian identity. Marcion's canon consisted of ten letters of Paul and the Gospel of Luke. It was to replace

the Jewish scriptures, to which he applied harsh content criticism (in this he was not alone, sharing the enterprise with many gnostic Christian interpreters). However, Marcion's attempted reform failed to convince his peers in Rome. By inviting the leaders of the Roman Christian communities to an open debate on his innovations (instead of quietly interpreting scripture and tradition in his own way in his own group, as Valentinus did), Marcion himself initiated a process that led to his exclusion (or perhaps to his voluntary departure). It was a daring endeavor to try to get rid of the scriptures, on which the identity of the Christian movement largely rested and to which it constantly appealed in order to prove that it had ancient roots and was not just a novel superstition. So thorough a break with the past and with the inveterate use of the Septuagint in the church aroused opposition, and the development of the canon inevitably proceeded via other routes in non-Marcionite circles. But the church that Marcion founded remained in existence and flourished for centuries. It might even have won the battle about Christian identity had its members not been adamant supporters of celibacy. No doubt its identity was to a large extent based on its own distinctive canon.

Marcion also tried to canonize one single Gospel, that of Luke (apparently "purged" from what he took to be "judaizing" additions). From the beginning, Christians had attributed the highest authority to "the Lord," preserving in memory and transmitting orally accounts of his words and deeds. The earliest Gospels are partial deposits of this oral tradition that persisted alongside the written Gospels, and was often even preferred to them, until about the mid-second century. Gospels continued to be written in the second century, but it was at first customary for a given Christian community to use only one Gospel (not necessarily one of the four which later became canonical);[7] often more than one such work may not even have been known to the congregation.[8] Indeed, there is no evidence before Tatian that a congregation would have taken efforts to come into possession of all four canonical-to-be Gospels.[9] For a long time the Gospels were not regarded as sacrosanct: Matthew and Luke could retell and reinterpret Mark's story; Tatian could work out his *Diatessaron*; the *Protevangelium of James* could rework the infancy narratives of Matthew and Luke; copyists could make significant alterations to the texts;[10] and so on. The collection of the four Gospels that were to gain canonical status arose only near the end of the second century, first in the Western church. Irenaeus (*Haer.* 3.11.8-9) had to argue inventively for it, while in the Eastern church other Gospels were also used, for example, the *Gospel of Peter* (Bishop Serapion of Antioch received a report of its use at a nearby congregation).[11] The four-Gospel collection was a compromise, striking a balance between an indefinite plurality of Gospels and an exclusive use of just one.[12]

When Christian communities became acquainted with multiple Gospels, the discrepancies between them became a problem. The desire for a single, self-sufficient Gospel worked to reduce the number, either by advocating one Gospel against the others (Marcion's solution) or by conflating several Gospels into one. The prime example of this latter tendency is Tatian's *Diatessaron* (c. 170), which weaves together most of Matthew, Mark, Luke, and John; it was used as the standard Gospel of the Syrian churches down to the fifth century. The popularity of this effort underlines the problem posed by the existence of different Gospels. A different solution was attempted by proto-orthodox church fathers, who relied on the four-Gospel collec-

tion: they took every effort to explain away the discrepancies between the Gospels.[13] Clearly the church did not *intend* to canonize plurality.[14]

Of the Catholic Epistles, only 1 Peter and 1 John had much currency in the second and third centuries. A collection of seven Catholic Epistles probably arose only in the third century. Justin is the first writer to show any knowledge of Acts, and it was only near the end of the second century that real importance began to accrue to it, possibly as the result of conflicts of the proto-orthodox with Marcionite and gnostic groups: Acts served to underline the view that the apostles acted and taught in complete harmony. The book of Revelation was well received in the West, but Eastern Christians tended for a long time to reject it. Many other writings were widely used and attained in some areas the status of scripture without making it to the mainstream canon in the end: *Apocalypse of Peter*, *Shepherd of Hermas*, *Gospel of Thomas*, *Gospel of Peter*, *1 Clement*, *Epistle of Barnabas*, and *Acts of Paul*.

Only in the fourth century did attempts begin to determine precisely what documents were to be regarded as supremely authoritative: the fourth and fifth centuries are the period of canon formation proper, when actual lists were drawn up.[15] Of special note is the Easter letter of Athanasius (letter 39), for it is the first list to name as exclusively authoritative precisely those twenty-seven documents that finally came to constitute the New Testament as we know it (though this letter certainly did not put an end to the disagreements). But no ecumenical council ever undertook to define the exact scope of the canon. Criteria of canonicity were set up in the process: the writing should be apostolic, catholic, orthodox, and in traditional use. None of these criteria was absolutely definitive, and, in retrospect, the first three seem rather deceptive.

304   The one that was most fully operative was simply traditional use.[16]

The problem remained that the writings that eventually gained canonical status were heterogeneous in themselves and open to different interpretations. Tertullian admitted that exegesis of scripture was of little help in the battle with heretics, as the latter were very clever in their use of scripture, and scripture itself seemed to offer material that lent itself to exploitation by them. He ended up by trying to deny heretics the right of arguing from scripture.[17] Indeed, the canon did little to solve the problem that doctrinal diversity posed to Christian identity; in doctrinal controversies all parties, including (say) Arians and Pelagians, were able to appeal to scripture.[18] Obviously, at least as important as possessing a canon was its "correct" interpretation—which

quite often meant replacing the literal meaning of the text with an allegorical one. Consequently, what came to be called the "rule of faith" was to be crucial for defining Christian identity in the proto-orthodox church.

AUTHORITATIVE TRADITION

Christians shared with Jews the confession of the Creator, who was the only true God (Rom. 3:30; 1 Tim. 1:17; and elsewhere), so they could accept the Shema, but they complemented it with claims about what this God had now done in and through Jesus. Precise, fixed creeds, however, are not found until the third or fourth century. Early Christians crystallized their conviction—in worship,[19] proclamation,[20] and confrontation with outsiders[21]—in brief slogans: "Jesus (Christ) is Lord" (Rom. 10:9; 1 Cor. 12:3; Phil. 2:11); God "raised Jesus from the dead" (Rom. 4:25); "Christ died for our sins" (1 Cor. 15:3); and so on. They transmitted summarizing accounts of important events (1 Cor. 11:23-25; 15:3-7) and celebrated Jesus in exalted hymns (Phil. 2:6-11). The sermons attributed to Peter and Paul in Acts suggest that in missionary propaganda a flexible traditional pattern was used, focused on Jesus' messiahship, death, and resurrection or exaltation. There are recurring motifs, but nothing like fixed creeds or doctrinal definitions is in evidence. The initial flexibility probably upheld a sense of unity—and concealed tensions that would make themselves felt when Christian intellectuals later worked out their particular understandings of the basic motifs. James Dunn observes that "any slogan is an *over*simplification" and that "fuller definition quickly becomes divisive."[22] The history of Christian doctrine during

12.1   Page from Codex Vaticanus containing the end of Romans and the beginning of the Letter to the Hebrews, from c. 350 C.E.

the following centuries (and after) fully confirms his point.

Paul already appeals to traditions handed on to him, when he sets out to refute a Corinthian understanding of resurrection that differs from his (1 Cor. 15:3-7). Appeals to tradition increase during the next generations. The Deutero-Pauline author of Colossians polemicizes against some Christians of a different persuasion[23] by calling their religious ideology a "philosophy" that amounts to "empty deceit, according to human tradition," implying that his own tradition "according to Christ" has a divine foundation (Col. 2:8). His addressees are to continue to live their lives "established in the faith, just as you were taught" (2:7). The Pastoral Epistles go further in emphasizing the role of tradition as a weapon against dissenters, contrasting the "deposit of faith" entrusted to the leader of a congregation with "what is falsely called knowledge," a phrase that possibly refers to the views of some gnostic Christians (1 Tim. 6:20; cf. 2 Tim. 1:14). "Pauline" traditions are dealt with as a closed doctrinal construction that one only has to guard.[24] The Epistle of Jude (v. 3) likewise stresses that one is to "contend for the faith that was once for all entrusted to the saints" (cf. 2 Pet. 1:12; 3:2).[25]

The Gospel of John, roughly contemporary with the Deutero-Paulines, testifies to a different milieu. Here the voice of the spirit is not bound to a deposit of beliefs, and there is no once-and-for-all fixed tradition. The only hallmark of authentic tradition is that Jesus' voice is heard in it; time and again, this voice will lead the congregation to "all the truth." The notion of the spirit (Paraclete), who reminds of Jesus' words and guides the congregation, enables the evangelist to creatively reinterpret the tradition in new situations. In this he comes close to the authors of gnostic Christian writings, and it is no surprise that his work was highly esteemed and much used by them.[26]

By the time of 1 John, however, the Johannine community had moved several steps closer to proto-orthodox Christianity. The author of the epistle stresses the need to "test the spirits" to find out who are "false prophets," the litmus test being the confession that Jesus is the Christ who has "come in the flesh" (1 John 4:2); 2 John 7 likewise warns of "deceivers" who do not subscribe to this confession. Attempts to refute a false view of Jesus here amount to a rudimentary "creed" intended to safeguard one's own Christology and to exclude from the community those who set forth a rival view—apparently a somewhat different interpretation of the Christology of the Gospel of John. More developed christological summaries with a polemical aim are then found in Ignatius. In the second century, the combination of single motifs into more comprehensive creedal statements came increasingly to be part of inner-Christian boundary-drawing. But neither the hymnlike confessions of Ignatius nor the tripartite creed of Justin (which explicitly subordinates the Son to the Creator and the spirit to the Son, 1 Apol. 13), nor even Irenaeus's rule of faith that he puts forward with universal claims are repetitions of fixed texts; both Ignatius and Irenaeus express their faith in different words in different contexts. The actual creeds (such as the Apostles' Creed, still recited in many churches) developed probably during the third century (or even later) from questions addressed to those about to be baptized.

Irenaeus (Haer. 1.10) lists the main objects of Christian faith: Christians believe in God, the almighty Creator; in Christ Jesus, the Son of God who became flesh for our salvation, and in the holy spirit that has proclaimed God's deeds

306 through the prophets. After this tripartite (*not trinitarian!*) statement, a fuller list of Christ's activities follows: the two comings, the virgin birth, the passion, the bodily resurrection, the bodily ascent to heaven, the return to restore everything and to resurrect the flesh (!) of all humanity. Irenaeus presents this summary of correct belief in order to refute the understanding of faith current among Marcionite and gnostic Christians. Scripture was to be interpreted in line with the tradition that the God of Israel was also the Father of Jesus, and through his spirit this same God had inspired the prophecies. But many of Irenaeus's "orthodox" tenets would have been highly controversial during the first century[27] (and, on the other hand, would have seemed crude and insufficient to the orthodox opinion leaders of the next centuries).

In his own time, Marcion's followers were formidable opponents to someone like Irenaeus, claiming that *they* were the only true church. Like Irenaeus after him, but unlike his contemporaries in early-second-century Rome, Marcion had emphasized uniformity of doctrine. He had also put his program into practice, creating a church of his own with a relatively unified doctrine. Irenaeus could blame Marcion for mutilating the tradition and use his own rule of faith as a weapon against the "wolf from Pontus," but the Valentinians were more difficult to deal with. Irenaeus himself tells that the creed that effectively excluded Marcionites proved useless against the Valentinians, for they joined in the orthodox confessions with other Christians. The majority of Christians did not disapprove of the followers of Valentinus, and the latter themselves were puzzled: why should anyone wish to expel them as heretics? But Irenaeus claims that although they verbally confessed the one God, they did so with mental reservations.

Proto-orthodox apologists held up gnostic Christians for contempt; some gnostic Christians did the same with regard to various teachings and practices of other Christian groups. For example, the *Gospel of Philip* (55.23-27) ridicules the virgin birth by pointing out that no woman can impregnate another, and the same writing asserts that baptism by other Christian groups is worthless (66.22-31).[28] How vague the boundary lines could be is shown by the fact that the author of *Testimony of Truth* can lump together as equally wrongheaded the teachings of both the proto-orthodox and the Valentinians, since both allow marriage.[29]

In the end, even the "rule of faith" could not quite perform what was hoped; different Christians leaned on different traditions or interpreted the same tradition in different ways. Whose rule was to be cherished? The need for trustworthy persons who could tell the genuine from the false was obvious. Irenaeus declares that "one must obey the priests who are in the church. . . . those who possess the succession from the apostles. For they receive simultaneously with the episcopal succession the sure gift of truth" (*Haer.* 4.26.2). The heretics depart from common tradition and meet without the bishop's approval.

AUTHORITATIVE PERSONS

Neither the collection and selection of texts to be publicly used in the church nor the crystallization of a tradition that was expected to be authoritative happened by itself. Such processes must have been driven forward by leading members of local congregations. Indeed, the said processes coincide with the formation of authoritative offices in the church, in particular of the office of an "overseer" or "bishop" (*episkopos*). The processes also affect each other: the leader gains authority from the conviction that the treasured tradition is entrusted to him; the tradition is considered reliable, as it is administered by a trustworthy person, who stands in a succession of authoritative leaders. Increasingly, guarding the pure doctrine or the "deposit of faith" receives pride of place among the duties of the overseer. His is largely a teaching office; he is supposed faithfully to transmit what the apostles once taught.

The apostles were regarded as foundational figures for the community. The term had undergone a development; in the early years it did not yet have a fixed content.[30] Jesus had sent out a group of followers, "wandering charismatics," to heal and to preach the kingdom (cf. Mark 6:7-13 par.), though apparently without using the term *apostle* (or its Aramaic equivalent). When Luke and Matthew term the Twelve, who were called by Jesus to be rulers of the restored Israel, *apostles* (Mark does not), they project a later designation into their accounts (Luke 6:13; Matt. 10:2). The term *apostolos* ("envoy") seems to have come to use in the Jerusalem congregation and may originally have connoted witnesses to resurrection appearances, but it was soon generally used of missionaries sent by a congregation (as Barnabas and Paul were sent by the congregation of Antioch). Paul emphatically applies the title to himself, being aware that his apostleship was controversial. The *Didache* still knows of wandering apostles (and prophets) whose sincerity needs to be tested by the congregation—obviously the apostles were not a well-known, closed circle. But in Jerusalem the meaning of the term came to be narrowed down to the Twelve, who had been witnesses both to Jesus' life and to the Easter appearances,

and Luke shares this understanding, excluding in Acts even his own great hero Paul from the group of the apostles.[31] Subsequently a synthesis emerged: the apostles who made up the foundation of the church were the Twelve *and Paul* (Ephesians, *1 Clement*, Ignatius).

In early times, there had been serious conflicts among apostles. Paul had challenged Peter in the notorious incident in Antioch (Gal. 2:11-14), which seems to have caused a definitive break between him and the congregation there. Paul was also engaged in conflict with other, unnamed apostles, who interfered with his work

12.2 Christ and the twelve apostles. Byzantine ivory relief, sixth century. Musée des Beaux-Arts, Dijon, France. Photo: © Giraudon/Art Resource, NY.

308 in Corinth (2 Cor. 10–13). Paul's uneasy relations with the other apostles were an embarrassment both in his own time and later; only when Acts provided an account of Christian beginnings in which peace and unanimity reigned and conflicts were peacefully solved in harmonious discussions, Paul appearing more Jewish and more conservative than any of the others, could Paul be elevated to the pedestal of a saint. Since then, the proto-orthodox church looked to the apostles as a unanimous collective whose teachings people believed that they cherished.[32] One increasingly appealed to traditions that were (mostly fictitiously) traced back to them; Acts 2:42 projects devotion to the "apostolic teaching" back to the earliest community in Jerusalem. The stamp of apostolicity (on anything) became crucial. Writings were attributed to various apostles (Matthew, John, Thomas, Philip) and their pupils (Mark, Luke); others were intentionally written in the name of apostles (Paul, Peter) or brothers of the Lord (James, Jude). The maverick Gospel of John was probably able to get a hearing outside the boundaries of the community within which it arose only because of its attribution to the fictitious "beloved disciple,"[33] subsequently tortuously identified with the apostle John.

Even the developing administrative structures of the congregations were traced back to initiatives of the apostles. In the beginning there were no fixed offices. The designation *ekklesia* that Paul uses for the local house churches is the name used in Greek cities of the plenary assembly of the free citizens, though in the Christian *ekklesia* even women and slaves participated as equals. Communities were founded by wandering preachers, who were held in great esteem; their word counted, and they also formed a symbolic bond that tied the small local communities together into one "church." But when the preachers moved on, the congregations had to trust in local leaders. Paul suggests that charismatic freedom flourishes in his congregations. He speaks of the many charismas within the one body of Christ; along with extraordinary "spiritual gifts" (such as glossolalia or prophecy), these also include ordinary services for the congregation (1 Cor. 12:28-29; Rom. 12:7-8; cf. Rom. 16:1, 6-7, 12; 1 Thess. 5:12-13). The true "leadership" is ascribed to the spirit's spontaneous activity (1 Cor. 12; 1 Thess. 5:19-20); to it correspond on the human side decisions made in the plenum of the congregation (cf. 1 Cor. 5:1-5).[34] In practice, though, the life of a community would have been steered by strong individuals, empowered either by their personal charisma (for example, Christian "prophets") or by their social status. Those who were in a position to provide a meeting place for a house church would obviously have a say in the way the affairs of the community were conducted. Paul himself, for all his appeals to the spirit, can make full use of his personal authority (cf. 1 Cor. 7:40). Second Corinthians documents a fierce battle, at times desperate, in which he engaged in order to retain his status and honor.

In some communities a similar situation prevailed still at the end of the century. Matthew seems to maintain the ideal of a small, house-church assembly in changing circumstances. In his community, teachers seem to possess the greatest authority (cf. Matt. 23:8-12, 34), and the meeting of the congregation has the power to excommunicate (18:15-18); apparently there are no specialists for administration.[35] The Johannine community likewise considers that it is guided by the spirit (John 16:13). The judgment of the congregation as a whole is important (1 John 2:20; 4:1); the Johannine circle does not participate in the tendency of the time to create fixed structures (on which see below).

Paul mentions officeholders with a title only in Philippi (Phil. 1:1): overseers and servants ("bishops and deacons"), both of them in the plural. What sort of duties they may have had is not clear, but these probably involved some kind of practical management.[36] We do not hear of "elders" in these congregations. By contrast, following a Jewish custom, the congregation of Jerusalem seems to have possessed a collegium of elders or "presbyters" (Acts 11:30; 15:2; 21:18) along with its strong leader, James. First Peter and the Epistle of James also presuppose that the congregations addressed are led by a group of elders (1 Pet. 5:1-4; Jas. 5:14). By the end of the first century, an assimilation of the two orders has taken place in various congregations. Clement of Rome implies that even the churches of Corinth and Rome are now led by a group of elders (1 Clem. 44.5 and elsewhere), who are also called overseers, and Luke gives a similar picture of the congregation in Ephesus (Acts 20:17-35: Paul invites "the elders of the church to meet him," v. 17, but calls them overseers and shepherds of the flock in v. 28). The Pastoral Epistles contain in one and the same letter directions both for the elders (1 Tim. 5:17-19; Titus 1:5-6) and for the overseer/bishop (Titus 1:7) or for one who "aspires to the office of bishop" (1 Tim. 3:1-7). In Titus 1, the author moves smoothly from speaking of the presbyters to speaking of "the bishop"; the conclusion suggests itself that we are witnessing a process that was to lead to the establishment of the office of a "monarchic bishop": an overseer emerges from the collegium of the elders and rises to be the sole leader of a congregation.[37]

In proto-orthodox congregations of the late first and early second century the administrative structure was attributed to measures taken by the apostles. Luke claims (Acts 14:23) that Paul and Barnabas installed elders (presbyters); Titus is told by "Paul" to do the same "in every town" (Titus 1:5). Clement of Rome states that "the apostles" tested their "firstfruits" in the spirit and then appointed them as overseers and deacons (1 Clem. 42.4) and even made preparations for the succession of these leaders in later times (44.1-2). The apostles had been sent by Jesus Christ, and he by God, so the present order established by them undoubtedly corresponds to the will of God (42.1-2). According to 2 Tim. 1:6, Paul installed Timothy by laying on of hands (though 1 Tim. 4:14 shows that actually the presbyters of the congregation had laid their hands on him).

To the fictions of apostolic writings and apostolic teaching was thus joined the fiction of apostolic succession. Appeal to this succession became important in the controversy of the proto-orthodox with gnostic Christians: Irenaeus claimed that all Gnostics "are much later than the bishops to whom the apostles have entrusted the churches" (Haer. 5.20.1). Lists of bishops in different localities were composed.[38] But gnostic Christians appealed to secret revelations by the Risen One to the apostles and could likewise speak of "apostolic tradition received from our predecessors" (Ptolemy, Flor. 7.9), though putting forward tradition lines that were different from the proto-orthodox ones.[39] The value that Basilides (or his followers) attributed to the "apostolic tradition" is attested in reports according to which his teacher was Peter's interpreter, Glaucias, or that he received "secret words" of the Savior from the apostle Matthias; Valentinus for his part was said to have based his teaching on Paul through a certain Theudas.[40]

310

Paul informs us that the charismatic gifts in his congregations (or at least in some of them) included those granted to "teachers" (1 Cor. 12:28-29; Rom. 12:6). Luke gives a list of "prophets and teachers" (among whom were Barnabas and Paul) at an early stage in Antioch (Acts 13:1-2). What exactly the task of the teachers was is difficult to tell,[41] but in any case the task of leadership is clearly distinguished from it in both 1 Corinthians and Romans.[42] In the Pastorals, however, leadership and teaching have merged; the overseer or bishop is to take care of *both* tasks.[43] The concentration of duties, and of power, is conspicuous. The task of the leaders is increasingly that of teaching the congregation and of defending the doctrine against "false teachers" (cf. 2 Pet. 2:1-2; Justin, *Dial.* 82.1; Hermas, *Sim.* 9.19.2-3; 22.1-3) who are said to pervert the scriptures at their own discretion. The author of 2 Peter emphasizes that "no prophecy of scripture is a matter of one's own interpretation" (2 Pet. 1:20-21); scripture has come about through people moved by the holy spirit and can therefore only be rightly interpreted by those who possess the spirit. But, typically, in the Pastorals the only person said to possess the gift of the spirit is the bishop. The charisma has thus been thoroughly routinized; the body of Christ has become a replica of the patriarchal household.[44]

Ignatius fights for the absolute authority of the (one single) local bishop. For him, there is no church without the bishop's office; without the bishop one is not allowed to do anything in the church. Ignatius gives up the "historical" argument (apostolic origin) for the bishop's special status (*Phld.* 1.1: *Eph.* 6.1) and appeals to direct divine legitimation. The bishop is installed by God; the earthly hierarchy is a replica of the heavenly one (*Magn.* 6.1; *Trall.* 3.1). For Ignatius, what has come to be called the "monarchic episcopate" is still a somewhat utopian ideal rather than an existing fact;[45] a few decades after him, however, the order proclaimed by him was making a breakthrough in the proto-orthodox church. For the first time, many Christian communities were organizing themselves into a strict order of hierarchical "ranks." The bishop was emerging as a "monarch" with a growing power even to exercise discipline.

Some texts from outside proto-orthodox circles reflect resistance to this process that provided the officeholders with increasing power. The *Gospel of Thomas* does not encourage seeking Jesus' presence in a community of believers at all; "it is the 'aloneness' of a single person which may be directly linked to the universal cosmos" (*Gos. Thom.* 30 + 77.2).[46] Still, "the internal logic of the Gospel seems to presuppose some sort of loosely structured school in which the sayings of Jesus were read and meditated upon."[47] "In a sense the Thomasine Jesus resembles the Stoic teacher who encourages his pupils to become their own teachers."[48]

The *Apocalypse of Peter* from Nag Hammadi laments that a faithful remnant is oppressed by "others of those outside our number who call themselves bishops and deacons, as if they have received their authority from God, but they bow before the judgment of leaders. These people are dry canals" (*Apoc. Pet.* 79.22-30).[49]

Some groups evidently wished to follow the principle of strict equality. According to Irenaeus (*Haer.* 1.13), every initiate in the Valentinian group of Marcosians was assumed to have received the gift of direct inspiration through the spirit; members decided by casting lots who should prophesy in the meeting at hand. Tertullian rages against the "overthrow of discipline" among the "heretics": "It comes to pass that today one man is their bishop, tomorrow another;

today he is a deacon who tomorrow is a reader; today he is a presbyter who tomorrow is a layman." Tertullian singles out the active participation of women in particular: "They are bold enough to teach, to dispute, to enact exorcisms, to undertake cures—it may be even to baptize" (*Praescr.* 41).

On the other hand, gnostic egalitarianism should not be exaggerated or idealized. As Ismo Dunderberg points out, for the Valentinian author of the *Interpretation of Knowledge* an ideal situation in the congregation is "that only those who have the spiritual gift are entitled to speak"; he "advocates a clear and unquestioned hierarchy based upon a division between the haves and have-nots" (*Interp. Know.* 15-17). "Thus his position is not much more egalitarian than one emphasizing the authority of the bishops and demanding unquestioned submission to them. The two viewpoints about the Christian community only differ from each other in their assessment as to *whom* authority belongs to."[50]

WOMEN AS LEADERS

The leadership of women, a scandal in the eyes of Tertullian, had already been strictly opposed in the Pastorals: "Let a woman learn in silence with full submission. I permit no woman to teach or to have authority over a man; she is to keep silent" (1 Tim. 2:11-12).[51] The author adds the argument that Eve, not Adam, was the first to be deceived and claims that women "will be saved through childbearing (!), provided they continue in faith and love and holiness" (vv. 14-15).

Here the values of patriarchal society triumph over earlier Christian practice that did not deny spiritual authority and, in many cases, ac-

tual leadership to women. A wealth of evidence suggests that women had significant roles in the early phases, even though that evidence is buried under stories that celebrate men's achievements.[52] Paul mentions several female coworkers of whom he thinks highly. Prisca (Rom. 16:3; 1 Cor. 16:19; cf. Acts 18:2, 18, 26; 2 Tim. 4:19) seems to have been a more prominent missionary than her husband, Aquila. Junia even receives the title of "apostle" (Rom. 16:7).[53] Phoebe, the deacon of the church at Cenchreae, is called a *prostatis* of many, which suggests a role as a patroness who may have provided a meeting place for the congregation.[54] Such resources easily go together with leadership. During the first and second centuries it was natural for women to act as leaders; their established social roles as household managers made them well suited for this task. In particular, women with relatively more wealth or higher status could easily assume the role of a patron of a group.[55] Revelation informs us of an influential prophetess and patron in Thyatira, scourged by the seer for her open attitude to Greco-Roman culture (probably for eating sacrificial meat on social occasions).[56]

During the second century the leadership of women came under attack in some circles, as the strict stance of the Pastorals shows. A reaction was not wanting. The *Acts of Thecla* depict an able female preacher who overshadows the great Paul, her teacher.[57] Tertullian had reason to complain that women appealed to the example of Thecla in support of their freedom to teach and baptize (*Bapt* 1.17.5).

While the position of women declined in proto-orthodox congregations, at least in some other groups women played a prominent role for quite some time. Marcion appointed women on an equal basis with men as priests and bishops. The Montanists honored, along with Montanus,

312 two women, Priscilla and Maximilla, as founders of the movement.[58] Marcellina was a well-known teacher who traveled to Rome to represent the Carpocratian group (Irenaeus, *Haer.* 1.25.6) that appealed to secret tradition transmitted through women (Mary, Salome, and Martha). "The casualness with which the 'powerless vessels capable of becoming strong through the gnosis' are mentioned in *1 Apoc. Jas.* (38.21-23) may very well be taken as an indication of an authentic reflection of strong and perceptive women who taught

12.3   Mary Magdalene by the Master of the Palazzo Venezia Madonna (fourteenth century). Photo: © National Gallery, London/Art Resource, NY.

and proclaimed the Christian message among the Gnostics the author of the writing knew."[59] In such circles women may have been able to *preserve* the position which they had been long used to having, without problems, in Pauline congregations.[60] Although far-reaching conclusions have been drawn about the egalitarianism of gnostic communities and about the privileged place of women in them,[61] some caveats are in order. The references to active women in leading positions among gnostic Christians "do not automatically mean that we are talking about a widespread phenomenon."[62]

In this connection, the figure of Mary Magdalene has aroused considerable interest. Whether the historical Magdalene ever had a prominent ecclesiastical role beyond being a source for the tradition of the empty tomb[63] we do not know; she abruptly disappears from sources pertaining to the early times. But she does put up an impressive reappearance in mystical and gnostic Christian sources, sometimes functioning as a role model, a prototype of a Christian who perceives deeper spiritual truths. In the *Gospel of Mary* a controversy between her and Peter is described that seems to reflect a disagreement over the position of women. Mary Magdalene, whom the Savior loved more than the other disciples (*Gos. Mary* 10.1-3; 18.10-15), takes the place of the leader in a difficult situation, consoling and encouraging the male disciples (9.12-24). She emerges as "a supreme spiritual authority who is courageous enough to challenge old traditions if they tend to discourage and intimidate the followers of Savior because of irrelevant issues, such as gender or restraining rules (18,7-21)."[64] Undoubtedly this Gospel—which is no longer generally characterized as gnostic, however— "was at least partly written as a defence of the women wanting to take part in spiritual leadership but being prevented by those who regarded it as an illegitimate enterprise."[65] More clearly gnostic Christian texts in which Mary Magdalene appears do *not*, however, seem to use her figure in such a way.[66] In the *Gospel of Philip* it is told that the Savior loved her more than other disciples and used to kiss her (63.34-37),[67] but the envy of the others does not really lead to a conflict with Mary. The question whether her special position affects the way women in general are valued in this writing remains open. "We simply do not know whether Mary Magdalene is merely a heroine of the past . . . or whether, as a woman who better than anybody else understood the reality of Jesus, she gave the later readers of the Gospel of Philip a model for identification that in turn affected their position in the community and the cult."[68]

From the third century on, as "the processes of institutionalization gradually transformed the house churches . . . into a political body," the position of women declined.[69] "As Christianity entered the public sphere, male leaders began to demand the same subjugation of women in the churches as prevailed in Greco-Roman society at large."[70] There are indications that women in roles of leadership came to be marginalized not only in orthodox circles but among gnostic Christians as well.[71]

INNER-CHRISTIAN (IN)TOLERANCE

The coming centuries would show, however, that the bishops themselves were able to disagree quite heavily. In the end, it took the authority of a monarch much more powerful than any bishop

to settle the (now mainly christological) disputes and to dictate definitively who was orthodox and who a heretic.

The measures taken in these inner-Christian quarrels were harsh. Robin Lane Fox notes that pagans had been intolerant of Jews and Christians, but that "the rise of Christianity induced a much sharper rise in religious intolerance and the open coercion of religious belief," and that "Christians were quick to mobilize force against the pagan cults and against their own unorthodox Christian brethren."[72] The violent, authoritarian intolerance that has characterized much of subsequent church history as well is, in part at least, to be traced back to the early documents of the Jesus movement.[73] Paul had set the tone (for example, Gal. 1:8-9; Phil. 3:2, 19; 2 Cor. 11:14-15;

12.4   The Nicene Council, which established the official doctrine of the person of Christ in 325 C.E. Byzantine icon.

314 Rom. 16:17-20);[74] other writers followed suit.[75] The Pastorals, Jude, and Revelation may be singled out as the extreme cases.

Some were concerned about this. Early on, the author of *2 Clement* puts forward sincere self-criticism, complaining that when pagans hear Christians talk about loving enemies, "they admire this abundant goodness. But when they then see that we do not love even those who love us, not to speak of those who hate us, they laugh at us and the name of the Lord is mocked" (13.3-4). Vicious polemic is definitely not the whole story. As our sources mainly come from the intellectual leaders, they tend to give a one-sided picture. Christians were widely praised for the love they showed to one another and, in critical situations, to others.[76] While many leaders were concerned to draw clear boundaries, rank-and-file members often tended to be far more careless—as the worries they caused to the guardians of pure doctrine and correct practice eloquently show. Grassroots Christianity has probably always found itself at some distance from the theoretical passions of ecclesiastical authorities.

Common Ground and Diversity in Early Christian Thought

The process that was to lead to the emergence of Christianity as an independent religion started when Jesus of Nazareth proclaimed the imminent coming of the "kingdom of God." He probably expected that this kingdom would be established on the earth, signaling a crucial turn in the history of humankind in general and the history of the people of Israel in particular. The terrestrial expectation was maintained by some branches of his Jewish Christian followers, among whom the author of Revelation with his belief in a concrete millennium stands out. In the following centuries, this belief was shared by many non-Jewish believers as well, including theologians of the stature of Irenaeus and Tertullian, who held that the justice of God required a concrete fulfillment of his promises on the earth. Many others, however, abandoned the earthly expectation, which they replaced by the hope for postmortem life in heaven. Such a spiritualized view that showed no interest in the future destiny of the world was held, for instance, by the authors of the Gospel of John

and of the *Gospel of Thomas*, as well as by gnostic Christians. Paul and the authors of the Synoptic Gospels combine aspects of both alternatives, which combination brings about a remarkable amount of tension in their views. What all positions have in common is the trustful conviction that one day evil will be overcome and the righteous will get justice, whether on this earth or in a new existence in the beyond.

Jesus probably also expected a concrete bodily resurrection of the dead believers; certainly this was the hope of subsequent millenarian theologians. A resurrection of material bodies only makes sense in the framework of an earthly existence in a time-space world. Those who replaced the latter with a spiritualized view also replaced the "crude" notion of a bodily resurrection with more refined ideas of the survival of the person (the immortality of the soul). But in this case, too, some tried to reconcile (consciously or unconsciously) the alternatives that in themselves seem incompatible. Paul's peculiar idea of a "spiritual body" was a notable attempt

316 in this direction. The apostle pays lip service to the notion of a bodily resurrection, while actually moving quite some way in the direction of the immortality of the soul (a concept that he never mentions in so many words). What unites the different views on a deeper level is the sure hope that the person's identity would survive in the hereafter.

Jesus and most of his early followers shared the general Jewish view that all humans sin, but this does not make the human condition hopeless in any way. Sinning can be resisted with some success, and there are God-given ways of dealing with lapses; transgressions can be passed over and forgiven. Much of the time this seems to be Paul's view as well, but in certain theologically charged contexts he moves on to speak of sin as a power under which humanity is tragically enslaved. This gloomy picture is a consequence of Paul's axiom that Christ alone saves. He reaches his notion of sin as a mighty power by thinking backward, from the solution to the plight: humanity *has to be* a hopeless victim of sin, so that nothing but God's new act in Christ can rescue it. A related view is expressed in John's Gospel: non-Christian humanity is hopelessly entangled in sin, for the essence of sin is that one does not believe in Jesus. Behind both Paul's and John's picture, a factional polemic shines through: "the others" are slaves of sin, whereas "we" have been freed from it. Gnostically inclined Christians held a genuinely pessimistic view of humanity enslaved to hostile powers (due to the necessity of living in a material body); the essence of sin is ignorance of this plight. The differences notwithstanding, all Christians seem to have agreed that one has to fight the temptations to sin and to prove worthy of one's call by a blameless life in accordance with God's will.

Jesus called his hearers to repentance and to a renewal of life in view of the imminent judgment and the establishment of God's kingdom. He implied that true repentance involved acknowledgment of his message and person. Jesus' followers held fast (in rather different ways, to be sure) to both parts of the challenge: in order to be saved one had both to repent and to acknowledge Jesus. The latter meant different things to different people: to accept Jesus' interpretation of the Torah (Matthew, James); to accept in faith that Jesus' death and resurrection had happened for the benefit of others, so that a sinner could start a new life in union with the risen Christ (Paul); to accept Jesus as revealer of what true life means (John, *Thomas*, gnostic Christians). The actual significance of Jesus differed dramatically from case to case; yet all agreed that a change of life and obedience to God's will were necessary prerequisites of salvation, and also that in one way or other salvation was connected with what Jesus had done or what he stood for.

The question of Jesus' self-understanding is particularly controversial. With due caution one may say that he regarded himself as the last herald of the coming kingdom, who also had a task in its establishment in the near future, a task that one may call messianic. His early followers openly called him the "Messiah" ("Christ") and the "Son of God," emphasizing that God had chosen him for his specific task (an adoption of sorts), which included a role as the judge at his second coming. Some emphasized the unchanging continuity of God's plan and applied to Jesus current notions of God's Wisdom and Logos, thus adumbrating the thought of Jesus' preexistence with God before his earthly career. The combination of the notion of preexistence with the story of Jesus' earthly life produced the picture of a divine being walking on the earth, one who lived in a human body ("flesh") but was at bottom different from humans because of his omniscience, divine power, and sinlessness. In some cases this led to the idea that a divine element had been implanted on the man Jesus and that this part left when the man died. Theologians tend to be highly critical of the docetism of such a view (Jesus being only seemingly a true man), held by many gnostic Christians. Yet a shadow of doubt is no less cast on the *true* humanity of Jesus in many orthodox writings, in particular the Gospel of John, the letters of Ignatius, or the work of Clement of Alexandria. All the same, even in the case of Christology, a common denominator may be found if one moves to a sufficiently abstract level: all early Christians held Jesus to be of unique significance, whether because of his God-given task or because of his own divine nature.

A battle about the legacy of Israel characterizes most of early Christianity. Despite some liberties in his interpretation of the Sabbath, Jesus seems to have observed Jewish practice; this is what a number of his Jewish-born followers certainly did. Others crossed the boundary between Jew and Gentile and relaxed their observance of the Torah during the process: circumcision was not required of Gentile converts; liberties were taken in the observance of food laws (Paul in particular). But the relaxation of the practice was combined with lip service to ideological continuity. It was important even to Gentile Christians to be able to appeal to the scriptures of Israel as an authority that supposedly witnessed to Christ and even legitimized their liberal practice. The Christians allegedly fulfilled in the spirit what the Torah aimed at even when they ignored many of its actual commandments. The Chris-

tians came to claim that they, not the Jews, were now God's chosen people. This process of separation looks different in different sources. Some (in addition to Marcion and gnostic Christians, even John, Ignatius, and *Epistle of Barnabas*) distinguish very clearly between Jews and Christians. Others maintain a conservative outlook but nevertheless drift in the direction of separation (Matthew, Luke, Epistle of James). A common ground exists in that few Christians could avoid the problem posed by the Jewish religion. Israel's traditions could hardly be simply ignored (even though some gnostic Christians did just that); somehow one had to come to grips with them—whether by maintaining, selectively reinterpreting, or polemically criticizing them.

A related problem was posed by the Greco-Roman tradition with its polytheistic civic cult that most branches of early Christianity condemned as idolatry; on the other hand, much of its standard ethics was acknowledged. Greco-Roman philosophy was rejected by some but positively used by others. The attitude to the Roman state could vary from fierce opposition (Revelation) to lavish praise (Luke). The solutions differed, but a common problem was obvious and inevitable: how to relate to pagan culture and politics in light of the new convictions?

Whichever of the themes discussed in this book one explores, it seems clear that a great diversity of attitudes and ideas reigns. The future of Christianity was completely open at least during the two first centuries. In the above paragraphs I pointed to some common ground or general principles that may be found behind the diversity. But it must have struck the reader that in order to do this I was forced to move to a fairly high level of abstraction. The common denominators seem rather vague. I for one remain much more

318 impressed by the colorful diversity connected with and nurtured by the different traditions, life situations, experiences, and insights of different groups and individuals who contributed to the rise of Christian beliefs. Anyone who, from whatever perspective, wrestles with Christian tradition, trying to make sense (or nonsense) of it, will do well to reflect on this diversity. While it may be welcome ammunition for critics, it is my experience-based conviction that recognition of the original diversity can also be a stimulus to creative new interpretations and constructive applications of this tradition.

Introduction

1. The closest counterparts are the works of Teeple, *Christianity*, and Theissen, *Theory*. Teeple's work is characterized by somewhat exaggerated historical skepticism, but deserves more attention than it has received; cf. Räisänen, *Beyond*, 138–39; Zeller, "Entstehung," 3 with n. 8. Theissen shares the comparative-religion starting point; his work stands out (and differs from mine) through ample use of theoretical models and an emphasis given to the New Testament canon. The latter concern leads Theissen eventually to establish a hidden theological unity behind the plurality of early Christianity (though he has himself first described it as a "seething chaos"). For my assessment of the work see *Beyond*, 142–46; also Räisänen, "Kathedrale?"

2. For example, Conzelmann, *History*; Fischer, *Urchristentum*; Vouga, *Geschichte*; Zeller, ed., *Christentum*; Wedderburn, *History*; Ebner, "Von den Anfängen." Rowland, *Origins*, is closer to the present work in its approach; cf. Räisänen, *Beyond*, 108–9. See now also Knight, *Origins*. N. T. Wright (*New Testament and the People of God*) and Dunn (*Christianity in the Making*) are working on huge multivolume projects in the area.

3. For example, Esler, ed., *Early Christian World*; Stark, *Rise of Christianity* (for an evaluation see J. T. Sanders, *Charisma*, 135–59).

4. For example, Vielhauer, *Geschichte*; Koester, *Introduction*; White, *From Jesus to Christianity*; L. T. Johnson, *Writings*; Theissen *Entstehung*; and the numerous introductions to the New Testament.

5. *Religion*, too, is a notoriously ambiguous term; Stegemann, "Much Ado," 230–42, provides a critical discussion of its use in the present connection. In itself, the term is not crucial for my purposes; what really counts is the reinterpretation of traditions in new situations (see p. 5). I myself doubt that religious experience can be distinguished as a category of its own from all other experience (cf. Räisänen, *Beyond*, 191–92). I take *religion* to denote practices and ideas that assume the existence of superhuman agents (such as Gods or angels) that demand respect and are understood to affect human life in significant ways. Grabbe, *Judaic Religion*, 3–5, presents helpful reflections (and a defense) of the use of the term in an ancient context.

6. Cf. Wedderburn, *History*, 4.

7. Smart, *Religions*, 12–21, distinguishes seven different dimensions.

8. Theissen, *Theory*, laudably discusses "mythical," ritual, and ethical aspects of early Christian religion. On rituals see now DeMaris, *New Testament*.

9. Smart, *Religions*, 17.

10. Wedderburn, *History*, x (my italics). Cf. Stroumsa, "Postscript," 360: one should "remember that the world of theological ideas is not quite distinct from the

320

world of day-to-day life and action. It certainly influences it as much as it is shaped by it." See also Grabbe, *Judaic Religion*, 8.

11. Cf. my discussion with Moxnes ("From Theology to Identity") in Räisänen, "What I Meant," 438–40. For the influence of ideas consider, for example, the role of millenarian theology in American politics (p. 112) or the possible role of the idea of predestination in the development of modern capitalism (p. 182).

12. Marshall, *Theology*, 17, singles me out as "the most vocal contemporary critic" of the enterprise of writing a theology of the New Testament, ascribing to me the view that "it must not and cannot be done" (18). My actual claim is that New Testament theology as currently conceived "may be a legitimate part of self-consciously *ecclesial* theology," whereas "those of us who work in a broader *academic* context might want to abandon such an enterprise"; "New Testament theology" could be replaced, in this academic context, with two different projects, the history of early Christian thought on one hand and critical philosophical or theological reflection on the New Testament on the other; see Räisänen, *Beyond*, 8. A more nuanced critique of my program from an evangelical perspective is presented by Thielman, *Theology*, 25–34.

13. Wrede ("Tasks and Methods") proposed that the discipline of New Testament Theology be replaced with "History of Early Christian Religion (and Theology)." The rise of neo-orthodox dialectical theology in the aftermath of World War I caused the proposal to be set aside for almost a century; the twentieth-century classic of Bultmann (*Theology*) presents a peculiar combination of *Religionswissenschaft* and existentialist theology. The first overall accounts consciously designed to realize Wrede's program were written in the 1990s by Berger (*Theologiegeschichte*) and Theissen (*Theory*). For a brief history of the discipline see Räisänen, *Beyond*, where I also give a programmatic account of the principles applied in the present book. For discussions of my program see Barr, *Concept*, 530–40; Balla, *Challenges*; and the numerous contributions in Penner and Vander Stichele, *Moving*; for my response see Räisänen, "What I Meant."

14. Theissen, *Theory*, xiii. Cf. Räisänen, *Beyond*, 151–56.

15. Cf. n. 26 (Gerstenberger); also Räisänen, *Beyond*, 203–9.

16. I have criticized New Testament theologies for using theological language and conceptual tools that are bound to be strange in the nonconfessional atmosphere of modern universities (though I do realize that different academic traditions exist): "We hear a good deal of God revealing himself definitively in Christ and speaking to us through the New Testament texts . . . [the authors] also make an effort to make the texts speak to modern men and women in their present situation. . . . Divine revelation is spoken of as if its existence were self-evident. The recourse to theistic God-talk (not just on a descriptive level) is a matter of course" (Räisänen, *Beyond*, 2). That this has not changed is borne out by the most recent New Testament theologies, which, despite the rather different theological persuasions of their authors, agree on the necessity of a faith perspective. For instance, Wilckens, *Theologie*, vi, claims that a theological work (like his New Testament theology) is to aid the church to speak publicly and clearly *about God*; cf. ibid., 55. Thielman, *Theology*, 34, states that when New Testament theology is "pursued within the church and under the authority of the text, it can provide the means through which the prophetic voice of the texts is heard clearly in the modern church and, through the church, in the world." Hahn, *Theologie*, 1:1, opens his work by saying that theology (including New Testament theology) is reflection on the truth claim, acknowledged as valid, of the Christian message. Cf. further Marshall, *Theology*; Matera, *Theology* (especially xxvii); Schnelle, *Theologie* (especially 36–37). For general discussions of the problems of New Testament theology see, for example, Morgan, "Theology (NT)" and the numerous essays in Rowland and Tuckett, eds., *Nature*; and Breytenbach and Frey, eds., *Aufgabe*.

17. Various English renderings for the German term are in use: Comparative Religion, Science of Religion, Religious Studies; different nuances may (but need not) be associated with different names. The discipline of *Religionswissenschaft* itself is in a process, continuously struggling for its identity (which includes sorting out its relation to theology). For my purposes it is sufficient to adopt a "descriptive" and "objective" approach that avoids metaempirical tools of interpretation and does not succumb to the absolute truth claims of any tradition. For a brief discussion of earlier debates concerning principles within comparative religion itself see Räisänen, *Neutestamentliche Theologie?* 67–73.

18. Theissen, "Widersprüche," 187 n. 4, estimates that comparative religion and theology overlap as much as 80 percent. Theology is bound to a religious confession and searches for religious truth, which it expects

to find in a given religion. Comparative religion investigates *all* religious sign systems in order to provide all members of the society with such knowledge as is necessary for dealing with religions. It is not bound to a confession (neither to a religious nor to an antireligious confession)—which does not mean that it is value-free; it is open to many value systems.

19. Consider, for example, Schüssler Fiorenza's claim that what she calls the scientific positivist paradigm strives to establish a single true meaning of the text in order to claim universality for its interpretations, determined to hold strictly to facts and evidence, to tell the simple truth (*Rhetoric*, 41–42); for my comments see Räisänen, *Beyond*, 118–19; idem, "What I Meant," 420–22. For more examples of caricatures see Räisänen, "Biblical Critics," 284–85.

20. See Räisänen, "What I Meant," 420–25.

21. Cf. also Stenström, "Fair Play?" 128.

22. Dunn, "Theologizing," attempting to vitalize New Testament theology, is critical of the demand to replace prescription with description (225) and emphasizes that "we need to see the text as a testimony to and expressive of the flow and movement of experience, thought and praxis in earliest Christianity" (227). But it is quite possible (and desirable!) to combine this insight with a descriptive task as I see it.

23. Stendahl (who emphasized the "descriptive" character of historical exegesis in his seminal article "Biblical Theology" in 1962) notes that "also description is a creative and imaginative task" but goes on to state that he remains "critical of those who use the impossibility of objectivity as a license for not trying" (Stendahl, "Dethroning," 63).

24. In doing this, the scholar does not necessarily deny a priori that some human thoughts may be divinely inspired (whatever that means)—whether they be found in Christian, Jewish, Muslim, or any other religious texts. Nevertheless, the application of a similar methodology to all religious texts inevitably narrows down the area in which speaking of a special revelation might make sense; it certainly makes it very difficult to any tradition to claim absolute authority for its truths.

25. Burkett, *Introduction*, 9.

26. Gerstenberger, *Theologies*, 2, makes a similar claim even for Old Testament theology, pointing out that theology "has exclusively to do with time-conditioned experiences of faith, statements and systems, in short with ideas of God and not with God in person or essence. Old Testament theology—formulated as

orientation for our day—should be content with the contextual images of God in the Hebrew Bible and in a similarly provisional and time-conditioned way venture to make binding statements or statements which nevertheless have only limited validity."

27. Cf. P. R. Davies, *Whose Bible?* 51: the academy is not a social space "in which gods [can] walk unchallenged around the vocabulary"; "the conflict is not about what you believe, but what you may be allowed to assume in your professional discourse."

28. Barclay, *Jews*, 15 with n. 6.

29. Wrede, "Tasks and Methods," 70; cf. J. Becker, "Theologiegeschichte," 126–33.

30. Thielman, *Theology*, 28–29, admits (criticizing Balla, *Challenges*, on this point) that the methodological decision to study New Testament theology, rather than the history of early Christian religion, results from the perspective of the Christian community.

31. A consistently canon-oriented approach will lead to the construction of a pan-biblical theology that deals with the Old and New Testaments together from a confessional Christian point of view. This is the position taken by Watson, who starts from the assertion that Christianity possesses the truth in the incarnate Word, mediated through texts (*Text and Truth*, 1), claims that the whole Bible is to be treated as a christocentric book in the vein of classic systematic theology (ibid., 2) and deems the impact of the historical-critical method "notoriously destructive" (ibid., 4). This last statement is all the more perplexing, as Watson himself is known as the author of an excellent historical-critical work that contains hard-hitting criticisms of Paul (*Paul, Judaism, and the Gentiles*). In the second edition of this latter book (2007), Watson tones down some of his sharper statements on Paul (no improvement, in my opinion); nevertheless, even this edition may be taken as a praiseworthy exercise precisely in historical criticism. In any case, Watson's publications on biblical theology (see also his *Text, Church, and World*) serve to clarify the methodological issue: if one refuses to take a history-of-religions approach and wants instead to construct a self-consciously Christian biblical theology, *this* is the logical outcome—the whole Bible would then have to be read from a patristic perspective, for it was in a patristic atmosphere that the canon was created. This is as Christian (in a traditional sense) as it can get. Yet those who plead for a Christian biblical theology have in general refrained from so strict a logic (see Räisänen, *Beyond*, 120–25,

322

32. Even Theissen, *Theory*, 209–48, speaks of "crises" (Judaistic, Gnostic, prophetic: traditional Jews brought about a crisis in which Paul saved the autonomy of the new religion, and so on; cf. Knight, *Origins*, 320, on the "threat" of Gnosticism), while a less biased account has to speak, say, of conflicts. Franzmann's point ("Complete History," 127) is appropriate (she is writing about gnostic Christians in particular): "Scholars must take seriously that heretics believed in their experiences of the heavenly Jesus and knew something of him from those experiences, just as orthodox groups believed in their own experiences of the risen Jesus and reflected on those experiences in subsequent generations."

33. A classic (if extreme) case is Bultmann, *Theology*: he asserts that New Testament theology in the real sense consists only of the theologies of Paul and John.

34. True, we can only reconstruct possible glimpses of their positions, but it is heuristically important to confront Paul with as plausible reconstructions of the "teachers" in Galatia or of the "deniers of resurrection" in Corinth as we can produce.

35. Pyysiäinen, "Intuition," 298.

36. At this point I fully agree with Dunn, "Theologizing," while rejecting his assumption that a descriptive task would be unable to take this dynamism into account. Dunn's proposal is that instead of "New Testament theology" one might better speak of "New Testament theologizing." Were it not for the stylistic inelegance, I might indeed just as well have entitled this book *Early Christian Theologizing*!

37. For a description of this interpretive model see Räisänen, *Beyond*, 189–202.

38. The word *experience* is in fact routinely used all the time, so that I am only making explicit what is going on all over the place. Cf., for example, Gerstenberger, *Theologies*, 1: the Old Testament "is a conglomerate of experiences of faith from very different historical and social situations." For a random example of the occurrence of a formula identical with mine see Kysar, "John," 931: "The methodology of the Evangelist [John] was to interpret tradition in the light of experience."

39. The recent works by Marshall, *Theology*, and Thielman, *Theology*, try to overcome this shortcoming by inserting chapters in which different sections are compared, as well as adding a final chapter dedicated to comparison (from the point of view of the "unity or diversity" problem).

40. See on this question, for example, Wedderburn, *History*, 4–7.

41. Berger, *Theologiegeschichte*, abounds in them.

42. Markschies, "Lehrer," 98, quoted by King, *Gospel of Mary*, 6.

43. King, *Gospel of Mary*, 6. It would indeed be desirable to make full use of nonliterary archaeological data. Unfortunately, such data are scarce before the time of Constantine; only about 180 C.E. does the Christian faith begin to "produce symbols and language that could be designated as Christian" and are distinguishable from the general culture; see Snyder, *Ante Pacem*, 2 and passim.

44. In a sense, it would be ideal to treat the material *both* from a tradition-historical *and* from a thematic perspective; this is done by Hahn, *Theologie*. The problem is that the work so constructed will grow to unmanageable size; Hahn's two volumes fill 1,700 pages.

45. According to Thielman, *Theology*, 38, claims about contradictions can be met with "reasonable counter-arguments" that are, in part, based on the "insight that the New Testament texts are the Word of God." "The resolution to some theological tensions within the New Testament probably lies . . . beyond the ability of human reasoning, tainted as it is by sin and infirmity, to understand" (39); reference is made to Paul's doxology in Rom. 11:33-36 as a New Testament precedent for "this way of understanding aspects of God's revelation that appear to be in tension with one another" (40). Cf. Matera, *Theology*, 480: the unity of New Testament theology "expresses itself in a multiplicity of ways because no one way can fully capture the mystery that is God in Christ." By contrast, Strecker, *Theologie*, 2–3, rejects the assumption of a theological unity in the New Testament; cf. also Schnelle, *Theologie*, 37–42.

46. Kümmel, *Theology*, 322–23. Cf. Matera, *Theology*, 423: "the unity of the New Testament is a presupposition of faith"; there must be an underlying unity "because each writing witnesses to God's self-revelation in Christ."

47. This is what happens, in my view, even in such critical works as Hahn's *Theologie* and Theissen's *Theory*. On Hahn see Räisänen, "What's Happening," 448–49; on Theissen, above, n. 1. On the earlier work of Dunn, *Unity*, see Räisänen, *Beyond*, 99–101. J. Becker, "The-

ologiegeschichte," 120, also contends for a remarkable original unity, but his list of topics common to all early Christians shares some of the abstract vagueness of Theissen's "basic motifs."

48. Dunn, "Theologizing," 236, caricatures a descriptive approach that finds inconsistencies in Paul: "It is only when we abstract texts from the particularities of their initial composition and reception that the variations of content and emphasis become problems as 'inconsistencies' and 'contradictions.' Rather . . . we should see in such variations the expression of living theology, not treat the letters as so many cadavers laid out in the pathology laboratory for dissection (!)." Why would someone engaged in "living" theologizing not be capable of inconsistencies? It seems to be an incontrovertible postulate for theologians like Dunn that a "great theological mind" such as Paul's cannot contradict itself. For a discussion of the issue see Räisänen, "Controversial Jew," 323–26.

49. See Räisänen, "Matthäus und die Hölle," 107–11. It is, however, a gross generalization to claim that, in my view, "the humanitarian value" of the historical task of the exegete "will emerge as texts once thought to be authoritative are exposed as oppressive and people are liberated from them" (Thielman, *Theology*, 25). While this seems to be the experience of many people with *some* texts, I am naturally not claiming that all (or even most) New Testament texts are "oppressive."

50. See Räisänen, "What I Meant," 432–35.

51. Here and there I offer brief comments on present-day matters. While they indicate my sympathies, they are not prescriptive; unlike New Testament theologies, the present work does not take "Christian truth" for granted as its point of departure. I just wish to point out some connections between the past and the present, and to stimulate the readers to think for themselves what these ancient attempts to make sense of life and experience might mean today.

52. Eschatology does not have a central position in existing New Testament theologies; it is more or less explained away. It is difficult to avoid suspecting apologetical motives here, as history as the arena of God's action has become a problem for modernity. Even Theissen's *religionswissenschaftlich* synthesis melts all early Christian expectations together into expressions of *one* "basic motif," the motif of renewal (*Theory*, 277). But to take the book of Revelation and the *Gospel of Thomas* to represent one motif is to move on a very abstract level.

53. Rowland, *Origins*, takes such a course; cf. Knight, *Origins*, 227–33.

54. The chapter reflects the conviction that there was nothing inevitable or preordained in this development. It could have taken a different course. In that case subsequent world history might have been different. In what ways—who knows?

1. Second Temple Judaism

1. For an overall picture see Gerstenberger, *Theologies*, 207–72.

2. Cf. von Rad, "Israel," 357–59.

3. Today many scholars prefer to speak of "Judeans" rather than "Jews" even when discussing Hellenistic and Roman times, since historically the name *Ioudaioi* first applied to the inhabitants of the territory of Judah. Yet, as Freyne, *Jesus*, 15, notes, "gradually it came to be applied to all those who adhered to the customs and practices of the Judeans, irrespective of their place of origin or residence"; therefore I see no urgent reason to abandon the traditional nomenclature.

4. Some have argued that the temple was actually established several decades later; cf. Pakkala, "Nomistic Roots," 258–59.

5. Other terms are, or have been, in use; each implies a particular view of the formation of Judaism. "Late Judaism," at one time a common designation, has largely ceded to "early Judaism," and even "middle Judaism" has been proposed (Boccaccini, *Middle Judaism*). As a more neutral term, "Second Temple Judaism" seems preferable; cf. Cohen, *Maccabees*, 7.

6. Still, some features of the preexilic religion may have contributed to the later development, for in comparison with the rest of the ancient Near East, Israel's religion was very much centered on its main God; a special relationship was thought to exist between Israel and Yahweh. See Pakkala, *Intolerant Monolatry*, 225–27. For more information on the religion of Israel during the monarchy, see Zevit, *Religions*; M. S. Smith, *Origins*.

7. The great work of the school, the Deuteronomistic History (as scholars call it), consists of the books of Deuteronomy, Joshua, Judges, 1–2 Samuel, and 1–2 Kings. Scholars continue to debate the issue, but meticulous analyses have, with some plausibility,

brought to light different stages in the growth of the work, among them a comprehensive nomistic redaction that sets great value on God's statutes and decrees. For an overview, see, for example, Pakkala, *Intolerant Monolatry*, 11–14; Römer, *Deuteronomistic History*.

8. For tolerant and intolerant monolatry see Pakkala, *Intolerant Monolatry*. For xenophobic tendencies in Deuteronomy (for example, Deut. 13) see Lang, "Segregation," especially 115: in order to strengthen the boundary between Jew and non-Jew, the Deuteronomist authors rewrote the history of Israel in the spirit of intolerant monolatry, publishing "their fantasies about a military powerful people who would annihilate polytheistic nations that threatened its unique religion." Cf. Collins, "Zeal," 7: "ethnic cleansing is the way to ensure cultic purity."

9. Pakkala, "Nomistic Roots," 255; cf. 266: the nomistic editors "created a new religion." See also, for example, Nissinen, "Elemente," 162–67.

10. Pakkala, "Nomistic Roots," 264–65.

11. Some have argued that it was in the interests of the (Achaemenid) Persian regime to help to stabilize the situation in the various parts of the empire by strengthening the power of local ruling classes (in this case, in Jerusalem) and creating a legal basis that would unite the population under a unified ideology. Cf. Hoglund, *Imperial Administration*; Berquist, *Judaism*; Runesson, *Origins*. However, Pakkala, *Ezra the Scribe*, argues persuasively that "Artaxerxes' rescript" in Ezra 7 in its final form "can only be unauthentic," a conclusion that "makes it more difficult to find a background for Ezra's mission in Achemenid political interests" and also "undermines attempts to find an Achemenid authorization in the activity of Ezra or in the introduction of the Torah in Judah/ Yehud" (ibid., 297; the authenticity of the text is discussed on 46–49). Cf. 76: "the text [the "rescript"] does not provide any evidence that there had been a connection between Ezra and the Achemenid rulers or administration."

12. Cf. Veijola, *Moses Erben*, 192–240.

13. Cf. Veijola, *5. Buch Mose*, 230. The notion of a text given by the Deity seems influenced by the older Near Eastern notion of destiny books held in heaven and passing into the possession of the king at his enthronement: Rochberg, *Heavenly Writing*, 209–36.

14. An acronym from *Torah* (law), *Nebiim* (prophets), *Ketubim* (writings).

15. Cohen, *Maccabees*, 167.

16. Cf. the reference to the tripartite scripture in Luke 24:44.

17. For the users of the Qumran scrolls, *Jubilees* and parts of *1 Enoch* seem to have possessed some kind of authoritative status. The scrolls suggest, for their part, that the limits of the canon were not fixed and also demonstrate a fluidity in the texts of the biblical books. See, for example, Nickelsburg, *Ancient Judaism*, 10–12, 20–21.

18. Nickelsburg, *Ancient Judaism*, 21.

19. Grabbe, *Judaic Religion*, 56, considers it to have been probably the most significant event of all in Second Temple Judaism.

20. The story is told in the *Letter of Aristeas*; the light cast by this writing on the origins of the Septuagint is discussed by Sollamo, "Letter of Aristeas."

21. See, for example, Schürer, *History*, 125–557; Grabbe, *Judaism*; Koester, *Introduction*, 1:197–217.

22. Cohen, *Maccabees*, 28–29.

23. Ibid., 22.

24. Yet Herod was probably *not* guilty of the "slaughter of the innocents" (Matt. 2:16-18). This legend is reported only by Matthew. Even Luke does not know of it, and there is no room for such an event in the chronology of his narrative of Jesus' infancy.

25. Grabbe, *Judaism*, 2:362–66; idem, *Judaic Religion*, 330–31.

26. Grabbe, *Introduction*, 18, notes that "Herod had his taxes, but there was some tangible benefit for the people. Roman taxes were for Roman good, and the tax burden was certainly not going to be any less."

27. E. P. Sanders, "Jesus' Galilee," 34–35.

28. E. P. Sanders, *Judaism*, 41.

29. Some Jews had asked Pompey that they not be ruled by a (Hasmonean) king; another deputation asked Augustus that he not give power to any of Herod's sons.

30. Cohen, *Maccabees*, 24.

31. Ibid., 24, 26.

32. E. P. Sanders, "Jesus' Galilee," 9–13.

33. The appearance of a centurion in Capernaum in a gospel story cannot count as evidence, as the officer is not even said to have been a Roman. He could have been a non-Jewish (Syrian?) officer in Antipas's army (if the story is based on a historical event).

34. Rappaport, "Anti-Roman," 101–2.

35. Ibid., 101: "This atmosphere did not prevail in Galilee, and the local leadership generally was able to restrain public resentment. Any tension created by Herod

Antipas' construction of Tiberias was contained, and resentment of his behavior could not be easily turned against Rome."

36. Funk, *Honest*, 33–34, is typical: "Jesus' home was semi-pagan Galilee, whose inhabitants, because they were often of mixed blood and open to foreign influence, were despised by the ethnically pure Judeans living to the south."

37. See p. 63.

38. Mack, *Myth*, 73; idem, *Lost Gospel*, 203; Crossan, *Historical Jesus*, 421–22.

39. Mack, *Lost Gospel*, 214.

40. Chancey, *Myth*, 167.

41. Ibid.; also Chancey, *Greco-Roman Culture*.

42. Both the Romans and Herod and his heirs distinguished between Jewish and non-Jewish parts of Palestine. Herod did build pagan temples, but not in Jewish cities (for example, in Sepphoris). See E. P. Sanders, "Jesus in Historical Context," 434–38; idem, "Jesus' Galilee," 16–22, 36.

43. There is a marked contrast between Antipas's modest urbanization at Sepphoris and Tiberias on one hand, and the more intensive Roman-styled architecture of these cities after the second century c.e. on the other hand. Most evidence for Greco-Roman culture in Galilee dates to after Hadrian.

44. This seems to have been the case since the Hasmonean times; see Chancey, *Myth*, 28–62, on the demographic history. The present state of the archaeological record suggests that the Galilean *Ioudaioi* were "Judean settlers with strong southern affinities from the time of the Maccabean conquests" (Freyne, *Galilee and Gospel*, 176–82; idem, "Jesus in Jewish Galilee," 198–99 [quotation]).

45. On the Galileans and the temple, see Chancey, *Myth*, 54–55; Freyne, "Jesus in Jewish Galilee," 200–203.

46. Horsley, *Spiral*, 237. In this scenario, the wealthy lent them money they could not repay, charged very high rates of interest, and then foreclosed on the property, so that estates grew larger and larger while more and more people were forced off the land; see Horsley, ibid., 232–33; Horsley and Hanson, *Bandits*, 60–61; cf. Borg, *Vision*, 84–86.

47. E. P. Sanders, *Judaism*, 159, 168.

48. E. P. Sanders, "Jesus in Historical Context," 447: "All other peasants in the Mediterranean world of the period had the same or similar expenses. With a very few exceptions, they all had two layers of government as well as religious establishments to support." Cf. the

reflections of Grabbe, *Judaism*, 19, on the problems connected with "assumptions about the tax burden on the average person"; ibid., 336, on Herod's time.

49. E. P. Sanders, *Judaism*, 168–69.

50. E. P. Sanders, "Jesus in Historical Context," 446.

51. Edwards, "Ethos," 63–65.

52. See, for example, Horsley and Hanson, *Bandits*, 164–72.

53. That the Zealots set fire to the city archives that contained the debt records shows that financial burdens were felt to be grave.

54. Grabbe, *Introduction*, 61. Grabbe, *Judaic Religion*, 112, emphasizes the role of upper-class leaders in the revolt.

55. To be sure, it is possible that this happened already before the rebellion and was one of its causes rather than its consequence.

56. Grabbe, *Introduction*, 30.

57. Cohen, *Maccabees*, 56.

58. The Gospels provide evidence for the existence of synagogue worship in Galilee in Jesus' time. Josephus refers to synagogues in several Jewish cities; Acts 6:9 mentions several synagogues in Jerusalem; a first-century c.e. Greek inscription from Jerusalem commemorates one Theodotus who had built a synagogue. For the Diaspora, synagogues are well attested in the first century c.e. On synagogues, see in particular Levine, *Ancient Synagogue*.

59. This is argued by Runesson, *Origins*, for example, 477–78. In his scenario, public Torah reading originated in Palestine, having developed from the public assemblies held at city gates in Persian times, and spread from there into Diaspora synagogues. Conversely, influences from the Diaspora contributed to the new organizational pattern of local, semipublic institutions dedicated to communal reading and study of the Torah (ibid., 479–80). The origins of the synagogue institution continue to be intensely debated.

60. According to Runesson, groups such as Pharisees, Essenes, and the Jesus movement formed voluntary associations (which might be called semipublic "synagogues"); but both the Pharisees and the followers of Jesus also tried to make their voices heard in the town or village assemblies, that is, in the "public synagogues." "Here anyone could put forward his (and her?) views in connection with the sabbath reading of the torah," which often resulted in discussion (Runesson, *Origins*, 483–84).

61. Grabbe, *Introduction*, 30–31.

326

62. The rendering is somewhat inaccurate, but in any case the notion of binding God-given decrees is a major part of the Torah.

63. In a great number of publications; note, for example, the title of the volume *Judaisms and Their Messiahs*, edited by Neusner and Green.

64. Luomanen, "Sociology," 118.

65. Hakola, "Social Identities."

66. Cohen, *Maccabees*, 14: "for all their disagreements and rivalries, ancient Jews were united by a common set of practices and beliefs that characterized virtually all segments of Jewry." See now also Cohen, "Common Judaism," esp. 82.

67. Cohen, *Maccabees*, 12–13.

68. A term used by E. P. Sanders, *Judaism*, 47–303, to denote what the priests and the mass of the people agreed on.

69. Grabbe, *Judaism*, 487; idem, *Introduction*, 46; differently E. P. Sanders, *Judaism*, 318: all Sadducees may have been aristocrats.

70. E. P. Sanders, *Judaism*, 340.

71. For an informative discussion that involves a spirited attack on the standard view that the Pharisees separated from other people, trying to reproduce the temple cult in their own homes, see E. P. Sanders, *Judaism*, 413–52, esp. 438–43.

72. E. P. Sanders, *Figure*, 44. It is possible that the name of the party did not originally mean "the separate ones" (the usual explanation), but was derived from another possible meaning, "specify," of the verb *parash*: the Pharisees may have been regarded as *paroshim*, "specifiers" or "the strict ones." See Baumgarten, "Name."

73. The traditional notion that they appealed to an oral law that was traced back to Sinai has been challenged in recent research; cf. Neusner, *Torah*; E. P. Sanders, *Jewish Law*, 97–130; also Grabbe, *Judaism*, 480; idem, *Introduction*, 44. The Pharisees did appeal to the antiquity of their traditions, but, unlike the Essenes, they did not elevate them to the status of scripture (E. P. Sanders, *Jewish Law*, 108).

74. An example of interpretive flexibility is their tradition of *'erubin*, the "fusion of Sabbath limits": all the houses in a courtyard could be made one "house" within which one could then carry pots and dishes from house to house even on a Sabbath, thus permitting communal dining on the Sabbath despite Jeremiah's ruling that Jews were not to carry burdens out of their houses on that day (Jer. 17:19-27).

75. They had considerable political influence during the Hasmoneans, especially during the reign of Queen Salome Alexandra (76–67 b.c.e.), but had shrunk in influence after her time.

76. On the influence of the Pharisees see E. P. Sanders, *Judaism*, 448–51.

77. See, for example, Collins, "Essenes," 619–22.

78. Pliny (*Nat. hist.* 5.73) locates the "solitary tribe of the Essenes" that "has no women and has renounced sexual desire, has no money, and has only palm trees for company," on the west side of the Dead Sea.

79. See, for example, Collins, *Scepter*, 6–7; García Martínez, *Dead Sea Scrolls Translated*, xlix–li. The identification has not gone unchallenged. For instance, Golb, *Who Wrote?*, suggests that the library is not sectarian, but belonged to the Jerusalem temple and was hidden in the desert before the onslaught of the Romans. He fails to account for the communal life described in 1QS or for Pliny's location of an Essene settlement to the Dead Sea area. Collins refers to the lack of writings that could be described as Pharisaic or conform to the teaching of the later Tannaim (early rabbinic sages), as well as to the paucity of pro-Hasmonean literature among the scrolls; he finds it plausible that the people who collected the scrolls had a quarrel with both the Hasmoneans and the Pharisees. The relation of the material remains at Qumran to the contents of the scrolls is discussed by Saukkonen, "Dwellers."

80. An excellent one-volume translation (followed in this book) is available: García Martinez, *Dead Sea Scrolls*.

81. The numbers in the reference codes refer to the cave from which the scroll or fragment in question was found; thus the *Community Rule* stems from cave 1 (but numerous fragments are found from cave 4).

82. See Metso, *Textual Development*.

83. The exceptional reference code is due to the fact that two manuscripts of this writing, found in a storeroom of the synagogue in Cairo (hence the "C") were known half a century before the discovery of Qumran. Fragments from some Qumran caves have shown that the "Cairo Document(s)" were copies of Qumranic originals.

84. Cf. the classic introduction: Knibb, *Qumran Community*.

85. The Groningen hypothesis holds that the Qumran community represented a splinter movement, born from an internal conflict in the older Essene movement; the group that stayed loyal to the Teacher of Righteousness finally moved to Qumran.

86. CD 11.17-22. Nevertheless, the temple and its priests were viewed as defiled; only those within the sect

could validly use the temple services (CD 6.11-16), and the "Damascus community" may have used them to a limited extent only. One can argue that CD no less than 1QS displays high tension with the greater society and that even the urban Damascus community created, in effect, "a society within society" (Wassen and Jokiranta, "Groups in Tension," 249–52; see furthermore Jokiranta, *Identity*, 73–79, on the "shared outlook" of both documents).

87. Magness, *Archeology*, 47–69.

88. The Teacher of Righteousness was not the founder of the movement, but he had been of great importance in its early phase and was later viewed as a prototypical teacher and group member; see Jokiranta, "Prototypical Teacher."

89. Wassen and Jokiranta, "Groups in Tension," 212 n. 5.

90. Collins, "Yahad," 96: We have "reached a point where it is no longer helpful to characterize any part of the textual evidence as describing the 'Qumran community.'"

91. Collins, "Yahad," 82. He continues by stating that there is no evidence in the scrolls either "that 'the Qumran community' had split off from the Essenes or that it ever ceased to be part of a broader sectarian movement" (contra the Groningen hypothesis mentioned above, n. 85.) In Collins's view, the term *yahad* does not refer to the Qumran settlement, but is an umbrella term for many smaller local groups; the specific community centered at Qumran should be viewed as an elite group *within* the *yahad*.

92. For a response to Collins, see Metso, "Term Yahad."

93. Vermes, *Dead Sea Scrolls*, 48, maintains, however, that "the severity of their judgement of the wicked was more dogmatic than practical, as appears from their insistence that vengeance is for God alone."

94. E. P. Sanders, *Judaism*, 374.

95. Ibid., 379.

96. No doubt the origin of these circles, too, lies in the tumults of Maccabean times. Moreover, the contents of the Enoch literature indicate that it originated with learned scribes, who had a great interest both in eschatological visions and in astrological speculation. A number of Enochic fragments have been found in Qumran.

97. On apocalypticism see pp. 81–82.

98. The *Book of Watchers* (chs. 1–36); the *Similitudes* (37–71); the *Astronomical Book* (72–82); the *Book of Dreams* (83–90); and the *Epistle of Enoch* (91–108), which contains the *Apocalypse of Weeks* (93.1–10; 91.11–17).

99. After the recognition that the extant fragments of the Enoch scrolls from Qumran do not contain any material from this part of the Enoch literature (parts of all other sources of *1 Enoch* are found in Qumran), the *Similitudes* are most often dated to the first century C.E. The issue of dating is far from settled, however (given the paucity of preserved material, the missing of the *Similitudes* in Qumran might be accidental; for comparison, note that only one of the half-dozen Enoch manuscripts has preserved a fragment from the section *1 En.* 90–105). The *Similitudes* are still dated to the first century B.C.E., for example, by VanderKam, "Messianism," 205.

100. Josephus describes John basically as a preacher of a moral message. The Synoptic Gospels are the only evidence for the eschatological content of his message and should be used with due caution when attempts are made to reconstruct John's proclamation; see Uro, "John the Baptist." It is not clear that John was "the gloomiest preacher of repentance within Judaism"; thus J. Becker, *Johannes der Täufer*, 25, criticized by Uro, "John the Baptist," 255. Cf. p. 341 n. 57.

101. In Acts 21:38 Paul is suspected of being one (though Luke mistakenly connects the Sicarii with the "Egyptian" mentioned above, p. 27); for a discussion of Luke and Josephus on this point, see Mason, *Josephus and the New Testament*, 211–13. Josephus may have lumped together a larger variety of rebellious movements into one "school"; cf. Mason, ibid., 206.

102. According to Num. 25, Phinehas had killed an Israelite man involved with a pagan woman and thus turned back God's wrath from the people of Israel.

103. Contrary to a view long popular among biblical scholars, the rabbis seem not yet to have dominated Jewish communities at the turn of the century. See, for example, Cohen, *Maccabees*, 109–10, 213–16; and the summary of the scholarly discussion in Hakola, *Identity Matters*, 61–65.

104. The origins of "rabbinic" Judaism are connected with the small town of Yavneh/Jamnia, where the Romans allowed Yohanan ben Zakkai to establish a study center of some sort.

105. Jewish synagogues had been granted special permission for assembly by Julius Caesar (Josephus, *Ant.* 14.213-16); in addition, they could be regarded as funerary collegia, which were permitted (see above, pp. 30, 42). One should, however, avoid the oft-used term *religio licita* ("permitted religion"), which first crops up in Tertullian.

328   106. Grabbe points out that Jews were officially *not* exempt from the cult of the emperor, yet for practical purposes they did not have to take part in it; the sacrifices for the emperor in the temple of Jerusalem and the inscriptions dedicated to him in many local synagogues were seen as fulfilling the requirement of loyalty to the state (*Judaic Religion*, 309–10, 331).

107. Cf. the events in Adiabene (Josephus, *Ant.* 20.38-48); some Pharisees carried out mission work according to Matt. 23:15. The scholarly discussion is briefly summarized by Grabbe, *Judaic Religion*, 296–97.

108. The concept of God-fearers has been questioned by Kraabel ("Disappearance") in particular. For a summary of the discussion see Zetterholm, *Formation*, 122–23; he concludes with Overman that "there is every reason to assume that the presence of a class of Gentiles associated with the synagogue is an authentic reflection of the diverse composition of diaspora Judaism in the late first century." Cf. also Svartvik, *Mark*, 325–33.

109. Cohen, *Maccabees*, 38.

110. Charlesworth, ed., *Old Testament Pseudepigrapha*, 1–2, is an invaluable collection of translations (followed in this book) with comprehensive introductions. For overviews of this whole body of literature see Nickelsburg, *Jewish Literature*; Stone, ed., *Jewish Writings*.

111. The work (that was preserved in Latin translation among the works of Philo) is often referred to by the Latin title *Liber Antiquitatum Biblicarum* (*L.A.B*).

112. A one-volume translation is available (Yonge, *Works of Philo*), though the Loeb translations by Colson and others remain the best in English. For a useful brief introduction see Schenck, *Philo*; comprehensive standard works include Wolfson, *Philo*, 1–2; Sandmel, *Philo of Alexandria*; Borgen, *Philo of Alexandria*.

113. An old (eighteenth-century!) one-volume translation is available (Whiston; reprinted over 200 times), but the multivolume translation in the Loeb Classical Library edition is preferable. On Josephus in general see, for example, Rajak, *Josephus*; Feldman, "Josephus"; Mason, *Josephus and the New Testament*.

114. Collins, "Testaments," 344.

115. Cf. Cohen, *Maccabees*, 207. A full new translation is available in Neusner, *Mishnah*. For an introduction to the contents of the Mishnah see Neusner, *Mishnah*, xiii–xliii; Strack and Stemberger, *Introduction*.

116. See, for example, Alexander, "Targum, Targumim."

117. Grabbe, *Judaic Religion*, 175, concludes that "there is no evidence that targums or targumizing had a place in the pre-70 synagogues"; cf. ibid., 164.

2. Greco-Roman Religion
and Philosophy

1. I am deeply indebted to Klauck, *Context*, throughout this chapter.

2. Lane Fox, *Pagans*, 67–68, observes that "at the level of the procession, the impact of a pagan cult can still be sensed in the journeys of the Christian images through the cities of southern Spain during Holy Week."

3. Klauck, *Context*, 12.

4. Strong, "Images," 97–98.

5. Cf. Propertius, *Eleg.* 2.28.46; Gladigow, "Roman Religion," 810.

6. Among the Romans the mythical stories of the Gods did not play the same central role as among the Greeks.

7. Klauck, *Context*, 28, following H. Kleinknecht.

8. Gladigow, "Roman Religion," 815.

9. Nock, *Conversion*, 12.

10. A major concern of Paul is the tense relations between Jewish and Gentile Christ-believers, apparently due to a change in the leadership of the church: due to the edict of Claudius, it had lost its Jewish-born leaders, and those born Gentiles had apparently taken over; see the discussion in Jewett, *Romans*, 59–61.

11. Klauck, *Context*, 88.

12. Burkert, *Mystery Cults*, 11.

13. As Klauck, *Context*, 122, correctly points out, "one can scarcely call this a 'resurrection' of Attis, although it is possible that this is how it was seen in late antiquity in the confrontation with Christianity."

14. People were eager to look to the Egyptian spiritual world for ancient, hidden wisdom that would explain life's mysteries.

15. Klauck, *Context*, 131.

16. Justin and Tertullian attribute the similarity to a device of demons.

17. The Cynic Diogenes put it trenchantly: "It would be ridiculous if Agesilaus and Epaminondas trashed about in the mud while useless people dwelt on the island of the blessed merely because they had undergone an initiation" (Diogenes Laertius, *Vit. Phil.* 6.39).

18. This group of scholars, keen on history-of-religion comparisons, was very influential in the late nineteenth and early twentieth century in religious studies, including the study of Christian origins.

19. Rudolph, "Mystery Religions," 274.

20. Wedderburn, *Baptism*, 394.

21. Cf. Zeller, "Entstehung," 103–4, 110–15.

22. M. W. Meyer, "Mystery Religions," 944. Cf. J. T. Sanders, *Charisma*, 134: "Christianity, the Isis religion, and the mysteries generally offered their adherents freedom from the fear of either annihilation or a miserable existence after death." Cf. also Rudolph, "Mystery Religions," 282.

23. For example, Klauck presents them in a chapter on "Popular Belief" (*Context*, 153–249), while noting himself that the nomenclature is open to criticism.

24. It was told that Asclepius, a hero who attained the status of a God after his death, had been born in this sanctuary and healed the sick and raised the dead there already in his boyhood.

25. Empedocles is reported to have said about himself: "I journey around as an immortal God, no longer mortal" (Diels, *Fragmente* 31B112). "Little more than a century after his death, stories were already in circulation which told how he had stayed the winds by his magic, how he had restored to life a woman who no longer breathed, and how he then vanished bodily from this mortal world and became a god" (Dodds, *Greeks and the Irrational*, 145, referring to Diogenes Laertius, *Vit. Phil.* 8.60-61, 67-68).

26. Apollonius was a Pythagorean philosopher and itinerant preacher of religious reform who lived in the first century C.E.; his life is narrated in a biography by Philostratus (222 C.E.). Philostratus's own interests color the account, but he may draw on earlier sources and local traditions. Accounts of miracles are not very common in the book, but an exorcism and the raising of a dead person in a funeral procession are depicted. Apollonius is called a "divine man" (*theios aner*, *Vit. Apoll.* 2.17; 8.15), and the crowd in Egypt look up to him "as to a God" (*theos*, ibid., 5.24).

27. To be sure, in philosophical circles miracles were not regarded as authenticating criteria of divinity; what was valued was the wisdom and virtue of the figure in question. But in less cultivated circles popular heroes were "remembered with awe for their possession of miraculous powers which defy sensibility" (Tiede, *Charismatic Figure*, 291).

28. Cf. the critical survey of scholarship by Koskenniemi, *Apollonius*, who rejects the category. Klauck, *Context*, 175–77, takes a more moderate stand.

29. Dillon, "Fate," 778.

30. Klauck, *Context*, 214.

31. Ibid., 211.

32. If one tries to preserve a distinction between religion and magic, one may say that coercion is typical of magic and petition typical of religion But the boundaries are vague; "ideal types seldom occur in their pure form in reality" (Klauck, *Context*, 218).

33. Ibid., 254–55.

34. Differently from the normal sacrificial usage, the blood of the animal was led to a pit in the earth as nourishment for the dead hero.

35. Klauck, *Context*, 265.

36. Klauck, *Context*, 274. Plutarch tells in his biography various versions of the legend that Alexander was begotten, in the form of a snake, by the God Zeus-Ammon, who had intercourse with his mother. Great miracles happened on the day of his birth. Alexander's entire body diffused a most delightful fragrance (*euodia*), a term sometimes used of the epiphanies of Deities. As a boy, Alexander received ambassadors in the absence of his father and astonished them with his intelligent questions.

37. Price, *Rituals*, 23–52, 174–75, followed by Klauck, *Context*, 284.

38. The inscription (quoted in Klauck, *Context*, 290) is from Ephesus; its occasion was Caesar's new regulation of the crushing system of taxes.

39. Klauck, *Context*, 299. Suetonius presents a telling anecdote: toward the end of his life, when Augustus passed by the Bay of Puteoli, passengers and sailors from a ship that had just arrived from Alexandria overwhelmed him, "clothed with white robes and garlands, and burning incense, with wishes that he might live a happy life and with boundless acclamation of praise: it was thanks to him that they lived, thanks to him that they put out to sea, and thanks to him that they enjoyed freedom and prosperity" (*Aug.* 98.2).

40. This *Nero redivivus* myth is hinted at also in the book of Revelation (Rev. 17:8, 11).

41. See Thompson, *Book of Revelation*, 104–7; Klauck, *Context*, 310. The issue is of relevance for the assessment of the historical context of the book of Revelation; see pp. 291–92. Pliny attacks Domitian's divine status during his lifetime, but his tendency is obvious: by putting Domitian in a bad light, he is enabled to present Trajan, the object of new hopes, in the most glorious light possible. Pliny promised Trajan that he would receive divinization as his future heavenly reward, but these reservations had no effect on the cultic veneration of Trajan in the provinces (Klauck, *Context*, 311–12). And his successor Hadrian was honored, for example, as the new Dionysus and as the Olympian Zeus.

330

42. Thompson, *Book of Revelation*, 104–7. The evidence is contradictory; Thompson relies on evidence from Domitian's own time, such as the poet Statius, who wrote that when Domitian was once acclaimed *dominus*, he forbade this. For a different view (based on the testimony of Suetonius, who wrote in Trajan's time), see, for example, D. L. Jones, "Roman Imperial Cult," 807.

43. For a balanced picture see B. W. Jones, "Domitian."

44. Price, *Rituals*, 233; cf. 212–13. Price (ibid., 233) concludes that the practices and language of the imperial cult give an ambiguous "picture of the emperor between human and divine. . . . Standing at the apex of the hierarchy of the Roman empire the emperor offered the hope of order and stability and was assimilated to the traditional Olympian deities. But he also needed the divine protection which came from sacrifices made to the gods on his behalf. The emperor stood at the focal point between human and divine."

45. Ibid., 213.

46. "If one speaks of a conversion experience in antiquity outside the Jewish/Christian sphere, what is meant is the adoption of one particular philosophical worldview with all its consequences for existential praxis. No one needed to 'convert' in this sense to a belief in the gods or to a mystery cult" (Klauck, *Context*, 334).

47. See Dillon, "Platonism," 379–80.

48. Tertullian stated that Seneca is often "one of us" (*Seneca saepe noster*); Jerome regarded him as the perfect example of the "fact" that a human soul is by nature Christian (*anima naturaliter christiana*).

49. This world principle can be given various other names as well, such as *physis* (nature), *heimarmene* (fate), and *pronoia* (providence).

50. Schmeller, "Stoics," 211.

51. Downing, *Cynics and Christian Origins*; Mack, *Myth* and *Lost Gospel*; Vaage, *Galilean Upstarts*. For a critical discussion of the "Cynic Q" hypothesis of these authors, see Tuckett, *Q*, 368–91.

52. See Asmis, "Epicureanism."

53. Klauck, *Context*, 390.

54. See Thom, "Pythagoreanism"; Koester, *Introduction*, 1:358–60.

55. The term never appears in the Nag Hammadi writings.

56. Impressive and influential was above all Jonas, *Gnosis*; see further Rudolph, *Gnosis*; Filoramo, *History of Gnosticism*.

57. A pioneering analysis is M. A. Williams, *Rethinking "Gnosticism."* For the ongoing debate see, in particular, King, *Gnosticism*; Marjanen, ed., *Was There a Gnostic Religion*; Marjanen, "Gnosticism."

58. Dunderberg, *Beyond Gnosticism*, 17. M. A. Williams, "Gnostic Religion," 77, suggests that one should be open to the possibility that some of the similarities "were less a matter of communal or school continuity than merely the recycling and adaptation of certain motifs by *different* groups or individuals" (his italics).

59. But not all! Even the limitation of the defining criteria to two (as here) rules out some texts that used to be regarded as "gnostic," such as the *Gospel of Thomas*, in which the world is not claimed to be evil, created by an evil or ignorant demiurge.

60. Marjanen, "Gnosticism," 210.

61. Cf. Dunderberg, *Beyond Gnosticism*, 31: it seems justified to use the term *Gnosticism* as an indication of a family resemblance between certain traditions; in light of their mythic teaching, Valentinians and Sethians seem more like "siblings" in comparison with "cousins" such as Marcion or Philo (and, one might add, John).

62. In a Platonic way, differing from the Hebrew Bible, Philo had explained that God had relegated some "negative" tasks (apparently not regarded as appropriate to God by Philo), such as the punishment of sinners, to angels. From here the way is not far to the gnostic view that a demonic demiurge, or demiurges, is to be distinguished from the highest God (even though Philo himself did not go all the way).

63. So-called Simonian gnosis may, however, have developed in *competition* with emerging Christianity. Irenaeus mentions Simon Magus (described in Acts 8 as a magician with a considerable following in Samaria) as the first gnostic, from whom all others descended. Simon seems to have had adherents, who paid some sort of divine worship to him; Justin Martyr knows of them in Rome in the mid-second century. The gnostically oriented system of the Simonians cannot be regarded as Christian; on the contrary, it contains "a kind of counter-scheme to the Christian doctrine of redemption" (Markschies, *Gnosis*, 76–77). The same seems to be true of Menander, another Samaritan, a disciple of Simon according to Irenaeus; cf. ibid., 77.

64. Pearson, *Gnosticism*.

65. The Hermetic tractates are too late (third century C.E.?) to count as evidence, and it has even been argued (though the question remains open) that they show Christian influence. The Nag Hammadi tractate *Eugnostos* (which has been used, and christianized, by

the author[s] of the *Sophia of Jesus Christ*) is a (vulgar) philosophical document without apparent Christian features. Scholars have conjectured that a similar process may have been responsible for other Christian gnostic writings, such as the *Apocryphon of John*, but no direct evidence is available. Moreover, *Eugnostos* "cannot be considered gnostic in any classic sense" (Parrott, "Eugnostos," 221).

3. EVENTS, PERSONS, SOURCES

1. Or perhaps one should say, with John the Baptist, to whose circle Jesus belonged for some time.
2. Admittedly, this claim is more controversial in today's scholarship than it was a generation ago. See the discussion in ch. 4.
3. See Fredriksen, *Jesus of Nazareth*, 241–59.
4. Jesus' message can even be characterized as "quietistic" (Zeller, "Entstehung," 32).
5. Crossan and Reed, *Excavating Jesus*, propose that Jesus' teachings represent a response to a crisis caused by "Romanization, urbanization and commercialization" of Galilee; but whether the urbanization of Sepphoris and Tiberias really brought about a profound economic crisis remains debated. Mark 12:17 ("give to the emperor the things that are the emperor's") hardly comes from someone who wishes to condemn Rome's economic exploitation of God's land. In any case, the parable in Q 14:16-24 portrays a man of tremendous wealth, but nowhere censures him; Luke 12:13-21 faults another wealthy man not for exploiting others but for not trusting God.
6. Neither the issue of the law in general nor that of the Sabbath in particular crops up in the passion narratives—contrary to what Mark 3:6 makes one expect.
7. It is not clear, either, that Jesus challenged the validity of the temple cult, whatever he may have said about destruction coming upon the temple; cf. Wedderburn, *History*, 31.
8. Luke's rather wooden mention of the appearance to Peter (Luke 24:34) shows "how far down the stream of development the gospel traditions as we have them are. For well-nigh all traces of (this) constitutive character of the appearance to Peter have been lost, and the story which would have expressed it has disappeared" (Evans, *Resurrection*, 107). Some scholars believe that

traces of such a story are found in the transfiguration story (Mark 9:2-8).
9. There is a late fictitious account in a fragment of the *Gospel of the Hebrews*, preserved by Jerome.
10. Strauss, *Life*, 727, quoted by Wedderburn, *Beyond Resurrection*, 24–25.
11. See p. 125.
12. It is only Luke's earthly realism that makes the separate event of ascension necessary (Luke had to explain why a particular appearance was final); see Wedderburn, *Beyond Resurrection*, 32.
13. Evans, *Resurrection*, 83, comments on the scene depicted in Matt. 28:16-20: "There is nothing temporary about it, and an ascension to an exalted state after it in the Lukan or even the Johannine sense, or any subsequent movement from Galilee to Jerusalem, would be unthinkable." This is a Matthean construction that would be "as out of place at the end of any other gospel as it is completely in place here" (ibid., 84).
14. Ibid., 130.
15. Ibid.; contra N. T. Wright, *Resurrection*, 478 and passim. Wright mounts a massive rescue operation in defense of the basic reliability of the appearance accounts of the canonical Gospels, but fails to meet the challenge posed by their heterogeneous variety.
16. Lüdemann, *Resurrection of Christ*, 36; cf. Wedderburn, *History*, 19–21. It follows that the tradition that Jesus first appeared to Mary Magdalene must be disputed (contra Theissen, *Erleben*, 161, who relies on the late story in John 20:11-18 and speculates that Mark 16:1-8 may originally have been a story about an apparition of Jesus, not of an angelophany).
17. Notably those who would constitute the nucleus of the Q group; see p. 63.
18. For a careful discussion of the options, see Myllykoski, "What Happened"; his conjecture is that Joseph of Arimathea (who buries Jesus according to Mark 15:42-47 par.) "had something to do with the burial of those crucified so that later Christians could imagine that he could take care of the body of Jesus" (ibid., 82). Yarbro Collins, *Beginning*, 119–48, and Lüdemann, *Resurrection of Christ*, 87, think that Mark created the story of the empty tomb; according to Lüdemann, the evangelist's comment on the silence of the women (Mark 16:8) betrays that the story is an innovation and that no such tradition existed before Mark. By contrast, Wedderburn (*Beyond Resurrection*, 48–65) surmises that the fixation on the "third day" as a central

332

19. Cf. Myllykoski, "What Happened," 46–47: "If both the disciples and the executors of Jesus knew where the respected Joseph of Arimathea had buried the body of Jesus, and acknowledged the testimony of the women who found this tomb empty on Sunday morning, then we have surprisingly few traces left of this major evidence for the resurrection of Jesus. Early traditions do not indicate the need for a proof of an empty tomb." If the early community in Jerusalem had known the place of the tomb, "they probably would have paid at least some attention to it and we could follow the traces of this interest back to the earliest stage of the tradition. . . . For James the Just, Peter, Stephen, Paul and others, the empty tomb was no argument for the miracle of resurrection, nor did they feel pressed by outsiders to defend such a piece of evidence. In Acts Luke merely tells us that the Jewish leaders took Jesus down from the cross and put him in a tomb (Acts 13:29). Polemic against the story of the empty tomb belongs only to a later time (Matt. 27:62-66; 28:2-4, 11-15), and the concrete identification of the tomb of Jesus in Jerusalem stems from the early 4th century."

20. Phenomenologically, there is probably no difference between these visions and, say, the apparitions of the Virgin Mary experienced by numerous people throughout church history; cf. Lüdemann, *Resurrection of Christ*, 48–49. For a thorough and balanced discussion of the visions from a psychological point of view, see Theissen, *Erleben*, 140–63. He concludes that the visions of the disciples after Jesus' death are not without analogies, and thus there is no reason to deny their subjective authenticity (ibid., 155; cf. 158–59).

21. Cf. Ebner, "Von den Anfängen," 17–18.

22. Cf. Wedderburn, *History*, 26–28, noting that Paul identifies in 1 Cor. 15:45 the risen Jesus as a "living spirit." For an analysis of the "mass ecstasy," see Lüdemann, *Resurrection of Christ*, 73–81.

23. The appearance of the expression "the firstborn of the dead" as a title of Jesus in Revelation shows that Paul's calling Jesus "the first fruits of those who have died" was not his own idea; the notion of Jesus as the first-

born (Rom. 8:29) of those to be resurrected probably came to him from older tradition.

24. The report in Acts is guided by legendary and idealizing tendencies.

25. This is not to say that all Hellenists would have shared the same views; one should single out Stephen and his friends as a more liberal group among them. But since it is this group that is of significance in the further history of early Christians, in what follows the designation "Hellenists" will refer to them.

26. Reconstructing the history and ideology of the Hellenists is a hypothetical and controversial issue. Some scholars (in particular, C. C. Hill, *Hellenists*, followed by Hurtado, *Lord*, 211–14) deny any real rift within the Jerusalem congregation; some have doubted even the historicity of Stephen (Matthews, "Need"). I follow the lines suggested in my earlier comprehensive articles (Räisänen, "Hellenists"; idem, "Hellenisten," with bibliographies), where I modify the groundbreaking work of Hengel, *Between Jesus and Paul*. For some criticisms of Hill see Räisänen, "Hellenisten," 1475–76. Emphasizing the source-critical problems and highlighting Luke's rhetorical purposes, Penner pleads for complete agnosticism (*In Praise*, 331). No doubt the problems are legion. However, the quick rise of a more or less liberal ideology and practice in the Christian congregation in Antioch, and their wide dissemination independently of Paul's mission and alongside it, cries for an explanation: here is a gap that is admirably filled by the Hellenists—despite all disagreements between modern reconstructions of their activities. Neither Hill nor Penner tackles this issue adequately.

27. Luke claims that the accusations were false, but this may be his somewhat forced interpretation of charges that he found in the tradition; see Walter, "Apostelgeschichte 6.1," 371; cf. Wedderburn, *History*, 47.

28. The name may stem from the Roman authorities; cf. Ebner, "Von den Anfängen," 29–31.

29. Cf. the story about Jesus and the Gentile woman (Mark 7:24-30 par. Matt. 15:21-28). The persevering *faith* (in Jesus' ability to cure) of the woman overcomes Jesus' original reluctance to help her. Yet the stimulus to the acceptance of Gentiles hardly comes from the historical Jesus (in that case it would have been difficult to ascribe such sayings as Matt. 10:5-6 and 15:24 to him).

30. In Gal. 3:2-5, Paul asks his converts polemically: "Did you receive the spirit by doing the works of the law,

or by believing what you heard? . . . Does God supply you with the spirit and work miracles among you by your doing the works of the law, or by your believing what you heard?" (The NRSV capitalizes "Spirit"; here and in other quotations, where I take the spirit to be an impersonal force [see ch. 9], I have deviated from this practice.) In Acts 10:44-48, Peter's decision to baptize his Gentile hearers right away depends on their having begun to speak in tongues, a phenomenon interpreted as a proof that a person had received God's spirit. The story is largely fictional (see n. 42), but it is nevertheless quite probable that it was incidents of this kind that made some Jewish Christ-believers take the step of accepting uncircumcised converts. The case is argued by Esler, "Glossolalia."

31. At the very least, he must have been engaged in violent polemics; probably he also tried to have measures of discipline applied to Christians. Lashing, even stoning, may have been included. Scholars disagree on the nature and setting of Paul's persecuting activity: many doubt Luke's account that portrays him as participating in the stoning of Stephen (Acts 7:58; 8:1). Galatians 1:22-23 suggests instead that Paul was not in Jerusalem shortly before his conversion experience.

32. Cf. Acts 8.

33. On Antiochian theology cf. J. Becker, *Paul*, 102–12.

34. Cf. Reinbold, *Propaganda und Mission*, especially 342–47, on this type of "mission," which was probably the usual way already in the first century. "The spread of the Christian faith was probably far more haphazard and unplanned" than the author of Acts would have us believe, largely dependent on "factors like trade-routes, the slave-trade or the directions taken by those fleeing from persecution" (Wedderburn, *History*, 61).

35. See the list in Räisänen, "Hellenists," 159–60.

36. Lüdemann, *Founder*.

37. There are some indications of an ecstatic inclination in Paul's letters. His foundational vision seems akin to (later) rabbinic visions connected with the experiences known as Merkabah (chariot) mysticism. See the seminal work of Segal, *Paul the Convert*.

38. This is the designation used by Wedderburn, *History*, 104, with reference to the likelihood that the meeting was in fact "a very small-scale affair" (ibid., 105).

39. For accounts of the meeting and its somewhat ambiguous outcome, see, for example, Haenchen, *Acts*, 455–72; Wedderburn, *History*, 104–10; Lüdemann, *Acts*, 186–92.

40. Cf. H. Leppä, *Luke's Critical Use*, 125–32. Paul would have been spared a lot of argumentative effort had he had such a stipulation at his disposal when dictating 1 Cor. 8–10; cf. Ebner, "Von den Anfängen," 32.

41. Acts passes over the conflict in silence.

42. This shows that the Cornelius story in Acts 10 (referred to above, n. 30) cannot be taken at face value: "So clear a guidance of God on the matter of eating with Gentiles should surely have prevented Peter from ever acceding to the demands of James's emissaries" (Wedderburn, *History*, 74).

43. For a summary of the recent discussion (important contributions include those of Dunn, Sanders, and Esler in particular) see Zetterholm, *Formation*, 130–34.

44. By contrast, they were undoubtedly able to exercise table fellowship in *Jewish* conditions in Jerusalem.

45. Wedderburn, *History*, 117.

46. Cf. Ebner, "Von den Anfängen," 35.

47. Cf. Wilson, *Luke and the Law*, 84–94.

48. See the discussion by Wedderburn, *History*, 110–14.

49. Pehkonen, "Rejoicing?" suggests that Paul's later attack on judaizing opponents in Phil. 3:2-11 is part of an attempt to cope with the disappointment caused by his visit to Jerusalem, and that even the more lenient-sounding critique in Phil. 1:15-18 belongs to the same context.

50. Second Corinthians is probably a composite document that consists of several separate letters; see, for example, L. Aejmelaeus, *Streit*; idem, *Schwachheit*, 19–26.

51. Other "Pauline" letters are generally rightly regarded as pseudonymous: 2 Thessalonians, Colossians, Ephesians, and the Pastoral Epistles.

52. Nothing is known of the personal views of Paul's fellow workers, such as Timothy, Titus, Prisca, or Aquila. Did Tertius, who wrote down Romans at Paul's dictation, or Phoebe, who delivered the letter to Rome, share Paul's views—or were they at all able to follow the flight of his arguments? One would like to know.

53. For a comprehensive discussion of scholarship on James, see Myllykoski, "James."

54. Josephus, *Ant.* 20.197-203; cf. Eusebius, *Hist. eccl.* 2.23.4-18, reporting Hegesippus. James's contact with a notorious "apostate" like Paul may well have been a factor; cf. Theissen, "Unglücksstifter," 237–38.

55. Writings attributed to James include not only the Hellenistic Jewish Christian *Epistle of James* and a popular infancy gospel (*Protevangelium of James*), but also two Valentinian *Apocalypses of James* and an ideologically

334

related *Apocryphon of James*. Both the *Gospel of Thomas* (saying 12) and the *Second Apocalypse of James* regard him as the greatest Christian leader, even though the status of James in comparison with Thomas in *Gos. Thom.* 12–13 remains a puzzle and may reflect the priorities of a pre-Thomasine tradition (for a comprehensive discussion of the matter, see Uro, *Thomas*, 80–105).

56. The First and Second Epistles of Peter, the *Gospel of Peter*, the *Preaching of Peter*, two different *Apocalypses of Peter*, *Acts of Peter*, and others.

57. "Q" is a hypothetical document reconstructed from the material common to Matthew and Luke over against Mark. Its existence is still denied by some prominent scholars, notably Goulder (especially *Luke*). I join the majority who find the Two Source Hypothesis the most plausible solution to the Synoptic problem (Mark wrote first; Matthew and Luke used, independently of each other, Mark and Q). Goulder thinks that Luke used Matthew, a hypothesis that requires one to believe, for example, that Luke dissected Matthew's Sermon on the Mount and dispersed its parts here and there in his own work.

58. Kloppenborg, *Excavating Q*, 171–75, and numerous others. But Theissen, *Entstehung*, 63, notes that, while a Galilean location is not impossible, it is "much less certain than many think"; other places in Palestine or Syria may fit just as well.

59. Q is usually dated shortly before the Jewish War, but Myllykoski ("Social History") gives grounds for situating it after the war (c. 75 C.E.). Kloppenborg's (*Formation*; *Excavating*) thesis of three strata of Q has been very influential, especially in the United States. He distinguishes between an earlier "sapiential" collection (Q¹) that later underwent a "deuteronomistically" oriented redaction; to the product thus formed (Q²) were later added the story of Jesus' temptation and a couple of short "nomistic" clauses. There are indeed clear traces of redaction in Q, but critics of the hypothesis point out that the material on which the editors have put their stamp does not seem to have formed an earlier collection; according to this view, there was no Q at all before Kloppenborg's Q². See, for example, Zeller, "Grundschrift"; P. Hoffmann, "Mutmassungen"; Tuckett, *Q*, 69–74.

60. Kloppenborg, *Excavating Q*, 183–84; also Uro, *Sheep*, 242.

61. Kloppenborg, *Excavating Q*, 200–201; Arnal, *Village Scribes* (who may go too far, however, in his claim that

originally radical sayings have been "domesticated" by the scribes).

62. In my references to Q passages, the numbering of the verses follows the Gospel of Luke (the standard practice): thus, for example, "Q 13:28-29" refers to the wording reconstructed by way of comparing Matt. 8:11-12 and Luke 13:28-29. In the reconstructions I rely on Robinson et al., eds., *Critical Edition of Q*.

63. An early (c. 125 C.E.?) papyrus fragment from a writing sometimes called the *Egerton Gospel* strikingly combines passages to which close parallels are found both in the Synoptic Gospels and in the Gospel of John. The question of its independence of the canonical Gospels is controversial, but the burden of proof would seem to rest on those who argue for dependence.

64. Wedderburn, *History*, 163. Cf. Painter, "James and Peter," 209: "Had the way of James prevailed it is unlikely that Christianity would have emerged as a religion separate from Judaism."

65. Two brief excerpts from a *Secret Gospel of Mark*, purportedly a more spiritual version of Mark's Gospel used by Alexandrian Christians, are included in a letter by Clement of Alexandria, found by Morton Smith in the monastery of Mar Saba in the Judean Desert in 1958. Koester, *Gospels*, 302, argues that the *Secret Gospel* was the original version of Mark's Gospel, the canonical Gospel being an edited later version; cf. S. G. Brown, *Mark's Other Gospel*. The thesis has received little support and even the authenticity of the letter has been called into question. Recently Carlson, *Gospel Hoax*, has claimed that it is a falsification by Smith himself, but the case is far from closed.

66. Theissen, *Entstehung*, 84–85.

67. E.-M. Becker, *Markus-Evangelium*.

68. The Gospels of Matthew, Mark, and Luke are called "Synoptic" because most of their materials can be viewed together (that is, synoptically) in parallel columns.

69. On the question of authorship, see, for example, Lührmann, *Markusevangelium*, 3–7; Marcus, *Mark 1–8*, 17–24. The name of the author may well have been Mark (Marcus, a common Roman name), but it is unlikely that he is identical with John Mark, once a coworker of Paul (for example, Acts 12:25) and Peter (1 Pet. 5:13).

70. The radical saying on food in Mark 7:15 and its even more radical interpretation in 7:19 (which lets Jesus proclaim all food clean) may even be derived from

Paul's teaching in Rom. 14:14 (rather than vice versa; see Räisänen, "Jesus and the Food Laws," 140–42). Svartvik, *Mark and Mission*, 344–48, describes Mark as a "Pauline gospel," emphasizing the importance of the cross of Christ for both Paul and Mark.

71. For arguments against Rome and for Syria see Theissen, *Lokalkolorit*, 246–61, 270–84; Marcus, *Mark 1–8*, 30–37.

72. See O. Leppä, *Making*.

73. Perhaps this is what the unknown author wished: the final salutations (Heb. 13:22-25) look like a conscious effort to imitate a Pauline letter.

74. The writing is included in the New Testament in Codex Sinaiticus (as an appendix at the end of the manuscript).

75. It was earlier common to give the letter an exact date, namely, 95/96 c.e. Yet this dating seems mistaken (and may be too early), since it depends on identifying the author with a Senator Flavius Clemens, possibly executed by Domitian, who on dubious grounds has been regarded as a Christian. See White, *From Jesus to Christianity*, 336–37.

76. *First Clement* is included in the New Testament in a relatively early manuscript (Codex Alexandrinus) and in some other early Christian Bibles. It was retained in the Syriac New Testament all through the Middle Ages.

77. The attribution is secondary; the real author is unknown.

78. Luz, *Matthäus*, 1:89–90, defends the thesis that Matthew's community was founded by wandering missionaries of the Q community.

79. The particularist command in Matt. 10:5b-6, 23 in the mouth of the earthly Jesus may reflect an earlier stance of Matthew's community.

80. Matthew's Gospel takes a critical stance to liberal attempts to mitigate the Torah (cf. Matt. 5:19). As Hengel puts it, if Matthew had the first (or the last) word in Christian theology, Paul would be a heretic ("Bergpredigt," 254).

81. It is customary in scholarship to find in a given Gospel indications of the life situation of the community in whose midst it originated and to interpret the writing with regard to this situation: the Gospel of Matthew, for example, reflects the problems of Matthew's community, and part of the purpose of the author is to address those problems. This (standard) approach is challenged by Bauckham and a circle around him (Bauckham, *Gospels for All Christians*); they argue that the (canonical) Gospels were probably "written for general circulation around the churches and so envisaged a very general Christian audience" (Bauckham, "Introduction," 1). The bottom line is that "the Matthean, Markan, Lukan, and Johannine communities should disappear from the terminology of Gospels scholarship" (ibid., 4). No, they should not! Even if (as is quite plausible) the authors wished to reach far beyond their own circle with their books, it is evident that the actual social context colors each work in numerous ways. Notably, even Marshall, while finding Bauckham's thesis attractive, notes that "it may still leave room for the individual Evangelists being affected by the communities in which they lived and writing more particularly for them and their needs rather than deliberately trying to be catholic in their approach" (Marshall, *Theology*, 21 n. 8). For criticisms of Bauckham's thesis, see, for example, Marcus, *Mark 1–8*, 25–28; Mitchell, "Patristic Counter-evidence"; Kazen, "Sectarian Gospels."

82. This is convincingly argued by Luz, *Matthäus*, 1:96–97.

83. See the discussion of the options in ibid., 100–103.

84. Should this be correct, the Gospel can be seen to reflect the importance that Peter and his mediating position came to enjoy in the Christian congregation of Antioch (or rather in some Christian communities: so great a city could doubtless accommodate several cells of Jesus-believers). Note the enhanced position given to Peter as a foundational figure in Matt. 16:17-19.

85. This is disputed by some scholars who consider *Didache* to be earlier than Matthew or even think that it was used by Matthew; cf. Draper, "Christian Judaism," 281.

86. *Didache* came to be regarded as canonical in some circles; it is counted among the controversial writings by Eusebius.

87. John does *not* mount a "social justice" argument against an oppressive empire; see p. 292.

88. De Jonge, "Patriarchs," 184–85.

89. See Trafton, "Isaiah, Martyrdom"; Knibb, "Martyrdom," 149–50. The work divides in two sections: the *Martyrdom of Isaiah* (chs. 1–5) is a Jewish work that includes a large Christian interpolation often called the *Testament of Hezekiah* (3.13—4.22, probably from the late first century); the *Vision of Isaiah* (chs. 6–11) is a Christian addition from the (early?) second century.

336

90. To be sure, recent American research is inclined to move Acts well into the second century.

91. Contrary to the common view, Luke seems to have known some Pauline letters, even Galatians, but he plays down the radicalism of the latter. On Luke's knowledge and use of Paul's letters in general, see L. Aejmelaeus, *Rezeption*; on his treatment of Galatians in particular, see H. Leppä, *Luke's Critical Use*.

92. Irenaeus, *Haer.* 1.26.2; 3.11.7; 3.21.1; 4.33.4; 5.1.3.

93. See Häkkinen, "Ebionites"; Skarsaune, "Ebionites"; Luomanen, "Ebionites and Nazarenes." The name is derived from Hebrew *'ebyon*, "poor." It may well be an authentic self-designation; the idea that the poor stand in a special relationship to God has a long history in Jewish tradition. It is also thinkable that the term was intended to underline a connection with the early community, the "poor of Jerusalem" (cf. Rom. 15:26). Cf. Luomanen, "Ebionites and Nazarenes," 89.

94. See Luomanen, "Ebionites and Nazarenes." Along with similarities, there are conspicuous differences between the Ebionites described by Irenaeus (late second century) and those described by Epiphanius (late fourth century)—so much so that Luomanen concludes that the Ebionites of Epiphanius cannot stand in direct continuity to those of Irenaeus.

95. In this I follow, for the sake of convenience, the usage of Dunn, *Unity*, 239–45 and passim (explained ibid., 409 n. 6).

96. In the *Pseudo-Clementines* (see n. 99), the "enemy" of Matt. 13:28 is equated with Paul; reference is made to the "lawless and senseless teaching of the enemy" that has been favored by some of the Gentiles (*Ps.-Clem. Ep. Petri* 2.3). Paul is even identified with Simon Magus.

97. At least some of them seem, however, to have distinguished between the man Jesus and the preexistent heavenly Christ who entered him at his baptism.

98. This Gospel was not considered heretical by church fathers, although it differs in some respects from the canonical-to-be Gospels. In addition, scholars have traditionally posited a *Gospel to the Nazarenes*, but it seems very uncertain whether such a writing actually existed (Luomanen, "Nazarenes' Gospel."). On the problem of the number see also Gregory, "Jewish-Christian Gospels," 56–59 (who leaves the question open). Scholars have also assumed the existence of a somewhat different movement of "heretical Jewish Christians" called Nazarenes (cf. recently Kinzig, "Nazoreans"), but Luomanen, "Nazarenes," persuasively argues that the notion of such a sect is a fic-

tion created by Epiphanius in the late fourth century. "Nazarenes" was simply the standard designation for Christians in Syriac.

99. This is a fictitious story about Clement of Rome and his experiences as a disciple of Peter, who is here seen as the representative of a law-abiding mission to the Gentiles; Peter explicitly denies that he had ever taught the abolishment of the law. The novel is preserved in two different versions: the Greek *Homilies* and the Latin *Recognitions*, both of which are based on a common source. The *Homilies* are introduced by a cover letter from Peter to James (*Epistula Petri*).

100. A reconstruction is given by F. S. Jones, *Source*.

101. Some scholars identify this source with the *Ascents of James*, a Jewish Christian writing known to have existed, but the identification is doubtful. Stanton, "Jewish Christian Elements," 317–23, opts for "An Apologia for Jewish Believers in Jesus."

102. F. S. Jones, *Source*, 165.

103. F. S. Jones, "Jewish Christianity."

104. See Luttikhuizen, "Elchasaites," and, for a somewhat different view, af Hällström and Skarsaune, "Cerinthus," 496–502. The traditions concerning the Elchasaites are very confused. The book itself may be dated to the time of Trajan's Parthian war (114–117 C.E.). According to a recently published biography of Mani, Mani's parents were Elchasaites and this founder of a new world religion himself received his first religious impressions in this movement; see Koester, *Introduction*, 2:205.

105. I follow Myllykoski's ("Cerinthus") characterization of Cerinthus. The patristic information is contradictory; Cerinthus is also made to appear a gnostic, and this view is tenaciously upheld by many modern scholars; cf. recently af Hällström and Skarsaune, "Cerinthus," 488–95.

106. See, for example, Kysar, "John," 919.

107. Thus Dunderberg, *Beloved Disciple*, 199–204.

108. J. Becker, "Verhältnis," 495.

109. J. Becker, *Johanneisches Christentum*, 46–56; idem, "Verhältnis," 484–85.

110. John's Gospel actually seems much closer in spirit to the *Gospel of Thomas* than to the Synoptics; see the list of ideas common to both in Dunderberg, *Beloved Disciple*, 6–8.

111. Problems in the flow of the narrative as well as theological tensions indicate that the present Gospel has been put together in several stages. See J. Becker, "Das vierte Evangelium."

112. Chapter 21 is in any case an addition, and clear indications of secondary revision can be detected, for example, in the farewell speech (chs. 13–17) and in ch. 6. The later layers may presuppose some knowledge of the Synoptic Gospels; cf. Dunderberg, *Johannes und die Synoptiker*.

113. Some scholars assume that the epistles were written before the Gospel (thus Strecker, *Theologie*, 441–42; Frey, *Eschatologie*, 3:55–60), but it is more plausible to assume that the Gospel is earlier: in it the Christ-believers are confronted with nonbelieving Jews, but there is no trace of this conflict in 1 John, where the congregation itself is divided on the issue of Christology. See, for example, R. E. Brown, *Community*, 93–97; J. Becker, *Johanneisches Christentum*, 39.

114. Kysar, "John," 904–6.

115. In 2 John, the author urges the readers to deny hospitality to the "separatists" in order to prevent them from propagating their influence. In 3 John the schism is connected with a conflict of authority between two leaders in a community, but it is very difficult to unravel the actual situation. Scholars have produced widely differing hypotheses concerning the date, chronological order, and mutual relationship of the three Johannine letters. An instructive overview is given by Kysar, "John," 907–9.

116. The question of the original language is controversial; Greek is also a possibility.

117. Charlesworth, "Odes," 725; cf. idem, "Solomon, Odes of," 114–15.

118. The early date is contested by some scholars who regard the letters as fictional and date them ca. 170. See ch. 12.

119. Uro, *Thomas*, 134–36; Dunderberg, *Beloved Disciple*, 5. The dating depends on whether one or more of the (written) Synoptic Gospels has been used, which is a controversial issue.

120. Earlier often considered gnostic, *Thomas* is hardly more (or less) gnostic than the Gospel of John; cf. Marjanen, "Gnostic Gospel?" 138–39.

121. This writing, too, was earlier generally regarded as gnostic (a view still held by Tuckett, *Gospel of Mary*, 42–54 and passim), but it would seem that it does not meet both of the criteria presented above (p. 54). *Pace* Tuckett, ibid., 140, 146, it is not clear that the *Gospel of Mary* implies a negative attitude to the material world.

122. MacRae, "Authoritative Teaching," 304.

123. Wilson, *Related Strangers*, 208.

124. See, for example, Vielhauer, *Geschichte*, 641–48. Some scholars have argued that the *Gospel of Peter* contains independent traditions. Crossan even posits an early "Cross Gospel" independent of the canonical passion narratives and empty tomb stories that was used by the authors of these Gospels; the final editor of the *Gospel of Peter* combined the original passion narrative of the Cross Gospel with elements from the canonical Gospels (Crossan, *Four Other Gospels*; idem, *Cross*). For criticisms see, for example, R. E. Brown, "Gospel of Peter." Koester, *Gospels*, 216–40, argues for independence from the canonical Gospels; both they and the *Gospel of Peter* would have drawn on a common tradition that told of Jesus' passion in scriptural diction.

125. Vielhauer, *Geschichte*, 676–77.

126. This term is used by White, *From Jesus to Christianity*, 398.

127. The author was deposed of his office when the work was recognized as a falsification, but it remained popular and was never suspected of doctrinal heresy (even though its teaching on abstinence runs squarely counter to that of the Pastorals); cf. Lau, "Enthaltsamkeit," 90. It is listed as canonical in Codex Claromontanus and as controversial in Eusebius.

128. Even the historical Paul had preferred continence to marriage, though without making this a general requirement (1 Cor. 7). In *Acts of Thecla*, continence has become the ideal for all Christians. This stance converges with a contemporary trend in the society: men tried to live as continent as possible in order to remain vital and virile; the Stoics advised married couples to limit sexual union to the procreation of children. Cf. Ebner, "Gemeindestrukturen," 184–85.

129. Another major part of the *Acts of Paul* is a fictitious correspondence between Paul and the Corinthian congregation known as *3 Corinthians*.

130. These novels were preserved by the Manicheans, who found their dualistic-pessimistic worldview confirmed in them.

131. The work is listed in the Muratorian canon (see p. 402, n. 15) as well as in the list of canonical books in Codex Claromontanus, and was commented on by Clement of Alexandria as holy scripture.

132. Evidently the writing has been composed in stages over a long period of time, a preferred date for the final version being c. 140; see Snyder, "Hermas," 148.

133. Koester, *Introduction*, 2:258–61. In some Christian circles, notably in Alexandria, the *Shepherd* came to be considered part of the New Testament. It is contained

338

in Codex Sinaiticus (as an appendix, along with the *Epistle of Barnabas*) and early versions of the Vulgate; Clement of Alexandria and Tertullian treat it as scripture.

134. Yet another factor was the salaries that the Montanists paid to their leaders in Asia Minor. By doing so they were shaking the prevailing church-political power structures (as the large city churches were led by wealthy individuals); see Marjanen, "Montanism," 209–10. Lane Fox, *Pagans*, 505, notes that "salaries are the heretics' one lasting legacy to Christian life"!

135. Ehrman, *Corruption*, 13. The term was taken over by Hurtado, who gave a more comprehensive description (*Lord*, 494): the reference is to "early examples and stages of the sorts of beliefs and practices that, across the next couple centuries, succeeded in becoming characteristic of classical, 'orthodox' Christianity, and came to be widely affirmed in Christian circles over against the alternatives." I prefer "proto-orthodox" to "mainstream," as we actually do not know about the numbers; cf. Dunderberg, *Beyond Gnosticism*, 18–20.

136. White, *From Jesus to Christianity*, 424–25.

137. Koester, *Introduction*, 2:297, suggests that the author "belonged to those orthodox Christians who named Paul as an authority of the church, but secretly wished that the great apostle had not written any letters—or at least not such letters as those that were causing so many interpretive problems in the effort to defend true faith against heresy."

138. Hills, "Apostles, Epistle of," 312, characterizes the work as "witness to the flowering of an ecclesiastical self-consciousness in an environment of competing Christian groups, but before the emergence of the 'Great [or Catholic] Church.'"

139. Corley, "Preaching," 282. The primary source of the fragments is Clement of Alexandria, and the work itself probably also stems from Egypt.

140. Translations are available in Robinson, ed., *Nag Hammadi Library*; and M. Meyer, ed., *Nag Hammadi Scriptures*. I follow those of the Robinson volume, with occasional adaptations to Meyer's somewhat freer renderings.

141. The assumption of two Gods is further fuelled by commonsense observations on the less-than-perfect character of the biblical God in many stories. Other interpreters tried different methods of dealing with such features (for example, allegorical exegesis).

142. Another Syrian, Cerdo, was active in the early second century in Rome, teaching a doctrine of two Gods and possibly influencing Marcion. On Simon Magus, who is singled out as the ancestor of all gnostics by the church fathers, and on his disciple Menander (neither of whom represents *Christian* gnosis), see above, p. 330, n. 63.

143. It included a 24-volume commentary on the Gospel of Luke.

144. Löhr, *Basilides*; cf. Markschies, *Gnosis*, 79–81.

145. Tertullian, *Val.* 4.1–2. The historical reliability of this information may be doubted, but its existence shows that Valentinus certainly enjoyed some popularity in Rome.

146. Dunderberg, "School of Valentinus," 64.

147. The *Gospel of Truth* is often ascribed to him too, but this attribution is uncertain.

148. Dunderberg, "School of Valentinus," 75.

149. See the discussion in Dunderberg, *Beyond Gnosticism*, 90–92.

150. However, the Valentinian "system" described by Irenaeus is basically his own construction that did not exist anywhere in such a form. Irenaeus "pulled together one body of thought from diverse written and oral sources" and "tends to give a more unitarian and systematic picture of Valentinian theology than it really had" (Dunderberg, "School of Valentinus," 66). Still, the cosmogonic myth described by Irenaeus was not his own invention; the Valentinian *Tripartite Tractate* provides a lengthy firsthand account of it (ibid., 71).

151. Dunderberg, "School of Valentinus," 81–82.

152. Dunderberg, *Beyond Gnosticism*, 3.

153. The dates suggested are highly tentative.

154. In this writing, however, faith is emphasized more than knowledge as a precondition of salvation; *pistis* with derivatives occurs nine times in the brief text.

155. The Sethian version seems more archaic: its appallingly demonlike picture of the demiurge has apparently been somewhat toned down in the Valentinian version. See Dunderberg, "School of Valentinus," 71.

156. The latter half of the third century? Cf. Isenberg, "Gospel of Philip," 141. Scopello, "Gospel of Philip," 160, suggests the second half of the second century or the first decades of the third.

157. Layton, *Gnostic Scriptures*, 5–214. Rasimus, *Paradise*, argues that instead of one Sethian corpus one should talk about a wider "classic gnostic" tradition that consists of three clusters of mythological ideas (Ophite, Barbeloite, and Sethian).

158. M. A. Williams, "Sethianism," 56–57.

159. Ibid., 32–33. See Williams's account of the *Holy Book of the Great Invisible Spirit* (ibid., 36–42), a third-century writing a little too late for our purposes.

160. No less than four early Coptic manuscripts have been preserved.

161. The work thus testifies to the struggle over the interpretation of the Gospel of John, in which the Johannine Epistles, too, are involved. See Turner, "Trimorphic Protennoia," 512–13; idem, *Sethian Gnosticism*, 146–47.

162. To be sure, the interpretation of the figure of Judas in this writing is controversial; some scholars think that the author intended to portray Judas in a negative light. Thus, for example, DeConick, *Thirteenth Apostle*. For the discussion see Dunderberg, "Judas' Anger."

163. The text is a Christian revision of a non-Christian (and essentially nongnostic) treatise called *Eugnostos the Blessed*.

164. Von Campenhausen, *Formation*, 182.

165. White, *From Jesus to Christianity*, 440.

4. LAST THINGS FIRST: GOD, HISTORY, AND BEYOND

1. W. C. Smith, *Scripture*, 246 n. 15. To be sure, Hindu eschatology does assume a catastrophic end of history, but this lies incomprehensibly far in the future. History consists of immensely long cycles of time (in which a catastrophic end is followed by a rebirth of the world) lasting millions of years.

2. W. C. Smith, *Scripture*, 9–10. Not that teleological views of history were lacking in the East either. Buddhism (here probably influenced by the same Zoroastrian tradition, which had a crucial impact on Jewish and Christian eschatology, as we shall see) knows the important figure of Maitreya, the future Buddha, whose coming will establish universal peace and concord.

3. The view, characteristic of much previous scholarship, that this is a unique vision that distinguishes the religion of Israel from that of its neighbors, is disproved by such evidence as the Mesha stele and the Esarhaddon treaties.

4. The Song of Moses in Exod. 15 (in its present form probably exilic) combines the different traditions: the whole song celebrates Yahweh as a "man of war" (v. 4), but mention is made also of the holy mountain where Yahweh has "planted" his people (v. 17); the song ends with the affirmation that "Yahweh will reign forever and ever" (v. 18).

5. Carroll, *Prophecy*, 150. See, for example, the lament psalms 74, 77, and 89.

6. See on the role of Persia: Isa. 45:1-3; on the return: 40:9-11; 43:1-7; on the gathering of the tribes: 49:6; on the new exodus: 51:11; on the renewal of Israel: 54:11-14; on that of the nations: 45:22-25; 49:6; 55:5; on the new creation, depicted as combat with chaos monsters: 51:9-11.

7. Nickelsburg, "Eschatology," 581.

8. Carroll, *Prophecy*, 13.

9. See on universal peace, for example, Isa. 2:2-4 (Mic. 4:1-3); Zech. 9:10; Ps. 46:10; *1 En.* 10; cf. also Isa. 9:4; 11:6-9; 65:25; on destruction Joel 3:9-10. Isaiah 60:3-6 envisages the pilgrimage of the nations to Zion, but 60:12 also states that nations that do not submit to Israel will be destroyed.

10. Isaiah 13:10, 13; 24:1-7, 18-23; 34:4; Jer. 4:23-28.

11. At least the descriptions of cosmic catastrophes and of the destruction of historical powers are intertwined, for example, in Isa. 13 (oracles against Babylon) and Isa. 24 (against Edom). Already in Judg. 5:20 the stars fight "from their courses" against the enemy in a hymn, the bulk of which celebrates the military actions of Israel's heroes.

12. It seems unviable to isolate "apocalyptic eschatology" as a distinct category. Future hopes similar to those displayed in works that can be classified as "apocalypses" are also found in works belonging to other genres. In a presentation focused on the formation of religious ideas, it is neither possible nor necessary to penetrate into the literary problems of apocalypticism (which are many). Apocalypses are not only eschatological works, and eschatological views similar to those found in apocalypses are found elsewhere too. The questions of the bearers and social settings of the apocalypses are largely unsettled problems.

13. Cf. the "Demotic Oracle" and the "Potter's Oracle"; see Collins, *Imagination*, 27–28.

14. The so-called Akkadian literary predictive texts; see Nissinen, "Neither Prophecies nor Apocalypses."

15. Collins, *Imagination*, 28.

16. Yet, contrary to a persistent scholarly claim, exact timetables are rare in apocalypticism, the book of Daniel being the exception rather than the rule.

340

17. In Ezek. 38–39 the process of dividing history into periods is already at work.

18. The "wicked" may have been members of aristocracy who had grown insensitive to the situation of the poor and thus forfeited faithfulness to the covenant of Yahweh; see Albertz, *Religionsgeschichte*, 543–49.

19. Cf. the role of the archangel Michael in Dan. 10:21; 12:1. Here too the age-old motif of a God's combat with chaos monsters is adapted to new historical circumstances.

20. Yet the great judgment scene in Dan. 7 actually describes "the judgment which the God of Israel passes on the nations that had oppressed his people." This "myopic outlook" naturally stems from the conviction that Yahweh was primarily interested in Israel and that he "shaped world-history for the achievement of Israel's destiny; so far as the fate of other nations was considered, it was generally in terms of their ultimate overthrow for their oppression of Israel" (Brandon, *Judgment*, 67–68).

21. Gowan, *Eschatology*, 91.

22. The ambiguous cases include Isa. 26:19 and 25:8; cf. also 4Q 521. Ezekiel 37 gives a drastic depiction of the revivification of dead bones as an image for national restoration. A few centuries later bodily resurrection ceased to be a metaphor.

23. This is convincingly argued by Hultgård, "Persian Apocalypticism." While the mass of apocalyptic Persian material occurs only in late sources, Greek authors such as Plutarch (who used the writings of Theopompos from the fourth century b.c.e.) show that the eschatological worldview did exist in Persia in the Achaemenid period. Contacts between Jews and Persians were frequent and friendly in those times.

24. Hultgård, "Persian Apocalypticism," 80. As for the intra-Jewish beginnings, the conviction of Yahweh's unlimited power that showed itself in the revivification of dead people by such men of God as Elijah or Elisha may be seen as a step on the road that was to lead to the belief in a general resurrection, effected by Yahweh.

25. Cf. Lehtipuu, *Afterlife Imagery*, 129. Postmortem life is presupposed in *1 En.* 22 (this is part of the *Book of Watchers*, which predates Maccabean times) in a context not colored by a situation of persecution. Enoch is shown the souls of the dead that are kept (the souls of the righteous being clearly distinguished from those of the wicked) to await a final judgment that will be executed on every individual (see ch. 5). This book

describes a "world out of joint," being perhaps written "as a response to a cultural trauma" caused by the collision of Western culture with traditional Near Eastern society, offering "an alternative reality in its visions of hidden places and life beyond death" (Collins, "Afterlife," 127). Even the *Book of Watchers* (see especially *1 En.* 25) assumes, however, that the judgment will be followed by a paradisal life on the earth in the vein of Isa. 65.

26. Collins, *Imagination*, 90.

27. It is possible that the final Hebrew version of Daniel (in chs. 8, 10-12) seeks to neutralize the political implications of the earlier Aramaic version, where the reign of God is equated with the realization of the political power of Israel (3:31, 33; 4:31-32; 6:26, 28; and, in particular, 7:27); see Albertz, *Religionsgeschichte*, 670.

28. Thus, for example, Nickelsburg, "Eschatology," 585: Dan. 12:1-3, "presuming the scenario in *1 Enoch* 24–27, allude to the long life of the righteous in the new Jerusalem and to the ongoing contempt to be heaped on the apostates." Cf. Fohrer, *Geschichte*, 401–2; Moore, *Judaism*, 2:297; Cohn, *Cosmos*, 174–75.

29. On *1 En.* 90, see ch. 5.

30. See *1 En.* 51.5: "The earth shall rejoice, and the righteous shall dwell upon it, and the elect shall walk thereon." Verse 4 states that the earth will be renewed.

31. Cavallin, *Life*, 27. The idea of heaven as a postmortem place for humans seems to have been an Egyptian invention that gained ground in Israel only in the Hellenistic period (J. E. Wright, *Heaven*, 50–51, 96–97).

32. Should "the wise" refer to the whole group of the righteous, it is even less likely that a heavenly existence is in view. Daniel 11:40-45 and 12:1 depict a time of a deep historical crisis (during Antiochus Epiphanes) from which the archangel Michael will finally rescue the people of Israel. It would be a strained reading to infer that the people are rescued away from the earth, and the connection with the earlier chapters reinforces this.

33. Cf. Nickelsburg, *Resurrection*, 26: "Perhaps the light imagery is intended to describe the theophanic glory that will envelope the new Jerusalem. . . . The righteous will live a long life in the new Jerusalem. There in the glorious light of the eschatological community, the wise teachers will shine with particular brilliance."

34. Nickelsburg, "Eschatology," 584–85. N. T. Wright, *New Testament*, 305–6, takes the text figuratively, but this is artificial.

35. For a summary see E. P. Sanders, *Judaism*, 289–303, though he somewhat devalues the testimony of apocalyptic literature.

36. See on the return of the tribes: *Pss. Sol.* 11.2-3; 17.28-31; 1QM 2.2-3; on the subjugation of Gentiles: *Pss. Sol.* 17.24; 1QM; on their conversion: *Sib. Or.* 3; Philo, *Praem.* 93-97, 164; on the renewed temple: 11QT 29.8-10; *Sib. Or.* 5.420-25.

37. Among the unliterary population, militant national aspirations were strong; cf. *Sib. Or.* 5.

38. This idea (of unmistakably Zoroastrian origin) looms large in *1 Enoch*, in *Jubilees*, and in Qumran.

39. Collins, *Imagination*, 29, points out that "Daniel 7–12 was written in the heat of persecution, but this seems to be rather exceptional."

40. Collins, "From Prophecy," 134.

41. For a critique of theories of deprivation as explanations of millenarianism in general see Cook, *Prophecy*.

42. For example, in *Psalms of Solomon*; 1QM; the activities of first-century c.e. sign prophets such as Theudas and "the Egyptian."

43. Rowland, *Origins*, 17. According to Josephus (*B.J.* 6.312), what incited the Jews to the war was "an ambiguous oracle" in the scriptures (Dan. 7?) "to the effect that at that time one from their country would become ruler of the world."

44. Collins, "From Prophecy," 147. See especially *1 En.* 104.

45. Nickelsburg, "Eschatology," 590.

46. Cavallin, *Life*, 123.

47. Ibid., 97.

48. Ibid., 139.

49. Ibid., 130, 132–33, with special reference to Wis. 5:15-16: "The righteous live [present tense!] forever and their reward is in the Lord."

50. Cavallin, *Life*, 130.

51. Even within the just mentioned section Wis. 3:1-9, vv. 7-8 seem to maintain a different, earthly eschatology (in that the righteous are said, "in the moment of their visitation" in which they will like sparks "kindle into flame," to be "judges and rulers over the nations of the world"). Two types of eschatology seem here to be juxtaposed "without very much reflection on the tension between them" (Cavallin, *Life*, 128). Differently N. T. Wright, *Resurrection*, 167–71: Wisdom presupposes an intermediate state for the souls before bodily resurrection and return to the earth.

52. In *Praem.* 79-172, Philo presents an eschatological scenario of events that will take place in the world.

Still, the drama is remarkably dehistoricized: the battle fought is bloodless, the enemies conquered are unnamed abstractions, and the unexpected liberation of the exiles arises because of their mass conversion to virtue. Even here Philo presents a spiritualized individualistic soteriology (only those Jews who maintain their "nobility" will participate in the future salvation). See Hecht, "Philo and Messiah."

53. The expression "kingdom of God" is very rare in Jewish literature (*basileia tou theou* occurs in *Pss. Sol.* 17.3), but references to God as king and to his kingdom or reign are not infrequent. Key occurrences include Ps. 145:10-13 (several references to "your kingdom"), Dan. 2:44, and *T. Mos.* 10.1-10. See, for example, Duling, "Kingdom." Meier, *Marginal Jew*, 2:269, summarizes his discussion of the background of "the kingdom of God" in Jesus' message (ibid., 237–70) by stating that the symbol of God's rule "was especially prominent in eschatological or apocalyptic contexts, conjuring up hopes of Israel's definitive salvation in the future."

54. The same sort of people are said to have waited for the "consolation of Israel" or for "the redemption of Jerusalem" (Luke 2:25, 38; cf. 24:21).

55. Notably by Crossan, *Historical Jesus* and *Revolutionary Biography*: the kingdom of God was, for Jesus, "a process of open commensality" (*Revolutionary Biography*, 70) that symbolized and embodied "radical egalitarianism" (71ff.); see further, for example, Borg, *Conflict*; idem, *Jesus*; idem, "Portraits"; Funk and Hoover, *Five Gospels*; Mack, *Myth*, 73; Funk, *Honest*, 143–216. For Horsley, *Jesus*, 170, the kingdom means a "renewal of social life" already under way.

56. Presented in different versions, for example, by E. P. Sanders, *Jesus and Judaism*; Allison, *Jesus*; Ehrman, *Jesus*; Meier, *Marginal Jew*, 2:337–38; Laaksonen, *Jesus*; cf. also the stimulating if at times speculative account of Freyne, *Jesus*. Rowland even presents Jesus as "the supreme example of the chiliastic mentality" (Rowland and Corner, *Liberating Exegesis*, 119).

57. To be sure, Josephus is silent about any eschatological dimension in John's message (but then he might have had good reasons for keeping quiet); caution is further called for due to the fact that it is only a couple of texts from Q that present John as a fiery preacher of eschatological judgment, and these pieces fit well with the general tenor of Q (Uro, "John the Baptist"). But while Uro successfully refutes assertions to the effect that John was "the gloomiest preacher of repentance within Judaism," he expressly

342

refrains from claiming that John lacked all apocalyptic imagery, nor is he willing to "go as far as those who want to replace the apocalyptic paradigm with pictures of John and Jesus as Cynic preachers" ("John the Baptist," 254–55).

58. Thus, with strong reasons, Meier, *Marginal Jew,* 2:339–48.

59. I would include among such sayings also Luke 17:21: the kingdom does not come by observing signs but is "within you" (*entos hymon*). On the meaning of *entos hymon,* see Holmén, "Alternatives." It is often rendered with phrases like "in your midst," but mainly because scholars try to understand the saying as an authentic word of Jesus (in which case a reference to a kingdom inside the hearers would make little sense). I think Zeller, "Entstehung," 34–35 n. 13, is right: the plausible rendering for *entos* is "within," which means that we have to do with a secondary fragment akin to *Gos. Thom.* 3. The expression *meta paratereseos* ("by observing signs") recalls the kind of signs and portents recounted in, say, Mark 13.

60. The not uncommon idea that Jewish leaders would have wished to kill someone for the reason that he spoke of God's love, or mixed with people of ill repute, is nothing short of absurd; cf. E. P. Sanders, *Jesus and Judaism,* 326–27.

61. The Romans were hardly a problem in Galilee. The possession of land and the economic situation could have been the problem, but Jesus does not seem concerned with the mundane causes of poverty either; what he does is to promise the kingdom to the poor.

62. The (wild) theory that Jesus planned an armed rebellion does not explain why he alone was arrested, but his followers were not searched.

63. Allison, *Jesus,* 146.

64. If the reference to the patriarchs is taken literally, they are "alive" already now; that is, one would have to reckon with an immediate "resurrection" (in the beyond!) after death. (But the patriarchs, like the martyrs, may have been a special case.)

65. See ch. 7 on Q 11:31-32.

66. I believe Q 17:24 is authentic, but does not (originally) identify the Son of Man with Jesus; see p. 197.

67. Jesus does not count himself among the twelve rulers over the tribes of Israel, but reserves a higher role for himself. "Viceroy" is the term used by E. P. Sanders, *Jesus and Judaism,* 234.

68. Kloppenborg, *Formation;* his analysis is followed, for example, by Mack.

69. Kloppenborg's stratigraphic analysis rests on too uncertain a foundation; cf. above, p. 334 n. 59.

70. Freyne, *Jesus,* 137, notes that wisdom texts from Qumran show that wisdom and apocalyptic are not antithetically opposed worldviews; cf. ibid., 140.

71. Cf. Zeller, "Grundschrift," 401.

72. It has been designed with a view to Q 11:19, itself a secondary saying. The majority of scholars favor authenticity, but see my arguments against this near-consensus in Räisänen, "Exorcisms"; cf. also Zeller, "Entstehung," 34.

73. The saying is, in context, not aimed at those healed (although commentators routinely understand it so) but at Jesus' critics and may therefore be construed as a warning: "the kingdom is now bearing down upon you," "if you maintain your present stance you will regret it" (E. P. Sanders, *Figure,* 177).

74. To be sure, many parables do reckon with eschatological expectation, but as they try to cope with the delay of the reversal, they betray their secondary origin.

75. Yet Meier, *Marginal Jew,* 2:338, points out that "the symbolizing of the final coming of the kingdom as the full growth and/or harvest coming from the initial seed . . . naturally conjures up a *relatively near consummation,* organically tied to the present, rather than a distant event in a vague future" (my italics).

76. Jeremias, *Parables,* 146–53.

77. The use of the image of "leaven" may in addition imply an element of threat, as "leaven" generally stood in Jewish (and early Christian) tradition for something evil that was about to spread. This would tie with the connotations of violent power found in the parables of the conquering of the strong man (Mark 3:23-27 par.) or the inbreaking thief (Q 12:39), or in the enigmatic saying about the kingdom that will, according to one interpretation, force its way through with violence (Q 16:16; the *Critical Edition of Q* interprets differently: "the kingdom of God is violated"). The kingdom will not only stand in contrast to the present state of things: it will amount to a violent change—brought about by God, not humans—of the present order.

78. Meier, *Marginal Jew,* 2:338.

79. Thus Mack, *Myth,* 73.

80. One cannot be absolutely certain that, according to this saying, the restoration has to take place on earth. *Testament of Judah* 25.1-2 predicts that the twelve patriarchs shall rise to act as princes of their tribes, but it remains unclear whether this would happen on earth or in the transcendence (some of the patriarchs

are given stars to rule over!). Also *T. Zeb.* 10.2-3 can be interpreted in both ways.

81. Contrast Mark 13:26-27, where the tradition of people coming from the different cardinal points to Zion is transcendentalized to signify a rapture to the beyond.

82. Laaksonen, *Jesus*, 248–53.

83. Cf. *2 Bar.* 29.6: "those who have hungered shall rejoice," a statement made in a millenarian context.

84. Cf. *2 Bar.* 73.2, a millenarian context.

85. The exorcisms gave Jesus the reputation of being out of his mind, if not in league with Satan (Mark 3:21, 22-30).

86. However, the explicit connection of exorcisms and healings with the (in some sense, present) kingdom seems to be a specialty of Q, taken over by Matthew and Luke, but not shared by Mark.

87. A visionary experience of the fall of Satan from heaven, referred to in Luke 10:18, may well have been the initial stimulus to Jesus' proclamation of the nearness of the kingdom, coupled with his battle against demons.

88. I find it hard to follow those interpreters who regard Jesus' exorcisms as "a serious challenge to the prevailing norms and values" (thus Freyne, *Jesus*, 148) or even intended to heal "the almost split-personality position of a colonial people" (Crossan, *Revolutionary Biography*, 91). Fredriksen, "What You See," 84, wryly comments: "Illness is really about ostracism, and demonic possession about colonial oppression. Evidently the only demons this Jesus can exorcize are our own." Freyne states quite rightly that by ridding the possessed of the demon, "Jesus was restoring them again to the social world from which they had been excluded," but continues that "in doing so he was calling into question the norms by which they were deemed to be deviant in the first place." Yet it would seem that in undertaking the exorcism Jesus rather accepted the norm: the person in question *was* deviant and had to be freed from his or her illness.

89. Twelftree, *Jesus the Exorcist*; cf. Theissen and Merz, *Historical Jesus*, 279.

90. E. P. Sanders, *Figure*, 170.

91. If this event is to be sudden and a surprise, the sequence of signs in Mark 13 can hardly be authentic.

92. These verses from Q recall Paul's vision of the rapture in 1 Thessalonians 4 that is paralleled by Mark 13:27, the gathering of the elect by angels.

93. Even E. P. Sanders (*Figure*, 171) acknowledges that in

Mark 9:47 and 10:17-27 the kingdom of God is "in heaven: it is a transcendent realm" into which people "will individually enter at death or at the great judgement." Sanders fails to show how this idea can be combined with the expectation that the kingdom will come to earth in the imminent future.

94. Cf. Schlosser, "Vollendung," 72–73.

95. Cf. ibid., 75–78.

96. Allison, *Jesus*, 155.

97. Apart from Cerinthus, whose connection with Jewish Christianity is doubtful, the only explicit reference to millenarian expectation of Jewish Christians in patristic sources is a late and untrustworthy statement in Jerome (*Comm. Jer.* 66.20). Eusebius (*Hist. eccl.* 3.20.4) has preserved a report of Hegesippus concerning a statement made by the grandsons of Jude, brother of Jesus, before the emperor Domitian. This seems, on the face of it, to testify to a fully transcendent kingdom: it was to be "neither of the world nor earthly, but heavenly and angelic, and it would be at the end of the world when he (Christ) would come in glory to judge the living and the dead to reward every man according to his deeds." Yet this confession tells us only that the two brothers denied any sort of *political* kingdom. The kingdom of Christ was presently located in heaven; it would be realized in the parousia at the end of the world. What exactly that would imply is not stated. Cf. Justin's analogous explanation in *1 Apol.* 11 that the kingdom is "with God" and not human; the *Dialogue* reveals that Justin nevertheless had an earthly kingdom in mind.

98. See above, p. 67.

99. Translation in F. S. Jones, *Source*, 95–96. The Latin version differs slightly in wording but not in content.

100. This designation notwithstanding, an earthly kingdom is clearly envisaged. The Syriac text runs: "One who is not baptized not only is rejected from the kingdom of heaven but also is in danger at the resurrection of the dead and . . . will fall short of eternal life." The Latin differs only in not mentioning "eternal life" here. See F. S. Jones, *Source*, 89.

101. Revelation 17:8 and 11 allude to the lore about the emperor Nero, whom many expected still to return either from the dead or from hiding in the East with the Parthians; cf. above, p. 49.

102. "Christ is in all likelihood thought to be personally present on earth" (Bousset, *Offenbarung*, 503).

103. This location is implied in Rev. 20:7-8: when the millennium is finally over, the nations will come "from

344

the four corners of the earth" and "march up over the broad earth and surround the camp of the saints and *the beloved city.*" An earthly reign is denied by some interpreters, who find the author simply putting forward a symbolical description of the martyrs' victory and reward, underlining "God's determination to correct the abuses that Christians have experienced at the hands of Satan" (Rome); thus Thielman, *Theology*, 645. There is indeed a difficulty in that, for example, in 11:15-19 the consummation is visualized as one movement, not two. Nevertheless, Rev. 20 is emphatic about *two* resurrections (vv. 5-6), so that atemporal, purely symbolical interpretations must be rejected. An earthly reign is promised already in 5:10 ("they will reign on earth"; cf. 2:26-27).

104. Over other nations? According to one reading, all nonbelievers have been destroyed in Rev. 19:11-21, but such a difficulty is by no means singular in Revelation (for example, where do the nations of 21:24 come from after 20:12-15? Or where is the judgment in 20:12 held after 20:11?). Other nations are in any case a more plausible object of reigning than is "the creation" (plants and animals). And 19:11-21 may not presuppose more than the destruction of the armies of the beast and the kings of the earth. The problem of "determining where the nations come from" is not grave enough to rule out a literal interpretation of the millennium (contra Marshall, *Theology*, 558–59), nor can a temporary kingdom of Christ be deemed simply as "utterly pointless" (ibid.), since there clearly was a tendency in eschatological thought toward a two-step fulfillment; I agree with, for example, Zeller, "Konsolidierung," 165.

105. Contrast the vivid depiction of the conflagration in 2 Pet. 3:10-14.

106. The seer follows an older tradition about a rebuilt Jerusalem that starts from Ezek. 40–48 and Deutero-Isaiah (Isa. 54:11-12; 60); cf. Tob. 13:16-20; *Sib. Or.* 5.247-56, 420-34.

107. The apocalypse in Mark 13 lists as signs: wars, court processes against Christians, splits of families, hatred against everybody, the "desolating sacrifice," the flight of the faithful to the mountains, pseudomessiahs and pseudoprophets. All of these probably hang together with experiences connected with the war against Rome.

108. Revelation draws on Ezekiel and Daniel, combining the earthly signs with "events" in heaven, thus producing a thoroughly mythical scenario.

109. For a discussion of the problem and the alternatives, see, for example, Best, *Thessalonians*, 294–302 (who hesitantly opts for "the hostile occupying power").

110. Myllykoski, "Cerinthus," argues persuasively that the references to chiliasm (and to possessionist Christology) are likely to be the trustworthy elements in the contradictory patristic accounts of Cerinthus's teaching, whereas the gnostic ideas ascribed to him are suspect. Nor is there reliable evidence to connect him with those Jewish Christians who followed Jewish halakah.

111. It has been customary to regard the Montanists as millenarians as well, but recent scholarship has shown that the basis for this assumption is rather thin. For discussion see Marjanen, "Montanism," 203–6. Still, "it cannot be ruled out that some early Montanist teachers included chiliastic emphases in their proclamation" (ibid., 206).

112. Nepos's millenarian interpretation of Revelation was refuted after his death by Dionysius of Alexandria in discussions with his adherents in the mid-third century. Millenarianism had a long tradition in Egypt already before Nepos; see G. Maier, *Johannesoffenbarung*, 87–96, 104.

113. The banquet of Matt. 8:11 is located in the millennium by Irenaeus, *Haer.* 5.30.4.

114. Justin, *Dial.* 81.2, cites Isa. 65:23, a statement on offspring that he seems to understand literally; cf. Nepos (Eusebius, *Hist. eccl.* 7.24); Lactantius.

115. See pp. 291–92.

116. Cf. Justin, *Dial.* 119.5; 139.4-5: the promise about the land, given to Abraham, is fulfilled in the generation of the millennium. The same is true of the promises given to the followers of Jesus who left everything (Matt. 19:29); see Irenaeus, *Haer.* 5.33.2.

117. "For God is rich in all things, and all things are his. It is fitting, therefore, that the creation itself, being restored to its primeval condition, should without qualification be under the dominion of the righteous" (*Haer.* 5.32.1).

118. Daley, "Patristische Eschatologie," 116–17 (the authenticity of the work is not quite certain, however).

119. In *Dial.* 81 the millennium is regarded merely as a prelude to the last judgment (after it, "the general, that is, eternal, resurrection for all will take place"); but in ch. 113 the possession of the holy land by the saints "after the holy resurrection" is regarded as of eternal duration (Daley, "Patristische Eschatologie," 99–100). A curious alternative is given by Lactantius (see Daley,

ibid., 140): rather than letting the two modes of existence follow each other, he locates both of them simultaneously in the millennium. Those believers who are alive at the parousia will continue their earthly life in the millennium, whereas those then resurrected will live in a new mode of existence in the same millennium (*Inst.* 7.24). No less curiously, Irenaeus (*Haer.* 5.36.2; Daley, ibid., 109) thinks that there are three levels of places in the final reign of the Father for the saved, depending on their "dignity": the most worthy dwell in heaven, others in paradise (between heaven and earth?), while those less worthy live in the heavenly city that has descended onto earth; still, all groups will see God all the time.

120. af Hällström, *Fides*, 89.

121. Cf. Irenaeus, *Haer.* 5.28.3.

122. The antichrist's setting himself in the temple of Jerusalem (*Haer.* 5.25.2) implies that the temple must first have been rebuilt.

123. This interpretation of 1 Thess. 4, once expressed by E. P. Sanders (*Jesus and Judaism*, 230), still seems persuasive to me, though Sanders himself gave it up later. See Räisänen, "Did Paul Expect?"

124. Cf. the allusions to "reigning" in 1 Cor. 4:8; Rom. 5:17.

125. Nor does he say (as Revelation does) that the heavenly Jerusalem will come down; it is "above" (Gal. 4:26).

126. It is not the point of the passage to provide eschatological teaching. Paul is rather recommending himself to the Corinthians by describing his confidence amid adversities; cf. Lindgård, *Line of Thought*. Yet what he thereby in passing discloses of his postmortem hopes is all the more revealing. On this passage see further, p. 128.

127. It is customary today to detect references to the parousia throughout the passage. With Walter, "Hellenistische Eschatologie"; and Haufe, "Individuelle Eschatologie," I think that those older scholars who interpreted the passage in a more Platonic vein were better on target.

128. "We wish not to be unclothed but to be further clothed, so that what is mortal may be swallowed up by life" (v. 4b). The allusion is oblique at best and could only be detected by readers familiar with the language of 1 Cor. 15.

129. "We look not at what can be seen but at what cannot be seen; for what can be seen is temporary, but what cannot be seen is eternal."

130. Some interpreters read into the text the notion of an interim state for souls, but v. 8 hardly gives the impression that the being-with-the-Lord could be a temporary phase.

131. It would seem that, according to v. 10, the individual Christian will on her or his death appear before the judgment seat of Christ; a private act seems envisaged. Having stood the test, he or she will have reached the state of being "away from the body and at home with the Lord" (v. 8).

132. This is the view of, for example, Knight, *Origins*, 209–15; for earlier representatives of it see Räisänen, "Did Paul Expect?" 2–6.

133. Cf. Lindgård, *Line of Thought*, 2, 222–25. He concludes from his analysis of 2 Cor. 4–5 that "Paul never ended up with a coherent concept on the relation between death and parousia." This text "does not support the view that Paul has changed or at least modified his eschatology." Instead, "the distinct pieces in the 'puzzle' were there all the time . . . in one situation Paul chose one piece, in another situation, another piece" (2).

134. Cf. Chester, "Expectations," 68. A good account of Paul's spiritualized eschatology is given by Fredriksen, *From Jesus to Christ*, 170–76. Although Paul, in a Jewish way, sees God definitively intervening in history, Paul does not praise "the future Jerusalem or the eschatological Temple. Images of earthly fecundity or social harmony do not figure in his presentation. . . . His vision of the End is no drama of national liberation writ large." Paul "denationalizes" both Jewish restoration theology and Christ. For when Christ at the parousia executes "his military duties in the final battle against evil, exactly as the Davidic messiah would. . . . he destroys cosmic foes, 'every rule and every authority and power,' not the apocalyptic Babylon (1 Cor. 15:24). . . . Paul radically redefines the concept of redemption as he does the concepts of Kingdom and Christ: through the originally political vocabulary of liberation, he praises a reality that is utterly spiritual" (Fredriksen, *From Jesus to Christ*, 171–73). All this has to be clearly stated against the fashionable trend that, informed by liberation theology, sees Paul (openly or covertly) fighting the Roman Empire. This Paul seems to me a product of wishful thinking. It is another matter that responsible modern theology may subject Paul's approach to a critical evaluation.

135. Cf. J. Becker, *Paul*, 448: Paul does *not* raise the question of compensational justice ("ausgleichende Gerechtigkeit") at the close of world history; that is not for him the crowning climax of history.

346

136. Second Thessalonians cannot be from his hand.

137. Cf. Mark 4:14, 20; the emphasis is on mission. Perhaps 4:11 too is to be seen in this light. The seed growing secretly in 4:26-29 could refer to the unassuming presence of the kingdom in the church, but the image of harvest refers to the final emergence of the kingdom in the eschatological judgment. Mark 14:25 is a piece of tradition that seems out of place in this Gospel. As Mark apparently does not envisage an earthly consummation, the verse must belong to very old tradition, quite possibly reflecting the voice of Jesus himself.

138. The programmatic verse "the kingdom of God is at hand" (1:15) can be interpreted in either way.

139. Kloppenborg, *Formation*, 165.

140. Unlike 1 Thess. 4, Mark is not concerned about the destiny of dead believers. Their resurrection is not mentioned, but elsewhere in the Gospel resurrection is presupposed. Precisely how parousia, resurrection, and (eternal) life relate to one another we are not told. *Martyrdom of Polycarp* 22.3 seems to allude to Mark 13:27 in expressing the hope of the author "that the Lord Jesus Christ may gather (*synagein*) me with his elect into his heavenly kingdom."

141. Equally strange is the explanation of N. T. Wright, *Jesus*, 516: the reference is, he claims, to the destruction of the temple.

142. See Myllykoski, "Social History."

143. Kloppenborg, *Formation*, 165–66.

144. The idea of the righteous shining like the sun after they have been gathered from the earth recalls *T. Mos.* 10.9, where the revelation of the kingdom of God involves that God raises the people to the heaven of the stars, the place of his habitation.

145. Matthew 6:10b ("Your will be done, on earth as it is in heaven") should hardly be counted here, however, for the verse probably refers to present human behavior (cf. 6:33).

146. In the great judgment scene in Matt. 25:31-46, the language of which recalls 19:28, the Son of Man is the only judge.

147. Cf. also Luke 20:38: all people (now) live (like the patriarchs) for God.

148. See the discussion in Lehtipuu, *Afterlife Imagery*, 256–64.

149. *Pace* Tannehill, *Narrative Unity*; see Räisänen, "Redemption."

150. On the speeches of Acts, in particular Acts 2:39-40; 3:20-21; 13:32-33; 26:6-7 (passages appealed to by Tannehill), see Räisänen, "Redemption," 67–71.

151. Still, even Luke does speak of eating and drinking with Jesus at his table in his kingdom: Luke 22:29-30.

152. Rowland, *Origins*, 295.

153. According to one theory, this group of believers reinterpreted traditional eschatology in accordance with an Alexandrian Jewish wisdom theology that had been introduced to Corinth by the prominent preacher Apollos. See, for example, Sellin, "Hauptprobleme," 3010–11, 3021–22.

154. It should be noted, however, that the author of 2 Timothy himself, though holding fast to the expectation of the parousia (4:1, 8), clearly expects the final salvation to take place in God's *heavenly* kingdom (4:18).

155. See Oberlinner, *2 Timotheusbrief*, 97–98; and, even more emphatically, Weiser, *2 Timotheus*, 195, 332–33. If the names are names of real persons, they must have been contemporaries of Paul, not of the author of the Pastorals (who could not have disclosed the pseudepigraphic character of his work in this way).

156. Cf. Wedderburn, *History*, 172–73: "Their view shows an uncomfortable similarity to the readiness of the authors of Colossians and Ephesians to speak of Christians as already raised with Christ and, in the case of Ephesians, as already in the heavenly regions."

157. The coming wrath of God is still there: Col. 3:6.

158. Ephesians 2:7 still refers to the "ages to come" so that the present bliss does not mean salvation in its fullness. Ephesians 4:30 mentions "the [coming] day of redemption," and 5:5 looks forward to a future kingdom of Christ.

159. Lindemann, *Aufhebung*, 239.

160. Rowland, *Origins*, 295. Rowland also claims that "such an outlook contrasts with the bulk of New Testament eschatology," but this is clearly not the case; large parts of the New Testament share the hope of a heavenly, rather than earthly, consummation.

161. For Walter, Hebrews is "the most important witness to an explicitly Hellenistic eschatology in the New Testament" ("Hellenistische Eschatologie," 351–55).

162. In a singular sentence (Heb. 6:2), "resurrection of the dead" and "eternal judgment" are mentioned—as part of the elementary teaching from which the author wants to proceed "toward perfection."

163. Such references (especially John 5:28-29; 6:39-40, 44, 54; 12:48b) are often ascribed to a late redactional layer. Frey, *Johanneische Eschatologie*, 1:69–71, argues against such a procedure.

164. Rowland, *Origins*, 255 (his emphasis).

165. The same verb is used in Q 17:34-35; cf. p. 103.

166. Cf. also John 16:16-22.

167. The apocalyptic notion of the "Son of Man" is emptied from connotations with the parousia and reinterpreted: Jesus qua Son of Man is a figure who ascends to heaven—to the place from which he has previously descended (John 3:13; 6:62; cf. 1:51: the Son of Man acts as the link by which heaven and earth are connected).

168. The only content given to eternal life is that the believers will *know the only true God and Jesus Christ whom he has sent*" (John 17:3).

169. Aune, *Cultic Setting*, 194.

170. Some scholars assume a conflict between the communities behind the two Gospels. For a critique of this assumption see Dunderberg, *Beloved Disciple*.

171. This statement amounts to a major obstacle to the thesis that, according to *Thomas*, salvation is acquired through heavenly journeys (prior to death) during which the Thomasine Christian experiences a mystical vision of God (thus DeConick, *Voices*); see Dunderberg, *Beloved Disciple*, 36 (and his whole discussion, 33–40).

172. Cf. Luke 17:21; *Gos. Mary* 8.15-21 ("the Son of Man is within you").

173. The expression "outside you" is problematic. It has been taken to mean that the crucial insight is available even to those outside the narrow circle of Jesus' close associates (cf. Fieger, *Thomasevangelium*, 27) or that it "leads to a new understanding of the mundane world" (Valantasis, *Gospel of Thomas*, 59).

174. In what is known as the "Unknown Berlin Gospel" (Papyrus Berolinensis 22220, published in 2000), Jesus introduces his disciples even before his death into higher mysteries. The apostles experience together with him a journey to heaven, reaching even the hall with God's throne.

175. Uro, "Encratite Gospel?" 155. Cf. *Gos. Thom.* 91 against those who try to discover signs of the end. The "scoffers" attacked in 2 Peter may have held a similar view.

176. Except once, in *Gos. Thom.* 113, a saying that *refutes* a visible coming.

177. Uro, "Neither Here Nor There," 18–19.

178. Uro, "Encratite Gospel?" 156. Cf. the future references, for example, in the following sayings (referred to, along with some other logia, by Uro, "Encratite Gospel?" 155 n. 57): *Gos. Thom.* 11: "When you come to dwell in the light, what will you do?"; in the context, the disappearance of the cosmos is envisaged; *Gos. Thom.* 18: the one who stands at the beginning will know the end and will not taste death; *Gos. Thom.* 27: only if one has the right attitude will one "find the kingdom" or "see the Father"; *Gos. Thom.* 75: "Many are standing at the door, but it is the solitary who will enter the bridal chamber." Cf. also sayings 4, 23, 44, 57, 60, 70, 79, and 106.

179. Marjanen, "Gnostic Gospel?" 129–30.

180. On gnostic eschatology see, for example, Peel, "Gnostic Eschatology"; Rudolph, *Gnosis*, 184–219.

181. Irenaeus, *Haer.* 1.23.5.

182. Dunderberg, *Beloved Disciple*, 126 n. 22.

183. Presented as a word of "the Apostle"; cf. Rom. 8:17; Eph. 2:5-6.

184. Peel, "Treatise," 53.

185. This tractate is late (and essentially non-Christian), perhaps from the fourth century C.E. (Bethge, "On the Origin," 170), but it may be based on earlier, second-century material (M. Meyer, "On the Origin," 202). The conflagration is already mentioned in Irenaeus's description of the Valentinian system (*Haer.* 1.7.1) and suggested in his account of the teaching of Marcus the "magician" (1.14.1; cf. Förster, *Marcus*, 201–6, 394–95).

186. Cf. MacRae, "Apocalyptic Eschatology," 323.

187. See the list in Peel, "Gnostic Eschatology," 156–58.

188. Daley, "Patristische Eschatologie," 121. In his popular writings Clement can refer to items of more traditional expectation, though without putting any special emphasis on them.

189. Daley, ibid., 123.

190. Daley, "Apocalypticism," 16.

191. Royalty, "Dwelling on Visions," 353–56, argues that already Colossians reveals a conflict between realized and futurist eschatology, represented by the deutero-Pauline author and the circle of John the seer, respectively. The "triumphal militarism" of Col. 2:15 could well be a deliberate response to such violent visions as we find in Revelation. According to Colossians, God *has* "disarmed the rulers and authorities"; he has, through Christ, already defeated all rulers and powers, earthly or heavenly. Revelation, by contrast, describes nothing but future battles in which the powers have yet to be defeated.

192. Käsemann, "Apologia," 194, points out, with characteristic relentlessness, that the author's collection of "disconnected" arguments is "not without internal tensions nor without tensions in regard to the epistle as a whole" and "betrays embarrassment"; the epistle thus

348

tacitly admits "that the doctrine of the Last Things is already landing the Church in difficulties, and her apologia is in fact the demonstration of a logical absurdity."

193. Gaius (c. 200 C.E.) attacked the view that the kingdom of Christ is "earthly."

194. On Augustine's eschatology, see Daley, "Patristische Eschatologie," 193–207.

195. To be sure, Augustine preserved a surprising amount of realistic eschatology in his system.

196. Cohn, *Pursuit*.

197. McGinn, "Apocalypticism and Church Reform."

198. The tradition of millenarianism even influenced the thought of the intellectuals of the French Enlightenment, although they avoided explicitly using it. See Baumgartner, *Longing for the End*, 133.

199. Zimdars-Schwarz and Zimdars-Schwarz, "Apocalypticism," 284.

200. Cf. Kovacs and Rowland, *Revelation*, 247–50 and passim.

201. Collins, McGinn, and Stein, "General Introduction," x.

202. "With the crusades, violence became a common part of millennialism" (Baumgartner, *Longing for the End*, 62). An extreme example of millennial violence is provided by the Münster Anabaptists (ibid., 95). Again, "the notorious St. Bartholomew's Massacre of August 1572 in Paris was so bloody . . . in part because Parisian Catholics believed that they were acting to eliminate Antichrist's hordes and thereby would bring about the endtime" (ibid., 97). Something amazingly similar took place in the French Revolution, since the same goal of creating a new people motivated the behavior of the Jacobins. "Lacking a belief in God who will begin the Millennium in his own good time, the Jacobins had to take a more direct role than did most millenialists" (ibid., 138).

203. Thomas Müntzer, who was convinced that the saints had to destroy the godless in order to prepare the world for the kingdom, signed his letters, "with the sword of Gideon."

204. Baumgartner, *Longing for the End*, 201–2, points out that most Bolsheviks had a Christian or Jewish upbringing, Stalin being a former seminary student. They "were familiar with biblical apocalyptic, and their rhetoric and expectations drew heavily on that literature. . . . The rhetoric of the Soviet state pronounced that its citizens were the new people living in the new age." On the other hand, Christians persecuted by the Soviet regime drew comfort from an interpretation

of their situation in apocalyptic terms, hoping for an imminent turn (Clay, "Apocalypticism," 314–15).

205. According to Marx, "history is predetermined to move through a series of events until a great catastrophe signals the time to return to a golden age. There will follow a period of transformation until the endtime is reached, at which point history ends" (Baumgartner, *Longing for the End*, 148).

206. Consider the American Civil War. "In the North, many Protestant leaders argued that the struggle to preserve the Union was a holy war fraught with millennial significance. . . . The war was purging the nation of its sin, providing a moral rebirth through a baptism of blood, and preparing the way for America to resume a grand millennial mission. . . . No less than their northern counterparts, southern clergy viewed the Confederate cause as sacred. . . . Some preachers popular with the troops asserted that God might use the Confederacy to inaugurate the kingdom of God on earth" (Moorhead, "Apocalypticism," 85–86). See further Räisänen, "Revelation," summarizing the work of Tuveson and Jewett.

207. Or, ultimately, even to the notion of the primordial battle against the chaos monster.

208. Tuveson, *Redeemer Nation*, 50–51.

209. Jewett and Lawrence, *Captain America*, 54. In his speeches, President George W. Bush regularly invoked divine guidance in setting aside the United States as the power to wage and win the decisive war. "The road of Providence is uneven and unpredictable," he concluded a speech in February 2005, "yet we know where it leads: It leads to freedom." See H. O. Maier, "President's Revelation."

210. According to Baumgartner, *Longing for the End*, 208ff., much of the Nazi appeal may have been due to the fact that Hitler and others succeeded "in framing their ideas in millennial rhetoric and apocalyptic symbolism." Germany becoming the Third Reich meant that one was entering the millennial age.

211. Ibid., 211.

212. D. Brown, *Discipleship*, 103–4.

213. Moltmann, *God in Creation*, 170. D. Brown, *Discipleship*, 104, comments that Moltmann in effect makes "heaven exclusively the destiny of this world rather than an alternative to it."

214. Rubenstein, *After Auschwitz*.

215. A survey among leading American rabbis and theologians in 1996 revealed that many influential Jewish thinkers in United States today do not share a tradi-

tional faith in a personal God who still guides humanity's and individual humans' destinies.

216. "To see any purpose in the death camps, the traditional believer is forced to regard the most demonic, antihuman explosion in all history as a meaningful expression of God's purposes. That is simply too obscene for me to accept" (Rubenstein, "Answer," 200; cf. idem, *After Auschwitz*, 171). Rubenstein ("Answer," 201) goes on to state that a theistic God is not necessary for Jewish religious life (while the Torah is).

217. Not for all, though! One can only wonder at the incredible popularity of "prophecy belief" literature, especially in the United States, which produces ever new mosaics of biblical predictions about events of our time and of the near future. See, for example, the devastating analysis of Boyer, *Time*.

218. Kehl, *Eschatologie*, 245.

219. Cf. W. C. Smith's comment on the view of his Hindu friend, quoted at the beginning of this chapter (*Scripture*, 246 n. 15): "In the early years of the twentieth century, most Western intellectuals and Western religious persons both would have found such a stance remote, even pitiable; at the end of the century, it may seem to many to make much more sense."

220. Cf., for example, the reflections of Walter, "Hellenistische Eschatologie," 355–56. He sides with pluriformity: Christians should not reject either alternative (earthly or spiritualized) to the advantage of the other. But neither should they try to construct an overall compromise that seeks to accommodate the contradictory views within a single larger framework, to "combine in one 'system' what is structurally incompatible." Precisely the plurality of eschatological language could "stimulate to ever new contemporizations."

5. After Death:
The Destiny of the Individual

1. Whether ancient Israelites practiced actual ancestor worship is debated; see, e.g., Lewis, "How Far?"

2. McDannell and Lang, *Heaven*, 10–11.

3. Cf., for example, Ps. 88:6-7, 11; Job 10:21-22; Sir. 17:27-28.

4. Brandon, *Judgment*, 58.

5. See the thorough discussion in Lehtipuu, *Afterlife Imagery*.

6. These included the three mythical criminals (Tityus, Tantalus, and Sisyphus) in Hades, the Titans in Tartarus (another place of punishment, a terrible prison), and some heroes and favorites of the Gods in Elysium. There may have been more of this dualism in popular notions. On the other hand, grave inscriptions seem to indicate that, for a great number of people in the Greco-Roman world, death was the end of everything.

7. The Homeric hymn to Demeter already distinguishes between the initiates (in Eleusis) and the noninitiated; partaking of the mysteries guarantees one a better lot in the beyond.

8. Cf. *Gorg.* 525b-526b; *Phaed.* 113d-114c; *Resp.* 614b-621b. However, the philosopher hardly meant his (inconsistent) imagery to be taken literally; actually his Socrates remains uncertain as regards postmortem life. Tartarus is portrayed in the same vein by Plutarch; the depiction was not meant literally, but as an "improving myth," yet obviously many readers took it seriously. Quite likely "the philosophers utilized well-known popular images to color their literary myths" (Lehtipuu, *Afterlife Imagery*, 110).

9. Apparently normal mortals had to repeat this cycle ten times before they could reach the final bliss with the Gods, whereas three times were sufficient for the (Orphic) pious. A third group, the incurable sinners, were permanently enclosed in Tartarus as warning examples.

10. Lehtipuu, *Afterlife Imagery*, 97. She concludes that "the belief in individual rewards and/or punishments was not restricted only to esoteric mystery cults or obscure philosophical speculations but was more common than often admitted in scholarly works" (ibid., 117). Christian apologetes from Justin on (*1 Apol.* 8) argued that Plato's references to the postmortem judgment were a preparation for Christian beliefs. In a sense they were right.

11. Lehtipuu, *Afterlife Imagery*, 94–96, 112–13. Plutarch (*Suav. viv.* 1105a-b) also claims that not very many people in his time fear the fabulous doctrines "of mothers and nurses." Those who do are those who believe that mystical rituals offer a remedy for the terrors of the afterlife. Plutarch thinks that fear of such terrors benefits the wicked, for they are thus "shocked into a state of greater honesty and restraint" (1104b). Lucian (*Luct.* 2), however, gives the impression that fear of punishments was more widespread among the masses.

350

12. Brandon, *Judgment*, 59–60.

13. For an analysis of the section, see Lehtipuu, *Afterlife Imagery*, 130–35.

14. The idea of a forensic judgment can be traced back to the Egyptian notion of weighing the souls of the dead; in Egypt, for the first time, a happy afterlife seems to have been connected with the moral quality of the person's earthly life; see Brandon, *Judgment*, 41, 69. The acceptance and development of this notion in Israel may have been aided by the older idea that Yahweh was the judge of inner hearts.

15. For punishments that involve fire, see, for example, *Sib. Or.* 4.184-86; *4 Ezra* 7.36-38; *L.A.B.* 23.6; *4 Macc.* 9:9. For *Ge Hinnom* as a place for child sacrifices see, for example, 2 Kgs. 23:1; 2 Chr. 28:3; 33:6; Jer. 7:31; 19:2-5.

16. Lehtipuu, *Afterlife Imagery*, 138.

17. Ibid., 141.

18. 2 Macc. 7:14 denies "resurrection to life" to the tyrant; 4 Macc. 10:15 threatens him with "eternal destruction" (*olethros*). *Psalms of Solomon* 3.11-12 extends this fate to "sinners" in general: "The destruction (*apoleia*) of the sinner is forever, and he will not be remembered when [God] looks after the righteous. This is the share of sinners forever, but those who fear the Lord shall rise up to eternal life."

19. For example, *T. Zeb.* 10.2: "the Lord shall bring down fire on the impious and will destroy them to all generations"; *L.A.B* 16.3; 1QpHab 13; CD 2.5-7.

20. "Day" remains a key word in eschatological texts (the day of wrath, of tribulation, of the judgment, of the Lord, and so on).

21. The pious rabbi wept, knowing that two ways would be before him, one to paradise, the other to Gehenna, and he did not know which way he would be led.

22. It is not clear (partly because the last pages of the text are missing) whether the prayer is heard, but God's mercy is emphasized in several places (for example, *Apoc. Zeph.* 2.9; 7.8; 11.2).

23. It is said that "the wise" will shine like the stars of heaven. Yet it is hard to see that this should necessarily mean that the wise have here become "companions of the host of heaven," in which case resurrection would even here be "a resurrection of the spirit from Sheol," as it seems to be in the *Epistle of Enoch* rather than a physical one; thus, for example, Collins, "Afterlife," 126; but see above, p. 83.

24. Collins, "Afterlife," 131.

25. The schools of Hillel and Shammai are said to have debated the form of resurrection, the Shammaites arguing that the resurrected body would be exactly the same as the present one, the Hillelites holding that it would be differently formed.

26. Collins, "Afterlife," 124. A similar notion is also found in *Jub.* 23.26-31. N. T. Wright assumes the idea of an intermediate state at least in *1 En.* 104 (*Resurrection*, 156–57).

27. Riley, *Resurrection*, 28.

28. Whether one can speak of Orphic influence, as is commonly done, is debated.

29. Riley, *Resurrection*, 59 n. 147.

30. Martin, *Corinthian Body*, 115.

31. Clytemnestra could show the wounds in her heart; Eurydice still limped; see Riley, *Resurrection*, 48–51.

32. One could even claim that bodily resurrection would mean chastisement for Philo; see Puech, *Croyance*, 165.

33. Riley, *Resurrection*, 42–43 n. 106, with reference to *Cher.* 115.

34. Nickelsburg, "Judgment," 151.

35. Cf. Theissen, *Erleben*, 172–76, on the "explosion of anxiety" in early Christianity as the backdrop for the joy of the "glad tidings."

36. See Räisänen, "Jesus and Hell."

37. The parallels to this section include Matt. 5:29-30, a string of logia apparently taken from another source so that the criterion of double attestation applies. The emphatic threefold threatening of the disciples with hell is all the more striking, as Mark lacks a judgment scene in his depiction of the parousia (Mark 13) and does not mention judgment even in his report on the proclamation of John the Baptist (Mark 1:4-8). The appeals to hellfire go against the author's tendency, which strengthens the case for authenticity.

38. Wolter, "'Gericht' und 'Heil,'" 384. Cf. also Q 12:4-5.

39. The word *telos* in v. 24 cannot here mean "the rest." It refers to "the end" that will take place after the parousia.

40. 1 Cor. 15:18 states that if Christ had not been resurrected, all the dead would perish (*apolonto*), probably being annihilated. The implication is that this is the destiny of those who do not belong to Christ. In this long chapter that is all about resurrection, Paul does not say a word about the resurrection of non-Christians; the impression is that they will remain dead.

41. Rom. 1:32; 2:3, 16; 3:19.

42. See the thorough discussion in Bernstein, *Hell*, 207–24.

43. Some would rather infer from this that Paul is after all inclined toward the idea of *apokatastasis*. By contrast, the pseudonymous 2 Thessalonians (1:7-9) suggests an eternal punishment: Jesus is revealed from heaven "in flaming fire," inflicting on the disobedient the "punishment of eternal destruction" (*olethros*), which means that they are "separated from the presence of the Lord and from the glory of his might."

44. For example, 1 Thess. 5:1-11: the day of the Lord is the moment of the great test, and Paul passionately hopes that his congregations will be found blameless.

45. Phil. 3:18-19: many (Christians!) live as enemies of the cross of Christ; "their end is destruction."

46. Still other Lukan passages are in tension with the notion of a resurrection altogether.

47. In his very long letter, Clement never once refers to the eternal fire or any other traditional characteristics of hell, although his whole writing has a serious warning tone. If taken at face value, his scriptural quotations (*1 Clem.* 14.4-5; 22.6) might suggest that he thought of the extinction of sinners, but all references to a future judgment are vague at best. Eschatological punishment is not a central conviction of Clement, who bases his exhortation on a theology of creation.

48. Cf. Herm. *Vis.* 3.7.2; *Sim.* 6.2.4; 9.18.2; 9.19.1; 9.20.4; 9.23.4.

49. Bernstein, *Hell*, 225, 227.

50. For a rebuttal of the numerous attempts of modern interpreters (including many evangelical interpreters, for example, Powys, *Hell*) to explain away the notion of eternal torment, see Räisänen, "Jesus and Hell." New Testament theologies in particular tend to be silent on hell (cf. Räisänen, "Matthäus und die Hölle," 107–11); an exception is the evangelical work of Guthrie, *Theology*, 887–92.

51. Acts 17:31 states that a day is set when Christ will judge the whole world in justice (cf. 24:15). John 5:28-29 refers to a day when all those who are in graves will rise, either to life or to judgment, in stark contrast to the general thrust of the eschatology of this Gospel.

52. The motif of a final day of judgment is not prominent in Mark, who mentions instead the gathering of the elect at the parousia. In Q, both the notion of "rapture" (one person will be "taken" and the other "left": Q 17:34-35) and the notion of a general judgment (Q 10:13-15; 11:31-32) are found.

53. Matt. 13:42, 50; 22:13; 24:51; 25:30.

54. Matthew's view is reminiscent of the rigorism of *4 Ezra* (there are only a few righteous people).

55. It is generally claimed that Luke does not intend to provide information of the postmortem world, but Lehtipuu, *Afterlife Imagery*, shows that there is no reason to deny that this was one of his aims in telling this story.

56. The case is argued by Lehtipuu, *Afterlife Imagery*, 265–75.

57. Hell is here envisaged in accordance with the Acherusian fiery lake known from the accounts of Plato and Plutarch.

58. The author states that if we "willfully persist in sin," what remains is "a fearful prospect of judgment, and a fury of fire that will consume the adversaries. Anyone who has violated the law of Moses dies without mercy. . . . How much worse punishment . . . will be deserved by those who have spurned the Son of God. . . . It is a fearful thing to fall into the hands of the living God" (Heb. 10:26-31). Cf. 12:18-29.

59. See further, for example, *Diogn.* 10.7; *2 Clem.* 17.5, 7; *Thom. Cont.* 142-43; *Gos. Phil.* 66.30—67.1.

60. Likewise *1 Apol.* 17.4; 21.6; *2 Apol.* 1.2; 2.2; 7.5; 44.5; 60.8; *Dial.* 35.8; 45.4; 47.4; 117.5; 120.5 (quoting Matt. 8:12). Cf. the "realms of fire" in Athenagoras, *Leg.* 31.

61. The *Apocalypse of Peter* was probably written in Egypt. Cruel torture in hell was, of old, a conspicuous feature of Egyptian notions of afterlife, but it was apparently not conceived of as everlasting; eventually evil was to be annihilated.

62. In *2 Apoc. Jas.* 62-63, James, the brother of Jesus, who is just about to be martyred, is quite worried about the consequences of his sin. Although this man, called "righteous" six times in the work, considers himself to be "saved from this dead hope" and "filled with God's grace," he is still afraid of meeting "a judge who is severe with sin." "This is not the prayer of a man who is confident and assured of resting soon with the Father" (Desjardins, *Sin*, 113).

63. Lane Fox, *Pagans*, 327, observes that "terrors in the next world were not unfamiliar to pagans, but Christians insisted on their certainty and imminent realization." There was "an ample place . . . for plain fear in Christian conversions, and Christian authors did not neglect it: their martyrs' words on hell and the coming judgment were believed to be an advertisement every bit as effective as their example at the stake. . . . Acquaintance with the Apocalypse of 'Peter' would make anyone think twice before leaving the Church. If fears for Eternity brought converts to the faith, one

suspects that they did even more to keep existing converts in it" (326–27).

64. Cf. *1 En.* 27.3-4.

65. Cf. *4 Ezra's* moving questioning, for example, 7.132-39; 8.4-18; 7.102-5; 8.19-36, 42-45.

66. Cf. the ideas of Plutarch, see above, p. 115. *Sibylline Oracles* 2.330-38 adds to the depiction of hell and heaven an oracle to the effect that intercession by saints in heaven can reverse the fate of some of the damned. This section could be part of the Jewish original or an interpolation by a Christian editor. One group of manuscripts contains a gloss in which this doctrine is ascribed to Origen (and condemned).

67. Daley, "Patristische Eschatologie," 131–34.

68. Brandon, *Judgment*, 133.

69. Even many evangelical theologians are disturbed by traditional notions of hell and can use surprisingly harsh language about this: "Unending torment speaks to me of sadism, not justice" (Wenham, *Facing Hell*, 254); "Surely a God who would do such a thing is more nearly like Satan" (Pinnock, "Destruction," 247). The solution for these scholars is a doctrine of annihilation. This is strongly opposed by another wing of evangelicals, who appeal to the testimony of the New Testament.

70. Kehl, *Eschatologie*, 294, 297. Similarly an official report by the Church of England: *Mystery of Salvation*, 199.

71. King, *Gnosticism*, 211, with reference to such writings as the *Apocryphon of James*, which encourages believers to face suffering.

72. Yet see also *Ep. Apos.* 24 [35] and *3 Cor.* 24.

73. For example, *1 Clem.* 26.3; Herm. *Sim.* 5.6-7; *2 Clem.* 9.1-2; 14.5. Cf. Ign. *Smyrn.* 7.1: the 'flesh' of Christ was raised by the Father."

74. But cf. *Res.* 17: the souls of the wicked go to Hades, where they, being corporeal, already burn and suffer!

75. See Hultgård, "Persian Apocalypticism."

76. Daley, "Apocalypticism," 8. *Dialogue* 80 mentions the millennium and the fleshly resurrection in the same breath.

77. Differently, however, John 20:17: do not touch! Cf. Ign. *Smyrn.* 3.1-3 (Jesus says not to touch him, since he is not "a bodiless demon").

78. Christ is here presented as an unknown traveler in simple human garb; cf., for example, Gen. 18 and the story of Philemon and Baucis (Lüdemann, *Resurrection of Christ*, 107).

79. Therefore it seems logical to infer from 1 Cor. 15 (with, for example, Wedderburn, *Beyond Resurrec-*

tion, 87) that Paul may well have thought that Jesus' "former body remained sown in the ground," for "so great is the stress upon the newness and the difference of the resurrection existence."

80. Matt. 28:16-20 "might be more easily reconciled with the manner of the appearance to Paul"; the mention of the "doubt" of some "suggests that this is no mere mundane encounter," and "what they 'see' also induces worship (v. 17)" (Wedderburn, *Beyond Resurrection*, 71). In Luke's hands, even elsewhere "what one might think were otherworldly phenomena take on a remarkably tangible form" (Wedderburn, *Beyond Resurrection*, 36): Luke specifies that the dove/spirit descends on Jesus in "bodily form" (Luke 3:22); in Acts 2, the spirit manifests itself in tongues of fire.

81. Cf. *Apoc. Pet.* 72.23-26. See Robinson, "Easter," 10–17.

82. The Savior then introduces himself as the triad of Father, Mother, and Son (*Apoc. John* 2.14). According to Layton, *Gnostic Scriptures*, 29, the texts originally referred to the "First Thought" (Protennoia; cf. *Apoc. John* 30.11-12); it is the only framing story that makes Jesus the speaker.

83. Riley, *Resurrection*, 67. He even adds that any soul could, and often did, eat with friends and relatives in the repasts of the cult of the dead, but this does not seem a real parallel to the risen Jesus eating fish, for those dining at the tombs would hardly have *seen* the dead eat with them.

84. Riley, *Resurrection*, 41. Some such understanding of Jesus' resurrection may be preserved in a fragment of tradition used in 1 Pet. 3:18: Christ "was put to death in flesh (= as a 'fleshly person'), but made alive in the spirit (= as a 'spirit person')"; see Karrer, *Jesus Christus*, 32. The author of 1 Peter has then given the formula a new interpretation; for him, "in the spirit" (*pneumati*) means "by God's spirit."

85. Such a view would connect these Corinthians with the Epicureans, who were notorious for their denial of any postmortem existence of the soul.

86. Martin, *Corinthian Body*, 123; cf. 122: it would have been "natural for the Corinthians to imagine a bringing to life of human corpses along lines familiar from popular myths and folklore."

87. See, for example, Sandelin, *Auseinandersetzung*, 134; Sellin, *Streit*; idem, "Hauptprobleme," 3011.

88. Such a position, which comes close to an eschatological *creatio ex nihilo*, was still held by the "simple believers" criticized by Origen; cf. af Hällström, *Fides*, 81.

89. This is a dichotomy derived from an exegesis of Gen. 2:7, where Adam is called "a living soul," and from a comparison between the first and the last Adam (the latter being, of course, Christ; cf. Rom. 5).

90. Rom. 8:9-11 suggests that the stuff *pneuma* found in the bodies of Christ-believers is a precondition for such a change to take place.

91. Wedderburn, *Beyond Resurrection*, 31.

92. Interpreters struggle in trying to characterize the *soma pneumatikon*: it is claimed that it does not consist of *pneuma*, but is rather determined by the *pneuma*, or animated by the spirit, or it belongs to the sphere of the spirit. See N. T. Wright, *Resurrection*, 347–56, in particular. But what does such a body then consist of? Martin persuasively pleads for the view that *pneuma* does, in the argument of 1 Cor. 15, denote a kind of stuff after all, a "celestial substance" (*Corinthian Body*, 129), in agreement with educated Greek views of the composition of human (and astral!) bodies.

93. Wedderburn, *Beyond Resurrection*, 118 (my italics).

94. Boyarin, *Radical Jew*, 61–62.

95. Wedderburn, *Beyond Resurrection*, 119.

96. Cf. Martin, *Corinthian Body*, 129–30.

97. Contrast Knight, *Origins*, 183, 211–12: the future bodies of believers are already present in heaven and will be superimposed on them at the parousia.

98. Cf. the balanced assessment of the situation by Lindgård, *Line of Thought*, 224: "The inexact imagery makes it possible that there may, to a certain degree, exist some continuity between the old and the new body though it is perfectly clear that Paul in 2 Cor. 5:1-10 emphasizes the discontinuity."

99. Cf. Boyarin, *Radical Jew*, 60: although Paul "considers some kind of a body necessary in order that the human being not be naked," his image of the human being "is of a soul dwelling in or clothed by a body, and, however valuable the garment, it is less essential than that which it clothes. . . . The body, while necessary and positively valued by Paul, is, as in Philo, not the human being but only his or her house or garment."

100. The generalizing words *pantas* (all) and *hekastos* (each) show that Paul is not thinking just of himself here, even though he has been using plural verb forms mainly of himself since 2:14.

101. Lindgård, *Line of Thought*, 223, points out that Paul's idea of moving to the Lord at death in 2 Cor. 5:8, besides being unconnected with the concept of the parousia, does not seem to be combined with the concept of the heavenly body (5:1) either.

102. In 2 Cor. 4:16—5:10, Paul is not consistent, but "switches back and forth between the dualistic and holistic perspective"; yet "the dominating feature in the section is dualism" (Lindgård, *Line of Thought*, 225).

103. Cf. Seneca, *Hercul. Oet.* 1703-4, 1725-26: "take my spirit . . . up to the stars . . . my father calls me and opens the heaven; I am coming, father." In *Apoc. Mos.* 42.8, Eve asks after Adam's death: "God of all, receive my spirit"; then "immediately she gave up her spirit to God."

104. Acts 2:31 (Peter's speech) presents a different picture: David states in the psalm that God will not leave his soul (!) in Hades nor let his "holy one see corruption." According to "Peter," David cannot speak of himself, for he died and was buried, and his tomb can still be seen. By contrast, Christ (of whom David is supposed to be speaking) was not left in Hades, nor did his flesh "see corruption," for God raised him, and he was exalted to the right hand of God. Jesus' fleshly body, then, did not decay in the grave. Here a resurrection of the "flesh" is envisaged. Does Luke think that other people go to heaven (or Hades) when they die, while Jesus was a special case? We get no clear answer.

105. See the thorough discussion by Uro, "Encratite Gospel?" 151–56.

106. For the equation image = body, based on Hellenistic Jewish exegesis of Gen. 1–2 as in Philo, *Opif.* 134, see Uro, "Encratite Gospel?" 150.

107. Uro, "Encratite Gospel?" 153 (my italics). Cf. *Gos. Thom.* 4: "The man old in days will not hesitate to ask a little child . . . about the place of life, and he will live. For many of the first will be last . . . and they will become one and the same." "Becoming one and the same" is "something that will finally come true only in the future" (though the saying does not tell when; Uro, "Encratite Gospel?" 154). Cf. *Gos. Thom.* 106.

108. Uro, *Thomas*, 76.

109. According to the Valentinian *Gospel of Philip*, too, the Christian is said to put on heavenly "garments" (for example, *Gos. Phil.* 57.19-22) at the hour of the departure of the *pneuma* from the body.

110. Peel, "Gnostic Eschatology," 159. That the resurrection will not be a purely "spiritual" event is suggested by 47.2-8 in particular: "Never doubt the resurrection, my son Rheginos! . . . you received flesh when you entered this world. Why would you not receive flesh when you ascend into the Aeon?" The interpretation of this and the other relevant passages is controversial; a different

354

interpretation is put forward, for example, by Layton, *Gnostic Scriptures*, 317. My reading is informed by a Finnish article by Outi Lehtipuu, in which she agrees with Peel ("Ruumiin ylösnousemus," 8–12).

111. Peel, "Gnostic Eschatology," 160.

112. Ibid.; cf. Dunn, *Unity*, 290. For a fresh discussion of the second- and third-century debates on resurrection, in which opposing parties appealed to Paul's authority, see now Lehtipuu, "Flesh and Blood."

113. Lehtipuu, "Flesh and Blood," 175–76.

114. Irenaeus, *Haer.* 1.30.

115. Peel, "Gnostic Eschatology," 162. Such absorption has been taken as the common "gnostic" view of the destiny of the self. This view *is* found, for example, in the *Tripartite Tractate* (124.13-25) and in Irenaeus's report on Saturninus (*Haer.* 1.24.1).

116. Riley, *Resurrection*, 66.

117. But does it really? Martin, *Corinthian Body*, 132, comments on Paul's "assumptions about identity through participation": "The transformation expected at the eschaton will cause the Christian body to shed the lower parts of its current nature and be left with the purer, transformed part of the pneuma. Christians will have bodies without flesh, blood, or soul—composed solely of pneumatic substance—light, airy, luminous bodies. The presupposition underwriting Paul's argument here is that the nature of any body is due to its participation in some particular sphere of existence. It gets its identity only through participation. *It is difficult to imagine how any kind of individuality as we conceive it today could exist in such a world view*" (my italics).

118. I discussed Paul's "spiritualized" expectation of the end in ch. 4 above.

119. Basilides, according to Origen, *Comm. Rom.* 5.1 (Löhr's frg. 18); *Apoc. John* 27.20-21; *Apoc. Paul* 21.19-21. An ineradicable popular misunderstanding holds that the doctrine of reincarnation was generally accepted in the early church, until the second council of Constantinople (553 C.E.) condemned it. What was condemned in that council was Origen's view of the *preexistence* of souls.

120. Thus Irenaeus in *Haer.* 5.31.2 (though earlier in his work Irenaeus assumes that dead believers go to a waiting place in heaven; see C. E. Hill, *Regnum Caeli*, 16–20).

121. Something like this seems to be assumed in *1 Clem.* 50.3-4.

122. This idea was once made popular especially by Cull-

mann, *Immortality*; on the discussion see Barr, *Garden of Eden*, 1–3.

123. One even makes an untranslatable and hardly comprehensible distinction between *Leib* and *Körper*, affirming the survival of the former (in some sense) and denying that of the latter.

124. Kehl, *Eschatologie*; Greshake, *Resurrectio*. Cf. above, pp. 112–13, on the analogous spiritualization of the parousia in this current of thought. Kehl, who pleads for the view in question, asks the very reasonable question (which critics have also asked), Is the subject of the fulfillment on this view in reality anything more than an immortal soul? He admits that his view may seem too spiritualizing, but points out that there is no alternative theory in sight able to combine the diverse viewpoints of Christian hope any more adequately than this model does (*Eschatologie*, 279).

125. Kehl, *Eschatologie*, 266, admits that in patristic time this modern Catholic position would have been considered gnostic.

126. It is not, of course, a Catholic view only.

6. Sold Under Sin?
The Human Condition

1. Cf. recently H.-M. Barth, *Dogmatik*, 489–96.

2. Fohrer, *Geschichte*, 192. To be sure, in early times the measures could occasionally be quite drastic; cf. 2 Sam. 21:1-9.

3. Cover, "Sin," 32–33.

4. Ibid., 32.

5. Cf. Ps. 78:38-39; 1 Kgs. 8:46; consider further the plead for leniency in an early Sumerian wisdom text, quoted by Cover, "Sin," 32: "Never has a sinless child been born to its mother . . . a sinless workman has not existed from of old."

6. Cover, "Sin," 33.

7. Barr, *Garden of Eden*, 7. See, for example, Ps. 18:22-28. Psalm 14, later quoted by Paul in Rom. 3:12, is a case in point. The context shows that, despite the sweeping language ("there is no one who does good" in v. 3 seems to refer to "humankind" in v. 2), the psalmist is actually only criticizing the corrupt fools who say "There is no God" (v. 1), "the evildoers who eat up my people" (v. 4).

8. Barr, *Garden of Eden*, 8 (my italics).

9. Ibid. (his italics).

10. See ibid., 5–14, especially 11–14; Westermann, *Genesis*, 374–80.

11. Barr, *Garden of Eden*, 11; cf. 12: "The story has a mildly ironic and comic character rather than one of unrelieved tragedy and catastrophe."

12. Ibid., 13. Genesis 3 is an obscure aetiological story, telling why the serpent crawls on its belly, why making a living is an effort, and so on. God forbids the humans to eat from "the tree of the knowledge of good and evil." Adam and Eve transgress, since they want to eat. The humans are not seeking omniscience, but an understanding of what is good and what is not. This knowledge God is not willing to grant them. No wonder some gnostics later thought that this was a story about an unwise creator who was not aware of ultimate reality. It is possible that behind the story lies an older mythical narrative that did speak of hubris and fall (cf. Ezek. 28—a story far better suited to illustrate a human wish to "be like God" that is so often erroneously detected in the story of Adam and Eve), but in Gen. 3 as it has come down to us these elements are lacking.

13. D. Brown, *Discipleship*, 178.

14. Cf. Westermann, *Genesis*, 376–77.

15. Winninge, *Sinners*, 212.

16. Ibid., 131–34, 181–84, and elsewhere.

17. Cf. Longenecker, *Eschatology*, 23–27.

18. This way of thinking was normal in the ancient Near East. Esarhaddon's report of the downfall of Babylon a century before ignores the political realities and regards the event as a punishment for the sins of the Babylonians, who had become excessively evil, eventually inciting the raging anger of Marduk; see Cover, "Sin," 39.

19. Cf. Neusner, *Judaism*, 19–20: "No generation in the history of Jewry has been so roundly, universally condemned by posterity as that of Yohanan ben Zakkai. . . . This was supposed to be a sinning generation. It was not a sinning generation, but one deeply faithful to the covenant . . . perhaps more so than many who have since condemned it. First-century Israelites sinned only by their failure. Had they overcome Rome . . . they would have found high praise. . . . Since they lost, later generations looked for their sin, for none could believe that the omnipotent God would permit his Temple to be destroyed for no reason." As after 586 B.C.E., so after 70 C.E. the alternative was this: "Either our fathers greatly sinned, or God is not just." A simi-

lar logic was followed, when the defeat by the Israeli army in 1967 was explained in Arab countries to be a consequence of insufficient observance of the will of God revealed in the Qur'an.

20. A parallel to his thought can be seen in the early Christian view that the destruction of the Holy City was the divine punishment for the killing of Jesus (Matt. 27:25-26) or of James the Just (Eusebius, *Hist. eccl.* 2.23.19-20).

21. For example, 1QH 9.21-27; 12.29-37; 17.14-15; 20.24-33. Luz, *Geschichtsverständnis*, 162 n. 102, observes that Luther's insight of human corruption, reached via introspection, is more reminiscent of Qumran than of Paul.

22. E. P. Sanders, *Paul and Palestinian Judaism*, 289. When the covenanters compared themselves to one another, let alone to outsiders, they were perfectly capable of making distinctions and appreciating moral strength.

23. This phrase "heralds a shift in focus away from a wondering acknowledgment of the marvelous mysteries of God in the preceding lines to a recognition of the sinful unworthiness of the psalmist" (Carter, *Paul*, 196).

24. Ibid. See also Newsom, *Self*, for example, 173, 220, 348–51.

25. E. P. Sanders, *Paul and Palestinian Judaism*, 284.

26. "The sin of Adam is noted in *1 En.* 32:6, but it is accorded no importance in the Enochic literature. The descent of the Watchers is depicted as a far more momentous event in the history of humanity" (Collins, "Sons of God," 269). The Enoch tradition is not unanimous, however. The *Epistle of Enoch* (*1 En.* 98.4) states that "sin was *not* sent on the earth, but man of himself created it" (ibid., 270).

27. Collins, *Imagination*, 39.

28. Thus Wis. 2:24: "the envy of the devil" brought death into the world.

29. Eliade, *Religious Ideas*, 2:270.

30. Barr, *Garden of Eden*, 18.

31. The rabbis, by contrast, later emphasized that study of the Torah was a means to oppose the evil inclination.

32. Some texts come close, though; cf. *T. Zeb.* 1.4-5: "I am not aware, my children, that I have sinned in all my days, except in my mind, nor do I recall having committed a transgression, except what I did to Joseph in ignorance."

33. Nickelsburg, *Origins*, 43.

34. Cover, "Sin," 37.

35. See Neale, *Sinners*, 68–97.

36. For example, Ps. 9:15-17; *Pss. Sol.* 7.1-6; 17.24-25;

356

Jub. 23.23-24. To be sure, this was not the only view of Gentiles.

37. Dunn, *Jesus*, 76. See, for example, 1QH 10.9-12.

38. For polemics by Jews against other Jews, see, for example, *1 En.* 82.4-7; *Pss. Sol.* 1.8; 2.3; 8.12-13; 17.5-8; CD 1.13-21; 1QS 4.9-14.

39. L. T. Johnson, "Anti-Jewish Slander" (quotation: 433). He demonstrates the universality of the "rhetoric of slander" both in the polemic between different Jewish groups and in that between philosophical schools in Greco-Roman antiquity. Cynics and early Stoics underlined the isolation of the sage by dividing humankind into only two classes: wise persons and fools; there was no middle ground (Meeks, *Moral World*, 50). Later Stoics, though, were more lenient.

40. To this day; cf. H.-M. Barth, *Dogmatik*, 489, 514, 521. The same heritage survives in Islam; cf. ibid., 501–2, 515, 521.

41. For an excellent overall account see E. P. Sanders, "Sin," who, however, pays scant attention to John and none to gnostic Christians.

42. Jesus does not assume anything like a general, hopeless sinfulness of humans; even in Luke 13:1-5 the necessity and possibility of repentance is underlined.

43. Later, of course, this became a problem; cf. Matt. 3:14-15 and the *Gospel of the Hebrews*, in which Jesus asks, "What sin have I so that I should go and be baptized by him?" (Jerome, *Pelag.* 3.2).

44. Jesus' rejoinder to the man's address ("no one is good but God") simply restates the old wisdom that humans (like Jesus himself) cannot be compared to their Creator. The discussion concerning the greatest commandment in Mark 12:28-34 likewise presupposes that the commandments can be fulfilled.

45. Contra Hahn, *Theologie*, 2:322–23. No doubt some sort of connection is established between illness and sin (cf. Mark 2:5-11; John 5:14): something in the life of a person may have caused his or her illness (cf. 1 Cor. 11:30). But this is a question of individual sinning, not of a general state of slavery to Sin or Satan. In connection with the exorcisms, where a battle against Satan *is* going on, we do not hear of sin.

46. "The underlying assumption appears to be a traditional Jewish one: if God commands something to be done, it must be within the power of humans to do it" (Mohrlang, *Matthew and Paul*, 114).

47. Theissen, *Erleben*, 71, comments: "The view of humans is bright."

48. Mohrlang, *Matthew and Paul*, 123; cf. 113–14.

49. Pernveden, *Concept*, 156.

50. Elsewhere (*Sim.* 9.23.4) Hermas presupposes the traditional notion of humans' creaturely sinfulness in comparison with God.

51. In a seminal article, Stendahl ("Introspective Conscience") coined the expression (Paul's) "robust conscience," countering the tradition of interpreting Paul as a representative of the post-Augustinian "introspective conscience of the West."

52. Matthew alone (21:32) mentions prostitutes—but only in connection with the Baptist's (not Jesus') preaching.

53. Thus in different ways, for example, Jeremias, *Jerusalem*, 303–12; E. P. Sanders, *Jesus*, 198–206; Borg, *Jesus*; cf. the survey in Pesonen, *Luke*, 3-12.

54. Without Luke's Gospel, the theme of sinners "would hardly have attracted so much attention, being but a minor theme in the other canonical Gospels." Luke did find the theme in his tradition, but "without him the matter would never loom so large in Christian preaching or, indeed, in critical Jesus scholarship." Pesonen, *Luke*, 1; cf.ibid., 239.

55. Neale, *Sinners*, 193, concludes that he was unable to find ways to understand the offense caused by Jesus' association with "sinners" at a strictly historical level.

56. Pesonen argues that, for Luke, "the toll collectors and sinners who followed Jesus are the forerunners of converted Gentiles"; what the evangelist really aims at in Luke 15 (the great chapter on the "lost") is the legitimation of Gentile Christianity and the mutual reconciliation of Jewish and Gentile Christians (*Luke*, 162); cf. Neale, *Sinners*, 189–90; Räisänen, "Prodigal Gentile," 44–48, 57.

57. Cf. Matt. 5:46-47; Mark 14:41 par.; *Herm. Sim.* 4.4.4.

58. There are indications that these Christians placed Paul, too, among the sinners, since he had given up parts of the Torah (Gal. 2:17; Rom. 3:8; 6:1).

59. Cf. Rev. 21:8; 22:15; and Rom. 1:18-32.

60. 1 John 5:16-17 agrees that there is mortal sin about which prayer is useless.

61. Bultmann, *Theology*, 2:25, interprets even John 8:44 on a very abstract level: "having the devil as one's father is a term to describe the sinner's existence. Or, said in another way, sin is not an occasional evil occurrence; rather, in sin it comes to light that man in his essence is a sinner, that he is determined by unreality, Nothing." On 16:8-9 Bultmann comments: "What is sin? It is the unbelief in which the world anchors itself to itself" (ibid., 31).

62. Cf. van der Watt, "Salvation," 107: "The essence of their sin is clear: it is not expressed in terms of individual deeds or guilt, but in terms of not accepting (believing in) God as he is revealed in and through Jesus"; cf. Hultgren, *Christ*, 153.

63. "The Jews" are not just the Jewish leaders, as a well-meant ecumenical trend in present-day exegesis would have it; see also p. 274 and Hakola, *Identity Matters*, 225–31.

64. Bultmann, *Theology*, 2:28: "One might almost say: the sin of 'the Jews' lies not in their ethics, as in Paul, but in their dogmatics." Bultmann, however, artificially connects this "dogmatic" sin with "self-security" (ibid.).

65. Hakola, *Identity Matters*, 210.

66. Dunderberg, "Sin and Sinlessness."

67. For what follows, see E. P. Sanders, "Sin," 45.

68. Cf. the similar statement in a spurious section, John 8:11.

69. Jesus is regarded as the great exception: Rom. 8:3; Heb. 4:15; and elsewhere.

70. Hultgren, *Christ*, 94–95.

71. Ibid., 93.

72. Ibid., 109.

73. Nickelsburg, *Ancient Judaism*, 81–82, 88.

74. Laato, *Paul*, 214.

75. Vollenweider, *Freiheit*, 349–60; Zeller, "Konsolidierung," 200–201, 217.

76. Since Euripides' tragedy of the same name, Medea who killed her children was the classic model of the conflict between willing and doing; cf. Hommel, "Das 7. Kapitel"; Theissen, *Psychologische Aspekte*, 214–20.

77. Ovid, *Metam.* 7.16-20. It is to some extent paralleled by the confessions of sin found at Qumran, and rabbinic speculations about the power of the evil inclination come rather close to it too. To be sure, sometimes the "evil inclination" relates to the normal human drive that is not sinful.

78. Seeley, *Deconstructing*, 150.

79. Philo (*Her.* 57) draws on the same tradition, even stating that humanity is divided in "the race of those who live by the divine spirit and reason" and "those who exist according to blood and the pleasure of the flesh." Taken out of context this sounds very Pauline, yet the opposition is here of a physical nature. Plutarch, who quoted the famous case of Medea to illustrate his conviction that even though we know what is right we often do not do it (*Vit. pud.* 533d), also painted a picture of the philosopher that mutatis mutandis corresponds to the picture of the *redeemed* person in Paul: philosophy "makes a man harmonious with himself, free from blame from himself . . . there is no passion disobedient to reason" (*Max. princ.* 776a, quoted in Boring, Berger, and Colpe, *Hellenistic Commentary*, 373–74). But Plutarch does not pretend that he, or anyone else, has attained this ideal: "Nowhere and never has the Wise Man existed" (*Comm. not.* 1076b; similarly Seneca, *Tranq. An.* 7.4.).

80. Wernle, *Beginnings*, 1:231, 232.

81. In Rom. 6, the slavery under Sin clearly belongs to the past of the Christ-believers: "you were slaves of sin" (v. 20), but now "you have been freed from sin and enslaved to God" (v. 22). Romans 7:5 likewise states in the past tense that "while we were living in the flesh, our sinful passions . . . were at work in our members to bear fruit for death," whereas we are now "dead to that which held us captive" (v. 6). Chapter 8 for its part makes a sharp distinction between "us, who walk not according to the flesh but according to the spirit," and "those who live according to the flesh" (vv. 4-8).

82. See the summary of the discussion in Jewett, *Romans*, 441–45. The "I" is still taken as a Christian, for example, by Laato, *Paul*, 109–45; cf. Dunn, *Romans*, 1:411–12.

83. Cf. Philo, *Virt.* 182: proselytes at once become prudent, temperate, modest, gentle, merciful, humane, venerable, just, magnanimous, lovers of truth and "superior to all considerations of money and pleasure," whereas Jewish apostates are "intemperate, shameless, unjust, disreputable, weak-minded, quarrelsome," and so on.

84. See p. 261.

85. Bultmann (for example, *Theology*, 1:247–48) claimed that Rom. 7:15-20 does not describe a person's empirically perceptible inner conflict at all; the conflict is of a "trans-subjective" type: a person desires what is good (life), but actually achieves what is evil (death). Not only are central terms of the passage ("doing," "good," "evil") interpreted in a strange way in this exegesis; the crux of the argument is Bultmann's understanding of "covetousness" or "desire" (*epithymia*) in 7:7-8 and elsewhere "nomistically" as a false zeal for fulfilling the law. For a rebuttal of this once influential interpretation, see Räisänen, "Use of *epithymia*." "Covetousness" means, here and elsewhere in Paul, the inclination to transgress the law, not the desire to fulfill it! A somewhat different version of Bultmann's interpretation is presented by Jewett, *Romans*, 462–73 (who takes Paul to be speaking also of himself): in his zeal for

358

the law that led him to persecute the Christians, Paul intended to bring about good (the messianic reign of peace), but effected evil.

86. Cf. E. P. Sanders, *Paul, Law, and Jewish People*, 75: "The human plight, without Christ, is so hopeless in this section that one wonders what happened to the doctrine that the creation was good. Those who see here a profound analysis of why the law is not an answer to the plight of humanity may miss the criticism of God the creator and giver of the law which can easily be derived from Rom. 7:10 and 7:14-25." Sanders notes (ibid., 78) that the "extreme presentation of human inability" in 7:14-25 does not express a view that Paul consistently maintains elsewhere but is "unique in the Pauline corpus."

87. Paul here avails himself of the Stoic theory of natural law; see, for example, Huttunen, "Greco-Roman Philosophy," 81–82. Naturally many theories have been developed to deny that these verses really speak of Gentiles fulfilling the requirements of the law (for example, Paul is referring to Gentile *Christians*: Cranfield, *Romans*, 1:155–56; Jewett, *Romans*, 213–14). For a refutation of such attempts to reconcile these statements with Paul's main concern, see Räisänen, *Paul and the Law*, 103–6; Longenecker, *Eschatology*, 186; Kuula, *Law*, 2:93–94.

88. Seeley, *Deconstructing*, 130.

89. Jewish views on homosexuality were decisively influenced from the stern condemnation in Lev. 18:22. Cf. Nissinen, *Homoeroticism*.

90. Paul does not speak of motives, as modern Christian sensitivities might lead one to expect, but of gross concrete acts.

91. In Rom. 3:3 Paul himself refers to his preceding argument by stating that "some" (rather than "all") have been disobedient—as if he were half conscious of the limited force of his evidence.

92. E. P. Sanders, "Sin," 45. One may add the observation, in itself trivial, that Paul's concluding appeal to scripture (Rom. 3:10-18) twists the original meaning of the biblical verses: Paul uses a catena of citations that originally described the sinfulness of the impious as opposed to the pious (cf., for example, Ps. 14:1, 4).

93. The expression *eph᾽ ho* here means "because," not "in whom" (as Augustine later read in the Latin translation [*in quo*]).

94. *Justin*, too, suggests that sinning is a potentiality that all human beings themselves activate (*Dial.* 124.4).

95. Seeley, *Deconstructing*, 139–40.

96. In Rom. 5:13, Paul offers another (even more artificial) explanation for the power of Sin, tracing it back to the (God-given!) law. Verses 13-14 also contradict 7:8, where Sin is said to be "dead" (that is, inactive) until the coming of the law.

97. E. P. Sanders, "Sin," 45.

98. Seeley, *Deconstructing*, 150.

99. For what follows, see E. P. Sanders, "Sin," 45–46.

100. The name Beliar appears in Paul only in 2 Cor. 6:15, in what is probably an unauthentic passage.

101. Thus E. P. Sanders, "Sin," 46. Galatians 3:22 reads: "But the scripture has imprisoned all things under the power of sin, so that what was promised through faith in Jesus Christ might be given to those who believe."

102. E. P. Sanders, *Paul and Palestinian Judaism*, 474–75, and elsewhere.

103. Wernle, *Beginnings*, 1:236–37.

104. Cf. Carter, *Paul*, 176–78, especially 178: "By locating sin in the body in this way, Paul is able to portray the problem of sin as being too deep-rooted for it to be dealt with by acceptance of the Jewish law."

105. Kuula, *Law*, 2:137.

106. Winninge, *Sinners*, 305.

107. Ibid., 309. Winninge, ibid., 310, notes that Paul is "unconvincing" in his depiction of the human plight. From the perspective of doctrinal history, it is ironic that the standard Jewish (and non-Pauline early Christian) view seems (roughly) to correspond to the notion of *simul iustus et peccator*, whereas Paul, of all people, seems to deny this idea.

108. Kuula, *Law*, 2:138.

109. Paul had after all been informed of such sexual transgressions as were "not found even among pagans (!)" but were tolerated by the Corinthian Christians (1 Cor. 5:1-5). Paul reckons with the possibility that "a brother" can be "sexually immoral or greedy, or [be] an idolater, reviler, drunkard, or robber" (5:9-13). Some members visit prostitutes (6:12-20); grievances within the congregation are taken to worldly courts (6:1-11). Still in 2 Cor. 12:20-21, Paul expresses his fear that he may find among the Corinthians precisely those vices that he had in Galatians listed as "works of the flesh" ("jealousy, anger, selfishness, slander, gossip, conceit, and disorder").

110. Cf. also Col. 3:5-8.

111. This point is rightly stressed by Carter, *Paul*, even if his constant appeal to Mary Douglas's anthropological model causes him to paint a coolly calculating Paul,

whose statements are dictated simply by his will to influence the social situation in his congregations.

112. Winninge, *Sinners*, 306, notes that "the prevalence of the idea about sin as an active power in the Pauline letters should not be overemphasized. The power notion is not worked out consistently until Romans."

113. The only comparable case outside the letters of Paul is Heb. 3:13: Christians are to take care that none are "hardened by the deceitfulness of sin." But unlike Paul, this author sees sin as a threatening active agent even in the life of Christians. Hahn, *Theologie*, 2:323–24, connects Revelation with Paul on this issue. But those fatefully involved with the power of evil in Revelation are those who *refuse* to follow the Lamb on the way of martyrdom and *willingly* worship the beast. Bultmann, *Theology*, 2:207, notes that "practically never is sin mentioned as a power that dominates man" in the post-Pauline church.

114. Marjanen, "Gnostic Gospel?" 138.

115. King, *Gospel of Mary*, 50. The metaphor of adultery means "an illegitimate mixing of one's true spiritual nature with the lower passions of the material body."

116. Filoramo, *Gnosticism*, 104.

117. These involve the Father of All or a primordial divine triad; other eternal beings that look like hypostatized qualities of the ineffable Father; lesser powers, "aeons"; lower entities that include the demiurge and his companions who create humans and imprison them in the body; a Sophia figure that becomes involved in a fall; and others. It is easy to deride (caricatures of) these myths, but they should be read with the practice of such authors as Plato and Plutarch in mind, who used myths for didactic purposes to attract the attention of readers not trained in philosophy. See the discussion on "Why All This Mythmaking?" in Dunderberg, *Beyond Gnosticism*, 24–30.

118. King, *Gnosticism*, 159.

119. Pagels, *Adam*, 74.

120. Bullard, "Hypostasis," 162.

121. Connecting wrong behavior with ignorance is also part of the Greek philosophical tradition.

122. Desjardins, *Sin*.

123. See *Gos. Truth* 32-33, where the argument is "far more 'Christian' than 'gnostic'" (Desjardins, *Sin*, 80); *Interp. Know.* 9.27-38, a section perhaps meant "to serve as a corrective for those who placed too much emphasis on salvation through faith (and knowledge) alone" (faith being a theme of the introductory section; cf. *Interp. Know.* 1-2) (Desjardins, *Sin*, 101).

124. Desjardins, *Sin*, 118.

125. Here too the patristic polemic has to be corrected that attached to pneumatic Christians the notion that they cannot sin.

126. Cf. above, p. 351 n. 62.

127. Desjardins, *Sin*, 118–19.

128. Devil: *Gos. Truth* 33.19-20; Error: *Gos. Truth* 17.14-15; Evil: *Tri. Trac.* 117.1-4.

129. Cf. Paul's talk of Sin dwelling in the flesh.

130. Desjardins, *Sin*, 119.

131. Ibid., 120–26.

132. Cf. Kelly, *Doctrines*, 357–66.

133. The tradition provided, in his view, yet another proof: the practice of baptizing infants with exorcisms and a solemn renunciation of the devil showed that they were in the power of the devil from the very first. A classic case of reasoning backward!

134. On Augustine's obsession (as it appears from a modern point of view) on this point, see P. Brown, *Augustine*, 388–90, with drastic examples.

135. Kelly, Doctrines, 365, with references.

136. Ibid., 387.

137. D. W. Johnson, "Pelagius," 255: "P[elagius] stressed the gratuitous character of salvation and maintained the Pauline emphasis on justification by faith alone. . . . To represent P[elagius] as denying the need for any kind of grace whatsoever for salvation is a caricature."

138. Pelagius did not imagine, of course, that anyone would live such a life from childhood to death; he envisaged a state that is attained by strenuous efforts of the will.

139. P. Brown, *Augustine*, 350.

140. Pagels, *Adam*, 99 (see her whole discussion, 98–150). Pagels finds both political and psychological reasons for the surprising success of Augustine's "idiosyncratic" theory of original sin.

7. What Must I Do to Be Saved? Different Paths to Salvation

1. If the jailer at Philippi used the phrase ascribed to him by Luke ("What must I do to be saved?" Acts 16:30), such a man could have meant only "What am I to do in order to avoid any unpleasant consequences of the situation created by this earthquake?" See Nock, *Conversion*, 9.

360

2. Cf. the story of Gideon's victory over the Midianites in Judg. 7: Yahweh demands Gideon to reduce his troops to the utmost, lest Israel can boast, "My own hand has delivered me" (v. 2). Cf. further 2 Chr. 25:7-8; 16:8; and Niditch, *War*, 143–44.

3. M. A. Elliott, *Survivors*, demonstrates that "remnant groups" were more common in Second Temple Judaism than has been thought; features of a remnant theology abound, for example, in *1 Enoch* and *Jubilees*.

4. In this vein, early Christians, too, came to divide people into saved and damned individuals.

5. The rabbinic dictum in *m. Sanh.* 10:1 is the classic statement of this viewpoint, but it is already presupposed by John the Baptist, who rejects it (Q 3:8), and by Paul, who, at the end of a tortuous argument, falls back upon it (Rom. 11:25-32): God's loyalty to the promise he gave to Israel's patriarchs eventually outweighs the failure of the people in keeping the covenant.

6. Westerholm, *Perspectives*, 350.

7. In addition to E. P. Sanders, *Paul and Palestinian Judaism*, see his more recent statement in *Judaism*, 262–75. Note the caveat that "covenantal nomism does not cover the entirety of Jewish theology, much less the entirety of Judaism. It deals with the theological understanding of the constitution of God's people: how they get that way, how they stay that way" (*Judaism*, 262).

8. Westerholm, *Perspectives*, 341–51. For criticisms of Sanders's position, see, for example, Carson et al., eds., *Justification and Variegated Nomism*; K. Müller, "Judentum." But see now Sanders's response in "Covenantal Nomism Revisited."

9. Thus Dunn, "Justice of God," 193.

10. Westerholm, *Perspectives*, 351 (his italics).

11. Nickelsburg, *Ancient Judaism*, 65.

12. See E. P. Sanders, *Judaism*, 252–56.

13. References to specific passages are listed in Nickelsburg, *Ancient Judaism*, 213 n. 14.

14. For an impressive account of the importance and meaning of repentance see Moore, *Judaism*, 1:507–34.

15. Some texts assume that members of the Essene movement were the only ones who had remained loyal to the (one and only) covenant (for example, CD 15.5-11), whereas other passages speak of a *new* covenant (for example, CD 6.19).

16. Occasionally the deeds specifically required by the Torah are called "works of the law," an exact verbal parallel to Paul's *erga nomou* (4Q398 frg. 2, 2.2-4).

17. It is noteworthy that a Hellenistic Jew like Philo displays a basically similar pattern of grace and effort: God's grace empowers the soul to rise to the mystic vision of God. Philo insists (against Stoic moralism) that the attainment of virtue, while rightly striven for, is ultimately a gift from God (for example, *All.* 3.136-37); see Barclay, *Jews*, 165 with n. 90.

18. At least this is how Q and, in its wake, Matthew and Luke present his message; but see the caveats in Uro, "John the Baptist."

19. There were, however, Jewish "baptismal movements"; cf. *Sib. Or.* 4.165 (but note that this is half a century later than John the Baptist's activity).

20. The evangelist adds: "and believe in the gospel!"

21. Yet the significance of such meals tends to be hugely overestimated; for a critique see Zeller, "Entstehung," 37–38. Certainly Jesus himself, a poor wandering preacher, could not afford to arrange great feasts.

22. See above, p. 141.

23. For the authenticity of the saying see J. Becker, *Jesus*, 79; Reiser, *Gerichtspredigt*, 214–15; cautiously Luz, *Matthäus*, 2:192. Differently, for example, E. P. Sanders, *Jesus*, 110; Funk and Hoover, *Five Gospels*, 181, 320 (on the a priori ground that one who spoke of love of enemies could not utter such words of condemnation).

24. For the authenticity of Q 11:31-32: J. Becker, *Jesus*, 81; Reiser, *Gerichtspredigt*, 205–6; Allison, *Jesus*, 138; Dunn, *Jesus Remembered*, 440–41; Luz, *Matthäus*, 2:275. Differently E. P. Sanders, *Jesus*, 114; Funk and Hoover, *Five Gospels*, 188, 332. Q 10:23-24 is regarded as a word of Jesus by J. Becker, *Jesus*, 135–36; Luz, *Matthäus*, 2:302.

25. For authenticity see J. Becker, *Jesus*, 261–67; Luz, *Matthäus*, 2:124. Becker, *Jesus*, 265, notes an analogy to the claims made by the speaker(s) in some hymns from Qumran: "at the judgment you pronounce as guilty all those who harass me, separating the just from the wicked through me" (1QH 15.12); "I am a trap for offenders, medicine for everyone who turns away from sin" (1QH 10.8). Becker senses in these hymns the prophetic self-claim of the "Teacher of Righteousness." Recent Qumran scholarship is more reserved on the issue of authorship; cf. Newsom, *Self*, 288. But even if the speaker is taken to be the current leader of the group rather than the historical "Teacher," the hymns do emphasize that opposition to him will make one "an outsider and a sinner" (Newsom, *Self*, 306).

26. Allison, *Jesus*, 171: Jesus "linked the judgment with response to himself and his itinerants." Luz, *Matthäus*, 2:150 cautiously assumes the authenticity of the saying.

27. See, for example, E. P. Sanders, *Jesus*, 333; J. Becker, *Jesus*, 417–18; Theissen and Merz, *Historical Jesus*, 100; Zager, *Jesus*, 36–41; Hahn, *Theologie*, 1:153; even Dunn, *Jesus Remembered*, 813–14, inclines to this view.

28. See, for example, Theissen and Merz, *Historical Jesus*, 420–23; Zager, *Jesus*, 41–45; Hahn, *Theologie*, 2:537–44. Mark 14:22 ("this is my body," without a "for you" formula) seems an early version of the bread saying, and Mark 14:25 (Jesus will drink wine "new" in the kingdom of God) the earliest accessible form of the cup saying.

29. In general, the existing New Testament theologies do not give an adequate picture of the diversity of the paths to salvation, partly because their author-by-author arrangement does not allow for convenient comparison and partly because the differences tend to be glossed over. See, however, Braun's brief comments on the actual contradictions ("Problematik," 406–7).

30. In an analogous way, 2 Peter later exhorts the readers to make "every effort" to support their faith with virtues that the author lists in 1:5-7. In this way, they may become "sharers of the divine nature" (1:4); this phrase that on the face of it suggests deification scarcely means in its context more than a life "in holiness and goodness" in face of the coming day of God (3:11-12; see Starr, *Sharers*).

31. In that passage it is stressed that whoever gives even a cup of cold water "to one of these little ones in the name of a disciple" will receive his or her reward (Matt. 10:42).

32. Cf. Luomanen, *Entering*, 184–93.

33. Seeley, *Deconstructing*, 48.

34. Note the subtle changes in the dialogue: ibid., 43.

35. See Luomanen's analysis of Matthew's view of salvation as compared to Jewish covenantal nomism: *Entering*, 281–84.

36. Ibid., 285.

37. Hippolytus leans on Irenaeus, *Haer.* 1.26.2. Cf. also Origen, *Cels.* 2.1; 5.61; Eusebius, *Hist. eccl.* 3.27.2; 6.17.

38. Hippolytus, *Haer.* 10.22; cf. 7.34.

39. Two different books are opened at the judgment according to Rev. 20:12, one of them being "the book of life." Some interpreters think that to be inscribed in this book equals predestinarian election. But even if the verse may imply God's foreknowledge of those whose deeds acquire salvation for them, it is clear that in their case, as well as in that of the rest of humankind, the sentence is "according to works"; cf. 2:23; 22:12. Cf. Stuhlmacher, *Theologie*, 2:252.

40. Luke's Jesus promises eschatological reward for the poor (4:18; 6:20-21; 14:21); the rich must distribute their possessions to the poor and take care of them (14:13; 18:22; 19:8). The rich man of Luke 16 does not use his worldly goods as he should have done and is therefore punished. Lazarus does not need to be particularly pious; since he is poor and has no one to help him, God takes care of him. Cf. the description of the righteous as poor and lowly in the *Epistle of Enoch* (*1 En.* 103.9-15); here too the inequity on earth will be compensated in the world to come. Cf. Lehtipuu, *Afterlife Imagery*, 175–83.

41. Cf. the discussion in Seeley, *Deconstructing*, 81–102, which leads to the conclusion that "Luke shows the superfluity of Jesus vis-à-vis the issues of salvation through generosity and continuity between the prophets' and Jesus' preaching" (ibid., 101).

42. Salo, *Treatment*, 29–31; Lehtipuu, *Afterlife Imagery*, 167.

43. Salo, *Ydin*, 306–7.

44. See, for example, Lehtipuu, *Afterlife Imagery*, 246–50.

45. John says to the crowd: "Whoever has two coats must share with anyone that has none; and whoever has food must do likewise"; to toll collectors: "Collect no more than the amount prescribed for you"; to soldiers: "Do not extort money from anyone by threats or false accusation, and be satisfied with your wages."

46. Many translations, anxious to avoid the idea that a human act can effect forgiveness, turn the causal relation on its head (thus the NRSV: "her sins . . . have been forgiven, *hence* she has shown great love").

47. See Räisänen, "Prodigal Gentile."

48. Cf. also Luke 12:33; 14:12-14.

49. In addition, see, for example, Luke 5:31-32 (Luke adds the clarifying words "to repentance" to Mark 2:17); Luke 15:7, 10; 18:9-14 (the toll collector in the temple, contrasted with the Pharisee); Acts 20:21; 26:20.

50. Lehtipuu, *Afterlife Imagery*, 246.

51. There is a faint echo of a ransom theology (here characteristically attributed to Paul) in Acts 20:28; of course, Luke knew that many Christians interpreted Jesus' death in redemptive terms, but he chose not to

362

emphasize this theology in his own work. In addition, Luke has preserved the references to the sacrifice of Jesus' body and blood on behalf of others in the story of the Lord's Supper in Luke 22:15-20 (vv. 19b-20 are missing from certain manuscripts, but this is probably due to a copyist's error).

52. Syreeni, "Matthew, Luke, and the Law," 148.

53. The Romans fade out of the Lukan picture!

54. The usual translation is "whatever has been strangled," but the meaning of the word is far from clear.

55. On the decree see further, p. 286.

56. No doubt he partly misunderstood Paul, but then one may ask: was it at all possible not to misunderstand him? And did not Paul on his part distort a Jewish and Jewish Christian position like that of James?

57. Syreeni, "James," 404.

58. Nickelsburg, *Ancient Judaism*, 52.

59. Ibid., 52–53.

60. On Jesus' death in Hebrews see p. 169.

61. The motif of opportunity to repentance is also emphasized in *2 Clement*. The author states that, as long as we are still in this world, we should "repent with our whole heart of the evil deeds we have done in the flesh, that we may be saved by the Lord, while we have yet an opportunity of repentance . . . by doing the will of the Father, and keeping the flesh holy, and observing the commandments of the Lord, we shall obtain eternal life" (*2 Clem.* 8.2-4). Human repentance (combined with obedience) and salvation through the Lord are self-evidently two sides of the same coin. See further, for example, *2 Clem.* 6.7; 9.7; 10.1; 11.7; 13.1; 19.3. The notion of Christ's atoning death is lacking.

62. Cf. Räisänen, "Righteousness by Works," especially 215.

63. A number of passages make clear that, for Clement, everything rests on the goodness and mercy of the Creator, for example, *1 Clem.* 20.11—21.1; 35–36. See Räisänen, "Righteousness by Works," 205–11.

64. Pernveden, *Concept*, 157.

65. Cf. *Mand.* 4.4.4; 7.1, 8; 12.3.6; and elsewhere.

66. Pernveden, *Concept*, 76–79. The peculiar Christology set forth in this section is discussed on p. 199.

67. 1 Thess. 4:14: "Since we believe that Jesus died and rose again, even so, through Jesus, God will bring with him those who have died."

68. On the soteriological significance ascribed to Jesus' resurrection (independently of the idea that his death had such significance) see Hahn, *Theologie*, 2:376–81, 403.

69. Matthew makes the connection even clearer by adding that the wine was "mixed with gall" (Matt. 27:34), which corresponds to the Septuagint reading of Ps. 69:22.

70. On the Jewish tradition about the inevitable sufferings of the righteous, crystallized in the words "Many are the afflictions of the righteous, but the Lord rescues them from them all" (Ps. 34:19), see Ruppert, *Leidende Gerechte*; G. Barth, *Tod*, 28–32.

71. In Jewish thought a "Deuteronomistic" tradition of prophets killed by their Israelite compatriots had developed, not based on any actual accounts in earlier layers of the Hebrew Bible but first found in Neh. 9:26. See the classic study of Steck, *Israel*.

72. This battle and Husayn's death are seen as the climax of world history: all previous history had aimed at that event, which will color the rest of all history with Husayn's blood. God had in advance revealed the event to all prophets from Adam on and they had mourned over Husayn's coming fate. As in the passion stories in the Gospels, the whole creation participated in the mourning: the sun eclipsed and the earth shook. See Ayoub, *Redemptive Suffering*, 145.

73. Ibid., 142–47, 198–216. I owe these references to Prof. Jaakko Hämeen-Anttila.

74. Scholem, *Sabbatai Sevi*, 799–802.

75. Ibid., 720; cf. 795–99. The crisis that the Sabbatians had to face was more serious: a renegade Messiah is certainly far more problematical than one who has suffered a martyr's death. Like the early Christians they too searched scripture and tradition "for intimations, hints, and indications of the extraordinary and bewildering events" (ibid., 802). Scholem goes on to note that readers of Paul can learn a great deal from Sabbatian writings, "composed in a very similar psychological situation"; in the Sabbatians' "audacious and novel" interpretations (reached, however, by methods not very different from those traditionally employed in rabbinic literature), "the clash between the old and the new, which is so conspicuous a feature in Paul's thinking, manifests itself in a more traditionally Jewish, though no less radical, fashion" (ibid., 803).

76. Ibid., 795.

77. Many of the authors who have preserved these formulations emphasize themselves other aspects of Jesus' work more, yet apparently cannot avoid including the idea of his dying for others in their writings (Mark, Matthew, John, 1 Clement).

78. Though not everywhere: see *Did.* 9–10.

79. Van der Watt, "Soteriology," 510, correctly notes: "Little or no apparent emphasis is placed on the atoning value of the cross in John's Gospel, although Jesus is pictured as the Lamb of God (1:29)."

80. In the same vein, Jesus dies in John's Gospel at the time when the lambs are slaughtered (John 19:14); that none of his bones is broken is said to fulfill scripture, probably the instruction about killing the Passover lambs (19:36; cf. Exod. 12:46).

81. See also John 10:11-18; 11:51; 15:13; the idea has so much traditional weight that it occurs in several contexts in this Gospel whose soteriology is thoroughly governed by a different idea, salvation as revelation.

82. The moral drawn is that the readers, too, should radiate such "fragrance" by walking in love, just as Christ did in giving himself as sacrifice.

83. Walter, "Hellenistische Eschatologie," 354.

84. Tuckett, "Atonement," 519. Discussions about the meaning of the blood sacrifice are summarized in Grabbe, *Judaic Religion*, 131–32.

85. See G. Barth, *Tod*, 50–56; Röhser, *Stellvertretung*, 58–63. It is not the killing of the animal that effects expiation, but the sprinkling of its blood on the altar or on the interior of the temple. Objects, too (altars, the shrine), are "expiated" with blood. (And people are not; their sins are taken away in the scapegoat ritual; see Theissen, "Kreuz," 435.) The animal sacrifice can be replaced with a flour offering that likewise effects expiation. "Thus one should not necessarily subsume every reference to Jesus' death as sacrifice under the category of sin-offering" (Tuckett, "Atonement," 519). Moreover, a sin offering is often also required when no forgiveness is needed: after cultic defilement resulting from giving birth, ejaculation, and so on.

86. G. Barth, *Tod*, 56; cf. Tuckett, "Atonement," 519.

87. Fitzer, "Ort," 179.

88. Thus recently A. Aejmelaeus in a tightly argued article ("Suffering Servant").

89. Collins, *Scepter*, 26, points out that there is no evidence that anyone in first-century Judaism expected a suffering Messiah, whether in fulfillment of Isa. 53 or on any other basis. The alleged allusions to such a figure in 4Q541 (who is said to "atone for the children of his generation," yet not by his death) do not bear scrutiny (ibid., 123–26). In the *Targum of Isaiah* the Song is given a messianic interpretation, but only as regards the high claims made for the servant; statements on his humility, suffering, or death are *not* applied to the Messiah.

90. In Acts 8:32-35, the Gentile courtier studies Isa. 53 and converts when Philip explains that the reference is to Jesus; Luke thus indicates that Isa. 53 was used as a common proof text—at least in his time.

91. Cf. G. Barth, *Tod*, 56–59.

92. Cf. ibid., 45, 58. The influence of Isa. 53 on Rom. 4:25 is doubted by S. K. Williams, *Jesus' Death*, 225. Others find an allusion to it even in the terse "according to the scriptures" in 1 Cor. 15:3; thus A. Aejmelaeus, "Suffering Servant," 478–84, who argues that a text (like Isa. 53) can serve as an "intertext" even if there are no verbal similarities between it and the text(s) where it is employed. Her point is that Isa. 53 is the only text in scripture on which the claim "according to the scriptures" *could* be based in the first place. But the counterargument, presented for example by G. Barth, still stands: other texts (for example, Mark 14:49; Luke 24:26-27) show that it was possible to claim harmony with scripture a priori, without any explicit references in mind. At some point Isa. 53 was discovered as a text that could be made to testify to Jesus—but not necessarily "in the beginning."

93. S. K. Williams, *Jesus' Death*; Seeley, *Noble Death*; G. Barth, *Tod*, 59–64.

94. *Hilasterion* probably does not refer to the lid of the ark ("mercy seat," Hebrew *kapporet*) in the temple; cf. Friedrich, *Verkündigung*, 61–65; Zeller, *Römer*, 87.

95. But there is a twist: the notion of vicarious dying becomes in the Jewish world "always bound up with the *hope* for a new life"; "the death is only accepted as saving death for others when it is seen in the light of the promise of life" (Theissen, *Theory*, 149–50).

96. However, 4 Maccabees is probably too late to have functioned as a direct source (contra S. K. Williams, *Jesus' Death*); one has rather to think of a common tradition behind both this work and, say, Romans (Rom. 3:25-26).

97. The present wording is shot through with Paul's own interpretive comments that probably include at least vv. 24 and 26b plus the words "through faith" in v. 25. See, for example, Dunn, *Romans*, 1:163–64; Jewett, *Romans*, 270–71.

98. It should be noted that it is a question of expiating sins previously committed. The notion of atoning even subsequent sins is hardly implied.

99. This docetic-sounding formulation is Paul's way of combining two incompatible convictions: that Jesus was fully human and that he nevertheless had no sin; cf. chapter 8.

100. In the Septuagint, and in the quotations in Heb. 10:6, 8, *peri hamartias* is a technical term for cultic sin offering. It is not clear, however, that this meaning is intended in Rom. 8:3. Even if it were, Paul uses the idea in a different way.

101. In light of the parallelism between "sin" and "righteousness" in 2 Cor. 5:21 (two abstract nouns, both used to denote two categories of people, sinners and/or the righteous), it is not feasible to take *hamartia* in the sense of cultic sin offering.

102. Theissen, *Theory*, 146. This is clearly the case in 1 Cor. 6:19-20. Yet the categories are not "pure." In 4 Maccabees the martyrs become a ransom for the sin of the people (see above).

103. Christ speaks: "Sheol saw me and was shattered, and Death ejected me and many with me.... And I made a congregation of living among his dead; and I spoke with them by living lips.... And those who had died ran toward me; and they cried out and said, 'Son of God, have pity on us. And deal with us according to your kindness, and bring us out from the bonds of darkness.'"

104. G. Barth, *Tod*, 85–97; Daniélou, *Theology*, 239–48. The idea occurs even in the Eucharist liturgy of Hippolytus's church order.

105. Breytenbach, *Versöhnung*.

106. Kuula, *Law*, 2:77–81.

107. J. Becker, *Paul*, 206–9; Theissen, "Kreuz," 431, 444–51.

108. See Kelly, *Doctrines*, 164–65.

109. Tuckett, "Atonement," 522.

110. Repentance is hardly mentioned at all. Paul suggests that right action will evolve almost automatically from the union with Christ—if one lives in the spirit, one will "walk" in the spirit. That life was not so simple became later painfully clear to Paul, and he had earnestly to exhort his converts to live up to their calling.

111. Christian interpreters have wrestled with the realism of Paul's language. Bultmann went farthest in translating Paul's union with Christ into existential categories. See the critical discussion in E. P. Sanders, *Paul and Palestinian Judaism*, 520–23, which leads to the conclusion that Paul really meant what he said and that "to an appreciable degree, what Paul concretely thought cannot be directly appropriated by Christians today" (ibid., 523).

112. Tuckett, *Christology*, 61. Paul has apparently received the notion from the baptismal tradition of the community in Antioch; see J. Becker, *Paul*, 104–5; cf. Schnelle, *Paulus*, 548.

113. Cf. Zeller, "Entstehung," 103–4.

114. Tuckett, *Christology*, 80.

115. Ibid., 83. In the Pastoral Epistles, too, the phrase occurs quite frequently, but almost without exception the writer speaks of abstract entities, rather than people, being in Christ: faith and love (1 Tim. 1:14; 2 Tim. 1:14), grace (2 Tim. 2:1), salvation (2 Tim. 2:10). Second Tim. 2:11-12 comes closer to Paul's idea ("if we have died with him, we will also live with him; if we endure, we will also reign with him"), but precisely the "in Christ" formula is missing; the fellowship with Christ is that of one individual alongside another, and in any case a matter of future hope rather than present reality (Tuckett, *Christology*, 85).

116. Schoedel, *Ignatius*, 19.

117. Dunn, *Unity*, 118.

118. Charlesworth, "Odes of Solomon," 730.

119. Uro, *Thomas*, 93 n. 63, refers to Gal. 2:20 as a Pauline analogy.

120. Peel, "Treatise," 53.

121. Cf. the usage in Hermas: "those who have believed" is "the ever-recurring description of those who belong to the Church" (Pernveden, *Concept*, 157).

122. Some of them may have found a terminological point of contact in the Jesus tradition, where *pistis* denotes faith in the healing power of the miracle worker.

123. Cf. Nickelsburg, *Ancient Judaism*, 39.

124. Only if one accepts this arbitrary interpretive device can one avoid the conclusion that "Paul has led himself into a curious cul-de-sac: if Abraham gained righteousness simply by trusting God, then Christ is unnecessary.... Abraham gains righteousness centuries before Jesus and, presumably, in perfect ignorance of him" (Seeley, *Deconstructing*, 138).

125. Slightly ironically, this emphasis on faith in Christianity from Paul on has produced the tendency to make right or wrong *doctrine* the touchstone of true religion. Cf. Weiss, *Earliest Christianity*, 426.

126. Cf. Westerholm, *Perspectives*; Wedderburn, "Paulusperspektive?"; Watson, *Paul* (2d ed.).

127. Bultmann, *Glauben*, 2:32–41; idem, *Theology*, 1:259-69, 281. Key texts for Bultmann are Rom. 3:27; 4:2-5; 7:7-13; 10:2-3; and Phil. 3:4-11. Strikingly, passages from Galatians are absent from this list.

128. To what extent it can be traced back to Luther himself is controversial. Saarinen, "Pauline Luther," argues that Luther's own theology is actually much closer to the New Perspective than is usually thought.

129. Westerholm, *Perspectives*, 444.

130. For representative quotations see the collection put to together by Westerholm, *Perspectives*, 249–58, who wittily calls it "The Quotable Anti-'Lutheran' Paul." It should be noted, however, that the New Perspective is far from being a harmonious unity, a point now stressed by Watson, *Paul* (2d ed.), xii, and passim. Scholars gathered under that umbrella hold rather different views of Paul's actual relation to Judaism. I discussed this in an early article comparing Sanders's and Dunn's views: Räisänen, "Galatians 2.16." See now also Räisänen, "Controversial Jew."

131. However, for Paul's own soteriology the notion of participation in Christ or in his "body," or emphasizing the spirit of God or of Christ as an experienced power, are more central. Therefore, even in Galatians, having proposed his thesis of justification by faith (Gal. 2:15-16), Paul immediately moves to speak of salvation and the law in terms of "participation in Christ" (2:19-20).

132. On Gal. 3:10-12, see Räisänen, *Paul and the Law*, 94–96, and the literature cited there; Donaldson, *Paul and the Gentiles*, 132; Kuula, *Law*, 1:65–73.

133. The sentence is read differently from the Hebrew Bible and given a specifically Pauline interpretation. Contrast Heb. 10:38-39, where the application is closer to the original.

134. Marshall, *Theology*, 439.

135. At most, Paul may have secondarily expanded his criticism of the religion of his compatriots to include the charge of zealous legalism, a charge understandable in light of the actions of some of his conservative opponents, but perhaps even more as a projection of his own past as an (atypical) overachiever in nomistic piety (Gal. 1:14) onto Judaism as a whole; cf. Phil. 3:4-9. See Wedderburn, "Paulusperspektive," 64.

136. Cf. Westerholm, *Perspectives*, 404–6, who states that Eph. 2:8-10, though post-Pauline, "remains as fine a statement as any of Paul's 'Lutheranism'" (405).

137. The "boasting" declined is not that of a Jew proud of fulfilling the Torah, but rather the pride of *Gentile* Christians over against Jewish Christians; see Fischer, *Tendenz*, 79–80.

138. Cf. Boccaccini, *Middle Judaism*, 265.

139. For example, Gaston, *Paul*; Gager, *Reinventing*. For a recent critique of this view, which flies in the face of crucial evidence, see Wedderburn, "Paulusperspektive."

140. For a fuller critique see Räisänen, "Paul, God, and Israel," 189–92.

141. Clearly James does not limit "works" to those that sep-

arate Jew from Gentile; he does not speak of "works *of the law*," but simply of "works."

142. James "puts forward the precise antithesis of Paul's formula" as stated in Gal. 2:16 and Rom. 3:28, and he intends this, too; "Paul's contention is proved wrong, the opposite case is shown" (Syreeni, "James," 402–3; cf. the argumentative *horate*, "so there you see," in v. 24).

143. Watson, *Paul*, 64–65 (cf. 2d ed., 122–23). Watson, *Paul*, 140, states (correctly, in my opinion) that in Rom. 4:18-25 "Abraham's trust is seen as a steadfast and heroic trust in God to fulfil his promises, despite unfavourable outward circumstances. According to v. 22, it was because Abraham had this kind of faith that righteousness was reckoned to him. 4:18ff is thus incompatible with the view that for Paul salvation is by grace alone. Grace is presupposed here in the form of the promise, but a strenuous human response, encompassing one's whole life, is required." This insightful passage is omitted from the second edition.

144. Cf. further the threat against the licentious and quarreling Corinthians in 1 Cor. 6:9 and the warning against an understanding that baptism is an automatic guarantee of salvation in 1 Cor. 10:1-13.

145. Jewish soteriology (as opposed to Paul's) is called synergistic by, for example, Laato, *Paul*, 167; Eskola, *Theodicy*, 44 and passim. Contrast Kuula, *Law*, 2:134.

146. For grace and effort in gnostic Christianity see later in this chapter.

147. See Räisänen, "Ringen"; idem, "Paul, God, and Israel"; idem, "Torn Between Two Loyalties."

148. Cf. Kuss, *Römerbrief*, 3:709; Hübner, *Gottes Ich*, 24–25.

149. Verse 14 shows that Paul is not insensitive to the problematic nature of this thesis. He even tries to refute some predictable objections, but all he can do is to assert that the Almighty cannot be unjust, since he has the power to do whatever he wants.

150. The hardening passage has evoked sharp but justified criticism from many commentators. Dodd's comment is famous: Paul takes "a false step" and "pushes what we must describe as an unethical determinism to its logical extreme"; the comparison with the potter represents God "as a non-moral despot" (Dodd, *Romans*, 157–58, 159). Cf. O'Neill, *Romans*, 157-58: Rom. 9:18 contains "a thoroughly immoral doctrine"; Kuss, *Römerbrief*, 3:730: the picture of God given in these verses has "despotic, tyrannical, Sultanic" traits.

151. McGrath, *Calvin*, 241.

152. Cf. Röhser, *Prädestination*, 179–92.

366

153. A popular proof text in early Christianity, Isa. 6:9-10 is quoted in a comparable context for example in Mark 4:11-12 par. and Acts 28:26-27.

154. In fact, the most normal passage in the self-contradictory section Rom. 9–11 is, in light of the total picture that emerges from Paul's letters, the middle part (9:30—10:21) that stresses the crucial nature of a faith decision (10:9-13). Cf. Kuula, *Law*, 2:331.

155. See Boring, "Language"; Hillert, *Salvation*. On Rom. 11:32, cf. Dunn, *Romans*, 2:697; Jewett, *Romans*, 712: "The expectation of universal salvation in this verse is indisputable, regardless of the logical problems it poses for systematic theologians."

156. The next verse speaks of "many," not of "all," but even here the respective acts of Adam and Christ are said to have equally comprehensive effects.

157. Cf. King, *Gnosticism*, 27; Dunderberg, "Judas' Anger." The reservation about apostates (on which compare Hebrews) reveals more of the bitter disappointment in a social conflict than it does a thought-out theological position.

158. That is, they cause this soul to be imprisoned in other bodies in cycles of reincarnation; see Layton, *Gnostic Scriptures*, 48.

159. King, *Gnosticism*, 160, 193.

160. Wilson, *Strangers*, 107.

161. Has the author only believing Gentiles in view?

162. Wilson, *Strangers*, 107.

163. Nickelsburg, *Ancient Judaism*, 74–75.

164. Cf. also *Jubilees*, and see the detailed discussion in M. A. Elliott, *Survivors*, 118–78.

165. Paul does rely on special mysteries revealed to him concerning eschatological events (1 Cor. 15:51; Rom. 11:25), yet this is not identical with founding salvation itself on the revelation of secrets. The same can be said of the book of Revelation, which parallels *1 Enoch* in the claim to reveal an imminent judgment that will be enacted by mechanisms already established in hidden places (cf. Nickelsburg, *Ancient Judaism*, 84), but emphasizes that salvation depends on one's behavior in the coming tribulation.

166. In the *Gospel of the Hebrews*, the holy spirit, which descends on Jesus at his baptism, finds in Jesus the rest it has searched in vain. The spirit here displays traits of God's personified Wisdom (cf. Sir. 24:6-7), so that Jesus comes to be seen as the bearer of this wisdom.

167. Nickelsburg, *Ancient Judaism*, 84; cf. Tuckett, "Atonement," 521.

168. "The salvific power of the cross lies in its revelatory power" (van der Watt, "Salvation," 113).

169. Ibid., 107.

170. His role is akin to that of the figure of Jewish Wisdom, "descended to call her children to their created purpose" (King, *Gnosticism*, 197).

171. The Thomasine Jesus here resembles a Stoic teacher; see Uro, *Thomas*, 100–101.

172. Cf. *Dial. Sav.* 35.

173. "In Valentinian mythology the primary role of savior is played by Christ, whereas Sethian myth presents a number of saviors, including many female figures" (King, *Gnosticism*, 159).

174. Ibid., 27.

175. The notion of Christ as physician receives a peculiar twist in the view, cherished in the school of Valentinus, that Christ heals the soul of noxious emotions. On this "christocentric therapy of emotions" that resembles the "cures" aimed at in philosophical schools of antiquity, see Dunderberg, *Beyond Gnosticism*, 95–118.

176. Jesus was persecuted for his teaching and nailed to the tree. The crucifixion is interpreted allegorically: Jesus is the fruit of the tree of knowledge and the Word of revelation, posted like a public notice on a wooden pole and read like the Book of Life (*Gos. Truth* 20). But "nothing suggests that the author would have considered the suffering of Christ to be ostensible or that someone else would have died on the cross instead of Christ" (Dunderberg, "School of Valentinus," 85).

177. King, *Gnosticism*, 155.

178. "The polemicists attacked their opponents as elitist determinists because the opponents purportedly said that the basis of salvation lies in the spiritual nature of humanity. From the polemicists' perspective this position undermines the doctrine of divine grace in the face of human sin" (King, *Gnosticism*, 282–83 n. 18). The old view is still perpetuated, for example, by Hultgren, *Rise*, 93.

179. King, *Gnosticism*, 207.

180. Rudolph, *Gnosis*, 117.

181. Ibid.

182. Desjardins, *Sin*, 119.

183. Church fathers had to wrestle with the question of why Christ came so late to accomplish his saving work.

184. See on the passage Achtemeier, *1 Peter*, 240–74, especially 244–46.

185. The related verse 1 Pet. 4:6 seems to envisage proclamation of the gospel (without specifying who carried

out the task, or when) to those who had died before Christ.

186. 1 Peter 3, too, came to be interpreted along such lines.

187. See also, for example, Justin, *Dial.* 72.4 (quoting the *Apocryphon of Jeremiah*); Irenaeus, *Haer.* 4.27.2.

188. A slightly different solution to the same problem was found by those members of the congregation in Corinth who undertook vicarious baptisms for the dead (1 Cor. 15:29). Today the Latter Day Saints continue this tradition in their own way.

189. Luke wrestles with the issue in the great Areopagus speech that he ascribes to Paul in Acts 17; see pp. 296–97.

190. Matt. 28:18-20 presents baptism (in connection with the Gentile mission) as a practice decreed by the risen Jesus, but this is a later interpretation; interestingly, the command to baptize is missing from the Lukan "command to mission" (Luke 24:47). Within the Matthean command, the threefold baptismal formula (which deviates from the early usage of baptizing "in[to] the name of Jesus" alone) is a problem in itself. But baptism in the threefold name is likewise mentioned in *Did.* 7.1-3. No trinitarian reflection is as yet connected with the formula; see Hahn, *Theologie*, 2:525.

191. John 4:2 ("it was not Jesus himself but his disciples who baptized") seems an apologetic correction. Did Jesus perhaps himself baptize some of the Twelve?

192. A proselyte baptism seems to have been in use during the first century in Judaism, but probably not before 70 c.e.; see Grabbe, *Judaic Religion*, 295–96. It was not a passive rite (for one immersed oneself) nor was it connected with remission of sins; see Hartman, "Baptism," 585.

193. On the phrase "into the name of," see, for example, Hartman, "Baptism," 586–87.

194. Cf. the words of Ananias to Saul/Paul in Acts 22:16: "Rise, be baptized and *wash away your sins*, calling on his name"; also Herm. *Mand.* 4.3.1-2.

195. Cf. the addition in many manuscripts to Luke's text in Acts 8:37 and the statement Mark 16:16 in the secondary, longer ending to Mark.

196. It is, however, remarkably casual in comparison with the later formal ceremony. Acts mentions several baptisms that were performed spontaneously as an immediate consequence of the person's response to the preaching (Acts 8:36, 38; 10:47-48; 16:14-15). Contrast the long and exacting catechumenate as described in Hippolytus's *Apostolic Traditions*.

197. Cf. Schnelle, *Paulus*, 545–49.

198. When Paul "recalled his readers to their beginnings as Christians, the recall was most often to the gift of the Spirit itself, and not to baptism" (Dunn, "Baptism," 85). Galatians 3:2-5 is a case in point. In 1 Cor. 12:13, where Paul states that "in the spirit we were all baptized into one body," the reference seems to be to the Corinthians' experience of receiving the spirit, the verb "baptize" being used as a metaphor; see Dunn, "Baptism," 95–96.

199. Zeller, "Entstehung," 111.

200. Dunn, "Baptism," 81, rightly speaks of "a rite triggered by human request and implemented by human action."

201. Cf. ibid., 101.

202. Ibid.

203. For references, see Kelly, *Doctrines*, 194–95, 207–8, 430. Whether infants were baptized before the end of the second century is controversial.

204. Exceptions include the *Gospel of Thomas*, which does not make much of rituals, such as baptism, and certainly does not create baptismal theology; see Uro, *Thomas*, 72. Cf. n. 208.

205. For fresh discussions of rituals in the Valentinian movement see Thomassen, *Seed*, 133–90, 333–414, and passim; Uro, "Bridal Chamber."

206. On the importance placed on baptism by Theodotus and other Valentinians see p. 240.

207. Desjardins, *Sin*, 119–20.

208. However, it is also possible according to the *Gospel of Philip* that a person is baptized but does not profit at all from the rite (*Gos. Phil.* 64.22-25). Baptism does not save *ex opere operato*. The *Gospel of Judas* goes further in its criticism of the overestimation of the rite, regarding baptism as a sign of false Christianity (*Gos. Jud.* 55-56). Layton, *Gnostic Scriptures*, 19, raises doubts about the practice of baptizing among gnostic Christians altogether, asking whether references to baptism are not mere metaphor (as clearly seems to be the case in *Apoc. Adam* 85.19-31: the hidden knowledge that Adam passed to Seth is the "holy baptism for people who have eternal knowledge"). He asks the same question with regard to the bridal chamber in the *Gospel of Philip* (ibid., 326).

209. On Sethian baptismal rites, including the "Five Seals" (presented in *Trimorphic Protennoia* as a five-stage ritual symbolizing the celestial ascent of the soul and bringing enlightening knowledge and total salvation), see Turner, *Sethian Gnosticism*, 238–42.

210. Rudolph, *Gnosis*, 227.

211. Ritual anointing was used in proto-orthodox communities as well (cf. 1 John 2:20; Jas. 5:14), often in connection with baptism. In any case, long before Tertullian (to whom we owe our first treatise on baptism), the rite of baptism consisted of three separate parts: immersion, unction, and the laying on of hands.

212. It is then a "kind of extreme unction" (Rudolph, *Gnosis*, 229).

213. Cf. Dunderberg, "School of Valentinus," 83.

214. Rudolph, *Gnosis*, 245.

215. Ibid., 246. Cf. *Gos. Phil.* 86.4-9: "If anyone becomes a son of the bridal chamber, he will receive the light. If anyone does not receive it while he is here, he will not be able to receive it in the other place He who will receive that light [in the bridal chamber] will not be seen [at his ascent], nor can he be detained."

216. Subsequently it became an established doctrine that the bread and wine are actually changed into the flesh and blood of Christ in the course of the ritual.

217. Kelly, *Doctrines*, 94.

218. Rudolph, *Gnosis*, 241.

219. Cf. ibid. The *Gospel of Philip* is explicit in establishing an "indispensable correlation between the image-character of earthly (and cultic) activities . . . and their realization in the next world": "Truth did not come into the world naked, but it came in types and images. The world will not receive truth in any other way. There is a rebirth and an image of rebirth. It is certainly necessary to be born again through the 'image'" (*Gos. Phil.* 67.9-18; Rudolph, *Gnosis*, 246). The "symbolic transformation of gnostic wisdom into cultic practices" (Rudolph, ibid., 247) could in some circles lead to scandalous practices to which older studies of Gnosticism gave great attention, such as the Ophites' alleged practice of using sperm and menstrual blood at their eucharistic meals.

220. Ruether, *Faith and Fratricide*, 244–45.

221. Ibid., 244.

8. TRUE MAN OR TRUE GOD? THE MEDIATOR OF SALVATION

1. These were especially developed in Egypt. In the person of Pharaoh, the son of Re, "a superhuman being had taken charge of the affairs of man. . . . The monarchy then was as old as the world, for the creator himself had assumed kingly office on the day of creation" (Frankfort, *Egyptian Religion*, 30).

2. The prophet himself is the one who is anointed (Isa. 61:1). By contrast, Haggai (2:23) and Zechariah (3:8; 4:6-10; 6:12) do tie their hopes to a Davidide (Zerubbabel).

3. Collins, "Pre-Christian Jewish Messianism," 1. The term *mashiah* occurs 38 times, but it never once designates an eschatological figure. For a qualification of this general thesis, see, however, Horbury, *Messianism*.

4. The term is also applied to the people of Israel (for example, Exod. 4:22-23; Hos. 11:1) and later to the righteous individual Israelite, too (for example, Wis. 2:17-18). In the plural it is also used of angelic beings (for example, Gen. 6:1-4; Job 1:6; 2:1).

5. The identity of the person called by others "son of God" and "son of the Most High" in 4Q246 is controversial.

6. Cf. Collins, *Scepter*, 165–66.

7. Collins, ibid., 56–73, shows that the expectation of a Davidic Messiah is more widely represented in the scrolls than used to be thought. His portrait is "sketchy but consistent." Presumably a human figure, he is "the scepter who will smite the nations" (Num. 24:17), "slay the wicked with the breath of his lips, and restore the Davidic dynasty" (ibid., 67). In 4Q174, the promise of 2 Sam. 7:14 is applied to the Davidic Messiah: God calls him his "son" (cf. Collins, *Scepter*, 164). On the priestly Messiah in the texts of Qumran and related literature, see ibid., 74–101.

8. Such as Judas ben Hezekiah, Simon and Athronges after the death of Herod (for example, Josephus, *B.J.* 2.56-65), as well as Menahem (*B.J.* 2.433-48) and Simon bar Giora (for example, *B.J.* 4.508) during the Roman war. On their messianic pretensions, see Horsley and Hanson, *Bandits*, 111–27.

9. Such as Theudas (Josephus, *Ant.* 20.97-99) or "the Egyptian" (Josephus, *B.J.* 2.261-63; *Ant.* 20.168-72). On these "sign prophets," see E. P. Sanders, *Jesus*, 170–72, 303; Horsley and Hanson, *Bandits*, 164–70.

10. Horsley and Hanson, *Bandits*, 127–29.

11. "Speedily cause the offspring of David, your servant, to flourish, and lift up his glory by your divine help because we wait for your salvation all the day."

12. Collins, "Messianism in the Maccabean Period," 106. In the vein of Deutero-Isaiah (where Cyrus is a messianic figure), *Sib. Or.* 3 "hails a Ptolemaic king as a virtual messiah" ("the king from the sun"; Collins,

Apocalyptic Imagination, 97) to pave the way for a utopian Jewish state. In 1 Macc. 14, the hymn in praise of Simon "strongly suggests that the time of fulfillment of the prophecies of Israel's glory had begun in the years of Simon's rule" (Nickelsburg, "Eschatology," 589). No future consummation is mentioned.

13. A different view is represented, for example, by Collins, *Encounters*, 180–82: a (semi-)divine figure, while "riding on the clouds" like the Canaanite Baal, to be identified with the archangel Michael (cf. Dan. 10).

14. Cf. Nickelsburg, "Son of Man," 138–42. This is so independently of the issue whether "Son of Man" was known as a fixed *title* in some apocalyptic circles. Of such a use there is no evidence (in *1 Enoch* it is not the question of a title)—unless the Gospels can qualify as such. This would not be a unique case: without the evidence of the Gospels we could not be sure that either "kingdom of God" or "Messiah" belonged to the central eschatological vocabulary of some Jewish circles; the extant Jewish sources give a rather different picture.

15. Nickelsburg, "Salvation," 63.

16. As Chester, "Messianic Expectations," 32, notes, this is hardly surprising in a "largely despondent work, directed against Rome in the immediate aftermath of the catastrophe of 66–70"; thus it is "obvious why the texts portray the Messiah not as a military figure but as destroying his enemies with the Torah/fire."

17. See also the reference to a savior figure in *Sib. Or.* 5.414-15: "a blessed man [will come] from the expanses of heaven with a scepter in his hands which God gave him."

18. Cf. Chester, "Messianic Expectations," 45–47; Collins, *Scepter*, 189.

19. Chester, "Messianic Expectations," 55–56.

20. He is described as "Iaoel of the same name, by virtue of my ineffable name" (*Apoc. Ab.* 10.3; cf. 10.8; 17.13). The name seems to be made up of the divine names Yahweh and El. In the *Apocalypse of Zephaniah* (probably from Egypt, early first century c.e.), a great angel Eremiel is described whose splendor is so shining that the seer mistakes him for God (*Apoc. Zeph.* 6).

21. Abraham sees "a wondrous man" sitting on a "terrifying throne" (*T. Ab.* 12.4-5). He is identified as Abel, "the son of the first-formed Adam," and he "sits here to judge the whole creation, examining both righteous and sinners" (13.3).

22. Collins, *Scepter*, 146; see his analysis of the text, 136–39, 146–53.

23. In the framework of the drama this happens in a dream of Moses, but undoubtedly the dream reflects wider traditions about Moses; see Collins, *Encounters*, 183. Cf. Philo, *Mos.* 1.155: Moses "was named god and king of the whole nation. And he was said to have entered into the darkness where God was."

24. Collins, *Scepter*, 149.

25. Young, "Two Roots," 113.

26. Cf. Collins, *Encounters*, 185: "Philo does not seem to regard the use of 'God' as a designation for the Logos as improper, although he clearly distinguishes between the supreme God and the intermediary deity."

27. Hurtado, *Lord*, emphasizes the boundary line between "honorific rhetoric" and cultic worship. On the likelihood of "some form of venerative behaviour" with regard to angels see Stuckenbruck, *Angel Veneration*, 103.

28. Segal, *Two Powers*.

29. Cf. Casey, *Jewish Prophet*, 175. For purposes of comparison one may consider the role of Virgin Mary in popular (in principle, monotheistic) Catholicism. Conversely, a Hindu author can state that "there is no polytheism in Hinduism," as "Siva, Vishnu, Brahma and Sakti are different aspects of one Lord" (Sivananda, *All About Hinduism*, 109).

30. Cf. Dunn, *Jesus Remembered*, 374–75.

31. Yet not as conventional exegesis of scripture, but on the basis of popular wisdom. The *Testimonium Flavianum* (Josephus, *Ant.* 18.63-64) calls Jesus a "wise man" and "teacher"; but see next note.

32. Josephus (see previous note) recognizes Jesus also as a "miracle worker."

33. Sabbatai Zevi, who posed as Messiah in the seventeenth century, elected twelve rabbis to represent the restored Israel (Scholem, *Sabbatai*, 222–23).

34. The individual stories may be open to historical doubt, but "the motif of surprise at the authority implicitly claimed by Jesus" must be well rooted in the reactions actually evoked by Jesus' teaching (Dunn, *Jesus Remembered*, 699).

35. The story of Jesus' ride to Jerusalem on an ass (Mark 11:1-10 par.) might reflect a claim on his part to be the hoped-for king, though not of the sort commonly expected; yet the historicity of this incident is controversial. Cf. the discussion in Collins, *Scepter*, 206–7.

36. Ignatius later picks it up from the Gospel vocabulary, but (mis)understands it as simply referring to the humanity of Jesus.

370

37. Apparently a memory of Jesus' idiolect was preserved in Christian usage (cf. *amen* in the expression "truly, [truly], I say to you," which likewise occurs only in words attributed to Jesus).

38. See, for example, the clear and comprehensive discussion of the problems and the interpretive options in Dunn, *Jesus Remembered*, 724–62 (though I disagree with his final conclusion).

39. Cf. Nickelsburg, "Son of Man," 142–49 (conclusion: 149).

40. For example, Hahn, *Hoheitstitel*, 32–42; J. Becker, *Jesus*, 249–67.

41. Vermes, *Jesus the Jew*, has called attention to the traditions of Honi the "circle-drawer" (first century B.C.E.), who is said to have made rain fall down and who prayed to God "like a son of the house" (*m. Taʿan* 3:8), and of Hanina ben Dosa, a wonder-working rabbi from the mid-first century C.E.

42. The significance of this address for Jesus' image of God has often been exaggerated, for example, by Jeremias, *Theology*, 66–67. God was frequently called Father in Jewish tradition (for example, Sir. 23:1, 4; 3 Macc. 6:3, 8) and so was Zeus in Greek tradition (for example, Homer, *Il.* 24.308; Dio Chrysostom, *Or.* 12, 74-75). Nor does *abba* mean "daddy"; cf. Barr, "'Abba' Isn't 'Daddy.'" Cf. Ashton, "Abba," 7: the use of *abba* by Christians (Gal. 4:6; Rom. 8:15; Mark 14:36) suggests that "the personal sense of the fatherhood of God was a typically Christian development of the Judaic tradition, and that this probably originated in a recollection of Jesus' teaching and of the example of his own prayer." But: "Since the address was taken over by Christians in their own prayer, they cannot have seen it as evidence of an *exclusive* relationship between Jesus and God" (his italics).

43. A pagan audience might have thought of the deification of distinguished men, such as Heracles, because of their merits.

44. The text is quoted in full in Mark 12:35-37 and Acts 2:34-35; allusions to it are found, for example, in Rom. 8:34-35 and 1 Cor. 15:25. For other references, see, for example, Hengel, "Psalm 110," 44. This is the most-quoted biblical text in the New Testament.

45. See Hahn, *Theologie*, 1:249–51.

46. Tuckett, *Christology*, 50.

47. Translation according to Dunn, *Romans*. Paul prefixes the formula with a mention of "the gospel of his (God's) Son," thus adapting it to a Christology of pre-existence that he himself holds.

48. M. Müller, "Son of God," 710. Cf. the short creedal statement (possibly dependent on Rom. 1:3-4) in 2 Tim. 2:8: "Remember Jesus Christ, raised from the dead, a descendant of David."

49. Hurtado stresses that "high" Christology is very early in evidence, but fails to seriously consider the phenomenon of "low" Christology at all. He does not discuss the "appointment in resurrection" in Acts (he has only brief references in *Lord*, 178–79, 344), or Rom. 1:3-4. Acts 13:32-33 does not appear in Hurtado's index at all.

50. Cf. Jervell, *Apostelgeschichte*, 152–53.

51. Tuckett, *Christology*, 143–44. For a critique of some attempts to find a higher Christology in Luke, see Tuckett, "Christology of Luke–Acts," 149–57. Recently, Rowe, *Narrative Christology*, has argued for a high Christology in Luke throughout, but I fail to see how Luke's use of *kyrios* in his Gospel could offset the numerous indications of Jesus' subordination to God in Luke's portrait of him.

52. Hurtado, *Lord*, 191–92. For more references, see ibid., 191 n. 70.

53. Ibid., 192–93.

54. The author uses this speculation to make a practical point: the Lord is an example for Hermas to keep his "flesh pure and stainless, that the spirit which inhabits it may bear witness to it, and your flesh may be justified" (*Sim.* 5.7.1). The passage may not be *intended* to make a christological point, but it does seem to *presuppose* (at least vestiges of) an archaic adoptionist Christology (contra Hurtado, *Lord*, 604). Cf. Brox, *Hirt*, 485–95, especially 487–88.

55. Kelly, *Doctrines*, 94. *Similitudes* 9.12.2 refers to the pre-existence of the Son, who advised the Father in the creation, but even here the "Son of God" is probably the spirit.

56. Hahn, *Theologie*, 1:566. The unusual expressions "times of refreshing" and "time of universal restoration" both refer to the parousia.

57. Oepke, "*parousia*," 857–58.

58. Even if the blood on Christ's robe (v. 13) were his own (which I consider unlikely), the rabid violence carried out by the "Word of God" cannot be explained away from the scene. The rod of iron, the winepress of wrath, and, not least, the invitation to the birds to eat the flesh of all and sundry, make abundantly clear that a horrible event is in view; against ameliorating interpretations, cf. Räisänen, "Revelation."

59. Hurtado, *Lord*, 250.

60. Cf. Tuckett, *Christology*, 86.

61. Long ago, Holtzmann underlined the idea of Christ's definite subordination to God (as opposed to any kind of coordination or *homoousia*) in Paul's thought (*Theologie*, 2:98–99). He pointed out that, on the basis of Paul's Christology, an Arian creed would be more natural than a Nicene one (ibid., 243).

62. Dunn, *Theology of Paul*, 251–52.

63. In Greco-Roman cults, many of the Deities were called *kyrioi* (cf. 1 Cor. 8:5), especially Serapis. In the framework of the developing ruler cult, emperors also came to be thus called. But 1 Cor. 16:22 (*maranatha*) indicates that the initial background of the Christian usage is Jewish (cf. *Did.* 10.6). There is some evidence that Greek-speaking Jews did use *kyrios* to refer to Yahweh (Fitzmyer, *Wandering Aramean*, 119–23), and even the absolute use of the Aramaic *mar* to refer to God is attested in the texts of Qumran. In calling Jesus *kyrios*, Christians used the same word that many Jews used to refer to God himself. This need not imply, however, that Jesus would have been thought to be on a par with Yahweh. Fitzmyer, ibid., 130–31, comments that Jesus was regarded "as sharing *in some sense* in the transcendence of Yahweh" and "*somehow* regarded as worthy of the same title" (my italics); but he was spoken of as *kyrios*, not as *theos*. Cf. Gen. 18:12-13 in the Septuagint: both Yahweh and Abraham are called *kyrios*.

64. Zeller, "Entstehung," 81; he traces this linguistic innovation back to the congregation in Antioch.

65. This is strongly emphasized by Hurtado, *Lord*, who, however, exaggerates the diffusion of overwhelming devotion to Jesus among his early followers. In Q in particular there is nothing comparable to what we find in Paul's letters.

66. See Dunn, *Theology of Paul*, 260; Hurtado, *Lord*, 151–52.

67. Contra the NRSV, which translates: "we wait for the . . . manifestation of the glory of our great God and Savior, Jesus Christ."

68. Tuckett, *Christology*, 87–88.

69. Hurtado calls the worship of Jesus "binitarian," stressing that it is "not ditheism" (*Lord*, 151). The distinction seems strained; Hurtado himself points out that "there are two distinct figures, God and Jesus."

70. Isis is called "the mistress of heaven, earth, and underworld" on the obelisk dedicated to her in Beneventum.

71. Zeller, "Entstehung," 79.

72. Tuckett, *Christology*, 180–82.

73. Note also Jesus' attributes in Rev. 22:13: "the Alpha and the Omega, the first and the last, the beginning and the end." Cf. Rev. 1:8; 21:6.

74. Cf. Luz, *Matthäus*, 1:150: without identifying Jesus with God, Matthew has put his Jesus story under a "high christological perspective." Jesus is the figure in whom God will be present among his people and later among all peoples.

75. Perhaps this is also indicated by the triadic (not yet trinitarian!) formula in 28:19.

76. Tuckett, *Christology*, 54.

77. Thus Wedderburn, *Baptism*, who also notes (356) that the idea behind Paul's usage may be less novel than his language. Even Paul's Gentile readers would have seen their own rulers and leaders as playing a representative role, upon which their own destinies and well-being depended.

78. Tuckett, *Christology*, 65.

79. Some find full divinity ascribed to Jesus in Heb. 1:8, 10. In Heb. 1:8, Ps. 44:7 LXX is quoted and Jesus seems to be addressed as God; in Heb. 1:10, verses from Ps. 101:26-28 LXX, originally predicated of God, are referred to Jesus. Yet in the context, the Son is wholly dependent on God. The Son, who is called "God" in v. 8, is in v. 9 reminded that "*your God* has anointed you with the oil of gladness beyond your companions," the point being that the Son will have a position over the angels. Psalm 101 is reinterpreted as an address by God *to* the Son, and here too the main thrust seems to be that the status of the Son will not change in the future. See Tuckett, *Christology*, 97.

80. In Mark 14:62, Jesus states that "you will see the Son of Man seated at the right hand of the Power and coming with the clouds of heaven"; Luke 22:69 changes this to "*from now on* the Son of Man will be seated at the right hand of the power of God," deleting the reference to the parousia.

81. In this, Luke comes close to John, for whom the Paraclete has replaced Jesus; see Tuckett, *Christology*, 144.

82. The paradox is enhanced in the singularly incongruous imagery of Revelation: Jesus is portrayed as the slaughtered Lamb, but the "wrath of the Lamb" (!) is extremely terrible, and in the end Christ the victim turns into the terror-provoking "King of the kings and Lord of the lords" (Rev. 19:16).

83. For Mark's elaboration of the "suffering" theme, see p. 206.

84. Tuckett, *Christology*, 142.

372

85. The docetically inclined efforts to deal with Jesus' death are discussed, pp. 222–23.

86. Cf. also John 6:14; 7:40.

87. For example, *Hom.* 1.19.1; *Rec.* 1.16.1; 2.22.1.

88. F. S. Jones, *Source*, 161, notes that it is not quite clear whether the author also presupposes the preexistence of Christ.

89. John's Jesus, by contrast, has nothing to do with exorcisms (though he does produce massive miracles, like the raising of dead Lazarus, as "signs" for something greater).

90. Note the parallel in the *Messianic Apocalypse* from Qumran (4Q521 frg. 2 II, 1-13) that likewise draws on the Isaiah passages: "[the heav]ens and the earth will listen to his Messiah. . . . for the Lord will place his spirit upon the poor, and the faithful he will renew with his strength. For he will honor the devout upon the throne of eternal royalty, freeing prisoners, giving sight to the blind, straightening out the twis[ted]. . . . the Lord will perform marvellous acts . . . he will heal the badly wounded and will make the dead live, he will proclaim good news to the meek, give lavishly [to the need]y, lead the exiled and enrich the hungry." Here, however, the healer is not the Messiah but God himself.

91. Theissen, *Theory*, 172. This impression is enhanced in Matthew's rendering of the story of Jesus walking on the sea: the disciples, who remain obtuse in Mark's version (Mark 6:51-52), venerate and acclaim Jesus as the "Son of God" (Matt. 14:33).

92. Weeden, *Mark*, has argued that Mark considers Peter's confession false, as it is based on Jesus' miracles; this is why Jesus silences him (Mark 8:30). On this (influential) interpretation, the disciples stand for some charismatics in Mark's community, who hold a "divine man" Christology, thinking that the presence of Jesus can be seen in their miracles; Mark attacks them by presenting the disciples in a bad light. However, the (truly striking) incomprehension of the disciples (for example, in 8:4 they do not know that Jesus might feed a crowd with a few loaves, although they have shortly before, in ch. 6, seen this happen) is only one side in their portrait in Mark; in other parts of the Gospel, they are presented in a completely positive light (1:16-20; 6:7-13). For a critique of Weeden and those who have followed him, see Räisänen, *Messianic Secret*, 211–14.

93. An alternative interpretation is that Jesus "from his *origin* belongs to the heavenly world"; thus Zeller, "Christology," 326. Yarbro Collins, "Messiah," 25–26,

also notes that, if the account is read from a traditional Greek point of view, it looks like the self-manifestation of a Deity. Read in this way, the account would be in tension with the description of the baptism, and it may be more plausible to take the transfiguration, on the level of Mark, as a "preview of the resurrection of Jesus." See also Dunn, *Christology*, 47–48.

94. In art, the Jesus of the pre-Constantine era is portrayed as a miracle worker who touches the diseased person with his hand, or miraculously multiplies the loaves and fishes, or changes water into wine. His suffering or death is not a theme. The faith of Christians as displayed in this art "centers on his delivering power"; "their Christology fits more the heroic figure of Mark (without a cross) than the self-giving Christ of the Apostle Paul" (Snyder, *Ante Pacem*, 109–10; cf. 298).

95. The notion of secrecy is not carried through consistently; the special honor and authority of Jesus is repeatedly revealed (first in Mark 2:10). See Räisänen, *Messianic Secret*, 224–41.

96. Most scholars would probably establish much more firmly a connection between the repeated injunctions to silence and the emphasis that suffering is an inevitable and central part of Jesus' calling. Yet the role of the "messianic secret" in Mark, once made famous by Wrede (*Messianic Secret*), is elusive; see the critical discussion in Räisänen, *Messianic Secret*, and the rejoinder by Tuckett, "Disciples." While it is clear that Jesus' suffering is strongly emphasized, even as an example to be followed if need be, especially in the central section 8:27-38, it is not clear what the specific contribution of the injunction to silence in 8:30 to the overall picture might be. Perhaps such injunctions simply indicate that humans could not yet know who or what Jesus was during his earthly life (as if Mark is half-aware of a post-Easter veneer in his own portrait of Jesus).

97. The reference is to the above-mentioned list of miracles in Q 7:22, taken up in Matt. 11:4-5.

98. Tuckett, *Christology*, 125.

99. Häkkinen, "Baptism," 75 n. 5, notes that he is not aware of any English translation of the Bible that translates the *eis* in Mark 1:10 properly with "into" (rather than with "[up]on," a rendering that is appropriate in the cases of Matthew and Luke, who have *epi*).

100. The phrase "Son of God" in Mark 1:1 is, however, probably a later scribal addition; see Yarbro Collins, "Establishing the Text."

101. Häkkinen, "Baptism," 75. In Christian art, the baptism of Jesus was still in the third and fourth century one of the most popular biblical scenes; see Snyder, *Ante Pacem*, 111. Snyder, 112, unnecessarily denies that the dove in these pictures represents the holy spirit as in the Gospel accounts; for criticisms see L. T. Johnson, *Religious Experience*, 151–53.

102. The *Gospel of the Ebionites* (according to Epiphanius, *Pan.* 30.13.7) combines Isa. 42:1 and Ps. 2:7 and preserves Mark's "into him."

103. On their notion that the sonship begins with Jesus' birth, see pp. 210–11. Mark describes the descending of the spirit as if it were a private vision ("*he saw* the heavens torn apart") and the heavenly voice ("*you are* my Son") as a private audition of Jesus. Matthew and Luke make public events of both: Luke states that "the heaven *was* opened," and Matthew lets the voice speak in the third person: "*This is* my Son." For Mark, unlike Matthew and Luke, possessionist Christology was not problematic; see Häkkinen, "Baptism," 87–88.

104. Cited in Jerome, *Comm. Isa.* 11.1-3.

105. Häkkinen, "Baptism," 79.

106. It is unlikely that Theodotus had any connection to the Ebionites; see Häkkinen, "Ebionites," 252.

107. See Kelly, *Doctrines*, 140. A peculiar twist was given to the baptism narrative in the thought of some Valentinians. At his descent from the Fullness, that is, in his incarnation, the Savior had to enter the human realm of imperfection in order to accomplish his mission; as a consequence, he was himself in need of redemption. He received his redemption in the baptism, when the "Name" (his divine nature) "came down upon Jesus in the dove and redeemed him" (*Exc. Theod.* 22.6; cf. Hippolytus, *Haer.* 6.35.5-6). See the discussion in Thomassen, *Seed*, 31–45.

108. Kelly, *Doctrines*, 117.

109. Goulder, *Tale*, 107–13, 128–42, does not make this distinction; his possessionist Christology (in the vein of Cerinthus) corresponds to what is here called the separationist view. Goulder thinks that the Cerinthian view is very early; Mark (who disapproves of it) has inadvertently retained traces of it, especially in the "into" of 1:10 and in the cry "My God, my God (*eloi eloi*), why did you forsake me!" (15:34; Goulder, *Tale*, 132–33, unconvincingly takes this to refer originally to "a divine spirit other than God himself," like Hebrew *elohim* in 1 Sam. 28:13, where it denotes Samuel's ghost). I do not see why the view that the spirit—God's power—entered Jesus at baptism (Mark, the Ebionites) should necessarily be connected with the idea that this spirit—now regarded as an independent agent, which is a different notion!—left Jesus at death (Cerinthus). The two notions should be kept apart, in which case the "into" in Mark 1:10 need not be an "oversight" (thus Goulder, *Tale*, 130) but may well correspond to Mark's own possessionist (but not separationist) view.

110. On Jesus' authority in the Gospels, see Hahn, *Theologie*, 2:230–33.

111. John develops the topic further, see John 5:10-18.

112. The provocative statements in Mark 2:10 and 28 are probably to be attributed to the evangelist Mark himself; thus, for example, Kiilunen, *Vollmacht*, 117–19, 197–98; Lührmann, *Markus*, 58, 64; Sariola, *Markus und das Gesetz*, 80–81.

113. Mark emphasizes several times that Jesus was active as a teacher, but transmits relatively little of the actual contents of his teaching (Mark 4:1-32; 7:1-23; 9:33-50; 10:2-12; 12:1-40; 13:1-37).

114. Cf. Tuckett, *Christology*, 128, who also points out that no idea of preexistence is implied.

115. Hurtado, *Lord*, 337.

116. King, *Gnosticism*, 197.

117. Bultmann, *Theology*, 2:66.

118. See Räisänen, "Begotten."

119. Sometimes one has sought indications of a knowledge of the miraculous birth tradition in the works of Mark and John, a knowledge that they could even presuppose their readers to possess so that they could content themselves with oblique hints. For example, Hurtado, *Lord*, 319–25, underlines that in Mark 6:3 Jesus is called "son of Mary" by the villagers and that in John 8:41 his Jewish opponents state that "we are not illegitimate children," implying—so the argument goes—that Jesus is illegitimate. The opponents would thus turn the Christian conviction of a miraculous birth into malevolent slander. But this is overly subtle; see Räisänen, "Begotten," 323–26.

120. For a thorough and balanced discussion of these stories, see R. E. Brown, *Birth*.

121. The Lukan Mary experiences an angelophany, while in Matthew Joseph receives the badly needed information (he has intended to abandon Mary) in a dream. Further dreams later guide him to protect the life of the newborn infant.

122. Unlike Luke, Matthew does not bring a story that initiates the reader into the mystery of Jesus' birth. He seems to assume that that his readers already know it;

374

cf., for example, Luz, *Matthäus*, 1:142.

123. Jesus' Davidic descent is presupposed in the old formula in Rom. 1:3, but rejected in Mark 12:35-37.

124. Four women (Tamar, Rahab, Ruth, and "the wife of Uriah") appear in the genealogy. The inclusion of women is striking in itself, but more surprising is the selection of precisely these four (instead, say, of the great foremothers Sarah and Rebekah). One has mostly taken the women as some kind of anticipatory types of Mary, with particular reference to sexual "irregularity" in the biblical stories about them (for example, R. E. Brown, *Birth*, 74). Yet the existence of such deviation is not clear in all cases (least of all in that of Ruth). It is hard to find a plausible common denominator for all these women; the interpretation that causes least difficulties is that they were all conceived to be Gentiles (H. Stegemann, "Die des Uria")—in which case any intended connection with Mary disappears.

125. Melchizedek's mother was barren. In old age, "she conceived in her womb, but Nir the priest [her husband] had not slept with her" (*2 En.* 71.1-2). Nir did not believe in the innocence of his wife and wanted, rather like the Matthean Joseph, to dismiss her. Suddenly the wife died; a baby was born from her corpse—a prodigious child, fully developed physically, who spoke and blessed God. Eventually Nir, too, praises the Lord "because by his word he has created a great priest, in the womb of Safonim, my wife. For I have no descendants. So let this child take the place of my descendants and become as my own son" (71.30-31 in manuscript A).

126. The Hellenistic influence is still visible in the motif of the abstinence of the father between conception and birth (thus also in the infancy stories of Heracles, Plato, and Alexander).

127. In the *Life of Numa* (4), Plutarch states that the Egyptians believe, plausibly in his view, that "it is not impossible for the *spirit* of a God to approach a woman and procure in her certain beginnings of parturition." In *Table Talk* (*Quaest. conv.* 717d), Plutarch mentions the tale of Plato's begetting by Apollo; he rejects it, since he finds it incompatible with the immutability of God. He reinterprets the issue: as in the creation of the world, the God activates a principle of becoming in matter, though not after the manner of human begetting (718a).

128. Diogenes Laertius, *Vit. phil.* 3.2; Philostratus, *Vit. Apoll.* 1.4.

129. Matthew does have a view of Jesus as "Son of God" with transcendent connotations (cf. 2:15; 3:17; 14:33; 17:5; 21:37; "the Son" in 11:27; 21:38; 24:36; 28:19), but it is not clear that he connects this with the miraculous birth. Theissen, *Theory*, 175, is positive: "Jesus is a divine being by virtue of his conception through the Spirit and his virgin birth"; but Stendahl, *Meanings*, 77, plausibly states that "in Matthew the virgin birth story is theologically mute: no christological argument or insight is deduced from this great divine intervention." Yarbro Collins, "Messiah," 29, infers from the Emmanuel prophecy (Matt. 1:23) that, for Matthew, "Jesus is divine, yet subordinated to God."

130. Even the stories in Luke 2:21-52 do not presuppose a virginal conception. In the story of Jesus' presentation in the temple (2:22-40), the narrator speaks quite innocently of his "parents" (v. 27) or of his "father and mother" (v. 33, in this order!). Also in the story of the boy Jesus in the temple (2:41-52), the expression "his parents" is used (v. 41), and the mother even employs the notable words "*your father* and I have been searching for you" (v. 48). This usage has worried some copyists, who changed v. 33 to read "Joseph and his mother" and v. 41 to read "Joseph and Mary."

131. Along with his portrait of Jesus as the heroic man and role model for Christians (cf. Luke's frequent references to Jesus at prayer, for example, Luke 3:21; 5:16; 6:12), Luke also "projects a very high view of Jesus' transcendent significance" into his account of Jesus' earthly life (Hurtado, *Lord*, 345). Much more frequently than other Gospel writers, he refers to the earthly Jesus as "the Lord" (for example, 7:13; 10:1; 12:42). Luke even has Peter, in his first encounter with Jesus, fall down at Jesus' feet in awe and ask, "Go away from me, Lord, for I am a sinful man!" (Luke 5:8). At the very least, Jesus is seen here as a rather extraordinary human.

132. The Qur'an (no doubt influenced by Jewish Christian notions) has developed this emphasis. The Qur'an accepts Jesus' virgin birth, but denies that it has anything to do with divinity. It is a sign of God's omnipotence: "God creates what He will. When He decrees a thing He does but say to it 'Be,' and it is" (3:47). A parallel is established between Jesus and Adam: "Truly, the likeness of Jesus, in God's sight, is as Adam's likeness; He created him of dust, then said He unto him, 'Be,' and he was" (3:59). With this emphasis, the Qur'an may be closer to the ideas of those who first brought forward the notion of Jesus'

virginal conception than is later ecclesiastical thought on this matter.

133. To be sure, the accuracy of this statement depends on the dating of the *Odes of Solomon*, where the combination also occurs (the virgin birth in 19.6-11; preexistence, for example, in 7.4-7; 41.11-15).

134. It may have been felt to be plausible as an argument against those who claimed that Jesus was not born at all (see p. 223)—though one would have thought a normal birth to have been a stronger proof.

135. See von Campenhausen, *Jungfrauengeburt*, 15–40.

136. See, for example, Justin, *Dial.* 48.4; Epiphanius, *Pan.* 30.2.2.

137. "Some said, 'Mary conceived by the holy spirit.' They are wrong and do not know what they are saying. When did a woman ever conceive by a woman? Mary is the virgin whom none of the powers defiled. This is greatly repugnant to the Hebrews, who are the apostles and apostolic men." The holy spirit, or Sophia Echamoth, is here a female character. The following section (*Gos. Phil.* 55.33-36) suggests that Jesus did have an earthly father.

138. Räisänen, *Mutter*; R. E. Brown et al., *Mary*.

139. Räisänen, *Mutter*, 118–24.

140. The "woman clothed with the sun" in Rev. 12 is not the mother of Jesus; the symbolic image stands for the church.

141. Gaventa, *Mary*, 119.

142. Cf. *Testim. Truth* 45.6-18: "John was begotten by the word through a woman, Elizabeth; and Christ was begotten by the word through a virgin, Mary. . . . John was begotten through a womb worn with age, but *Christ passed through a virgin's womb.* When she [Mary] . . . had given birth to the Savior, . . . she was found to be a virgin again." Another popular tradition has it that Mary did not need a midwife at all, since the birth was totally painless (*Odes Sol.* 19; *Ascen. Isa.* 11.1-16).

143. The new Eve motif is also found in Justin, *Dial.* 100.4-6.

144. The rapidity of the process is emphasized, for example, by Hengel, *Son of God*, 2 (though he exaggerates not a little in suggesting that "more happened in this period of less than two decades than in the whole of the next seven centuries").

145. Cf. ibid., 57: "Ancient man did not think analytically or make differentiations in the realm of myth in the way that we do, but combined and accumulated his ideas in a 'multiplicity of approximations.'"

146. Hengel, ibid., 69, referring, for example, to the preex-

istence of the Son of Man and of his name in *1 En.* 48.3, 6; 62.7; to the preexistence of the name of the Messiah in rabbinic sources; and to traditions about Wisdom. I fail to see, however, the allegedly "radical *trinitarian* character" of the "combination of Jewish ideas of history, time and creation with the certainty that God had disclosed himself fully in his Messiah Jesus of Nazareth" (ibid., 72).

147. Knox, *Humanity*, 12.

148. Christ is distinguished from God: all things exist "through" (*dia*) Christ, but "from" (*ex*) God.

149. Cf. also Rev. 3:14 ("the beginning of God's creation") and the statements on Christ as the Alpha and the Omega (Rev. 1:8, 21:6, 22:13); *Odes Sol.* 41.10, 15: Christ was begotten by the "riches" of the Father and "the thought of his heart. . . . He was known before the foundations of the world, that he might give life to persons forever by the truth of his name."

150. This passage is generally regarded as a traditional hymn, but O. Leppä, *Making*, 89–98, argues that it (like most of the letter) is a cento of biblical and Pauline expressions put together by the author.

151. For Paul the goal is God: Rom. 11:36; 1 Cor. 8:6.

152. The addition "the church" in one way makes the passage more "Pauline," though it is no longer the local community but the universal church that is the body of Christ.

153. The language suggests inspiration: Jesus is uniquely inspired by God, or filled with God's spirit. See Tuckett, *Christology*, 78.

154. Ibid., 79.

155. Ephesians takes over from Colossians the idea of the cosmic role of Christ. Yet the focus is shifted: Christ is made head over all things "for the church" (Eph. 1:22). This shift results in a marked *lessening* on any protological role of Christ; the explicit reference to Jesus as God's agent in creation—for example, Col. 1:16—is one of the few elements not taken over from Colossians. Whether Ephesians thinks of Jesus as actually preexistent is not entirely clear; see Tuckett, *Christology*, 82.

156. Kuschel, *Born*, 25.

157. Van Ess, "Islamic Perspectives," 18. In some (marginal) Shi'a cults the astonishing belief is held that Ali (Muhammad's cousin and son-in-law, the fourth caliph) and the imams are "incarnations of the Godhead, partakers of his attributes and powers, their bodies being but accidents inseparable from their visible forms" (Guillaume, *Islam*, 118).

376

158. Dunn, *Christology*, 182, followed by Kuschel, *Born*, 291. See further, for example, Dunn, *Christology*, 190, 194; and Kuschel, *Born*, 335 on Col. 1, as well as Kuschel's summary (303–8) on Paul ("no pre-existence christology"); Dunn, *Theology of Paul*, 266–93. Contrast, for example, Hahn, *Theologie*, 2:215–19.

159. It continues, for example, in 1 Tim. 3:16 and 1 Pet. 1:20.

160. Cf. Conzelmann, *1 Corinthians*, 167: Paul and his predecessors use a tradition already used by Philo *All.* 2.86), which equated the rock with God's Wisdom. Contrast the minimalist interpretation of Dunn, *Christology*, 184: "Paul's readers should see the rock then as an equivalent to Christ now."

161. See, for example, Vollenweider, "Metamorphose," 120–21. In the *Prayer of Joseph*, the patriarch Jacob is regarded as the incarnation of an archangel; see above, p. 195.

162. See Vollenweider, "Metamorphose," 116–31. A growing trend in scholarship, represented, for example, by Gieschen, *Angelomorphic Christology*, and taken up to some degree by Hurtado, *Lord*, emphasizes the role of angelological traditions as a crucial factor in the development of high Christology. Surely speculations about angels, say, as personified aspects of God, will have helped, though sometimes the connections suggested seem strained (see below, n. 197, on the notions of "divine name" and "glory" in John).

163. Zeller, "Entstehung," 85–87; Schnelle, *Theologie*, 157–59.

164. Vollenweider, "Metamorphose," 119–22.

165. Zeller, "Christology," 324, citing evidence.

166. Lüdemann, *Acts*, 118–19. Justin later confirms that "almost all the Samaritans, but also a few among other nations, confess him [Simon] as the first God and worship him" (*1 Apol.* 26.3).

167. Cf. Behm, "*morphe*," 746–48.

168. Zeller, "Entstehung," 85; idem, "Menschwerdung," 159–63. Cf. also *Odes Sol.* 7: the Lord "became like me, that I might receive him. In form he was considered like me, that I might put him on" (v. 4); "like my nature he became, that I might understand him, and like my form, that I might not turn away from him" (v. 6). That these statements do not imply full identification with mortals is shown by 28.17-18 and 41.8; see n. 171 and p. 223.

169. Knox, *Humanity*, 33. The point was made (and slightly overplayed) already by Weiss, *Earliest Christianity*, 489–90: "It cannot be denied that, for Paul,

the human body which Christ possessed upon earth means something like a disguise, appropriate to a rôle which he played here; he avoids, even purposely, the more direct and more powerful expression 'he became man,' because he still does not dare to express the complete humanity of Christ. . . . He permitted himself . . . to waver more or less in the balance between an actual humanity and a merely external assumption of a human body, as a result of which the inner being of the personality of Christ remains untouched by actual earthly humanity and sinfulness. In this Paul grazes the later heresy of 'Docetism.'" Cf. Nineham, *Use and Abuse*, 150.

170. Knox, *Humanity*, 51.

171. Cf. *Odes Sol.* 41.12: the singer refers to Christ as "the Man who humbled himself, but was raised because of his own righteousness"; yet the "Man" does not seem to be an ordinary man, for he says: "All those who see me will be amazed, because *I am from another race*" (41.8); cf. 17.6.

172. Apart from the *Odes of Solomon* (see above), note the appearance of similar terminology in *Acts of John*, *Ascension of Isaiah*, *Gospel of Truth*, *Apocalypse of Peter*, and in the work of Marcion (pp. 220–23).

173. It seems that, spurred by Ps. 110:4, the author has delved into Gen. 14, the only other biblical reference to Melchizedek, producing a novel christological reading. 11QMelch suggests that there may have been a varied body of speculation about Melchizedek in Jewish tradition, on which even the author of Hebrews could draw (Hurtado, *Lord*, 501). Cf. also the Nag Hammadi tractate *Melchizedek*.

174. Tuckett, *Christology*, 95–96.

175. Ibid., 101.

176. Kelly, *Doctrines*, 147–48, my italics.

177. Similarly, the *Dialogue of the Savior* states that the First Logos "established the cosmos and inhabited it and inhaled fragrance from it" (*Dial. Sav.* 34); cf. Uro, *Thomas*, 39, 44–45. For a different interpretation of *Gos. Thom.* 77, see, however, Marjanen, "Gnostic Gospel?" 121–24.

178. This must refer to the Father (Marjanen, "Portrait," 211).

179. Ibid.

180. Uro, *Thomas*, 45. See further Marjanen, "Portrait," 217–19, who also refers to other early Christian texts that contain the same idea of the common divine origin of Jesus and the rest of humanity.

181. Uro, *Thomas*, 53.

182. At the head of this development is the liturgy: doxologies are directed to Christ (2 Tim. 4:18; 2 Pet. 3:18; Rev. 1:5-6); psalms are sung to the Lord (cf. Eph. 5:19). Pliny, *Ep.* 10.96.7, takes this to mean that the Christians sing to Christ as to their God.

183. Some scholars hold that one or more of the Synoptic Gospels does presuppose the preexistence of Jesus; thus Stuhlmacher, *Theologie*, 2:137 (on Mark), 161 (on Matthew), 192 (on Luke). The case is argued at length by Gathercole, *Pre-existence*; for a trenchant critique of this work see Dunn, "Review."

184. Apart, of course, from his death and, in the case of Paul, a few of his sayings.

185. Kuschel, *Born*, 364.

186. Knox, *Humanity*, 16.

187. As Tuckett, *Christology*, 162, points out, the idea of agency enriches these ideas further: "an agent is like the one who sent him"; cf. John 13:20; 12:44–45; 14:9.

188. Dunn, *Christology*, 62. Dunn's subsequent remark that we should "not overestimate the significance of the differences" between New Testament Christologies seems totally unwarranted in light of his own discussion of the matter.

189. Knox, *Humanity*, 37. Cf. Wiles, "Reflections," 95: John radically changes the use of "Son of God" language, for "if *personal* pre-existence is anything more than a highly pictorial way of saying the same thing as the earlier . . . Christologies, then it cannot coexist with the other christological formulations. It is bound in the long run to distort and to devour them." Contrast Hengel, *Son of God*, 73: "the christological climaxes of the Fourth Gospel" [like John 1:1 or 10:30] mark the goal and consummation of New Testament christology."

190. Knox, *Humanity*, 26.

191. Cf. Ashton, *Understanding*, 501: "The Johannine Jesus carries his glory with him and his garments are always 'glistening intensely white.'"

192. There are hints in this direction in the Synoptic Gospels, in particular in the passion predictions (for example, Mark 8:31 par.); on the other hand it is suggested that there are things that the Son does not know (Mark 13:32 par. Matt. 24:36).

193. Consonant with this, the word *suffer* (almost a technical term with regard to Jesus' destiny in the Synoptic Gospels, where "the Son of man has to suffer much") does not occur at all.

194. Ashton, *Understanding*, 489; see his whole discussion of the "passion": ibid., 485–90.

195. To be sure, he does not say, "The Father and I have created the world"; cf. Kuschel, *Born*, 383; contrast *Gos. Thom.* 77.

196. Isaiah saw the glory of the preexistent Christ (John 12:41; cf. Isa. 6). Cf. the similar notion in 1 Pet. 1:10-11.

197. Hurtado, *Lord*, 374–92, discusses at length the significance of the notions of the glory of God and the name of God in John's Christology. But one should not press Johannine verses to the point of claiming that Jesus is *identified* as the Divine Name or the Glory. Thus Gieschen, *Angelomorphic Christology*, 271–80, commenting on, for example, John 12:28; 1:14; 5:43-44; cf. Hurtado, *Lord*, 386 on 12:28. This is not a natural reading of these verses. The meditation on Jesus as the Father's "name" is developed further in *Gos. Truth* 38.7—41.14. In this writing, the emphasis on Jesus as uniquely manifesting the proper name of the Father serves to distinguish this true Deity from the inferior, cruel God of the Old Testament (42.4-9).

198. Bultmann, *Theology*, 2:62, drew from this the modernizing and apologetic conclusion (accepted by Kuschel, *Born*, 383) that "Jesus is not presented in literal seriousness as a pre-existent divine being," but "the mythological terminology is intended to express the absolute and decisive significance of his word."

199. Hurtado, *Lord*, 398.

200. Nineham, *Use and Abuse*, 153–54; cf. Hultgren, *Christ*, 186–87.

201. Käsemann, *Letzter Wille*, 22–52 (especially 22–30, 51–52), 82–83. Hurtado's (*Lord*, 394–96) criticism of Käsemann misses the point, as he does not discuss, for example, John's "passion" story (without actual suffering!) at all (though he stresses Jesus' death as the pivotal demonstration of the reality of the incarnation), nor does he seem to perceive the meaning of "naive" in Käsemann's formulation. Of course, it is not a question of "real" (reflective or "formal") docetism; cf. Knox, *Humanity*, 25–27, who speaks of a "process of qualifying the humanity of Jesus" that has proceeded as far as it could go short of a final, formal denial of the human reality (27). This is why the fact that John knows of Jesus' human origins and "shares a concern to embed Jesus fully within a specific geographical, cultural, religious, political, chronological, and ethnic setting" (Hurtado, *Lord*, 395) is no weighty counterargument. No doubt the Gospel of John does affirm a genuinely human Jesus "in its own terms" (Hurtado, *Lord*, 394)—but it is these terms that are the problem.

378

202. Käsemann, *Letzter Wille*, 29.

203. Goulder, "Two Roots," 81. Wernle, *Beginnings*, 2:119, long ago asked in his forthright manner: is John's Jesus "much else than a phantom?"

204. Wiles, "Debate," 331–32 (my italics). Cf. Käsemann, *Letzter Wille*, 29: the Johannine Son of Man "is after all not a human being among others," but "God who descends into the human sphere and manifests himself there."

205. In both cases the result is that the cardboard Jews of the story want to stone Jesus to death.

206. Wilson, *Strangers*, 79. Dunn, *Christology*, xxxi–xxxii, states frankly that if the preexistent Word of God, the Son of God, is a person in the sense that Jesus of Nazareth was a person, "then Christianity is unavoidably tritheistic"; he tries to avoid this conclusion by explaining away, as we saw, the notion of a real preexistence of Jesus from New Testament texts.

207. Scholem, *Messianic Idea*, 123. According to one view, when the redemption began, God removed himself upward and Sabbatai "ascended to be God in His place"; others taught that the "Holy King" had himself been incarnated in the person of the Messiah (ibid., 124).

208. Even though he does not seem to suffer pain on the cross, and it is not completely beyond doubt that he *really* needs to eat; cf. John 4:31-34 and Käsemann, *Letzter Wille*, 22; Knox, *Humanity*, 26.

209. See on the *Gospel of Thomas* above, pp. 216–17.

210. First John itself underlines that Jesus' suffering was real and belonged to his being the "Christ" (5:6); cf. the reference of Pol. *Phil.* 7.1 to the "testimony of the cross."

211. Cf. Goulder, *Tale*, 122–23. Another possibility, described by Hurtado, *Lord*, 419–21, is that Jewish angelological traditions inspired some Christians to interpret Jesus' earthly life as an "appearance," analogous to the angelic visits to the earth. However, the Cerinthian interpretation better explains the issue of confessing or not confessing the identification of Jesus with the Christ.

212. Pagels, *Gnostic Gospels*, 73.

213. Turner, "Trimorphic Protennoia," 512–13; idem, *Sethian Gnosticism*, 147.

214. Some stories portray Jesus as an arrogant child: for example, when slighted by other children, he causes them to die (*Inf. Gos. Thom.* 3.1-4; 4.1-4)!

215. Hurtado, *Lord*, 451.

216. Ibid., 598.

217. Cf. the view of some Valentinians of the "Eastern" branch of the school, who held that the Savior was born from the Virgin Mary "as through a pipe," without any physical contact with her (Hippolytus, *Haer.* 6.35.5-7); Dunderberg, "School," 76.

218. Contra Hurtado, *Lord*, 598.

219. Ibid., 600.

220. Cf. *Tripartite Tractate* (see p. 225). Thomassen, *Seed*, 154–55, points to the ambiguity attached to the notion of the Savior's incarnation in the *Gospel of Truth* (and other Valentinian texts): on one hand "incorruptibility" is seen as something which the Savior had when he incarnated; on the other hand it is something that he "put on" after his incarnation, suffering, and death. Thomassen (ibid., 155 n. 19) rightly points out that "the question of docetism versus a 'real' incarnation in *Gos. Truth* is not one that can be answered in terms of either-or" and that the orthodox doctrine of the two natures of Christ is beset with the same problems; "the difference is more a matter of emphasis than of absolute distinctions."

221. The Ethiopic version continues: "and have grown up like unto you that were born in flesh."

222. Irenaeus, *Haer.* 1.26.1, with some obviously secondary features removed; thus Myllykoski, "Cerinthus," 233. The *Gospel of Peter* (19) has Jesus cry on the cross: "My power, my power, you have left me!" This could be taken as a trace of separationist Christology. The *Gospel* itself, however, hardly represents such a view. The Jesus who died and was raised is said to have returned to from where he had been sent (56): the preexistence of Jesus is implied.

223. Irenaeus (*Haer.* 1.26.2) states that the Ebionites shared Cerinthus's view of Christ. Epiphanius, too, connects the Ebionites with Cerinthus (*Pan.* 30.3.6; 30.14; 30.16.3; 30.34.6), yet without mentioning the separation of "Christ" from Jesus. In my view, it remains uncertain whether the Ebionites held a separationist or just a possessionist Christology (regarding Jesus as a man who gained a diviner power at his baptism). Of course there may have been different views among Ebionites, some holding the former, others the latter view.

224. Cf. Koschorke, *Polemik*, 44.

225. The view that Jesus did not really die on the cross later reappears, somewhat surprisingly, in an ambiguous verse of the Qur'an: "they did not slay him, neither crucified him, only *a likeness of that was shown to them*" (Qur'an 4:157, trans. Arberry).

226. See on the passage Koschorke, *Polemik*, 18–27. He

points out that it is quite imprecise to brand the view put forward in this text as "docetic" (ibid., 26).

227. See King, *Gnosticism*, 209.

228. See Löhr, *Basilides*, 255–73, on the report as a whole; and ibid., 272, on the present passage.

229. "It was another, their father, who drank the gall and the vinegar; it was not I. They were striking me with a scourge, but someone else, Simon, bore the cross on his shoulder. Someone else wore the crown of thorns" (*Treat. Seth* 56.6-13).

230. Pearson, "Basilides," 23.

231. A quotation of Basilides (Clement of Alexandria, *Strom.* 4.83.1; Löhr's frg. 7) seems to presuppose that Jesus did in fact suffer; see Pearson, "Basilides," 26.

232. Cf. Marjanen, "Suffering." In the *Letter of Peter to Philip*, the suffering of Jesus even has an exemplary and consolatory function; the author and the readers of this text have apparently been persecuted (ibid., 497–98). Cf. *Apoc. Jas.* 5.33—6.6; 13.23-25; and King, *Gnosticism*, 209–10.

233. Gnostic mythology is found in *Melch.* 8–9 and a gnostic interpretation of the paradise story in 9.28—10.11.

234. "They will say of him, he was unbegotten, though he was begotten; he does not eat even though he does eat; he does not drink, though he does drink; he is not circumcised, though he was circumcised; he is unfleshly, though he came in the flesh; he did not come to suffering, (though) he did endure suffering; he did not rise from the dead, (though) he did rise from dead."

235. Marcion regarded the material "flesh" as extremely evil; a strict ascetic, he could not imagine that the Savior would have subjected himself to the disgraceful order of reproduction. Nevertheless, it is a delicate issue to define whether Christ suffered and died only apparently according to Marcion; see the discussion in Harnack, *Marcion*, 125–26, with the paradoxical-sounding conclusion that Christ really suffered in the likeness of human form that he had adopted.

236. "Jesus practiced divinity; he ate and drank in a special way, without excreting his solids . . . the nourishment within him was not corrupted, for he did not experience corruption." The same claim is made elsewhere of Pythagoras; Valentinus's idea may be based on earlier stories about this legendary Greek sage; see Dunderberg, "School of Valentinus," 74.

237. The Qur'an (5:79) still appeals to it to prove that Jesus was merely human.

238. Dunderberg, "School of Valentinus," 74.

239. Zeller, "Konsolidierung," 136.

240. Schoedel, "Ignatius," 385–86. Intriguingly, however, *Smyrn.* 5.2 seems to indicate that those whom Ignatius so violently attacks were admirers of his courage in face of martyrdom; "docetism did not necessarily imply a lack of respect for martyrs and martyrdom" (Schoedel, *Ignatius*, 234).

241. Cf. *Treat. Res.* 44.12-32: the Lord existed *in the flesh*, being both Son of God and Son of Man. He possessed "humanity and divinity, so that by being Son of God he might conquer death, and that by his being the Son of Man Fullness might be restored." For an interpretation of the passage, see Thomassen, *Seed*, 83–85.

242. Cf. Thomassen, *Seed*, 49: "The Saviour needs to share in the condition of the ones he has come to save. He must take their physical existence on himself in order to save them from it. . . . He remains, to be sure, superhuman in so far as his birth is without sin and defilement, but the incarnation must be in some sense 'real' as well in order to be meaningful as a soteriological idea."

243. Pagels, *Gnostic Gospels*, 96.

244. Hurtado, *Lord*, 528–29.

245. Cf. Nineham (quoted above, p. 219); J. T. Sanders, *Charisma*, 131.

246. Knox, *Humanity*, 63. He also refers to John 6:35; 10:30; and 11:25.

247. Young, "Cloud," 23.

248. Ibid., 28.

249. Tuckett, *Christology*, 7.

250. Hick, *Metaphor*, 48, 45.

251. Knox, *Humanity*, 103–4. The same is, of course, true of the doctrine of the virginal conception, which is "'docetic' in its implications." "In the light of our biological knowledge," it is "impossible to see how Jesus could be said to share our human nature, if he came into existence by a virginal conception of the kind traditionally proposed" (Peacocke, "DNA," 65).

252. Knox, *Humanity*, 106.

253. Wiles, "Christianity without Incarnation?" 4. Hick, *Metaphor*, offers a detailed critique of some modern attempts to give an intelligible meaning to the idea of divine incarnation. For a spirited attack on the John-Chalcedon trajectory, see Casey, *Jewish Prophet*, 162–81. "If Christianity is to remain a viable option for honest and well-informed people, it should surely undo that process of development, and emerge as something nearer to the religion of Jesus of Nazareth" (ibid., 178).

254. Küng, *Islam*, 606.

255. Ibid., 606–7. Houlden, *Jesus*, 120 (retorting to the allegation that the classic pattern of Christology simply brings out the implications of New Testament belief within a new framework of ideas), points out that it "need to be recognized how strange and blasphemous the first Christians would have found the ascription to Jesus of divinity as later conceived." Young now takes a more positive view of the efforts of "orthodox" thinkers than she did in "Cloud," pleading that "the New Testament is to be read Christianly" and claiming that "it may be true that only hindsight covers the true significance of things" ("Trinity," 301); but even so she has to concede that there was "nothing inevitable" about trinitarian theology. "The doctrine of the Trinity is the outcome of reading the scriptural texts with particular questions in mind, questions which do not seem to have occurred to the earliest Christians at all" ("Trinity," 288).

256. Küng, *Islam*, 596–97. Note, for example, the hierarchy assumed by Justin, *1 Apol.* 13.3-4: "We reasonably worship Him [Jesus Christ], having learned that He is the Son of the true God Himself, and holding Him in the *second* place, and the prophetic spirit in the *third*."

257. Young, "Cloud," 23.

258. For what follows, see ibid., 24–30.

259. Ibid., 25. Logically there was no room in this scheme for the Holy Spirit as part of the Godhead.

260. See Groh, "Arius," 385.

261. Ibid. On Arius, see also Young, *Nicaea*, 58–64; the "arch-heretic" turns out to be "a rather literal-minded conservative" (Young, *Nicaea*, 64), whose views had their clear starting point in scripture.

262. However, many (the "spirit-fighters") would not have ascribed this kind of preexistence to the Spirit; against them, the Council of Constantinople (381 C.E.) asserted the divinity of the Holy Spirit as well. The Cappadocians finally produced the terminology (three persons—one nature) that came to prevail. See Küng, *Islam*, 612.

263. Young, "Cloud," 27.

264. Cf., for example, Davis et al., *Incarnation*.

265. Scroggs, *Christology*, ix (my italics).

266. Hick, ed., *Myth*, ix. That even this formulation assumes for Jesus a uniqueness that is hard to defend historically is shown in Nineham's "Epilogue" to Hick's volume.

267. Hick, ed., *Myth*, x, ix (my italics). See also Lindeskog, *Problem*, 191–92; cf. 27–29.

268. In a more recent work, Hick speaks programmatically of the *Metaphor of God Incarnate* (the title of the work).

9. The Empowering Presence: Experiences and Doctrines of the Spirit

1. The phrase "holy spirit" (Isa. 63:10-11; Ps. 51:13) is rare in the Hebrew Bible. It becomes frequent in rabbinic literature, generally in relation to prophetic activity.

2. The spirit sent by Yahweh can even be "evil" (1 Sam. 16:14) or lying (1 Kgs. 22:22); cf. Judg. 9:23.

3. On Greco-Roman prophecy, see Aune, *Prophecy*, 23–48; Flower, *Seer*.

4. Kleinknecht, "*pneuma*," 346; cf. Aune, *Prophecy*, 33.

5. "The prophetess at Delphi and the priestesses at Dodona when out of their senses have conferred great benefits on Hellas, both in public and private life, but when in their senses few or none" (*Phaedr.* 244).

6. See, for example, Plato, *Apol.* 22c; *Ion* 534d; *Meno* 99d; *Phaedr.* 244 a-c. In the first three cases Plato is comparing the inspiration of poets and administrators (!) to that of the mantic prophets.

7. See, however, Mic. 3:8.

8. Moore, *Judaism*, 1:237.

9. Aune, *Prophecy*, 103–6; Grabbe, *Judaic Religion*, 236–39; Boring, "Prophecy," 497. Josephus reports on the (in his view, false) "sign prophets" (Theudas: *Ant.* 20.97-99; "the Egyptian": *B.J.* 2.261-63; *Ant.* 20.168-72); on Essenes, who were able to foretell the future (*Ant.* 13.311-12; *B.J.* 1.68-69; 2.159) and on the unlettered peasant Joshua ben Ananiah, who constantly repeated a doom oracle against Jerusalem (*B.J.* 6.300-309); Josephus even represents himself acting as a prophet (without using the term) sent from God to announce that Vespasian would become emperor (*B.J.* 3.400–402).

10. Rowland, *Open Heaven*, 21.

11. "Ezra" prays God to send his "holy spirit" into him, so that he may write again the books of the Bible that had been lost in the destruction of Jerusalem (v. 22). He is given a cup to drink "full of something like water, but its color was like fire" (v. 39). When Ezra has drunk

from the cup, God's spirit lights "the lamp of understanding" in his heart. See the excursus on inspiration in Stone, *Fourth Ezra*, 119–24.

12. Stone, "Apocalyptic Literature," 429; cf. Russell, *Method and Message*, 158–59. On the relative frequency of visionary experiences in Greek culture, see Dodds, *Greeks and the Irrational*, 102–21, especially 116–17.

13. Job gives his daughters miraculous "cords"; placing them on one's breast gives the daughters "a new heart" so that they no longer care for mundane things and start speaking in the language of angels. The spirit is mentioned in *T. Job* 48.3: as the first daughter "spoke ecstatically, she allowed 'the spirit' to be inscribed on her garment." One manuscript also states (51.2) that the holy spirit was present at Job's bed. Although the meaning of the verse is uncertain, 51.3 may suggest that the daughters were also granted the gift to interpret their speech.

14. Thus Newsom, *Songs*, 15, 17.

15. Dautzenberg, *Prophetie*, 69, 207–13.

16. Aune, *Prophecy*, 152.

17. Philo says that he has experienced this intellectual "intoxication" "ten thousand times"; contrast Lane Fox's dry comment that "careful study of Philo's writings shows how rare and faint these scholarly 'flashes' were" (*Pagans and Christians*, 313). The first writer we know to have talked about poetic ecstasy under "a holy spirit" was Democritus; see Dodds, *Greeks and the Irrational*, 82. On Philo see now Levison, "Philo's Personal Experience," esp. 197–202.

18. Cf. the enigmatic "Servant of Yahweh" in Isa. 42:2; cf. 61:1.

19. Cf. Albertz, *Religionsgeschichte*, 514–15.

20. Yahweh had filled Bezalel "with divine spirit, with ability, intelligence, and knowledge in every kind of craft, to devise artistic designs . . . in every kind of craft," just as he had "given skill to all the skillful" to work on the construction of the tent of meeting (Exod. 31:1-11). Philo emphatically refers to this passage (*Gig.* 23).

21. The "less extraordinary" effects of the spirit parallel those ascribed to other attributes of God, such as Wisdom. In Prov. 8, Wisdom (personified) calls people to learn from her and provides the same virtues as the spirit (and the law): truth, righteousness, knowledge. Wisdom 7:25 describes Wisdom in terms that would fit the spirit even better: it is "a breath of the power of God." Humans can find right knowledge and gain salvation only if God gives them wisdom and

sends his holy spirit from on high (Wis. 9:17-18).

22. Cf. *T. Jud.* 24.3: God will pour out his spirit on the Messiah (cf. Isa. 11:2), who will "pour the spirit of grace on you. And you shall be sons in truth, and you will walk in his first and final decrees." This passage may, however, come from a Christian.

23. Sjöberg, "*pneuma*," 385, connects the Qumranic mentions of possession of the spirit with Josephus's mention of pneumatic phenomena (foretelling of the future) by some Essenes (see above, n. 9).

24. Luke 11:20 speaks of the "finger of God," which was probably the original reading in Q. As stated above, I doubt that Q 11:20 is a saying of the historical Jesus, but the notion that with divine aid Jesus fought the forces of Satan (Mark 3:22-30) was surely his own conviction. Jesus' ability to heal is ascribed to "the power of the Lord (God)," without specific mention of the spirit, in Luke 5:17; cf. 4:36. "Power" (*dynamis*) and "spirit" (*pneuma*) are explicitly identified by Luke in 1:35 and 24:49; cf. Acts 1:8; 6:8; 10:38. If the saying that equates polemic against Jesus' exorcisms with blasphemy of the holy spirit (Mark 3:29 in conjunction with 3:22) were authentic, that would suggest that Jesus explicitly ascribed his exorcistic ability to the spirit (thus Dunn, *Remembering Jesus*, 694–95; Rowland, *Origins*, 171–72); yet such an assumption is problematic (cf. Luz, *Matthäus*, 2:257).

25. Thus even Dunn, *Remembering Jesus*, 374–75, though he admits that it is entirely possible that Jesus experienced a commissioning at the Jordan (ibid., 377).

26. See Lüdemann, *Resurrection of Jesus*, 100–108; differently N. T. Wright, *Resurrection*, 324–25.

27. Lüdemann, *Acts*, 50; cf. Fischer, *Urchristentum*, 64–65: Luke's account, in itself unhistorical, suggests that one has to reckon with outbursts of glossolalia in the early period. Schenke, *Urchristentum*, 20, locates the event in Galilee (in Jerusalem the only place with enough space for such a mass experience would be the temple area), but such an event there should have left more traces in the tradition.

28. Luke thereby creates a story that parallels Jewish accounts of the giving of the Torah (cf. Philo, *Decal.* 46).

29. By contrast, the Gospel of John does not refer to a general reception of the spirit; in John's story, the risen Jesus breathes his spirit right after the resurrection (rather than at Pentecost, John 20:22) on the *apostles*, commissioning them to exercise church discipline (forgive sins or deny forgiveness; cf. Matt. 18). What is

382

common to Acts and John is that *Jesus* is the bestower of the spirit (cf. Acts 2:33).

30. Apart from Paul in a special situation in Corinth, one probably did not distinguish sharply between glossolalia and prophecy; see Jervell, *Apostelgeschichte*, 138; cf. Dautzenberg, *Prophetie*, 229.

31. Paul probably inherited the notion from the traditions of the "Hellenists," who, however, presumably did not differ decisively from the "Hebrew" part of the community on this point; contra Horn, "Holy Spirit," 270–71; see, for example, Conzelmann, *Grundriss*, 116–17.

32. The nature of the rite as a bath hints at a more negative content: purification from sin(s).

33. Strangely enough, the baptism conducted by the spirit-guided wonder-worker Philip (Acts 8:5-13) had not given the spirit to the baptized Samaritans; Peter and John have to complete his work (8:15-17).

34. While Luke has some obvious church-political aims in Acts 8:15-17, the story seems also to reflect the fact that not every baptism was accompanied by spectacular phenomena. One is tempted to assume that in reality such signs were not the rule, and Bultmann, *Theology*, 1:160, suggests indeed that only *occasionally* may the individuals baptized have had special "spiritual" or emotional experiences. Paul testifies that all Christians did not possess extraordinary abilities even in Corinth, where "spiritual gifts" abounded (1 Cor. 12:8-11, 29-30); the pneumatics may have been in the minority. See also Meeks, *Urban Christians*, 151–52.

35. Cf. Dautzenberg, *Prophetie*, 214, discussing 1QM 10.10-11: extraordinary visionary experiences were probably limited to a small group of especially "gifted" persons, and yet they are regarded as characteristic of the whole community, the "people of the holy covenant" and its election.

36. For this definition, see Boring, "Prophecy," 496.

37. Boring, "Prophecy," 500, suggests that the abundance of prophetic phenomena in the Lukan birth story (Luke 1:35, 41-45, 67-69; 2:29-35) may also "preserve memories and materials from early Christian prophets."

38. See Eusebius, *Hist. eccl.* 3.31.3-4; 3.39.9; 5.24.2.

39. For Q and Matthew, see Boring, "Prophecy," 499.

40. He writes words of prophecy (Rev. 1:3; 19:20; 22:7, 10, 18-19) and belongs to a group of prophets (22:9).

41. Klauck, "Sendschreiben," 179–80.

42. 1 Thess. 4:15-17 may well be another example of such an utterance, this time preserved in a letter of Paul.

43. Boring, "Prophecy," 500; cf. Aune, *Prophecy*, 296–99.

44. See Förster, *Marcus*, 135. Marcus's activity is probably to be dated c. 160–180 c.e. (ibid., 390).

45. Thomassen, *Seed*, 499. Thomassen calls attention to the fact that Marcus operated in Asia Minor, the birthplace of Montanism and an area strongly associated with ecstatic (especially female) prophecy even earlier. Clement of Alexandria, *Exc. Theod.* 24, indicates that prophecy may not have been an alien feature in Valentinian worship: "The Spirit which each of the prophets received individually for his ministry is poured out upon all those who belong to the Church. That is why the signs of the Spirit—healings and prophesyings—are accomplished by the Church" (ibid., 499 n. 30).

46. Förster, *Marcus*, 123–26, 136–38, argues convincingly that Irenaeus's allegation is probably without foundation. Contra Filoramo, *History*, 168, who calls Marcus a "Gnostic Casanova."

47. See, for example, Lüdemann, *Acts*, 144–46.

48. Peter did accept the decision, though, as his behavior in Antioch before the arrival of the "men from James" shows (Gal. 2:11-12).

49. Cf. Esler, *Galatians*, 107; Dunn, *Theology of Paul*, 418–19; idem, *Galatians*, 153–54.

50. Cf. Lüdemann, *Acts*, 144.

51. 2 Cor. 5:13 and 12:7 imply that the experience hinted at in 12:2-4 was not an isolated event in Paul's life; see Dunn, *Unity*, 191.

52. Aune, *Prophecy*, 249.

53. Often the revelation that John receives "in the spirit" is mediated through an angel (for example, Rev. 17:3; 21:10). The seer's use of traditional materials and stereotyped forms in describing his visions is no objection to the reality of his experiences; see Boring, "Prophecy," 500.

54. Boring, "Prophecy," 501, is typical.

55. Lane Fox, *Pagans*, 381, calls the work a "jewel of the non-canonical writings" and says that Hermas's "visionary odyssey is surely the work of a 'prophet' as the early Church orders knew one: a Christian, gifted with the Spirit, who deserved the community's highest respect" (ibid., 388). On the institutionalized church life at Rome as the context of the work, see White, *From Jesus to Christianity*, 344. That Hermas does not regard himself as a "prophet" in a traditional sense is another matter. Cf. also Aune, *Prophecy*, 218.

56. Filoramo, *History*, 155–56; he states that "the psychological origin of Gnosticism cannot be detached from phenomena of possession and religious enthusiasm typical of the period."

57. Ibid., 117. The reference is to Hippolytus, *Haer.* 6.42: Valentinus "alleges that he had seen an infant child lately born; and questioning (this child), he proceeded to inquire who it might be. And (the child) replied, saying that he himself is the Logos, and then subjoined a sort of tragic legend; and out of this (Valentinus) wishes the heresy attempted by him to consist." Yet both the reliability of the report and the interpretation of the passage are uncertain; see the lengthy discussion in Markschies, *Valentinus*, 205–15.

58. The author uses Paul's body metaphor (1 Cor. 12), but applies it differently, to solidify a hierarchy between those who have the "prophetic gift" and those who have not; see Dunderberg, *Beyond Gnosticism*, 149–58.

59. Note the analogy with the Pythia, whose utterances had to be interpreted; cf. Kleinknecht, "*pneuma*," 348.

60. Paul suggests that the one who speaks in tongues may also act as interpreter, but has to pray for the power to interpret the speech (1 Cor. 14:13).

61. Conzelmann, *1 Corinthians*, 204 n. 7; Esler, "Glossolalia," 47–48.

62. Dunn, *Unity*, 179. In 1 Cor. 14:23, too, Paul's choice of words (outsiders would conclude that a congregation speaking in tongues is "raving," *mainesthe*) suggests that he saw a connection between glossolalia and Greek mantic prophecy; cf. L. T. Johnson, *Religious Experience*, 115.

63. See Schüssler Fiorenza, *In Memory*, 227–28.

64. L. T. Johnson, *Religious Experience*, 132–33.

65. Ibid., 130–31. On the issue of veiling, see Martin, *Corinthian Body*, 239–49.

66. L. T. Johnson, *Religious Experience*, 117. Horn, *Angeld*, 201–6, considers the phenomenon to be only a Corinthian peculiarity.

67. L. T. Johnson, *Religious Experience*, 118.

68. Cf. Dautzenberg, *Prophetie*, 214–15.

69. See on this Marjanen, "Montanism," 196–99.

70. L. T. Johnson, *Religious Experience*, 133, with reference to the polemical account of Eusebius, *Hist. eccl.* 5.16.7-10.

71. L. T. Johnson, *Religious Experience*, 134; Irenaeus, *Haer.* 1.13.4. Förster, *Marcus*, 117–18, rejects the thesis that the prophecies of the Marcosians can be regarded as cases of glossolalia.

72. John Chrysostom does not understand the passage about tongues in 1 Corinthians, and Augustine "dismisses the significance of tongues as a special dispensation of the primitive church, no longer of pertinence to the church in his day" (L. T. Johnson, *Religious Experience*, 135).

73. "Gifts of healing by the spirit" and "the working of miracles" (is the latter a reference to exorcisms?) are mentioned among the "spiritual gifts" that were in evidence in Paul's Corinth (1 Cor. 12:9-10, 28-30; cf. 13:2), though they seem to have had a less central place than glossolalia and prophecy (they are not mentioned in ch. 14).

74. 1 Pet. 4:13-14 also connects sharing Christ's sufferings (understood as suffering for the name of Christ) and the presence of God's spirit; cf. Dunn, *Unity*, 196.

75. The notion of Peter and Simon engaged in a conflict has its roots in Acts 8:9-24.

76. Bultmann, *Theology*, 1:157-60, analyzes "inconsistencies or contradictions" in some early Christian notions.

77. "Prophecy, in fact, is the only constant in Paul's 'lists' of charismata" (Boring, "Prophecy," 498). Paul himself could well be classified as a Christian prophet (depending on one's definition of the term); cf. Aune, *Prophecy*, 248–49. Paul does not apply the title to himself, but he places himself squarely in a prophetic succession by alluding to scriptural expressions of the consciousness of a prophetic vocation (Jer. 1:5; Isa. 49:1) in his short reference to his "call" (Gal. 1:15-16).

78. Dautzenberg, *Prophetie*, 122–48, argues that *diakrisis* does not mean "discernment" but "interpretation." Criticisms against this view are presented, for example, by Wolff, *Korinther*, 2:104–5.

79. "The others" may mean "the other prophets" (Conzelmann, *1 Corinthians*, 245), but even this reading would not remove the underlying problem.

80. In this case, too, the implication is that all spiritual or prophetic utterances that occur are not good, that is, God-given.

81. In Thessalonica, too, prophecy had obviously created some kind of problem.

82. Paul puts a special weight on the gift of wisdom, of which he himself is a bearer, in 1 Cor. 2:6-16.

83. Wernle, *Beginnings*, 1:262. Cf. Weiss, *Earliest Christianity*, 626–27: in Paul's hands, the ancient animistic idea of a temporary seizure by supernatural powers changes to that of a permanent "gift" (as in 1 Cor. 12:28), but "the concept is completely changed when mention is made of the 'indwelling' of the Spirit (Rom. 8:9, 11), of the lifelong control of the Spirit (Rom. 8:4-5)."

84. Cf. Wernle, *Beginnings*, 1:263: "a theory of Christian life as it should be is here built up upon isolated great experiences."

384

85. In 1 Thess. 4:8, Paul inserts a reference to God's bestowing his spirit upon the addressees, and precisely the mention of the spirit seems "to imply that they should have known better" (Shaw, *Cost*, 32).

86. In this connection, Paul even seems to divide the believers in two classes: those with and those without the spirit (1 Cor. 2:10—3:4). Paul is engaged in polemics against a group of members in the congregation: "Even though they are Spirit people, he could not address them as such because both their thinking and behavior are contrary to the Spirit. . . . even though they do have the Spirit, they are acting like 'mere human beings'!" (Fee, *Presence*, 96–97; cf. Conzelmann, *1 Corinthians*, 72). Despite his branding the Corinthians as fleshly, Paul states a little later that God's spirit dwells in them after all (1 Cor. 3:16).

87. This corresponds to Stoic notions; cf. Nock, *Conversion*, 221: "Stoicism had taught that there was in man a particle of the divine spirit as a thing inherently bound to be present in his nature. But this was in a sense something up to which he must live rather than something by which he must live. In any case, it was supposed to be present in all men." Valentinus, in his poem *Harvest* (frg. 8), says that all is suspended and carried by the spirit (leaning on the pantheistic Stoic notion of the all-pervasive spirit that permeates the world).

88. Some fail to do such good works even though the spirit has descended on them, but they will still be saved because they possess the spirit. The idea seems to be that "once you have received the Spirit you *cannot* avoid making progress, though you may fall short of true perfection" (Dunderberg, "Judas' Anger"). On receiving the spirit, see also *Gos. Truth* 26.35—27.8; 31.17-20. In the last passage "the powerful spirit" is mentioned along with thought, understanding, mercy, and salvation as a gift by the Savior "from the infiniteness and sweetness of the Father." The spirit thus continues Christ's revelatory work and brings knowledge; cf. Hauschild, *Gottes Geist*, 274–75 n. 2.

89. Hauschild, *Gottes Geist*, 178–79; Desjardins, *Sin*, 38–39.

90. Desjardins, *Sin*, 39–40. Cf. the importance placed on baptism in *Tri. Trac.* 127.28—128.5: Desjardins, *Sin*, 86; Thomassen, *Seed*, 171.

91. Desjardins, *Sin*, 96.

92. Ibid., 120–26.

93. "There are more visions recorded in Acts than in the rest of the New Testament put together (Revelation apart)" (Dunn, *Unity*, 181).

94. In this rendering, *pneumatikois* is understood as neuter; thus, for example, Conzelmann, *1 Corinthians*, 67; Fee, *Presence*, 104–5. If the word is understood as masculine (thus, for example, Horn, *Angeld*, 185–86), Paul is saying that he interprets spiritual truths to those who possess the spirit.

95. Eph. 3:3 also ascribes to Paul knowledge of a mystery received through revelation.

96. For example, Acts 1:16; 4:25 (through David); 28:25-26 (through Isaiah). According to 1 Pet. 1:10-11, the Old Testament prophets had "the spirit of *Christ* within them." In 2 Tim. 3:16, the whole scripture is *theopneustos*, inspired by God's spirit (and therefore useful and of educational value, enabling believers to perfect and virtuous life).

97. "He approaches the Holy Scriptures with a fundamental conviction that God has placed concealed secrets in them, which only the eye enlightened by the Spirit can discover" (Weiss, *Earliest Christianity*, 436).

98. On Paul's freedom with regard to the wording of the scriptural texts quoted by him, see Koch, *Schrift*, 186–90.

99. To be sure, 1 John 4:1-3 presupposes that cases of prophecy occur in the congregation.

100. Cf. Bultmann, *Theology*, 2:88. Dunn notes that "John is no enthusiast: he is not a protagonist of tangible spirituality" (*Unity*, 199).

101. R. E. Brown, *John*, 2:643. John 7:39 states that the exaltation of Jesus was a precondition of the coming of the spirit.

102. Cf. Käsemann, *Letzter Wille*, 71.

103. Schnelle, *Theologie*, 667. Whether this exposition is at least partly based on spontaneous outbursts in worship, in that some members spoke in the name of the risen Lord (thus, for example, J. Becker, *Evangelium des Johannes*, 209–10), cannot be ascertained.

104. No wonder charismatic persons such as Montanus or Mani could seize on the Paraclete passages. Some early Muslim interpreters even applied them to Muhammad.

105. According to 1 John 2:20, 27, the anointing with the spirit provides members of the congregation with true knowledge.

106. Boring, "Prophecy," 500.

107. Dunn, *Unity*, 197.

108. Carroll, *Prophecy*, 184–204.

109. Ibid., 198–204.

110. Teeple, *How Christianity*, 217, comments that "humility was not one of Paul's virtues."

111. For a trenchant critique (sometimes exaggerated, but quite often to the point) of Paul's manipulating rhetoric throughout his letters, see Shaw, *Cost*, 29–185 (on 1 Cor. 2, see 65–66; on 2 Cor. 1, see 114).

112. Cf. Dunn, *Unity*, 182.

113. Of the guardians of Paul's legacy, the author of Colossians seems very reserved toward prophecy. Ephesians looks back to prophets as authoritative figures but does not show knowledge of them as a living reality. See Boring, "Prophets," 499.

114. Mark displays considerable open-mindedness in his recognition of the maverick exorcist who uses Jesus' name without joining his disciples (Mark 9:38-40). This passage is omitted by Matthew, who also reverses the positive saying in Mark 9:40 ("whoever is not against us is for us") (Matt. 12:30).

115. Boring, "Prophets," 499.

116. Cf. ibid.

117. See the discussion of the options in Luz, *Matthäus*, 1:524–25.

118. Shaw, *Cost*, 65–66, commenting on 1 Cor. 2:14.

119. Cf. Bauer, *Orthodoxy*, 77–78; Thompson, *Revelation*, 132; Klauck, *Sendschreiben*, 170.

120. Mohrlang, *Matthew and Paul*, 112–13, 123–24.

121. Ibid., 111–12. Jesus was, of course, a bearer of the spirit, understood in the vein of the Hebrew Bible as a special endowment of power upon a chosen individual for a divinely appointed task. The spirit is mentioned as a helper in courts (Matt. 10:20; 24:20).

122. As far as we can discern, "extraordinary" manifestations of the spirit play no part in the communal life of the Ebionites; cf. von Campenhausen, *Kirchliches Amt*, 196–97.

123. Cf. Bultmann, *Theology*, 1:334.

124. On an analogous process of the spirit becoming independent in rabbinic Judaism, see Sjöberg, "*pneuma*," 386–87; he emphatically notes that this does not make the spirit a heavenly being, but rather presents it as a divine reality that encounters and challenges a person.

125. In connection with worship and rituals, tripartite formulas established themselves, in which God, Christ, and the spirit were connected in various ways (for example, 2 Cor. 13:13; 1 Cor. 12:4-6). The connection was particularly firm in baptismal liturgy (Matt. 28:19; *Did.* 7.1, 3; Justin, *1 Apol.* 61.3, 13). These and other triadic formulations are often overinterpreted in trinitarian terms (for example, Fee, *Presence*, 839–

42). For criticisms, see Hahn, *Theologie*, 2:290–94. Hahn points out that they do not imply the notion of a personal Spirit, let alone of a divine Trinity—in contrast to the so-called *Comma Johanneum* ("there are three that testify in heaven, the Father, the Word [or: Son], and the Holy Spirit, and these three are one," 1 John 5:7-8 in some manuscripts), which is a late interpolation. Matthew 28:19 came later to be used as the most important New Testament support for the doctrine of the Trinity. Cf. also Schowalter, "Trinity."

126. Kelly, *Doctrines*, 94–95, with a list of the relevant passages. Hermas's views on the topic are, however, confused, and it is also possible that the identification of Michael as the Son of God is meant to equate him with Christ; thus Brox, *Hirt*, 490.

127. According to Brox, *Hirt*, 542, Hermas distinguishes between the Spirit as a preexistent heavenly person and the spirit as a power that dwelled in Jesus and is given to all Christians.

128. Justin attributes the inspiration of the prophets both to the spirit and to the Logos (for the latter see *1 Apol.* 33.9; 36.1), and so does Theophilus; see Kelly, *Doctrines*, 103.

129. In the less sophisticated thought world of the Christian editor of the *Ascension of Isaiah*, Christ the Lord and the "angel of the holy spirit" are worshiped by other heavenly beings both before and after the incarnation; both are clearly different from and subordinated to the Father (see above, pp. 221–22).

130. See Kelly, *Doctrines*, 102.

131. Ibid.

132. Ibid., 122.

133. M. A. Williams, "Sethianism," 44.

134. Cf. Pagels, *Gnostic Gospels*, 52.

135. For a (relatively cautious) critique of the doctrine of the Trinity, see Küng, *Islam*, 604–17. He notes that the doctrine is largely passed over in practical Christian preaching.

136. Muhammad once received from his Christian contacts the impression that the Christian Trinity (to him, an idolatrous abomination) actually consists of God, Jesus, and Mary (cf. Qur'an 5:116).

137. Or a place in the Godhead along with the Three: "In Latin American Catholicism the Virgin's importance was such that she came, always unofficially, to be seen as a member of a *quaternity* that challenged the Trinity stipulated by orthodox theology" (Pike, "Latin America," 431–32, my italics).

10. True Israel? From Jewish to Christian Identity

1. Contrast Boyarin's (*Dying*, 8) extreme suggestion that we should not think of Christianity and Judaism in late antiquity as different religions at all, but only as "points on a continuum."

2. Exclusive monotheism was a late development in the history of Israelite religion, a product of the Babylonian exile (see above). The famous "discovery of monotheism" by Second Isaiah can be viewed as "an exaggeration of patriotism" (M. Smith, "Common Theology," 147; Goldenberg, *Nations*, 18). "Motivated by a potent combination of national pride and religious devotion, biblical writers as a rule were convinced that their own god was the strongest" (Goldenberg, *Nations*, 20).

3. Social identity can be defined as "that part of an individual's self-concept, which derives from his knowledge of his membership of a social group (or groups) together with the value and emotional significance attached to that membership" (Tajfel, *Human Groups*, 255). It indicates one's perception of being similar to other members of the in-group and different from members of the out-group.

4. The Shema consists of three scriptural passages: Deut. 6:4-9; 11:13-21; Num. 15:37-41. The original meaning (including the proper rendering) of Deut. 6:4 is controversial; it is quite likely that the formula was first understood in a monolatric rather than monotheistic sense (Israel was to worship Yahweh alone). But in the time of the Second Temple, the Shema was undoubtedly conceived of as a monotheistic confession of the one and only God.

5. The Greeks drew an analogous distinction between themselves and the unenlightened "barbarians." The analogy ceases, however, at the point where the Jews insist that a convert deny all other Gods and affirm exclusive loyalty to the God of the Jews.

6. Sometimes a special value of the people was stressed, though; for example, it could be held that Israel alone had accepted the covenant and the law offered by God.

7. This latter "deed" seems a rather arbitrary dispossession of peoples defending their own territory, which, seen from a nonpartisan perspective, "endangers Yahweh's claim to be a just God of all nations" (Patrick, "Election," 437). The editors of Deuteronomy have felt the need to provide a justification: the alleged wickedness of these nations (Deut. 9:4-5).

8. Philo uses slightly different language: without using the term *covenant* at all, he speaks of the Jewish community as "a commonwealth (*politeia*) of true life" (*Virt.* 219) that is the special possession of God. But being a member of this commonwealth, or being "initiated into the mystery of Moses" (*Virt.* 179), seems in effect equivalent to having entered the Jewish covenant; cf. E. P. Sanders, "Covenant," 31–32.

9. From a slightly different perspective, one could call it "ethnocentric covenantalism"; thus Longenecker, *Eschatology*, 34.

10. Levinson, "You Must Not Add," 13–15. Juha Pakkala (personal communication) points out that elsewhere in the ancient Near East laws were given by the king (even if their origin was claimed to lie with the Gods); the striking fact that the king plays no part whatsoever in the legislation in the Hebrew Bible shows that its collections of legal material (including the oldest core of Deuteronomy) were born only after the time of the monarchy.

11. K. Müller, "Gesetz," 13–16.

12. Interpreters tend to claim that no innovative activity is involved in their efforts; the interpreter only elucidates the truth already latent in the authoritative text. Nevertheless, exegesis had provided a strategy for actual religious renewal already in ancient Israel (and the process continued in Second Temple Judaism). But "renewal and innovation are almost always covert rather than explicit," though in many cases exegesis involves nothing less than "the radical subversion of prior authoritative texts" (Levinson, "You Must Not Add," 12; for examples from Deuteronomy see ibid., 36–44).

13. Due to conflicts within the restoration community, Trito-Isaiah already speaks of only one group within Israel as "my elect"; over against this group stands another group that has proven faithless and arrogant (Isa. 65).

14. Zetterholm, *Formation*, 114.

15. Zetterholm, ibid., 124–27, emphasizes the potential significance of synagogal charitable activities in a city like Antioch that was populated largely by newcomers lacking social stability and interpersonal attachments.

16. Barclay, *Jews*, 408–9.

17. Barclay, ibid., 429.

18. Cultic images of Gods are subjected to unrestrained mockery in some prophetic passages, especially Isa. 44:9-20.

19. Barclay, *Jews*, 429–31; Sandelin, "Danger."
20. Barclay, *Jews*, 432. There seems to have been something of a gap between statements of principle and actual practice, however. Goodman, *Mission*, 49–59, argues that, in general, Jews would have shown tolerance toward Gentile worship outside the land of Israel. Inscriptions testify to God-fearers who are members of a city council, which must have involved Gentile cultic activities; see Zetterholm, *Formation*, 129. On the other hand, the writings of Philo show that Gentile cults could be experienced as a danger (enticement to idolatry); see Sandelin, "Danger," especially 123–31.
21. E. P. Sanders, *Judaism*, 52. The one exception is *Sib. Or.* 4.24-30; this author seems to have opposed all temples and all animal sacrifices.
22. Barclay, *Jews*, 420.
23. In fact, Gen. 17 is one of the few places in the Bible where circumcision figures prominently; "the Bible as a whole generally ignores it and nowhere regards it as the essential mark of Jewish identity or as the sine qua non for membership in the Jewish polity. It attained this status only in Maccabean times" (Cohen, *Maccabees*, 43).
24. Barclay, *Jews*, 434–37.
25. Ibid., 435–36.
26. Ibid., 437.
27. Ibid., 440.
28. E. P. Sanders, *Judaism*, 266. Pseudo-Philo is vigorously opposed to marriages with Gentiles (*L.A.B.* 9.5; 18.13-14; and elsewhere).
29. Ezra is claimed to have expelled from Jerusalem more than a hundred foreign wives and their children (Ezra 10); *Jubilees*, a text of the Maccabean period, speaks of intermarriage as a capital crime (*Jub.* 30). Even Philo explains that intermarriage leads to impiety (*Spec.* 3.29). Still, intermarriage occasionally happened, as the case of Timothy shows (a son of a Jewish mother and a Greek father, according to Acts 16:1). For a very nuanced account see now Hayes, *Gentile Impurities*.
30. Since, however, what Jews regarded as idolatry was part and parcel of Gentile civic religion, very few non-Jews could in practice be free from idolatry. Therefore the notion of righteous Gentiles in the framework of a Noahide covenant is less generous toward Gentiles than it may at first appear.
31. *Jub.* 15.26: anyone who is not circumcised belongs to the "children of destruction," destined "to be destroyed and annihilated from the earth and to be uprooted from the earth because he has broken the covenant of the Lord our God"; cf. 22.22.
32. The exception is the *Testament of Abraham* (from Egypt), where there is "no distinction between Jew and gentile." The sins mentioned are "heinous by anyone's definition" (no specifically Jewish transgressions are singled out); "everyone is judged by the same standard, whether the majority of his deeds be good or evil" (E. P. Sanders, "Testament of Abraham," 877).
33. On the other hand, Donaldson, *Paul*, 65, suggests that Philo and others "were implicitly making a distinction—between full proselytes and what could be called 'natural law proselytes'—for which they did not yet have the categories or the vocabulary"; when Philo discusses proselytes, he never mentions circumcision or other specific Torah requirements, defining conversion primarily in terms of the abandonment of idolatry and the acceptance of monotheism and virtue (cf. *Virt.* 102, 181–82, 212–19; *Spec.* 1.51; 4.78; Donaldson, *Paul*, 64).
34. E. P. Sanders, "Covenant," 42.
35. Boyarin, *Radical Jew*, 52.
36. Ibid., 39.
37. Fredriksen, *From Jesus to Christ*, 149–50; Donaldson, *Paul*, 69–74. Donaldson (74) points out, however, that the texts are ambiguous on the issue whether the saved Gentiles are expected to have adopted the Torah. The central concern is the vindication of Israel; "wherever Gentiles appear in this tradition, their treatment, positive or negative, is subservient to this central theme."
38. Barclay, *Jews*, 170–73.
39. Ibid., 177.
40. Wolfson, *Philo*, 1:69; cf. Wilson, *Leaving*, 39: "it appears that they, like Philo, were interpreters of their tradition, not defectors from it."
41. Barclay, *Jews*, 177.
42. *Spec.* 1.56-57, 315-16; cf. Sandelin, "Danger," 122–23. Philo, leaning on biblical precedents, supports the execution of apostates who participate in a pagan cult (obviously a trespass much more serious than that of the allegorists). In *Life of Moses* 1.300-304, he admires the zeal of Phinehas, who killed an Israelite chieftain for consorting with a Midianite woman. May one speculate that such zeal reveals Philo's hidden need to defend his own liberalism?
43. Thus the "renegades" in 1 Macc. 1:11 to whom the proposal is ascribed, "Let us go and make a covenant with the Gentiles around us, for since we separated from them many disasters have come upon us."

388

44. In the same vein, in Pseudo-Philo (*L.A.B.* 16.1) the rebellious Korah objects to the "unbearable law" of the tassels (on the corners of the garments of the Israelites; cf. Num. 15:37-41); in *L.A.B.* 25.13, there is a reference to people who wanted to "investigate the book of the Law, whether God had really written what was in it or Moses had taught these things by himself."

45. See Laaksonen, *Jesus und das Land*, 353.

46. On Jesus and the Jewish identity markers in general, see Holmén, *Jesus and Covenant Thinking*.

47. Regarding circumcision, we have nothing to go on in the Jesus tradition.

48. For the *Wirkungsgeschichte* of Mark 7:15 down to the fourth century, see Svartvik, *Mark and Mission*, 109–204; he concludes that "early Christian writers could not make up their mind whether Jesus taught or fought the Law" (203).

49. I pleaded for that interpretation in "Jesus and the Food Laws."

50. In that case, the original meaning would have been something like: "a person is not defiled *so much* by that which goes into him from outside as he is defiled by that which comes out of him"; cf., for example, Kazen, *Jesus*, 65–67, 228–31; Holmén, *Jesus and Covenant Thinking*, 241–49. See further Fredriksen, *Jesus of Nazareth*, 104–10, for an excellent discussion of Jesus and the Law.

51. E. P. Sanders, *Jewish Law*, 6–23. Meier, "Historical Jesus," persuasively argues that "none of the Gospel stories of Jesus being accused of violating the Sabbath by healing goes back to the historical Jesus" (304), partly for the reason that no Jewish source before 70 CE states that healing activity is a violation of the Sabbath (303).

52. For different explanations, see, for example, E. P. Sanders, *Jesus*, 61–71; Neusner, "Money-Changers"; Buchanan, "Symbolic Money-Changers?"; Seeley, "Jesus' Temple Act"; Fredriksen, "Gospel Chronologies," esp. 274-75. Fredriksen doubts the historicity of the act; Buchanan and Seeley deny it altogether.

53. Cf. Wedderburn, *History*, 31.

54. E. P. Sanders, *Jesus*, 218–21 (quotation 221). The only solid evidence of Jesus' dealings with Gentiles consists of two healings from a distance (Mark 7:24-30 par.; Q 7:1-10).

55. James "was holy from his mother's womb, drank neither wine nor intoxicating drink and ate no animal food. No razor came upon his head, he did not anoint himself with oil, and he did not use the bath. He alone was permitted to enter the holy place, for his garments were not of wool but of linen. He used to enter the temple alone, and was often found on his knees beseeching forgiveness for the people, so that his knees became hard like those of a camel from his constantly bending them in his worship of God, and beseeching forgiveness for the people" (reported in Eusebius, *Hist. eccl.* 2.23.5-6). The image of James as high priest is certainly unhistorical.

56. Myllykoski, "James," 71.

57. Cf. Chilton, "James," 8. In Acts 15, Luke attributes the Apostolic Decree (15:20, 29), which apparently sets forth a minimum of Jewish religious obligations that Gentile converts would have to observe, to James's initiative. This, however, seems to be part of Luke's playing down the conflicts in early Christianity.

58. Cf. Berger, *Theologiegeschichte*, 506.

59. Cf. Manson, *Sayings*, 25; Luz, *Matthäus*, 1:308, 317–18.

60. Theissen, "Paulus—der Unglücksstifter," 231–38.

61. F. S. Jones, "Jewish Christianity," 332.

62. The *Circuits* is not concerned with who is truly a Jew, but who is a "worshiper of God" (*theosebes*)—"a word derived from Hellenistic piety but carrying heavy Jewish overtones and simultaneously being adopted by gentile Christians" (F. S. Jones, "Jewish Christianity," 331–32).

63. *Hom.* 8.5-7; cf. *Rec.* 4.5.

64. See *Rec.* 6.8-10; *Hom.* 11.25-28; F. S. Jones, "Jewish Christianity," 328. Wilson (*Strangers*, 141) calls attention to the "magnanimous" view in *Hom.* 8.6-7: God "accepts him who has believed either of these"—either Moses or Jesus; the passage seems to contain "a two-covenant theory, in which both are rooted in the same God but one revealed to the Jews through Moses and the other to the Gentiles through Christ. Equally valid and equally valuable, the parallel covenants are available to those who do not hate or oppose the other." Wilson follows Georg Strecker in tracing back *Hom.* 8.6-7 to an earlier source, *Kerygmata Petrou*, the existence of which is, however, doubted in recent research. If Jones is correct in his source analysis, this startlingly generous view belongs to the "Homilist" who wrote in the early fourth century; *he* does not require baptism for Jews to be saved (F. S. Jones, "Jewish Christianity," 330–31). On the other hand, Wilson, *Strangers*, 152, states that even if we doubt the existence of *Kerygmata Petrou*, there is no reason automatically to assign the passage in question to some later period. "It could rep-

resent a strain of Christian conviction that had deeper roots, and the parallel sentiment known to the author of *Barnabas* [*Barn.* 3.6, 4.6] is one good reason for thinking this." But to whatever period this ecumenical high point in early Christian literature is dated, it seems to reflect the attitude of some *Gentile* Christians.

65. F. S. Jones, "Jewish Christianity," 329.
66. Myllykoski, "James," 74.
67. Cf. Zeller, "Konsolidierung," 144.
68. F. S. Jones, *Source*, 159–60.
69. The sequel, Q 16:18, goes beyond the Torah in prohibiting divorce altogether, but then again "greater stringency than the law requires is not illegal" (E. P. Sanders, *Jesus*, 256). "With the arrival of John and Jesus a new era has dawned, but this is not one where the Law loses any of its validity" (Tuckett, *Q*, 408–9).
70. Tuckett, *Q*, 425; see his whole discussion, 404–24. Kloppenborg Verbin, *Excavating Q*, 152–53, 212–13, maintains that the Torah (and the temple) appear in a positive light only in what he takes to be a last redactional layer, consisting of the temptation story (Q 4:1-13) and of two law-affirming glosses by a "nervous redactor" (Q 11:42c; 16:17). He finds "no evidence of a nomistic piety, and indeed, no special interest in the Torah at all" within the "larger compositional units of Q" (*Excavating Q*, 153). It is not obvious, however, that one can relegate the temptation story, where "the Torah is a self-evidently appropriate basis for argument" and the temple a holy place (*Excavating Q*, 152, 212) to the margins of Q; on the contrary, it would seem to represent a programmatic prologue to this Gospel. Kloppenborg Verbin himself states that "it is likely that the Q people [not just the "nervous redactor"] took for granted the principal distinguishing marks of Israelite identity—circumcision, some form of Sabbath observance, and probably certain dietary observances" (*Excavating Q*, 256); however, he finds in the bulk of the document "popular resistance to any extension of practice designed specifically in support of the Temple in the south" (257). Both the assumption of general suspicion of the temple in Galilee and the assumed role of the Pharisees as representatives of the temple may be doubted.
71. Tuckett, *Q*, 436, 435.
72. Ibid., 431, 426. The question whether the Q people were involved in the Gentile mission is controversial and the evidence ambiguous; for different positions see, for example, Tuckett, *Q*, 393–404 (Q is aware of the Gentile mission but not actively engaged in it); and Uro, *Sheep*, 210–23 (the Gentile mission is practiced in Q communities). What seems clear is that Q is *not opposed* to the Gentile mission. In fact, apart from Matt. 10:5b-6 (a saying in itself open to different interpretations), there is no evidence at all for outright opposition to the Gentile mission in the Jesus movement. What was debated was the conditions of the inclusion of Gentiles (circumcision or not?) and, above all, of their living together with Jewish-born believers.
73. Cf. Q 3:7-9 (John the Baptist's polemical preaching); 10:12-15; 13:28-29 ("you" will be excluded from the kingdom, while Gentiles stream in).
74. Particularly intense hostility prevails between the Q group and the Pharisees. But as the woe on the Pharisees as "*unmarked* graves" (Q 11:44) shows, the dangerous nature of the Pharisees was something hidden, clearly visible only to those who shared the faith in Jesus as a prophet sent by God. Therefore, the decisive reason for the Q attack against the Pharisees is perhaps not their interpretation of the Torah but their rejection of the preaching of the Q people. Thus Hakola, "Q People." Tuckett assumes that Q may have "emanated from a Christian community in close touch with Pharisaism, experiencing some hostile suspicion from non-Christian Pharisees" (Tuckett, *Q*, 447). The controversies with Pharisees (too deeply embedded in the gospel tradition to be all post-70) indicate that the Q movement and the Pharisaic movement were close to each other; the Christian group may have been claiming to be a genuine part of the latter (Tuckett, *Q*, 448–49).
75. Tuckett, *Q*, 322; see his whole analysis on 283–323.
76. Wilson, *Strangers*, 137.
77. Zetterholm, *Formation*, 93–94.
78. Schrage, "Ekklesia." Paul's statements on his having "persecuted the *ekklesia* of God" (1 Cor. 15:9; Gal. 1:13; cf. Phil. 3:6) may indicate that the term was known to him from his pre-Christian time.
79. If Paul's persecution of them consisted in synagogal disciplinary measures, as is likely, this confirms that the Hellenists had not separated themselves from the synagogue.
80. Already at this early stage Paul betrays nearness to and distance from Judaism at the same time: terms like *election* link up with Jewish covenantal tradition, but no long salvation history is in view. The Christ-believers "orient themselves toward the imminent judgment,

390

the coming Lord, the Spirit of the end time. The most remote past event of significance is the fate of Jesus" (J. Becker, *Paul*, 139). In this connection Paul neither mentions Israel nor cites the scriptures.

81. Boyarin, *Radical Jew*, 39, 44; cf. Cf. Theissen, *Theory*, 164: "What later gained its independence as primitive Christianity was originally an attempt to open up Judaism to all non-Jews."

82. Cf. Barclay, *Jews*, 385: "In the intimate atmosphere of his house-churches Paul and his (mostly Gentile) converts shared common meals, joined in prayer and worship, exchanged spiritual gifts and greeted each other with the holy kiss. . . . To associate with gentiles in such intimacy without requiring that they come under the authority of the Jewish law was to stretch Jewish openness to 'strangers' far beyond its usual limits."

83. The interpretation of Paul's view of the Torah is extremely controversial in scholarship. I follow the course outlined in Räisänen, *Paul and the Law*. For a fresh discussion see now Kuula's two volumes, *Law*.

84. Boyarin, *Radical Jew*, 10. Cf. Boyarin's (155–56) comment on Gal. 4:12, where Paul says that he has become as one of the Galatians: Paul "has given up his specific Jewish identity in order to . . . create the new spiritual People of God. . . . It is difficult for me to understand how scholars can assume that Paul remained Law-observant given this verse."

85. E. P. Sanders, *Paul, Law, Jewish People*, 171–79 (quotations: 176, 178). In Rom. 14–15 Paul tries, on the face of it, to protect the identity of Jewish-born Christians, granting them the right to keep observing kosher laws. But by calling them "weak" and those who ignore food laws "strong," he in effect endorses the perspective of the "strong." Barclay concludes that "while, *on the surface and in the short term*, Paul protects the Law-observant Christians, in the long term and at a deeper level he seriously undermines their social and cultural integrity. . . . While accepting their right to remain attached to the Jewish community, Paul requires from the weak a deep social commitment to their fellow Christians, even if they do not respect the Jewish law in their conduct" (Barclay, "Do We Undermine?" 306, his italics; see the whole discussion, ibid., 299–308 and cf. n. 93).

86. Barclay, *Jews*, 386.

87. Houlden, *Public Face*, 32.

88. Cf. also Reinbold, *Propaganda und Mission*, 29–30: Paul is *nolens volens* about to break with his Jewish-

ness. Reinbold adds the observation that it is Paul's Jewish brothers and sisters *in the Lord* who are his true "relatives" (Rom. 16:7, 11, 21), while unbelieving Jews are his "kindred *according to the flesh*" (Rom. 9:3). J. Becker, *Paul*, 75–76, takes a more radical position, defining Paul as an apostate from Judaism; he also draws a totally negative picture of Paul's view of the law (394–98).

89. Nanos, *Mystery*, 8, 23 n. 5, and passim. According to Nanos, Paul held that Christian Gentiles were obliged to follow the purity rules of the law as reformulated in the Apostolic Decree (Acts 15:20, 29) when they were associated with Jews. This leads to a number of strange explanations: for Nanos, the expression "obedience of faith" (Rom. 1:5) refers to the Apostolic Decree (*Mystery*, 218–22, 237–38); Rom. 11:26 to Paul himself, coming from Jerusalem (ibid., 278–79), and so on. Building on the work of Gaston and Stowers, Gager, *Reinventing Paul*, argues passionately that Paul presented no criticism at all of the Torah. All critical points about curse, condemnation, and death concern the Torah only in the case that it is imposed on Gentiles: when Paul appears to say something about the law and Jews that is unthinkable from a Jewish perspective, he is probably not talking about Jews at all, but is talking about the law and Gentiles (ibid., 58). Gager's view is accepted as axiomatic by Zetterholm, *Formation*. This "new Paul" is, however, a highly unlikely creation. See, for example, Wedderburn, "Paulusperspektive?" esp. 53–62.

90. Nanos, *Mystery*, 344, admits that if the traditional reading of the Antiochian incident is correct, then Paul compromised, and faith indeed nullified the Torah. Consequently, he presents a tortuous and lengthy exegesis of the passage (the conclusions: 362–66). Cf. Tomson's problems with the same passage: *Paul and Jewish Law*, 222–30.

91. The expression "through the law" in v. 19 is unclear, but it probably means that Paul's giving up full observance was not an arbitrary decision of his own, but conformed to God's will.

92. Barrett notes that Paul is nowhere more un-Jewish than here ("Things," 146) and that he "had in fact ceased to be a practising Jew" (*1 Corinthians*, 240).

93. Barclay, "Do We Undermine?" 301, is outspoken: "The certainty and candour with which Paul here expresses his freedom from the law is quite breathtaking. In principle, it appears, he could see no objection to eating shellfish, hare or pork. Do we have reason to doubt

that his diet was sometimes as scandalously 'free' as his principles?"

94. Many Christian interpreters still seem to think that circumcision and food laws were minor issues anyway, so that Paul was plainly right in suggesting that the whole law *is* fulfilled, if only the command of mutual love is observed. Thurén even writes that "if obedience is counted as circumcision [as is the case in Rom. 2:26], then the ritual requirements of the law are met *expressis verbis*"; interpreting Gal. 6:15, he calls circumcision "a minor surgical operation," which "as such means nothing" (*Derhetorizing Paul*, 109, 171).

95. Dunn, *Galatians*, 291. Dunn even claims that "Paul's interpretation of covenant and promise was a legitimate option for Jews (and Judaism)" (*Jesus*, 208).

96. We should not be "over-impressed by the traditional and scriptural content" of his theology (Barclay, "Paul among Diaspora Jews," 114) or even by possible "halakic" concerns (emphasized, for example, by Tomson, *Paul and Jewish Law*) in his ethics.

97. Barclay, "Paul among Diaspora Jews," 93.

98. Riddle, "Jewishness," 244.

99. Barclay, "Paul among Diaspora Jews," 119.

100. Segal, *Paul*, 277, with reference to Rom. 9:6-29.

101. That Jesus-believing Jews are in focus here does not make a real difference, for it is precisely their traditional Jewish identity that is at stake.

102. For a perceptive exegesis of the difficult verses Gal. 3:19-20, see Kuula, *Law*, 1:104–21.

103. Ibid., 1:195.

104. Cf. his reference to those who insist on circumcision as "those who *mutilate* the flesh" in Phil. 3:2.

105. Kuula, *Law*, 1:82.

106. Boyarin, *Radical Jew*, 156.

107. Betz, *Galatians*, 323; Lüdemann, *Paulus und das Judentum*, 29; Kuula, *Law*, 1:88–89; Schnelle, *Theologie*, 307, 327–28. Galatians 6:15-16 reads: "For neither circumcision counts for anything, nor uncircumcision, but a new creation. Peace and mercy be upon all who walk by this rule, and upon the Israel of God."

108. Kuula, *Law*, 1:94.

109. For example, Dunn, *Jesus*, 197, and elsewhere.

110. The Hebrew term for "assembly" (of the Lord), *qahal*, is rendered with *ekklesia* in the Septuagint: Deut. 23:2-4; Num. 16:3; 20:4; Mic. 2:5; 1 Chr. 28:8.

111. This word occurs very often in the openings of the letters, for example in 1 Cor. 1:2; 2 Cor. 1:1.

112. Schnelle, *Theologie*, 307.

113. A prominent representative of the former view is Cranfield, *Romans*, 2:851–62; of the latter, Dunn, *Theology of Paul*, 159–61 and elsewhere. I have devoted an extensive critique to Cranfield's position in Räisänen, *Paul and the Law*, 42–50; the arguments set forth there also apply to Dunn's view (cf. Räisänen, *Paul and the Law*, xxx).

114. Von der Osten-Sacken, *Römer 8*, 245.

115. Hübner, *Law*, 139. Recent representatives of such interpretations include Longenecker, *Eschatology*, 207–11, 243–44; Dunn, *Theology of Paul*, 638–39, 645–46. I have criticized this trend in two comprehensive articles: "'Law' of Faith" and "Paul's Word-Play"; for a summary see *Paul and the Law*, 50–52. I am followed, for example, by Zeller, *Römer*, 92–93, 152; Ziesler, *Romans*, 118, 202; Westerholm, *Perspectives*, 323–25. The discussion has now been carried forward by Sundkvist, *Christian Laws*, who gains a fresh perspective by investigating the reception of the phrases in question (he also considers Gal. 6:2 and 1 Cor. 9:21) by early Greek interpreters.

116. For the evidence see Räisänen, "Paul's Word-Play." For possible (indirect) influences on Paul's thought on the law from popular Greek philosophy see F. S. Jones, *Freiheit*; Huttunen, *Paul and Epictetus*. Engberg-Pedersen, *Paul and the Stoics*, finds remarkable similarities between Paul and Stoic thought, but his discussion of the matter moves on a very abstract level.

117. Sundkvist, *Christian Laws*, 287; cf. 288–89: Rom. 8:2 "implies that the Law's true purpose, to promote life through obedience to its precepts, has been realized by the Spirit in a way tantamount to a fundamental affirmation of this intent." Yet the *nomos* expressions in question "do not allow the Mosaic law to remain in force." To be sure, Sundkvist does not allow a wordplay; for all its ambiguity, *nomos* contains here a reference to the Mosaic law, and a polemical reference at that. I still do not see why a wordplay should (or even could!) be excluded, given the difficulty of understanding the extremely active role given to the *nomos* in the salvific event according to Rom. 8:2 in particular. How could Paul suggest that the Torah (in whatever way understood) would be the *subject* that has liberated Christians? But we agree on the main point: the allusions to the Torah are ambiguous and polemical. Sundkvist's interpretation of Rom. 3:27 was anticipated by Kuula, *Law*, 2:126–27, who, however, also accepts the metaphorical (wordplay) interpretation (though it "remains incomplete"). According to Kuula (*Law*, 2:127), Paul's purpose is "to forge a continuity

between faith and the law redefined as scripture" (cf. 3:21), "yet the continuity remains on a merely terminological level."

118. Cf. Gal. 3:19; Rom. 3:20; 5:2; 1 Cor. 15:56; and Räisänen, *Paul and the Law*, 140–50.

119. Strecker, *Theologie*, 216, comments on Phil. 3:7 that "it is hardly possible to express the break with Judaism in a more radical manner."

120. The expression *telos nomou* could also be translated "the goal of the law," and many interpreters take it in this positive sense. While Paul could perfectly well speak of Christ as the goal on the law (see next paragraph), the context of Rom. 10:4 indicates that in this particular case "termination" is the more likely rendering; see Räisänen, *Paul and the Law*, 53–56.

121. In more than half of his quotations, Paul makes changes that make the text better suit his argument; see Koch, *Schrift*, 186–90.

122. Fredriksen, "Law," 423. She notes that Paul's conviction of the imminent return of Christ, "the one consistent theme" in his letters, "spared him having to work out a 'theology' of the Law."

123. Barclay, *Jews*, 387. Cf. Theissen, "Römer 9–11," 311: Paul's "thought is full of contradictions. One does more justice to him, when one does not explain them away, but interprets them historically and psychologically." For a less empathetic estimation see Goulder, *Tale*, 33–34: Paul believed contradictory things, he was "in an impossible position," and he was "reduced to offering a series of arguments which were weak and contradictory."

124. The verses are often regarded as an interpolation (see, for example, Pearson, "1 Thessalonians 2:13-16"), and indeed they would seem to make more sense if the events of 70 c.e. were in view in v. 16c. However, the contents and vocabulary of v. 16a (the Jews "are hindering us from speaking to the Gentiles so that they may be saved") point to Paul himself as the author. If this outburst is genuinely Pauline, it must be due to anger caused by some concrete event (though the statement that the definitive punishment has taken place remains mysterious).

125. Hübner, *Gottes Ich*, 17.

126. It is inadequate to summarize the point of Rom. 9:6-13 as Dunn, *Jesus*, 148, does: "Those who are Israelites, but who *fail to recognize* the covenant character of their status as Israelites, have to that extent sold their own birthright" (my italics); cf. Dunn, *Romans*, 2:540: "Paul's argument concerns the character and mode

rather than the fact of election." No, it concerns precisely the "fact"!

127. It is often thought that this is the problem that Paul sets out to tackle in the section; thus, for example, Gaston, *Paul*, 97; Gager, *Reinventing*, 132; Nanos, *Mystery*, 263.

128. For instance, E. E. Johnson, *Function*, 147–50, and N. T. Wright, *Climax*, 238–39, do not take this negative side seriously enough.

129. This lesson is drawn from the biblical example of God's dealing with Pharaoh in Exodus; astonishingly, this classical enemy of Israel here stands for the Jews of Paul's time; see Hübner, *Gottes Ich*, 45.

130. Elsewhere (2 Cor. 4:3-4) Paul occasionally attributes the blindness of the unbelievers not to the God of Israel but to the "god of this aeon." This fact shows for its part how far he is from possessing a consistent doctrine of divine hardening. The introduction of Satan into Rom. 9 as the cause of Israel's stubbornness would have totally destroyed the argument based on God's sovereignty.

131. Strikingly, Abraham here appears in a role quite different from Gal. 3 or Rom. 4: as "the ancestor—a crucial figure back in Israel's story, into which gentiles have been incorporated" (Houlden, *Public Face*, 37).

132. Contra, for example, Schnelle, *Theologie*, 329, who takes "all Israel" to mean only the believing remnant (as in 9:27), and Marshall, *Theology*, 326 (referring to Rom. 11:23): only all who believe.

133. Kuss, *Römerbrief*, 3:792; similarly Sanders, *Paul, Law, and Jewish People*, 198; Kuula, *Law*, 2:344. Strecker, *Theologie*, 216–22, devalues the idea as a merely tactical church-political concession.

134. However, the idea is analogous to the Jewish notion of the eschatological pilgrimage of the nations: Gentiles will be saved, since they eventually become Jews—or at least adopt Jewish values and abandon their own Gods.

135. Boyarin, *Radical Jew*, 151: the idea is at bottom "supersessionist," and it may have done a lot of *harm* to Jews, as it has kindled Christian hopes for their large-scale conversion. Since this has not happened, the disappointment has been ever so great, playing a part in the hardening of Luther's attitude, for instance.

136. In a similar vein, for example, Ruether, *Faith and Fratricide*, 105–6; Kuss, *Römerbrief*, 3:825; Sanders, *Paul, Law, and Jewish People*, 197–99; Theissen, "Römer 9–11"; Walter, "Interpretation," 173, 176: Paul is attempting to "square the circle"; Schnelle, *Paulus*, 390; Lüdemann, *Paul*, 162. Marshall's struggle with the

passage (*Theology*, 331–36) shows how difficult it is to make sense of it when one is not prepared to reckon with the possibility that the apostle might sometimes contradict himself.

137. Houlden, *Public Face*, 35.

138. In reality, the quotation is a mixture (possibly put together by someone before Mark) from Exod. 23:20; Mal. 3:1; and Isa. 40:3. See further, for example, Mark 12:10-11; 13:26-27; 14:62.

139. On Mark's unsystematic view of the law see Dautzenberg, "Gesetzeskritik," 54–61; and Sariola, *Markus und das Gesetz*, especially 248–61; on Mark's relation to Jews and Judaism as a whole, see Wilson, *Strangers*, 36–46.

140. On the generalizing nature of Mark's remark see E. P. Sanders, *Jewish Law*, 262. Even the (Jewish) *Letter of Aristeas* (304–6) generalizes, claiming that "all Jews" washed their hands "in the sea" (!), but they are said to have done this before praying, not before eating (cf. *Sib. Or.* 3.591-93).

141. This means that he is either a Gentile Christian or a Hellenistic Jewish Christian alienated from his Jewish heritage somewhat in the manner of Paul; Mark 7:19 is comparable to the sarcasm of Gal. 5:12 and Phil. 3:2.

142. In 1:44, Mark's Jesus even obligates the healed leper to fulfill a commandment of Moses by showing himself to a priest.

143. In light of Mark 15:38 (the curtain of the temple is torn in two when Jesus dies, thus opening the way to God's presence), this may be taken as a rejection of the temple cult; in 11:17, Jesus, having driven out the sellers and buyers, teaches that the temple ought to be "a house of *prayer* for all the nations," a statement that likewise seems to deny the significance of the sacrifices. In 13:2, Jesus' prediction of the destruction of the temple opens the apocalyptic discourse, which has its climax in the promise of the parousia of the Son of Man. Mark seems, however, more interested in the significance of the fate of the temple for Christian eschatology (it is the prelude to the imminent end) than in interpreting it as a judgment over the Jews; see Wilson, *Strangers*, 44–45.

144. Note also his humane interpretation of the Sabbath in Mark 2:27, followed by the emphasis on the authority of the "Son of Man" to make decisions about the Sabbath in 2:28.

145. It is exaggerated to claim that, for Mark, the Torah is abrogated by Jesus; thus, for example, Hübner, *Gesetz in der synoptischen Tradition*, 223.

146. Cf. the analogous distancing from the Jewish adversaries in Mark 7:13b: "*you* do many things like this."

147. Wilson, *Strangers*, 45–46.

148. Seeley, *Deconstructing*, 71–72, comments on the "frightful maliciousness" of the tenants, whose motives do not make sense in terms of the parable itself. In the imagery of the parable, the Jewish leaders become the real executioners of Jesus. Cf. ibid., 66–67: as early as Mark 3:6 (immediately after conflicts about the Sabbath), Mark's Pharisees merely want to kill Jesus, without any real concern for the Sabbath.

149. Jesus' strange act of cursing a fig tree that had no fruit (because it was not "the season for figs"!) in Mark 11:12-14 is often taken as an allegory for cursing the temple and the people of Israel; the cleansing of the temple in 11:15-19 is sandwiched between the cursing of the fig tree and its observed result in 11:20-21.

150. The glaring exception is the action of the crowd in Mark 15:11-15, when they (stirred up by the priests, to be sure) demand Jesus to be crucified.

151. Wrede, *Messianic Secret*, 62.

152. On the Markan "parable theory," see Räisänen, *Messianic Secret*, 76–143 and the literature discussed there. Not surprisingly, Matthew (Matt. 13:13) replaces Mark's final conjunction "in order that" (*hina*) with the causal "because" (*hoti*); the hardening of the listeners is no longer due to a divine plan but a punishment for their own incomprehension. Luke (8:12) for his part tries to shift the responsibility from God to the devil.

153. Syreeni, "Matthew, Luke, and the Law," 141.

154. Ibid.; in the last sentence he quotes the Jewish author G. Friedlander (1911).

155. Luomanen, *Entering*, 88.

156. Ibid., 87.

157. Syreeni, "Matthew, Luke, and the Law," 141.

158. Matthew deletes Mark's "thus he declared all foods clean" (Mark 7:19b) and adds to the end of the section the remark "to eat with unwashed hands does not defile" (Matt. 15:20b), implying that the issue has all the time been the "tradition of the elders" about washing hands (v. 2) rather than food. Matthew also inserts vv. 12-14: the criticized custom is to be uprooted, because it is a "plant" not planted by God.

159. Even Matthew's Jesus states that "it is not what goes into the mouth that defiles" (Matt. 15:11) and (worse!) that "whatever goes into the mouth enters the stomach, and goes out into the sewer" (15:17).

160. Syreeni, "Matthew, Luke, and the Law," 145; he also notes that "a strongly ambivalent attitude to the law"

is common to Matthew and Paul, despite all their differences.

161. While earlier tradition (Paul and the tradition on which he relies, say, in 1 Cor. 15:3-4) already reflects efforts to understand the career of Jesus in terms of the scriptures, Matthew "seems to have reversed the process: now the scriptures are to be explained in terms of Jesus" (Fredriksen, *From Jesus to Christ*, 43).

162. W. S. Green, "Introduction," 6.

163. See Luz, *Matthäus*, 2:227. Konradt, *Israel*, 191–200, distinguishes probably too sharply between the leaders and the people.

164. Luz, *Matthäus*, 2:228. Very often, though, Christian scholars refuse to recognize the supersessionism in Matthew's position; see, for example, Marshall, *Theology*, 124–25 with n. 65.

165. Scholars disagree on the social setting of Matthew: had his group already left the synagogue, or were they still part of it, in the middle of a process that would lead to separation? See on the options Luz, *Matthäus*, 1:94–99. In agreement with Luz, 96–97, I find the latter the more likely alternative, for in the Gospel the synagogue is viewed through the eyes of an outsider.

166. One should not think, however, that Matthew's group had to leave the synagogue because of "persecution" by Jewish leaders; the separation seems due to its own decision, and the harshness of the polemic against the Pharisees can be understood in terms of a "postdecision conflict": the rejected alternative is presented as bad in order to legitimate one's own decision. Thus Luz, *Matthäus*, 3:400, followed by Hakola, "Social Identity," 135.

167. Cf. Syreeni, "James," 416 with n. 51. James 1:14-15 can be read as "directed against Paul's insinuation that God (by giving the law) is the initiator of lust and sin" (ibid., 412).

168. Vielhauer, *Geschichte*, 575. This is one of the many indications that James the brother of the Lord cannot be the author of the letter. The author's famous critique of Paul's "faith versus works" antithesis does not concern the Torah as such ("works of the law" in the Pauline sense); the issue is the Christian way of life as James sees it.

169. Seitz, "James and the Law," 485. Konradt, *Existenz* 203–5, is more cautious, but even he admits that all commandments were probably not observed in practice.

170. Syreeni, "James," 420, also noting that "the emphasis laid on baptismal 'birth' hardly complies with a programme of circumcision."

171. This assimilation is best revealed in Jas. 2:8-13, where, within the same train of thought, "the royal law" (v. 8) and "the law of liberty," through which the readers are to be judged (v. 12), suggest the Christian ethical norms, whereas the "whole law" (v. 10) is seen as consisting characteristically of the Decalogue (v. 11).

172. Cf. Syreeni, "James," 417 (referring to Konradt, *Existenz*, 67–74). "With some systematization, it can be inferred that in Jas *nomos* is the ethical or imperative aspect of the life-giving *logos* that was 'planted in your hearts' and that 'can bring you salvation' (1:21)." The exhortation to be "doers of the *word* and not merely hearers" (1:22-25) takes up and transforms the contrast between doers and hearers of the *law* from Rom. 2:13.

173. Syreeni, "James," 420 n. 63, with reference to Konradt, *Existenz*, 318. Theissen, *Das Neue Testament*, 93, even speaks of "*liberal* Jewish Christianity."

174. In this passage, the argument runs as follows. An offering of firstfruits is necessary *because of the biblical law*. In the author's community, prophets take the place of the high priests in the biblical text. But even if there are no prophets there, *the commandment has to be fulfilled*; and then "the poor" take the place of the priests who, according to the law, are entitled to receive the firstfruits; see Schweizer, *Church*, 140 n. 506.

175. Wilson, *Strangers*, 224.

176. Schweizer, *Church*, 141.

177. Wilson, *Strangers*, 162.

178. Räisänen, "Nicolaitans," 150–51.

179. That local Jews are meant is likely; thus, for example, Klauck, "Sendschreiben," 163; Thompson, *Revelation*, 68; Aune, *Revelation*, 1:162. Differently Wilson, *Strangers*, 163: some Gentile "Judaizers" are the target of the author here. But Rev. 11:8, where the earthly Jerusalem is prophetically unmasked as Sodom and Egypt, suggests for its part that the author does take a radically critical stance toward unbelieving Jews.

180. Also *T. Benj.* 11.2; cf. *T. Jud.* 24.3.

181. Wilson, *Strangers*, 105–6.

182. Ibid., 107.

183. The importance of "listening to Moses and the prophets" (Luke 16:29-31) illustrates the previous statement (from Q) that no stroke will disappear from the law (Luke 16:17).

184. Salo, *Treatment*, 63.

185. Syreeni, "Matthew, Luke, and the Law," 148, 149.

186. See Jervell, *Luke*, 185–99.

187. Syreeni, "Matthew, Luke, and the Law," 147.

188. The usual translation is "whatever has been strangled," but the meaning of the word is far from clear.
189. Syreeni, "Matthew, Luke, and the Law," 148.
190. Ibid., 145.
191. Ibid., 150.
192. Wilson, *Strangers*, 57.
193. Gaston, "Anti-Judaism," 153; cf. Wilson, *Strangers*, 57.
194. Cf. Qur'an 4:157.
195. R. E. Brown, "Gospel of Peter," 338–39.
196. Schnelle, *Theologie*, 575.
197. Wilson, *Strangers*, 74.
198. It is commonly held that the Christians had been violently expelled from the synagogue (cf. John 9:22; 12:42; 16:2), but this has been questioned on good grounds by Hakola, *Identity Matters*. The traditional view presupposes that the early rabbinic movement had great power and influence within Judaism. It is claimed that the rabbis emerged as the new leaders after 70 C.E. and defined in a new way what it meant to be a Jew. They no longer tolerated such groups as the Johannine Christians, and so they began to harass them, which finally led to their expulsion from the synagogue. This view is no longer tenable. Recent research has shown that the rabbis did not have that kind of power at all (see above, p. 327 n. 103).
199. Hakola, *Identity Matters*, 109.
200. Ibid., 110.
201. Ibid., 97.
202. It is not at all clear that the healing as such violates the Sabbath, since Jesus heals by his word, but the command to carry the mat (John 5:10) certainly does (according to a common Jewish understanding).
203. Meeks, "Divine Agent," 58; Hakola, *Identity Matters*, 152.
204. Cf. Paul's statement that the letter of the law kills (2 Cor. 3:6).
205. Cf. Wilson, *Strangers*, 78: "The law may point to Christ, but that is its sole remaining function, and not one that looms large in John's world. At best it points away from itself to the superior revelation through Christ."
206. On John 1:17, see, for example, Pancaro, *Law*, 534–46.
207. J. Becker, "Verhältnis," 491.
208. Hakola, *Identity Matters*, 176.
209. The expression is used of the Jewish authorities (for example, John 1:19; 7:13), but also of the crowds (for example, 6:41, 52) or of the national religious community as a whole (2:13). Jesus himself con-

trasts his disciples with "the Jews" in 13:33. Wilson, *Strangers*, 76, correctly notes that when John's narrative proceeds, "*hoi Ioudaioi* have become the Jews in general."
210. Hakola, *Identity Matters*, 226, 231.
211. Wilson, *Strangers*, 80. Cf. 334 n. 165: the fact that John lifts the conflict to a cosmological level does not mitigate his view of the Jews but "compounds the anti-Judaism and pushes it in a disastrous direction."
212. Hakola, *Identity Matters*, 218.
213. Ibid., 181, following Haenchen, *Johannesevangelium*, 369–70. "Because their own identity was at stake, the Johannine Christians may have played down the role of more sympathetic Jews in their symbolic universe" (Hakola, *Identity Matters*, 185), for "if Jews are sensible and fair-minded, their refusal of Christianity becomes more problematic than if they are hardhearted, vicious and ignorant of their own Scripture" (Setzer, *Jewish Responses*, 168, followed by Hakola, *Identity Matters*, 186).
214. Yet Jesus is worthy of more glory than Moses (Heb. 3:3), and he is "a priest forever according to the order of Melchizedek," the mysterious king to whom Abraham paid tithes (7:1-4, 15-20).
215. Yet "God had provided something better so that they would not, apart from us, be made perfect" (Heb. 11:40).
216. Cf. Attridge, *Hebrews*, 203: the abrogation of the law "does not point to its relative inferiority, but to a fundamental disability deriving from its essential 'fleshiness,' which proverbially entails weakness." The point is not that sinful people have not been able to administer the law properly; the law itself is seriously deficient. Cf. Heb. 9:9-10.
217. Cf. Bultmann, *Theology*, 1:111.
218. O. Leppä, "Useless Command," 189. Cf. White, *From Jesus to Christianity*, 323: "perhaps the first thoroughgoing effort to work out a Christian supersessionist theology. . . . God had all along intended Jesus to replace Judaism."
219. Wilson, *Strangers*, 123.
220. Rese, "Church and Israel," 30. Colossians 3:11 draws on Gal. 3:28 ("there is no longer Jew and Greek . . . slave and free . . .") but adds that there is "no longer . . . circumcised and uncircumcised."
221. The Israelites once had Christ "as the future redeemer they were hoping for"; Eph. 1:12 shows that in their pre-Christian times the Jewish Christians hoped in Christ; see Rese, "Church and Israel," 26.

222. Ibid., 29; similarly Beker, *Heirs*, 90; Hübner, *Epheser*, 182–83; Stuhlmacher, *Theologie*, 2:47.

223. Behind 2 Tim. 3:15-16 lies the assumption that the scriptures now belong to the Christians; see Richardson, *Israel*, 159 n. 6; Rese, "Church and Israel," 31.

224. Rese, "Church and Israel," 31.

225. Sometimes a political need to dissociate themselves from Judaism may be involved in the new circumstances: the establishment of the *fiscus Judaicus*, or the poll tax imposed on Jews by Vespasian after the Jewish War, emphasized, for example, by Zetterholm, *Formation*, 198–200, 223.

226. King, *Gnosticism*, 41.

227. Correspondingly, the apologist Aristides views the observance of the ritual law as a service rendered (through ignorance) to angels, not to God (*Apol.* 14 in the Syriac text).

228. The promised land refers to Christians (*Barn.* 6.8-19); the milk and honey that is in store in the land means Christian possession of faith and the word (6.17), and the Sabbath is the Christians' heavenly rest (6.15).

229. Wilson, *Strangers*, 232, regards it as the earliest secure reference to the Christian Sunday, but this depends on his early dating of *Barnabas* to 96–98 C.E.

230. The relevance of the early mention of the first day of the week in Paul (1 Cor. 16:2) is not clear; see Wilson, *Strangers*, 230.

231. Ibid., 235; see his whole discussion (230–35).

232. On this, see ibid., 235–41. The issue remained controversial among Christians for centuries, however, as the Quartodecimans insisted on celebrating on the fourteenth of Nisan, the Jewish Passover day. But naturally even these Christians celebrated the feast for partly (and significantly) different motives than Jews—and could display a quite hostile attitude to Jews, as the case of Melito shows (see pp. 280–81).

233. In light of Ignatius's other statements on the subject, "this is not a comment on the preparatory role of the people of God in the Old Testament period," but must mean something like "Judaism yielded to Christianity, not Christianity to Judaism" (Schoedel, *Ignatius*, 126).

234. Zetterholm, *Formation*, 221.

235. Ibid., 204–7.

236. Ibid., 235.

237. In what follows, fun is made of the observation of the moon: "and if no moon be seen, they do not celebrate what is called the first Sabbath, nor keep the new moon, nor the days of unleavened bread, nor the feast (of tabernacles?), nor the great day (of atonement?)."

238. For the interpretation of the fragment, see Pilhofer, *Presbyteron*, 228–30.

239. Marjanen, "Religious Practices," 180.

240. Valantasis, *Gospel of Thomas*, 101; Marjanen, "Religious Practices," 173–74, 177–78.

241. "His disciples said to him, 'Twenty-four prophets have spoken in Israel, and they all spoke of you.' He said to them, 'You have disregarded the living one who is in your presence and have spoken of the dead.'"

242. Marjanen, "Religious Practices," 180; cf. Valantasis, *Gospel of Thomas*, 130.

243. Moreland, "Thomas 52," 91.

244. Marjanen, "Religious Practices," 181.

245. Even this move, however, can be seen as a continuation of the Jewish (and early Christian) tradition that held various phenomena to be pre-existent. Thomassen gives a comprehensive discussion on protology in Valentinianism (*Seed*, 146–90, 315–29; the latter section is characteristically entitled "The Transformation of Eschatology to Protology").

246. The paradise story, for instance, if taken literally, contained crude anthropomorphisms and descriptions of even morally dubious behavior on the part of the Creator, and it therefore "clearly held the potential to be truly offensive for many ancient readers" (M. A. Williams, *Rethinking*, 72).

247. Cf. ibid., 76, with reference to the *Testimony of Truth*.

248. See Räisänen, "Marcion," 107–13.

249. For instance, Joshua, a "prophet of the creator," conquered the Holy Land with violence and cruelty; Christ prohibits all violence and preaches mercy and peace. Joshua stopped the sun so that it would not set before the people had revenged their enemies; the Lord says, "Do not let the sun go down on your anger." Moses stretched out his arms toward God in order to kill many in war (Exod. 17:11-13); the Lord stretched out his hands on the cross to save people. Documentation in Harnack, *Marcion*, 272*–73*, 281*–82*.

250. See Greschat, *Apelles*.

251. Cf. the mocking comment of Celsus (Origen, *Cels.* 7.18): "Whether is it Moses or Jesus who teaches falsely? Did the Father, when he sent Jesus, forget the commands which he had given to Moses? Or did he change his mind, condemn his own laws, and send forth a messenger with counter instructions?"

252. Ptolemy seems to have intended his writing also as a partial (and relatively mild) criticism of Marcion; cf. Dunderberg, *Beyond Gnosticism*, 87–90.

253. The perfect God could not have given an imperfect law

that needed to be fulfilled by someone else and contained precepts incompatible with his own being and will (*Flor.* 3.4).

254. Note, however, that although this distinction is implicit in Justin's writing, he never spells it out. Possibly his "high regard for the authority of Scripture unconsciously prevented him from working out a bolder . . . breakdown of the unity of Scripture in the manner of Ptolemy" (Stylianopoulos, *Justin Martyr*, 74–75; cf. Räisänen, *Paul and the Law*, 32).

255. The command of circumcision had a special purpose: to assist the Romans in identifying Jews in order to punish them (*Dial.* 16.2).

256. Justin even accuses the Jews of cutting predictions of Christ out of their text of scripture—but he is actually comparing their texts with a version of the Septuagint to which Christians had made additions of their own.

257. To be sure, Jesus had personally warned Christians about this Messiah of the creator (Luke 21:8; *Marc.* 4.39).

258. See Räisänen, "Marcion and the Origins."

259. Chadwick, *Early Church*, 85. For a comprehensive treatment of Melito's sermon, see Wilson, *Strangers*, 241–57.

260. Syreeni, "Matthew, Luke, and the Law," 148–49: old Simeon's "portrait is so impressively painted that only an attentive reader of the story may recognize how thoughtful of him it was to depart (Lk 2,29) as the time of fulfilment began."

261. Ruether, *Faith and Fratricide*.

262. Wilson, *Strangers*, 221.

263. Wilson, "Marcion and the Jews," 58; cf. Wilson, *Strangers*, 221, but see also the reservation made on 297.

264. Reventlow, "Role of the Old Testament," 145–46.

265. Others, such as the Greek philosopher Celsus, tended to agree, charging Christians with innovation and impiety.

266. For example, Rubenstein, *After Auschwitz*, 14–28.

267. Propp, "Chosen People," 110.

11. STRANGERS IN A TRANSITORY WORLD: CHRISTIANS AND PAGANS

1. Nock, *Conversion*, 84.

2. Celsus notes that only someone utterly childish can think that "the stone, wood, brass, or gold which has been wrought by this or that workman" are Gods and not images representing Gods (in Origen, *Cels.* 7.92). Yet the idea seems to have been popular among simple folk that images of Gods are more than mere images; they stand in a relation to the God and possess supernatural power. Even earlier philosophers like Plato had believed that images could be filled with divine power. See Markschies, *Valentinus*, 41.

3. Celsus pointed out this discrepancy: if, as the Christians maintain, the idols are nothing, then there should be nothing to prevent them, say, from participating in the public festivals (in Origen, *Cels.* 8.21).

4. For example, Barrett, *Romans*, 37, speaks of "the manifest decadence of the pagan world"; Dodd, *Romans*, 25, of "the grossest form of superstition and immorality." Contrast Shaw, *Cost*, 143: the passage is "one of the most violent and hate-filled in Scripture."

5. Lane Fox, *Pagans*, 345–46.

6. Cf. Aristides, *Apol.* 8-13; Justin, *1 Apol.* 9.2-5; Athenagoras, *Leg.* 27.

7. Cf. Markschies, *Valentinus*, 39–42.

8. Wischmeyer, "Paul's Religion," 82.

9. Cf. ibid.: "His astonishingly frequent and urgent warnings against idolatry in the Corinthian correspondence show the power he ascribes to the realm of the *eidola* in spite of his 'enlightened' Jewish polemics against idols." From later times (for example, Cyprian's sermon on the lapsed), we know that Christians could take the presence of the Gods at a sacrifice very literally: Christians who had eaten a sacrifice had eaten demons with it, often with disastrous consequences; see Lane Fox, *Pagans*, 444.

10. Theissen, *Soziologie*, 275.

11. Ibid., 280. On the discussion concerning the person of Erastus, see Gillman, "Erastus"; Jewett, *Romans*, 981–83.

12. Romans 14–15 reflects a related conflict between "strong" and "weak" Christians in Rome. Sacrificial meat or wine is not mentioned in so many words, but it is a fair assumption that those who ate no meat or drank no wine did so in order to avoid contact with idols.

13. Cf. O. Leppä, "Debates."

14. E. Meyer, *Ursprung*, 2:194.

15. In patristic tradition, the Nicolaitans are said to have traced their ideas back to Nicolaus of Antioch, one of the members of the Stephen group (Acts 6:5). Most scholars deny such a connection, but it makes sense, as a free attitude toward food was part of the Hellen-

ist legacy. For a full discussion of the Nicolaitans, see Räisänen, "Nicolaitans."

16. In view of the similarities of the charges, I extend (in accordance with standard practice) the term *Nicolaitans* to apply even to the "Jezebel" group, though the name itself does not appear in Rev. 2:18-29.

17. In Rev. 2:24, the term *burden* (*baros*) is used; it is plausible to connect this with similar usage in Acts 15:28; cf. Räisänen, "Nicolaitans," 150–51.

18. Duff, *Who Rides*, 69, argues that "Jezebel's" followers were people engaged in trade and commerce, whereas John's supporters consisted of day laborers, the unemployed, and the underemployed.

19. The battle is indeed mainly ideological, for, contrary to a common opinion, there is little evidence for a widespread persecution of the Christians at the end of the first century; see later in this chapter.

20. Yarbro Collins, "Persecution," 740–41.

21. Duff, *Who Rides*, 61; cf. 131.

22. Ibid., 132.

23. Thompson, *Book of Revelation*, 125. However, we have no information concerning the attitude of the Nicolaitans to actual pagan cults or religious festivals.

24. Minucius Felix, *Oct.* 36.6; Eusebius, *Hist. eccl.* 5.1.26 (the martyr Biblis in Lyon); Tertullian, *Apol.* 9.13.

25. Theissen, *Soziologie*, 285; M. A. Williams, *Rethinking "Gnosticism."*

26. Suetonius, *Nero* 16.2; *Claudius* 25.3; Pliny, *Ep.* 10.96; Tacitus, *Ann.* 15.44.

27. Cf. also Eph. 4:17-19; Titus 3:3; and elsewhere.

28. R. J. Hoffmann, *Celsus*, 44, summarizing the view of Celsus.

29. Lane Fox, *Pagans*, 95.

30. Tertullian, *Apol.* 7.8; Aristides, *Apol.* 17.2; Athenagoras, *Leg.* 3; 32; 35; Justin, 1 *Apol.* 26.

31. Tacitus, *Ann.* 15.44, narrates that Nero attempted to get rid of the rumor that he himself had ordered the fire to be set in that he "fastened the guilt and inflicted the most exquisite tortures on a class hated for their abominations, called Christians by the populace. . . . An arrest was first made of all who confessed; then, upon their information, an immense multitude was convicted, not so much of the crime of arson, as of hatred of the human race."

32. Lane Fox, *Pagans*, 434, notes that it is "one of the unrecognized effects of Paul's later career that it caused Christians to be persecuted by Romans." Theissen, "Unglücksstifter," 243–44, arrives at a similar conclusion.

33. See above, p. 36.

34. Cf. Wedderburn, *History*, 189.

35. In a similar vein, even philosophers who criticized public rites and made missionary propaganda were blamed for withdrawing themselves from public life and, at times, persecuted.

36. In some early Christian martyrdom stories, Jews are blamed for instigating pagans to persecute Christians, but such insinuations should not be uncritically accepted.

37. Exceptions were made that permitted some clubs (professional, social, or burial societies) to exist.

38. Zeller, "Konsolidierung," 221.

39. Klauck, *Context*, 329.

40. Price, *Rituals*, 233 (my italics), followed by Thompson, *Book of Revelation*, 163. See above, p. 50.

41. Lane Fox, *Pagans*, 40.

42. Cf. Price, *Rituals*, 124–25: "The difficulties which the Christians posed for their contemporaries lay firstly with their threat to traditional cults in general and only secondarily with an allegedly subversive attitude to the emperor."

43. Lane Fox, *Pagans*, 426. The authorities seem always to have been more interested in persuading Christians to recant than in executing them.

44. For the state of the question see the critical survey by Duff, *Who Rides*, 3–16; cf. also Mayordomo, "Gewalt," 54–59.

45. Yarbro Collins, "Persecution," 746; cf. Klauck, "Sendschreiben," 153–56, 160–64.

46. The martyrs of Rev. 6:9-11, whose souls thirst for vengeance, are probably victims of Nero's persecution a generation earlier, if not Old Testament martyrs; see Kraft, *Offenbarung*, 119; Aune, *Revelation*, 2:406.

47. This marking would seem to refer to tattoos (Thompson, *Revelation*, 143). As it is not known that tattoos would have been required for buying and selling, Rev. 13:16-17 is often taken to refer to coins with images, but this "stretches the tattoos beyond recognition" (ibid.). The visions give expression to the dark expectations of the seer rather than to the empirical reality of his environment.

48. See above, p. 50.

49. Klauck, "Sendschreiben," 181; idem, *Context*, 329–30.

50. Contra Schüssler Fiorenza, *Revelation*; cf. the discussion in Räisänen, "Biblical Critics," 289–92.

51. Duff, *Who Rides*, 64 (my italics). Duff is leaning on Ramsay MacMullen.

52. The cities of Asia Minor often took the initiative

to establish a cult of the emperor; cf. Mayordomo, "Gewalt," 56–57; and above, p. 48.

53. Theissen, *Theory*, 244.

54. Lane Fox, *Pagans*, 423.

55. When Ignatius, condemned to death as a Christian, was brought to Rome, at each stop he was allowed to preach and meet with local Christians, "none of whom was in any apparent danger although their Christian identity was obvious" (Stark, *Rise*, 180).

56. Frend, *Martyrdom*, 413.

57. White, *From Jesus to Christianity*, 362, gives a table that lists the number of known victims during the century from Trajan (111/112 C.E.) to Caracalla (212 C.E.). The sum total for the thirteen events, for which figures can be inferred, is 47. In four additional cases the numbers are lacking.

58. Lane Fox, *Pagans*, 441. Archaeological evidence, too, suggests that the Christians' conflict with the state "has been overemphasized by later generations." There were persecutions, but "if anything, the data reflect a lack of concern for police or State activities. . . . One must temper the later scenario with the apparent fact that local Christians were fairly open about their faith and its public ramifications." Some letters show that "Christians were engaged in buying, selling and banking, *qua* Christians" (Snyder, *Ante Pacem*, 304).

59. Eusebius (*Hist. eccl.* 5.16.20-21) cites a second-century text that asserts that persecutions experienced by Marcionites or Montanists are no proof whatsoever of their faith. Therefore those who in prison prepared themselves to die for the "true faith" did not consent to mix with Montanist martyrs who found themselves in the same plight.

60. On *Apoc. Jas.* 5-6 see above, p. 160; and cf. Pagels, *Gnostic Gospels*, 90–91 (though she regards the writing as gnostic).

61. Dunderberg, *Beyond Gnosticism*, 12, 168–73.

62. Cf. M. Meyer, "Second Discourse," 475, 480. Whatever the real-life background of these insinuations may have been, persecutions of gnostics by other Christians certainly took place from the fourth century on, when varieties of Christianity labeled heretical were attacked by orthodox believers supported by the emperor. Property of heretics was confiscated, their texts destroyed, and their meetinghouses burned by angry monks.

63. An early instance is the celebration of the anniversary of Polycarp's death in the place where his bones were deposited (*Mart. Pol.* 18.2-3).

64. Ignatius often refers to his prospective death as sacrifice (*Rom.* 2.2; 4.2) or ransom (*Smyrn.* 10.2). In the background of his fanatic longing for martyrdom looms 4 Maccabees, with its idealization of the Jewish heroes of faith.

65. Lane Fox, *Pagans*, 445.

66. According to Clement (*Strom.* 4.71-72), the Valentinian teacher Heracleon disparaged martyrdom, arguing that it was useless to confess Christ with death if one had denied him by one's conduct. Cf. *Testim. Truth* 33.25—34.25.

67. These could even be sins committed in a former life, as Basilides held a doctrine of reincarnation. He strongly believed (in a Stoic way) in the goodness of divine Providence, including the punishments imposed by it (*Strom.* 4.86.1).

68. Cf. Luttikhuizen, "Elchasaites," 345. Similar views were put forward by some Jewish sages, although they were highly controversial: according to Rabbi Ishmael, it was permissible for a Jew even to sacrifice to idols to save his life, unless more than ten Jews were present.

69. The *Gospel of Judas* (38) claims that apostolic leaders allow men to sacrifice their wives and children; this can be interpreted as criticism of martyrdom. Cf. Pagels and King, *Reading Judas*.

70. Klauck, *Context*, 329; contra, for example, Horsley, ed., *Paul and Empire*; N. Elliott, *Liberating Paul*.

71. Vollenweider, "Politische Theologie?" scrutinizes Philippians from this point of view and concludes (ibid., 468) that it is not necessary to enter "the minefield of Rom. 13:1-7" to dismantle the picture of Paul as a radical representative of resistance to Rome: Philippians (which envisages a heavenly commonwealth for the Christians: Phil. 3:20) contains little that contemporary readers could have taken as signs of a counterprogram against the Roman system. Paul turns out to be more interested in the life of the cities than in the emperor and the empire; rather than attacking their administration, he offers a "better alternative," claiming that what a *polis* ought to be (a seat of concord, peace, and freedom) is realized in the Christian congregations (ibid., 469).

72. Cf. Meeks, *Urban Christians*, 189: in Paul's letters, "there is no hint anywhere that Roman imperialism is a cause of the evil state of the present age." Fredriksen, *From Jesus to Christ*, 173, correctly notes that Paul radically redefines the concepts of kingdom, Christ, and redemption: "through the originally political vocabulary of liberation, he praises a reality that

400

is utterly spiritual." Dunn, *Theology of Paul*, 679–80, speaks of Paul's "political quietism"; his advice in Rom. 13 "is in fact a call to good citizenship, on the assumption, no doubt partly at least, that civil disorder and strife benefits no one (least of all the little people). . . . Paul of all people will have been well aware that good citizenship was also a missionary strategy which commended the gospel to those of good will." Huttunen, "Greco-Roman Philosophy," 87–88, compares Paul with Epictetus and finds a difference in that Paul does not make any division between political and moral authority; in the overall context of Rom. 12–13, especially of 13:10, one even gets the impression that "authorities enforce people to do the good the Torah and Christian ethics require. In a word: the sword compels to love." Recognizing that Paul was not a revolutionary does not, of course, mean that one should turn a blind eye to the atrocities done under the cover of his exhortation to obey the authorities, as it "has been used to justify a host of horrendous abuses of individual human rights" (O'Neill, *Romans*, 209; N. Elliott, *Liberating Paul*, 217). But it would be unfair to make Paul, who expected the parousia of Christ within a few years' time, responsible for this tendentious reception history.

73. Mark states that Pilate handed Jesus over to be crucified, after which the soldiers mocked him and led him out to Golgotha (Mark 15:15-20), but Luke modifies this: Pilate handed Jesus over "as they wished" (Luke 23:25). Luke also "omits the Marcan passage which describes the mockery and physical violence to which the Roman soldiers subjected Jesus in the Praetorium (Mk 15.16-20), while introducing a new section in which Jesus receives similar treatment from Herod and his Jewish soldiers (23.6-12)" (Esler, *Community*, 203). The omission of Mark 15:16-20 produces the impression that those who lead Jesus out to be crucified are the Jewish leaders.

74. Esler, *Community*, 222.

75. Cf. Merkt, "Profilierung," 424. Even the Valentinian *Tripartite Tractate*, in which the "lust for power" comes in for comprehensive criticism, considers earthly power to be necessary for the administration of *oikonomia*. Power can be possessed and used in a right way, too; "those who do exercise power only need to recognize that their ruling is temporary." Dunderberg, *Beyond Gnosticism*, 173, concludes that an ancient Christian reader may have found in these affirmations "justification for taking part, even more actively than

some other early Christians did, in public life and in the duties involved with it."

76. See the outline of different positions in Dunderberg, *Beyond Gnosticism*, 182–84.

77. Barclay, *Jews*, 391, contrasts Paul's attitude with Aristeas's appreciation of the Greek *paideia*. Shaw, *Cost*, 63, notes that the subsequent importance of the Corinthians passage has been immense, "as it is the first attempt in Christian writing to define the relationship between religious authority and secular reason. It informs both the agonized attempts of the Church Fathers to express a coherent attitude to the heritage of classical literature and the more recent dilemmas of church leaders in relation to science."

78. Vices: Rom. 1:29-31; 13:13; 1 Cor. 5:10-11; 6:9-10; 2 Cor. 12:20; Gal. 5:19-20. Virtues: Gal. 5:22-23; Phil. 4:8. In the Pauline school: Col. 3:5, 8; Eph. 4:31; 1 Tim. 6:11. Note also the household codes in Col. 3:18—4:1; Eph. 5:22—6:9.

79. The significance of this speech has been assessed in diametrically opposite ways, either supporting tolerant "inclusivism" or pleading for outright "exclusivism"; see Räisänen, *Marcion, Muhammad and the Mahatma*, 9–12.

80. No such altar is known to have existed.

81. Dibelius, *Studies*, 63.

82. Pregeant, *Christology*, 151.

83. On the argument from antiquity, which the Christians adopted from Jewish authors (who, in turn, had it from ancient Greek writers), see Pilhofer, *Presbyteron Kreitton*. Notably, some early apologists did not resort to this argument, but emphasized instead the newness of Christianity, which distinguished it from Jews and pagans alike; thus the *Preaching of Peter*, Aristides, and the *Letter to Diognetus*; see ibid., 226–34.

84. Theophilus of Antioch, *Autol.* 3.16.1

85. For example, Justin, *1 Apol.* 44.8-10; cf. 60.6.

86. See Dunderberg, *Beyond Gnosticism*, 176–85.

87. Cf. Clement of Alexandria, *Strom.* 1.94.1-3. Once again the Christian view had been preceded by Philo (*Congr.* 11).

88. Justin, *1 Apol.* 46.3; *2 Apol.* 10, 13. Minucius Felix (*Oct.* 20) affirmed that "either the Christians of today are philosophers, or . . . the philosophers of old were already Christians." Athenagoras, for his part, argued that poets and philosophers had found something of the truth "by guesswork," "each of them moved by his own soul through some affinity with the spirit of God" (*Leg.* 7), whereas Christians had

their teachings directly from God, who had inspired the prophets.

89. Hurtado, *Lord*, 645.

90. King, *Gnosticism*, 49.

91. Pearson, "Basilides," 28.

92. On the Valentinians as a "school," see now Dunderberg, *Beyond Gnosticism*.

93. Lampe, *Die stadtrömischen Christen*, 254.

94. Ibid., 255–57. Lampe (ibid., 257) emphasizes, however, that although the gnostic leaders belonged to the cultural elite, the flock of their followers was more mixed; cf. Irenaeus, *Haer*. 3.15.2.

95. Dunderberg, *Beyond Gnosticism*, 97.

96. M. Williams, *Rethinking "Gnosticism*," 107. Cf. the "Naassene" source used by Hippolytus, where scripture, Homeric poetry, and the rites and symbols of various cults are presented as witnesses to the Naassene (Ophite) truth (understood as universal truth); see Frickel, *Hellenistische Erlösung*, 65.

97. See Denzey, "Bardaisan."

98. Weltin, *Athens and Jerusalem*, 78.

99. Ibid., 79.

100. A prime witness would be the doctrine of Trinity; cf. above, pp. 254–55.

101. Hanson, *Studies*, 211; cf. Stroumsa, "Postscript."

102. Boccaccini, *Middle Judaism*, 265, points out: "if universalism means the capacity of attaching value to being different, then its opposite is not particularism or nationalism, but dogmatism and intolerance, namely, the pretense of possessing the whole truth or having the only key to salvation. By this definition, some middle Judaisms were undoubtedly sectarian and intolerant; others were able to develop mature positions that were much more universalistic than those of early Christianity. Early Christians, in fact, were quite willing to accept pagan proselytes, but much less willing to recognize the possibility of salvation for nonbelievers, be they Jews or Gentiles." Cf. Boyarin, *Radical Jew*, 232–33.

103. One could add: "and Muslim."

104. W. C. Smith, "Idolatry," 54–55. Smith's appreciation of the "spiritual life of communities served by images" stems from his experience in India, where the closest present-day analogies to image-worship in the Greco-Roman world can probably be found. Writing in the context of interreligious dialogue, Smith (57) concludes that "we had good reasons to dismiss 'idolatry' as a concept. As an interpretation of others' religious life . . . it has been intellectually wrong, and morally

wrong." Cf. Räisänen, *Marcion, Muhammad and the Mahatma*, 46–48.

105. Soares-Prabhu, "Laughing," 129–31.

12. TOWARD CHRISTIAN ORTHODOXY

1. On this topic, see in particular Gamble, "Canon." "Canon" (originally "a tool for measurement") is a closed list of authoritative writings.

2. Some, notably Paul, apparently did not have access to a great treasure of the Lord's sayings, but the few times Paul does appeal to them show that he too regarded them as authoritative (even though he did not shrink from modifying the scope of a saying when it suited him: 1 Cor. 7:11; 9:14).

3. Theissen, *Theory*, 368 n. 4, adopts a confusingly wide notion of canon, suggesting that "the New Testament writings had 'canonical' quality from the start by participating in the charism of their authors." Contrast J. Becker, "Theologiegeschichte," 126–33.

4. Contra Theissen, who claims that "there was a *deliberate* decision to put other writings alongside" the given Septuagint (*Theory*, 261; my italics). Scholars used to suppose, though, that the canon had virtually reached its full form by the end of the second century. This assumption went together with a tendency to see the chief causes of canon formation in the conflicts of that century. It was thought, for example, that Marcion forced the proto-orthodox church to form its own canon as a reaction to his, or that the gnostics were opposed to shaping a canon that excluded their documents, or that the Montanists provided the motivation for the proto-orthodox church to close its canon. These notions have been seriously challenged; see Gamble, "Canon," 857. Gnostic groups valued much the same literature as other Christians and differed rather in the assumptions and methods with which they approached these writings. Nor did the proto-orthodox church deny the continuing activity of the spirit in response to the Montanists.

5. Cf. Gamble, "Canon," 853; but see also the caveats in J. Becker, "Theologiegeschichte," 130–32.

6. Cf. Trobisch, *Entstehung*; Theissen, *Entstehung*, 136–45.

7. For example, *2 Clem.* 8.5 refers to a "gospel," from which the author quotes a saying that resembles Luke

16:10-12 but appears not to be derived from the Gospel of Luke; see Koester, *Ancient Gospels*, 353–55.

8. On the claim of Bauckham and others who hold that the (canonical) Gospels were addressed to "all Christians," see above, p. 335 n. 81.

9. J. Becker, "Theologiegeschichte," 133.

10. For example, John 7:53—8:11 and the various "longer endings" after Mark 16:8.

11. Eusebius, *Hist. eccl.* 6.12.2-6.

12. Gamble, "Canon," 855.

13. Cf. Merkel, *Widersprüche*.

14. Contra Theissen, *Theory*, 250, who claims that the canon consciously affirms the "multiplicity in primitive Christianity" (but that behind this multiplicity there is a unity that alone explains the formation of the canon).

15. The Muratorian canon (long regarded as a Roman product of the late second century) may be best considered an Eastern list of the fourth century. So Sundberg, "Canon Muratori," followed by G. Robbins, "Muratorian Fragment"; Gamble, "Canon," 856. It lists four Gospels, Acts, thirteen letters of Paul (omitting Hebrews), Jude, 1–2 John, Wisdom of Solomon (!), Revelation, and *Apocalypse of Peter*; it omits the majority of the Catholic Letters. Eusebius (*Hist. eccl.* 3.25) for his part divides authoritative writings into three categories: acknowledged books (the four Gospels, Acts, fourteen letters of Paul [including Hebrews], 1 John, 1 Peter, and possibly Revelation); disputed books (James, Jude, 2 Peter, 2–3 John, *Acts of Paul*, Hermas, *Apocalypse of Peter*, *Barnabas*, *Didache*, and possibly Revelation); and rejected books (*Gospel of Peter*, *Gospel of Thomas*, *Gospel of Matthias*, *Acts of Andrew*, and so on).

16. Gamble, "Canon," 857–58.

17. Tertullian, *Praescr.* 14, 15, 18, 19.

18. Thus Johannine sayings such as "I and the Father are one" (John 10:30) and "the Father is greater than I" (John 14:28) "were gifts to opposing sides in the Arian controversy." "If 10.30 seemed to support the orthodox Nicene Christians . . . , the Arians could claim that it merely implied 'an exact harmony in all words and works' (i.e., not essential being) between Father and Son; and 14.28, so apparently Arian, could be taken by the orthodox to refer simply to Jesus in his incarnate life on earth" (Houlden, "John," 361).

19. 1 Cor. 12:3; 16:22; Phil. 2:11; 1 John 4:1-3; and so on.

20. Cf. Dunn, *Unity*, 54–55.

21. 1 Cor. 8:5-6; Acts 9:22; and so on.

22. Dunn, *Unity*, 59.

23. Royalty, "Dwelling on Visions," argues that Colossians is reacting to John of Patmos and his followers, "who were dwelling on their visions of heavenly worship within the Asian Christian communities" (335 and passim). Whether or not this thesis is valid (is the term *philosophia* really so vague that it can be applied to John's revelations?), it is appropriate to look for Colossians' opponents among those Christians whose writings also made it to the New Testament (thus also O. Leppä, "Debates").

24. Strikingly, however, Paul seems to be the exclusive authority for the Pastorals; in marked contrast to Acts, there is no appeal to any other apostolic leaders; see Beker, *Heirs*, 37–39.

25. Cf. the statements on confession in Hebrews (4:14; 10:23) and on the "teaching of Christ" in 2 John 9; cf. 1 John 2:27.

26. Heracleon, a Valentinian, wrote the first extant commentary on the Gospel; the Fourth Gospel is quoted in the *Gospel of Philip*, possibly also in the *Gospel of Truth*.

27. Most early Christians could have agreed that Jesus was "the Christ" and the "Son of God"—for the simple reason that these designations are not defined more closely. The virgin birth was largely accepted in the second century, but would have been foreign to most Christians during the first two generations or so. That Jesus became "flesh" is, of course, a Johannine formulation; a sending Christology "from above" was not shared by all (it is absent from the Synoptic Gospels). The slogan "for our salvation" is too general to be controversial, and the fact of Jesus' passion was believed by most—only not by those who held docetist or possessionist views. Jesus' resurrection was not in doubt, but its nature would have been controversial, so much so that it is difficult to know on which side Paul, with his idea of a "spiritual body," should be placed. In any case, Irenaeus's "crude" formulation about the resurrection of the "flesh" runs counter to more spiritual notions of resurrection, including Paul's. Jesus' bodily ascension is mentioned only by Luke before the second century. His return from heaven was expected by many, but even the author of the Fourth Gospel has replaced it with an internalized notion of the parousia. And if Irenaeus's phrase "to bring together everything" refers to an earthly millennium (in which he certainly believed), he has included in his "universal" rule of faith a belief that, though old, had from the start been controversial.

28. See Franzmann, "Complete History," 120–21.
29. King, *Gnosticism*, 53; cf. 178.
30. For what follows see Frey, "Paulus und die Apostel"; Reinbold, *Propaganda und Mission*, 32–116.
31. Acts does not use the term of Paul, except in 14:4, 14, where the usage probably stems from the source used.
32. This view finds its climax in Irenaeus (*Haer.* 3.1.1): after the resurrection all apostles were endowed with the holy spirit and each of them equally received the whole gospel.
33. On the fictive nature of the Beloved Disciple, cf. Dunderberg, *Beloved Disciple*, 147–48 and passim.
34. J. Becker, "Verhältnis," 489.
35. One might argue that Matthew's ambivalent presentation of Peter as both the "rock" on which the church is built and the "stumbling block" (16:13-23) reflects Matthew's attitude toward emerging Christian leadership; Peter's authority is democratized, as it were, in 18:18. Cf. Uro, *Thomas*, 99.
36. The task of the *diakonos* is surely older than that of the overseer: it must have grown spontaneously from the needs of the community (cf. 1 Cor. 16:15) and has then been gradually acknowledged as a formal title. The title *episkopos* sounds more official. It has its roots probably in the Greek association system and suggests a person with some administrative tasks given by the community rather than a leader of the community.
37. Cf. Zeller, "Konsolidierung," 189–90.
38. An example is Irenaeus's list of Roman bishops that includes thirteen names from Peter to Irenaeus's contemporary, Eleutheros (175–189 C.E.).
39. Marcion took an exceptional course in suggesting that early on the original apostles had falsified the gospel. For him, Paul was the only legitimate apostle.
40. Clement of Alexandria, *Strom.* 7.106.4—107.1; 7.108.1; Hippolytus, *Haer.* 7.20.1
41. Wolff, *1 Korinther*, 2:115, lists baptismal instruction, transmission of tradition, and pneumatic exegesis of scripture.
42. The *Didache* still knows of wandering (prophets and) teachers who may in some cases settle down in a congregation (*Did.* 13.1-2). The seer of Patmos, himself a latter-day wandering charismatic, claims sovereign prophetic authority, even speaking to the congregations as "Christ" (Rev. 2–3), but also engaged in battle against another bearer of the spirit, the prophetic woman leader in Thyatira. Conflicts between wandering prophets and settled leaders are in evidence in 3 John and in Matt. 7:15-23.

43. *Did.* 15 (a chapter added to the writing later, in changed circumstances) also shows that local bishops and deacons have adopted the tasks hitherto fulfilled by prophets and teachers.
44. Yet in the second century, independent Christian teachers, who founded schools after the model of philosophical schools, appear on both sides: Justin on the proto-orthodox, Valentinus on the gnostic side. Even later there was some tension between bishops and independent teachers, such as Clement of Alexandria or Origen, as doctrinal authorities.
45. The letters of Ignatius are the earliest evidence for the ideal of monarchic episcopate, which is one reason why some scholars regard the letters as a falsification from around 165–175 C.E. But for Ignatius such an order is still more an ideal than a fact, and the Pastoral Epistles help to fill in the gap in the history of the monarchic episcopate between Ignatius's time and the end of the century.
46. Uro, *Thomas*, 103.
47. Ibid., 104.
48. Ibid., 100–101.
49. Cf. Pagels, *Gnostic Gospels*, 40.
50. Dunderberg, *Beyond Gnosticism*, 195.
51. On the face of it, 1 Tim. 2:8-12 seems to agree with a Pauline passage, 1 Cor. 14:33-36, where the apostle states that "women should be silent in the churches," as it is "shameful for a woman to speak in church." This passage is, however, suspect of being an interpolation (made in the spirit of 1 Timothy), both on text-critical grounds and because a few chapters earlier (1 Cor. 11) Paul approves of the practice of women acting as prophets in the church of Corinth, provided that they cover their heads properly (revealing that he was somewhat ambivalent about women prophets, though not opposed to them; Torjesen, *Priests*, 42). Moreover, what is known of Paul's relation to his female coworkers puts the passage in 1 Cor. 14 in a dubious light. The passage is regarded as an interpolation for example by Conzelmann, *1 Corinthians*, 246. Should it nevertheless be authentic, it must refer to some practical trifle, such as disturbances caused by some curious women loudly asking questions in the meetings; thus Wolff, *Korinther*, 2:140–43.
52. "In New Testament passages where women leaders played prominent roles, the male authors muted their contributions by the way they wrote their stories" (Torjesen, *Priests*, 13). One of these authors is Luke, who, for all the attention he pays to women (from the

infancy stories on), in Acts carefully plays down their achievements as leaders and missionaries. See Seim, *Double Message*.

53. Notoriously, her gender changed in the course of the history of interpretation, and many translations still have a male "Junias" in Rom. 16:7. But John Chrysostom had preached eloquently about Junia, the female apostle, whom the Christian women in Constantinople were to emulate, and commentators down to the twelfth century referred to her as a female. On the discussion, see Jewett, *Romans*, 961–65.

54. Further early figures include Euodia and Syntyche in Philippi (Phil. 4:2), the Corinthian female prophets (1 Cor. 11), Lydia (Acts 16), and the four daughters of Philip (Acts 21:8-9). Inscriptions from the second and third centuries bear witness that Christian women have borne the title "elder" (Torjesen, *Priests*, 10, 20)—and even a Theodora Episcopa is said to be attested in a Roman basilica (ibid., 9-10).

55. Women's leadership in some Jewish synagogues (for example, as "ruler of the synagogue") is attested by inscriptions; see Brooten, *Women Leaders*.

56. See above, p. 287. In the larger society, women were excluded from the political sphere; decisions concerning the government of the *polis* were made by free men only. But women had influential roles in working life and business, including the associations (*collegia*).

57. The *Acts of Thecla* fight with the aid of the figure of Thecla for the right of women to act as Christian missionaries; see Ebner and Lau, "Überlieferung," 3. The presbyter who composed the *Acts of Paul* tried apparently to make Thecla a subsidiary minor figure, inserting the narrative about her into the framework of Paul's feats—but the sympathy of readers remained on the side of Thecla: the *Acts of Thecla* were copied much more often than the *Acts of Paul* en bloc, and in Christian iconography she appears quite independently of Paul, for example as the "Lady of the animals"; see Ebner and Lau, ibid., 4. The stories used by the presbyter had perhaps been generated and were cultivated among celibate women involved in Christian ministry.

58. According to Epiphanius, they appealed to the prophetess Miriam (Moses' sister) and to the daughters of Philip in support for their practice of appointing women to the clergy (*Pan.* 49).

59. Marjanen, *Woman*, 224.

60. Ebner, "Von den Anfängen," 50.

61. See Rudolph, *Gnosis*, 211; Pagels, *Gnostic Gospels*, 66; Filoramo, *History*, 176.

62. Marjanen, "How Egalitarian," 781.

63. She is often taken to be also an early witness to a vision of the risen Jesus, but this is unlikely, as the first appearances probably took place in Galilee; see above, pp. 58 and 331 n. 16.

64. Marjanen, "Mary Magdalene," 58.

65. Marjanen, *Woman*, 225. King states that Mary here represents "those Christians who question the validity of any apostolic authority that challenges the truth of their own experience of the Living Lord"; for them, authority is based on spiritual qualifications alone, and women who have those qualifications are allowed to exercise authority (King, "Gospel of Mary," 623–24). But see also the more cautious assessment of the significance of the gender issue by Tuckett, *Gospel of Mary*, 194–203 (especially 200).

66. Pagels, *Gnostic Gospels*, 64–69, argues that gnostic texts (among which she includes the *Gospel of Mary*) use the figure of the Magdalene "to suggest that women's activity challenged the leaders of the orthodox community, who regarded Peter as their spokesman" (64). But such a generalization has to be qualified. It is not altogether clear that the position represented by Mary (and by his defender Levi) in the *Gospel of Mary* is gnostic, and in any case the picture of the Magdalene in the *Gospel of Mary* differs markedly from that in the other pertinent texts. For example, in the *Pistis Sophia* (cf. ibid., 65) the cause of the quarrel between Peter and Mary is not the position of women in general, but the credibility of Mary as a transmitter of traditions; Peter's ideas are just as gnostic as Mary's, so that he can hardly represent "orthodox" Christianity (see Marjanen, *Woman*, 222–23). It seems that "the discussion about women's role in religious groups was also a matter of *inner-Gnostic debate*" (Marjanen, "How Egalitarian," 791; my italics).

67. Marjanen, *Woman*, 156–60, shows that neither these statements nor the designation companion (*koinonos*) used in Gos. Phil. 59.6-10 are to be taken in a sexual sense. Kissing was a well-known metaphor for transmitting a special spiritual power.

68. Marjanen, "How Egalitarian," 786.

69. Torjesen, *Priests*, 6.

70. Ibid., 38.

71. Marjanen, *Woman*, 224; he finds that the portrayal of Mary Magdalene in *Pistis Sophia* (see n. 66) may mirror such a trend within gnostic Christianity.

72. Lane Fox, *Pagans*, 23; cf. Stroumsa, "Postscript," 357, 360.

73. Cf. Desjardins, *Peace*, 100–108, on "the insider-outsider mentality."

74. Shaw, *Cost*, 44, notes that Gal. 1:8-9 is "the first recorded anathema in Christian history." Jewett, *Romans*, 1014, finds in Rom. 16:17-20 "the violent impulse of identifying heretics and destroying them," which has proved so disastrous in church history, but he regards these verses as an interpolation (ibid., 985–96), in sharp contrast to Stuhlmacher, *Römer*, 252, who finds them quite consistent with the argumentation in Romans. Jewett, *Romans*, 988, ascribes

the putative interpolation to the group that produced the Pastorals. But if the verses are not an interpolation, they provide a good starting point for the kind of polemic practiced by the Pastorals.

75. The presbyter who wrote 2 and 3 John denies hospitality to dissenters, eliciting from Theissen, *Das Neue Testament*, 109, the comment that even the Johannine "theology of love" contains "inquisitorial potential."

76. Cf. Stark, *Rise*, 73–94, on the "humanitarian" actions of many Christians toward both insiders and outsiders during the disastrous epidemics in the second and third centuries c.e.

Achtemeier, Paul J. *1 Peter: A Commentary on First Peter.* Hermeneia. Minneapolis: Fortress Press, 1996.

Aejmelaeus, Anneli. "The Suffering Servant: Isaiah 53 as an Intertext in the New Testament." Pages 475–94 in *Lux Humana, Lux Aeterna: Essays on Biblical and Related Themes in Honour of Lars Aejmelaeus.* Edited by Antti Mustakallio. Publications of the Finnish Exegetical Society 89. Helsinki: Finnish Exegetical Society/Göttingen: Vandenhoeck & Ruprecht, 2005.

Aejmelaeus, Lars. *Die Rezeption der Paulusbriefe in der Miletrede (Apg 20:18-35).* AASF, series B, 232. Helsinki: Suomalainen tiedeakatemia, 1987.

———. *Schwachheit als Waffe: Die Argumentation des Paulus im "Tränenbrief" (2. Kor. 10–12).* Publications of the Finnish Exegetical Society 78. Helsinki: Finnish Exegetical Society/Göttingen: Vandenhoeck & Ruprecht, 2000.

———. *Streit und Versöhnung: Das Problem der Zusammensetzung des 2. Korintherbriefes.* Publications of the Finnish Exegetical Society 46. Helsinki: Finnish Exegetical Society, 1987.

Albertz, Rainer. *Religionsgeschichte Israels in alttestamentlicher Zeit.* Grundrisse zum Alten Testament. ATD Ergänzungsreihe 8/1. Göttingen: Vandenhoeck & Ruprecht, 1992. [ET: *A History of Israelite Religion in the Old Testament Period.* Translated by John Bowden. 2 vols. Louisville: Westminster John Knox, 1992.]

Alexander, Philip S. "Targum, Targumim." *ABD* 6 (1992): 320–31.

Allison, Dale C. *Jesus of Nazareth: Millenarian Prophet.* Minneapolis: Fortress Press, 1998.

Arberry, Arthur J., trans. *The Koran Interpreted.* Reprint. Oxford: Oxford University Press, 1986.

Arnal, William E. *Jesus and the Village Scribes: Galilean Conflicts and the Setting of Q.* Minneapolis: Fortress Press, 2001.

Ashton, John. "Abba." *ABD* 1 (1992): 7–8.

———. *Understanding the Fourth Gospel.* Oxford: Clarendon, 1991.

Attridge, Harold W. *Hebrews: A Commentary on the Epistle to the Hebrews.* Hermeneia. Philadelphia: Fortress Press, 1989.

Aune, David E. *The Cultic Setting of Realized Eschatology in Early Christianity.* NovTSup 28. Leiden: Brill, 1972.

———. *Prophecy in Early Christianity and the Ancient Mediterranean World.* Grand Rapids, Mich.: Eerdmans, 1983.

———. *Revelation 1–5.* WBC 52A. Dallas: Word, 1997.

———. *Revelation 6–16.* WBC 52B. Nashville: Nelson, 1998.

———. *Revelation 17–22.* WBC 52C. Nashville: Nelson, 1998.

Ayoub, Mahmoud M. *Redemptive Suffering in Islam: A Study of the Devotional Aspects of Ashura in Twelver Shi'ism.* The Hague: Mouton, 1978.

408   Balla, Peter. *Challenges to New Testament Theology: An Attempt to Justify the Enterprise.* WUNT 2/95. Tübingen: Mohr Siebeck, 1997.

Barclay. John M. G. "'Do We Undermine the Law?' A Study of Romans 14.1—15.6." Pages 287–308 in *Paul and the Mosaic Law.* Edited by J. D. G. Dunn. WUNT 89. Tübingen: Mohr Siebeck, 1996.

———. *Jews in the Mediterranean Diaspora from Alexander to Trajan (323 BCE–117 CE).* Edinburgh: T. & T. Clark, 1996.

———. "Paul among Diaspora Jews: Anomaly or Apostate?" *JSNT* 60 (1995): 89–120.

Barr, James. "'Abba' Isn't 'Daddy.'" *JTS* 39 (1988): 28–47.

———. *The Concept of Biblical Theology: An Old Testament Perspective.* London: SCM, 1999.

———. *The Garden of Eden and the Hope of Immortality.* London: SCM, 1992.

Barrett, C. K. *A Commentary on the First Epistle to the Corinthians.* BNTC. London: Black, 1968.

———. *A Commentary on the First Epistle to the Romans.* BNTC. London: Black, 1973.

———. "'Things Sacrificed to Idols.'" Pages 40–59 in *Essays on Paul* by C. K. Barrett. London: SPCK, 1982.

Barth, Gerhard. *Der Tod Jesu im Verständnis des Neuen Testaments.* Neukirchen-Vluyn: Neukirchener, 1992.

Barth, Hans-Martin. *Dogmatik: Evangelischer Glaube im Kontext der Weltreligionen.* 2d ed. Gütersloh: Chr. Kaiser/Gütersloher Verlaghaus, 2002.

Bauckham, Richard, ed. *The Gospels for All Christians: Rethinking the Gospel Audiences.* Edinburgh: T. & T. Clark, 1998.

———. "Introduction." Pages 1–7 in *The Gospels for All Christians: Rethinking the Gospel Audiences.* Edited by Richard Bauckham. Edinburgh: T. & T. Clark, 1998.

Bauer, Walter. *Orthodoxy and Heresy in Earliest Christianity.* Translated and edited by Robert A. Kraft and Gerhard Krodel. London: SCM, 1972.

Baumgarten, Albert I. "The name of the Pharisees." *JBL* 102 (1983): 411–28.

Baumgartner, Frederic J. *Longing for the End: A History of Millennialism in Western Civilization.* New York: St. Martin's Press, 1999.

Becker, Eve-Marie. *Das Markus-Evangelium im Rahmen antiker Historiographie.* *WUNT 194. Tübingen: Mohr Siebeck, 2006.

Becker, Jürgen. *Das Evangelium des Johannes, Kapitel 1-10.* Ökumenischer Taschenkommentar zum Neuen Testament 4/1. Gütersloh: Gütersloher Verlagshaus Gerd Mohn/Würzburg: Echter, 1979.

———. *Jesus von Nazaret.* Berlin: Walter de Gruyter, 1996. [ET: *Jesus of Nazareth.* Translated by James E. Crouch. New York: Walter de Gruyter, 1998.]

———. *Johanneisches Christentum: Seine Geschichte und Theologie im Überblick.* Tübingen: Mohr Siebeck, 2004.

———. *Johannes der Täufer und Jesus von Nazareth.* Neukirchen-Vluyn: Neukirchener, 1972.

———. *Paul: Apostle to the Gentiles.* Translated by O. C. Dean Jr. Louisville: Westminster John Knox, 1993.

———. "Theologiegeschichte des Urchristentums—Theologie des Neuen Testaments—Frühchristliche Religionsgeschichte." Pages 115–33 in *Aufgabe und Durchführung einer Theologie des Neuen Testaments.* Edited by Cilliers Breytenbach and Jörg Frey. WUNT 205. Tübingen: Mohr Siebeck, 2007.

———. "Das Verhältnis des johanneischen Kreises zum Paulinismus: Anregungen zur Belebung einer Diskussion." Pages 473–95 in *Paulus und Johannes: Exegetische Studien zur paulinischen und johanneischen Theologie und Literatur.* Edited by Dieter Sänger and Ulrich Mell. WUNT 198. Tübingen: Mohr Siebeck, 2006.

———. "Das vierte Evangelium und die Frage nach seinen externen und internen Quellen." Pages 203–41 in *Fair Play: Diversity and Conflicts in Early Christianity: Essays in Honour of Heikki Räisänen.* Edited by Ismo Dunderberg, Christopher Tuckett, and Kari Syreeni. NovTSup 103. Boston: Brill, 2002.

Behm, Johannes. "*morphe*, etc." *TDNT* 4 (1967): 742-59.

Beker, J. Christiaan. *Heirs of Paul: Paul's Legacy in the New Testament and in the Church Today.* Edinburgh: T. & T. Clark, 1992.

———. *Paul the Apostle: The Triumph of God in Life and Thought.* Philadelphia: Fortress Press, 1984.

Berger, Klaus. *Theologiegeschichte des Urchristentum: Theologie des Neuen Testaments.* Uni-Taschenbücher, Grosse Reihe. 2d ed. Tübingen/Basel: Francke, 1995.

Bernstein, Alan E. *The Formation of Hell: Death and Retribution in the Ancient and Early Christian Worlds.* Ithaca: Cornell University Press, 1993.

Berquist, Jon L. *Judaism in Persia's Shadow: A Social and Historical Approach.* Eugene, Ore.: Wipf and Stock, 2003.

Best, Ernest. *The First and Second Epistles to the Thessalonians.* BNTC. London: Black, 1977.

Bethge, Hans-Gebhard. Introduction to *On the Origin of the World.* Pages 170–71 in *The Nag Hammadi Library in English.* Edited by James M. Robinson. 3d ed. San Francisco: HarperSanFrancisco, 1990.

Betz, Hans Dieter. *Galatians: A Commentary on Paul's Letter to the Churches in Galatia*. Hermeneia. Philadelphia: Fortress Press, 1979.

Boccaccini, Gabriele. *Middle Judaism: Jewish Thought, 300 B.C.E. to 200 C.E.* Minneapolis: Fortress Press, 1991.

Borg, Marcus J. *Conflict, Holiness, and Politics in the Teaching of Jesus*. Harrisburg, Pa.: Trinity Press International, 1998. First published 1984 by Edwin Mellen.

———. *Jesus, a New Vision: Spirit, Culture, and the Life of Discipleship*. San Francisco: Harper & Row, 1987.

———. "Portraits of Jesus in Contemporary North American Scholarship." *HTR* 84 (1991): 1–22.

Borgen, Peder. *Philo of Alexandria: An Exegete for His Time*. NovTSup 86. Leiden: Brill, 1997.

Boring, M. Eugene. "The Language of Universal Salvation in Paul." *JBL* 105 (1986): 269–92.

———. "Prophecy (Early Christian)." *ABD* 5 (1992): 495–502.

Boring, M. Eugene, Klaus Berger, and Carsten Colpe, eds. *Hellenistic Commentary to the New Testament*. Nashville: Abingdon, 1995.

Bousset, Wilhelm. *Die Offenbarung Johannis*. 2d ed. KEK 16. Göttingen: Vandenhoeck & Ruprecht, 1906.

Boyarin, Daniel. *Dying for God: Martyrdom and the Making of Christianity and Judaism*. Stanford: Stanford University Press, 1999.

———. *A Radical Jew: Paul and the Politics of Identity*. Berkeley: University of California Press, 1994.

Boyer, Paul. *When Time Shall Be No More: Prophecy Belief in Modern American Culture*. Cambridge, Mass.: Belknap, 2000.

Brandon, S. G. F. *The Judgment of the Dead: The Idea of Life after Death in the Major Religions*. New York: Scribner, 1967.

Braun, Herbert. "Die Problematik einer Theologie des Neuen Testaments." Pages 405–24 in *Das Problem der Theologie des Neuen Testaments*. Edited by Georg Strecker. Wege der Forschung 367. Darmstadt: Wissenschaftliche Buchgesellschaft, 1975.

Breytenbach, Cilliers. *Versöhnung: Eine Studie zur paulinischen Soteriologie*. WMANT 60. Neukirchen-Vluyn: Neukirchener, 1989.

Breytenbach, Cilliers, and Jörg Frey, eds. *Aufgabe und Durchführung einer Theologie des Neuen Testaments*. WUNT 205. Tübingen: Mohr Siebeck, 2007.

Brooten, Bernadette J. *Women Leaders in the Ancient Synagogue: Inscriptional Evidence and Background Issues*. BJS 36. Atlanta: Scholars Press, 1982.

Brown, David. *Tradition and Imagination: Revelation and Change*. Oxford: Oxford University Press, 1999.

———. *Discipleship and Imagination: Christian Tradition and Truth*. Oxford: Oxford University Press, 2000.

Brown, Peter. *Augustine: A Biography*. Berkeley: California University Press, 1969.

Brown, Raymond E. *The Birth of the Messiah: A Commentary on the Infancy Narratives in Matthew and Luke*. Garden City, N.Y.: Doubleday, 1977.

———. *The Community of the Beloved Disciple: The Life, Loves, and Hates of an Individual Church in New Testament Times*. Mahwah, N.J.: Paulist, 1979.

———. *The Gospel according to John*. 2 vols. AB 29/29A. Garden City, N.Y.: Doubleday, 1966–70.

———. "The *Gospel of Peter* and Canonical Gospel Priority." *NTS* 33 (1987): 321–43.

Brown, Raymond E., Karl P. Donfried, Joseph A. Fitzmyer, and John Reumann, eds. *Mary in the New Testament: A Collaborative Assessment by Protestant and Roman Catholic Scholars*. Philadelphia: Fortress Press, 1978.

Brown, Scott G. *Mark's Other Gospel: Rethinking Morton Smith's Controversial Discovery*. Waterloo, Ont.: Wilfrid Laurier University Press, 2005.

Brox, Norbert. *Der Hirt des Hermas*. KEKSup 7. Göttingen: Vandenhoeck & Ruprecht, 1991.

Buchanan, George Wesley. "Symbolic Money-Changers in the Temple?" *NTS* 37 (1991): 280–90.

Bullard, Roger A. Introduction to *Hypostasis of the Archons*. Pages 161–62 in *The Nag Hammadi Library in English*. Edited by James M. Robinson. 3d ed. San Francisco: HarperSanFrancisco, 1990.

Bultmann, Rudolf. *Glauben und Verstehen 2: Gesammelte Aufsätze*. 3d ed. Tübingen: Mohr Siebeck, 1967.

———. *Theology of the New Testament*. Translated by Kendrick Grobel. 2 vols. New York: Scribner, 1951–55.

Burkert, Walter. *Ancient Mystery Cults*. Cambridge, Mass.: Harvard University Press, 1987.

Burkett, Delbert R. *An Introduction to the New Testament and the Origins of Christianity*. Cambridge: Cambridge University Press, 2002.

Campenhausen, Hans von. *The Formation of the Christian Bible*. 2d ed. Philadelphia: Fortress Press, 1984.

———. *Die Jungfrauengeburt in der Theologie der alten Kirche*. SHAW. Heidelberg: Carl Winter, 1962.

———. *Kirchliches Amt und geistliche Vollmacht in den ersten drei Jahrhunderten*. BHT 14. Tübingen: Mohr Siebeck, 1963.

410 Carlson, Stephen C. *The Gospel Hoax: Morton Smith's Invention of Secret Mark.* Waco: Baylor University Press, 2005.

Carroll, Robert P. *When Prophecy Failed: Reactions and Responses to Failure in the Old Testament Prophetic Traditions.* London: SCM, 1979.

Carson, D. A., Peter T. O'Brien, and Mark A. Seifrid, eds. *Justification and Variegated Nomism.* 2 vols. WUNT 2/140; WUNT 2/181. Tübingen: Mohr Siebeck, 2001, 2004.

Carter, T. L. *Paul and the Power of Sin: Redefining "Beyond the Pale."* SNTSMS 115. Cambridge: Cambridge University Press, 2002.

Casey, P. M. *From Jewish Prophet to Gentile God: The Origins and Development of New Testament Christology.* Cambridge: James Clarke, 1991.

Cavallin, Hans Clemens Caesarius. *Life after Death: Paul's Argument for the Resurrection of the Dead in 1 Cor. 15. Part I: An Enquiry into the Jewish Background.* ConBNT 7/1. Lund: CWK Gleerup, 1974.

Chadwick, Henry. *The Early Church.* Vol. 1 of *The Pelican History of the Church.* Reprint. Harmondsworth: Penguin, 1978.

Chancey, Mark A. *Greco-Roman Culture and the Galilee of Jesus.* SNTSMS 134. Cambridge: Cambridge University Press, 2006.

———. *The Myth of a Gentile Galilee.* SNTSMS 118. Cambridge: Cambridge University Press, 2002.

Charlesworth, James H. "Odes of Solomon." Pages 725–71 in *The Old Testament Pseudepigrapha.* Vol. 2, *Apocalyptic Literature and Testaments.* Edited by James H. Charlesworth. New York: Doubleday, 1985.

———. "Solomon, Odes of." *ABD* 6 (1992): 114–15.

Chester, Andrew. "Jewish Messianic Expectations and Mediatorial Figures and Pauline Christology." Pages 17–89 in *Paulus und das antike Judentum.* Edited by Martin Hengel and Ulrich Heckel. WUNT 58. Tübingen: Mohr Siebeck 1991.

Childs, Brevard S. *Biblical Theology of the Old and New Testaments: Theological Reflection on the Christian Bible.* London: SCM, 1992.

Chilton, Bruce. "James, Peter, Paul, and the Formation of the Gospels." Pages 3–28 in *The Missions of James, Peter and Paul: Tensions in Early Christianity.* Edited by Bruce Chilton and Craig A. Evans. NovTSup 115. Leiden: Brill, 2005.

Clay, J. Eugene. "Apocalypticism in Eastern Europe." Pages 293–321 in *The Encyclopedia of Apocalypticism.* Vol. 3, *Apocalypticism in the Modern Period and the Con-temporary Age.* Edited by Stephen J. Stein. London: Continuum, 2000.

Cohen, Shaye J. D. "Common Judaism in Greek and Latin Authors." Pages 69–87 in *Redefining First-Century Jewish and Christian Identities*, Essays in Honor of E. P. Sanders. Edited by Fabian E. Udoh, et al. Christianity and Judaism in Antiquity Series 16. Notre Dame, Ind.: Notre Dame University Press, 2008.

———. *From the Maccabees to the Mishnah.* 2d ed. Louisville: Westminster John Knox, 2006.

Cohn, Norman. *Cosmos, Chaos, and the World to Come: The Ancient Roots of Apocalyptic Faith.* New Haven: Yale University Press, 1993.

———. *The Pursuit of the Millennium: Revolutionary Millenarians and Mystical Anarchists of the Middle Ages.* Revised ed. New York: Oxford University Press, 1970.

Collins, John J. "The Afterlife in Apocalyptic Literature." Pages 119–39 in *Death, Life-after-Death, Resurrection and the World-to-Come in the Judaisms of Antiquity.* Edited by Alan J. Avery-Peck and Jacob Neusner. Leiden: Brill, 2000.

———. *The Apocalyptic Imagination: An Introduction to the Jewish Matrix of Christianity.* New York: Crossroad, 1992.

———. *Encounters with Biblical Theology.* Minneapolis: Fortress Press, 2005.

———. "Essenes." *ABD* 2 (1992): 619–26.

———. "Forms of Community in the Dead Sea Scrolls." Pages 97–111 in *Emanuel: Studies in Hebrew Bible, Septuagint, and Dead Sea Scrolls.* Essays in Honour of Emanuel Tov. Edited by Shalom M. Paul, Robart A. Kraft, and Lawrence H. Schiffman. VTSup 94. Leiden: Brill, 2003.

———. "From Prophecy to Apocalypticism: The Expectation of the End." Pages 129–61 in *The Encyclopedia of Apocalypticism.* Vol. 1, *The Origins of Apocalypticism in Judaism and Christianity.* Edited by John J. Collins. London: Continuum, 2000.

———. "Messianism in the Maccabean Period." Pages 97–109 in *Judaisms and Their Messiahs at the Turn of the Christian Era.* Edited by Jacob Neusner, William Scott Green, and Ernest S. Frerichs. New York: Cambridge University Press, 1987.

———. "Pre-Christian Jewish Messianism: An Overview." Pages 1–20 in *The Messiah in Early Judaism and Christianity.* Edited by Magnus Zetterholm. Minneapolis: Fortress Press, 2007.

———. *The Scepter and the Star: The Messiahs of the Dead*

Sea Scrolls and Other Ancient Literature. New York: Doubleday, 1995.

———. "The Sons of God and the Daughters of Men." Pages 259–74 in *Sacred Marriages: The Divine-Human Sexual Metaphor from Sumer to Early Christianity.* Edited by Martti Nissinen and Risto Uro. Winona Lake, Ind.: Eisenbrauns, 2008.

———. "Testaments." Pages 325–55 in *Jewish Writings of the Second Temple Period: Apocrypha, Pseudepigrapha, Qumran Sectarian Writings, Philo, Josephus.* Edited by M. E. Stone. CRINT 2/2. Assen: Van Gorcum/ Philadelphia: Fortress Press, 1984.

———. "The Yahad and the 'Qumran Community.'" Pages 81–96 in *Biblical Traditions in Transmission: Essays in Honour of Michale A. Knibb.* Edited by Charlotte Hempel and Judith M. Lieu. JSJSup 111. Leiden: Brill, 2006.

———. "The Zeal of Phinehas: The Bible and the Legitimation of Violence." *JBL* 122 (2003): 3–21.

Collins, John J., Bernard McGinn, and Stephen J. Stein. "General Introduction." Pages vii–xi in *The Encyclopedia of Apocalypticism.* Vol. 1, *The Origins of Apocalypticism in Judaism and Christianity.* Edited by John J. Collins. London: Continuum, 2000.

Conzelmann, Hans. *1 Corinthians: A Commentary on the First Epistle to the Corinthians.* Translated by J. W. Leitch. Hermeneia. Philadelphia: Fortress Press, 1975.

———. *Grundriss der Theologie des Neuen Testaments.* Uni-Taschenbücher 1446. 4th ed. Tübingen: Mohr Siebeck, 1987. [ET: *An Outline of the Theology of the New Testament.* Translated by John Bowden. New York: Harper & Row, 1969.]

———. *History of Primitive Christianity.* Translated by J. E. Steely. Nashville: Abingdon, 1973.

Cook, Stephen L. *Prophecy and Apocalypticism: The Postexilic Social Setting.* Minneapolis: Fortress Press, 1995.

Corley, Kathleen E. "Peter, Preaching of." *ABD* 5 (1992): 282.

Cover, Robin C. "Sin, Sinners (Old Testament)." *ABD* 6 (1992): 31–40.

Cranfield, Charles E. B. *A Critical and Exegetical Commentary on the Epistle to the Romans.* 2 vols. ICC. Edinburgh: T. & T. Clark, 1975–79.

Crossan, John Dominic. *The Cross That Spoke: The Origins of the Passion Narrative.* San Francisco: Harper & Row, 1988.

———. *Four Other Gospels: Shadows on the Contours of Canon.* Minneapolis: Winston, 1985.

———. *The Historical Jesus: The Life of a Mediterranean Jewish Peasant.* Edinburgh: T. & T. Clark, 1991.

———. *Jesus: A Revolutionary Biography.* San Francisco: Harper Collins, 1994.

Crossan, John Dominic, and Jonathan L. Reed. *Excavating Jesus: Beneath the Stones, Behind the Texts.* New York: HarperSanFrancisco, 2001.

Cullmann, Oscar. *Immortality of the Soul or Resurrection of the Dead? The Witness of the New Testament.* London: Epworth, 1958.

Daley, Brian E. "Apocalypticism in Early Christian Theology." Pages 3–47 in *The Encyclopedia of Apocalypticism.* Vol. 2, *Apocalypticism in Western History and Culture.* Edited by Bernard McGinn. London: Continuum, 2000.

———. "Patristische Eschatologie." Pages 84–119 in *Handbuch der Dogmengeschichte* 4/7a. Edited by Michael Schmaus, et al. Freiburg: Herder, 1986.

Daniélou, Jean. *A History of Early Christian Doctrine before the Council of Nicaea.* Vol. 1, *The Theology of Jewish Christianity.* Translated by J. A. Baker. London: Darton, Longman, & Todd, 1964.

Dautzenberg, Gerhard. "Gesetzeskritik und Gesetzesgehorsam in der Jesustradition." Pages 46–70 in *Das Gesetz im Neuen Testament.* Edited by Karl Kertelge. QD 108. Freiburg: Herder, 1986.

———. *Urchristliche Prophetie: Ihre Erforschung, ihre Voraussetzungen im Judentum und ihre Struktur im ersten Korintherbrief.* BWANT 6/4 = 104. Stuttgart: Kohlhammer, 1975.

Davies, Philip R. *Whose Bible Is It Anyway?* JSOTSup 204. Sheffield: Sheffield Academic Press, 1995.

Davis, Stephen, Daniel Kendall, and Gerald O'Collins, eds. *Incarnation: An International Symposium on the Incarnation of the Son of God.* Oxford: Oxford University Press, 2002.

DeConick, April D. *The Thirteenth Apostle: What the Gospel of Judas Really Says.* London: Continuum, 2007.

———. *Voices of the Mystics: Early Christian Discourse in the Gospels of John and Thomas and Other Ancient Christian Literature.* JSNTSup 157. Sheffield: Sheffield Academic Press, 2001.

de Jonge, Marinus. "Patriarchs, Testaments of the Twelve." *ABD* 5 (1992): 181–86.

DeMaris, Richard E. *The New Testament in Its Ritual World.* London: Routledge, 2008.

Denzey, Nicola. "Bardaisan of Edessa." Pages 159–84 in *A Companion to Second-Century Christian "Heretics."* Edited by Antti Marjanen and Petri Luomanen. VCSup 76. Leiden/Boston: Brill, 2005.

412   Desjardins, Michel R. *Peace, Violence and the New Testament.* Biblical Seminar 46. Sheffield: Sheffield Academic Press, 1997.

————. *Sin in Valentinianism.* SBLDS 108. Atlanta: Scholars Press, 1990.

Dibelius, Martin. *Studies in the Acts of Apostles.* Translated by M. Ling. London: SCM, 1956.

Diels, Hermann. *Fragmente der Vorsokratiker griechisch und deutsch.* 3 vols. Reprint. Berlin: Weidmannsche Buchhandlung, 1960-61.

Dillon, John M. "Fate, Greek Conception of." *ABD* 2 (1992): 776–78.

————. "Platonism." *ABD* 5 (1992): 378–81.

Dodd, C. H. *The Epistle of Paul to the Romans.* MNTC. Reprint. London: Hodder and Stoughton, 1947.

Dodds, E. R. *The Greeks and the Irrational.* Berkeley: University of California Press, 1951.

Donaldson, Terence L. *Paul and the Gentiles: Remapping the Apostle's Convictional World.* Minneapolis: Fortress Press, 1997.

Downing, F. Gerald. *Cynics and Christian Origins.* Edinburgh: T. & T. Clark, 1992.

Draper, J. A. "The Holy Vine of David Made Known to the Gentiles through God's Servant Jesus: 'Christian Judaism' in the *Didache*." Pages 257–83 in *Jewish Christianity Reconsidered: Rethinking Ancient Groups and Texts.* Edited by Matt Jackson-McCabe. Minneapolis: Fortress Press, 2007.

Duff, Paul B. *Who Rides the Beast? Prophetic Rivalry and the Rhetoric of Crisis in the Churches of the Apocalypse.* Oxford: Oxford University Press, 2001.

Duling, Dennis C. "Kingdom of God, Kingdom of Heaven." *ABD* 4 (1992): 49–69.

Dunderberg, Ismo. *The Beloved Disciple in Conflict? Revisiting the Gospels of John and Thomas.* Oxford: Oxford University Press, 2006.

————. *Beyond Gnosticism: Myth, Lifestyle, and Society in the School of Valentinus.* New York: Columbia University Press, 2008.

————. *Johannes und die Synoptiker: Studien zu Joh 1–9.* AASF Diss. Hum. 69. Helsinki: Suomalainen tiedeakatemia, 1994.

————. "Judas' Anger and the Perfect Human in the *Gospel of Judas*." In *The Judas Codex.* Edited by April DeConick. Forthcoming.

————. "The School of Valentinus." Pages 64–99 in *A Companion to Second-Century Christian "Heretics."* Edited by Antti Marjanen and Petri Luomanen. VCSup 76. Leiden/Boston: Brill, 2005.

————. "Sin and Sinlessness in 1 John: Theory and Practice." A paper read in the Johannine Literature Section at the SBL 2008 annual meeting in Boston, 2008.

Dunn, James D. G. "Baptism and the Unity of the Church in the New Testament." Pages 78–103 in *Baptism and the Unity of the Church.* Edited by Michael Root and Risto Saarinen. Grand Rapids: Eerdmans, 1998.

————. *Christology in the Making: An Inquiry into the Origins of the Doctrine of the Incarnation.* 2d ed. London: SCM, 1989.

————. *Galatians.* BNTC. London: Black, 1993.

————. *Jesus, Paul, and the Law: Studies in Mark and Galatians.* London: SPCK, 1990.

————. *Jesus Remembered.* Vol. 1 of *Christianity in the Making.* Grand Rapids: Eerdmans, 2003.

————. "The Justice of God: A Renewed Perspective on Justification by Faith." Pages 187–205 in *The New Perspective on Paul: Collected Essays.* Edited by James D. G. Dunn. WUNT 185. Tübingen: Mohr Siebeck, 2005.

————. "Not so much 'New Testament Theology' as 'New Testament Theologizing.'" Pages 225–46 in *Aufgabe und Durchführung einer Theologie des Neuen Testaments.* Edited by Cilliers Breytenbach and Jörg Frey. WUNT 205. Tübingen: Mohr Siebeck, 2007.

————. Review of Simon J. Gathercole's *The Pre-existent Son: Recovering the Christologies of Matthew, Mark, and Luke, Review of Biblical Literature.* RBL. April 28, 2007.

————. *Romans 1–8.* WBC 38A. Dallas: Word, 1988.

————. *Romans 9–16.* WBC 38B. Dallas: Word, 1988.

————. *The Theology of Paul the Apostle.* Grand Rapids: Eerdmans, 1998.

————. *Unity and Diversity in the New Testament: An Inquiry into the Character of Earliest Christianity.* 2d ed. London: SCM/Philadelphia: Trinity Press International, 1990.

Ebner, Martin. "Gemeindestrukturen in Exempeln: Eine eindeutig frauenfreundliche Kompromisslösung." Pages 180–86 in *Aus Liebe zu Paulus? Die Akte Thekla neu aufgerollt.* Edited by Martin Ebner. SBS 206. Stuttgart: Katholisches Bibelwerk, 2005.

————. "Von den Anfängen bis zur Mitte des 2. Jahrhunderts." Pages 15–57 in *Ökumenische Kirchengeschichte 1: Von den Anfängen bis zum Mittelalter.* Edited by Martin Ebner, et al. Darmstadt: Wissenschaftliche Buchgesellschaft, 2006.

Ebner, Martin, and Markus Lau. "Überlieferung, Gliederung und Komposition." Pages 1–11 in *Aus Liebe zu*

Paulus? Die Akte Thekla neu aufgerollt. Edited by Martin Ebner. SBS 206. Stuttgart: Katholisches Bibelwerk, 2005.

Edwards, Douglas R. "The Socio-Economic and Cultural Ethos of the Lower Galilee in the First Century: Implications for the Nascent Jesus Movement." Pages 53–73 in *The Galilee in Late Antiquity.* Edited by Lee I. Levine. New York: Jewish Theological Seminary of America, 1992.

Ehrman, Bart D. *Jesus: Apocalyptic Prophet of the New Millennium.* Oxford: Oxford University Press, 1999.

———. *The Orthodox Corruption of Scripture: The Effect of Early Christological Controversies on the Text of the New Testament.* Oxford: Oxford University Press, 1993.

Eliade, Mircea. *A History of Religious Ideas: From Gautama Buddha to the Triumph of Christianity.* Vol. 2. Translated by Willard R. Trask. Chicago: University of Chicago Press, 1984.

Elliott, Mark Adam. *The Survivors of Israel: A Reconsideration of the Theology of Pre-Christian Judaism.* Grand Rapids: Eerdmans, 2000.

Elliott, Neil. *Liberating Paul: The Justice of God and the Politics of the Apostle.* Biblical Seminar 27. Sheffield: Sheffield Academic Press, 1995.

Engberg-Pedersen, Troels. *Paul and the Stoics.* Edinburgh: T. & T. Clark, 2000.

Eskola, Timo. *Theodicy and Predestination in Paul's Soteriology.* WUNT 2/100. Tübingen: Mohr Siebeck, 1998.

Esler, Philip Francis. *Community and Gospel in Luke–Acts: The Social and Political Motivations of Lucan Theology.* SNTSMS 57. Cambridge: Cambridge University Press, 1987.

———. *Galatians.* New Testament Readings. New York: Routledge, 1998.

———. "Glossolalia and the Admission of Gentiles into the Early Christian Community." Pages 37–51 in Philip Francis Esler, *The First Christians in Their Social Worlds: Social-Scientific Approaches to New Testament Interpretation.* New York: Routledge, 1994.

Esler, Philip Francis, ed. *The Early Christian World.* Vol. 1. London: Routledge, 2000.

Evans, C. F. *Resurrection and the New Testament.* London: SCM, 1970.

———. *Saint Luke.* TPINTC. London: SCM, 1990.

Fee, Gordon D. *God's Empowering Presence: The Holy Spirit in the Letters of Paul.* Peabody, Mass.: Hendrickson, 1994.

Feldman, Louis H. "Josephus." *ABD* 3 (1992): 981–98.

Fieger, Michael. *Das Thomasevangelium: Einleitung, Kommentar und Systematik.* NTAbh 22. Münster: Aschendorff, 1991.

Filoramo, Giovanni. *A History of Gnosticism.* Translated by Anthony Alcock. Oxford: Blackwell, 1991.

Fischer, Karl Martin. *Tendenz und Absicht des Epheserbriefes.* FRLANT 111. Göttingen: Vandenhoeck & Ruprecht, 1973.

———. *Das Urchristentum: Kirchengeschichte in Einzeldarstellungen* 1/1. Berlin: Evangelische Verlagsanstalt, 1985.

Fitzer, Gottfried. "Der Ort der Versöhnung nach Paulus." *TZ* 22 (1966): 161–83.

Fitzmyer, Joseph A. *A Wandering Aramean: Collected Aramaic Essays.* SBLMS 25. Chico, Calif.: Scholars, 1979.

Flower, Michael Attyah. *The Seer in Ancient Greece.* Berkeley: University of California Press, 2008.

Fohrer, Georg. *Geschichte der israelitischen Religion.* Berlin: Walter de Gruyter, 1969. ET: *History of Israelite Religion.* Translated by David E. Green. London: SPCK, 1973.

Förster, Niclas. *Marcus Magus: Kult, Lehre und Gemeindeleben einer valentinianischen Gnostikergruppe.* WUNT 114. Tübingen: Mohr Siebeck, 1999.

Frankfort, Henri. *Ancient Egyptian Religion: An Interpretation.* New York: Harper & Row, 1961.

Franzmann, Majella. "A Complete History of Early Christianity: Taking the 'Heretics' Seriously." *JRH* 29 (2005): 117–28.

———. *Jesus in the Nag Hammadi Writings.* Edinburgh: T. & T. Clark, 1996.

Fredriksen, Paula. *From Jesus to Christ: The Origins of the New Testament Images of Jesus.* New Haven: Yale University Press, 1988.

———. "Gospel Chronologies, the Scene in the Temple, and the Crucifixion of Jesus." Pages 246–82 in *Redefining First-Century Jewish and Christian Identities, Essays in Honor of E.P. Sanders.* Edited by Fabian E. Udoh, et al. Christianity and Judaism in Antiquity Series 16. Notre Dame: Notre Dame University Press, 2008.

———. *Jesus of Nazareth, King of the Jews: A Jewish Life and the Emergence of Christianity.* New York: Knopf, 2000.

———. "Law: New Testament Views." Pages 423–24 in *The Oxford Companion to the Bible.* Edited by Bruce M. Metzger and Michael David Coogan. Oxford: Oxford University Press, 1993.

———. "What You See Is What You Get: Context and Content in Current Research on the Historical Jesus." *ThTo* 52 (1995): 75–97.

414 Frend, William H. C. *Martyrdom and Persecution in the Early Church: A Study of a Conflict from the Maccabees to Donatus.* Oxford: Blackwell, 1965.

Frey, Jörg. *Johanneische Eschatologie 1: Ihre Probleme im Spiegel der Forschung seit Reimarus.* WUNT 96. Tübingen: Mohr Siebeck, 1997.

———. "Paulus und die Apostel: Zur Entwicklung des paulinischen Apostelbegriffs und zum Verhältnis des Heidenapostels zu seinen 'Kollegen.'" Pages 192–227 in *Biographie und Persönlichkeit des Paulus.* Edited by Eve-Marie Becker and Peter Pilhofer. WUNT 187. Tübingen: Mohr Siebeck, 2005.

Freyne, Sean. *Jesus, a Jewish Galilean: A New Reading of the Jesus Story.* New York: T. & T. Clark, 2005.

———. "Jesus in Jewish Galilee." Pages 197–212 in *Redefining First-Century Jewish and Christian Identities: Essays in Honor of Ed Parish Sanders.* Edited by Fabian E. Udoh. Notre Dame, Ind.: Notre Dame University Press, 2008.

Frickel, Joseph. *Hellenistische Erlösung in christlicher Deutung: Die gnostische Naassenerschrift.* NHS 19. Leiden: Brill, 1984.

Friedrich, Gerhard. *Die Verkündigung des Todes Jesu im Neuen Testament.* Biblisch-theologische Studien 6. Neukirchen-Vluyn: Neukirchener, 1982.

Funk, Robert W. *Honest to Jesus: Jesus for a New Millennium.* San Francisco: HarperCollins, 1996.

Funk, Robert W., and Roy W. Hoover. *The Five Gospels: The Search for the Authentic Words of Jesus.* New Translation and Commentary by Robert W. Funk, Roy W. Hoover, and the Jesus Seminar. New York: Polebridge, 1993.

Gager, John G. *The Origins of Anti-Semitism: Attitudes toward Judaism in Pagan and Christian Antiquity.* Oxford: Oxford University Press, 1983.

———. *Reinventing Paul.* New York: Oxford University Press, 2000.

Gamble, Harry Y. "Canon, New Testament." *ABD* 1 (1992): 852–61.

García Martínez, Florentino. *The Dead Sea Scrolls Translated: The Qumran Texts in English.* Translated by Wilfred G. E. Watson. 2d ed. Boston: Brill, 1996.

Gaston, Lloyd. "Anti-Judaism and the Passion Narrative in Luke and Acts." Pages 127–53 in *Anti-Judaism in Early Christianity.* Vol. 1, *Paul and the Gospels.* Edited by Peter Richardson and David Granskou. Studies in Christianity and Judaism 2. Waterloo, Ont.: Wilfrid Laurier University Press, 1986.

———. *Paul and the Torah.* Vancouver: University of British Columbia Press, 1987.

Gathercole, Simon J. *The Pre-existent Son: Recovering the Christologies of Matthew, Mark, and Luke.* Grand Rapids: Eerdmans, 2006.

Gaventa, Beverly Roberts. *Mary: Glimpses of the Mother of Jesus.* Edinburgh: T. & T. Clark, 1999.

Gerstenberger, Erhard S. *Theologies in the Old Testament.* Translated by John Bowden. New York: T. & T. Clark, 2002.

Gieschen, Charles A. *Angelomorphic Christology: Antecedents and Early Evidence.* AGJU 42. Leiden/New York: Brill, 1998.

Gillman, Florence Morgan. "Erastus." *ABD* 2 (1992): 571.

Gladigow, Burkhard. "Roman Religion." *ABD* 5 (1992): 809–16.

Golb, Norman. *Who Wrote the Dead Sea Scrolls? The Search for the Secret of Qumran.* New York: Scribner, 1995.

Goldenberg, Robert. *The Nations That Know Thee Not: Ancient Jewish Attitudes toward Other Religions.* Biblical Seminar 52. Sheffield: Sheffield Academic Press, 1997.

Goodman, Martin. *Mission and Conversion: Proselytizing in the Religious History of the Roman Empire.* Oxford: Clarendon, 1994.

Goulder, Michael. *Luke: A New Paradigm.* JSNTSup 20. Sheffield: Sheffield Academic Press, 1989.

———. *A Tale of Two Missions.* London: SCM, 1994.

———. "The Two Roots of the Christian Myth." Pages 64–86 in *The Myth of God Incarnate.* Edited by John Hick. London: SCM, 1977.

Gowan, Donald E. *Eschatology in the Old Testament.* Edinburgh: T. & T. Clark, 1987.

Grabbe, Lester L. *An Introduction to First Century Judaism: Jewish Religion and History in the Second Temple Period.* New York: T. & T. Clark. 2003.

———. *Judaic Religion in the Second Temple Period: Belief and Practice from the Exile to Yavneh.* London: Routledge, 2000.

———. *Judaism: From Cyrus to Hadrian.* 2 vols. Minneapolis: Fortress Press, 1992.

Green, William Scott. "Introduction: Messiah in Judaism, Rethinking the Question." Pages 1–13 in *Judaisms and Their Messiahs at the Turn of the Christian Era.* Edited by Jacob Neusner, William Scott Green, and Ernest S. Frerichs. Cambridge: Cambridge University Press, 1987.

Gregory, Andrew. "Jewish-Christian Gospels." Pages 54–67 in *The Non-Canonical Gospels.* Edited by Paul Foster. London/New York: T. & T. Clark, 2008.

Greschat, Katharina. *Apelles und Hermogenes: Zwei theologische Lehrer des zweiten Jahrhunderts.* VCSup 48. Leiden: Brill, 2000.

Greshake, Gisbert. *Resurrectio mortuorum: Zum theologischen Verständnis der leiblichen Auferstehung.* Darmstadt: Wissenschaftliche Buchgesellschaft, 1986.

Groh, Dennis E. "Arius, Arianism." *ABD* 1 (1992): 384–86.

Guillaume, Alfred. *Islam.* Reprint. Harmondsworth: Penguin, 1968.

Guthrie, Donald. *New Testament Theology.* Downers Grove, Ill.: InterVarsity Press, 1981.

Haenchen, Ernst. *The Acts of the Apostles: A Commentary.* Oxford: Blackwell, 1982.

———. *Das Johannesevangelium: Ein Kommentar.* Edited by Ulrich Busse. Tübingen: Mohr Siebeck, 1980. [ET: *John: A Commentary on the Gospel of John.* 2 vols. Hermeneia. Minneapolis: Fortress Press, 1988.]

Hahn, Ferdinand. *Christologische Hoheitstitel: Ihre Geschichte im frühen Christentum.* FRLANT 83. Göttingen: Vandenhoeck & Ruprecht, 1966. [ET: *The Titles of Jesus in Christology: Their History in Early Christianity.* Cambridge: James Clark, 2002.]

———. *Theologie des Neuen Testaments.* 2 vols. Tübingen: Mohr Siebeck, 2002.

Häkkinen, Sakari. "The Baptism of Jesus." Pages 73–91 in *Lux Humana, Lux Aeterna: Essays on Biblical and Related Themes in Honour of Lars Aejmelaeus.* Edited by Antti Mustakallio. Publications of the Finnish Exegetical Society 89. Helsinki: Finnish Exegetical Society/Göttingen: Vandenhoeck & Ruprecht, 2005.

———. "Ebionites." Pages 247–78 in *A Companion to Second-Century Christian "Heretics."* Edited by Antti Marjanen and Petri Luomanen. VCSup 76. Boston: Brill, 2005.

———. *Köyhät kerettiläiset: Ebionit kirkkoisien teksteissä.* Suomalaisen Teologisen Kirjallisuusseuran julkaisuja 223. Helsinki: Suomalainen Teologinen Kirjallisuusseura, 1999.

Hakola, Raimo. *Identity Matters: John, the Jews and Jewishness.* NovTSup 118. Boston: Brill. 2005.

———. "The Q People and Burdens Hard to Bear: Polemic against the Pharisees and the Lawyers in Q 11:39-52." Paper read in November 2007 at the SBL annual meeting in San Diego.

———. "Social Identities and Group Phenomena in Second Temple Judaism." Pages 259–76 in *Explaining Christian Origins and Early Judaism: Contributions from Cognitive and Social Science.* Edited by Petri Luomanen, Ilkka Pyysiäinen, and Risto Uro. BibInt 89. Leiden: Brill, 2007.

———. "Social Identity and a Stereotype in the Making: The Pharisees as Hypocrites in Matt 23." Pages 123–39 in *Identity Formation in the New Testament.* Edited by Bengt Holmberg and Mikael Winninge. WUNT 227. Tübingen: Mohr Siebeck, 2008.

Hällström, Gunnar af. *Fides Simpliciorum according to Origen of Alexandria.* Commentationes Humanarum Litterarum 76. Helsinki: Societas Scientiarum Fennica, 1984.

Hällström, Gunnar af, and Oskar Skarsaune. "Cerinthus, Elxai, and Other Alleged Jewish Christian Teachers or Groups." Pages 488–502 in *Jewish Believers in Jesus: The Early Centuries.* Edited by Oskar Skarsaune and Reidar Hvalvik. Peabody, Mass.: Hendrickson, 2007.

Hanson, Richard P. C. *Studies in Christian Antiquity.* Edinburgh: T. & T. Clark, 1985.

Harnack, Adolf von. *Marcion: Das Evangelium vom fremden Gott: Eine Monographie zur Geschichte der Grundlegung der katholischen Kirche; Neue Studien zu Marcion.* 1921. Reprint. Darmstadt: Wissenschaftliche Buchgesellschaft, 1985.

Hartman, Lars. "Baptism." *ABD* 1 (1992): 583–94.

Haufe, Günter. "Individuelle Eschatologie des Neuen Testaments." *ZTK* 83 (1986): 436–63.

Hauschild, Wolf-Dieter. *Gottes Geist und der Mensch: Studien zur frühchristlichen Pneumatologie.* BEvT 63. Munich: Chr. Kaiser, 1972.

Hayes, Christine E. *Gentile Impurities and Jewish Identities: Intermarriage and Conversion from the Bible to the Talmud.* Oxford: Oxford University Press, 2002.

Hecht, Richard D. "Philo and Messiah." Pages 139–68 in *Judaisms and Their Messiahs at the Turn of the Christian Era.* Edited by Jacob Neusner, William Scott Green, and Ernest S. Frerichs. Cambridge: Cambridge University Press, 1987.

Hengel, Martin. *Between Jesus and Paul: Studies in the Earliest History of Christianity.* London: SCM Press, 1983.

———. *Judaism and Hellenism: Studies in Their Encounter in Palestine during the Early Hellenistic Period.* Vol. 1. Translated by John Bowden. 2d ed. London: SCM, 1981.

———. "Psalm 110 und die Erhöhung des Auferstandenen zur Rechten Gottes." Pages 43–73 in *Anfänge der Christologie.* Festschrift for Ferdinand Hahn. Edited by Cilliers Breytenbach and Henning Paulsen. Göttingen: Vandenhoeck & Ruprecht, 1991.

416 ———. *The Son of God: The Origin of Christology and the History of Jewish-Hellenistic Religion.* Translated by John Bowden. Philadelphia: Fortress Press, 1976.

———. "Zur matthäischen Bergpredigt in ihrem jüdischen Hintergrund." Pages 219–92 in idem, *Kleine Schriften.* Vol. 2, *Judaica, Hellenistica et Christiana.* WUNT 109. Tübingen: Mohr Siebeck, 1999.

Hick, John. *The Metaphor of God Incarnate: Christology in a Pluralistic Age.* 2d ed. London: SCM, 2005.

———. "Preface." Pages ix–xi in *The Myth of God Incarnate.* Edited by John Hick. London: SCM, 1977.

Hick, John, ed. *The Myth of God Incarnate.* London: SCM, 1977.

Hill, Charles E. *Regnum Caelorum: Patterns of Millennial Thought in Early Christianity.* 2d ed. Grand Rapids: Eerdmans, 2001.

Hill, Craig C. *Hellenists and Hebrews: Reappraising a Division within the Earliest Church.* Philadelphia: Fortress Press, 1992.

Hillert, Sven. *Limited and Universal Salvation: A Text-Oriented and Hermeneutical Study of Two Perspectives in Paul.* ConBNT 31. Stockholm: Almqvist & Wiksell, 1999.

Hills, Julian V. "Apostles, Epistle of." *ABD* 1 (1992): 311–12.

Hoffmann, Paul. "Mutmassungen über Q: Zum Problem der literarischen Genese von Q." Pages 255–88 in *The Sayings Source Q and the Historical Jesus.* Edited by Andreas Lindemann. BETL 98. Leuven: Leuven University Press, 2001.

Hoffmann, R. Joseph, trans. *Celsus: On the True Doctrine, A Discourse against the Christians.* Oxford: Oxford University Press, 1987.

———. *Marcion: On the Restitution of Christianity: An Essay on the Development of Radical Paulinist Theology in the Second Century.* AAR Academy Series 46. Chico, Calif.: Scholars Press, 1984.

Hoglund, Kenneth G. *Achemenid Imperial Administration in Syria-Palestine and the Missions of Ezra and Nehemiah.* SBLDS 125. Atlanta: Scholars Press, 1992.

Holmén, Tom. "The Alternatives of the Kingdom: Encountering the Semantic Restrictions of Luke 17, 20–21 (*entos hymon*)." *ZNW* 87 (1996): 204–29.

———. *Jesus and Jewish Covenant Thinking.* BibInt 55. Boston: Brill, 2001.

Holtzmann, Heinrich Julius. *Lehrbuch der neutestamentlichen Theologie.* Vol. 1. Sammlung Theologischer Lehrbücher. 2d ed. Freiburg/Leipzig: Mohr Siebeck, 1911.

Horbury, William. *Jewish Messianism and the Cult of Christ.* London: SCM, 1998.

Horn, Friedrich Wilhelm. *Das Angeld das Geistes: Studien zur paulinischen Pneumatologie.* FRLANT 154. Göttingen: Vandenhoeck & Ruprecht, 1992.

———. "Holy Spirit." *ABD* 3 (1992): 260-80.

Horsley, Richard. A. *Jesus and the Spiral of Violence: Popular Jewish Resistance in Roman Palestine.* San Francisco: Harper & Row, 1987.

Horsley, Richard A., ed. *Paul and Empire: Religion and Power in Roman Imperial Society.* Valley Forge, Pa.: Trinity Press International, 1997.

Horsley, Richard A., and John S. Hanson. *Bandits, Prophets, and Messiahs: Popular Movements at the Time of Jesus.* San Francisco: Harper & Row, 1985.

Houlden, J. L. *Jesus: A Question of Identity.* London: SPCK, 1992.

———. "John, Gospel of." Pages 361–63 in *A Dictionary of Biblical Interpretation.* Edited by R. J. Coggins and J. L. Houlden. Philadelphia: Trinity Press International, 1990.

———. *The Public Face of the Gospel: New Testament Ideas of the Church.* London: SCM, 1997.

Hübner. Hans. *Biblische Theologie des Neuen Testaments.* 3 volumes. Göttingen: Vandenhoeck & Ruprecht, 1990–1995.

———. "An die Epheser." Pages 127–277 in Hans Hübner, *An Philemon, An die Kolosser, An die Epheser.* HNT 12. Tübingen: Mohr Siebeck, 1997.

———. *Das Gesetz in der synoptischen Tradition: Studien zur These einer progressiven Qumranisierung und Judaisierung innerhalb der synoptischen Tradition.* 2d ed. Göttingen: Vandenhoeck & Ruprecht, 1986.

———. *Gottes Ich und Israel: Zum Schriftgebrauch des Paulus in Römer 9–11.* FRLANT 136. Göttingen: Vandenhoeck & Ruprecht, 1984.

———. *Law in Paul's Thought: A Contribution to the Development of Paul's Theology.* Translated by J. C. G. Greig. Studies of the New Testament and Its World. Edinburgh: T. & T. Clark, 1986.

Hultgård, Anders. "Persian Apocalypticism." Pages 39–83 in *The Encyclopedia of Apocalypticism.* Vol. 1, *The Origins of Apocalypticism in Judaism and Christianity.* Edited by John J. Collins. London: Continuum, 2000.

Hultgren, Arland J. *Christ and His Benefits: Christology and Redemption in the New Testament.* Philadelphia: Fortress Press, 1987.

———. *The Rise of Normative Christianity.* Minneapolis: Fortress Press, 1994.

Hurtado, Larry W. *Lord Jesus Christ: Devotion to Jesus in Earliest Christianity.* Grand Rapids: Eerdmans, 2003.

Huttunen, Niko. "Greco-Roman Philosophy and Paul's Teaching on Law." Pages 74–89 in *The Nordic Paul: Finnish Approaches to Pauline Theology*. Edited by Lars Aejmelaeus and Antti Mustakallio. Library of New Testament Studies 374. London: T. & T. Clark, 2008.

———. *Paul and Epictetus on Law*. Library of New Testament Studies. London: T. & T. Clark, 2009.

Isenberg, Wesley W. Introduction to the *Gospel of Philip*. Pages 139–41 in *The Nag Hammadi Library in English*. Edited by James M. Robinson. 3d ed. San Francisco: HarperSanFrancisco, 1990.

Jeremias, Joachim. *Jerusalem zur Zeit Jesu: Eine kulturgeschichtliche Untersuchung zur neutestamentlichen Zeitgeschichte*. 3d ed. Göttingen: Vandenhoeck & Ruprecht, 1962. [ET: *Jerusalem in the Time of Jesus*. Translated by C. H. Cave and F. H. Cave. Philadelphia: Fortress Press, 1975.]

———. *New Testament Theology*. Vol. 1, *The Proclamation of Jesus*. Translated by John Bowden. 5th ed. New Testament Library. London: SCM, 1978.

———. *The Parables of Jesus*. Translated by S. H. Hooke. 2d ed. New York: Scribner, 1972.

Jervell, Jacob. *Die Apostelgeschichte*. KEK 3. Göttingen: Vandenhoeck & Ruprecht, 1998.

———. *Luke and the People of God: A New Look at Luke–Acts*. Minneapolis: Augsburg, 1972.

Jewett, Robert. *Romans: A Commentary*. Hermeneia. Minneapolis: Fortress Press, 2007.

Jewett, Robert, and John Shelton Lawrence. *Captain America and the Crusade against Evil: The Dilemma of Zealous Nationalism*. Grand Rapids: Eerdmans, 2003.

Johnson, D. W. "Pelagius (c. 354–c. 425)." Pages 255–56 in vol. 2 of *Dictionary of Biblical Interpretation*. Edited by John H. Hayes. Nashville: Abingdon, 1999.

Johnson, E. Elizabeth. *The Function of Apocalyptic and Wisdom Traditions in Romans 9–11*. SBLDS 109. Atlanta: Scholars Press, 1989.

Johnson, Luke Timothy. "The New Testament's Anti-Jewish Slander and the Conventions of Ancient Polemic." *JBL* 108 (1989): 419–41.

———. *Religious Experience in Earliest Christianity: A Missing Dimension in New Testament Studies*. Minneapolis: Fortress Press, 1998.

———. *The Writings of the New Testament*. Philadelphia: Fortress Press, 1986.

Jokiranta, Jutta. "Identity on a Continuum: Constructing and Expressing Sectarian Social Identity in Qumran *Serakhim* and *Pesharim*." Ph.D. diss. University of Helsinki, 2005.

———. "Prototypical Teacher in the Qumran Pesharim: A Social Identity Approach." Pages 309–28 in Jutta Jokiranta, "Identity on a Continuum: Constructing and Expressing Sectarian Social Identity in Qumran *Serakhim* and *Pesharim*." Ph.D. diss. University of Helsinki, 2005.

Jones, Brian W. "Domitian." *ABD* 2 (1992): 221–22.

Jones, Donald L. "Roman Imperial Cult." *ABD* 5 (1992): 806–9.

Jones, F. Stanley. *An Ancient Jewish Christian Source on the History of Christianity: Pseudo-Clementine Recognitions 1.27–71*. Texts and Translations 37. Christian Apocrypha Series 2. Atlanta: Scholars Press, 1995.

———. "'Freiheit' in den Briefen des Apostels Paulus: Eine historische, exegetische und religionsgeschichtliche Studie. GTA 34. Göttingen: Vandenhoeck & Ruprecht, 1987.

———. "Jewish-Christian Chiliastic Restoration in Pseudo-Clementine *Recognitions* 1.27–71." Pages 529–47 in *Restoration: Old Testament, Jewish, and Christian Perspectives*. Edited by James M. Scott. JSJSup 72. Leiden: Brill, 2001.

———. "Jewish Christianity of the *Pseudo-Clementines*." Pages 315–34 in *A Companion to Second-Century Christian "Heretics."* Edited by Antti Marjanen and Petri Luomanen. VCSup 76. Leiden/Boston: Brill, 2005.

Karrer, Martin. *Jesus Christus im Neuen Testament*. Grundrisse zum Neuen Testament. NTD Ergänzungsreihe 11. Göttingen: Vandenhoeck & Ruprecht, 1998.

Käsemann, Ernst. "An Apologia for Primitive Christian Eschatology." Pages 169–95 in Ernst Käsemann, *Essays on New Testament Themes*. London: SCM, 1964.

———. *Jesu letzter Wille nach Johannes 17*. Tübingen: Mohr Siebeck, 1966.

Kazen, Thomas. *Jesus and Purity Halakhah: Was Jesus Indifferent to Impurity?* ConBNT 38. Stockholm: Almqvist & Wiksell, 2002.

———. "Sectarian Gospels for Some Christians? Intention and Mirror Reading in the Light of Extra-Canonical Texts." *NTS* 51 (2005): 561–78.

Kehl, Medard. *Eschatologie*. Würzburg: Echter, 1986.

Kelly, J. N. D. *Early Christian Doctrines*. 2d ed. London: Black, 1960.

Kiilunen, Jarmo. *Die Vollmacht im Widerstreit: Untersuchungen zum Werdegang von Mk 2,1—3,6*. AASF Diss. Hum. 40. Helsinki: Suomalainen Tiedeakatemia, 1985.

King, Karen L. "Gospel of Mary." Pages 601–34 in *Searching the Scriptures 2: A Feminist Commentary*. Edited by Elisabeth Schüssler Fiorenza. London: SCM, 1995.

418 ————. *The Gospel of Mary of Magdala: Jesus and the First Woman Apostle.* Santa Rosa, Calif.: Polebridge, 2003.

————. *What Is Gnosticism?* Cambridge, Mass./ London: Belknap, 2003.

Kinzig, Wolfram. "The Nazoreans." Pages 463–87 in *Jewish Believers in Jesus: The Early Centuries.* Edited by Oskar Skarsaune and Reidar Hvalvik. Peabody, Mass.: Hendrickson, 2007.

Klauck, Hans-Josef. *The Religious Context of Early Christianity: A Guide to Graeco-Roman Religions.* Translated by Brian McNeil. Studies of the New Testament and Its World. London/New York: T. & T. Clark, 2000.

————. "Das Sendschreiben nach Pergamon und der Kaiserkult in der Johannesoffenbarung." *Bib* 73 (1992): 153–82.

Kleinknecht, Hermann. "*pneuma* etc.: A. *pneuma* in the Greek world." *TDNT* 6:334–59.

Kloppenborg, John S. *The Formation of Q: Trajectories in Ancient Wisdom Collections.* SAC. Philadelphia: Fortress Press, 1987.

Kloppenborg Verbin, John S. *Excavating Q: The History and Setting of the Sayings Gospel.* Minneapolis: Fortress Press, 2000.

Knibb, Michael A. "Martyrdom and Ascension of Isaiah: Introduction." Pages 143–55 in *The Old Testament Pseudepigrapha.* Vol. 2. Edited by James H. Charlesworth. New York: Doubleday, 1985.

————. *The Qumran Community.* Cambridge Commentaries on Writings of the Jewish and Christian World 2. Cambridge: Cambridge University Press, 1987.

Knight, Jonathan. *Christian Origins.* London/New York: T. & T. Clark, 2008.

Knox, John. *The Humanity and Divinity of Christ: A Study of Pattern in Christology.* Cambridge: Cambridge University Press, 1967.

Koch, Dietrich-Alex. *Die Schrift als Zeuge des Evangeliums: Untersuchungen zur Verwendung und zum Verständnis der Schrift bei Paulus.* BHT 69. Tübingen: Mohr Siebeck, 1986.

Koester, Helmut. *Ancient Christian Gospels: Their History and Development.* Philadelphia: Trinity Press International, 1990.

————. *Introduction to the New Testament.* Vol. 1, *History, Culture, and Religion of the Hellenistic Age.* 2d ed. New York/Berlin: Walter de Gruyter, 1995.

————. *Introduction to the New Testament.* Vol. 2, *History and Literature of Early Christianity.* Reprint. New York/ Berlin: Walter de Gruyter, 1987.

Konradt, Matthias. *Christliche Existenz nach dem Jakobusbrief: Eine Studie zu seiner soteriologischen und ethischen Konzeption.* SUNT 22. Göttingen: Vandenhoeck & Ruprecht, 1998.

————. *Israel, Kirche und die Völker im Matthäusevangelium.* WUNT 215. Tübingen: Mohr Siebeck, 2007.

Koschorke, Klaus. *Die Polemik der Gnostiker gegen das kirchliche Christentum unter besonderer Berücksichtigung der Nag Hammadi-Traktate "Apokalypse des Petrus" (NHC VII,3) und "Testimonium Veritatis" (NHC IX,3).* NHS 12. Leiden: Brill, 1978.

Koskenniemi, Erkki. *Apollonios von Tyana in der neutestamentlichen Exegese: Forschungsbericht und Weiterführung der Diskussion.* WUNT 2/61. Tübingen: Mohr Siebeck, 1994.

Kovacs, Judith, and Christopher Rowland. *Revelation.* Blackwell Bible Commentaries. Oxford: Blackwell, 2004.

Kraabel, A. Thomas. "The Disappearance of the 'God-Fearers.'" *Numen* 28 (1981): 113–26.

Kraft, Heinrich. *Die Offenbarung des Johannes.* HNT 16a. Tübingen: Mohr Siebeck, 1974.

Kümmel, Werner Georg. *The Theology of the New Testament according to Its Major Witnesses: Jesus—Paul—John.* Translated by John Bowden. London: SCM, 1976.

Küng, Hans. *Der Islam: Geschichte, Gegenwart, Zukunft.* 2d ed. Munich: Piper, 2006.

Kuschel, Karl-Joseph. *Born Before All Time? The Dispute over Christ's Origin.* Translated by John Bowden. New York: Crossroad, 1992.

Kuss, Otto. *Der Römerbrief 3.* Regensburg: Pustet, 1978.

Kuula, Kari. *Paul's Polemical Treatment of the Law in Galatians.* Vol. 1, *The Law, the Covenant, and God's Plan.* Publications of the Finnish Exegetical Society 72. Helsinki: Finnish Exegetical Society/Göttingen: Vandenhoeck & Ruprecht, 1999.

————. *The Law, the Covenant and God's Plan 2: Paul's Treatment of the Law in Romans.* Publications of the Finnish Exegetical Society 85. Helsinki: Finnish Exegetical Society/Göttingen: Vandenhoeck & Ruprecht, 2003.

Kysar, Robert. "John, the Gospel of." *ABD* 3 (1992): 912–31.

Laaksonen, Jari. *Jesus und das Land: Das Gelobte Land in der Verkündigung Jesu.* Åbo: Åbo Academy Press, 2002.

Laato, Timo. *Paul and Judaism: An Anthropological Approach.* Translated by T. McElwain. South Florida Studies in the History of Judaism 115. Atlanta: Scholars Press, 1995.

Lampe, Peter. *Die stadtrömischen Christen in den ersten beiden Jahrhunderten: Untersuchungen zur Sozialgeschichte.* 2d ed. WUNT 2/18. Tübingen: Mohr Siebeck, 1989. [ET: *From Paul to Valentinus: Christians at Rome in the First Two Centuries.* Edited by Marshall D. Johnson. Translated by Michael Steinhauser. Minneapolis: Fortress Press, 2003.]

Lane Fox, Robin. *Pagans and Christians.* New York: Knopf, 1989.

Lau, Markus. "Enthaltsamkeit und Auferstehung." Pages 80–90 in *Aus Liebe zu Paulus? Die Akte Thekla neu aufgerollt.* Edited by Martin Ebner. SBS 206. Stuttgart: Katholisches Bibelwerk, 2005.

Layton, Bentley. *The Gnostic Scriptures: A New Translation with Annotations and Introductions.* New York: Doubleday, 1987.

Lehtipuu, Outi. *The Afterlife Imagery in Luke's Story of the Rich Man and Lazarus.* NovTSup 123. Leiden/Boston: Brill, 2007.

———. "'Flesh and Blood Cannot Inherit the Kingdom of God:' Transformation of the Flesh in the Early Christian Debates Concerning Resurrection." Pages 159-80 in *Metamorphoses: Resurrection, Taxonomies and Transformative Practices in Early Christianity.* Edited by Turid Karlsen Seim and Jorunn Økland. Berlin: Walter de Gruyter (forthcoming).

———. "Ruumiin ylösnousemus Nag Hammadin kirjoituksissa." *Teologinen Aikakauskirja* 114 (2009): 3–20.

Leppä, Heikki. "Luke's Critical Use of Galatians." Th.D. diss. Helsinki, 2002.

Leppä, Outi. "Debates within the New Testament Canon." Pages 211–37 in *The Formation of the Early Church.* Edited by Jostein Ådna. WUNT 183. Tübingen: Mohr Siebeck, 2005.

———. *The Making of Colossians: A Study on the Formation and Purpose of a Deutero-Pauline Letter.* Publications of the Finnish Exegetical Society 86. Helsinki: Finnish Exegetical Society & Göttingen: Vandenhoeck & Ruprecht, 2003.

———. "Useless Commandment: Animosity toward the Earlier Covenant in Hebrews." Pages 177–197 in *Animosity, the Bible and Us: Some European, North American, and South African Perspectives.* Edited by John T. Fitzgerald, Fika J. van Rensburg, and H. F. van Rooy. Global Perspectives on Biblical Scholarship 12. Society of Biblical Literature: Atlanta, 2009.

Levine, Lee I. *The Ancient Synagogue: The First Thousand Years,* New Haven: Yale University Press, 2000.

Levinson, Bernard M. "You Must Not Add Anything to What I Command You: Paradoxes of Canon and Authorship in Ancient Israel." *Numen* 50 (2003): 1–51.

Levison, John R. "Philo's Personal Experience and the Persistence of Prophecy." Pages 194–209 in *Prophets, Prophecy, and Prophetic Texts in Second Temple Judaism.* Edited by Michael H. Floyd and Robert D. Haak. Library of Hebrew Bible/Old Testament Studies 427. London: T. & T. Clark, 2006.

Lewis, Theodore J. "How Far Can Texts Take Us? Evaluating Textual Sources for Reconstructing Ancient Israelite Beliefs about the Dead." Pages 169–217 in *Sacred Time, Sacred Place: Archaeology and the Religion of Israel.* Edited by Barry M. Gittlen. Winona Lake, Ind.: Eisenbrauns, 2002.

Lindemann, Andreas. *Die Aufhebung der Zeit: Geschichtsverständnis und Eschatologie im Epheserbrief.* SNT 12. Gütersloh: Mohn, 1975.

Lindeskog, Gösta. *Das jüdisch-christliche Problem: Randglossen zu einer Forschungsepoche.* Acta Universitatis Upsaliensis, Historia Religionum, 9. Uppsala/Stockholm: Almqvist & Wiksell, 1986.

Lindgård, Fredrik. *Paul's Line of Thought in 2 Corinthians 4:16—5:10.* WUNT 2/189. Tübingen: Mohr Siebeck, 2005.

Löhr, Winrich A. *Basilides und seine Schule: Eine Studie zur Theologie- und Kirchengeschichte des zweiten Jahrhunderts.* WUNT 83. Tübingen: Mohr Siebeck, 1996.

Longenecker, Bruce W. *Eschatology and the Covenant: A Comparison of 4 Ezra and Romans 1–11.* JSNTSup 57. Sheffield: Sheffield Academic Press, 1991.

Lüdemann, Gerd. *The Acts of the Apostles: What Really Happened in the Earliest Days of the Church.* Amherst, N.Y.: Prometheus, 2005.

———. *Paul: The Founder of Christianity.* Amherst, N.Y.: Prometheus, 2002.

———. *Paulus und das Judentum.* Theologische Existenz Heute 215. Munich: Chr. Kaiser, 1983.

———. *The Resurrection of Christ: A Historical Inquiry.* Amherst, N.Y.: Prometheus, 2004.

———. *The Resurrection of Jesus: History, Experience, Theology.* Translated by John Bowden. London: SCM, 1994. Minneapolis: Fortress Press, 1995.

Lührmann, Dieter. *Das Markusevangelium.* HNT 3. Tübingen: Mohr Siebeck, 1987.

Luomanen, Petri. "Ebionites and Nazarenes." Pages 81–118 in *Jewish Christianity Reconsidered: Rethinking Ancient Groups and Texts.* Edited by Matt Jackson-McCabe. Minneapolis: Fortress Press, 2007.

420 ———. *Entering the Kingdom of Heaven: A Study on the Structure of Matthew's View of Salvation.* WUNT 2/101. Tübingen: Mohr Siebeck, 1998.

———. "Nazarenes." Pages 279–314 in *A Companion to Second-Century Christian "Heretics."* Edited by Antti Marjanen and Petri Luomanen. VCSup 76. Leiden/Boston: Brill, 2005.

———. "The 'Sociology of Sectarianism' in Matthew: Modeling the Genesis of Early Jewish and Christian Communities." Pages 107–30 in *Fair Play: Diversity and Conflicts in Early Christianity: Essays in Honour of Heikki Räisänen.* Edited by Ismo Dunderberg, Christopher Tuckett, and Kari Syreeni. NovTSup 103. Boston: Brill, 2002.

———. "The Nazarenes' Gospel and Their Commentary on Isaiah Reconsidered." In *Bringing the Underground to the Foreground: New Perspectives on Jewish and Christian Apocryphal Texts and Traditions* (Proceedings of the Jewish Pseudepigrapha & Christian Apocrypha Section at the SBL International Meeting in Groningen, The Netherlands, July 25–28, 2004). Edited by Pierluigi Piovanelli. Turnhout: Brepols, 2007.

Luttikhuizen, G. P. "Elchasaites and Their Book." Pages 335–64 in *A Companion to Second-Century Christian "Heretics."* Edited by Antti Marjanen and Petri Luomanen. VCSup 76. Leiden/Boston: Brill, 2005.

Luz, Ulrich. *Das Evangelium nach Matthäus 1.* EKKNT 1/1. 5th ed. Düsseldorf/ Zürich: Benzinger & Neukirchener, 2002. [ET: *Matthew 1–7.* Hermeneia. Edited by Helmut Koester. Translated by James E. Crouch. Minneapolis: Fortress Press, 2007.]

———. *Das Evangelium nach Matthäus 2.* EKKNT 1/2. Zürich/ Neukirchen-Vluyn: Benzinger & Neukirchener, 1990. [ET: *Matthew 8–20.* Hermeneia. Edited by Helmut Koester. Translated by James E. Crouch. Minneapolis: Fortress Press, 2005.]

———. *Das Evangelium nach Matthäus 3.* EKKNT 1/3. Zürich/ Neukirchen-Vluyn: Benzinger & Neukirchener, 1997. [ET: *Matthew 21–28.* Hermeneia. Edited by Helmut Koester. Translated by James E. Crouch. Minneapolis: Fortress Press, 2005.]

———. *Das Geschichtsverständnis des Paulus.* BEvT 49. Munich: Chr. Kaiser, 1968.

Mack, Burton L. *A Myth of Innocence: Mark and Christian Origins.* Philadelphia: Fortress Press, 1988.

———. *The Lost Gospel: The Book of Q and Christian Origins.* San Francisco: Harper, 1993.

MacRae, George. "Apocalyptic Eschatology in Gnosticism." Pages 317–25 in *Apocalypticism in the Mediterranean World and the Near East.* Edited by David Hellholm. 2d ed. Tübingen: Mohr Siebeck, 1989.

———. Introduction to *The Authoritative Teaching.* Pages 304–5 in *The Nag Hammadi Library in English.* Edited by James M. Robinson. 3d ed. San Francisco: HarperSanFrancisco, 1990.

Magness, Jodi. *The Archaeology of Qumran and the Dead Sea Scrolls.* Grand Rapids: Eerdmans, 2002.

Maier, Gerhard. *Die Johannesoffenbarung und die Kirche.* WUNT 25. Tübingen: Mohr Siebeck, 1981.

Maier, Harry O. "The President's Revelation: The Apocalypse, American Providence, and the War on Terror." *WW* 25 (2005): 294–307.

Manson, T. W. *The Sayings of Jesus as Recorded in the Gospels according to St. Matthew and St. Luke.* London: SCM, 1949.

Marcus, Joel. *Mark 1–8.* AB 27. New York: Doubleday, 1999.

Marjanen, Antti. "Gnosticism." Pages 203–20 in *The Oxford Handbook of Early Christian Studies.* Edited by Susan Ashbrook Harvey and David G. Hunter. Oxford: Oxford University Press, 2008.

———. "How Egalitarian Was the Gnostic View of Women? Mary Magdalene Texts in the Nag Hammadi and Related Documents." Pages 779–91 in *Coptic Studies on the Threshold of a New Millennium.* Vol. 1. Edited by M. Immerzeel and J. van der Vliet, et al. Leuven: Peeters, 2004.

———. "Is *Thomas* a Gnostic Gospel?" Pages 107–39 in *Thomas at the Crossroads: Essays on the Gospel of Thomas.* Edited by Risto Uro. Studies of the New Testament and Its World. Edinburgh: T. & T. Clark, 1998.

———. "Mary Magdalene, a Beloved Disciple." Pages 49–61 in *Mariam, the Magdalene, and the Mother.* Edited by Deirdre Good. Bloomington, Ind.: Indiana University Press, 2005.

———. "Montanism: Egalitarian Ecstatic 'New Prophecy.'" Pages 185–212 in *A Companion to Second-Century Christian "Heretics."* Edited by Antti Marjanen and Petri Luomanen. VCSup 76. Leiden/Boston: Brill, 2005.

———. "The Portrait of Jesus in the *Gospel of Thomas.*" Pages 209–19 in *Thomasine Traditions in Antiquity: The Social and Cultural World of the Gospel of Thomas.* Edited by Jon Ma. Asgeirsson, April D. DeConick, and Risto Uro. Nag Hammadi and Manichean Studies 59. Leiden/Boston: Brill, 2006.

———. "The Suffering of One Who is a Stranger to Suffering: The Crucifixion of Jesus in the Letter of Peter to

Philip." Pages 487–98 in *Fair Play: Diversity and Conflicts in Early Christianity: Essays in Honour of Heikki Räisänen*. Edited by Ismo Dunderberg, Christopher Tuckett, and Kari Syreeni. NovTSup 103. Boston: Brill, 2002.

———. "Thomas and Jewish Religious Practices." Pages 163–82 in *Thomas at the Crossroads: Essays on the Gospel of Thomas*. Edited by Risto Uro. Studies of the New Testament and Its World. Edinburgh: T. & T. Clark, 1998.

———. *The Woman Jesus Loved: Mary Magdalene in the Nag Hammadi Library and Related Documents*. Nag Hammadi and Manichean Studies 40. Leiden: Brill, 1996.

Marjanen, Antti, ed. *Was There a Gnostic Religion?* Publications of the Finnish Exegetical Society 87. Helsinki: Finnish Exegetical Society/Göttingen: Vandenhoeck & Ruprecht, 2005.

Markschies, Christoph. *Gnosis: An Introduction*. Translated by John Bowden. London/ New York: T. & T. Clark, 2003.

———. "Lehrer, Schüler, Schule: Zur Bedeutung einer Institution für das antike Christentum." Pages 97–120 in *Religiöse Vereine in der römischen Antike: Untersuchungen zu Organisation, Ritual und Raumordnung*. Edited by Ulrike Egelhaaf and Alfred Schäfer. Tübingen: Mohr Siebeck, 2002.

———. *Valentinus Gnosticus? Untersuchungen zur valentinianischen Gnosis mit einem Kommentar zu den Fragmenten Valentins*. WUNT 65. Tübingen: Mohr Siebeck, 1992.

Marshall, I. Howard. *New Testament Theology*. Downers Grove, Ill.: InterVarsity, 2004.

Martin, Dale B. *The Corinthian Body*. New Haven/London: Yale University Press, 1995.

Mason, Steve. *Josephus and the New Testament*. 2d ed. Peabody, Mass.: Hendrickson, 1993.

Matera, Frank J. *New Testament Theology: Exploring Diversity and Unity*. Louisville: Westminster John Knox, 2007.

Matthews, Shelly. "The Need for the Stoning of Stephen." Pages 124–39 in *Violence in the New Testament*. Edited by Shelly Matthews and E. Leigh Gibson. New York/London: T. & T. Clark, 2005.

Mayordomo, Moisés. "Gewalt in der Johannesoffenbarung als Problem ethischer Kritik." Pages 45–69 in *Neutestamentliche Exegese im Dialog: Hermeneutik—Wirkungsgeschichte—Matthäusevangelium*. Festschrift for Ulrich Luz. Edited by Peter Lampe, Moisés Mayordomo, and Migaku Sato. Neukirchen-Vluyn: Neukirchener, 2008.

McDannell, Colleen, and Bernhard Lang. *Heaven: A History*. New Haven: Yale University Press, 1990.

McGinn, Bernard. "Apocalypticism and Church Reform: 1100–1500." Pages 74–109 in *The Encyclopedia of Apocalypticism*. Vol. 2, *Apocalypticism in Western History and Culture*. Edited by Bernard McGinn. London: Continuum, 2000.

McGrath, Alister E. *A Life of John Calvin: A Study in the Shaping of Western Culture*. Oxford: Blackwell, 1990.

Meeks, Wayne A. "The Divine Agent and His Counterfeit in Philo and the Fourth Gospel." Pages 43–67 in *Aspects of Religious Propaganda in Judaism and Early Christianity*. Edited by Elisabeth Schüssler Fiorenza. Notre Dame, Ind.: University of Notre Dame Press, 1976.

———. *The First Urban Christians: The Social World of the Apostle Paul*. New Haven: Yale University Press, 1983.

———. *The Origins of Christian Morality: The First Two Centuries*. New Haven: Yale University Press, 1993.

Meier, John P. "The Historical Jesus and the Historical Sabbath." Pages 297–307 in *Redefining First-Century Jewish and Christian Identities*, Essays in Honor of E. P. Sanders. Edited by Fabian E. Udoh, et al. Christianity and Judaism in Antiquity Series 16. Notre Dame, Ind.: Notre Dame University Press, 2008.

———. *A Marginal Jew: Rethinking the Historical Jesus: Mentor, Message and Miracles*. Vol. 2. AB Reference Library. New York: Doubleday, 1994.

Merkel, Helmut. *Widersprüche zwischen den Evangelien: Ihre polemische und apologetische Behandlung in der Alten Kirche bis zu Augustin*. WUNT 13. Tübingen: Mohr Siebeck, 1971.

Merkt, Andreas. "Selbstbehauptung und Inkulturation in feindlicher Umwelt: Von den Apologeten bis zur 'Konstantinischen Wende': 5. Die Profilierung des antiken Christentums angesichts von Polemik und Verfolgung." Pages 409–33 in *Christentum 1: Von den Anfängen bis zur Konstantinischen Wende*. Edited by Dieter Zeller. Die Religionen der Menschheit 28. Stuttgart: Kohlhammer, 2002.

Metso, Sarianna. "Whom Does the Term Yahad Identify?" Pages 63–84 in *Defining Identities: We, You, and the Other in the Dead Sea Scrolls*. Edited by Florentino García Martínez and Mladen Popovic. STDJ 70. Leiden/Boston: Brill, 2008.

———. *The Textual Development of the Qumran Community Rule*. STDJ 21. Leiden: Brill, 1997.

422

Meyer, Eduard. *Ursprung und Anfänge des Christentums.* Vol. 2, *Die Apostelgeschichte und die Anfänge des Christentums.* Stuttgart: Cotta, 1923.

Meyer, Marvin. "Mystery Religions." *ABD* 4 (1992): 941–45.

———. "On the Origin of the World." Pages 199–222 in *The Nag Hammadi Scriptures: The International Edition.* Edited by Marvin Meyer. New York: HarperOne, 2007.

———. "Second Discourse of the Great Seth." Pages 473–86 in *The Nag Hammadi Scriptures: The International Edition.* Edited by Marvin Meyer. New York: HarperOne, 2007.

Meyer, Marvin, ed. *The Nag Hammadi Scriptures: The International Edition.* New York: HarperOne, 2007.

Mitchell, Margaret M. "Patristic Counter-evidence to the Claim That the Gospels Were Written for All Christians." *NTS* 51 (2005): 36–79.

Mohrlang, Roger. *Matthew and Paul: A Comparison of Ethical Perspectives.* SNTSMS 48. Cambridge: Cambridge University Press, 1984.

Moltmann, Jürgen. *God in Creation: An Ecological Doctrine of Creation.* Translated by Margaret Kohl. London: SCM, 1985; Minneapolis: Fortress Press, 1993.

Moore, George Foot. *Judaism in the First Centuries of the Christian Era: The Age of Tannaim.* 2 vols. Reprint. New York: Schocken, 1971.

Moorhead, James H. "Apocalypticism in Mainstream Protestantism, 1800 to the Present." Pages 72–107 in *The Encyclopedia of Apocalypticism.* Vol. 3, *Apocalypticism in the Modern Period and the Contemporary Age.* Edited by Stephen J. Stein. London: Continuum, 2000.

Moreland, Milton. "The Twenty-Four Prophets of Israel Are Dead: Gospel of Thomas 52 as a Critique of Early Christian Hermeneutics." Pages 75–91 in *Thomasine Traditions in Antiquity: The Social and Cultural World of the Gospel of Thomas.* Edited by Jon Ma. Asgeirsson, April D. DeConick, and Risto Uro. Nag Hammadi and Manichean Studies 59. Leiden/Boston: Brill, 2006.

Morgan, Robert. "Theology (New Testament)." *ABD* 6 (1992): 473–83.

Moxnes, Halvor. "From Theology to Identity: The Problem of Constructing Early Christianity." Pages 264–81 in *Moving Beyond New Testament Theology? Essays in Conversation with Heikki Räisänen.* Edited by Todd Penner and Caroline Vander Stichele. Publications of the Finnish Exegetical Society 88. Helsinki: Finnish Exegetical Society/Göttingen: Vandenhoeck & Ruprecht, 2005.

Müller, Karlheinz. "Gesetz und Gesetzeserfüllung im Frühjudentum." Pages 11–27 in *Das Gesetz im Neuen Testament.* Edited by Karl Kertelge. QD 108. Freiburg: Herder, 1986.

———. "Gibt es ein Judentum hinter den Juden? Ein Nachtrag zu Ed Parish Sanders' Theorie vom 'Covenantal Nomism.'" Pages 473–86 in *Das Urchristentum in seiner literarischen Gechichte.* Festschrift for Jürgen Becker. Edited by Ulrich Mell and Ulrich B. Müller. BZAW 100. Berlin/New York: Walter de Gruyter, 1999.

Müller, Mogens. "Son of God." Pages 710–11 in *The Oxford Companion to the Bible.* Edited by Bruce M. Metzger and Michael D. Coogan. New York/Oxford: Oxford University Press, 1993.

Myllykoski, Matti. "Cerinthus." Pages 213–46 in *A Companion to Second-Century Christian "Heretics."* Edited by Antti Marjanen and Petri Luomanen. VCSup 76. Leiden/Boston: Brill, 2005.

———. "James the Just in History and Tradition: Perspectives of Past and Present Scholarship (Part 1)." *Currents in Biblical Research* 5 (2006): 73–122.

———. "The Social History of Q and the Jewish War." Pages 144–99 in *Symbols and Strata: Essays on the Sayings Gospel Q* Edited by Risto Uro. Publications of the Finnish Exegetical Society 65. Helsinki: Finnish Exegetical Society, 1996.

———. "What Happened to the Body of Jesus?" Pages 43–82 in *Fair Play: Diversity and Conflicts in Early Christianity: Essays in Honour of Heikki Räisänen.* Edited by Ismo Dunderberg, Christopher Tuckett, and Kari Syreeni. NovTSup 103. Boston: Brill, 2002.

Mystery of Salvation, The: The Story of God's Gift. A Report by the Doctrine Commission of the General Synod of the Church of England. London: Church House Publishing, 1995.

Nanos, Mark D. *The Mystery of Romans: The Jewish Context of Paul's Letter.* Minneapolis: Fortress Press, 1996.

Neale, David A. *None but the Sinners: Religious Categories in the Gospel of Luke.* JSNTSup 58. Sheffield: Sheffield Academic Press, 1991.

Neusner, Jacob. "Money-Changers in the Temple: The Mishnah's Explanation." *NTS* 35 (1989): 287–90.

———. *Judaism in the Beginning of Christianity.* Philadelphia: Fortress Press, 1984.

———. *The Mishnah: A New Translation.* New Haven/London: Yale University Press, 1988.

———. *Torah: From Scroll to Symbol in Formative Judaism.* Philadelphia: Fortress Press, 1985.

Newsom, Carol Ann. *The Self as Symbolic Space: Constructing Identity and Community at Qumran*. STDJ 52. Leiden: Brill, 2004.

———. *Songs of the Sabbath Sacrifice: A Critical Edition*. HSS 27. Atlanta: Scholars Press, 1985.

Nickelsburg, George W. E. *Ancient Judaism and Christian Origins: Diversity, Continuity, and Transformation*. Minneapolis: Fortress Press, 2003.

———. "Eschatology (Early Jewish)." *ABD* 2 (1992): 579–94.

———. "Judgment, Life-after-Death, and Resurrection in the Apocrypha and the Non-Apocalyptic Pseudepigrapha." Pages 141–62 in *Judaism in Late Antiquity*. Part 4, *Death, Life after Death, Resurrection and the World-to-Come in the Judaisms of Antiquity*. Edited by Alan J. Avery-Peck and Jacob Neusner. Leiden: Brill, 2000.

———. *Resurrection, Immortality, and Eternal Life in Intertestamental Judaism and Early Christianity*. 2d ed. HTS 56. Cambridge, Mass.: Harvard University Press, 2006.

———. "Salvation without and with a Messiah: Developing Beliefs in Writings Ascribed to Enoch." Pages 49–68 in *Judaisms and Their Messiahs*. Edited by Jacob Neusner, William Scott Green, and Ernest Frerichs. New York: Cambridge University Press, 1987.

———. "Son of Man." *ABD* 6 (1992): 137–50.

Niditch, Susan. *War in the Hebrew Bible: A Study in the Ethics of Violence*. Oxford: Oxford University Press, 1993.

Nineham, Dennis. "Epilogue." Pages 186–204 in *The Myth of God Incarnate*. Edited by John Hick. London: SCM, 1977.

———. *The Use and Abuse of the Bible: A Study of the Bible in an Age of Rapid Cultural Change*. 2d ed. London: SPCK, 1985.

Nissinen, Martti. "Elemente sekundärer Religionserfahrung im postexilischen Juda? Erwiderung auf R. Schmitt." Pages 159–67 in *Primitive und sekundäre Religion als Kategorie der Religionsgeschichte des Alten Testaments*. Edited by Andreas Wagner. BZAW 364. Berlin/New York: Walter de Gruyter, 2006.

———. *Homoeroticism in the Biblical World: A Historical Perspective*. Translated by Kirsi Stjerna. Minneapolis: Fortress Press, 1998.

———. "Neither Prophecies nor Apocalypses: The Akkadian Literary Predictive Texts." Pages 134–48 in *Knowing the End from the Beginning: The Prophetic, the Apocalyptic, and Their Relationships*. Edited by Lester L. Grabbe and Robert Donel Haak. JSPSup 46. London/New York: T. & T. Clark, 2003.

Nock, Arthur Darby. *Conversion: The Old and the New in Religion from Alexander the Great to Augustine of Hippo*. Reprint. Oxford: Oxford University Press, 1969.

Oberlinner, Lorenz. *Kommentar zum zweiten Timotheusbrief*. HTKNT 11/2. Freiburg: Herder, 1995.

Oepke, Albrecht. "*parousia, pareimi*." *TDNT* 5:858–71.

O'Neill, J. C. *Paul's Letter to the Romans*. London: Penguin, 1975.

Osten-Sacken, Peter von der. *Römer 8 als Beispiel paulinischer Soteriologie*. FRLANT 112. Göttingen: Vandenhoeck & Ruprecht, 1975.

Pagels, Elaine. *Adam, Eve, and the Serpent*. New York: Random House, 1988.

———. *The Gnostic Gospels*. London: Weidenfeld & Nicholson, 1980.

Pagels, Elaine, and Karen L. King. *Reading Judas: The Gospel of Judas and the Shaping of Christianity*. New York: Viking, 2007.

Painter, John. "James and Peter: Models of Leadership and Mission." Pages 143–209 in *The Missions of James, Peter and Paul: Tensions in Early Christianity*. Edited by Bruce Chilton and Craig A. Evans. NovTSup 115. Leiden: Brill, 2005.

Pakkala, Juha. *Intolerant Monolatry*. Publications of the Finnish Exegetical Society 76. Helsinki: Finnish Exegetical Society/Göttingen: Vandenhoeck & Ruprecht, 1999.

———. *Ezra the Scribe: The Development of Ezra 7–10 and Nehemia 8*. BZAW 347. Berlin: Walter de Gruyter, 2004.

———. "The Nomistic Roots of Judaism." Pages 251–68 in *Houses Full of All Good Things: Essays in Memory of Timo Veijola*. Edited by Juha Pakkala and Martti Nissinen. Publications of the Finnish Exegetical Society 95. Helsinki: Finnish Exegetical Society/Vandenhoeck & Ruprecht, 2008.

Pancaro, Severino. *The Law in the Fourth Gospel: The Torah and the Gospel, Moses and Jesus, Judaism and Christianity according to John*. NovTSup 42. Leiden: Brill, 1975.

Parrott, Douglas M. Introduction to *Eugnostos the Blessed* and *The Sophia of Jesus Christ*. Pages 220–21 in *The Nag Hammadi Library in English*. Edited by James M. Robinson. 3d ed. San Francisco: HarperSanFrancisco, 1990.

Patrick, Dale. "Election: Old Testament." *ABD* 2 (1992): 434–41.

424

Peacocke, Arthur. "DNA of Our DNA." Pages 59–67 in *The Birth of Jesus: Biblical and Theological Reflections*. Edited by George J. Brooke. Edinburgh: T. & T. Clark, 2000.

Pearson, Birger A. "Basilides the Gnostic." Pages 1–31 in *A Companion to Second-Century Christian "Heretics."* Edited by Antti Marjanen and Petri Luomanen. VCSup 76. Leiden/Boston: Brill, 2005.

———. *Gnosticism, Judaism, and Egyptian Christianity*. SAC. Minneapolis: Fortress Press, 1990.

———. "1 Thessalonians 2:13-16: A Deutero-Pauline Interpolation." *HTR* 64 (1971): 79–94.

Peel, Malcolm L. "Gnostic Eschatology and the New Testament." *NovT* 12 (1970): 141–65.

———. Introduction to *The Treatise on Resurrection*. Pages 52–54 in *The Nag Hammadi Library in English*. Edited by James M. Robinson. 3d ed. San Francisco: HarperSanFrancisco, 1990.

Pehkonen, Nina. "Rejoicing in the Judaisers' Work? The Question of Paul's Opponents in Phil. 1.15-18a." Pages 132–55 in *The Nordic Paul: Finnish Approaches to Pauline Theology*. Edited by Lars Aejmelaeus and Antti Mustakallio. Library of New Testament Studies 374. London: T. & T. Clark, 2008.

Penner, Todd. *In Praise of Christian Origins: Stephen and the Hellenists in Lukan Apologetic Historiography*. Emory Studies in Early Christianity. New York/London: T. & T. Clark, 2004.

Penner, Todd, and Caroline Vander Stichele, eds. *Moving Beyond New Testament Theology? Essays in Conversation with Heikki Räisänen*. Publications of the Finnish Exegetical Society 88. Helsinki: Finnish Exegetical Society/Göttingen: Vandenhoeck & Ruprecht, 2005.

Pernveden, Lage. *The Concept of the Church in the Shepherd of Hermas*. Studia Theologica Lundensia 27. Lund: Gleerup, 1966.

Pesonen, Anni. "Luke, the Friend of Sinners." Th.D. diss. University of Helsinki, 2009.

Pike, Frederick B. "Latin America." Pages 420–54 in *The Oxford Illustrated History of Christianity*. Edited by John McManners. Oxford: Oxford University Press, 1990.

Pilhofer, Peter. *Presbyteron Kreitton: Der Altersbeweis der jüdischen und christlichen Apologeten und seine Vorgeschichte*. WUNT 2/39. Tübingen: Mohr Siebeck, 1990.

Pinnock, Clark. "The Destruction of the Finally Impenitent." *CTR* 4 (1990): 243–59.

Powys, David J. *"Hell": A Hard Look at a Hard Question: The Fate of the Unrighteous in New Testament Thought*. Paternoster Biblical and Theological Monographs. Carlisle: Paternoster, 1998.

Pregeant, Russell. *Christology beyond Dogma: Matthew's Christ in Process Hermeneutic*. Semeia Supplements. Philadelphia: Fortress Press, 1978.

Price, S. R. F. *Rituals and Power: The Roman Imperial Cult in Asia Minor*. Reprint. Cambridge: Cambridge University Press, 1998.

Propp, William H. "Chosen People." Pages 109–10 in *The Oxford Companion to the Bible*. Edited by Bruce M. Metzger and Michael David Coogan. Oxford: Oxford University Press, 1993.

Puech, Émile. *La Croyance des esséniens en la vie future: immortalité, résurrection, vie éternelle? Histoire d'une croyance dans le judaïsme ancien*. Volume 1, *La résurrection des morts et le contexte scripturaire*. EBib, Nouvelle série 21. Paris: Gabalda, 1993.

Pyysiäinen, Ilkka. "Intuition, Reflection, and the Evolution of Traditions." Pages 282–307 in *Moving Beyond New Testament Theology? Essays in Conversation with Heikki Räisänen*. Edited by Todd Penner and Caroline Vander Stichele. Publications of the Finnish Exegetical Society 88. Helsinki: The Finnish Exegetical Society/Göttingen: Vandenhoeck & Ruprecht, 2005.

Rad, Gerhard von. "*Israel* etc.: Israel, Judah and Hebrews in the Old Testament." *TDNT* 3:356–59.

Räisänen, Heikki. "Begotten by the Holy Spirit." Pages 321–41 in *Sacred Marriages: The Divine-Human Sexual Metaphor from Sumer to Early Christianity*. Edited by Martti Nissinen and Risto Uro. Winona Lake, Ind.: Eisenbrauns, 2008

———. *Beyond New Testament Theology: A Story and a Programme*. 2d ed. London: SCM, 2000.

———. "Biblical Critics in the Global Village." Pages 283–309 in Heikki Räisänen, *Challenges to Biblical Interpretation: Collected Essays, 1991–2001*. BibInt 59. Leiden: Brill, 2001.

———. *Challenges to Biblical Interpretation: Collected Essays, 1991–2001*. BibInt 59. Leiden: Brill, 2001.

———. "A Controversial Jew and his Conflicting Convictions: *Paul, the Law, and the Jewish People* Twenty Years After." Pages 319–35 in *Redefining First-Century Jewish and Christian Identities: Essays in Honor of E. P. Sanders*. Edited by Fabian E. Udoh. Notre Dame, Ind.: Notre Dame University Press, 2008.

———. "Did Paul Expect an Earthly Kingdom?" Pages 2–20 in *Paul, Luke and the Graeco-Roman World: Essays in Honour of Alexander J. M. Wedderburn*.

Edited by Alf Christophersen, et al. JSNTSup 217. Sheffield: Sheffield Academic Press, 2002.

———. "Exorcisms and the Kingdom: Is Q 11:20 a Saying of the Historical Jesus?" Pages 15–36 in Heikki Räisänen, *Challenges to Biblical Interpretation: Collected Essays, 1991–2001*. BibInt 59. Leiden: Brill, 2001.

———. "Galatians 2.16 and Paul's Break with Judaism." Pages 112–26 in *Jesus, Paul and Torah: Collected Essays*. Translated by David E. Orton. JSNTSup 43. Sheffield: Sheffield Academic Press, 1992.

———. "Die Hellenisten der Urgemeinde." *ARNW* 2.26.2 (1995): 1468–1514.

———. "The 'Hellenists': A Bridge Between Jesus and Paul?" Pages 149–202 in *Jesus, Paul and Torah: Collected Essays*. Translated by David E. Orton. JSNTSup 43. Sheffield: Sheffield Academic Press, 1992.

———. "Jesus and the Food Laws: Reflections on Mark 7.15." Pages 127–48 in *Jesus, Paul and Torah: Collected Essays*. Translated by David E. Orton. JSNTSup 43. Sheffield: Sheffield Academic Press, 1992.

———. "Jesus and Hell." In *Jesus in Continuum*. Edited by Tom Holmén. WUNT. Tübingen: Mohr Siebeck. Forthcoming.

———. *Jesus, Paul and Torah: Collected Essays*. Translated by David E. Orton. JSNTSup 43. Sheffield: Sheffield Academic Press, 1992.

———. "Eine Kathedrale aus dem Chaos? Ein Gespräch mit Gerd Theissen über Einheit und Vielfalt der urchristlichen Religion." Forthcoming.

———. "The 'Law' of Faith and the Spirit." Pages 48–68 in *Jesus, Paul and Torah: Collected Essays*. Translated by David E. Orton. JSNTSup 43. Sheffield: Sheffield Academic Press, 1992.

———. "Marcion." Pages 100–124 in *A Companion to Second-Century Christian "Heretics."* Edited by Antti Marjanen and Petri Luomanen. VCSup 76. Leiden/Boston: Brill, 2005.

———. *Marcion, Muhammad and the Mahatma: Exegetical Perspectives on the Encounter of Cultures and Faiths*. London: SCM, 1997.

———. "Marcion and the Origins of Christian Anti-Judaism: A Reappraisal." Pages 191–205 in Heikki Räisänen, *Challenges to Biblical Interpretation: Collected Essays, 1991–2001*. BibInt 59. Leiden: Brill, 2001.

———. "Matthäus und die Hölle." Pages 103–24 in *Die prägende Kraft der Texte: Hermeneutik und Wirkungsgeschichte des Neuen Testaments*. Edited by Moisés Mayordomo. Ein Symposium zu Ehren von Ulrich Luz. SBS 199. Stuttgart: Katholisches Bibelwerk, 2005.

———. *The Messianic Secret in Mark's Gospel*. Translated by Christopher Tuckett. Studies of the New Testament and Its World. Edinburgh: T. & T. Clark, 1990.

———. *Die Mutter Jesu im Neuen Testament*. 2d ed. AASF 247. Helsinki: Suomalainen Tiedeakatemia, 1989.

———. *Neutestamentliche Theologie? Eine religionswissenschaftliche Alternative*. SBS 186. Stuttgart: Katholisches Bibelwerk, 2000.

———. "The Nicolaitans: Apoc 2; Acta 6." Pages 141–89 in Heikki Räisänen, *Challenges to Biblical Interpretation: Collected Essays, 1991–2001*. BibInt 59. Leiden: Brill, 2001.

———. "Paul, God, and Israel: Romans 9–11 in Recent Research." Pages 178–206 in *The Social World of Formative Christianity and Judaism: Essays in Tribute to Howard Clark Kee*. Edited by Jacob Neusner, et al. Philadelphia: Fortress Press, 1988.

———. *Paul and the Law*. 2d ed. WUNT 29. Tübingen: Mohr Siebeck, 1987.

———. "Paul's Word-Play on *nomos*: A Linguistic Study." Pages 69–94 in *Jesus, Paul and Torah: Collected Essays*. Translated by David E. Orton. JSNTSup 43. Sheffield: Sheffield Academic Press, 1992.

———. "The Prodigal Gentile and His Jewish Christian Brother: Lk 15,11-32." Pages 37–60 in Heikki Räisänen, *Challenges to Biblical Interpretation: Collected Essays, 1991–2001*. BibInt 59. Leiden: Brill, 2001.

———. "The Redemption of Israel: A Salvation-Historical Problem in Luke–Acts." Pages 61–81 in Heikki Räisänen, *Challenges to Biblical Interpretation: Collected Essays, 1991–2001*. BibInt 59. Leiden: Brill, 2001.

———. "Revelation, Violence, and War: Glimpses of a Dark Side." Pages 151–65 in *The Way the World Ends? The Apocalypse of John in Culture and Ideology*. Edited by William John Lyons and Jorunn Økland. Sheffield: Sheffield Phoenix, 2009.

———. "'Righteousness by Works': An Early Catholic Doctrine? Thoughts on 1 Clement." Pages 203–24 in *Jesus, Paul and Torah: Collected Essays*. Translated by David E. Orton. JSNTSup 43. Sheffield: Sheffield Academic Press, 1992.

———. "Römer 9–11: Analyse eines geistigen Ringens." *ANRW* 2.25.4 (1987): 2891–939.

———. "Torn Between Two Loyalties: Romans 9–11 and Paul's Conflicting Convictions." Pages 19–39 in *The Nordic Paul: Finnish Approaches to Pauline Theology*. Edited by Lars Aejmelaeus and Antti Mustakallio. Library of New Testament Studies 374. London: T. & T. Clark, 2008.

426 ———. "The Use of *epithymia* and *epithymein* in Paul." Pages 95–111 in *Jesus, Paul and Torah: Collected Essays*. Translated by David E. Orton. JSNTSup 43. Sheffield: Sheffield Academic Press, 1992.

———. "What I Meant and What It Might Mean . . . An Attempt at Responding." Pages 400–443 in *Moving Beyond New Testament Theology? Essays in Conversation with Heikki Räisänen*. Edited by Todd Penner and Caroline Vander Stichele. Publications of the Finnish Exegetical Society 88. Helsinki: Finnish Exegetical Society/Göttingen: Vandenhoeck & Ruprecht, 2005.

———. "What's Happening in New Testament Theology?" Pages 439–58 in *Lux Humana, Lux Aeterna: Essays on Biblical and Related Themes in Honour of Lars Aejmelaeus*. Edited by Antti Mustakallio. Publications of the Finnish Exegetical Society 89. Helsinki: Finnish Exegetical Society/Göttingen: Vandenhoeck & Ruprecht, 2005.

Rajak, Tessa. *Josephus: The Historian and His Society*. Classical Life and Letters. London: Duckworth, 1983.

Rappaport, Uriel. "How Anti-Roman Was the Galilee?" Pages 95–102 in *The Galilee in Late Antiquity*. Edited by Lee I. Levine. New York: Jewish Theological Seminary of America, 1992.

Rasimus, Tuomas. "Paradise Reconsidered: A Study of the Ophite Myth and Ritual and Their Relationship to Sethianism." Th.D. diss. University of Helsinki, 2006.

Reinbold, Wolfgang. *Propaganda und Mission im ältesten Christentum: Eine Untersuchung zu den Modalitäten der Ausbreitung der frühen Kirche*. FRLANT 188. Göttingen: Vandenhoeck & Ruprecht, 2000.

Reiser, Marius. *Die Gerichtspredigt Jesu: Eine Untersuchung zur eschatologischen Verkündigung Jesu und ihrem frühjüdischen Hintergrund*. NTAbh 23. Münster: Aschendorff, 1990

Rese, Martin. "Church and Israel in the Deuteropauline Letters." *SJT* 43 (1990): 19–32.

Reventlow, Henning Graf. "The Role of the Old Testament in the German Liberal Protestant Theology of the Nineteenth Century." Pages 132–48 in *Biblical Studies and the Shifting of Paradigms: 1850–1914*. Edited by Henning Graf Reventlow and William Farmer. JSOTSup 192. Sheffield: Sheffield Academic Press, 1995.

Richardson, Peter. *Israel in the Apostolic Church*. SNTSMS 10. Cambridge: Cambridge University Press, 1969.

Riddle, Donald W. "The Jewishness of Paul." *JR* 23 (1943): 240–44.

Riley, Gregory J. *Resurrection Reconsidered: Thomas and John in Controversy*. Minneapolis: Fortress Press, 1995.

Robbins, Gregory Allen. "Muratorian Fragment." *ABD* 4 (1992): 928–29.

Robinson, James M. "Jesus—from Easter to Valentinus (or to the Apostles' Creed)." *JBL* 101 (1982): 5–37.

Robinson, James M., ed. *The Nag Hammadi Library in English*. 3d ed. San Francisco: HarperSanFrancisco, 1990.

Robinson, James M., Paul Hoffmann, and John S. Kloppenborg, eds. *The Critical Edition of Q: A Synopsis including the Gospels of Matthew and Luke and Thomas with English, German and French Translations of Q and Thomas*. Hermeneia. Minneapolis: Fortress Press, 2000.

Rochberg, Francesca. *The Heavenly Writing: Divination, Horoscopy, and Astronomy in Mesopotamian Culture*. Cambridge: Cambridge University Press, 2004.

Röhser, Gunter. *Metaphorik und Personifikation der Sünde: Antike Sündenvorstellungen und paulinische Hamartia*. WUNT 2/25. Tübingen: Mohr Siebeck, 1987.

———. *Prädestination und Verstockung: Studien zur frühjüdischen, paulinischen und johanneischen Theologie*. TANZ 14. Tübingen: Francke, 1994.

———. *Stellvertretung im Neuen Testament*. SBS 195. Stuttgart: Katholisches Bibelwerk, 2002.

Römer, Thomas. *The So-called Deuteronomistic History: A Sociological, Historical, and Literary Introduction*. London: T. & T. Clark, 2007.

Rowe, C. Kavin. *Early Narrative Christology: The Lord in the Gospel of Luke*. BZNW 139. Berlin: Walter de Gruyter, 2006.

Rowland, Christopher. *Christian Origins: An Account of the Setting and Character of the Most Important Messianic Sect of Judaism*. 2d ed. London: SPCK, 2002.

———. *The Open Heaven: A Study of Apocalyptic in Judaism and Early Christianity*. London: SPCK, 1982.

Rowland, Christopher, and Mark Corner. *Liberating Exegesis: The Challenge of Liberation Theology to Biblical Studies*. London: SPCK, 1990.

Rowland, Christopher, and Christopher Tuckett, eds. *The Nature of New Testament Theology: Essays in Honour of Robert Morgan*. Oxford: Blackwell, 2006.

Royalty, Robert M. "Dwelling on Visions: On the Nature of the So-called 'Colossians Heresy.'" *Bib* 83 (2002): 329–57.

Rubenstein, Richard L. *After Auschwitz: History, Theology, and Contemporary Judaism*. 2d ed. Johns Hopkins Jewish Studies. Baltimore: Johns Hopkins University Press, 1992.

———. "Answer." Pages 192–201 in *The Condition of Jew-*

ish Belief: A Symposium compiled by the editors of the Commentary Magazine. New York: Macmillan, 1966.

Rudolph, Kurt. *Gnosis: The Nature and History of an Ancient Religion.* Translated and edited by Robert McLachlan Wilson. Edinburgh: T. & T. Clark, 1983.

———. "Mystery Religions." Pages 272–85 in *Religions of Antiquity.* Edited by Robert M. Seltzer. New York: Macmillan, 1989.

Ruether, Rosemary Radford. *Faith and Fratricide: The Theological Roots of Anti-Semitism.* New York: Seabury, 1974.

Runesson, Anders. *The Origins of the Synagogue: A Socio-Historical Study.* ConBNT 37. Stockholm: Almqvist & Wiksell, 2001.

Ruppert, Lothar. *Der leidende Gerechte: Eine motivgeschichtliche Untersuchung zum Alten Testament und zwischentestamentlichen Judentum.* FB. Würzburg: Echter, 1972.

Russell, D. S. *The Method and Message of Jewish Apocalyptic, 200 B.C.–A.D. 100.* OTL. London: SCM/Philadelphia: Westminster, 1964.

Saarinen, Risto. "The Pauline Luther and the Law: Lutheran Theology Re-Engages the Study of Paul." Pages 90–113 in *The Nordic Paul: Finnish Approaches to Pauline Theology.* Edited by Lars Aejmelaeus and Antti Mustakallio. Library of New Testament Studies 374. London: T. & T. Clark, 2008.

Salo, Kalervo. *Luke's Treatment of the Law: A Redaction-Critical Investigation.* AASF Diss. Hum. 57. Helsinki: Suomalainen tiedekatemia, 1991.

———. *Luukkaan teologian ydin: Lukkaan evankeliumin ja Apostolien tekojen pelastuskäsitys.* Suomen Eksegeettisen Seuran julkaisuja 84. Helsinki: Suomen Eksegeettinen Seura, 2003.

Sandelin, Karl-Gustav. *Die Auseinandersetzung mit der Weisheit in 1. Korinther 15.* Publications of the Research Institute of the Åbo Akademi Foundation 12. Åbo: Åbo Akademi, 1976.

———. "The Danger of Idolatry according to Philo of Alexandria." *Temenos* 27 (1991): 109–50.

Sanders, E. P. "The Covenant as a Soteriological Category and the Nature of Salvation in Palestinian and Hellenistic Judaism." Pages 11–44 in *Jews, Greeks and Christians: Religious Cultures in Late Antiquity: Essays in Honor of William David Davies.* Edited by Robert Hamerton-Kelly and Robin Scroggs. SJLA 21. Leiden: Brill, 1976.

———. "Covenantal Nomism Revisited." Forthcoming in *JSQ.*

———. *The Historical Figure of Jesus.* London: Allen Lane/Penguin, 1993.

———. *Jesus and Judaism.* London: SCM/Philadelphia: Fortress Press, 1985.

———. "Jesus' Galilee." Pages 3–41 in *Fair Play: Diversity and Conflicts in Early Christianity: Essays in Honour of Heikki Räisänen.* Edited by Ismo Dunderberg, Christopher Tuckett, and Kari Syreeni. NovTSup 103. Boston: Brill, 2002.

———. "Jesus in Historical Context." *ThTo* 50 (1993): 429–48.

———. *Jewish Law from Jesus to the Mishnah: Five Studies.* London: SCM/Philadelphia: Trinity Press International, 1990.

———. *Judaism: Practice and Belief 63 BCE–66 CE.* London: SCM, 1992.

———. *Paul and Palestinian Judaism: A Comparison of Patterns of Religion.* London: SCM/Philadelphia: Fortress Press, 1977.

———. *Paul, the Law, and the Jewish People.* Philadelphia: Fortress Press, 1983.

———. *Paul: A Very Short Introduction.* Oxford: Oxford University Press, 2001.

———. "Sin, Sinners (New Testament)." *ABD* 6 (1992): 40–47.

———. "Testament of Abraham." Pages 871–902 in *The Old Testament Pseudepigrapha.* Vol. 1, *Apocalyptic Literature and Testaments.* Edited by James H. Charlesworth. New York: Doubleday, 1983.

Sanders, Jack T. *Charisma, Converts, Competitors: Societal and Sociological Factors in the Success of Early Christianity.* London: SCM, 2000.

Sandmel, Samuel. *Philo of Alexandria: An Introduction.* Oxford: Oxford University Press, 1979.

Sariola, Heikki. *Markus und das Gesetz.* AASF Diss. Hum. 56. Helsinki: Suomalainen tiedeakatemia, 1990.

Saukkonen, Juhana Markus. "Dwellers at Qumran: Reflections on Their Literacy, Social Status, and Identity." Pages 615–27 in *Scripture in Transition: Essays in Honour of Raija Sollamo.* Edited by Anssi Voitila and Jutta Jokiranta. JSJSup 126. Boston: Brill, 2008.

Schenck, Kenneth. *A Brief Guide to Philo.* Louisville: Westminster John Knox, 2005.

Schenke, Ludger. *Die Urgemeinde: Geschichtliche und theologische Entwicklung.* Stuttgart: Kohlhammer, 1990.

Schlosser, Jacques. "Die Vollendung des Heils in der Sicht Jesu." Pages 54–84 in *Weltgericht und Weltvollendung: Zukunftsbilder im Neuen Testament.* Edited by Hans-Josef Klauck. QD 150. Freiburg: Herder, 1994.

428

Schmeller, Thomas. "Stoics, Stoicism." *ABD* 6 (1992): 210–14.

Schnelle, Udo. *Paulus: Leben und Denken.* Berlin/New York: Walter de Gruyter, 2003.

———. *Theologie des Neuen Testaments.* Uni-Taschenbücher 2917. Göttingen: Vandenhoeck & Ruprecht, 2007.

Schoedel, William R. *Ignatius of Antioch: A Commentary on the Letters of Ignatius of Antioch.* Hermeneia. Philadelphia: Fortress Press, 1985.

———. "Ignatius, Epistles of." *ABD* 3 (1992): 384–87.

Scholem, Gershom. *The Messianic Idea in Judaism and Other Essays on Jewish Spirituality.* London: George Allen & Unwin, 1971.

———. *Sabbatai Sevi: The Mystical Messiah, 1626–1676.* Bollingen Series 93. Princeton: Princeton University Press, 1973.

Schowalter, Daniel N. "Trinity." Pages 781–82 in *The Oxford Companion to the Bible.* Edited by Bruce M. Metzger and Michael David Coogan. Oxford: Oxford University Press, 1993.

Schrage, Wolfgang. "'Ekklesia' und 'Synagoge': Zum Ursprung des urchristlichen Kirchenbegriffs." *ZTK* 60 (1963): 178–202.

Schürer, Emil. *The History of the Jewish People in the Age of Jesus Christ (175 B.C.–A.D. 135).* Vol. 1. Revised and edited by Geza Vermes and Fergus Millar. Edinburgh: T. & T. Clark, 1973.

Schüssler Fiorenza, Elisabeth. *In Memory of Her: A Feminist Theological Reconstruction of Christian Origins.* London: SCM, 1983.

———. *Revelation: Vision of a Just World.* Minneapolis: Fortress Press, 1991.

———. *Rhetoric and Ethic: The Politics of Biblical Studies.* Minneapolis: Fortress Press, 1999.

Schweizer, Eduard. *Church Order in the New Testament.* SBT 1/32. Translated by Frank Clarke. London: SCM, 1961.

Scopello, Madeleine. Introduction to the Gospel of Philip. Pages 157–60 in *The Nag Hammadi Scriptures: The International Edition.* Edited by Marvin Meyer. New York: HarperOne, 2007.

Scroggs, Robin. *Christology in Paul and John.* Proclamation Commentaries. Philadelphia: Fortress Press, 1988.

Seeley, David. *Deconstructing the New Testament.* BibInt 5. New York: Brill, 1994.

———. "Jesus' Temple Act." *CBQ* 55 (1993): 263–83.

———. *The Noble Death: Graeco-Roman Martyrology and Paul's Concept of Salvation.* JSNTSup 28. Sheffield: Sheffield Academic Press, 1990.

Segal, Alan F. *Paul the Convert: The Apostolate and Apostasy of Saul the Pharisee.* New Haven: Yale University Press, 1990.

———. *Two Powers in Heaven: Early Rabbinic Reports about Christianity and Gnosticism.* SJLA 25. Leiden: Brill, 1977.

Seim, Turid Karlsen. *The Double Message: Patterns of Gender in Luke–Acts.* Nashville: Abingdon, 1994.

Seitz, O. J. F. "James and the Law." *SE* 1 (TU 73): 1959, 472–86.

Sellin, Gerhard. " Hauptprobleme des ersten Korintherbriefes." *ANRW* 2.25.4 (1987): 2940–3044.

———. *Der Streit um die Auferstehung der Toten: Eine religionsgeschichtliche und exegetische Untersuchung von 1 Korinther 15.* FRLANT 138. Göttingen: Vandenhoeck & Ruprecht, 1986.

Setzer, Claudia. *Jewish Responses to Early Christians: History and Polemics, 30–150 C.E.* Minneapolis: Fortress Press, 1994.

Shaw, Graham. *The Cost of Authority: Manipulation and Freedom in the New Testament.* London: SCM, 1983.

Sivananda, Sri. *All About Hinduism.* Shivanandanagar: Divine Life Society, 1988.

Sjöberg, Erik. "pneuma etc.: pneuma in Palestinian Judaism." *TDNT* 6:375–89.

Skarsaune, Oskar. "The Ebionites." Pages 419–62 in *Jewish Believers in Jesus: The Early Centuries.* Edited by Oskar Skarsaune and Reidar Hvalvik. Peabody, Mass.: Hendrickson, 2007.

Smart, Ninian. *The World's Religions: Old Traditions and Modern Transformations.* Cambridge: Cambridge University Press, 1989.

Smith, Mark S. *The Origins of Biblical Monotheism: Israel's Polytheistic Background and the Ugaritic Texts.* New York: Oxford University Press, 2001.

Smith, Morton. "The Common Theology of the Ancient Near East." *JBL* 71 (1952): 135–47.

Smith, Wilfred Cantwell. "Idolatry in Comparative Perspective." Pages 53–68 in *The Myth of Christian Uniqueness.* Edited by John H. Hick and Paul. F. Knitter. Maryknoll, N.Y.: Orbis, 1987.

———. *What Is Scripture? A Comparative Approach.* London: SCM, 1993.

Snyder, Graydon F. *Ante Pacem: Archaeological Evidence of Church Life before Constantine.* Macon, Ga.: Mercer University Press, 2003.

———. "Hermas' The Shepherd." *ABD* 3 (1992): 148.

Soares-Prabhu, George M. "Laughing at Idols: The Dark Side of Biblical Monotheism (an Indian Reading of

Isaiah 44:9-20)." Pages 109–31 in *Reading from This Place*. Vol. 2, *Social Location and Biblical Interpretation in Global Perspective*. Edited by Fernando F. Segovia and Mary Ann Tolbert. Minneapolis: Fortress Press, 1995.

Sollamo, Raija. "The Letter of Aristeas and the Origin of the Septuagint." Pages 329–42 in *X Congress of the International Organization for Septuagint and Cognate Studies, Oslo, 1998*. Edited by Bernard A. Taylor. Septuagint and Cognate Studies 51. Atlanta: SBL, 2001.

Stanton, Graham. "Jewish Christian Elements in the Pseudo-Clementine Writings." Pages 305–24 in *Jewish Believers in Jesus: The Early Centuries*. Edited by Oskar Skarsaune and Reidar Hvalvik. Peabody, Mass.: Hendrickson, 2007.

Stark, Rodney. *The Rise of Christianity: How the Obscure, Marginal Jesus Movement Became the Dominant Religious Force in the Western World in a Few Centuries*. San Francisco: HarperSanFransisco, 1997.

Starr, James M. *Sharers in Divine Nature: 2 Peter 1:4 in Its Hellenistic Context*. ConBNT 33. Stockholm: Almquist & Wiksell, 2000.

Steck, O. H. *Israel und das gewaltsame Geschick des Propheten: Zur Überlieferung des deuteronomistischen Geschichtsbildes im Alten Testament, Spätjudentum und Urchristentum*. WMANT 23. Neukirchen-Vluyn: Neukirchener, 1967.

Stegemann, Hartmut. "'Die des Uria': Zur Bedeutung der Frauennamen in der Genealogie von Mt 1,1-17." Pages 246–76 in *Tradition und Glaube: Das frühe Christentum in seiner Umwelt*. Festschrift for K. G. Kuhn. Edited by Gert Jeremias, Heinz-Wolfgang Kuhn, and Hartmut Stegemann. Göttingen: Vandenhoeck & Ruprecht, 1971.

Stegemann, Wolfgang. "Much Ado about Nothing? Sceptical Inquiries into the Alternatives 'Theology' or 'Religious Studies.'" Pages 221–42 in *Moving Beyond New Testament Theology? Essays in Conversation with Heikki Räisänen*. Edited by Todd Penner and Caroline Vander Stichele. Publications of the Finnish Exegetical Society 88. Helsinki: Finnish Exegetical Society/ Göttingen: Vandenhoeck & Ruprecht, 2005.

Stendahl, Krister. "The Apostle Paul and the Introspective Conscience of the West." *HTR* 56 (1963): 199–215.

————. "Biblical Theology: A Program." Pages 11-44 in idem, *Meanings: The Bible as Document and as Guide*. Philadelphia: Fortress Press, 1984.

————. "Dethroning Biblical Imperialism in Theology." Pages 61–66 in Heikki Räisänen, et al., *Reading the Bible in the Global Village: Helsinki*. Atlanta: SBL, 2000.

————. "*Quis et Unde*—Who and Whence? Matthew's Christmas Gospel." Pages 71–83 in Krister Stendahl, *Meanings: The Bible as Document and as Guide*. Philadelphia: Fortress Press, 1984.

Stenström, Hanna. "Fair Play? Some Questions Evoked by Heikki Räisänen's *Beyond New Testament Theology*." Pages 105–32 in *Moving Beyond New Testament Theology? Essays in Conversation with Heikki Räisänen*. Edited by Todd Penner and Caroline Vander Stichele. Publications of the Finnish Exegetical Society 88. Helsinki: Finnish Exegetical Society/Göttingen: Vandenhoeck & Ruprecht, 2005.

Stone, Michael E. "Apocalyptic Literature." Pages 383–441 in *Jewish Writings of the Second Temple Period: Apocrypha, Pseudepigrapha, Qumran Sectarian Writings, Philo, Josephus*. Edited by Michael E. Stone. CRINT 2/2. Philadelphia: Fortress Press, 1984.

————. *Fourth Ezra*. Hermeneia. Minneapolis: Fortress Press, 1990.

Stone, Michael E., ed. *Jewish Writings of the Second Temple Period: Apocrypha, Pseudepigrapha, Qumran Sectarian Writings, Philo, Josephus*. CRINT 2/2. Assen: Van Gorcum & Philadelphia: Fortress Press, 1984.

Stowers, Stanley K. *A Rereading of Romans: Justice, Jews, and Gentiles*. New Haven: Yale University Press, 1994.

Strack, Hermann L., and Günter Stemberger. *Introduction to the Talmud and Midrash*. Translated by Markus Bockmuehl. Edinburgh: T. & T. Clark, 1996. Minneapolis: Fortress Press, 1992.

Strauss, David Friedrich. *The Life of Jesus Critically Examined*. First German edition in 1835. London: SCM, 1973.

Strecker, Georg. *Theologie des Neuen Testaments*. Berlin/ New York: Walter de Gruyter, 1996.

Strong, John S. "Images." *ER* 7 (1987): 97–104.

Stroumsa, Guy G. "Postscript: the Future of Intolerance." Pages 356–61 in *Tolerance and Intolerance in Early Judaism and Christianity*. Edited by Graham N. Stanton and Guy G. Stroumsa. Cambridge: Cambridge University Press, 1998.

Stuckenbruck, Loren T. *Angel Veneration and Christology: A Study in Early Judaism and in the Christology of the Apocalypse of John*. WUNT 2/70. Tübingen: Mohr Siebeck, 1995.

Stuhlmacher, Peter. *Biblische Theologie des Neuen Testaments*. 2 vols. Göttingen: Vandenhoeck & Ruprecht, 1992, 1999.

430 ———. *Der Brief an die Römer.* NTD 6. Göttingen: Vandenhoeck & Ruprecht, 1989.

Stylianopoulos, Theodore G. *Justin Martyr and the Mosaic Law.* SBLDS 20. Missoula, Mont.: Scholars Press, 1975.

Sundberg, Albert C. "Canon Muratori: A Fourth Century List." *HTR* 66 (1973): 1–41.

Sundkvist, Mikael. *The Christian Laws in Paul: Reading the Apostle with Early Greek Interpreters.* University of Joensuu Publications in Theology 20. Joensuu: University of Joensuu, 2008.

Svartvik, Jesper. *Mark and Mission: Mk 7:1-23 in Its Narrative and Historical Contexts.* ConBNT 32. Stockholm: Almqvist & Wiksell, 2000.

Syreeni, Kari. "James and the Pauline Legacy: Power Play in Corinth?" Pages 397–437 in *Fair Play: Diversity and Conflicts in Early Christianity: Essays in Honour of Heikki Räisänen.* Edited by Ismo Dunderberg, Christopher Tuckett, and Kari Syreeni. NovTSup 103. Boston: Brill, 2002.

———. "Matthew, Luke, and the Law: A Study in Hermeneutical Exegesis." Pages 126–55 in *The Law in the Bible and Its Environment.* Edited by Timo Veijola. Publications of the Finnish Exegetical Society 51. Helsinki: Finnish Exegetical Society/Göttingen: Vandenhoeck & Ruprecht, 1990.

Tajfel, Henri. *Human Groups and Social Categories: Studies in Social Psychology.* Cambridge: Camridge University Press, 1981.

Tannehill, Robert C. *The Narrative Unity of Luke–Acts.* Vol. 1, *A Literary Interpretation 1: The Gospel According to Luke.* Philadelphia: Fortress Press, 1986.

Teeple, Howard M. *How Did Christianity Really Begin? A Historical-Archaeological Approach.* Evanston: Religion and Ethics Institute, 1992.

Theissen, Gerd. *Die Entstehung des Neuen Testaments als literaturgeschichtliches Problem.* SHAW 40. Heidelberg: Universitätsverlag Winter, 2007.

———. *Erleben und Verhalten der ersten Christen: Eine Psychologie des Urchristentums.* Gütersloh: Gütersloher Verlagshaus, 2007.

———. "Das Kreuz als Sühne und Ärgernis: Zwei Deutungen des Todes Jesu bei Paulus." Pages 427–55 in *Paulus und Johannes: Exegetische Studien zur paulinischen und johanneischen Theologie und Literatur.* Edited by Dieter Sänger and Ulrich Mell. WUNT 198. Tübingen: Mohr Siebeck, 2006.

———. *Lokalkolorit und Zeitgeschichte in den Evangelien.* NTOA 8 Freiburg: Universitätsverlag/Göttingen: Vandenhoeck & Ruprecht, 1989. [ET: *The Gospels in Context.* Minneapolis: Fortress Press, 1991.]

———. *Das Neue Testament* (Beck'sche Reihe, 2192). Munich: Beck, 2002. [ET: *The New Testament: History, Literature, Religion.* Translated by John Bowden. London: T. & T. Clark, 2003.]

———. "Paulus—der Unglücksstifter: Paulus und die Verfolgung der Gemeinden in Jerusalem und Rom." Pages 228–44 in *Biographie und Persönlichkeit des Paulus.* Edited by Eve-Marie Becker and Peter Pilhofer. WUNT 187. Tübingen: Mohr Siebeck, 2005.

———. *Psychologische Aspekte paulinischer Theologie.* FRLANT 131. Göttingen: Vandenhoeck & Ruprecht, 1983. [ET: *Psychological Aspects of Pauline Theology.* Translated by John P. Gavin. Philadelphia: Fortress Press, 1987.]

———. "Röm 9–11—eine Auseinandersetzung des Paulus mit Israel und mit sich selbst: Versuch einer psychologischen Auslegung." Pages 311–41 in *Fair Play: Diversity and Conflicts in Early Christianity: Essays in Honour of Heikki Räisänen.* Edited by Ismo Dunderberg, Christopher Tuckett, and Kari Syreeni. NovTSup 103. Boston: Brill, 2002.

———. *Studien zur Soziologie des Urchristentums.* WUNT 19. Tübingen: Mohr Siebeck, 1979. [ET: *The Social Setting of Pauline Christianity.* Translated by John H. Schülz. Philadelphia: Fortress Press, 1982.]

———. *A Theory of Primitive Christian Religion.* Translated by John Bowden. London: SCM, 1999.

———. "Widersprüche in der urchristlichen Religion: Aporien als Leitfaden einer Theologie des Neuen Testaments." *EvT* 64 (2004): 187–200.

Theissen, Gerd, and Annette Merz. *The Historical Jesus: A Comprehensive Guide.* Translated by John Bowden. London: SCM/Minneapolis: Fortress Press, 1998.

Thielman, Frank. *Theology of the New Testament: A Canonic and Synthetic Approach.* Grand Rapids: Zondervan, 2005.

Thom, Johan C. "Pythagoreanism." *ABD* 5 (1992): 562–65.

Thomassen, Einar. *The Spiritual Seed: The Church of the Valentinians.* Nag Hammadi and Manichean Studies 60. Leiden: Brill, 2006.

Thompson, Leonard L. *The Book of Revelation: Apocalypse and Empire.* Oxford: Oxford University Press, 1990.

———. *Revelation.* Abingdon New Testament Commentaries. Nashville: Abingdon, 1998.

Thurén, Lauri. *Derhetorizing Paul: A Dynamic Perspective on Pauline Theology and the Law.* WUNT 124. Tübingen: Mohr Siebeck, 2000.

Tiede, David Lenz. *The Charismatic Figure as Miracle Worker*. SBLDS 1. Missoula, Mont.: SBL, 1973.

Tomson, Peter J. *Paul and the Jewish Law*. CRINT 3/1. Assen/Maastricht: Van Gorcum/Minneapolis: Fortress Press, 1990.

Torjesen, Karen J. *When Women Were Priests: Women's Leadership in the Early Church and the Scandal of their Subordination in the Rise of Christianity*. San Francisco: HarperSanFrancisco, 1995.

Trafton, Joseph L. "Isaiah, Martyrdom and Ascension of." *ABD* 3 (1992): 507–9.

Trobisch, David. *Die Entstehung der Paulusbriefsammlung: Studien zu den Anfängen christlicher Publizistik*. NTOA 10. Freiburg: Universitätsverlag/Göttingen: Vandenhoeck & Ruprecht, 1989.

Tuckett, Christopher M. "Atonement in the NT." *ABD* 1 (1992): 518–22.

———. *Christology and the New Testament: Jesus and His Earliest Followers*. Edinburgh: Edinburgh University Press, 2001.

———. "The Christology of Luke–Acts." Pages 133–64 in *The Unity of Luke–Acts*. Edited by Jozef Verheyden. BETL 142. Leuven: Leuven University Press, 1999.

———. "The Disciples and the Messianic Secret in Mark." Pages 131–49 in *Fair Play: Diversity and Conflicts in Early Christianity: Essays in Honour of Heikki Räisänen*. Edited by Ismo Dunderberg, Christopher Tuckett, and Kari Syreeni. NovTSup 103. Boston: Brill, 2002.

———. *Q and the History of Early Christianity: Studies on Q*. Edinburgh: T. & T. Clark, 1996.

Tuckett, Christopher M., ed. *The Gospel of Mary*. Oxford Early Christian Gospel Texts. Oxford: Oxford University Press, 2007.

Turner, John D. Introduction to *Trimorphic Protennoia*. Pages 511–13 in *The Nag Hammadi Library in English*. Edited by James M. Robinson. 3d ed. San Francisco: HarperSanFrancisco, 1990.

———. *Sethian Gnosticism and the Platonic Tradition*. Bibliothèque Copte de Nag Hammadi, Section Études 6. Quebec: Presses de l'Université Laval/Louvain/Paris: Peeters, 2001.

Tuveson, Ernest Lee. *Redeemer Nation: The Idea of America's Millennial Role*. Chicago: University of Chicago Press, 1968.

Twelftree, Graham H. *Jesus the Exorcist: A Contribution to the Study of the Historical Jesus*. WUNT 2/54. Tübingen: Mohr Siebeck, 1993.

Ulrich, Jörg. "Selbstbehauptung und Inkulturation in feindlicher Umwelt: Von den Apologeten bis zur 'Konstantinischen Wende': 1. Theologische Entwicklungen." Pages 223–300 in *Christentum 1: Von den Anfängen bis zur Konstantinischen Wende*. Edited by Dieter Zeller. Die Religionen der Menschheit 28. Stuttgart: Kohlhammer, 2002.

Uro, Risto. "The Bridal Chamber and Other Mysteries: Ritual System and Ritual Transmission in the Valentinian Movement." Pages 457–86 in *Sacred Marriages: The Divine-Human Sexual Metaphor from Sumer to Early Christianity*. Edited by Martti Nissinen and Risto Uro. Winona Lake, Ind.: Eisenbrauns, 2008.

———. "Is *Thomas* an Encratite Gospel?" Pages 140–62 in *Thomas at the Crossroads: Essays on the Gospel of Thomas*. Edited by Risto Uro. Studies of the New Testament and Its World. Edinburgh: T. & T. Clark, 1998.

———. "John the Baptist and the Jesus Movement: What Does Q Tell Us?" Pages 231–55 in *The Gospel Behind the Gospels: Current Studies on Q*. Edited by Ronald A. Piper. NovTSup 75. Leiden: Brill, 1995.

———. *Neither Here Nor There: Luke 17:20-21 and Related Sayings in Thomas, Mark, and Q*. Institute for Antiquity and Christianity, Occasional Papers 20. Claremont: Institute for Antiquity and Christianity, 1990.

———. *Sheep among the Wolves: A Study on the Mission Instructions of Q*. AASF Diss. Hum. 47. Helsinki: Suomalainen tiedeakatemia, 1987.

———. *Thomas: Seeking the Historical Context of the Gospel of Thomas*. London: T. & T. Clark, 2003.

Vaage, Leif E. *Galilean Upstarts: Jesus' First Followers according to Q*. Valley Forge, Pa.: Trinity Press International, 1994.

Valantasis, Richard. *Gospel of Thomas*. New Testament Readings. New York: Routledge, 2000.

VanderKam, James C. "Messianism and Apocalypticism." Pages 193–228 in *The Encyclopedia of Apocalypticism*. Vol. 1, *The Origins of Apocalypticism in Judaism and Christianity*. Edited by John J. Collins. London: Continuum, 2000.

van der Watt, Jan G. "Conclusion—Soteriology of the New Testament: Some Tentative Remarks." Pages 505–22 in *Salvation in the New Testamen: Perspectives on Soteriology*. Edited by Jan G. van der Watt. NovTSup 121. Leiden/Boston: Brill, 2005.

———. "Salvation in the Gospel according to John." Pages 101–31 in *Salvation in the New Testamen: Perspectives on Soteriology*. Edited by Jan G. van der Watt. NovTSup 121. Leiden/Boston: Brill, 2005.

432 van Ess, Josef. "Islamic Perspectives." Pages 5–18 in *Christianity and the World Religions: Paths of Dialogue with Islam, Hinduism, and Buddhism*. Edited by Hans Küng, et al. Translated by Peter Heinegg. London: Collins, 1987.

Veijola, Timo. "Die Deuteronomisten als Vorgänger der Schriftgelehrten: Ein Beitrag zur Entstehung des Judentums." Pages 192–240 in idem, *Moses Erben: Studien zum Dekalog, zum Deuteronomismus und zum Schriftgelehrtentum*. BWANT 8/9. Stuttgart: Kohlhammer, 2000.

———. *Das 5. Buch Mose, Deuteronomium: Kapitel 1,1—16,17*. ATD 8/1. Göttingen: Vandenhoeck & Ruprecht, 2004.

Vermes, Geza. *The Dead Sea Scrolls in English*. 2d ed. Harmondsworth: Penguin, 1976.

Vielhauer, Philipp. *Geschichte der urchristlichen Literatur*. Berlin: Walter de Gruyter, 1975.

Vollenweider, Samuel. *Freiheit als neue Schöpfung: Eine Untersuchung zur Eleutheria bei Paulus und in seiner Umwelt*. FRLANT 147. Göttingen: Vandenhoeck & Ruprecht, 1989.

———. "Die Metamorphose des Gottessohns: Zum epiphanialen Motivfeld in Phil 2.6-8." Pages 107–31 in *Das Urchristentum in seiner literarischen Geschichte*. Festschrift for Jürgen Becker. Edited by Ulrich Mell and Ulrich B. Müller. BZAW 100. Berlin/New York: Walter de Gruyter, 1999.

———. "Politische Theologie im Philipperbrief?" Pages 457–69 in *Paulus und Johannes: Exegetische Studien zur paulinischen und johanneischen Theologie und Literatur*. Edited by Dieter Sänger and Ulrich Mell. WUNT 198. Tübingen: Mohr Siebeck, 2006.

Vouga, François. *Geschichte des frühen Christentums*. Uni-Taschenbücher 1733. Tübingen/Basel: Francke, 1994

Walter, Nikolaus. "Apostelgeschichte 6.1 und die Anfänge der Urgemeinde in Jerusalem." *NTS* 29 (1983): 370–93.

———. "'Hellenistische Eschatologie' im Neuen Testament." Pages 335–56 in *Glaube und Eschatologie*. Festschrift for Werner Georg Kümmel. Edited by Erich Grässer and Otto Merk. Tübingen: Mohr Siebeck, 1985.

———. "Zur Interpretation von Römer 9–11." *ZTK* 81 (1984): 172–95.

Wassen, Cecilia, and Jutta Jokiranta, "Groups in Tension: Sectarianism in the Damascus Document and the Community Rule." Pages 209–58 in Jutta Jokiranta, "Identity on a Continuum: Constructing and Expressing Sectarian Social Identity in Qumran *Serakhim* and *Pesharim*." Ph.D. diss. University of Helsinki, 2005.

Watson, Francis. *Paul, Judaism, and the Gentiles: A Sociological Approach*. SNTSMS 56. Cambridge: Cambridge University Press, 1986.

———. *Paul, Judaism, and the Gentiles: Beyond the New Perspective*. Grand Rapids: Eerdmans, 2007. [2d ed. of previous work.]

———. *Text and Truth: Redefining Biblical Theology*. Edinburgh: T. & T. Clark, 1997.

———. *Text, Church and World: Biblical Interpretation in Theological Perspective*. Edinburgh: T. & T. Clark, 1994.

Wedderburn, Alexander J. M. *Baptism and Resurrection: Studies in Pauline Theology against Its Graeco-Roman Background*. WUNT 44. Tübingen: Mohr Siebeck, 1987.

———. *Beyond Resurrection*. London: SCM, 1999.

———. *A History of the First Christians*. London: T. & T. Clark, 2004.

———. "Eine neuere Paulusperspektive?" Pages 46–64 in *Biographie und Persönlichkeit des Paulus*. Edited by Eve-Marie Becker and Peter Pilhofer. WUNT 187. Tübingen: Mohr Siebeck, 2005.

Weeden, Theodore J. *Mark: Traditions in Conflict*. Philadelphia: Fortress Press, 1971.

Weiser, Alfons. *Der zweite Brief an Timotheus*. EKKNT 16/1. Neukirchen-Vluyn: Neukirchener, 2003.

Weiss, Johannes. *Earliest Christianity: A History of the Period A.D. 30–150*. Vol. 2. Translated and edited by Frederick C. Grant. New York: Harper, 1959. (German original 1917.)

Weltin, E. G. *Athens and Jerusalem: An Interpretive Essay on Christianity and Classical Culture*. Studies in Religion, AAR 49. Atlanta: Scholars Press, 1987.

Wenham, John. *Facing Hell: An Autobiography*. London: Paternoster, 1998.

Wernle, Paul. *The Beginnings of Christianity*. Translated by Gustav A. Bienemann. 2 vols. Theological Translation Library. New York: Putnam, 1914.

Westerholm, Stephen. *Perspectives Old and New on Paul: The "Lutheran" Paul and His Critics*. Grand Rapids: Eerdmans, 2004.

Westermann, Claus. *Genesis 1–11*. BKAT 1/1. Neukirchen-Vluyn: Neukirchener, 1974. [ET: *Genesis 1–11*. Continental Commentary. Translated by John J. Scullion. Philadelphia: Fortress Press, 1984.]

White, L. Michael. *From Jesus to Christianity*. San Francisco: Harper, 2004.

Wilckens, Ulrich. *Theologie des Neuen Testaments 1: Geschichte der urchristlichen Theologie, Teilband 1: Geschichte des Wirkens Jesu in Galiläa.* Neukirchen-Vluyn: Neukirchener, 2002.

Wiles, Maurice. "Christianity without Incarnation?" Pages 1–10 in *The Myth of God Incarnate.* Edited by John Hick. London: SCM, 1977.

———. "Christology—The Debate Continues." *Theology* 85 (1982): 324–32.

———. "Reflections on James Dunn's *Christology in the Making*." *Theology* 85 (1982): 92–96.

Williams, Michael A. *Rethinking "Gnosticism": An Argument for Dismantling a Dubious Category.* Princeton: Princeton University Press, 1996.

———. "Sethianism." Pages 32–63 in *A Companion to Second-Century Christian "Heretics."* Edited by Antti Marjanen and Petri Luomanen. VCSup 76. Leiden/Boston: Brill, 2005.

Williams, Sam K. *Jesus' Death as Saving Event: The Background and Origin of a Concept.* HDR 2. Missoula, Mont.: Scholars Press, 1975.

Wilson, Stephen G. *Leaving the Fold: Apostates and Defectors in Antiquity.* Minneapolis: Fortress Press, 2004.

———. *Luke and the Law.* SNTSMS 50. Cambridge: Cambridge University Press, 1983.

———. "Marcion and the Jews." Pages 45–58 in *Anti-Judaism in Early Christianity 2: Separation and Polemic.* Edited by Stephen G. Wilson. Studies in Christianity and Judaism 2. Waterloo, Ont.: Wilfrid Laurier University Press, 1986.

———. *Related Strangers: Jews and Christians, 70–170 C.E.* Minneapolis: Fortress Press, 1995.

Winninge, Mikael. *Sinners and the Righteous: A Comparative Study of the Psalms of Solomon and Paul's Letters.* ConBNT 26. Stockholm: Almqvist & Wiksell, 1995.

Wischmeyer, Oda. "Paul's Religion: A Review of the Problem." Pages 74–93 in *Paul, Luke and the Graeco-Roman World: Essays in Honour of Alexander J. M. Wedderburn.* Edited by Alf Christophersen, et al. JSNTSup 217. Sheffield: Sheffield Academic Press, 2002.

Wolff, Christian. *Der erste Brief des Paulus an die Korinther 2: Auslegung der Kapitel 9–16.* 2d ed. THKNT 7/2. Berlin: Evangelische Verlagsanstalt, 1982.

Wolfson, Henry A. *Philo: Foundations of Religious Philosophy in Judaism, Christianity, and Islam.* 2 vols. Cambridge, Mass.: Harvard University Press, 1948.

Wolter, Michael. "'Gericht' und 'Heil' bei Jesus von Nazareth und Johannes dem Täufer: Semantische und pragmatische Beobachtungen." Pages 354–92 in *Der historische Jesus: Tendenzen und Perspektiven der gegenwärtigen Forschung.* Edited by Jens Schröter and Ralph Brucker. BZNW 114. Berlin: Walter de Gruyter, 2002.

Wrede, William. *The Messianic Secret.* Translated by J. C. G. Greig. Cambridge/London: James Clarke, 1971. (German original 1901.)

———. "The Tasks and Methods of 'New Testament Theology.'" Pages 68–116 in Robert Morgan, *The Nature of New Testament Theology: The Contribution of William Wrede and Adolf Schlatter.* London: SCM Press, 1973. (German original 1897.)

Wright, J. Edward. *The Early History of Heaven.* Oxford: Oxford University Press, 2000.

Wright, N. T. *The Climax of the Covenant: Christ and the Law in Pauline Theology.* Edinburgh: T. & T. Clark, 1991. Minneapolis: Fortress Press, 1992.

———. *Jesus and the Victory of God.* Vol. 2 of *Christian Origins and the Question of God.* Minneapolis: Fortress Press, 1996.

———. *The New Testament and the People of God.* Vol. 1 of *Christian Origins and the Question of God.* Minneapolis: Fortress Press, 1992.

———. *The Resurrection of the Son of God.* Vol. 3 of *Christian Origins and the Question of God.* Minneapolis: Fortress Press, 1993.

Yarbro Collins, Adela. *The Beginning of the Gospel: Probings of Mark in Context.* Minneapolis: Augsburg Fortress, 1992.

———. "Establishing the Text: Mark 1:1." Pages 111–27 in *Texts and Contexts: Biblical Texts in Their Textual and Situational Contexts,* Essays in Honor of Lars Hartman. Edited by Tord Fornberg and David Hellholm. Oslo: Scandinavian University Press, 1995.

———. "The Messiah as Son of God in the Synoptic Gospels." Pages 21–32 in *The Messiah in Early Judaism and Christianity.* Edited by Magnus Zetterholm. Minneapolis: Fortress Press, 2007.

———. "Persecution and Vengeance in the Book of Revelation." Pages 729–49 in *Apocalypticism in the Mediterranean World and the Near East.* Edited by David Hellholm. 2d ed. Tübingen: Mohr Siebeck, 1989.

Yonge, Charles D., trans. *The Works of Philo: Complete and Unabridged.* New, updated edition. Peabody, Mass.: Hendrickson, 1993.

Young, Frances. "A Cloud of Witnesses." Pages 13–47 in *The Myth of God Incarnate.* Edited by John Hick. London: SCM, 1977.

434 ———. *From Nicaea to Chalcedon: A Guide to the Literature and Its Background*. London: SCM, 1983.

———. "The Trinity and the New Testament." Pages 286–305 in *The Nature of New Testament Theology: Essays in Honour of Robert Morgan*. Edited by Christopher Rowland and Christopher Tuckett. Oxford: Blackwell, 2006.

———. "Two Roots or a Tangled Mass." Pages 87–121 in *The Myth of God Incarnate*. Edited by John Hick. London: SCM, 1977.

Zager, Werner. *Jesus und die frühchristliche Verkündigung: Historische Rückfragen nach den Anfängen*. Neukirchen-Vluyn: Neukirchener, 1999.

Zeller, Dieter. *Der Brief an die Römer*. RNT. Regensburg: Pustet, 1985.

———. "Die Entstehung des Christentums." Pages 15–123 in *Christentum 1: Von den Anfängen bis zur Konstantinischen Wende*. Edited by Dieter Zeller. Die Religionen der Menschheit 28. Stuttgart: Kohlhammer, 2002.

———. "Konsolidierung in der 2./3. Generation." Pages 124–222 in *Christentum 1: Von den Anfängen bis zur Konstantinischen Wende*. Edited by Dieter Zeller. Die Religionen der Menschheit 28. Stuttgart: Kohlhammer, 2002.

———. "Die Menschwerdung des Sohnes Gottes im Neuen Testament und die antike Religionsgeschichte." Pages 141–76 in *Menschwerdung Gottes—Vergöttlichung von Menschen*. Edited by Dieter Zeller. NTOA 7. Göttingen: Vandenhoeck & Ruprecht, 1988.

———. "New Testament Christology in Its Hellenistic Reception." *NTS* 47 (2001): 312–33.

———. "Eine weisheitliche Grundschrift in der Logienquelle?" Pages 389–401 in *The Four Gospels 1992*. Festschrift for Frans Neirynck. Edited by Frans van Segbroeck, et al. Leuven: Leuven University Press, 1992.

Zetterholm, Magnus. *The Formation of Christianity in Antioch: A Social-Scientific Approach to the Separation between Judaism and Christianity*. New York: Routledge, 2003.

Zevit, Ziony. *The Religions of Ancient Israel: A Synthesis of Parallactic Approaches*. London: Continuum, 2001.

Ziesler, John. *Paul's Letter to the Romans*. TPINTC. London: Trinity Press, 1989.

Zimdars-Schwarz, Sandra L., and Paul Zimdars-Schwarz. "Apocalypticism in Modern Western Europe." Pages 265–92 in *The Encyclopedia of Apocalypticism*. Vol. 3, *Apocalypticism in the Modern Period and the Contemporary Age*. Edited by Stephen J. Stein. London: Continuum, 2000.

lifestyle, 288

442

466

*Asterisk indicates writings not included among the Nag Hammadi codices.

OTHER CHRISTIAN TEXTS